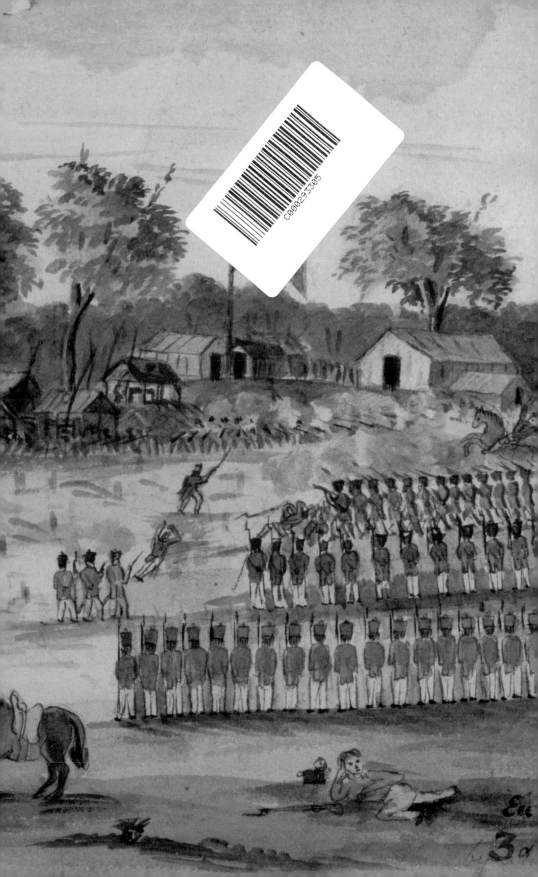

EUREKA

PETER FITZSIMONS

EUREKA

THE UNFINISHED REVOLUTION

WILLIAM HEINEMANN: AUSTRALIA

A William Heinemann book
Published by Random House Australia Pty Ltd
Level 3, 100 Pacific Highway, North Sydney NSW 2060
www.randomhouse.com.au

First published by William Heinemann in 2012

National Library of Australia
Cataloguing-in-Publication Entry

FitzSimons, Peter.
Eureka: the unfinished revolution/Peter FitzSimons.

ISBN 978 1 74275 525 0 (hbk.)

Eureka Stockade (Ballarat, Vic.)
Gold miners – Victoria – Ballarat – History.
Riots – Victoria – Ballarat – History.
Ballarat (Vic.) – History – 1851–1901.

994.57031

Jacket design by Adam Yazxhi/MAXCO
Front jacket: Eureka flag photo by Kate Morris; 'Swearing Allegiance to the "Southern Cross"' by Charles Doudiet, courtesy Art Gallery Ballarat. Back jacket: 'Eureka Slaughter, 3rd December 1854' by Charles Doudiet, courtesy Art Gallery Ballarat
Internal maps by Jane Macaulay
Internal design and typesetting by Xou Creative, Australia
Printed in Australia by Griffin Press, an accredited ISO AS/NZS 14001:2004 Environmental Management System printer

Random House Australia uses papers that are natural, renewable and recyclable products and made from wood grown in sustainable forests. The logging and manufacturing processes are expected to conform to the environmental regulations of the country of origin.

To Raffaello Carboni, Mrs Ellen Clacy, William Craig, Samuel
Huyghue, Samuel Lazarus and William Bramwell Withers, whose
contemporary – and, in the case of Withers, near-contemporary –
accounts I have most enjoyed and relied upon in the formation of
this book. And to all those diggers who fought so valiantly . . .

'By and by there was a result, and I think it may be called the finest thing in Australasian history. It was a revolution – small in size; but great politically; it was a strike for liberty, a struggle for principle, a stand against injustice and oppression . . . It is another instance of a victory won by a lost battle. It adds an honourable page to history; the people know it and are proud of it. They keep green the memory of the men who fell at the Eureka Stockade, and Peter has his monument.'

Mark Twain after visiting the Victorian goldfields in 1895

'Eureka was more than an incident or passing phase. It was greater in significance than the short-lived revolt against tyrannical authority would suggest. The permanency of Eureka in its impact on our development was that it was the first real affirmation of our determination to be masters of our own political destiny.'

Ben Chifley, Labor Prime Minister

'The revolt at Eureka is the one picturesque bloodstain on the white pages of Australian history. British officials referred to it as "a trifling affair" but the little fight was big with results, for it helped to shatter official tyranny and to establish democratic rule in Australia.'

The Lone Hand, January 1912

CONTENTS

Contents

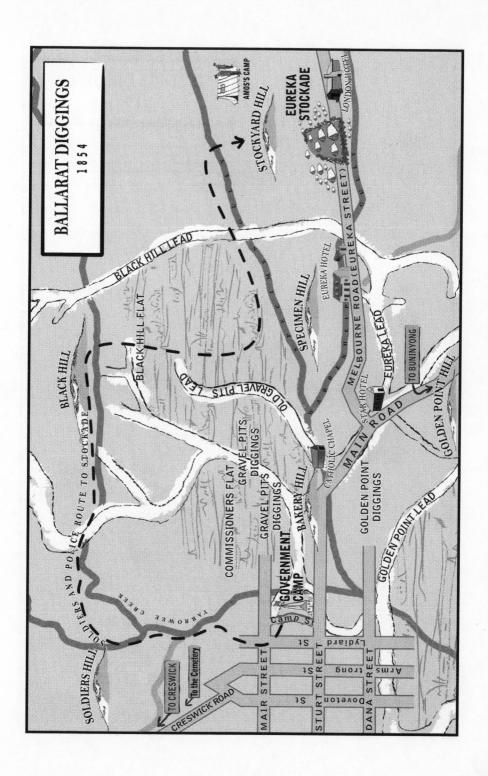

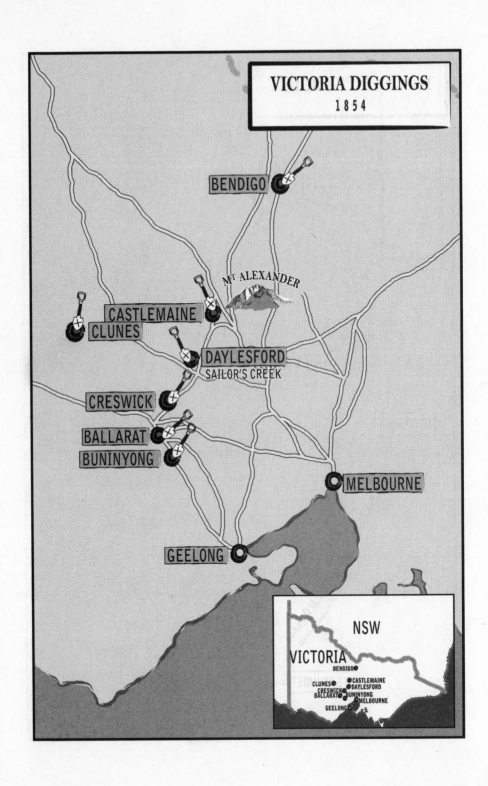

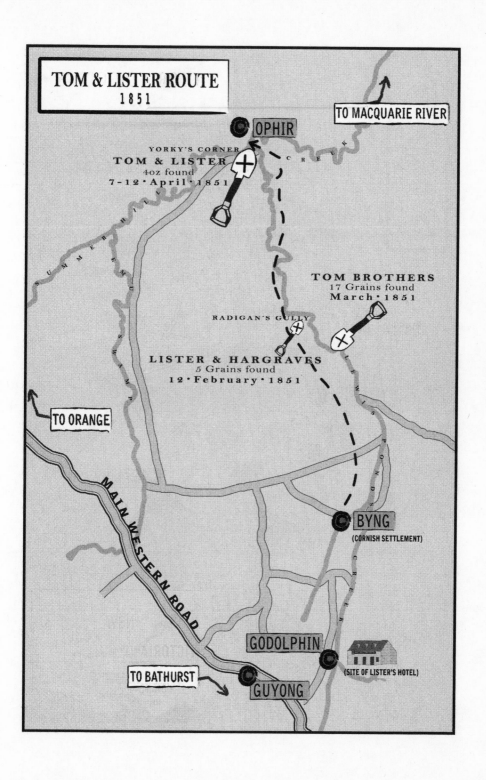

TOM & LISTER ROUTE
1851

TO MACQUARIE RIVER

OPHIR

YORKY'S CORNER
TOM & LISTER
4oz found
7·12·April·1851

CREEK

TOM BROTHERS
17 Grains found
March·1851

RADIGAN'S GULLY

LISTER & HARGRAVES
5 Grains found
12·February·1851

TO ORANGE

MAIN WESTERN ROAD

TO BATHURST

BYNG
(CORNISH SETTLEMENT)

GODOLPHIN

GUYONG

(SITE OF LISTER'S HOTEL)

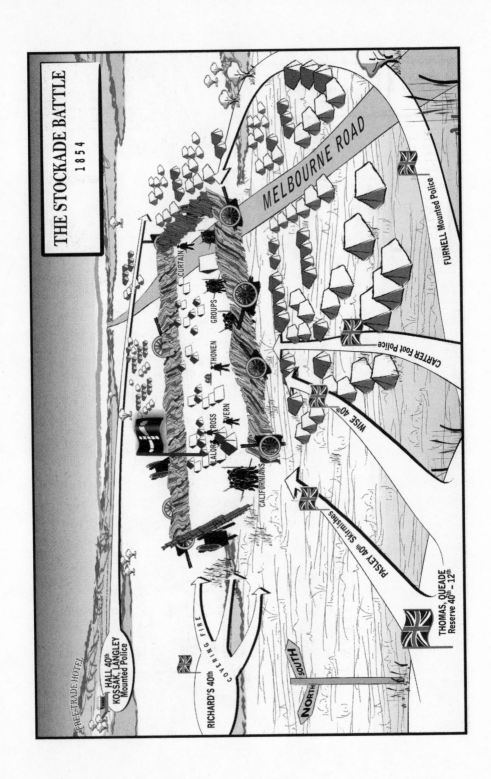

STOCKYARD HILL VIEW
1 8 5 4

BUNINYONG

MELBOURNE ROAD

WARRENHEIP ROAD

MT WARRENHEIP

LONDON HOTEL

STOCKYARD HILL

EAST
WEST
NORTH

BACKGROUND AND ACKNOWLEDGEMENTS

Like most Australians, the saga of the Eureka Stockade is in the very marrow of my bones. As a primary school kid in the late 1960s, I recall both the fun of participating in a mock Eureka Stockade re-enactment at the Mangrove Mountain Community Fair, and being pleased that I got to dress up as a good rebel and not in the red coat of a bad British soldier. We learnt about the subject briefly at Peats Ridge Public, and it was almost as much fun a legend from Australia's past as the bushrangers – not that I was particularly interested in the Eureka saga academically.

Nevertheless, in Mr Rex Ward's history class at high school in Sydney in the mid-70s, that changed. On one particular sleepy afternoon I was doing what I usually did in history class – multiplying the number of bricks on the wall from top to bottom, by the number of bricks from left to right – when Mr Ward started his lesson on the Eureka Stockade. Remembering Mangrove Mountain and the excitement of it all, my ears pricked up and, for the first time in months, I not only sat up straight but went further. Out of pure bloody-mindedness I began to *listen*, and it was right there and then that my love of Australian history began – my enthrallment with that particular story sparked a wider, burning passion. The action! The characters! The fact – and this was perhaps the key – that this was a real *Australian* story!

The leap forward to this book, however, was only relatively recent. A couple years ago, at a meeting of the directors of Ausflag in the Sydney suburb of Crows Nest, we were sifting through many worthy submissions from our fellow citizens of what a modern Australian flag should look like when the thought struck me: what a pity we Australians don't have our own version of the Americans' legendary Betsy Ross story, that country's purported maker of the first 'Stars and Stripes' flag during the Revolutionary War.

While the designs we were seeing were mostly admirable, I had my doubts as to whether the Australian people as a whole would ever choose a flag designed last Tuesday ahead of one designed at the beginning of the last century, one that had been fluttering ever since.

And that, of course, led me to thinking about the Eureka story as the possible subject for a book. Look, I certainly didn't think that the flag of the Southern Cross would ever be embraced as the answer – in the 21st century it is too associated with either right-wing racist rednecks who brandish it as a symbol of white Australia or hard left-wing members of the union movement who, far more admirably, wave it for workers' rights. But, against that, Eureka was certainly a saga that encompassed our oldest and best-known flag after the national flag, and so it might be worth exploring anyway. All this happened in roughly the same time frame that my friend and researcher Henry Barrkman started suggesting that Eureka would be a good subject for me, and a producer from SBS Radio in Melbourne, Yvonne Davis, wrote to me, pointing out that the multicultural aspects of the saga had never been truly explored. (Multicultural aspects? What multicultural aspects? I wasn't really aware that there were any?) And then, the breakthrough . . . Out of the blue, two brothers, Peter and Ron Craig, wrote to me saying they were the great-grandsons of William Craig, who had not only come out on the ship from Ireland with the hero of the piece, Peter Lalor, but also penned a long-forgotten book about Lalor and his experience in the Eureka Stockade. Given that I was interested in writing books on Australian history, they wondered if I would like to read their great-grandfather's original manuscript?

I would, and I did. We wined, we dined, we talked. I was hooked, and soon afterwards I began.

Rarely have I been so enthused while working on a book. Yes, I have been equally passionate about other stories, just as stories, but with this one I felt I was getting to uncover the very foundation stones of what it is to be an Australian – from multiculturalism to mateship, from our broad distrust of the elites who would seek to rule over us, to our wide embrace of egalitarianism and insistence on a 'fair go, mate', to the very use of the word 'mate'! In the diggers' willingness to roll up their sleeves and just get on with it, whatever the appalling conditions, and their propensity to pull together to overcome hardships, I recognised much of the spirit that the country was built on. In their refusal to cower before power – most particularly their loud insistence to the government of 'no taxation without representation' – and backing that up with their willingness to fight for their rights, even against overwhelming odds, I found fascinating parallels with the Boston Tea Party that I had never before appreciated.

And early on, to my shame, I realised I knew more about that Boston Tea Party than I did about this seminal episode in our own history. I had no idea, for example, that on the eve of the Eureka battle, an Australian 'Declaration of Independence' had been written and enunciated; that diggers from other goldfields had marched to the aid of the men on Ballarat behind a man brandishing a sword as the lightning cracked, while they all sang *'La Marseillaise'*! I simply didn't know that for the first part of the actual battle the rebels gave at least as good as they got; that Karl Marx himself had followed the Eureka uprising and written about it; and that the court cases after the battle, as they put 13 of the rebels on trial for High Treason, had been the seminal court cases in Australian history and nothing less than a triumph of Australian justice. How exciting I found it that, far from being an isolated 'local tax revolt' as some of its deriders would have it, the Eureka rebellion was nothing less than the flowering of a broad international movement towards democracy, a flowering that put Australia at the very prow of democratic change around the world.

In short, I soon became obsessed with the whole story, and

determined to blow the dust off the saga and try to bring it to life using every resource I had and could access.

In terms of making it accurate, the bad news was that there are so many layers of mythology surrounding what actually occurred, and even conflicting contemporary accounts, that it was frequently difficult to separate fact from fiction. However, the good news was that the source material – diaries, letters and newspapers – was bountiful beyond belief and rich in wonderful detail.

Of course, it will be for you, the reader, to judge whether or not I have managed to pull it off, but my aim at the outset was to take that rich detail and place it at the service of making this book feel like a novel – to take the thousand points of light represented by footnoted fact and place the reader in the moment, rather than in the 21st century looking back with a telescope on events long ago. It is the approach I have employed in my books since coming under the influence of the American writer Gary Smith in 2000, most particularly in *Kokoda, Tobruk, The Ballad of Les Darcy, Charles Kingsford Smith, Batavia* and *Mawson* – but only with Sir Douglas Mawson have I been as blessed with as much fine detail as was available on this book. For the sake of that novel-like feel, for the sake of the storytelling, I have very occasionally created a direct quote from reported speech in a newspaper, diary or letter. For the same reason, I have stayed with the imperial form of measurement and used the spelling of the day, as in 'Toorac', as opposed to 'Toorak'. In instances where two spellings were used at the time – i.e. 'Ballarat' and 'Ballaarat' – to avoid confusion I have chosen the modern version. And finally, in my attempts to make the story live and breathe, when no positive determination can be made as to which of many versions of the truth is correct – who designed and sewed the original Eureka flag, for example – I have put my reasons for choosing the version I did in the endnotes, rather than interrupt the narrative flow.

In terms of researching the book, it was, if you'll forgive the laboured metaphor, like finding myself in an entire goldfield of information, and I learnt very quickly where the most fertile fields, bearing the most valuable nuggets, were to be found.

As I note in my dedication, the most valuable of the accounts from the time that I drew upon, and certainly the most colourful memoir, is the one written by Raffaello Carboni, despite its oft-maddening chronological contradictions. I also cite the diaries of Samuel Huyghue, Samuel Lazarus, John Lynch and the later personal accounts of Godfrey Howitt, Ellen Clacy, Antoine Fauchery, Henry Nicholls, Charles D. Ferguson and the aforementioned William Craig. The letters of Charles Pasley to his father were invaluable, as were the government official reports to their superiors, for example, those written by both Commissioner Robert Rede and Lieutenant-Governor Sir Charles Hotham. A compilation of contemporary accounts, *Eureka: From the Official Records*, assembled and edited by Ian MacFarlane, was a wonderful resource. Similarly, I would not have completed this book to the standard I desired without the Victorian Government's collected papers – 'Correspondence Relative to the Recent Discovery of Gold in Australia (1852–1856)' which allowed me to gain better insight into the government's side of the story. As an addendum, *Historical Studies: Eureka Supplement*, a collection of significant academic articles published on the centenary of Eureka in 1954, was invaluable.

Of the historians who tackled the subject, William Bramwell Withers is the obvious stand-out in the 19th century, due to the fact that he lived at Ballarat and was able to draw on the memories and direct correspondence of many of the key players, who trusted him enough to tell him what they knew.

Of the modern writers, the book to which I most constantly referred was John Molony's *Eureka*. As to other books, the most valuable to me were Weston Bate's *Lucky City*, H. J. Stacpoole's *Gold at Ballarat* and, for a strong, clear overview of the whole story and excellent images, Geoff Hocking's *Eureka Stockade*. Gregory Blake's book, *To Pierce the Tyrant's Heart* was vital for the wonderfully colourful and accurate details it provided for the actual assault on the Stockade. As a man who worked for four years compiling that book, I was grateful when Greg agreed to work with me to ensure that my own detail was well founded. As it turns out, we did not agree on all things, as I drew different conclusions from the evidence presented on a couple of issues, but he remained a fantastic source of advice and detailed information on the whole Eureka saga, and I thank him warmly. Similarly, David Hill's book *The Gold Rush* provided a great overview of the history of gold digging in this country, including Eureka, and I am thankful that David was also a great source of advice throughout my writing of this book. Both Thomas Keneally and David Day have also covered Eureka in their own writings and were generous with their counsel, from which I profited, and I am in their debt. Beyond the aforementioned Craig brothers, I was contacted by many proud descendants of Eureka figures and they were universally helpful. But I particularly acknowledge the Noyce family, descended from Samuel Perry; Trevor Carroll, descended from Patrick Carroll; and Hazel Brombey, descended from Barnard Welch.

In all of my historical books since *Kokoda*, I have called on my friend Dr Michael Cooper's twin passions for medicine and history to help inform me on the medical aspects of the story, and in this book he was as valuable as ever, giving me detailed advice on everything from what a fresh bayonet wound would look like to how they amputated arms in Australia in 1854. I thank him warmly for his input, once again. I am indebted also to Dr Stephen Gale from the School of Geosciences at the University of Sydney for his expertise on matters geological, most particularly how gold was formed. Dr John Waugh of the University of Melbourne was wonderfully generous in lending his expertise on Australian constitutional history, as was my quasi-cousin, the former NSW Liberal parliamentarian Andrew Tink. I warmly thank them both. I am indebted to both Graham Fricke – the former County Court judge who practised at the Victorian Bar for 21 years before becoming an author on legal history – and Julian Burnside

QC for their input on my chapter concerning the Eureka trials. James Phillips, the noted heritage architect from Melbourne, provided useful information on architectural details from Melbourne at the time of Eureka, and I thank him. So, too, the noted vexillologist (a student of flags) Ralph Kelly – who is also on the board of Ausflag with me – was more than helpful putting his expertise at the service of this book, which I deeply appreciate. John Vaughn of Australiana Flags also gave me valuable input, and I very much appreciated being able to call on the knowledge of two Eureka experts in Dr Joseph Toscano of the Anarchist Media Institute and Dr Chris McConville of Victoria University. In London, Catherine Pope's input on the English angles was very useful. Both Mark Latham and Gerard Henderson were useful and knowledgeable sounding boards on the political angles of the story, and I thank them.

Way back when I wrote my first book in 1990, *Basking in Beirut*, my dear friend at *The Sydney Morning Herald*, Harriet Veitch, gave me wise counsel on every part of it and did the preliminary editing. Well, now 22 years and 25 books later, she still is, and I value more than ever her input into all things to do with the form and texture of this book. Similarly, I met my long-time researcher Sonja Goernitz at the Sydney Writers' Festival seven years ago, and when I found she was German-born I thought I could probably use her talents for, perhaps, a day or two as I researched and wrote *Tobruk*. She, too, has worked for me on every book since and has been invaluable in terms of general research for *Eureka*, most particularly on the parts of the story set in New South Wales.

I also thank Glenda Lynch of Canberra, who pursued leads in the National Archives; Megan Schlipalius of Perth, who handled the WA angles; my friend Julia Baird, who is writing her own biography on Queen Victoria and who helped me with that part of the story; and Jill Blee in Ballarat, who was a constant fount of detailed information on particular elements of the Eureka saga. Jane Macaulay designed the superb maps and illustrations in *Mawson*, and did so for this book as well – I am indebted to her. I also thank warmly Tim Sullivan, the Deputy CEO & Museums Director of The Sovereign Hill Museums Association, who went well above and beyond the call of duty in helping me out when I was in Ballarat – and also local mining historian Peter d'Auvergne.

In terms of really in-depth research on the Melbourne and Ballarat parts of the story, however – going for the rich mother lode that lay deep down below the surface – I was blessed with the best.

For this particular book, I knew I needed someone on the ground in Melbourne to trawl the archives of the State Library of Victoria and the Public Record Office Victoria to get to the primary documents that, ideally, would allow me to sort through the many previously referred to layers of legend that have wrapped themselves around Eureka, not to mention the conflicting accounts from those there at the time, and try to work out what actually happened.

In this regard, I could not have done better than PhD candidate in Sociology at Deakin University Libby Effeney, who retrieved countless treasures for me and resolved many of the aforementioned conflicting accounts. In contemplating her input, I am reminded of a line my old rugby coach Peter Fenton said after the Sydney team I had the honour to be a part of toured Europe in 1984.

'We thought,' he told people afterwards, 'we would take this kid Nick Farr-Jones along with us, to give him a bit of experience. But it turned out, he took us!'

Many people from many institutions were extremely helpful to both myself and my researchers in digging out information, but I particularly thank Bob Allen from the Eureka Centre in Ballarat, Tim Hogan and Chris Wade from the State Library of Victoria, the staff of the Public Record Office Victoria, the Mitchell Library in Sydney and those of The Royal Anglican Regiment Museum in England. A special thanks, too, to Jack Roberts and the team at Reason in Revolt, who digitised many of the existing issues of *The Ballarat Times*. Thank you, especially, to the online digital project

Trove, an initiative of the National Library of Australia, which has digitised many of the historical newspapers, in partnership with state libraries, used in the research of this book. What a resource that is – and what a privilege to be able to instantly access contemporary accounts from journalists on the ground at the time, compare them, and get ever closer to the truth.

I thank all at Random House, particularly Margie Seale, Nikki Christer and, as ever, Alison Urquhart for backing the project from the first. As to my editor, Brandon VanOver, he had a great feel for the story from the moment we began discussing it, and I am indebted to the thoroughness of his approach, his professionalism and skill in spotting inconsistencies, repetitive prose, and all the rest – and suggesting ways of fixing them.

Let me, most importantly, acknowledge the highly professional work of my dear friend and principal researcher on this book, Henry Barrkman, who also coordinated the work of many of the other researchers. His dedication to pursuing the highest degree of accuracy in any given matter was unwavering (read, obsessive to the point of needing medical help). This fanatical and high-energy streak was particularly useful in this book, as the mass of material of differing value required precisely his high level of skill and deep care to get it right. I am in your debt, Henry – as is this book.

Finally, I thank my wife, Lisa, a professional editor by background, who kept me sane through the toughest part of the writing and, as ever, provided unending encouragement and strength whenever I flagged. (Still, it was always a Eureka flag, now that I come to think of it.)

All up, I hope you enjoy reading the book at least half as much as I have enjoyed writing it.

Peter FitzSimons
Neutral Bay, Sydney
September 2012

Author's Note

For the sake of good storytelling, I have very occasionally created a direct quote from an indirect quote in a newspaper. However, this has required only changes to pronouns, word endings and the like, and I have always remained faithful to the original. I have certainly not created any words or concepts that do not appear in the original source. For example, the original, 'He protested against the whole of the proceedings; the meeting was more to enrich the rich, and oppress the poor man', now reads, 'I protest against the whole of the proceedings,' he finishes his address. 'This meeting is more to enrich the rich, and oppress the poor man.'

PROLOGUE

Gold? Yellow, glittering, precious gold?
. . .
This yellow slave
Will knit and break religions, bless th' accursed,
Make the hoar leprosy adored, place thieves
And give them title, knee and approbation
With senators on the bench . . .
William Shakespeare, *Timon of Athens*, Act IV, Scene III

In the time before Australia was Australia, all that we now see before
us of our brown and pleasant land consisted of fragments of solidi-
fied crust, colliding and crumpling. Molten rock was hurled out
across the constantly changing land surface, even as huge jets of
steam burst forth into the atmosphere . . .

In the bowels of the earth, at extremely high temperatures, the
most desirable element of all was dissolved in saline waters: gold.
These waters, too compressed to turn into steam, also shot upwards
ever upwards to the surface. Ever and always, that water streamed,
screamed, along the path of least resistance, through whatever cracks,
fissures and fault lines lay before it. And then, when the conditions
were just right, in certain very rare and scattered parts of Australia,
as the water cooled or indeed turned into steam, the dissolved gold
was deposited as veins in the surrounding rock, such as quartz and
slate. These veins could in turn be broken down by water, by ice, by
geological and chemical processes, and by erosion over hundreds of
millions of years, which could reduce whole thrusting mountains of
rock into shattered, scattered fragments. Frequently the gold released

from the veins settled as small specks in streams, mixing with sand and other mineral deposits. Sometimes it was left as whole nuggets just on or near the surface. In many places, ancient streams thick with such nuggets were later buried beneath brief volcanic outflows, and as the land continued to weather and change once more to cover those original streams, the gold was again buried deep beneath the surface of rich alluvial soil. In one particular spot, in the south-east corner of that emerging continent to be called Australia, the gold was laid thickly in a tight crisscross of streams on, around and beneath a curiously elongated, dome-like hill.

And there the gold lay for eons as plant life slowly began to appear, followed eventually by animals, birds, insects, fish and finally . . . people, as the land we know as Australia did indeed become exactly that.

To be sure, all that glittered was not gold, and in fact the gold glittered so little that the first of the continent's indigenous people, who arrived some 60,000 years ago, knew little and cared less about it. Oh yes, they loved the land alright, but contrary to the later notion of owning the land, the Aborigines felt that the land owned them, or at least that they were an inseparable part of it. Of the things they saw around them, far more interesting were the animals, fish, birds and creatures that they knew had come from the Dreamtime, and many of them embodied the spirits of their ancient ancestors. Those flecks of lustre here and there that the natives may have occasionally seen on various pebbles as they crossed the creeks, and even the nuggets, were a little interesting because they shone so, but, as gold was of no practical use, it was not particularly valued. They pushed on, pursued the songlines of their existence, prospered, and, as they thinly populated the land, named particular features as they went.

The local Wathaurong clan called one such place – a wide valley nestled amidst soft, rolling hills, graced by bubbling creeks and shaded by a thick and fragrant cover of eucalyptus trees – ballaarat, a place to recline on your balla, your elbow. After all, this place where

2

the flat met the bush by a curiously elongated hill that looked a little like an echidna was teeming with life. The food sources of kangaroos, wallabies, possums, echidnas, wombats and myriad others were never far away and the fresh water supply was constant – even at the height of the heat, after the flowers bloomed and before the snakes disappeared.

And yet one day, in the direction of the rising sun, a bizarrely white man by the name of Captain Cook had come with many other white men on a big ship they called *Endeavour*, eventually stopping in a bay before departing again. For eighteen summers the Gadigal people around Botany Bay had thought that it had been no more than a strange visitation by their ancestors in a curious form and there would be no more of it. After all, they had all been raised on tribal stories of spirit-creatures that wandered the land and the sea performing fantastic acts before just as quickly disappearing, and these extraordinary white men in their big canoe fitted exactly into their Dreaming – it was just the first time they had seen those stories for themselves.

But return the men did, and far more powerfully and numerously than before.

In January of 1788, many more strange white men came under the command of one 'Captain Phillip', and this time they did not go away. They stayed. They cut down trees. They brought strange animals and plants – and terrible diseases – with them. They did not understand or respect that the tribes were of the land. In fact, they started chasing them off it, putting up fences and scouring all over, exploring, looking for whatever easy treasures there might be upon it that they could plunder.

———

And there was some real treasure there! In August 1788, the convict James Daley begged to report that he had discovered something very interesting on some of the land he had been tilling down by the harbour near Government House in the new town of Sydney, something that glittered . . . maybe even gold!

As good as his word, Daley produced from a matchbox what indeed looked to be tiny pieces of the precious metal. Now, he informed the Lieutenant-Governor, Major Robert Ross, with amazing presumption for one who had been transported to New South Wales for seven years for being a criminal, in return for his and a particular female convict's freedom, together with their passage back to England on the next ship sailing, and a moderate amount of money . . . he was prepared to tell him where that gold was to be found. Upon the Lieutenant-Governor's counteroffer, however, that Daley either tell him immediately or receive 100 lashes, the convict decided, upon consideration, to accept. Strangely, however, after arriving on the spot in the company of an officer and some soldiers, Daley ran off! And things became stranger still. For after arriving back in the camp early in the afternoon, he informed all and sundry that he had left the officer in possession of a goldmine, and after grabbing a few things from his tent, disappeared once more. Where to?

Exactly. As a white man in a land populated by blacks, there was really nowhere but the settlement to go to, and 'the want of provisions soon brought him from his concealment'.[1] And now, another officer put a different deal to him. Purposefully loading his gun, he invited the miscreant to confess where the 'gold' had come from. Again, Daley decided to accept.

For you see, he stammered, strictly speaking it was not really quite gold at all. He had simply filed down a yellow belt buckle and mixed it with some gold from a guinea.

And that was that. Far from his freedom and a trip home with his love, Daley received 100 lashes from a cat-o'-nine-tails for his trouble, as well as being obliged to 'wear a canvas frock with the letter "R" cut and sewn upon it, to distinguish him more particularly from others as a rogue'.[2] Tragically, four months later, 'the poor wretch was executed for housebreaking'.[3]

Not that any of the excitement halted, for even a moment, the spread of white people across the land, pushing the Aboriginal people out as they went.

———————

Yet it wasn't as if the white men didn't have serious fights of their own, between themselves.

Some of the Irish convicts had been sent to the colonies specifically for their involvement in the Irish Rebellion of 1798, whereby the brave patriots had taken up such arms as they could get their hands on – mostly homemade pikes – and attempted to overthrow British rule from their lands. In the famed Battle of Vinegar Hill on 21 June of that year, some 20,000 of them had clashed with the same number of heavily armed British troops at a place called Vinegar Hill in County Wexford, Ireland, and acquitted themselves superbly well. True, the rebels lost the battle, but the way they had wielded their mere pikes against the artillery and rifles of the occupiers would gladden Irish hearts for generations to come.

In fact, and this was the point, Australia had its own mini-version of just such an uprising, led by some of the veterans of that campaign – and using 'Vinegar Hill' for a password – with plans for 200 convicts at Castle Hill to meet up with around 1000 supporters from the Hawkesbury and march on Sydney to gain their freedom. The signal for the uprising to begin occurred on the unseasonably hot and humid evening of 4 March 1804, when a 'vigorously rung bell' set 200 rebels to rise as one and a hut at Castle Hill was set ablaze. Thereafter, the raging 200, initially wielding their pikes, set off.

After breaking into Government Farm's armoury to steal guns and ammunition, they marched on Parramatta, raiding farm after farm along the way to get more weapons, shouting the cry of the insurgents in old Ireland six years earlier, 'Death or Liberty!', as they went. On the spot, the most notable veteran of the Irish Vinegar Hill battle who was among them, their leader Philip Cunningham, was unanimously voted by the other rebels as the 'King of the Australian Empire'. In short order they had 180 muskets, swords and pistols between them, as well as – and this proved enormously significant – more alcohol than they could possibly drink, though they tried hard enough . . . Their freedom was *intoxicating* in every way.

That night, in his gracious Parramatta home, the Reverend Samuel Marsden – otherwise known as 'the Flogging Parson' – was enjoying dinner with his wife and children and their distinguished guest, none other than Elizabeth Macarthur (wife of soldier, pioneer and entrepreneur John Macarthur and the first soldier's wife to arrive in New South Wales), when just after the clock on the mantelpiece had struck nine times their door was flung open. In an instant, a local settler, William Joyce, had burst into the room. As Mrs Macarthur would recall ever after, he was 'pale and in violent agitation'.

'Sir,' Mr Joyce gasped, 'come with me. And you, too, Madam.'[4]

In shattered fragments, his story soon emerged. Only a short time earlier, the Irish convicts had raided his Seven Hills farm, dragged him from his bed and taken him hostage. It had only been *in extremis* that he had managed to escape. Behind him, even as he spoke, the testament to the truth of his words was seen by the glow in the night sky to their north. The 'Croppies', as the convicts were known, really *were* rising. Within minutes panic gripped all of Parramatta's 1200 residents as the word spread. There was *menace* in that glow and the streets were now filled with settlers fleeing before the approaching mob of convicts. Run for your lives!

After a singularly anxious night, mercifully, the beat of a military drum was heard as dawn broke. Summoned from Sydney, the soldiers had marched through the night. Governor King had declared martial law and sent them out after the rebels!

And, just as had happened in ol' Ireland, the British forces proved equal to the task, ruthlessly crushing the insurrection. After 29 soldiers, backed by 50 armed civilians, caught up with the convicts, the battle lasted no longer than 30 minutes. When the smoke had cleared, 15 of the rebels had been killed, with another nine subsequently hanged for their trouble – including Cunningham, that very night, without trial.

Nevertheless, for a brief time those Irish rebels had indeed had their freedom and it, too, would inspire Irish people in Australia for generations to come.

————————

Generally, however, such disturbances were few, and the colony continued to grow – and well beyond Sydney, at that. Sometimes as the colony expanded, settlers discovered things that, while nothing to the natives, were potentially extremely valuable to them. A case in point came in 1823 when, after the white settlers had pushed through to get west of the Blue Mountains that book-ended the Sydney settlement on one side with the Pacific Ocean on the other, an Irish-born government surveyor by the name of James McBrien was surveying a new road 15 miles south-east of Bathurst, right by the Fish River, when his attention was caught by 'numerous particles of gold convenient to the river'.[5]

Look, if it had been an extraordinary amount of gold, or if he had not been on government business at the time, perhaps he might have followed up on it. As it was, it wasn't really that much gold to worry too much about, so he merely took some specimens and reported it to his masters when he returned to Sydney.

But for the authorities, too, it was problematic. They were running not just a colony but a penal colony, where the most important thing was a certain dull stability. Who knew what might happen if the convicts, and perhaps more particularly their guards, felt that a fortune in gold might be had if only they broke free of their shackles, or put down their guns and batons and took to the hills?

Already there was a growing gap between those who ruled in the colonies and those who were meant to be ruled. For there was something troubling about this growing generation of young people who had not been born in, or even been to, England. There was an increasingly distinctive way they had in dressing – sort of slovenly and uncaring – and of speaking – dashed ambivalent about pronouncing vowels for one thing. They tended to be bigger and more raw-boned than recent arrivals of the same age come from the motherland. They were darker for being more exposed to the sun and, while they were not necessarily insolent, there was a certain lack of automatic deference to their obvious betters.

Most troubling of all, more and more of them appeared to identify more with being from the colonies than with being the sons and daughters of Great Britain! They were, in short, disloyal ingrates best summed up by an editorial in a Sydney newspaper in 1826, which put its finger right on the rough nut of the problem: 'They have lost their English spirit and have degenerated into Australians.'[6]

This sneering aside, nothing altered the fact that there were more and more of these Australians, both born to that fatal shore and crossing the oceans to get there to make new lives.

The inevitable result was that down in the south-eastern part of the continent the 60,000 years of sole Aboriginal occupation was coming to an end. In those mid-1820s, two intrepid explorers, Hamilton Hume and William Hilton Hovell, had successfully trekked all the way from Appin in New South Wales down to Corio Bay in the south-western corner of that massive expanse of protected water named Port Phillip Bay to find hundreds of square miles of what was clearly arable land on its foreshores, stretching into the hinterland, and duly reported their discovery to the authorities. A decade later, the first of those who had settled in Van Diemen's Land, and had found the going tough, began to venture across Bass

Strait – becoming the 'Overstraiters' – and found a place where the only thing that lay between them and claiming huge swathes of land were a few easily-dealt-with natives.

One of the most significant Overstraiters was John Batman. A native of Sydney, born of a convict father of wild disposition – from whom he inherited his passions for drinking and womanising, though not necessarily in that order – he had worked variously as a farmer and bounty hunter, and in 1826 had even captured the infamous bushranger Matt Brady, known as 'the Wild Colonial Boy of Van Diemen's Land'. After tiring of farming without any success in an area near Launceston, Batman had thought to try his luck on the mainland.

In late May 1835, having formed the Port Phillip Association with four other settlers in Van Diemen's Land, Batman left Launceston with three domestic servants and seven Aboriginal workers and travelled across Bass Strait upon the sloop *Rebecca*. It was his hope that his Aborigines would be able to act as interpreters with the local Indigenous population so he could conduct the business he had in mind. For Batman did not want to just *occupy* the vast acreage of land that he knew awaited there. Not a bit of it. He wanted to buy it. And it was for that very reason that he was carrying lots of trinkets, some mirrors and many, many blankets.

After entering Port Phillip Bay on 29 May, *Rebecca* anchored in a small bay about twelve miles into the harbour and Batman made the first of several trips ashore.[7] Exploring the rich surrounding land on foot, he quickly fell in with fresh tracks of the 'locals' before coming across 'a beautiful plain about 3 to 400 Acres of as rich land as I ever saw'.[8]

The following day he saw the local natives for the first time from a distance and was awestruck by this potential pastoralist's paradise: 'A light black soil covered with Kangaroo Grass 2 feet high and as thick as it could stand . . . The land was as good as land could be – the whole appeared like land [laid] out in farms for some 100 years back.'[9]

On 31 May, Batman's Aboriginal scouts made contact with the Wurundjeri for the first time. There were 20 women toting heavy loads along with 24 children and four dingos, their men having gone up river. Batman – trying hard not to look at their naked breasts, though they didn't seem to mind – gave them blankets, necklaces, looking glasses, a tomahawk, some apples and handkerchiefs (in case they were caught short with a runny nose). In return, he was presented with some spears, a basket and a bucket.[10]

Over the ensuing days, Batman continued to sail towards the head of the bay, stopping off each day to walk the country. Each time he was more enamoured with the vast expanses of open land that at times extended 30 miles in every direction. The land near the rivers and creeks teemed with ducks and other waterfowl, and he noticed the Aborigines had constructed stone fish traps in the creeks.

On 3 June, Batman began an extended trek up the river the Wurundjeri men had followed.[11] He surveyed the land and discovered good supplies of fresh water in places away from the river, which itself had good drinking water. On sighting the Keilor Plains, he described it as 'the . . . most beautiful sheep pasturage I ever saw in my life'.[12] Wildlife was plentiful – kangaroos, emus, dingos and wild geese in glorious profusion. With such vast, open, well-grassed plains and rich black soil, the only deficiency for the grazier was that there were so few trees for firewood – just scattered she-oaks, wattle trees and small gums.

On 6 June, Batman was indeed able to make contact with eight elders of the Wurundjeri clan.[13] The three principal chiefs were brothers, all with the name Jaga-Jaga, and two of them were notably superb physical specimens, 'six feet high and very good looking' as Batman recorded in his diary. Many of their companions had daubed their faces with red, white and yellow clays.

An enormously significant exchange ceremony soon took place by the bank of a small stream, as the sounds of the Australian bush pressed close. Through sign language – for, of course, the language of the Aborigines from Van Diemen's Land was entirely different – Batman succeeded in making their elders understand that he and his people wished to settle on the very land in which the natives could trace their own origins to the Dreamtime. Furthermore, in return for the land stretching from where they stood to all natural barriers in view – amounting to 600,000 acres of land and delineated by marks made upon trees – he was prepared to give them many of the 'treasures' he had with him, which he was quick to display.

To make them properly understand what the deal entailed, Batman had the elders put some dirt in his hands to signify that the land now belonged him, while he physically put the treasures in their hands – 20 pairs of blankets, 30 tomahawks, 100 knives, 50 pairs of scissors, 30 looking glasses, 200 handkerchiefs and 100 pounds of flour and six shirts – to make them understand that this was a swap. A yearly rent of 100 pairs of blankets, 100 knives, 100 tomahawks, 50 suits of clothing, 50 looking glasses, 50 pairs of scissors and five tons of flour were also included in Batman's treaty.

The eight elders seemed to agree – although it is possible that they thought the deal was simply to allow Batman and his men safe passage across the land – and applied their marks to the treaty that Batman presented to them.

And so it was done. To celebrate, once it was all completed, the Aborigines who had come with Batman danced in a corroboree with the Wurundjeri, their joyous cries and stomping causing the kooka-burras and other birds for hundreds of yards around to take flight in fright. Or was it that they sensed what was about to overtake the superb natural habitat in which they had made their home?

On 7 June 1835, Batman took up his quill and carefully transcribed in triplicate copies of the deed of his land purchase from the Wurundjeri. That accomplished, he wandered over to another meeting by a nearby creek with the tribal elders to deliver more of the promised 'property'.[14] In turn, the two handsome principal elders presented Batman with a chieftain's mantle and took no small delight in his modelling the garment before them. Then, encouraged by the example of one of Batman's Aborigines who had (away from the women, as this was men's business) made his Sydney clan's mark upon a tree, the principal elder of the Wurundjeri inscribed the mark of his own country and tribe. This Batman excised and adhered to a copy of the deed.[15]

Business and pleasure concluded, Batman's party began their return trek by a different route, crossing and naming the creeks and valleys as they progressed towards the mouth of the river, where his vessel was waiting. Soon after rejoining the Saltwater River, he came upon a fecund march he quickly named Batman's Marsh, recording in his diary, 'I think at one time I can safely say I saw 1000 Quails flying at one time, quite a Cloud. I never saw anything like it before I shot two very large ones as I was walking along.'[16]

At one end of the marsh lay a huge space of open water – a small lake of near-perfect oval shape – at the other end of which the incoming river had turned into a large waterfall. Notwithstanding the myriad mosquitos and flies that were also here in abundance, the whole place looked at first blush as if Adam and Eve could happily have made their home there, and probably did once upon a sunlit time.

The Saltwater River they were travelling on now joined a much larger river from the east, that which the Wurundjeri call Birrarung: 'river of mists and shadows'. Two of Batman's Aborigines swam the seven miles to the head of the river to retrieve Batman's small boat. However, foul weather the following day prevented them heading down the Saltwater River. Instead, Batman recorded, 'The boat went up the large river . . . and . . . I am glad to state about six miles up found the River all good water and very deep. This will be the place for a village.'[17] He decided to call the whole place – what else? – 'Batmania'.

When Batman left on a brief trip to Launceston to gather his wife, Eliza, and seven daughters, he left behind his three white domestic servants and several of his Aboriginal workers, effectively to hold the fort. By that river, in the middle of that scrub, those white men felt that they were the only members of their race for many hundreds of miles in any direction.

And yet, on 6 July, while gathered around the fire eating their damper, they looked up to see the most extraordinary figure approaching. At least six foot six – perhaps there is something in the water at that extraordinary lake – the fellow was robed in kangaroo skins and carrying boomerangs and spears, but there was clearly something different about him . . .

'Hello . . .' he said, a little uncertainly.

He was a white man! Yes, a very dark white man and – truth be told – a very ugly one, with a heavy brow and deeply pockmarked face, but a white man nevertheless. A tattoo on his forearm read 'WB', giving credence to his claim that his name was William Buckley.

Little by little over the next few days, as his long-lost ahh-billl-itees in the English language started to return, the story came out. Though he at first claimed to have been a soldier who had survived a shipwreck, in short order he revealed the truth of the matter. He had, in fact, been a convict aboard the ship *Calcutta* that, with the good ship *Ocean,* had first attempted to settle these parts in 1803, with 308 convicts and half as many officers, soldiers and free settlers. Their troupe had landed on the southern shore of Port Phillip Bay, at a place they named 'Sullivan Bay',[18] after the undersecretary for the colonies, John Sullivan, and tried to make a go of it.

The venture had been a disaster from first to last and, just before the settlement was abandoned to retreat to Van Diemen's Land, he and several other convicts had escaped. Two were quickly recaptured and two others decided to try to walk to Sydney, never to be heard from again. But Buckley had decided to stay in the area, walking around the contours of the bay, at first living off berries and shellfish. One day he had seen what looked to be a spear planted in some freshly upturned earth and used it as a walking stick. Shortly thereafter he had come across native women who recognised the spear as belonging to the grave of their most revered, recently departed tribal elder, and they recognised him as that man's spirit returned to life!

'They called me Murrangurk,' he told the fascinated men, 'which I afterwards learnt was the name of a man formerly belonging to their tribe.'[19]

Yes, as a *ngamadjid,* one returned from the spirit world to which their dead had departed, he had to be cared for, and he soon became part of their tribe, learning their language, customs and ways, taking two wives and fathering one daughter. In return, he regaled them with grand stories about the English people across the seas, the way they lived, the ships they possessed, the guns they fired and so on.

The newcomers listened, *stupefied.* What were the chances that a man could have survived and prospered for that long among a people whose ways and language were so foreign to his own?

The men had an answer that would subsequently become part of Australian folklore: Buckley's and none.[20]

For all that, in the coming weeks and months, Buckley proved more than useful as a translator, managing to explain, to the chiefs most particularly, 'the consequences which might arise from any aggression on their part'.[21]

———

In the meantime, when Governor Bourke of New South Wales – which had Port Phillip Bay on its southern borders – found out about this so-called 'treaty', he was appalled. Despite Batman's claim that he was 'the greatest landowner in the world',[22] Bourke knew he was no such thing. For, as he declared on 6 August 1835, the land, as Crown land, belonged to King William IV of the United Kingdom and could not be sold and redistributed. The very *notion* of negotiating with the natives implied that they had some claim to it, which was outrageous. Batman and his people were nothing less than trespassers. Though Bourke was quick to declare the agreement null and void, by this time it was too late. Batman had merely been at the prow of other settlers and, within months of the natives' marks being put on the parchment, they had been hunted well away from their traditional lands and the new settlers had taken root and begun to grow.

One of these was a man by the name of John Pascoe Fawkner, who, after starting life as the son of a convict, had gone on to marry a convict, and then effectively became one himself! For his back was marked by the 500 lashes he had received for having tried to help seven convicts escape – a prelude to being sentenced to three years in gaol himself for 'committing some atrocious Robberies and Depredations'.

But that was all behind him now. Like many who had come to this settlement on the edge of the wilderness, he was determined to make a fresh start and, after arriving in the Port Phillip District on Friday, 16 October 1835, he wrote in his diary that evening: 'Warped up to the Basin, landed 2 cows, 2 calves and the 2 horses.'[23]

Yes, in some ways Fawkner and his fellow colonists were far better provided for, and prepared than, the first European arrivals three decades earlier. But even then their hold on this new settlement was so precarious that disaster was only narrowly averted when, on two occasions, 'Derrimut' – the headman of the Boonwurrung people – used William Buckley's translating skills to warn Fawkner of an intended forthcoming attack by 'up-country tribes', allowing the whites just enough time to arm and defend themselves.

'The Blacks we learnt intended to murder us for our goods,'[24] Fawkner wrote in his diary on 28 October. A further entry on 13 December 1835 was more detailed:

[Derrimut] came this day and told us that the natives intended to rush down upon us and plunder our goods and

murder us. we cleaned our pieces and prepared for them . . .
I and two others chased the Blacks away some distance.[25]

Curiously, Buckley – with his loyalties apparently torn – also mentioned to Fawkner that 'if he had his will he would spear [Derrimut] for giving the information',[26] though he at least appeared to have faithfully passed on the warnings.

However close-run those near-disasters had been, with yet more arrivals security improved and the process of colonisation, once begun, could not be stopped. In fact, so arable was the land, so vast the possibilities for settlers like Batman and Fawkner, that within a year the place where the treaty had been signed was unrecognisable, as the trees had been cut down, crops planted and rough kinds of huts constructed. For the first part of this process the key interpreter used by Batman and others remained William Buckley, who had received a pardon from George Arthur, the Lieutenant-Governor of Van Diemen's Land. Buckley did not last long, however. Feeling that he was now distrusted by both the blacks and the whites, he drifted to Van Diemen's Land to begin the next phase of his life.

Melbourne, however – for that is what 'Batmania' had been renamed by Governor Bourke (in honour of British Prime Minister William Lamb, the 2nd Viscount Melbourne), after going through other incarnations as Bearbrass, Bareport, Bareheep, Barehurp and Bareberp – continued to grow, which was fortunate as this was just in time to begin to soak up the population overflow from Sydney Town.

'This colony,' Governor Bourke proudly reported to Whitehall in October 1836, 'is like a healthy Child outgrowing its Clothes. We have to let out a tuck every month.'[27]

To help maintain government control of this newly established settlement, Bourke first sent a police superintendent from Sydney down only a few months after Batman and his first settlers had arrived. When the settlement continued to grow, all of it with free settlers only – no convicts – by the end of September 1836 he had sent 30 Redcoats of the 4th King's Own Regiment to build their own base.

And just as many were pouring into the new settlement, so, too, were others pouring into adjoining regions.

In early 1838, six intrepid colonists in the company of an Aboriginal guide had left Corio Bay – known to the Aboriginals as *Jilong*, while the land beside it became known to the settlers as Geelong – on the south-western shores of the far larger Port Phillip Bay.

Having come from Van Diemen's Land, they had found that all the best land within 25 miles of the coast had already been claimed, and so were obliged to journey farther afield, over hills, through valleys, around swamps and across many arid plains. Just four days and 50 miles later, they ascended the heavily wooded slopes of a small mount subsequently named Mt Buninyong[28] – from the local Aboriginal word *bunning* for knee, and *yowang*, hill, thus 'hill like a knee' – and gazed with wonder to the north-west. 'An ocean of forest with island hills, was all around them, but not a speck visible that spoke to them of civilisation.'

Within that ocean of forest they could also see huge swathes of grassy lands, some of it contained in a wide valley, nestled among the hills, which looked particularly promising. And beyond that still, they could see the as-yet-unnamed, far-distant Grampian ranges and Pyrenees. Some very limited exploration was possible, and yet, running out of supplies, they were soon enough obliged to make their famished way back to the big smoke.

Nevertheless, from January 1838 on, the first settlers migrated in the general direction of the promising country that had been spotted. Two Scots settlers, Henry Anderson and William Cross Yuille, just 19 years old, drove their flocks forward into that particular grassy valley to settle. The kangaroos didn't really bother bounding away, so placid was this invasion, while the emus barely blinked.

In short order, William Yuille began to cut down many of the scattered wattle and gum trees and build his home by the banks of a stream he called Yarrowee Creek. All around were many other creeks, gullies, patches of forest and grassy slopes. 'A pastoral quiet reigned everywhere.'[29]

Yuille decided to call his run Ballaarat, after the Wathaurong people's notion of *balla arat* – a great place to lean on your elbow. And within that run there was no more beautiful or picturesque resting place than a particular waterhole surrounded by wattles at the juncture of the Yarrowee and Gong Gong creeks, at the foot of a curiously elongated, dome-like hill, where the grass around always remained green, no matter how deep the drought, how long the summer, how rare the rains.

No sooner had these pioneers opened up the land than hundreds, then thousands, then millions of sheep and thousands of cattle began to flow into the central highlands' felicitous rolling grass country. It was the very area that the explorer Major Sir Thomas Livingstone Mitchell had first seen in 1836 when, upon reaching the junction of the Murray and Loddon rivers, he became so enchanted by the area and its pastoral possibilities that he called it Australia Felix.[30]

True, this was all Crown land, with all that lay upon it and beneath it belonging to His Majesty William IV, but the 1836 legislation passed by His Majesty's representative in Australia, the New South Wales Government, had already determined what they could do. So long as the squatters did not settle within three miles of each other – in practice giving each squatter about 6000 acres – and paid an annually renewed lease of £10 per annum to the government, they were allowed to 'squat' upon that land and have grazing rights. If there were any disputes, it was for the Commissioner of Crown lands – the official in formal charge of all of His Majesty's sovereign territory – to regulate it.

———

By 1839 the Port Phillip settlement and its surrounding regions were thriving to the point that, with no fewer than 5000 settlers, the Governor of New South Wales, Sir George Gipps, felt that it needed a full-time administrator, and this person proved to be a Londoner by the name of Charles Joseph La Trobe. An imposing man at six feet tall, he arrived on the last day of September that year, with his Swiss wife, their two-year-old daughter, Agnes, two servants and a prefabricated cottage that had first been put together in England before being dismantled, transported 10,000-odd miles and then reconstructed in Melbourne. Settling into that small, two-room cottage on a corner of the Government Paddock – an estate he soon renamed *Jolimont* – he was not long in getting to work. As one whose father had been a peripatetic missionary (Charles himself had considered entering the Church), and who, as an adult, had travelled through both North and South America as a tutor to the troubled young Swiss-based Frenchman Count Albert de Pourtalès, Charles La Trobe was nothing if not used to adapting to different climes, and he did well from the first in this benign pastoral outpost of the British Empire.

And yet, just as La Trobe accommodated his growing family by adding rooms onto his cottage – with a kitchen, library and servants' quarters constructed by local builders, even as they built stables out the back – so too had he taken over a colony whose settlers were already spilling into adjoining regions.

From the beginning, however, he was eager for this colony to be a place where far more than mere wealth was accumulated, as he noted in his first speech in Melbourne:

'It is not by individual aggrandisement, by the possession of numerous flocks or herds, or by costly acres, that the people shall secure for the country enduring prosperity and happiness, but by the acquisition and maintenance of sound religious and moral institutions without which no country can become truly great.'[31]

Though La Trobe set out from the first to build such institutions, the numbers of people who continued to arrive, seeking numerous flocks, herds, costly acres and all the rest, continued to swell . . .

There were soon so many squatters and the Port Phillip District was becoming so important that only six years after Batman had arrived, the Legislative Council of New South Wales was expanded so that six of 36 members could represent the southern settlement. Of course, you had to be a very wealthy landowner to be such a representative, because no person of even moderate means could afford the time and expense of travelling regularly to Sydney – only to be outvoted 30–six on most matters that would advantage Sydney as opposed to Port Phillip and its environs – but it was a start. The whole area was continuing to strengthen as the population grew and the land became ever more valuable.

As to the squatters around Yarrowee, they continued to prosper as their sheep grew fat. Only shortly after settlement, one of those squatters, Henry Anderson, was walking on his run with a friend when he picked up a small piece of quartz and noticed it had a curious, gleaming streak in it.

'This is gold,' he announced to his companion.

'Tut-tut, man,' his friend replied. 'Golden nonsense!'[32]

Feeling a fool, but not knowing the half of it, Anderson immediately threw the stone at a nearby donkey.

And, yes, there were occasionally problems from the devastated Aboriginal tribes that had been all but wiped out by this invasion into their territory, but the natives were neither numerous enough nor powerful enough for the settlers to worry about too much. Perhaps worst of all, from only a short time after the white invasion, their dispossession was aided by the newly formed body of the Native Police Corps, Aboriginal men – a 'Satanic Battalion of Black Guards'[33] – whose specific role was to move the 'uncivilised' natives off their land.

Much further to the north of the Port Phillip District, in 1839, a Polish immigrant, Paul Strzelecki, found traces of gold not far from Lithgow, west of Sydney. Five years later the Very Reverend William Braithwaite Clarke – a man of both God and geology – was chipping away at a rock face near Hartley in the Blue Mountains when he found particles of gold gleaming back at him – *gleaming* – in the bright sunshine. Over the next three years he widened his range of fossicking and soon formed the opinion that the whole region would be found 'abundantly rich in gold'.

Finally, he was ready. He had the evidence – a bag of samples – and journeyed to see his friend Governor George Gipps at the vice-regal country residence in Parramatta Park, an English manor in the classic style set in gracious gardens.

Alas, the governor was ailing when he arrived, but still not so sick that his wife would not let the Reverend see him. And yet, when Clarke excitedly opened his bag and laid the gold samples out before him, His Excellency pronounced himself something far less than impressed and a lot more than merely concerned. He quickly cut him short with a dismissive wave of the hand, saying, 'Put it away, Mr Clarke, before we all have our throats cut.'[34]

For Governor Gipps appreciated what the Reverend perhaps did not: the discovery of gold would change things. The whole continent was right at the point of transition from a penal colony to being something more, perhaps even a country in its own right. A country with its institutions, certainly, where a fair measure of its population was putting down roots, but those institutions are not so grand and those roots not so deep that a gold rush couldn't turn everything upside down, and the mob might rule. And so for the moment, that was where it was left . . .

———

In other parts of the world, within less than a decade, the challenge by the broad mass of people to the rule of the elite was not so easily averted.

In late 1847, a 29-year-old German philosopher and law graduate by the name of Karl Marx – at the time living in Brussels because his homeland had denied him freedom of speech in the press due to his dangerously revolutionary ideas – was putting the finishing touches to a pamphlet he had worked up with his great friend Friedrich Engels. Engels was the 27-year-old bon vivant eldest son of a wealthy German cotton manufacturer, who had recognised, he felt, a genius in Marx that perhaps even Marx himself was not aware of.

It was a pamphlet they called the Manifest der Kommunistischen Partei, which became known in the English-speaking world as *The Communist Manifesto*. Using analysis that was revolutionary in every sense of the word, their firm view was expressed in the manifesto's opening line: 'The history of all hitherto existing society is the history of class struggles.'[35] Most pointedly, they asserted that the working class was being exploited by those who owned the means of production and that the capitalist system was inherently unfair. They proposed an entirely new economic structure for the world, presenting a vision whereby the workers would and should rise against their oppressors, seize the means of production, and the world's wealth would thereafter be redistributed on a far more equal basis: *'Jeder nach seinen Fähigkeiten, jedem nach seinen Bedürfnissen'* – 'From each according to their means, to each according to their needs.'[36]

Workers of the world unite!

According to them, workers around the world were beginning to rise against their oppressors, and their chief hope was that their book would encourage others to do the same.

Within weeks – not because of Marx, but because of the forces he identified – that very thing began to happen across Europe, as a broad mass of the population in country after country rose up against the traditional establishment elites and challenged their iniquitous rule.

First, in February, the good citoyens of Paris, France, and most particularly the humble workers, flooded into the streets in revolt at the rule of 'Le Bourgeois Monarch,' King Louis-Philippe and his Prime Minister, François Pierre Guillaume Guizot. 'Down with Guizot!' they shouted. 'Down with the sold ones! Down with Louis-Philippe! *Vive la Réforme!*'

Erecting barricades, throwing pavement stones at the Parisian municipal guards – so fiery was their rage, so great their numbers, that Guizot resigned. Still, that did not quell the uprising and on the next day French soldiers fired directly into the milling crowd, killing 52 and wounding hundreds of others.

'Aux armes, citoyens! Formez vos bataillons!'

And so they did. In such numbers and with such fury – all of it concentrated on the royal palace – that within two days King Louis-Philippe put himself in a disguise and, travelling as 'Mr Smith', fled to England, a country that was itself in turmoil . . .

———————

In England, a little over a decade earlier – in a curious coalition of six liberal parliamentarians combining forces with six forward-thinking working men – a committee had been formed as the foundation of a movement that then and there was engaged in a fierce struggle for the nation's destiny. In 1838 they had published the People's Charter, which had six basic planks in its platform, calling for enormous political change in Great Britain: the vote for every man of sound mind over 21 not in gaol; secret ballot elections; no property qualifications for members of parliament; parliamentary members to be paid, enabling poor people to stand, too; equal constituencies so everyone's vote was worth the same amount; and annual parliaments, with all members elected for a year only.[37]

In the first instance, when there was a violent outbreak by 'Chartist' rioters in the North of England in support of these claims, that outbreak was put down by troops under the command of Sir Charles Napier.

When Sir Charles arrived in Manchester on 6 May 1839, it was to find handbills being handed out to the working people that included the seditious lines:

L et England's sons then prime her guns,
  And save each good man's daughter;
In tyrant's blood baptise your sons,
And every villain slaughter.
By pike and sword your freedom strive to gain,
Or make one bloody Moscow of old England's plain.[38]

Sir Charles – whose later recorded view was that, 'The best way to quiet a country is a good thrashing, followed by great kindness afterwards. Even the wildest chaps are thus tamed'[39] – proved up to the task of quelling the revolt. Going to see the Chartist leaders, he was nothing if not frank:

'I understand,' he told them, 'you are to have a great meeting on Kersal Moor, with a view to laying your grievances before Parliament. You are quite right to do so, and I will take care that neither soldier nor policeman shall be within sight to disturb you. But meet peaceably, for if there is the least disturbance I shall be amongst you and at the sacrifice of my life, if necessary, do my duty. Now go and do yours!'[40]

The meeting subsequently took place in perfect peace.

This was consistent with the proclamation of one of their original leaders, the parliamentarian William Lovett, who had always insisted that Chartism should 'inform the mind' rather than 'captivate the sense' and so succeed 'without commotion or violence'.[41] At this time most Chartists still held that the way to achieve their ends was not by armed insurrection but 'moral force': by making their case in a united and coherent fashion, frequently from a podium in front of massive 'monster meetings' and by petition, collectively persuading those who opposed them and those wavering on the virtues of their case. Together, united and forward! Another key was land, trying to ensure that by collective action the workers could join the propertied classes. The Chartist Cooperative Land Company was formed, where workers combined their resources to buy estates that could then be subdivided into two-, three- and four-acre lots and handed over to the lucky workers who won what was effectively a lottery.

They continued to be fond of mass meetings, and on one occasion a decade later, 10 April 1848 – at a time when 'physical force' Chartists were holding greater sway – no fewer than 150,000 Chartists turned up at Kennington Common to hear the speakers and then form a procession to try to deliver a petition to Parliament. This petition threatened that, if ignored, it would see the people create a separate national assembly, even as they pressed the Queen to dissolve Parliament until such a time as their charter was made law. The march on Parliament began well, but then the Redcoats again turned up in their own great numbers and threatened to shoot those at the front of the procession if they dared to try to cross the Thames.

Would they? Should they?

. . .

. . .

No.

Whatever the virtues of 'physical force', it was quite another matter when your enemies had more than you did. Ultimately, the Chartists were unwilling to take on this armed force with an armed insurrection of their own, and the march splintered and petered out. Nevertheless, the panicked Parliament immediately pushed through new legislation on sedition – *encouraging one's fellow subjects to rebel against their state* – and treason – *betraying one's country by aiding and abetting another state* – so that such massed meetings as had been witnessed were effectively banned. For the Treason Felony Act 1848 stated that any person levying war, 'by Force or Constraint to compel

Her or Them to change Her or Their measures or counsels, or in order to put any Force or Constraint upon or in order to intimidate or overawe both Houses or either House of Parliament, or to move or stir any Foreigner or Stranger with Force to invade the United Kingdom or any other of Her Majesty's Dominions or Countries under the Obeisance of Her Majesty, Her Heirs or Successors, and such Compassings, Imaginations, Inventions, Devices, or Intentions, or any of them, shall express, utter, or declare, by publishing any Printing or Writing, or by open and advised Speaking, or by any overt Act or Deed, every Person so offending shall be guilty of felony, and being convicted thereof shall be liable, at the Discretion of the Court, to be transported beyond the Seas for the Term of his or her natural Life.'[42] (By downgrading punishment from death to transportation to the colonies, it was hoped that juries would be more ready to convict.)

In this case, the heavy hand of the law did make the more outspoken elements of the Chartist movement back down as things began to calm.

Elsewhere the struggle went on, and nowhere was it fiercer than in Ireland, where for the previous two years the rains had barely stopped falling and potato blight had taken a terribly strong hold. All over the country, where green fields had once provided the vegetable in such quantity that the people could eat potato for breakfast, lunch and dinner – and did so – there was now a stinking black mess. Without potatoes the people began to starve and unrest took hold. Of course they could not blame the government for the rains or the blight, but there were other things for those suffering and starving to take aim at.

Right at the height of the starvation, when the exhausted priests were worked overtime providing last rites to the dying, Ireland was a net exporter of food. The grip of starvation was killing the people, but the political grip of Britain on the land was stronger. The need for commerce to continue, for the profits of the merchants buying and selling Irish produce, was more powerful than any other consideration – most particularly when the starving poor of Ireland had no money to buy the food anyway.

In the stately home of Tenakill, in the village of Raheen, Queen's County, a 42-year-old man by the name of Fintan Lalor was in the thick of the struggle for the people's rights from the beginning. Born of a family of wealthy tenant farmers, fiercely Catholic and nationalist to the core, Lalor was consumed with passion for nothing less than the Republican revolutionary cause: Ireland must throw off its wretched British shackles, return the country to its people and allow the land of the emerald green to be in charge of its own destiny. In this cause he was following in the footsteps of his father, Patrick, who twenty years earlier had not only actively advocated the repeal of the 1800 Act of Union that had created the United Kingdom of Great Britain and Ireland, but also led the charge against the iniquitous British practice of requiring Irish Catholics to pay a tithe – in part according to how much land you owned – to the newly installed Church of England for the upkeep of its clergy and maintenance of its assets.

The spirit of the anti-tithe movement was captured by a famous letter penned by the Bishop of Kildare and Leighlin, Dr James Doyle: 'There are many noble traits in the Irish character, mixed with failings which have always raised obstacles to their own well-being; but an innate love of justice, and an indomitable hatred of oppression, is like a gem upon the front of our nation, which no darkness can obscure. To this fine quality I trace their hatred of tithes. May it be as lasting as their love of justice!'[43]

Exactly. Patt Lalor – so the story goes – while attending a meeting in Maryborough on 10 February 1831, openly declared that he would never again pay tithes. He was proud to say that though the Tithe Men could take his property and put it on the market if they liked, he felt sure his countrymen had such high respect for his cause that no-one would put their hand up to buy it.

When the local clergyman sent his bailiff to take away 25 of Lalor's sheep, Lalor was able to get a brief enough legal intervention to have each animal branded with the word 'TITHE'. They were taken back and put on sale before a large crowd at the Mountrath fair, and not *one* hand was raised to buy them at any price! When the clergyman's agent, Mr Brough, suddenly bought them himself, the crowd surged forward, only to be stopped by Lalor. He was a man of peace, and there were other ways.

As no-one in the region would buy the sheep, Brough had them taken by a bailiff to Dublin, but that unfortunate bailiff found that all the way to that city, every time he stopped for food and shelter, doors were closed to him. He arrived at Dublin a shattered, exhausted man, only to find no-one would buy them there, either. The sheep were then shipped to Liverpool. 'However a priest of Irish origin and faithful to the cause warned the salesmen in Liverpool what had happened with the sheep in Ireland. The sheep weren't sold in Liverpool either and were then driven to Manchester where the story goes that they died on the road.' The Church of England never received a penny from Lalor's sheep, while, as the elected representative of the Queen's County (1832–35), Lalor was able to continue to fight the good fight in no less than the British House of Commons.

The eldest of Patrick Lalor's twelve children, Fintan, however, had no patience for such comparatively gentle means of protest. He had a rage within that drove him away from peaceful resolution and towards bloody revolution. To that end, despite being frequently ill, he continually displayed his eloquence and courage for the cause in the public domain, speaking at meetings and writing to journals, while also doing more clandestine work away from the gaze of the authorities. Inspiring passion in others is where he truly excelled. Absent rich British landlords taking rent from the poor Irish farmers working their land – Lalor described this as no more than: 'the robber's right by which the lands of this country are beholden in fee of the British Crown. I acknowledge no right of property in a small class which goes to abrogate the rights of a numerous people . . . I deny and challenge all such rights, howsoever founded or enforced. I challenge them as founded only on the code of the brigand, and enforced only by the sanction of the hangman.'[44]

Another thundering editorial published in *The Irish Felon* on 1 July 1848 was addressed directly to the British government: 'We hold the present existing government of this island, and all existing rights of property in our soil, to be mere usurpation and tyranny, and to be null and void as of moral effect; and our purpose is to abolish them utterly, or lose our lives in the attempt. The right founded on conquest and affirmed by laws made by the conquerors themselves, we regard as no other than the right of the robber on a larger scale. We owe no obedience to laws enacted by another nation without our assent; nor respect to assumed rights of property which are starving and exterminating our people.'[45]

Fintan Lalor was equally forthright in what he and his people intended to do about it:

'We have determined to set about creating, as speedily as possible, a military organisation.'[46]

And even then he was only warming up, urging Ireland to 'close for our final struggle with England' to ensure the country could be 'Ireland her own, and all therein, from the sod to the sky . . . without suit or service, faith or fealty, rent or render, to any power under Heaven'.[47]

'Remember this,' he famously wrote in another article for *The Irish Felon* on 22 July 1848, his words strong enough to echo through the ages, 'that *somewhere, somehow*, and by *somebody*, a beginning must be made . . . [48] Who strikes the first blow for Ireland? Who draws first blood for Ireland? Who wins a wreath that will be green for ever?'[49]

In the face of this passion made public – a very dangerous pursuit when being hanged for treason was a real possibility – Patrick Lalor's relationship with his son became so strained that it was close to rupture. The father feared the consequence of his son's revolutionary zeal.

Less than a week after publishing that last diatribe, brave Fintan Lalor was arrested and thrown into prison. His work, however, would go on. All over Ireland, others too had been rising.

In Tipperary, Irishmen of the Young Ireland movement had launched a nationalist revolt against English rule, standing their ground against British forces in nothing less than a cabbage patch, intent on declaring an independent Irish republic. True, the revolt had been crushed by the British forces and many of the local lads arrested, convicted and transported to Australia for sedition, but it was a start!

While the revolutionaries needed the Irish peasants to rise and join them in the revolt, the most urgent concern of the peasantry at this point was to simply feed themselves as the potato famine bit deeper and deeper, taking the lives of no fewer than one million Irish. For many, the only way out appeared to be to actually get out, sell their belongings for whatever they could and secure passage for themselves and their families on ships bound elsewhere – with the United States of America and Australia being favourites.

As to Fintan Lalor, though subsequently released from prison because he was so ill, he died not long afterwards and was buried an Irish hero. The famed Irish patriot Charles Gavan Duffy would describe him as 'the most original and intense of all the men who have preached revolutionary politics in Ireland'.[50]

Though the youngest Lalor had deeply admired his eldest brother's political passion, 21-year-old Peter was a far quieter type of man. Educated at Dublin's prestigious Trinity College (despite his Catholicism) where he studied hard to be a civil engineer – he really preferred building things to tearing them down – he had not the time, interest or disposition to become involved in the nuts and bolts, the cloak and dagger, the fire and brimstone needed to stoke a revolution. The last thing the Lalor family needed at this point was more trouble, and the quietly spoken Peter steered clear of it – well clear of it.

Like so many of his compatriots, Peter began to contemplate joining the millions of Irish who were leaving. In those new lands, there were apparently thousands of acres to spare, enough to build a whole new life upon, a place where a people could prosper.

————

In Italy, meanwhile, a close equivalent to the Young Ireland movement was La Giovine Italia – Young Italy – devoted to liberating the lands around Milan and Venice from the grip of the oppressive Austrian Empire so that a unified Italian republic could be formed.

In the latter part of the 1840s, the most legendary of the military leaders in this struggle was Giuseppe Garibaldi, who encouraged the people to rise and join him, before subsequently supporting, by force of arms, the Roman Republic.

One of his citizens-turned-soldier was a highly educated 32-year-old former seminarian by the name of Raffaello Carboni, hailing from the northern Italian town of Urbino. Physically, he was a small man, but some clues to his rather flamboyant passion for the cause at hand were provided by his flowing red hair and beard, the flashing quixotic look he had in his eyes and the fact that he generated such energy that he had a great deal of trouble keeping still. In times of peace, this energy led him to learn five languages and as many instruments, travel all over Europe, become an author, journalist and composer. In times of war, an activist on many political fronts, it led him to the battlefront under Garibaldi.

Where there was action, there was Carboni. In the course of battle he received no fewer than three wounds, including a particularly bad one to his left leg. He escaped with his life – just – and though there was no diminution in his passion for the cause, still he decided it would be wiser to leave Italy for a time.

———————

Now, if America was spared such uprisings it was because their own revolt against iniquitous rule had already occurred some three-quarters of a century earlier with the American War of Independence, and their own republic had taken a strong hold.

And yet there, too, something far more intoxicating than revolution was in the air.

In California in late January 1848, a building foreman named John Marshall was just completing construction on a sawmill by the American River for his boss John Sutter, at a place called Sutter's Mill, near Coloma, when something amazing happened. Having allowed the natural flow of the river to widen and deepen the tailrace overnight, the next morning he noticed a shiny metal in the channel bed. It was . . . sort of . . . golden.

Taking it to Sutter, the two had it tested and the news was confirmed: it was gold.

Marshall was elated, Sutter . . . deflated.

The joy that men have felt through the ages at finding buried treasure is all the more elevated when the treasure is a gift from Mother Nature herself. However, Sutter felt the equally familiar fear of one already wealthy who realises his whole world risks being upended at the hands of others, others less worthy, who are seeking an entirely different type of wealth.

For all that, because Sutter had huge plans in this area – not just for a lumber mill but for building an entire agricultural empire – he managed to convince Marshall to keep quiet about the discovery . . . for the moment.

Yet gold – *gold!* – and secrecy simply do not go together. Since forever, there has been something about that lustrous, shiny metal that makes men whisper excitedly to confidants, who inevitably whisper the news to others, and others still, until those whispers in the wind amount to a breeze, a blow and then a gale, until a full-blown storm is underway.

It was not long after the news reached San Francisco, a small outpost of just 1000 people, that newspaper publisher and merchant Samuel Brannan set up a store to sell gold prospecting supplies. 'A tall man, darkly handsome, whose hair fell in soft brown waves to his shoulders from under a broad-brimmed beaver hat, he was soon to be seen strutting down the main street clutching in his right hand a vial of gold. 'Gold! Gold! Gold from the American River!' announced Brannan.

He was a newspaper publisher – why not put it on the front page? The answer was simple: after the journalists and production staff found out what the following day's article was, they had all simply left for the goldfields and there was no-one left to put the paper out and . . .

And what is that sound?

What sound?

That . . . rushing sound!

It was the sound of vast swathes of humanity moving, by every means of locomotion imaginable, up every path, track and road they could find – coming from all directions – towards the spot on the American River where gold had been found. The 1849 gold rush had begun within days of Brannan broadcasting the news, and Sutter was soon proven quite right in his fears. For not only were his own workers among those who abandoned their posts on his lumber mills to pursue gold, but the once quiet spot was soon inundated with hundreds and then thousands of would-be miners – many of them veterans of the just finished war against Mexico – who stole his cattle, 'harvested' his crops and took over his land. He was soon ruined, not that anybody particularly noticed or cared. They were too busy going after gold, and finding it!

News of the find reached Europe in mid-October[51] 1848, where it caused a fevering of the brow of many men who immediately left for California, and a scratching of the brows of the two German intellectuals who had penned *The Communist Manifesto*: Karl Marx and Friedrich Engels. Their views of the economic world had simply not encompassed this.

As Engels put it in a letter to Marx, the discovery of gold was a case 'not provided for in the *Manifesto*: creation of large new markets out of nothing'.[52]

This would require some more analysis. Who knew what effect such a discovery would have on the war between the economic classes? One thing was certain: the world was indeed turning upside down now that the working class was suddenly becoming rich, and many a rich man who had previously become wealthy on the back of that working-class labour now denied him was going broke!

And all of it at a time when the oppressed classes across the world were getting themselves organised to *demand* the rights so long denied them. Who knew just what changes these two powerful forces – arising at the same time in history and both attacking the established order – would work on the world, even in its most remote parts?

CHAPTER ONE

FROM GOLDEN FLEECE TO GOLD ITSELF...

Potent as was the wonderful lamp of Aladdin, and magnificent as were its successes, the power of gold has equalled in its marvellous effects all that the warm orient fancy has pictured for us in the Arabian Nights. Gold has done even more than ever mere magician achieved. It certainly has operated magically in Australia, and in no part of the country has it created greater marvels than in Ballarat . . .[1]

W. B. Withers in *History of Ballarat*

Gold rush!

In Australia, the good tidings of what is happening in California breaks on 23 December 1848, when, under the banner headline NEW GOLD MINE, *The Sydney Morning Herald* announces:

We have received, per Euphemia, dates from California to the 20th of June . . . The only item of interest is the news from the gold diggers – other matters receive no attention. The whole country is in a state of turmoil, and everybody is flying to the gold region to reap a fortune. All the seaport towns are deserted. Out of a population of nearly one thousand, San Francisco only contains about fifty or sixty souls, and these would leave were it possible. The news of the gold discoveries has spread with lightning speed, and the minister, merchant, artisan,

mechanic, farmer, labourer, and loafer, have all gone
to seek their fortune. Farms and crops are deserted,
and all branches of business are at a stand . . .[2]

It is fascinating news, with one particular complication: where exactly is California? Most Australians have never heard of it. Quickly enough, consultation with the atlas reveals it is a region on the west coast of the United States of America, on the other side of the Pacific from the east coast of Australia. This is a tad problematic as no regular shipping lines run between the two coasts, but such is the clamour to cross over that within a bare few months there is many a ship seen splitting the heads of Sydney's Port Jackson and sailing into the swell directly north-east, laden with thousands of men eager to try their luck on these new diggings.

As a matter of fact, in time there are so many men leaving, even whole families, that it threatens the very stability of the colony. For without all those men, who will run the farms, the foundries and factories, the stores and silos, not to mention repair the roads and shepherd the sheep? Who will do the work necessary to make the colony grow and become strong in this oft-hostile continent? With just 200,000 people in the entire country, it simply cannot sustain the continued leaching of able-bodied men to foreign goldfields. There seems to be only one answer: Australia must find its own gold.

In the meantime, they would just have to put up with the heavy exodus of men.

11 November 1850, Melbourne, news is received at 'The Chalet'

If there is a little bit of Europe in Melbourne at this time, it is to be found at the end of the long carriage driveway on the estate of *Jolimont en Murs*, past the grotto, shrubberies and bountiful diamond-and-sickle-shaped garden beds in the latest style, to the flowering-creeper-adorned house where Charles La Trobe and his family live. It is a place known by many a loyal subject as 'The Chalet' for its uniquely Continental form.

'Small as our establishment is,' La Trobe had described it to his older sister Charlotte in England, 'I assure you that there is not a more comfortable, well regulated and more tasty one in this part of the world both without and within.'³

Though modest by London standards, the estate is really something compared to the rest of Melbourne and, though the setting is a triumph of taste rather than treasure, at least the glassware is crystal and the silverware actual silver. Invitations are highly prized and, on this particular night, while Charles La Trobe presides at the head of the table and one of the guests is regaling the assembly with a very jolly story of how in India – if you can *believe* it! – they use leaves of the banana plant for plates, he is interrupted by the sound of thundering hooves and carriage wheels coming to a halt on the gravel driveway. In an instant, the insistent pounding of at least *two* sticks comes on the door. Whoever has arrived is in a desperate hurry.

Charles La Trobe is not perturbed, however, and as one of the servants answers the summons he neatens up his neckerchief and comments that perhaps the pounding on the door has come from 'a new governor in search of a night's lodging!'⁴

Begging your leave, Your Honour, but the new arrivals prove to be the Lord Mayor of Melbourne, William Nicholson, and his immediate predecessor in the post, Augustus Frederick Adolphus Greeves. Nicholson, who for some reasons has a rag tied around one of his fingers, is flourishing an Adelaide newspaper that has just arrived – highly prized, for that city usually gets its news from England between five and eight days earlier than Melbourne.

'Your Honour,' he says, 'allow me to draw your attention to the fact that the Separation Bill has passed through both Houses. The news is spreading quickly, and I shall be unable to restrain the people.'⁵

La Trobe, of course, understands only too well the import of the revelation, that the British Parliament had actually passed this Separation Bill on 1 August, a little over three months earlier. It is what his colony has been straining towards for well over a decade: separation from New South Wales. It means that its six parliamentarians will return from the New South Wales Legislative Council in Sydney, and, if elected or appointed, instead be part of a separate Legislative Council set up in Melbourne . . .

They would have, as the other colonies would have, their own Constitution, their own Supreme Court! In the Port Phillip District – soon to be renamed 'Victoria' under the legislation, in honour of the Queen – they would no longer be subject to Sydney's capricious whims but would be able to rule themselves, to make laws and gain control over general revenue from taxes and levies on the colony's subjects (even if the Crown would retain control over the revenue from the sale of land).

La Trobe – who realises he is about to go from being a mere Superintendent to a Lieutenant-Governor, while the Governor of the senior colony, New South Wales, Sir Charles Augustus FitzRoy, will be installed as the 'Governor-General' – is gracious enough to allow that the people *may* celebrate that night, at which point the Lord Mayor thanks him profusely and immediately heads off to light his private bonfire, the signal the good people of Melbourne have been waiting for that their general jubilation may be unfettered.

And of course it does not stop there. For not only do those celebrations continue well into the night, but the general joy is so profound that they go on for many days more, too. *The Melbourne Morning Herald & General Daily Advertiser* sets the tone on its front page with its special-edition headline the next afternoon:

EXTRAORDINARY
GLORIOUS NEWS! SEPARATION AT LAST!![6]

7 January 1851, on the approaches to Port Jackson, impatience builds

He is a huge man, nervously twirling his black moustache and anxiously pacing the deck of the good ship *Emma* as it blow-bobs its way through the heads of Port Jackson and into Sydney Harbour. When he had left this same harbour two years earlier to try his luck on the Californian goldfields, it had been with the hope that he would return, travelling first class, laden with treasure. Instead, all he truly brings back is an idea – an idea that because the landscape of the Californian goldfields is reminiscent of a valley he had once seen 17 years earlier, up Bathurst way, perhaps that valley might have gold too! True, an American acquaintance in whom he had confided this view had been derisive.

'There's no gold in the country you're going to,' he'd said. 'And if there is, that darned Queen of yours won't let you dig it . . .'[7]

Rising to the occasion, 34-year-old Edward Hammond Hargraves had taken off his hat, adopted what he assumed to be a magisterial pose and replied, 'There's as much gold in the country I am going to as there is in California; and Her Most Gracious Majesty the Queen, God bless her, will make me one of her Gold Commissioners.'[8]

Hargraves remains so convinced he is right that, shortly after landing on the Sydney docks, he borrows £105 from a friend to buy a horse and some supplies, and on 5 February 1851 sets off from Sydney heading west.

Five days later Hargraves and his exhausted nag arrive in the rough region of their destination and pull into the Wellington Inn at Guyong, which he knows to be run by Captain John Lister of the ship *Wave*, the one that had brought him to Australian shores 18 years earlier.

Upon entering this rustic establishment, Hargraves learns that only a little more than six months earlier, alas, the good captain was killed when, on a trip to Bathurst, he was thrown from his gig.

The establishment, however, is still being run by Lister's widow (who remembers Hargraves at once after he mentions his name) and her 22-year-old son, John Hardman Australia Lister. Over dinner Hargraves decides to confide in her precisely why he has come, the theory he has nurtured for nearly a year now, that not far from where they are now seated there are riches beyond a man's imagining!

Yet, he would later write: 'It occurred to me that I could not prosecute my plans efficiently without assistance . . . After dinner, therefore, I disclosed to her the object of my visit, and begged her to procure a black fellow as a guide to the spot I wished to visit first . . . She entered with a woman's heartiness into my views, and offered me the assistance of her son . . . who, she assured me, knew the country well.'[9]

And so John Lister does – and neither is the young man a stranger to the idea that there is gold in this region. As a matter of fact, upon the mantelpiece of the inn are two chunks of quartz from the Upper Turon that he proudly shows Hargraves. On carefully examining the samples, Hargraves tells Lister that one of them resembles rock found near goldmines.

Thus acquainted, on the morning of 12 February 1851, the two head off with their two horses and a fresh packhorse. From the relatively open country around Guyong, within a very short time the gullies start to fall away, the trees close in, and the men are soon nudging and trudging their way down the summery, dry creek bed of Lewis Ponds Creek.

The further they go, the more excited Hargraves becomes as the country starts to resemble more and more the gold-bearing landscape he saw in California.

Some 14 miles on, Hargraves is beside himself with excitement as the familiar quartz, granite and slate outcrops become more apparent and, the tree-cover aside, the hills and gullies start to look exactly as they did in the Sierra Nevada.

'I felt myself surrounded by gold; and with tremendous anxiety panted for the moment of trial, when my magician's wand should transform this trackless wilderness into a region of countless wealth.'[10]

First things first, however . . . Not even gold should get between a 20-stone man and his luncheon. Two miles further up the creek bed, in the middle of the day, he and John arrive at a particularly pleasant spot where Lewis Ponds Creek intersects with Radigan's Gully, where water is easily obtained and the horses can slake their thirst. To this point, Hargraves has not shared his excitement with young Lister, but now is as good a time as any. After they wolf down their cold beef and damper, washed down by billy tea, he tells him straight.

All around them, right now, Hargraves begins, and right beneath them in the creek that Lister has just been wading through, there is gold – *gold!*

Lister stares back with complete astonishment, but Hargraves is quite serious.

'And now,' the older man announces portentously, 'I will find some gold.'[11]

The young man watches intently as Hargraves takes his pick and digs a small amount of dirt from a rock formation that runs at right angles to the creek before taking his trowel to fill a pan with sodden earth. The tin pan, which he has brought all the way from California, is some 18 inches across the top, 12 inches across the bottom, and its sloping sides run four inches deep. Taking a stick, he mixes the dirt into a fine batter and then begins his careful 'panning'. Slowly, bit by bit, he sluices the earth out of the pan with the water from the nearby creek. The soil thins and washes away, leaving . . . leaving . . . leaving some pebbles and . . . *there!* . . . a very small speck of glittering gold!

'Here it is!'[12] he exclaims.

The effect is instantaneous. This news is not just promising, not just good, not even great. This news, Hargraves knows from the moment he sees the gleam in his pan, is life-changing for him and his companion, and it will lift the entire country. The older man repeats the process five times and pans some specks of gold on four occasions.

Drawing himself up and puffing himself out, he makes a considered pronouncement to the stupefied John Lister, indeed to all the world, as if he is standing behind a pulpit: 'This is a memorable day in the history of New South Wales. I shall be a baronet, you will be knighted, and my old horse will be stuffed, put in a glass case, and sent to the British Museum.'[13]

Blank-faced, Lister blinks up at this self-proclaimed aristocrat. Hargraves is not joking, at least not totally. At this instant he really does feel himself 'to be a great man'.[14] All that is necessary now, he says, is for them to discover '[payable] gold, and it will be the luckiest day that has happened to New South Wales.'[15]

Once back at Lister's Inn, Hargraves is so excited he can barely speak. Already, above and beyond whatever personal fortune he might make at these diggings, he knows that if he can just follow up on this initial discovery by finding gold in greater quantities to prove that it is 'payable' – of sufficient quantity and accessibility to ensure economic profit – it will be of enormous benefit to the colony, and, far more importantly, of enormous benefit to *him*. Beyond seeking an appropriate reward for founding such an industry, he will surely have his dream realised and be made a commissioner of the goldfields, in the same way the government already has a commissioner of Crown lands. (The prestige! The *salary!*)

Oddly, when Hargraves and young John arrive back at Guyong, the rest of the Lister family remains quietly unimpressed with the 'discovery' – as a matter of fact, they say they can barely see it.

'There! *There!* Can you not see it *now?*' No, no . . . no, they can't. In the end, it is only with the aid of a glass tumbler placed upside down over the specks that they acknowledge they can see it after all. Just. If you say that really is gold.

Clearly, it is going to take something more than what the men have already found to impress the government.

Still, before turning in for the night at Mrs Lister's inn, Hargraves writes a 'memorandum of the discovery':[16]

> Wednesday 12th February, 1851
>   Discovered gold this day at - - -; named the Diggings
> Hargraves, who was the first Discoverer in New South
> Wales of the metal in the earth in a similar manner
> as found in California. This is a memorable day.[17]

The most obvious place to continue the search is towards the Macquarie River, in the area first penetrated by Europeans in the person of the great explorer Charles Sturt a little over two decades earlier. The following morning, young Lister suggests that his great friend James Tom, who lives over yonder at the Cornish Settlement, Byng, is the man who knows the land best.

Why not take him as their guide, John suggests, in the same way that John had been the guide along Lewis Ponds Creek? Hargraves is agreeable and makes what the other two would ever after swear is a firm commitment: 'Whatever arises from the discovery, we will share in it. It will be a very handsome thing if we find payable gold.'[18]

The trio search over the next eight days down Lewis Pond Creek towards its junction with Summer Hill Creek, itself a tributary of the Macquarie River in the area known as Yorkey's Corner. Although they find small particles of gold everywhere, they do not manage to find it in the greater, payable quantities they need. More than a little disappointed, they return to Guyong, where they come to another agreement: they will now split up. Lister and James Tom will continue searching in the area around the Upper Turon River, while Hargraves will set off[19] for the gullies around Dubbo.

———————

When Hargraves returns to Guyong a month later, not only is his horse stuffed, but so is he – and he has found no more traces of significant gold. For their part, Tom and Lister have found small traces of gold in several locations, though still nothing truly payable.

It is decided that the best thing now would be to construct a Californian gold cradle, called a 'rocker', designed to do the same job as panning, albeit on a much larger scale. With the assistance of Tom's younger brother, William, a skilled carpenter, the cradle is constructed in the front room of the Tom family residence.

A little like a sturdy version of a baby's cradle, the Californian cradle is a wooden box, about a yard long, inside of which is a series of ever longer trays. Above the top tray is a hopper, a box with one vertical side composed of bars that allow all but solid pieces to pass through.

By putting, hopefully, 'paydirt' into the hopper, pouring water upon it and using a lever to rock the cradle from side to side, the water rushes down and breaks up the dirt before cascading over the lower trays. The muddy paydirt becomes muddy water, becomes a tiny muddy waterfall and, because there is a small rim or 'riffle' at the end of each tray, whatever gold is in that muddy waterfall collects at the bottom riffle. Of course, one needs a ready water supply and a lot of labour, but this technique had been proven in California to be the most efficient way of extracting the gold. If the dirt is of the thick clay variety, sometimes it needs to undergo a process of 'puddling', whereby it is put into a large tub of water and broken up with a spade, or even the feet of a miner, before being fed into the cradle.

By this time Hargraves is quietly eager to report (and of course claim any reward and receive all accolades) to the New South Wales Government in Sydney unquestionable evidence of the existence of what will be the first payable goldfield in New South Wales. And he certainly feels that *he* personally has found it.

John Lister accompanies him for part of the way, and they stop to prospect on Campbells River and at Mutton Falls, south of Bathurst on the Fish River. When they again meet with no success, the two decide to part company. Before separating, however, they confirm their agreement once more – whoever finds payable gold will write the other, for they are all equal partners.

Lister then returns to Guyong to find that the Tom brothers have taken the cradle out for a trial run, and the machine works! Over three days they have found 17 grains of gold between them. No, it is not necessarily something to write home about, but it is certainly enough to write to Edward Hargraves about, as per their agreement.

20 March – 1 April 1851, a rough-looking character arrives in Macquarie Street, Sydney

Someone to see you, Mr Thomson. An enormous chap by the name of Edward Hargraves. Says he has something of the greatest importance to the colony to show you.

Well, Edward Deas Thomson, the Colonial Secretary of New South Wales, is far too busy and important to see him now. Hargraves will just have to wait until he has finished his duties with the Legislative Council of Parliament. And so wait Hargraves does. On the morning of their first of three meetings, a terrible downpour bursts upon Sydney Town in general and Hargraves in particular. No matter, in the vest of his pocket Hargraves has something that helps to keep him warm: a German matchbox containing the specks of gold he has gathered. True, the specks are not so numerous nor so weighty that they couldn't altogether be held 'on a threepenny bit',[20] but it is gold, alright. When at last Hargraves is granted his audience with the Colonial Secretary in his splendid office at Macquarie Place just off Bridge Street – all plush carpets, mahogany furniture, landscape paintings and portraits on the wall staring down on them – this time the discoverer is not told to put his scant gold samples away for fear of having their throats cut.

Rather, Thomson immediately if reluctantly recognises the significance of the find, if indeed that find is verified.

'If this is gold country, Mr Hargraves,' says he in tones of one whose utterances are mostly commands but is now moved to a rare moment of reflection, 'it will stop the Home Government from sending us any more convicts, and prevent emigration to California; but it comes on us like a clap of thunder, and we are scarcely prepared to credit it.'[21]

Once apprised of the news, Governor FitzRoy writes to the Secretary of State[22] in London, Lord Earl Grey, that he suspects the gold sample presented has come from California.

7–14 April 1851, at the junction of Summer Hill and Lewis Pond creeks, 30 miles due north of Guyong, the hand that rocks the cradle

After setting off on this morning of 7 April, John Lister and now William Tom Jnr decide to try their luck once more around Yorkey's Corner at the junction of the Summer Hill and Lewis Ponds creeks. It takes a day and a half to get to the site, guiding their horses along the bank of the creek bed, and not long after midday they arrive. Just as with Hargraves, they secure the horses and have a quick spot of lunch before beginning their search.

And . . . sure enough, just minutes after beginning their exploration of the creek bed a mile or so below its junction, William Tom suddenly stops and stares.

'I have found a bit of gold!' he calls excitedly to his companion.

'You are only joking . . .'[23] Lister replies, disbelieving that it could be this easy.

But no – there, indeed, sitting on the creek bed, is a small nugget that weighs 3/5 of an ounce. Success!

The following day they set up their cradle by the creek bed and as one man loads the hopper with what they hope is paydirt, another ladles water upon the top of the soil.

There! And there! And *there!*

Small specks of gold are shining back at them in the dappled light.

On 12 April the two young men set off for the Wellington Inn with no less than four ounces of gold carefully secured – enough to confirm beyond any doubt that, and this is the key, there is 'payable' gold here. As per their agreement with Hargraves, John Lister writes to the older man, bearing glad tidings of the success of the cradle and the location where they have found their four ounces of gold. Upon receipt of the letter, Hargraves immediately races back – here is the evidence he has been waiting for!

2 May 1851, Sydney Town stops with a start

Typically, beneath a banner headline, *The Sydney Morning Herald* is the first to confirm the rumours that have been swirling: 'THE GOLD DISCOVERY. It is no longer any secret that gold has been found in the earth in several places in the western country. The fact was first established on the 12th February, 1851, by Mr. E. H. Hargraves, a resident of Brisbane Water, who returned from California a few months since . . .

'Mr. Stutchbury, the Government Geologist, is now in the district, and Mr. Hargraves has proceeded there to communicate with him, and in a few weeks we may expect definite information. At present all that is known is that there is gold over a considerable district; whether it is in sufficient quantities to pay for the trouble of obtaining it remains to be ascertained. Should it be found in large quantities a strict system of licensing diggers will be immediately necessary.'[24]

5–6 May 1851, 'Springfield', a deal is done in the home of the Toms

In the scheme of things, it is an extremely important meeting. After arriving breathless back in Guyong, Edward Hargraves meets his partners in the home of the family Tom. By the end of the meeting Hargraves has bought all of the gold the other men have. He does so with a gleam in his eye, for with the gold in *his* possession *he* can be the one who presents the proof that the government seeks – that a serious find has been made.

8 May 1851, Bathurst, Hargraves holds court, and most of the cards

Tonight is a long way out of the usual for the sleepy town of Bathurst. On this evening, if you haven't heard, Edward Hammond Hargraves himself has come to speak with select gentlemen at the Carriers Arms Inn on a subject he knows will interest them all: gold.

It is to be found in their region! 'From the foot of the Big Hill to a considerable distance below Wellington, on the Macquarie,' he says, 'is *one vast gold field*.'[25]

There is one particular place where the gold is so plentiful that he has already established a company of nine miners who, right now, are digging at a 'point of the Summer Hill Creek near its junction with the Macquarie, about 50 miles from here, and 30 from Guyong. Ophir, from the "city of gold" in the Bible, is the name given to these diggings.'[26]

Upon the revelation of the gold's location, there is a stirring through the small assembly, like a strong gust of wind passing over a field of wheat. They shift, they sway, they lean in closer, hanging on his every word.

From the character of some of the country explored, Hargraves concludes, 'gold will be found in mass' and he 'would not be surprised if pieces of 30 or 40 lbs. should be discovered'.[27]

While Bathurst had been a sleepy town, it is now wide awake. Soon after the meeting breaks up late that night, all of the township is abuzz. In the wee hours, as the light of the lantern matches the strangely feverish gleam in their eyes, men closely scan local maps to work out that 'point of the Summer Hill Creek, near its junction with the Macquarie', where the gold apparently lies. The first of the rush begins the following day, as Bathurst begins to empty . . .

Even before the Bathurstians arrive, however, the diggings have received an interesting visitor in the form of the local Commissioner of Crown Lands, Charles Green. Having heard of Hargraves's boasts, he has realised that unlawful activity is taking place. And, sure enough, when he arrives at Ophir, there they are – eight men digging for gold! Alas, when he orders them off for trespassing, they barely look up.

Morning of 14 May 1851, the Ophir Diggings are rushed

Moses would have been no less pleased to show his people the Promised Land.

On this sparkling morning, a supremely proud Edward Hargraves leads no fewer than 37 horsemen – including the government geologist, Samuel Stutchbury – through the bush, around the hills and down into the gully to his now not-so-lost El Dorado. There they find William and James Tom as two relatively anonymous men – bar the fact that they are the only ones so furious they can barely raise spit – amongst *hundreds* of men similarly trying their luck. These include, as the *Bathurst Free Press* notes, so many men from so many walks of life, 'including magistrates plying their picks and cradles most laboriously' that 'there appears every probability of a complete social revolution in the course of time'.[28]

But not to worry about all that for now. This is Hargraves's big moment, and he turns in a bravura performance. Oh, people, surely Beethoven never played the piano, nor Stradivarius presented a newly made violin, nor Shakespeare taken up a quill with more pride than Hargraves now flourishing his pan as he sets to work on some soil by the creek to instantly produce, *voilá*, '21 grains of fine gold'![29]

On the spot, the impressed Samuel Stutchbury issues Hargraves a certificate to the effect that payable gold has been found, which will be forwarded to the Colonial Secretary.

Yet, even before the Colonial Secretary receives that report, the *Bathurst Free Press* has no hesitation in reporting on the matter of Stutchbury's visit: 'The fact of the existence of gold is therefore clearly established, and whatever credit or emolument may arise therefrom, Mr Hargraves is certainly the individual to whom it properly belongs.'[30]

Needless to say, John Lister and the Tom brothers are not equally convinced of their partner's greatness and, in fact, are seething. After all, they had an *agreement* with Hargraves to keep it all secret for the moment and he has *broken* it, all so he can claim to be the discoverer of the gold and get the reward.

15 May 1851, Sydney seethes with excitement

It is like a stone thrown into a pond where instead of the ripples getting smaller the wider they travel, they actually get larger. For on this clear, crisp, late autumnal dawn in Sydney Town, the stone comes in the form of the first edition of *The Sydney Morning Herald* thudding down on doorsteps in the city and handed by newsboys to the first of the city workers.

There! Have you seen it? *There!*

The magic headline comes on the top of page three:

DISCOVERY OF AN EXTENSIVE GOLDFIELD
(FROM THE BATHURST FREE PRESS)

THE existence of gold in the Wellington district
has for a long time been an ascertained fact,
but public attention has never until now been
seriously drawn to the circumstance.[31]

The story goes on to detail the information released by Hargraves,
including his magic phrase that the area around Bathurst is 'one vast
goldfield', and, for the first time, the exact location of where the gold
is to be found!

But, careful, everyone – the paper also gives a small word of
warning:

In the statements made we do not intend to incur
any responsibility. We tell the story as 'twas told
to us. The suddenness with which the announcement
of a discovery of such magnitude has come upon
us – a discovery which must, if true, be productive
of such gigantic results not only to the inhabitants
of these districts but to the whole colony, affects
the mind with astonishment and wonder in such a
manner as almost to unfit it for the deductions of
plain truth, sober reason, and common sense.[32]

And whatever else, the last part is most certainly true: the colony's
collective mind is indeed affected with such 'astonishment and
wonder' that 'sober reason and common sense' are soon in singularly
short supply. A collective madness appears to take hold, so much
so that on this very day people from all walks of life are seen to
leave their lives in the city, buy picks, shovels, wheelbarrows and
every digging implement they can get their hands on, and head up
Parramatta Road towards the Blue Mountains and beyond. Before
the week is out, that first small thud from the *Herald* dropping on

front verandahs across Sydney causes a growing thunder as whole human waves hit the diggings. First in their dozens, then in their hundreds, they come!

Rich man, poor man, beggar man, thief; tinker, tailor, soldier, spy, from the lowest of the low, right up to an aide of Governor FitzRoy himself – they answer the siren's call.

For, as they say in California, there really is *gold* in them thar hills! Each fresh discovery, each nugget, each story that circulates of someone who left their work on a Monday as a poor man only to be a rich man 'fore seven days have passed causes the excitement to grow.

The Sydney Morning Herald captures the mood on 20 May 1851: 'A complete mental madness appears to have seized every member of the community, and as a natural consequence there has been a universal rush to the diggings. Any attempt to describe the number-less scenes – grave, gay, and ludicrous – which have arisen out of this state of things, would require the graphic power of Dickens.'[33]

Only ten days after the announcement, no fewer than a *thousand* men are at Ophir.

When, just four months earlier, Hargraves had ventured up this very track he had looked like a lone man on a horse. In fact, as it now transpires, he had been something of a cross between a trailblazer and the vanguard for an entire gold-digging army.

What can the authorities do? The answer is very, very little, no matter how hard they try. Although Colonial Secretary Thomson replies to his Commissioner of Crown Lands, Charles Green, that he must take his Inspector of Police with some men to halt the dig-gings, it is the same as before – while Commissioner Green and the police do indeed hand out notices to desist, the diggers barely look up. The authorities will have to come up with a different system. One with teeth. What is certain is that, unable to stop the masses from digging, they're going to have to find a way to make them pay for the privilege.

The Sydney Morning Herald is also far from happy with the course of events, strongly editorialising: 'The mania for emigrating to the gold-fields of California, which at one time threatened to decimate our population and which naturally filled sober-minded colonists with an anxiety bordering on alarm, has often occupied our most serious alarm, but that mania, compared with the one which we are now menaced with by the discovery of gold within our own borders was as nothing . . .

'Should our gold prove to be abundant in quantity, rich in quality and easy of access, let the inhabitants of New South Wales and neighbouring colonies stand prepared for calamities more terrible than earthquakes and pestilence.'[34]

––––––––––––

The government geologist, Samuel Stutchbury, writes from the diggins at Summer Hill Creek to the Colonial Secretary. Mr Stutchbury begs to inform him that 'gold has been obtained in considerable quantity' and that 'the number of people at work and about the diggings (that is, occupying about one mile of the creek), cannot be less than 400, and of all classes'. The gold, he says, is not merely in the creek, but also on the ground all around it.

He also adds as a word of warning, 'I fear, unless something is done very quickly, that much confusion will arise in consequence of people setting up claims.'[35]

'Excuse this being written in pencil,' he concludes, 'as there is no ink yet in this city of Ophir.'

21 May 1851, the New South Wales Governor issues a proclamation

It is the equivalent of trying to stem a flood by planting a single stop sign in front of the rushing waters. For on this day a

'PROCLAMATION' appears in *The NSW Government Gazette*, to be picked up by other papers in the coming days, asserting that, as Australia is a British colony, all of its land is *Crown* land, meaning all gold found upon it belongs to Her Gracious Majesty Queen Victoria . . . and all those who want to dig for it will have to pay Her Majesty's Government 30 shillings a month, *in advance*, to work a claim of eight feet by eight feet, totalling 64 square feet.

And as the proclamation makes clear, the consequences of failure to pay that fee are serious: 'Therefore, I, Sir Charles Augustus FitzRoy, the Governor, aforesaid, on behalf of Her Majesty, do hereby publicly notify and declare, that all persons who shall take from any Lands within the said Territory, any Gold Metal, or Ore containing gold . . . without having been duly authorised in that behalf, by her Majesty's Colonial Government, will be prosecuted, both Criminally and Civilly, as the law allows.'[36]

Most importantly – for this is the major measure to try to ensure social stability, the measure insisted upon by the squattocracy – the license can only be granted to men who 'had been properly discharged from employment or were not otherwise improperly absent from hired service'.[37] And it has to be carried on that person at all times.

And yet . . . no-one cares.

They don't even care – can you *believe* it? – that Governor FitzRoy has the right to do this, as established by the sixteenth-century lawsuit *R. v. Earl of Northumberland* ('Case of Mines'), which was decided in 1568. They all keep digging regardless. And from Sydney, others keep heading out to join them.

Reports from letters to the editor of *The Sydney Morning Herald* over the next few days gives the flavour:

> **About 30 seamen as well as the mechanics and labourers at the new buildings in George Street left this morning for the diggings.**

> Sydney is going stark, staring mad. Gold, gold, gold is the one and only topic, from the merchant down to the chimney sweep. Little else is thought of or talked about. Labourers and tradesmen are striking for wages and leaving in all directions. Sailors are deserting their ships, and young men in good situations giving notice or throwing up employment at once.

> The population of Sydney is in a fearful state of commotion from the prevalence of the gold mania. Numbers come round the coach office, eager to catch the news on the arrival of the mail. The probable number who left Sydney for the diggings on Monday last was 1000, and in less than a week it is expected ten times the number will start for Bathurst.[38]

This proves a prescient prediction, for within days the roads leading out of Sydney are packed with an unending cavalcade of drays and carts, each more heavily laden than the last with 'tents, rockers, flour, tea, sugar, mining tools, etc. – each accompanied by from four to eight men, half of whom bore firearms'.[39] The less wealthy are seen to be pushing mere wheelbarrows with their supplies and implements, while one extraordinary conveyance is seen to be pulled along by four bulldogs!

Already the number of people on the streets of downtown Sydney is noticeably thinner, while Parramatta – that much closer to the diggings and therefore all the more tempting for its population – looks so deserted it may as well have dingos running down its main street.

Everywhere, the shops have adapted to the gold rush by putting in their front windows and on their principal display shelves everything that might attract the attention of a man heading off for the goldfields from the standing start of no provisions: shovels, picks, axes, saws, pots, pans, dungarees, heavy shirts and heavier boots, and most particularly . . . cradles.

'The gold washing machine, or Virginian "cradle",' runs one contemporary account, 'hitherto a stranger to our eyes, became in two days a familiar household utensil, for scores of them were paraded for purchase.'[40]

And, yes, the hands that rock those cradles are frantically grasping, reaching for ever more supplies, but it is not hard to see why it is so and why the rush is filled with people from all walks of life. The price of gold at this time is around £3 an ounce, while the average labourer is earning little more than £20 and certainly no more than £30 for an entire *year's* work. With just one nugget, one lucky find, you could earn many times more than your annual wage.

The Maitland Mercury sagely notes: 'Many persons are now going to dig for gold who are wholly unfit for such work; men who would hesitate to walk the length of George Street in a shower of rain are going, at the beginning of winter, to a district where the climate is almost English, and where they will not be able to get shelter in even the humblest hut.'[41]

Not for nothing does the alarmed Governor write to the Colonial Secretary in London, informing him that the rush is already 'unhinging the minds of all classes of society'.[42]

Will unhinged minds agree to pay the license fees? This is far from sure, and it is the Government Surveyor, Samuel Stutchbury, still on site at the diggings, who is the first to pinpoint the problem, in a letter to his masters in Sydney on 25 May: 'Up to this time the miners are quiet and peaceable, but almost to a man armed. With such numbers as will without doubt in a very short period be brought together, good order will very much depend upon the government adopting wise measures for collecting dues, which should be made as easy as possible in the mode of payment; as I fear that no police power could enforce the collection of dues against the feelings of the majority.'[43]

And there will be many more diggers coming, so extraordinarily munificent are these goldfields proving to be. He estimates there to be currently 1000 people there, 'and with few exceptions they appear to be doing well, many of them getting large quantities of gold. Lumps have been obtained varying in weight from 1 oz to 4 lbs, the latter being the heaviest I have heard of '.[44]

Upon reading such reports, the authorities are not long in concluding that the rush will soon get a whole lot *more* intense. Clearly something must be done to maintain order, as well as putting in a structure to collect the license fees, and on 23 May the government announces the appointment of its first Commissioner over the Gold Region, with the former Police Magistrate of Parramatta, Mr John Richard Hardy, being appointed to the post. It will be for him to oversee Her Majesty's peace and ensure that the law and regulations are being obeyed. As 'the Crown writ small', he will have the responsibility of issuing the licenses and, most importantly, collecting the fees.

The appointment of such a figure is an obvious course, but *The Sydney Morning Herald* thinks the authorities have picked the wrong man: 'We feel particularly curious to know upon what grounds Mr. Hargraves is overlooked [as Gold Commissioner], or if not overlooked, why his claims are the last to be considered [when] to Mr. Hargraves, and Mr. Hargraves principally, does the merit of the discovery belong . . .

'Already, a general feeling of indignation has been expressed, and more particularly at the diggings, at the apparent slight with which Mr. Hargraves has been treated in this matter.'[45]

Within a little over a week, the government caves in and agrees to appoint Edward Hargraves. Again, the *Herald* is honoured to report it, in an edition that also carries an apology for the fact that many recent editions have been delivered late, because 'our runners being found wanting, have rushed for the Diggings without leave or license, at least without ours'.[46]

The good news is that the *Herald* pronounces itself 'satisfied, as will be the Colony and the parent country, extreme gratification in learning that the local government, as a preliminary bonus to Mr. Hargraves, have presented that gentleman with the sum of £500, and the appointment of Commissioner of Crown Lands, for the purpose of exploring such districts as he may judge desirable of investigation for further discoveries of gold'.[47]

Hargraves himself is of course extremely gratified, not just with the remuneration and the position as Commissioner, with its handsome salary of £250 per annum, but with something else that rivals it for pleasure. The position also comes with a uniform, boasting a great deal of gold lace and a peaked cap, and on those goldfields he is always to be accompanied by two mounted policemen. *Heaven!*

Yes, there is an ongoing outcry from the squatters at the government's seeming accommodation of the mass of labourers who continue to leave their jobs to go to the diggings, but when their man on site, Samuel Stutchbury, reports that 'there is no doubt that auriferous deposits exist throughout a very great extent of country, and that very shortly the export of gold from this will rival that of San Francisco',[48] it is obvious that there is not a lot they can do.

'It would be madness,' Colonial Secretary Deas Thomson gravely tells pastoralist James Macarthur, 'to attempt to stop that which we have not physical force to put down'.[49]

CHAPTER TWO

VICTORIA

Population and wealth will flow in upon us in
copious, rapid and continuous streams . . .
A high and noble destiny awaits the long despised Australia,
and she must now be treated by her haughty mistress, not as
a child, but as an equal. In every point a great change must
be, or Australia will know how to vindicate her rights.[1]

The People's Advocate, 23 July 1851

Early June, 1851, Melbourne stirs

Devastating!

For those in the town of Melbourne and its regional surrounds, the news of the finds of gold in the north, up Bathurst way, is producing terrifying results. For though the new colony itself has been prospering, with over six million sheep now fattening and breeding on more than 1000 stations, animal raising is a labour-intensive exercise, and much of that labour is not long in downing tools, upping sticks and heading north to try their luck. So, too, in the principal towns of Melbourne and Geelong – the latter the heart of the rich farming land – as within days everyone from ex-convicts, policemen and judges to labourers, shepherds, carpenters, common merchants and men of the civil service have all thrown it in and are streaming to the goldfields near Bathurst. The consequence is that ships must go unloaded, furnaces unstoked, foundries and factories unmanned, and flocks unattended, while the few remaining authorities must find replacements for the departed police and judges wherever they can. So desperate is the situation that they even going so far as to employ the hated Vandemonians from across Bass Strait – always the lowest class of men, far more used to being *hit* with a truncheon than *wielding* one on the side of justice.

Most appalled with the turn of events is the squattocracy, the wealthy squatters who have already made a fortune by paying a pittance to collective thousands of men to run vast flocks of sheep upon the rolling grass flatlands. Many of their workers have simply gone in the night. Elsewhere, it is reported that farmers who had just sown their crops for the next season's harvest have also walked off their land and headed to the goldfields. *Something* must be done to prevent all the able-bodied men from going.

Early June 1851, Ophir under siege

A bare fortnight after the first mass of diggers arrive on site at Ophir, what was once a wonderfully secluded wooded gully, with a bubbling creek and ample birdlife, is being transformed by every new arrival. The undergrowth is trampled to make space for tents. Trees have been cut down both for firewood and to ensure that when their root-systems are exposed by the holes being dug all around they won't fall upon the miners.

One journalist reaches for his quill and describes it thus: 'The point was occupied by about fifteen parties cutting straight into the hill, and as we looked down upon their busy movements, digging, carrying earth, and working the cradles at the edge of the water, with the noise of the pick, the sound of voices, and the washing of the shingle in the iron boxes of the cradle, I could scarcely believe that barely two weeks ago, this was a quiet secluded gully in a far out cattle run.'[2]

It is far from secluded now. They are now part of a noisy swarm, not only loving finding the gold, but loving the prospecting life as well. As observed by one digger, James Bonwick, 'The wild, free and independent life appears the great charm. They have no masters. They go where they please and work when they will.'[3]

1 pm, Monday, 9 June 1851, passions rise in the Hall of the Mechanics' Institution, Collins Street

And *still* they stream in! It is one of the largest daytime gatherings yet seen in Melbourne. At five minutes past the hour the hall is already more than half full, and it continues to fill so rapidly that it soon goes from 'standing room only' to people who are listening outside continually shouting 'Speak up!' so that they, too, may follow proceedings. For the issue at hand is important: what can be done to prevent the colony from continually bleeding vast numbers of its workers to the New South Wales goldfields?

Upon the motion being put by one of the first settlers of the colony after Batman, the distinguished politician John Pascoe Fawkner, that the Mayor of Melbourne chair the meeting – and that motion being passed – that gentleman takes over.

William Nicholson begins by noting that the purpose of the gathering is to raise a significant amount of money, 'which can be offered as a reward to any person or persons who shall within a given time make known the locality of a gold mine, [in this region] capable of being worked to advantage'.[4]

Nearly all at the meeting are in furious agreement that the move is necessary, as many of the colony's finest step up to the podium to not only pledge their own money but to exhort others to do the same.

Councillor McCombie is blunt in stating outright that, 'If something is not done to prevent the present universal movement for the goldfield, property will suffer and be reduced in value, buildings will be stopped, and the city be almost denuded of its population.'[5]

For his part, Councillor Hodgson maintains, 'If we act properly, the discovery of gold in these parts will turn out to be one of great advantage to this colony, as it is no doubt one of the wise dispensations of Providence for bringing population to this country. We have seen that when there was famine in Great Britain numbers had departed from that country for Canada and America; but when gold was found in California, the tide of emigration went there. I think that gold being found in this colony is another means used by Providence to send population here.'[6]

Others take a less benign view of Providence, warning starkly that if they do 'not now make an effort and do something, our working men will all rush to Sydney'.[7]

Despite the general alarm, the gathering is not without some levity, with Councillor McCombie drawing great laughter when, after others suggest that a reward should also be offered for the finding of other valuable minerals, he sagely notes, 'No shrine, Pagan or Mahommedan, has drawn as many pilgrims as that of gold'.[8] He goes on: 'Should we succeed in finding gold, we will make this colony great, fully one hundred years before she could otherwise arrive at greatness.'[9]

Hear, *hear*. Hear, *HEAR!*

But wait, what's this? For among all the learned, distinguished and well-groomed gentlemen suddenly stands a poorly dressed fellow with the huge, rough hands that mark him as one who must bear a pick, shovel or some other rough tool for a living. Unbidden, he now steps to the podium and notes – in what is as pure a form of Chartism as you'll find after a six-day march in any direction – that, 'though a working man from Yorkshire, I have as good a right to speak as anybody else'.[10]

No, he doesn't! Stop him, someone, please!

No, let the man speak!

As reported in that rising force among Melbourne newspapers,

The Argus, this fellow's insistence on speaking occasions 'great confusion and cries of order'.

Order! *Order!*

Unbowed, however, the working man goes on: 'Why have you not taken steps before now to find these mines and minerals . . . ? I am perfectly prepared to worship gold too, but I personally am not carried away by the gold mania. I have occupied the same situation for three years, indeed ever since I have come to this colony, and I most earnestly impress upon my fellow workers that they should not leave their work and run away after gold-finding. But I do not believe that this meeting is really called for the advantage of the working classes. If those who had called it had wished to serve the working classes, they would have done something during the last three years, to remedy the dirty lanes and alleys, and the stagnant pools of Melbourne, for I can tell you that health is always gold to the working man. I see many of the [town council] coming forward now, but why had they not come forward to remedy these evils?'[11]

A stir of protest rolls through the meeting, eventually quelled by more cries of 'Order! *Order!*'

'I protest against the whole of the proceedings,' he finishes his address. 'This meeting is more to enrich the rich, and oppress the poor man.'[12]

Noteth *The Argus*: (*'Hisses and applause.'*)

And so it goes. At least by the time the meeting breaks up at four o'clock in the afternoon its principal aim has been realised. Two days later, the bottom right-hand corner of *The Argus* bears an announcement that is soon the talk of Melbourne:

TWO HUNDRED GUINEAS REWARD

THE Committee appointed by the General Meeting held in Melbourne on the 9th instant, are now prepared to offer a Reward of
TWO HUNDRED GUINEAS

To any person or persons who shall discover to them a
GOLD MINE,
Or **DEPOSIT** within 200 miles of Melbourne, capable of being; worked to advantage; this amount to be independent of any reward the Government may be disposed to grant.
WILLIAM NICHOLSON, Mayor, Chairman.[13]

29 June 1851, at Clunes, 90 miles north-west of Melbourne, a pick picks right

Though born in Ireland, in many ways James Esmond is a man just like Edward Hargraves. He, too, had been on the California goldfields, leaving Australia in June 1849, and has gained some experience as a gold prospector, even if he did arrive a little too late to really prosper. By then, all the best claims had been taken. And the 29-year-old is equally intrigued by the possibility that gold might be found in Australia, based on the remarkable similarities between the sort of country he is familiar with in Victoria – the Pyrenees Ranges – and the goldfields of California.

The odd thing is that, two years earlier, a shepherd by the name of Chapman, who had been working on a station in the central Pyrenees, had caused a small rush when he claimed to have found 38 ounces of gold. The disbelieving Esmond, however, had not joined in, going to California instead. But now he has returned, convinced that greater treasures might lie in these here Pyrenean hills.

Back in the Burnbank area, Esmond meets by chance the respected German physician turned geologist Dr George Herman Bruhn, who tells him of a promising quartz-bearing reef on Donald Cameron's property ten miles south-west at Clunes. Now, just as he had seen done in California, Esmond begins a systematic search for gold in this very place.

On this day, Esmond finds himself on the northern side of the hill opposite Cameron's property, at the eastern base of the Pyrenees, with his pick raised above his head, ready to strike a blow at a likely looking bit of quartz. What has propelled him to this place in time is much the same as what had first propelled him to leave Ireland a little over a decade earlier to work on sheep stations and then drive the weekly mail coach between Buninyong and the Horsham region, before propelling him all the way to California . . . and back. In part it is a restless nature, in part a sense of adventure and, perhaps mostly, it is a belief that there is a better life for him somewhere just up ahead, if he can only find it . . .

With the smooth, downward arc of the pick, wielded by a man who has done this many times before, the tip of the tool splinters the rock face – and what is the first thing he sees?

Splinters of quartz . . .

But wait. For there is something else, gleaming back at him in the sunshine, a wink from Mammon himself. *Gold!*

More excited than he has ever been in his life, Esmond continues fossicking, gathering samples. In no more than an hour he has enough gold to prove that his is a payable find.

A week later, on 5 July 1851, after at last tracking down his missing horse, Esmond takes his small sample of gold into the offices of the *Geelong Advertiser*, where, with a mind to claiming the substantial reward that has been offered for finding gold, he meets journalist Alfred Clarke and shows him the samples. The gold, as Clarke would recall, shows 'distinctly to the naked eye, embedded in the quartz, in small particles, varying from dust size to the size of a small pin's head'.[14]

Stunned, Clarke asks the obvious: where did you find it?

Up among the mountains, Esmond replies vaguely, with a nod of his head towards the distant Pyrenees, but will not be drawn further.

With Clarke in tow, however, he does allow for his gold to be *confirmed* as such by the equally stunned local jeweller and watchmaker, William Patterson.

And then, while Clarke prepares to write his truly ground-breaking story, Esmond heads off to Melbourne to buy the material he needs to build a cradle just like he used in California.

Late June 1851, up Mudgee way in New South Wales, a blackfella breaks through

Local lore has it that there are good blackfellas, bad blackfellas and tragic blackfellas. A good blackfella understands that no matter how they might feel about it, they have lost their land and their way of life, and adapts accordingly to fit in with the white man's way – even working for the white man to make his dispossession easier.

A bad blackfella doesn't accept the loss at all and continues to fight against it, up to and including committing terrible violence on law-abiding white people.

And a tragic blackfella is caught between the two: destroyed by a combination of the loss of his land and indulgence in the worst of the white man's vices, like alcohol.[15]

Jemmy Irving is a good blackfella. Raised and educated in the old mission school at Wellington, he had been working for many years as a stockman for the well-known squatter Dr William John Kerr from Wallowa, and had been treated well. The mostly merry Dr Kerr first came to Australia from Ireland as the doctor on a convict ship, and was a man of noted humanity and kindness. After starting a medical practice at Bathurst, he moved on to sheep farming on a run situated on the highlands between Macquarie River and Meroo Creek. The run was situated on very fertile land right by the Meroo Creek, about 53 miles from Bathurst and 18 miles from Mudgee, and he and his family prospered. Still, as the only medico within a hundred horizons, he has always been available to give free medical assistance to whomever needed him, including his workers, and his lovely wife frequently acts as his voluntary nurse.

Jemmy likes the Kerrs for their kindness and is happy to work for them, tending to a couple of flocks of their sheep.

On this particular day in late June, Jemmy is tending to one of those flocks in some of the wild scrub that lies next to Dr Kerr's land. For hours he wanders through the bush, beside the creek and in the shade of the towering stringybarks and white gums, a very remote place that once was within the songlines of his clan, but is now lost for the clan is no more. And yet, Jemmy still moves easily, a man in his element, even though he has lost his natural right to it and . . .

And there. What is that? Jemmy is just following the tail of a flock over a low ridge when he comes face to face with an enormous stump of white rock thrusting through the ridge's surface – the type of rock that the white man calls 'quartz' – and as the bright sun shines down upon it there is something gleaming from it, something embedded in the quartz. It looks like the same shiny metal that he had once seen on a gold sovereign.

The white men call the shiny metal 'gold', and Jemmy knows that in recent times it seems to be all the Doktah and his friends and relatives talk about. People have been finding it in creeks around here for the last few weeks, and every time they do it sets off another whole lot of conversations, along with people rushing out to see if they can find some themselves. There are a couple of smaller clumps beside the main outcrop, and when Jemmy turns one of them over he finds that the lower side is made up of the same metal. That clump is too heavy to move far, but a much smaller rock has the same properties, and he decides to take it with him. Perhaps it might please the Doktah.

Early the next morning, Doktah Kerr is walking up and down the verandah of his house in his slippers, enjoying his after-breakfast pipe, when his dogs suddenly start barking. Shortly afterwards, he sees Jemmy coming out of the bush.

The doctor likes Jemmy for his calm, quiet and dignified ways, and greets him warmly. But this time Jemmy does not seem so calm at all and immediately tells him has found something, something *important*, maybe even . . . 'gold'.

Laughing uproariously, the doctor replies delightedly, 'Fudge!'[16]

His laughter stops as suddenly as a shot duck when Jemmy shyly shows the small nugget he has carried all this way. That *does* rather look like gold, Doktah has to admit, and he examines it closely. True, it is not quite as lustrous as he imagines gold to be in its natural state – this is rather more like slightly tarnished brass – but it is certainly worth further investigation. So in short order the horses are saddled and the doctor and his good wife ride off, with Jemmy trotting along just in front, leading the way.

The doctor is unaccustomedly nervous in case Jemmy can't find the place again, but he shouldn't be. Jemmy knows this country, grew up on this country, could find his way back there with as much ease as Doktah could find his way around the streets of faraway Sydney, the big smoke that Doktah and his missus also talk about a lot.

And there it is there, Boss, the very rock.

Dr Kerr can barely breathe – and nor can his wife – for it is gold alright, and a huge amount. It looks, in fact, to be the biggest nugget he has ever heard of, let alone seen. It is so big, embedded across three big blocks of quartz, that the only thing he and Jemmy can do in the end – after returning to the homestead to get a horse-drawn dray and implements – is to take the sledgehammer and break the quartz blocks down to get to the nugget itself.

And so it is that the largest nugget found in the world – in the 1851 years since our Lord Jesus Christ was born – is broken into two large chunks and many smaller pieces. Then Dr Kerr and Jemmy must strain – good Lord above, but the larger two pieces, still encased in quartz, are amazingly heavy – to get them in the cart. The largest chunk is like a golden piece of honeycomb, spotted with holes of an entirely random nature. All put together, Jemmy's gold proves to weigh no less than 106 pounds, and the good Doctor is not long in selling 103 pounds of it for the princely sum of £4,140!

Now, a lesser man might have simply reckoned that as the gold had been found by his stockman, who was working on his property at the time, that fellow is due no part of the reward. But not Dr Kerr. Grateful for the find, he is sure to give his loyal servant Jemmy, together with two other Aboriginal workers he is close to, Long Tommy and Tommy Bumbo, 'two flocks of sheep, two saddle horses and a quantity of rations, and supply them with a team of bullocks to plough some land in which they are about to sow a crop of maize and potatoes'.[17]

7 July 1851, Victoria awakes to the news

It is the *Geelong Advertiser* that has the honour of breaking the news of James Esmond's stunning find to wider Melbourne:

GOLD IN THE PYRENEES

The long-sought treasure is at length found! Victoria is a gold country, and from Geelong goes forth the first glad tidings of the discovery. Mr Esmond arrived in Geelong on Saturday with some beautiful specimens of gold, in quartz, and gold-dust in a 'debris' of the same species of rock . . . The specimens shown are sufficient to satisfy the most sceptical, whilst the respectability of the discoverer, Mr Esmond, is a guarantee against the practice of any 'sham'.[18]

15 July 1851, Melbourne consecrates and celebrates a different success

A holiday for everyone! For today is the day, dear friends, 'to transform the chrysalis, "His Honour", into the gay butterfly "His

Excellency"',[19] and 'the Port Phillip of yesterday makes way for the Victoria of today'.[20] At half past ten, all of the troops, all the mounted and city police arrive at the Government Offices in the company of the heads of all the government departments, ready to witness Charles La Trobe, accompanied by His Honour the Resident Judge William à Beckett and the newly installed Attorney-General, William Foster Stawell, be so anointed. In the open space in front of the Treasury it is William Stawell himself – closely observed by Solicitor-General Redmond Barry among other leading officials – who has La Trobe repeat the sacred oaths, after which the Resident Judge declares that Charles Joseph La Trobe is now, officially, the Lieutenant-Governor of the colony. At this point the field battery fires its guns in celebration as a signal to the city, near and far, that the great event has occurred. The assembled multitude of the city's leading dignitaries bursts forth with three cheers, and the band strikes up with a stirring rendition of 'God Save the Queen'.

This is a very auspicious day in the colony of 'Victoria', as everyone is now delighted to call it. For on this day the impact of the Separation Bill passed by the British Parliament the year before is truly felt, as Victoria becomes a separate entity from New South Wales, one that will soon have its own Legislative Council – composed of 20 members elected by substantial property owners, together with ten members appointed by the Lieutenant-Governor – whose role it will be to advise the Lieutenant-Governor. True, this governing body is not going to be representative of the people at all, but only a certain section of the population, and that section will comprise the wealthiest and most powerful in Victoria: the squatters. But, for the moment, that fact is lost in the general celebrations of independence.

What it means, as *The Argus* has already noted in an editorial on the subject, is that, 'The depressing influence of our connexion with Sydney is at an end. Our laws have to be discussed and amended amongst ourselves.'[21] And yet, opines the paper, from those to whom much is given, much is expected: 'Let us remember this, in our aim to lift the dear land of our adoption into a high place in the scale of nations. Let us think of her in no lower light than that of the model colony, and strain our utmost nerve to justify the title. Let that be the Pole Star by which we ever steer; and even if we have to struggle with a baffling wind here, and an adverse current there, let us never falter in our course . . . We are one of the smallest, and youngest of British colonies, but we have that within us, which properly developed shall to some extent influence the destinies of the world.' [22]

18 July 1851, Bathurst is agog

The excitement in both colonies is now overwhelming. For, back at Bathurst, the almost unhinged exhilaration engendered by the find of the Kerr Nugget is staggering in its effect. On this day, *The Sydney Morning Herald*, relying on its colleagues at the *Bathurst Free Press*, report the news:

Bathurst is mad again! The delirium of golden fever has returned with increased intensity. Men meet together, stare stupidly at each other, talk incoherent nonsense, and wonder what will happen next. Everybody has a hundred times seen a hundred weight of flour; a hundred weight of sugar or potatoes, is an everyday fact, but a hundred weight of gold is a phrase scarcely known in the English language. It is beyond the range of our ordinary ideas – a sort of physical incomprehensibility – but that it is a material existence, our own eyes bore witness on Monday last.[23]

If the news of the find thrills the denizens of Bathurst and beyond, far beyond measure, it does not – with the exception of Dr Kerr himself – thrill the squatters. As their workers now leave in droves, there are urgent communications with the government, suggesting, sometimes *insisting*, that the diggings be stopped immediately.

Otherwise, they warn, their own operations will simply have to cease. In response, the government prevaricates – they are on the side of the squatters, but they also must be realistic. Such is the frenzy to get to the goldfields at any price, at any personal cost, that it is obvious no law the authorities might come up with would be able to stop the general flood.

25 July 1851, this way to paradise, from Geelong

While passing through Geelong once more, on the way back to his diggings, James Esmond had entrusted the journalist Clarke with the location of his find – on the condition that Clarke not publish it until Esmond has had time to buy his supplies and be back at Clunes. And on this day, after another find in the same locale confirms that Esmond is telling the truth, Clarke now gives specific directions in the *Geelong Advertiser* as to where the goldfield lies:[24]

> **F**rom Geelong to Buninyong is fifty miles; arrived there, Clunes Diggings are about twenty-seven miles further, to gain which make for Clarke's, and from Clarke's outstation turn off to Coghill – the 'Gold Field' is before you within a short distance – work! and success attend you![25]

On the same day, a letter to *The Argus* reports that in this location: 'The diggers are in great spirits – our old cook has gathered an ounce. When they are provided with proper implements, they expect ten times the present produce per man. In spite of the extreme severity of the weather there are daily arrivals. There are forty today on the ground. Warren, shoemaker, is so sanguine that he expects to realise £2000 by Christmas. "Will not put an awl in leather again." Such are his expressions. Esson is to commence cradling on Monday, under the direction of Esmond, who arrived today.

'P.S. Ten o'clock, Sunday. David Anderson has returned from the diggings, and says the cook has realised two and half ounces in a week.'[26]

The *cook!* Two and a half ounces in a week! The cobbler! £2000 before Christmas!

Though it is not yet a *rush* – the reports are too scattered and uncertain for men to throw it all in to pursue what is not yet truly confirmed – in short order gold – *gold!* – is the only subject anyone cares to talk about. Do you think it's real? Think this cove, Esmond, is on the up and up? At least fifty men do, and are soon on their way to Clunes, where they join the amazingly accommodating Esmond at the diggings.

Wednesday, 23 July 1851, *The Sydney Morning Herald* declares . . .

On this issue of the discovery of the Kerr Nugget, and *in* this issue, the *Herald* – rarely one to publish prose that is not as sober as a judge and as serious as the 1850 drought – simply cannot help itself and reaches for the purple ink as the ramifications continue to sink in:

> From the monarch on the throne to the peasant at the plough, there will be astonishment, wonder, and admiration. From the palace to the cottage, from the drawing-room to the nursery, from the philosopher and the statesman to the school-boy, this Lump of Gold and the land which produced it will for a while be the all-absorbing tonic.[27]

With this knowledge of the stunning riches that this brown land possesses comes a new-found confidence, a notion that perhaps Australia can be more than a mere offshoot of another country.

'We have within ourselves, in our own rich and prolific gold-fields,' proudly proclaims *The People's Advocate and New South Wales*

Vindicator shortly after the *Herald* article, 'the elements of all future greatness – the elements of future nationality, and of coming independence . . . Yes! We shall be a NATION; not a mere dependency of a far off country, which however we may venerate and love as a birth place of ourselves and our fore-fathers, has been to us in this our bright southern home, but a cruel step-mother.'[28]

RAH!

And yet, even as these words are being penned and distributed, the story of the ownership of the nugget still has some way to go. For who truly does own it? Dr Kerr had felt that it was his to sell; after all, *his* stockman had found it. (As to that Aboriginal stockman, no-one is so ludicrous as to suggest that he owns it because he found it on land that was in fact his ancestral home.) The gold-dealer from Sydney, Thacker, Daniel & Co., had come up to negotiate a sale, paying Dr Kerr £4140 for the privilege. The government, however, has an entirely different view. As the gold has been found on Crown land, by diggers unlicensed at the moment of discovery, the official view is that the nugget belongs to *them*, and it is so strong in this opinion that a 'demand for its surrender into the hands of the government was made by the newly installed Gold Commissioner, Mr Hardy'.[29]

When Messrs Thacker and Daniel take such a dim view of this demand that they refuse to comply, the government sends in the police and the gold is forcibly seized, causing great outrage, followed by lawyers, letters and great legal manoeuvring, even as the public at large cries out in outrage at the government's actions.

Finally, the government agrees to give the gold back to the finders, 'provided they enter into a bond to pay Her Majesty a royalty of ten per cent, should the home government, upon inquiry into the merits of the case, insist upon such payment'.[30]

The government is not without support in so doing, with *The Southern Cross* declaiming, 'It is, no doubt, very hard upon the Messrs Thacker, but the case is altogether a singular one . . . If royalties are to be enforced at all, we cannot but consider 5 per cent on private lands, and 10 per cent on Crown Lands, as an exceedingly moderate impost, more especially as mines, minerals, and ship-building timber are reserved to the Crown in all deeds of grant. A premium for permission to work gold-mines cannot reasonably be objected to by a people desirous of preserving order, regularity, and good government.'[31]

8–15 August 1851, gold fever spreads through Victoria

Now that it has been established that there is gold in the quartz country around Clunes, there are a number of other prospectors who wish to see if there might be gold in their own regions. One of them is an English-born blacksmith by the name of Thomas Hiscock, who now hails from the small settlement of Buninyong, just seven miles south of Ballarat. There would forever afterwards be speculation that perhaps James Esmond had talked to Hiscock as he made his way back from Geelong to Clunes, maybe even describing to him the kind of hills with quartz and surface gravel that gold could be found in . . . but for whatever reason, only shortly after Esmond had passed through Buninyong, Hiscock made a key decision. In the company of his son, Thomas Hiscock Jnr, and one of his son's friends, John Thomas, he decides to go looking for gold in any likely spots they can find within cooee of their Buninyong home.

For many days, the men return to their homes each night empty-handed. But on this bright, shining morning of 8 August 1851, high on a slope of the White Horse Range, Thomas Snr sees a promising quartz boulder – he has been told this is what to look for – takes his pick and swings . . .

Lower down on those same slopes, the two younger men hear a sudden exultant cry from the older man that he has found *gold* at last!

Neither young man budges. They've heard it all before when old Tom had got excited about discovering small chunks of mica. But when he charges down the slopes to show them that this time he really *has* done it, there is no mistaking it. It glints, it gleams, it glitters, it *glows*, its glory will never fade – it is gold!

And, as also follows the familiar pattern, the news is not long in getting out, allowing the rush to roar as it never has before.

While it had been one thing for a digger to try his luck at faraway Clunes, Buninyong is only a day's hard ride away from Geelong and well worth having a go at.

Within just a few days the roads leaving both Geelong and Melbourne are filled with men from all walks of life, now practically *running*, eager to try their luck as all of the Melbourne newspapers, including *The Herald* in Melbourne, *The Argus* and *Geelong Advertiser*, lead, day after day, with ever more breathless stories: 'GOLD!', 'OFF TO THE DIGGINGS', 'EUREKA', and most appropriately of all . . . 'MANIA'.

Writing on 15 August, the correspondent for *The Argus* sums it up neatly: 'Let all possible publicity be given to the great fuel, that an unlimited gold field exists in this, the finest colony in the Southern Hemisphere – the advantages we enjoy over our neighbours in Sydney cannot be too often repeated, or too glowingly penned.

'Our gold fields are in close proximity to our ports, one within four hours walk of Melbourne, another within one day's walk of Geelong, and others within one hard day's ride of either town; we have a superabundance of animal food; we have a superabundance of the richest land for agricultural purposes, only waiting for what the mother country has too much of – labour; we have a climate that cannot be surpassed under heaven. All we require is an ardent desire implanted in our breasts to make headway, and a determined resolve that we shall not lag behind.'[32]

As it happens, 'lagging' is one thing not apparent, as the flood of men leaving their other posts of work to get to the diggings thickens by the hour.

16 August 1851, La Trobe makes his move

Charles La Trobe feels he has no choice. While the results of the discovery of gold within his colony are to date as far as he can ascertain, 'but moderate',[33] he feels they are sufficient to do as Governor FitzRoy has done before him in New South Wales and declare that all the gold found belongs to Queen Victoria, and so issues a proclamation:

'Now I, Charles Joseph La Trobe, Esq., Lieutenant-Governor aforesaid, on behalf of Her Majesty, do hereby publicly notify and declare that all persons who shall take from any land within the said colony, any gold, metal, or ore containing gold, or who, within any waste lands which have not yet been alienated by the Crown, shall dig for and disturb the soil in search of such gold, metal, or ore, without having been duly authorised in that behalf by Her Majesty's Colonial Government, will be prosecuted both criminally and civilly as the law allows . . . GOD SAVE THE QUEEN!'[34]

This is shortly followed up with six key provisional regulations, 'under which Licenses may be obtained to dig for, search and remove the same', that include: from the first day of September 'no person [is] allowed to dig, search for or remove gold, on land, whether public or private, without first taking out or applying for a license'; the license fee is to be 'fixed at one pound ten shillings per month, paid in advance'; and, perhaps most crucially, 'No person will be eligible to obtain a license, or the renewal of a license, unless he shall produce some certificate of discharge from his last service, or prove to the satisfaction of the commissioner that he is not a person improperly absent from hired service.'[35]

And *that* should stop the flood of labour away from the squatters.

21 August 1851, reports come in from Buninyong, Clunes and . . . Ballarat

A man with a felicitous and evocative turn of phrase, *Geelong Advertiser* journalist Alfred Clarke – now out Buninyong way, where they are yet to hear of the recent proclamation – continues to tramp far and wide on the diggings on behalf of his paper, taking notes in his diary in elegant longhand.

A natural storyteller, he takes some pleasure in penning his thoughts, recording the feeling of this place, at this time:

> The scene presents a strange appearance, picturesque enough, but somewhat lugubrious during the heavy rains. Tents are pitched, fires are burning, trees are cut down, the sound of the axe is heard in all directions, cradles are rocking, and men crouching down to the water's edge are intent on exploring the golden sands, which like true modesty retires before undue advances.[36]

Everywhere he walks, he sees men he knows from Geelong, men who have deserted the solid brick and mortar of that town for the flapping tarpaulin of Buninyong, who have exchanged – yes, these are the perfect phrases to capture it – 'comfort for inconvenience, ease for hardship, ordinary travail for hard labour, and all is set at nought against the desire for gold, gold that is to be rent from the bowels of the earth. Neither rain or storm overpowers the desire; the cry is still "they come, they come!"'[37]

And so they do. Every hour, at least, a new party arrives, a few with swags on their backs; many with guns, acting as a kind of advance party to stake a claim before their group carrying the heavy supplies arrives many hours later; and here a lone man on a horse, eager to try his luck. And now, come the evening, 'the cradle rests, the dippers and the tin dishes are thrown aside for the night, the horses are turned adrift, and the busy workers have retired to their tents, the line of which may be soon be traced by blazing fires. Beef, biscuit, and damper, all, or some form the evening's repast, are then partaken of, pipes follow, and a deep slumber looms on the eventful day.'[38]

Just before they partake of this well-deserved rest, Alfred Clarke walks from tent to tent, documenting how they are faring.

'Good evening, Mr Richard!' says the journalist, 'What luck today?'

'Well, I don't know, come and look, here it is,' the digger replies, pouring the water from the pannikin to show the thin scattering of gold at the bottom.

'How much do you say?'

'Well, I don't know, shall I say two ounces and a half?'

'Don't say too much – suppose you state two and a quarter, and then you'll be within the mark.'

'Be it so,' replies Clarke. 'I want but the truth.'[39]

And so it goes. The next tent has a party of six who, after three days' labour, also have two ounces and a quarter of gold to boast of. The next one along, with four men, after three and a half days, have five ounces and a quarter. The next, a party of four, after two days' work, an ounce and a half. The last party of three, after a day and a half, has just an ounce.

In sum, such pickings for such work are only okay . . . and beyond those who actually have found gold, there are many others whose only reward has been blistered hands, aching backs and severely depleted savings. They had hoped for El Dorado and found very little indeed. And so Clarke now chooses his words carefully to fulfil his duty to his readers, to be their man on the ground, writing, 'And now one word before closing this despatch would advise all parties who have comfortable situations to stay at home, and "let well alone," make no sacrifices of the present for the future, but patiently await the result of the present experiments . . . I say wait awhile, rush not rashly to the christening of the gold-birth – there will be plenty without you at its baptism, and your time will be to celebrate its maturity . . . My last word is, "pause! before you plunge." [40]

And yet for those diggers who have already plunged, the abiding sense is that there *must* be gold in heavier concentrations in these parts. But where?

So it is that, just like dingos looking for easy meat, many of the disappointed diggers follow the creeks and gullies that spread out from Clunes and Buninyong in all directions until . . .

Until, on this 21st day of August, a 26-year-old Irishman by the name of James Regan finds himself making his way back from the Clunes diggings that he has been checking out to Buninyong, where he has been based with his 75-year-old friend, John Dunlop, a one-time dashing cavalry officer at the Battle of Waterloo. Regan's course takes him heading down a muddy gully and through the shadowy glades until he emerges onto the grassy slopes leading down into the valley they call 'Ballaarat'. This is heavily worked squatting country, a place within a fifteen mile radius of where William Yuille had first established himself and where there are now some 20 stations. An English visitor to the area a decade earlier had noted in his diary, 'What would the poor farmers at home think of having 150 and 300 square miles of excellent grazing or pasture land for £10 per annum?'[41]

Not that Regan cares about that! For now he comes to a nice 'gravelly slope with quartz boulders',[42] a little to the south of a heavily timbered and curiously dome-like hill on the northern end of Yuille's run. This'll do . . .

In his first attempt, he first takes a shovelful of soil from the slope before taking it to a nearby creek for some gentle panning and . . . meets all but instant success. The gold gleams in the bottom of his pan. A *lot* of gold. More gold in a few spades than he had been able to glean in whole hours of labouring at Buninyong . . . A good man,

Regan quickly packs up and returns to Buninyong for John Dunlop, and the two begin searching in earnest.

Over the next few days they gather in no fewer than 104 grains of gold, weighing a very handsome four ounces – worth over £12!

Are they entirely alone at this point? Two years later, in late 1853, Dunlop would be asked that very question by a Select Committee of the Victorian Parliament: 'When you arrived, you were sure there was no one there?' [43]

Dunlop would be very quick with his reply, as there was absolutely no doubt at the time and he can recall it clearly: 'No; there was no sign of anyone, only a few huts belonging to the natives.'[44]

25 August 1851, the Buninyong goldfields stir with revolt

If there is one thing worse than scratching just a few specks of gold around Buninyong and Clunes when you had been hoping to find fist-sized nuggets, it is hearing the news that the government expects you to pay 30 shillings a month for the privilege!

It is for that reason that the news of the Lieutenant-Governor's proclamation hits the nascent goldfields like a storm. Thirty shillings? *Thirty shillings?* A pound and a half? At a time when they have no guarantees of earning anything at all? For many of the miners it is thirty shillings expenditure for what may potentially be a month of nothing. Many have spent their last capital buying picks, shovels and supplies before getting themselves up here on the expectation that they will soon find gold – in the absence of that gold, they are now stony motherless broke.[45] What do you do when the government wants the value of half an ounce of gold out of you every month when you haven't found that much?[46]

It is for very good reason that 1 September, the day the tax is to begin, becomes known on the fields as 'BLACK MONDAY'.

The government's stated reasons for the introduction of the license fees are many, but a principal one is that to properly manage goldfields and keep law and order will require an enormous effort and *expense* on the part of the Civil Service, and who better to pay for that than the very diggers who are incurring the cost? All of the gold, whether on private or Crown land, belongs to Her Majesty anyway, and so the men must pay for the right to dig it.

That is not the way the diggers themselves see it. They see the Lieutenant-Governor caving into the demands of the squatters. The humble workers are *not* free to simply up and leave their jobs to try their luck on the goldfields – they need the permission of the boss cockies first. And that goes for soldiers, sailors, police and the public service, too. For the diggers, it is nothing less than an outrage. Most of the squatters in these parts had, like Yuille, claimed their lands 15 years and more earlier, meaning that for latecomers there is no land left to lease, let alone buy – even if they had the capital to do so. Only the squatters themselves can buy farming land from the government, because, under the 1847 Gipps Regulations, once squatters had occupied the land for five years they could purchase, at a cost of just one pound an acre, no fewer than 320 acres. And now the government wants the diggers to pay 30 shillings a month for merely the right to dig on an *infinitesimally smaller* patch of ground? For many diggers it reminds them of the appalling governments in Europe they have left behind.

At least, however, the outraged diggers have the support of many of the gentlemen of the press. As ever, Alfred Clarke is on top of the issue and fully on the diggers' side, sending a dispatch back to his paper, the *Geelong Advertiser*, before it is subsequently reprinted in *The Argus*:

'Thirty shillings a month, for twenty-six days' work, payable in advance, is the impost demanded by our Victorian Czar. Eighteen pounds sterling per annum, per head, is the merciless prospective exaction on an enterprise scarcely fourteen days old. It is a juggernaut tax to crush the poor, and if attempted against the richer and more powerful parts of the community, would be fatal to the domination that is, and La Trobism in one twelvemonth would be spoken of in the past tense. Why should a lawful occupation, promising so much, be strangled at its birth? I say unhesitatingly, fearlessly, and conscientiously, that there has not been a more gross attempt at injustice since the days of Wat Tyler; it is an insult to common sense, and if passed bye, by the journals of Port Phillip, without strict comment, it will be an indelible stain upon them. If such a thing as this tax be tolerated, it will be the first step to liberticide, for liberty cannot be where the foundation of all wealth is trammelled . . .

'It is hinted that a meeting of the diggers will take place, this afternoon, to consider upon the above question of the Gold Licenses.'[47]

And that meeting, a gathering of some 40 to 50 diggers, does indeed take place on the Buninyong diggings as miner after miner steps up to tell his story and express his views. One in particular who is warmly applauded lays it on the line from the first.

'I am a free man,' he says, 'and a hard-working man, willing to pay my fair share to the government, but I cannot and will not pay thirty shillings a month for a license.'[48]

The next man reports that, just to get to the diggings and buy the equipment he needed, '[I have] spent every halfpenny . . . and now I am to be taxed before I have been here a week, or had the opportunity of getting any of it back again'.

It is not right!

Another says he couldn't even scrape together enough to 'pay a shilling a day' to the commissioner, while a man who had been to California for their gold rush says, 'The Yankees don't do it in this here fashion.'[49]

All 50 of them agree that there has to be a better way of raising money and so pass a resolution calling on the government to withdraw the tax.

27 August 1851, Ballarat receives visitors

How can Dunlop and Regan keep the good pickings at Ballarat to themselves? It is impossible. Far from being pioneers a long way out on their own, they are no more than the vanguard of a whole swarm of other prospectors who, disappointed by the yield at both Clunes and Buninyong, are also looking elsewhere. In short, the same force that has propelled Regan and Dunlop to this golden point is also propelling everyone else with a pick, a shovel and hope in his heart – meaning that within just a few days several other groups have arrived and they, too, meet immediate success. Some of them even begin to find good-sized *nuggets*.

The whole situation is still manageable – for there is plenty of gold for everyone – just so long as the general word doesn't get out so that a real rush to this spot begins. But, of course, it cannot last.

———

Alfred Clarke is not long in hearing of the diggings at Ballarat and, in the company of a digger he has fallen in with at Buninyong, William Brownhill, has come to investigate. They head down the gully in the last few days of August to find Dunlop and Regan there, going strong, together with half a dozen other parties, now digging into the side of the hill and washing the result in the creek.

If the new arrivals are delighted to see how well it is all clearly going and pleased to be here, the reception they receive is not commensurately warm. Regan, his wealth growing by the hour and eager to keep the numbers down, looks up from a dish in which small pieces of gold are gleaming to see the friendly reporter from the *Geelong Advertiser* beaming down upon him – and he is shattered.

'I would rather have seen the devil than him,'[50] he would later record of his thoughts at the time.

Brownhill's welcome is equally unprepossessing. When he begins to follow the diggers' example, he is firmly told that this side of the hill is taken and he must go elsewhere. Reluctantly, Brownhill heads for the other side of the hill that, unfortunately for him, will soon become known as 'Poverty Point'. But, of course, this notion of 'our side of the hill' simply cannot last as the weight of numbers increases by the day, and then by the hour.

On 28 August, an old campaigner by the name of Henry Hennington turns up and, instead of merely scratching the surface as the others have been doing, actually sinks a small shaft on a spot on the slope where he has found some promising gold specks in the grass. And there they are, like a bunch of golden grapes, good-sized nuggets 'all over the bottom like a jeweller's shop'.[51]

Not long afterwards, Hennington digs another hole in a different spot, this one ten feet deep, and is rewarded once more with a similar crop of golden grapes. It is on the strength of such finds that this area at Ballarat becomes known as 'Golden Point' – a small hill so rich in alluvial gold, on or near the surface, that you can barely miss. Just start digging! And so the men do, pulling out ever more gold. And there, still recording it all, is the beaming face of Alfred Clarke, his trusty pencil scratching ever more copious notes in his notebook.

What a *story!* Even if suddenly the rain is tumbling down as never before. He starts to race back to Buninyong regardless, to write his report. 'I had a creek running down my vertebrae, a lagoon in each boot and a waterhole in my hat,' he would later say of this trip. 'I was in excellent condition for cradling.'[52]

In short order, his report is on its way to Geelong, secured in the satchel of a horseman heading that way . . .

Mid-September 1851, Melbourne goes mad

Since the time that gold has been discovered, all of Melbourne and much of the colony appear to have lost its senses. Government work, much of it reliant on contractors, is at a standstill. For anyone with get-up-and-go has already got-up-and-gone. Labourers, louts and lawyers, farmers and foundry workers, mechanics and magistrates – they all form part of a human tide moving from Melbourne and Geelong to the diggings, scouring the land as they go, looking for supplies that might help. At Geelong, a man is brought to a halt by an outraged priest, convinced that the cradle on the man's back was only a short time before his bloomin' *pulpit!*

Among the many other problems this gold fever engenders is the continued loss of labour from the worthy pursuits of agriculture, all at a time when the wool shearing season is drawing nigh. After the squatters have suffered the colossal indignity of seeing swarms of these diggers infesting the land that they rightly have leasehold over, they now must bear the humiliation of seeing their own workers abandoning their posts to join the swarm!

Are the squatters really expected to shear the sheep, herd the cattle and harvest the wheat *themselves*? There will soon be a lot more work to do and no pastoral workers left to do it. In panic, some squatters have already sold up and left their runs because they simply cannot work them without men.

Yes, it has really come to that! In Melbourne you can no longer get a cab unless you are a digger, in part because they give the biggest tips, even for the smallest trips, refusing to take change on their fares. These damn diggers are out to change *everything*.

And it is not just the people of Melbourne who are in an uproar. Down in Hobart, the Bishop of Tasmania is reduced to paddling out to his yacht on the Derwent River every night, as this is the only way he can protect that boat from being stolen by convicts who want to go to the diggings. Things are turning upside down in that fair town. The Governor's wife, Lady Denison, complains about a woman walking the wharves dressed in bright pink velvet for no apparent reason. Meanwhile, her husband, Sir William Denison, laments that, 'There is no longer the division of rich and poor.'[53]

CHAPTER THREE

THE GOLDEN GLOBE

*Generally young, shallow-brained fellows, proud of their
uniform, treating the diggers overbearingly, and bringing down
invectives upon the Government through its servants.*[1]

Mrs Andrew Campbell, wife of the Ballarat police magistrate, was not
flattering in her characterisation of the police on the diggings.

*But with all its golden advantages, Australia has yet greater for the
emigrant who prefers the comforts and decencies of life to bartering his soul
for gold. In Australia, as elsewhere, Mammon carries his curse with him,
and his worshippers must partake of it. Drunkenness, debauchery, crime,
and immorality, in every shape, are the characteristics of such a society as
is now gathering in the gold districts. There are thousands of respectable
families in England whose interest it would be to emigrate, but who would
not encounter such a condition for all the gold Australia contains.*[2]

George Butler Earp, *The Gold Colonies of Australia, and Gold Seeker's Manual*

2 September 1851, *The Times* of London reports

It is a lengthy editorial, and it appears on the fourth page of the most
venerable newspaper in all of Great Britain:

AUSTRALIAN GOLD

Gold is likely to prove a drug in the market.
There has been a fresh discovery of this

precious metal in New South Wales. Advice recently received from Sydney inform us that gold has been discovered in large quantities at Bathurst, 150 miles from that place . . .

There is no inherent improbability in the report. It comes to us confirmed by the strongest positive testimony, Australia may yet put California to shame. It is said that from the mountain ranges to an indefinite extent in the interior, the region named is one vast gold field.[3]

However great a stir such stories create in Britain, by now, of course, they are totally out of date, as even greater finds are afoot . . .

8 September 1851, *The Argus* breaks the news

Alfred Clarke has been having a good year of it, breaking story after story himself, and today his most important one yet is published.

THE NEW DIGGINGS
BUNINYONG. THURSDAY MORNING
(4 SEPTEMBER)

A prolific gold field has been discovered about seven miles from Buninyong . . . on Yuille's station.

The gold found here is of virgin purity – some of the pieces are as round as a shot; others have squared sides, and some present a laminated appearance, as though subjected to extreme pressure.

Again, Geelong may cry 'Eureka!' for there is no doubt but that the long-sought is at length found; and ere long we shall lay claim to the appellation of the 'Golden District'.[4]

And it keeps going. Within days Clarke is using that rarest of journalistic devices – capital letters – but nothing less will do to report that, 'The news from the Gold Field is exciting . . . The fact of

TWENTY-THREE OUNCES having been obtained by one party, on the first opening of a new "claim," will bear comparison with any of the successes of the first Bathurst diggers.'[5]

And further: 'Let me then say, that success has exceeded the expectations of the most sanguine, and that Geelong may proudly boast, without fear of contradiction, that she possesses a gold field as rich as any ever yet discovered . . .

'Out of a hundred and twenty on the ground, there is not one idle hand. I never witnessed such a cheerful untiring scene of industry in my life, carried on in silence, broken only by the rocking of the cradle, or the exclamations elicited by an occasional extraordinary yield, or the upturning of a "nugget".'[6]

Of course, locally, Clarke's story starts the rush to beat them all, with people from all walks of life, including doctors, ministers, merchants and others, continuing to pour into Ballarat. By now there is no more questioning whose side of 'Black Hill' – as it has recently become known – is whose, only where the boundary of your claim extends to. And there are many disputes therein, particularly if one claim strikes it rich. Those with experience in California know best where to look for the easiest gold – that is, on the gravelly slopes where quartz boulders are most apparent, and there the gold is so near the surface it is frequently found 'tangled in the roots of stumpy black-stemmed grass-trees and tough stringy-barks'.[7]

Among the first of the new wave to arrive is none other than James Esmond. Though he has been busily pursuing his diggings at Clunes since first discovering gold there two months earlier, he – like everyone – has heard of the better diggings at Ballarat and on 10 September turns up in the company of the brothers Cavanagh. In this game, having had gold-digging experience counts for a great deal – one of the hard-bitten and bushy-whiskered brothers had been digging in California, just as Esmond had – as it helps to guide a sense of where gold is likely to be found based on 'the lead', the trace of the ancient creek bed *beneath*. If gold has been found here and . . .

here . . . then there is every chance that it will also be found, say . . . here . . . and probably, too, right *there*, at an even greater depth than the others have gone, beneath the barren layer previously felt to be the 'floor' and into the blue clay below.

In the space of just two days, by digging to a depth of 30 feet, the three veterans manage to pull out of the ground a staggering 50 pounds of gold – the equivalent of *seven* years' wages for a simple labourer. Much of it is found in the form of nuggets, something that stupefies those who know of California. Over there, they don't have nuggets; they have grains. Over there, they weigh in ounces. Here, they are weighing their gold in *pounds*.

The staggering find by Esmond and the Cavanaghs unleashes even more energy than already apparent – there is now no more leaning on the elbow at *ballaarat*. Their experience has revealed even *more* gold here, at greater heights on the hill and greater depths in the ground than anyone had previously thought. So *keep digging*, Bluey! Did you hear me? Fifty pounds of gold in just two and a half days!

That amount being – at anything up to £4 per ounce – a king's ransom, it is sent back to Melbourne under armed escort, whereupon it becomes the first significant quantity of Victorian gold to be exported to England.

In Melbourne, only one question and one answer is on everyone's lips:

'When are you off to the diggings?'

'Immediately!'

If Bathurst is mad again, Melbourne is now even madder. As recorded by one contemporary Melbourne storekeeper, William Hall, who watches it all close up, aghast: 'I cannot describe the effect it had upon the sober, plodding, and industrious people of Melbourne . . . The excitement it created in Melbourne was so intense, so all absorbing, that men seemed bereft of their senses; magistrates and constables, parsons and priests, merchants and clerks, policemen and paupers, all hastened to Golden Point; the ships in the harbour were abandoned by many chief officers as well as by the seamen.'[8]

And yet, among these many men of abandoned work in the pursuit of gold, there is one of a newly minted profession who is about to come into his own. Francis Doveton is Victoria's first duly appointed Gold Commissioner, the man ultimately responsible for collecting the license fees, and it is only a couple of days after he arrives at Ballarat on 19 September in the company of five armed troopers – supported by Captain Dana and a pod of native police, who are delighted to be able to lord it over white folk for a change – that he has his first confrontation with miners on the Brownhill Diggings. They are as angry about the fee now as when the news first broke, and more than happy to tell him so.

But the 33-year-old Doveton, an Englishman with a ramrod for a spine and an ice cube for a heart, whose father was a Reverend and whose adult life has been spent first as an officer with the 51st Regiment of Foot and then as a police magistrate in Tasmania, gives them no quarter, sir – do you *hear?* NO *quarter!*

The law is the law, and you will *obey* it.

Nor is there the slightest relief from Assistant-Commissioner David Armstrong, a former blacksmith who, to follow Charles Dickens in *Great Expectations*, is wont to beat on miscreants 'with a vigour only to be equalled by the vigour which he *used* to beat on his anvil'. As a matter of fact, Armstrong carries a riding crop made of brass for that very purpose. No matter that after his time as a blacksmith he had been a digger himself, trying his luck in California in '49. The fact is he did not achieve any success there, and seems to bitterly resent those who are trying to do so here. And so it is on this occasion that Armstrong is every bit as forceful as Doveton, being the one to tell the diggers straight up, 'The license fee is to be enforced, and . . . as half of September is still to run, each man is required to pay fifteen shillings.'[9] Furthermore, as per the law of the land, each claim will be strictly limited to an eight-foot square of land – barely enough to swing a billy of tea in.

The diggers' response is as strong as it is immediate. The following day a particularly large digger by the name of Herbert Swindells – a man with the torso of a tree trunk and upper arms like other men's thighs – holds court in what will become the classic fashion of the diggings. Standing on the high stump of a recently felled gum tree, the bloody sap still seeping down its sides, he calls for one and all to come hear him speak.

And so they do, leaving their cradles, their picks, shovels and buckets to gather around.

Swindells wishes to know, and he wishes to know it at the top of his voice: Are we going to meekly GIVE IN to this cove, Doveton, and pay this license? Are we going to agree to RESTRICT our diggings to a tiny eight by eight feet square? Or are we going to RESIST?

We're going to RESIST!

Likely led by Swindells, as he flourishes a pistol over his head and roars, 'Before I am done with this business, I will shoot someone.'[10]

Two resolutions are passed, one calling for the license to be reduced to just five shillings a month and the other asserting that the men should be allowed a five-times larger portion of Crown land to mine on.

Alas, when a delegation of two men is sent to the Commissioner's tent to present these resolutions, Doveton, backed by Armstrong and their armed body of men, gives the delegation something a little shorter than short shrift.

'I am not here to make the law but to administer it,' Doveton declares baldly, a mini-king in his mini-kingdom. 'And if you don't pay the license, I'll damned soon *make* you pay it.'[11]

The delegation is sent packing. At least, however, the diggers have something of the power of the press behind them. In his own report on the issue in the *Geelong Advertiser* on 26 September, the redoubtable Alfred Clarke writes: 'Gold digging is now a regular occupation, and if the Government intends to suppress it – they must raise an army for the express purpose, for the people are fast spreading out in all directions, and as gold digging is an epidemic I should not feel the least surprise if the police were to drop musket and take to tin dishes – Captain Dana to his pick and the Commissioner to his cradle. For . . . if the truth be told the Government is the greatest Gold Digger after all, and the most lucky – for where they dig they find it in pockets and are saved the expense of outfit or license – work when they please, and sink a shaft in every man's purse – and, perhaps in his heart too.'[12]

One digger who disagrees, however, and is brave enough to say so, is the highly respected James Esmond. Having witnessed terrible lawlessness in California, he believes that, by handing over money for the license, the diggers are paying for the law to be enforced for their own protection and that it will be well worth it.

When all is said and done – a lot more of the former than the latter – it is of course Doveton and his men who win the fight. The vast majority of the diggers do indeed pay up, either the 15 shillings or quarter ounce of gold, as they see fit. Such is the government's in-built advantage in all negotiations with the diggers, however, that its fixed gold exchange price of £3 (60 shillings) per ounce in payment for a one-month license always makes a tidy profit when taking a half ounce of gold as payment rather than 30 shillings in currency as, of course, gold may be worth considerably more in the city. And it doesn't even stop there. As the fresh half-month licenses bear the date 21 September, the government still manages to obtain another six shillings out of every digger.[13]

While it is one thing for you to put your hand in the air for some-thing so simple as pronouncing yourself in favour of protesting to the Commissioner, it is quite another to stare down a bevy of armed policemen wanting to see your license when you don't have one. And this is more particularly so when you know that there is easy gold to be found, and a king's ransom might be buried just a few inches beneath the surface of your claim. And as most of the diggers have been daily mining gold worth between £3 and £5, it is not *that* hard to come up with the money necessary to get issued with the small piece of paper that allows them to dig legally:

VICTORIA GOLD LICENSE.
NO.---,
21 SEPTEMBER, 1851
THE BEARER _____, HAVING PAID TO ME THE FIFTEEN SHILLINGS, ON ACCOUNT OF THE TERRITORIAL REVENUE, I HEREBY LICENSE HIM TO DIG, SEARCH FOR, AND REMOVE GOLD ON AND FROM THE DISTRICT OF BUNINYONG AND LODDON, AS I SHALL ASSIGN TO HIM FOR THAT PURPOSE DURING THE MONTH OF SEPTEMBER, 1851. THE QUANTITY OF GROUND ALLOWED IS EIGHT FEET SQUARE. THE LICENSE TO BE PRODUCED WHEN DEMANDED BY ME, OR ANY OTHER PERSON ACTING UNDER THE AUTHORITY OF THE GOVERNMENT.
F.C. DOVETON,
COMMISSIONER.

No fewer than 400 of these pieces of paper are issued within the first few days, while within a month there are 1300 and a fortnight after that 2246! It is not long before Captain Dana runs out of the printed licenses and must have new ones hastily written by hand.

This, at least, is pleasing to the Victorian government as they bring the diggings under their control. Doveton and his hawks are at the prow of how it is to work across all the goldfields. For every newly opened field of major diggings, there will be a government outpost to house a Gold Commissioner, supported by police, to maintain the peace, arrest those who break the law *and* collect the license fees. Those outposts are to be in clearly defined camps separate from the diggers, replete with many tents to house the police and next to which the Union Jack will, more often than not, be wilting under the hot sun.

At the beginning of each month there is a crowd around the Commissioner's tent to get the license, and if some diggers find it onerous to trek the oft four or five miles from their diggings to line up, get papers, trek back and lose half a day in the process – and others simply can't afford it because their capital is gone and they haven't found gold yet – then that's just too damn bad. The lockup, usually no more than the stump of an old tree upon which 'the prisoners were attached by sundry chains, the handcuff being round one wrist and through a link of the chain',[14] awaits until such a time as they or their friends or family can pay for their license for them. As to the fine, this varies from £3 to £10, depending on how long it is judged they have been digging without one. And if they *still* can't pay, then they must work out on the roads like a common convict, forfeit their claim and perhaps even be sent to Melbourne to do time in gaol.

23 September 1851, London, Friedrich Engels to Karl Marx

The more that Friedrich Engels hears about what is happening in Britain's southern colonies, the more he is amazed, and he waxes lyrical in his predictions to his friend Karl Marx in London.

'The British will be thrown out and the united states of deported murderers, burglars, rapists and pickpockets will startle the world by demonstrating what wonders can be performed by a state consisting of undisguised rascals. They will beat California hollow. But whereas in California rascals are still lynched, in Australia they'll lynch the honnêtes gens [gentry], and Carlyle will see his aristocracy of rogues established in all its glory.'[15]

25 September 1851, *The Argus* asks the question

Whatever else, however, at least the diggers enjoy the broad support of certain members of the press, and no-one more than the Geelong correspondent of *The Argus*, Alfred Clarke, who on this day is straight to the point: 'The full amount of the gold licenses, nay more than the full amount of them, has been exacted; and once more the representative of royalty (I beg Her Majesty's pardon, for casting so base a slur on her fair name) has unfurled the banner of oppression, and calls on his myrmidons to rally round him, and support him in his attempt to establish a Reign of Terror . . .

'Mr La Trobe has always been particularly unfortunate in linking himself and the interests of the colony with bad advisers. A man possessed of no mind himself, he has hitherto been ready to confer honourable and responsible appointments on individuals assumed to be gentlemen, and has been in the habit of listening to them, but who are in reality useless foppish whipper snappers; a set of aristocrats reared on a democratic dung-heap; men devoid of common sense, and lost and dead to every sense but that which proclaims their own ignorance, and persuades them that they still are men in form, if not in mind. What would any community of freemen who were working hard for a living think to hear a puppy of an officer talk about "irons," and handcuffing those who did not pay for the privilege of being allowed to work!'[16]

Against such outrages the diggers have appealed to the people. Will the people answer them? That question remains to be answered, but having the press behind them would be a good start.

September 1851, Mt Alexander region, 50 miles north of Ballarat

As rich as the pickings at Ballarat prove to be, however, the foraging instinct of the diggers is, as ever, not just to dig *down* to the riches, but also like ripples on a pond, to spread *out* to see if there might be even better – or at least less crowded – pickings elsewhere. And it is at this time that the word spreads: some shepherd named Worley has discovered a piece of golden quartz four miles north of Castlemaine in Barkers Creek, lying at the southernmost ridges of Mount Alexander. Within days the first group of restless diggers from Ballarat swoops into the area, and within weeks they move along into the nearby, fabulously auriferous gully of Forrest Creek, which runs east towards Chewton and will give its name to the lucrative Forrest Creek diggings. Always, the search is for the easy alluvial gold, which doesn't require a great deal of digging.

Within weeks men are winning up to half a pound of gold per day and by November, 'two, three, and four pounds per day [is] common amongst the *luckies*' of Forrest Creek.[17] Another valuable goldfield has been discovered – one of many soon to be uncovered – that is so strong and so rich, in the early days particularly, that much of the flow of new chums from Melbourne to Ballarat is diverted instead to these Forrest Creek diggings. Just 6000 men had been a part of the first rush on Ballarat, but more than twice as many now race to Mount Alexander's quartz-covered ranges and what will become 15 square miles of adjoining goldfields centred on Chewton – a number that soon swells to 30,000. Within three months, the Ballarat fields are briefly left all but deserted. These are heady times, and with the growing realisation that it is frequently the first to arrive who get the easiest pickings, there is a constant frenzy to move from one set of goldfields to the next. Only on Sunday does the frantic labour stop, with the Commissioner strictly forbidding any work on the Sabbath.

The stories – and they are true – soon spread not only to the other diggings, but also, of course, to Melbourne, which is once more agog. One man managed to find 80 pounds of gold in a single hour! Another, using no more than his penknife, if you can believe it, filled a quart pot with nuggets in just one day's digging!

Prospectors quickly come to realise that this entire Mt Alexander Range is 'a prolongation of that of which Buninyong forms a part,'[18] and every nook and cranny of this fresh country, every ridge and gully, every hopeful outcrop of rock – all of it up for grabs! – is now being scoured by hopefuls.

The net result is that only a few weeks after Forrest Creek has been discovered, the blessed wives of two workers on the Mt Alexander North pastoral property, Mrs Kennedy and Mrs Farrell, find gold while camping next to Bendigo Creek, 24 miles north of Castlemaine. In short order, those diggings are soon opened up. Bendigo Creek proves particularly rich, and in the coming months no fewer than 40,000 diggers will be feverishly working both sides of its banks.

3–4 October 1851, the Ballarat goldfields receive two visitors . . .

Where once was a bubbling creek with no more than an occasional passing shepherd for company, all is changed. Now, a solid mass of men are as busy as ants, trekking back and forth up and down the recently denuded slopes, carrying buckets of dirt, rocking the cradle, ladling water from the creeks to wash it through and spasmodically emitting cries of joy as they gather the gold.

On this Tuesday, however, the diggers receive a visitor who is not there to join the diggings so much as to have some understanding of them, to inform his future decisions. William Westgarth is a senior member of the colony's first parliament, which is just about to sit, and the first president of Melbourne's Chamber of Commerce. He is impressed from the first.

Conducted to the right spot at Golden Point, he is given a spade and is met with success in an instant: 'Out of one pound weight of matrix which I removed on the corner of the spade, I picked out 7s 6d worth of gold.'[19]

It is a great deal of food for thought. On Westgarth's way back to Melbourne, he would recount, 'I mused over all I had seen, and long ere reaching home had concluded that £10,000 a day was being taken out of Ballarat.'[20] It is a staggering amount of wealth coming from a spot that previously produced next to nothing, and clearly the government is quite right to garner its fair share.

The next day, an even more important visitor arrives, with a name more than merely familiar to the diggers. Though in this rustic scene the signs of faraway Melbourne are few, for weeks now government notices warning of penalties for such offences as not having a fully paid license on you at all times have been pinned up and pasted all over the goldfield, always released by authority of 'His Excellency' Charles Joseph La Trobe.

And now, here is the man himself. Here is Lieutenant-Governor Charles Walter *Joseph* La Trobe, come on his first visit to the diggings and dressed in a frockcoat and tall hat for the occasion.

'Joe!' cries out a digger upon first sighting him, to the general merriment of all – with the exception of the Lieutenant-Governor, who stiffens at this presumption. But it is too late.

Joe! Joe! *Joe!* JOE! Somehow this nickname seems so perfect for Charles Walter Joseph La Trobe that it sticks, and soon it will become not only the sobriquet for La Trobe but indeed all those who represent his authority, from the Gold Districts Commissioners to their retinue of Assistant-Commissioners and clerks and assistants; from the captains who represent the armed might of the British Empire in these parts to their subalterns, sergeants and soldiers; from the police inspectors to their constables and native police who are charged with keeping Her Majesty's peace on the goldfields. The Joes are the officials, the authorities, the stuffed shirts, those who, without ever lifting a pick in anger or picking up a shovel, presume to rule over the diggers. By defining them, the diggers are also helping to define themselves, the valiant souls who have come here from all over the world to try thier luck. The diggers come from all walks of life, from all classes and levels of education and from many countries. And they're all equal here – no-one is better than anyone else, so don't try it on, because no-one cares.

On this day, though, the Joe in question – the original – goes for a walk around the diggings accompanied by some native police and their white commander, Captain Henry Dana, and is largely ignored by the diggers.

Still, it is instructional for him. The level of enthusiasm that the diggers have for their task is quickly apparent, and he can see why. He roughly counts 500 cradles being worked by about five times as many men, with another 500 or so men arriving every day – and just about all of them are making huge amounts of money! When he comes to the first shaft, that of William Brownhill, and observes the way he digs for the gold, La Trobe says to the miner pleasantly, 'Your mother did not think when you came to Australia that you were going to dig gold out of the ground in that manner.'[21]

What worries His Excellency, though, is where this labour is coming from, and who is doing the work they have left behind? He even raises with the diggers themselves the possibility of revoking their licenses for as long as two months, until such times as the harvest can be taken in, at which point they would be able to resume. But not to worry, La Trobe assures them, 'During that time, each man's allotted space would be carefully guarded, and returned to you.'[22]

Very kind of you, Joe. But do you not understand? We are neither convicts nor slaves, but free men. It may well suit **you** *to have us return to the farms to bring in the harvest. But it does not suit* **us**.

Like Westgarth, La Trobe is quick to notice how well the diggers are doing and at one point witnesses just two tin dishes of dirt producing a staggering eight pounds of gold, while he also hears of a party of diggers who find 16 pounds of gold in the morning and another 15 pounds in the afternoon!

La Trobe leaves the diggings with much to consider and, upon his return to Melbourne to find it even more abandoned, a growing sense of desperation. On 10 October he writes to the Secretary of State in London, Earl Grey, to update him on the situation:

'It is quite impossible for me to describe to your lordship the effect which these discoveries have had upon the whole community . . . Within the last three weeks the towns of Melbourne and Geelong and their large suburbs have been in appearance almost emptied of many classes of their male inhabitants . . . Not only have the idlers to be found in every community, and day labourers in town and the adjacent country, shopmen, artisans, and mechanics of every description thrown up their employments and in most cases leaving their employers and their wives and families to take care of themselves, run off to the workings, but responsible tradesmen, farmers, clerks of every grade, and not a few of the superior classes have followed; some, unable to withstand the mania and force of the stream, but others because they were, as employers of labour, left in the lurch, and had no other alternative. Cottages are deserted, houses to let, business is at a standstill, and even schools are closed. In some of the suburbs not a man is left, and the women are known, for self-protection, to group together to keep house. The ships in the harbour are in a great measure deserted . . . Even masters of vessels, like farmers, have made up parties with their men to go shares at the diggings . . . Both here and at Geelong all buildings and contract works, public and private, are at a stand-still.'[23]

For his part, Earl Grey – though perhaps drinking some calming tea with his famous father's name to it – is nothing if not alarmed to read the missive. Apart from everything else, the wool provided by the colonies is the staple that the British textile industry depends upon. Without it, that industry would struggle.

The solution for Charles Joseph La Trobe right now? Well, if it is not to revoke the licenses – both his experience on the gold-fields and subsequent advice received concur that the resistance to such a move would be overwhelming – then perhaps at least they should be more expensive? Perhaps even doubled in fee? That would simultaneously limit the number of would-be goldminers deserting to the fields and ensure that those who are mining generate more revenue for the government's coffers, which are becoming ever more depleted by the steadily increasing expenditure necessary to admin-ister the goldfields and the steeply rising wages that must be paid to those civil servants decent enough to remain in their workplaces and keep Victoria functioning. Compounding La Trobe's financial problems is the insistence by the Legislative Council that none of the colony's general revenue be spent on 'any services for anything which in its opinion is consequent on the discovery and search for gold'.[24] The heavy cost of administering and policing the goldfields, thus, can only come from the license fees themselves.

24 October 1851 *The Melbourne Morning Herald* reports . . .

A HOAX

Yesterday Mr George Say amused himself in cooking up a cock and bull story about gold being found in the gutter at the corner of Lonsdale and Swanston streets, and very near his late public house, the 'St George and Dragon'. He had the impudence to bring a specimen of it (as he called it) to our office, and told all manner of lies to induce us to perpetrate the hoax on the public. It appears that he procured a piece of quartz from some place or another, and over this lie had sprinkled some gold-beaten leaf, and had rubbed some of the leaf into the crevices of the 'sample' to form the delusion. If Mr Say gets his window smashed in some fine night for carrying on such vagaries, we will not pity him one bit.[25]

James Daley, the long-dead convict who had first faked the discovery of gold for his own ends to try to fool Governor Phillip would have been proud – and unsurprised that the ruse did not work.

1 November 1851, Melbourne, La Trobe worries

It is not quite that Victoria has fulfilled Governor Gipps's warning of 12 years before – that if gold fever takes hold then 'we will all have our throats cut'[26] – but things are still worrying Lieutenant-Governor La Trobe. For the general madness that has taken hold of Victoria is now *so* strong that, on this day, Charles La Trobe writes to Governor-General FitzRoy to request an increase to his small military force in Victoria. He later informs Earl Grey in the London Colonial Office of his hope that this action proves sufficient, 'happen what may', to safeguard the gaols, banks and public buildings.[27]

For its part, *The Melbourne Morning Herald* is quick to express the common mood among those of the better classes. 'It is sad,' it opines wearily, 'that the gentleman should change places with the lucky blackguard.'[28]

Early November 1851, the Ballarat goldfields widen, deepen . . . and rise

Meanwhile, the stream of people heading to the diggings continues to swell, to the point that it becomes first a river of humanity heading to specific spots and then nothing less than a flood as those people spread across the land, frantically fossicking for the treasures they know abound there, if only they can be the first to find them. On those goldfields, where there had been complete wilderness only months before, there are now entire tent *cities*, with some solid structures even sprouting among them.

Look there, now, at what used to be Yuille's Run. From the hilltops looking down into the valley at night, the hundreds and hundreds of fires make the new arrivals look like an occupying army, and in many ways that is exactly what they are. The diggers sit around these fires, warming themselves and smoking their pipes, even as they cook their meals of damper and mutton chops . . . and damper . . . with perhaps a little more damper after that, and boil their billies of tea.

The blackfellas, who had been in these parts for thousands of years, have almost all left for parts unknown, having been hunted off the rest of their traditional lands, with only the occasional group to be seen here and there on the fringes of the encampments, living in their 'humpies'. These structures consist of two forked sticks placed upright in the ground, with one horizontal stick perched between them, and upon that the Aborigines rest tree branches and large slabs of bark to give themselves partial protection from the weather.

'They lie all around their fires at night,' writes one digger to his family at home, 'and all the covering they wear is a possum rug or a blanket thrown around them. Their principal food is the possum which they find out by knocking on the trees, and where they find a hollow sound they cut open the tree and so catch the opossum. They also kill Turkeys, pigeons and parrots with the boomerang which they are very expert at throwing.'[29]

In truth, the diggers themselves are only marginally less nomadic than the natives, as the vast majority of them remain in calico tents and are capable of moving on short notice should news arrive of some other goldfield where the pickings are even greater. (Already, many have gone to try their luck at the new diggings at Forrest Creek.) True, a very few have constructed rough huts using split logs – known as 'slabs' – of eucalyptus trees and bark, but these are rudimentary shelters at best, and actually closer to rude.

Still, by now the settlement at Ballarat is starting to be established enough that some canvas saloons are even opening up for those who can afford a bit of fun. And many tents are in fact by now like small houses, frequently built around the solid structure of a large fireplace with a chimney, and a large hearth for cooking on.

The vast majority of diggers don't mind the Aborigines who remain around and about. As recorded in the diary of one digger, Thomas Pierson, 'They are given to theft otherwise inoffensive if not put up to be otherwise by whites, the bushrangers get them for guides.'[30]

The diggers mostly want what is *in* their land, not this particular bit of land itself, and that is a crucial difference. Many of the Aborigines manage to survive by trading with the diggers. They give the diggers the amazingly warm and light possum skin cloaks that only they know how to make; in return, the diggers give to them grog and some of their strange food. And sometimes the diggers will pay to see them get all painted up and perform corroborees or show how they throw their boomerangs, something they are also asked to do for visiting dignitaries.

From late 1851 onwards, there are even – and this is an enormous breakthrough when they first arrive – a few white women. At first, when a woman very occasionally appeared on the diggings, the cry would go up, 'There's a woman!',[31] and instantly the tents would empty and head after head would pop up from the mine-shaft to gaze longingly upon her fine form while the suddenly self-conscious lady walked past, usually behind her suddenly protective and glowering husband.

'There was no man, having the heart of a man, who did not bless the vision [of a woman],' one of the first chroniclers of the times, William Bramwell Withers, would record, 'while many an eye was moistened with the sudden tear as love, hope, disappointment, fear, struggled all at once in the homeless digger's bosom.'[32]

And, sure enough, where those women settle, the immediate area is soon brightened and practised eyes can spot her influence. The tins outside the tent are suddenly brighter; a suspended rope soon appears, on which is hung freshly washed laundry, including actual *sheets*; 'a pet cockatoo, chained to a perch, makes noise enough to keep the "missus" from feeling lonely when the good man is at work';[33] and, of course, that good man is seen to have a smile for the first time in weeks – even a gleam in his eye – as he heads back to his tent after a long day's digging.

As to grog, well, that is a little more problematic . . . but only a little. In an effort to keep good order, the government has placed a strict prohibition on the sale of liquors, but that is easily got around. For sly grog sellers are *everywhere*. They are men who either buy up big in Melbourne and smuggle it to the goldfields in the middle of drays carrying other supplies, or they have their own stills and make it themselves. Either way, if it is grog you want – nearly always hard liquor because wine and ales are far too bulky and expensive to cart – there is never a problem.

A nearby visitor noted, 'No official supervision could prevent the smuggling of liquors, mostly of the vilest description.'[34]

But it is still alcohol!

Drink up, lads, for tomorrow we may find gold!

6 November 1851, Geelong gets along

On this day a gold buyer in Geelong – an admittedly new occupation in this city – is just walking along, minding his own business, when a rather rough-looking character (who still can't be as bad as he smells) suddenly heaves into view, *looking right at him.* Is he about to be assaulted? Robbed?

'Mr . . .' the fellow addresses him. 'I hear you're a gold buyer.'

'Yes,' replies the Geelong man carefully, his nostrils twitching.

'What are you giving?'

Ah-hah! The fellow only wants to trade gold! Relieved, the buyer replies, 'Oh, if it's a good sample, £3 per ounce, but I don't care about buying very small lots. How much have you?'

'I suppose pretty handy – 60 pounds.'[35]

11 November 1851, *The Argus* reports . . .

It is not pretty reading. For this report, coming from Ballarat, informs the readers of Melbourne and wider Victoria what happens when a freshly arrived digger jumps into an abandoned hole to try his luck. Two government troopers arrive and ask him why he is in this hole. The digger, something of a 'larrikin', answers, 'To wear out my old clothes'.[36]

For his trouble, the unfortunate digger finds himself handcuffed and chained to a tree until the next morning! And now the correspondent of *The Argus* plaintively asks the question: 'Now I ask Mr La Trobe if this is conduct to be tolerated. Is this the way to secure the goodwill of diggers who have plenty of arms and ammunition with them? Was this man a slave? Was he a wild beast? What was he? A free man, and to be thus treated.'[37]

The reaction of the diggers themselves is reported to be equally savage, as placards soon appear all over the goldfields exhorting the diggers:

DOWN WITH LA TROBE! - - THE COMMISSIONERS! PAY NO LICENSES.

ATTEND THE MEETING TONIGHT. THE GOVERNMENT OFFICERS ARE - - - SCOUNDRELS.[38]

Such protests are deemed to be a good thing by *The Argus* correspondent, for, 'Where is the man who will try to vindicate the conduct of the Government officials? They have been charged with partiality, imbecility, fraud and ignorance from the commencement of their career, and there they still remain. Whose blood would not boil at such a disgraceful stretch of authority as is here exhibited! Or who would not rather support the man thus shamefully ill-treated, than use his tongue, much less his arm, in defence of this mockery of a Government!'[39]

The journalist goes further and takes direct aim at the irresponsible man who is most responsible for the coming disaster: 'If Mr La Trobe is courting future fame, he will very soon have the honour of having his name handed down to posterity as the man who [severed] the few remaining links that still bound Victoria to the Parent State, for no man will sanction such acts of tyranny as this and when the diggers once resist his authority, that moment he may take ship, and flee the country.'[40]

22 November 1851, the glad gold tidings spread to London and beyond

The news of the goldfields in Australia, particularly the staggering account of the finding of the Kerr Nugget, continues to spread throughout the world. On this day, *The Illustrated London News* has the headline story 'The Gold Discovery In Australia', and is beside itself with enthusiasm: 'We have accounts of the progress made at "the digging" which shows that Australia is likely to surpass California in the wonderful productiveness of its fields. We learn, for instance, by the present advices, that in one hole lumps of gold weighing altogether 106 lb were picked up by an individual.'[41]

Typical is the reaction of an 18-year-old Scotsman by the name of William Craig, whose entire soul comes alive as he reads the thrilling news from Australia.

'YES, that's the land for me!' he would later describe his feelings. 'A continent in itself, inhabited by only a few civilised beings and wild aborigines, while millions of acres of good land are waiting settlement by people of the right stamp.'[42]

Another who is impressed by the things he reads in *The Illustrated London News* is none other than that red-headed Latin man of action, former Italian revolutionary Raffaello Carboni.

After recovering as well as he could from the wounds he had received while fighting alongside Garibaldi, Carboni had been obliged to leave Italy for his own safety and, moving through all of France, Germany and Malta, finally finished here in London, where he has been working – far too hard, in his view, for far too little money – as a translator. The idea of finding golden nuggets in the Australian bush is really most appealing . . .

Other Europeans, like one Robert Rede, are luckier still. For they are already there. The well-educated 39-year-old son of a Royal Navy officer – who had once trained to be a medico at the Royal London College of Surgeons before drifting to Paris for nearly a decade – is a restless soul who just happens to arrive in Melbourne at this very time. Eager to try his luck in this new country, he soon makes his way to Bendigo and through both digging and doctoring – he becomes known as the 'little doctor',[43] despite the fact that he hadn't completed his medical studies – immediately does well.

29 November 1851, Victoria, the record is set straight

It is only a simple letter to the *Geelong Advertiser*, and at the time is barely remarked upon. Still, it is the very notion that inspired its writing – the desire to set the record straight – that, with the passage of the years, will turn the letter into an ever more important foundation stone of truth. For the author of the letter is one Archibald Yuille, William's cousin, and he is quickly to the point:

BALLÂRAT, 25TH NOVEMBER, 1851

Sir,
Perceiving that the name of the diggings here is usually pronounced incorrectly I beg to state that it is a native name, and that the accent is not on the last syllable, but on the one before it as written above.
It is a pity that Englishmen should spoil the euphony of the native language.
I am, Sir,
Your most obedient servant,
ARCHD. B. YUILLE[44]
Owner of the Run Ballârat.

Early December 1851, Melbourne, whither the withering police

His name is James Yarrow, and he used to be poor, earning just four shillings a day for the Victorian police. But that was then, in the distant past, just over six weeks ago. Now, *now* he is rich. And he has the proof! Marching into the dim, dingy and stifling barracks where he used to live – he can now barely comprehend how he was able to stand the sheer dullness of it – he meets up with his old comrades, who are still wearing the same drab blue uniforms as ever, and pulls out the largest wad of notes they have ever *seen*. There is £500 if there is a pound, and that is what he has earned in just six weeks on the diggings since he resigned! His former comrades couldn't get that kind of money in seven whole years of walking the beat in Melbourne, wrestling with Vandemonians, Aborigines, drunken Irishmen and wild Californians, and James has earned this in just *six weeks*! And it has all happened at a time when the price of bread has doubled and the price of wood and water has gone up five times, while their wages haven't changed.

In response, some of his former colleagues immediately give notice, even as they prepare to head to the diggings. Others wait as long as that afternoon. Only a very few of the more timid souls do nothing, but within days what's left of the Victorian police have a crisis at hand. It is so bad that the desperate Chief Commissioner of Police, Evelyn Sturt – the brother of the great explorer Charles Sturt, who was one of the first to penetrate the interior of the country – feels obliged to write two letters in quick succession to Lieutenant-Governor La Trobe, the second informing him that at a single muster, 50 out of his 55 city police had given notice and would cease service from 31 December 1851. And that, he claims, is 'notwithstanding the considerable increase to their pay I was instructed to offer them'.[45] In fact, he is soon authorised to offer his ordinary constables a 50 per cent increase – *six* shillings a day, for the next *12 months* – if they'll only stay! And yet they're simply not interested.

But what more can La Trobe do, beyond across-the-board civil service pay increases, to try to hold on to as many of his own employees as he can, as well as refuse licenses to men who have quit their jobs without notice? Not a lot.

Nowhere is the problem worse than sailors abandoning newly arrived ships. It is so bad that deeply alarmed ship-brokers send a letter to the Colonial Land and Emigrant Commissioners in London, urgently requesting that a few policemen and colonial soldiers can be placed on board each ship while in Port Phillip, with the specific task of ensuring no seamen try to steal away. Just to make the point, they also wonder if a warship posted nearby would also be helpful, not to mention some shuttle steamers to disembark emigrants so the ships themselves, with their precious sailors, can remain as far off shore as possible.

One measure La Trobe does take to encourage those police on the goldfields to stay at their posts is to institute a system whereby, when their arrests generate fines, such as for not having a gold license or selling sly grog, the arresting officers (typically an inspector with two constables) are to be given half of the proceeds once convictions are recorded and the license fee deducted.

Yes, it is obvious that such a system will encourage perjury, corruption and blackmail, and police will inevitably focus less on preventing crime and more on going after these mere misdemeanours – and then try to get convictions, come what may – but extreme times call for extreme measures. And how else, when police constables are being paid just six shillings per day, could they possibly be kept at their posts?

Personally, La Trobe tries to live as simply as possible, believing, as he had once written to Governor Gipps, that, 'It is my duty to set a good example & to show that it is possible to live moderately and contentedly even in the midst of a crowd of successful speculators who are making their thousands by the turn of every card.'[46] But it is now obvious that his is an example no-one wishes to follow. And what is most troubling is that the budget for maintaining law and order on the goldfields is blowing out. The wages and costs for civil servants on the Mt Alexander goldfields alone – including paying for Assistant-Commissioner Lydiard and his assistants to live on the goldfield and administer the license system, the police to maintain order, the magistrates in town to administer the law, and the armed escorts heading back and forth with the gold – is now around £1000 monthly. And that is in just one gold district, where for the month of November 1851 the diggers themselves pulled out a tad less than £94,000 of gold to be escorted to Melbourne!

It cannot go on, and La Trobe's fear is that because of the invading diggers and his lack of wherewithal to provide the military security that the goldfields, cities and ports need, Victoria risks descending into anarchy or worse – no longer being a British possession.

It is with this in mind that in the first days of December, at a time when he has just 44 soldiers in the entire colony to call upon, La Trobe writes to Secretary of State Earl Grey in London, earnestly requesting him to send troops: 'It is imperatively my duty to urge . . . that immediate steps should be taken to afford this security to the colony, both as respects internal disturbance or attack from without. Melbourne ought to be made the headquarters of one regiment at least.'[47]

Yes, that is it. With one solid regiment of men who *couldn't* just leave their posts if bitten by gold lust – because they would be shot for desertion if they did so – Melbourne might possibly be kept stable.

––––––––––

And so, the Redcoats are coming, are they? To our peaceful province?

That, at least, is the very strong view of *The Argus* when it catches wind of La Trobe's move, and it wastes no time in condemning the Lieutenant-Governor: 'The rumour that Mr La Trobe has sent for a supply of troops, has produced an extraordinary sensation, among many people down here . . . A man must be worse than a madman to venture on such an expedient at the present time; for the strength of the government consists most decidedly in the good sense and peaceable disposition of the diggers; if it once forfeits that, we are lost and the miserable display of a few hundred redcoats, among a population of 15,000 armed men, mad in their search for gold, will be the first thing to alienate their respect for the constituted authorities.'[48]

Which is as may be. In the meantime, however, La Trobe, in his urgent need to get at least a makeshift force for law and order onto the goldfields until the Redcoats can arrive, makes another desperate move. He writes to his fellow Lieutenant-Governor in Van Diemen's Land, Lord Denison, and asks him to send up soldiers, whether drawn from the 99th Regiment or some of the army pensioners who are known to have retired to his colony – men without the wherewithal to do anything else – so that the government can at least have *some* presence. It is all part of his insistence, as he assures Earl Grey, that 'every practicable means to secure the maintenance of good order and observance of the law in the country districts will be resorted to'.[49]

Maintaining that order is all the more difficult, not just for the numbers of men heading to the goldfields, but also for the diggers' growing resistance to paying the license fees, all at a time when La Trobe's advisers are very insistent that they actually should be paying *more*.

More? Just as a duck is to water, so is the digger to outraged protest at any mention of the license fee. Typical is the response of one contemporary writer and digger, William Howitt: '[The] Government, in fact, has done nothing forever for the diggers but tax them! The whole amount of taxation which the squatters, who hold the whole country in possession . . . pay to the Government, is £20,000 a-year. The diggers, on the contrary, pay in licenses more than half a million a-year.'[50]

But even if La Trobe did want to increase taxes on the squatters, who still paid just £10 annually apiece for their vast holdings, their resistance would be even more intense than the diggers'. For the truth of it is, the ruling class in Victoria, as in New South Wales, is the squattocracy. They are the people who have arrived here first, who settled the land and built it up, whose members crowd the Legislative Council. Getting more money out of them would be more than problematical; it would be nigh on impossible. It is a problem La Trobe continues to wrestle with, but there seems only one obvious way forward . . .

8 December 1851, across the cross Victorian goldfields

It is shocking. Outrageous. Breathtaking in its sheer bastardry. For it is on this day that the news from Melbourne reaches the diggings: the administration of Charles La Trobe has announced that from the first day of the New Year, the license fee will double to £3 per month! Even more appalling and infuriating to many is that this legal obligation to pay up will also apply to 'all persons on the goldfields who are in any manner concerned with the search for gold, as tent keepers, cooks, &c, on the same terms as those who are digging for it.'[51]

The outcry from the diggings is all but universal as plans are put in place to hold meetings among the angry miners to decide what to do. Typical is the large notice pinned to trees and stumps at the Forrest Creek diggings:

FELLOW DIGGERS!

The intelligence, has just arrived of the resolution of the Government to double the license fee. Will you tamely submit to the imposition or assert your rights as men?

You are called upon to pay a tax originated and concocted by the most heartless selfishness, a tax imposed by Legislators for the purpose of detaining you in their workshops, in their stable yards, and by their flocks and herds ...

Remember that union is strength, that though a single twig be bent or broken, a bundle of them tied together yields not nor breaks ...[52]

As a result of those meetings and subsequent communications between the goldfields, plans are put in place for a mass meeting for every digger who can get there, while all over it is noted that there is a sudden surge in demand from the diggers for guns, pistols, ammunitions and even cutlasses for the desperate. It is for very good reason that the correspondent of *The Argus* dryly asks of its Melbourne readers, 'What will save the Colony?' It is a question in everybody's mouth . . .[53]

Mid-December 1851, Ballarat proper takes shape

A careful, considered man is Government Surveyor William Swan Urquhart. And this is an important job. For no more than four months after gold was discovered, his superiors have sent the surveyor to Ballarat to lay out streets for a township and, most particularly, designate where government buildings should be built. Having received his instructions on 3 December, Mr Urquhart arrives at Ballarat on 11 December and the next day looks around to get his bearings. With it being obvious that no township can be laid where the diggings are taking place, while it still needs to be close to such diggings, he is not long in making his selection. The choice is obvious: the township shall be laid atop a small plateau just to the west of Yarrowee Creek, and for the next fortnight he sketches his plans on his huge sheets of paper. Other men build castles in the sky, but that has never appealed to Urquhart. He loves to see a town even before it is built, to form it up beneath his fingers, and he barely notices the days passing.

The basic plan is a grid of wide streets, and he also has the honour of baptising these thoroughfares, naming them after figures already significant in the short history of Ballarat since colonisation.

Yes, the place is unrecognisable since the days when the Aborigines had this broad valley to themselves, but Urquhart at least gives a nod to their traditional ownership by assigning some Aboriginal names to the physical features. The creek is *'Yarrowee'* and the swamp *'Wendouree'*, while the waterholes remain *'Quimidupakup'* and the hole further downstream *'Parmoompi'*.[54]

From Urquhart's map, with its precise measurements of distances and angles, it will be the job of the Royal Engineers and their workforce to actually build the streets, which will frame four large blocks containing 40 land lots that the government can eventually sell to raise revenue. No less than 20,000 acres of nearby agricultural land by Dowling Forest, Lake Learmonth and Lake Burrumbeet, Miners Rest and Glendaruel, in lots varying in size from 80 to 320 acres each, are also set aside for eventual sale, though for the moment at least the government has no interest in releasing it.

Four o'clock in the afternoon, 15 December 1851, at Forrest Creek just outside of Castlemaine, beside the Old Shepherd's Hut

Down tools, lads, no more rocking the cradle – let's get going and be quick about it. For the meeting has near started.

It is a meeting such as the goldfields have never seen, with men emerging from every shaft, every creek and gully, every hill for a radius as far as 20 miles, including Bendigo, and making their way to Old Shepherd's Hut, in a paddock at the small settlement of Chewton, just outside Castlemaine, east of the junction of Forrest and Wattle creeks. As a matter of fact, there are so many men, and the cause so similar, that they will ever after refer to it as the first 'monster meeting', just as such meetings used to be called in the great days of Chartism in old England. For these 15,000 miners present – together with brass bands and waving flags – have come to protest. They intend to *make* the government change its mind.

And that is certainly the theme that speaker after speaker warms to as they stand on the back of a dray and scale the heights of oratory, led by one of the key organisers, Laurence Potts, a radical Englishman well steeped in the rhetoric of Chartism:

'Brother diggers and fellow-citizens . . .' he begins in stirring cadences, the voice of a man who knows how to move a crowd with his words alone and . . . loves . . . every . . . *syll* . . . *a* . . . *ble* of it. He goes on: 'I see before me some 10,000, or 12,000 men which any country in the world would be proud to own as their sons, the very cream of Victoria and the sinews of her strength. Now, my friends, let it be seen this day whether you intend to be slaves of Britain, whether you would bow down your neck to the yoke or whether, like true *men,* you would support your rights . . !55 *(Cheers)*

'On this ground are collected . . . men, who have hitherto united in the bonds of friendship, discarded all distillation of nations and needs, and lived like brothers. Why then should we bear a grievous imposition, while it is in our power to avoid it? You must be aware, that the 30 shillings charged by the government is an illegal taxation, and that His Excellency has no power to tax us. We are willing to pay a small tax, but the question is, will we pay £36 a year? *(Voices from all parts, Never!)*

'The *Herald* describes us as a set of "cut-throats and scoundrels", from that journal little else could be expected . . . Talk of honesty! I defy the world to produce the same honesty among the same number as at Forrest Creek. Is there one of you who locks your door? *(Laughter)* When I retire to rest, the last inquiry I make of those in the tent is, whether they have put the skewer in the blanket. *(Renewed laughter)* Men go to work, leaving thousands of pounds in their boxes, without lock or guard, and nothing but a bit of calico between that and a robber, that is, if there is any. Do not fathers bring their daughters among us, husbands their wives and children, and where has there been a single case of one being insulted? You are living in better order here than they are in Melbourne, with all their blue coat force, pistols and carbines included. It is useless to talk of physical force, moral force is what is required. You are men, possessed of the same power of reason, strength of mind and body, as your would-be extorters. Now will you pay the £3 license . . .? *(Never!)*

'The Home Government do not require, nor do they possess the power to enforce unjust taxation. It was such taxation that lost Great Britain, America. *(A pause)*

'I hope brother diggers, as a Briton, such unjust taxation will not be the cause of separating these splendid Colonies from the Mother Country. But mind, if from any misgovernment, the feelings and affection we at present possess as Britons, are torn asunder by Government misrule, and 50,000 British hearts are estranged by misrule – then, and then only, must violence be talked of. *(Hear, hear!)* There are few here who would advocate separation, few who do not love the Country of their adoption, few who do not feel themselves free! And none, I trust, who will be slaves! *(Immense cheering)* I call upon you once more, to pledge yourselves to support one another – not only against taxation, but against disorder.'[56]

The subsequent roar, they say, can likely be heard in Melbourne, and with the help of the many journalists who are there to cover the meeting, it is. Every syll-a-ble of it.

And such is the power of Potts's words that by the time he reluctantly concludes, the mood has moved from bitter anger to something approaching joy, as the attendees begin to realise the collective power they possess, having turned up in such numbers. This point is made well by the next speaker, Mr Lineham.

'Now I will tell you what I intended to do, when the Commissioner came round. I should refuse to pay, and he would compel me to go with him. Now I should propose if one went, all went. *(Yes, yes)* Of course, we are too independent to walk, and it will take a curious number of horses to drag us to Melbourne. *(Laughter)* I am not an advocate for forcible resistance, nor do I think any of you are; we can gain the day without it, though the *Herald* should use its thunders.

I would advise, that until something definite is settled, pay nothing; it is the height of madness for Government to try the strength of a body of men like us, united as I believe we are; we can defy the whole colony put together if compelled to do so. I trust none will pay the £3 imposition or any royalty, though they were obtaining twenty-pound weight of gold per day . . .' *(Hear, hear! Hear hear!)*[57]

Mr Lineham then reads the key resolution, which is seconded by Mr Doyle, and carried: *'That this meeting while deprecating the use of physical force, and pledging itself not to resort to it except in case of self-defence; at the same time pledges itself to relieve or release any or all diggers that on account of non-payment of £3 license may be fined or confined by Government orders or Government agents, should Government temerity proceed to such illegal lengths.'*[58]

And there is another particularly impassioned speaker, a one-armed digger and former sea captain come all the way from the diggings at Bendigo Creek. It is Captain John Harrison, a former squatter already well known for his passion for republicanism and his participation in the Anti-Transportation League devoted to stopping the transportation of convicts to our continent.

He is greeted with three hearty cheers, and immediately gets to it: 'I am a little late, but you will bear in mind I have ridden 20 miles to address you. *(A voice: 'Put your cap on, Captain')* I took my cap off, my lads, to honour patriots, but I might not do so for Victoria or her myrmidons . . . What then are we paying for? We give a fee for protection, and get nothing in return . . . They say it's for the Queen. Has the Queen not enough, or does she want it to buy pinafores for the children? They will tell you her salary is small. I wish to God I had 1/20th for mine!

'Talk of doubling the fee, let them reduce it one-half of the present charge, instead of doubling, or they will find, like the tale of the golden egg, that in grasping all, they will get nothing. As for the statements of the *Herald* with respect to a royalty fee, it is only put in another and more obnoxious shape. They say, that according to law the Queen is entitled to royalty. The Colonies never cost the Queen or Government one shilling, and under those circumstances I consider that they are not entitled to the benefits of the land. It was a similar tax that lost Charles his head; it was unjust taxation that caused the United States to throw off the burden, and unless the Government learns a little wisdom, an additional tax might lead to the same result here.

'We ask but for justice! *(Cheers)* In America, the land sold, benefited the country. It caused immigration, repaired roads, and all and every part was fully and fairly accounted for. If Mr La Trobe has any foresight, he must see this tax ought to be appropriated to similar purposes and unfold the vast resources and manifest riches to the world. Why does he require it for the Queen, who will never receive a sixpence? Let him expend it to make the Colonies what they ought to be. Let him make it a Colony of virtuous and thriving people. We have been told that the poor man is starving, that work is scarce, and they have nothing. Now the scale may be turned. The poor man may be elevated, the independency so much desired is within his grasp . . .

'Is it not as fair to give the poor man a chance as the squatter, when wool is up? Why should so much favour be shown them? What attention have they paid to the comforts of their men – bad huts, bad food, and often bad treatment, while they were lolling in their mansions. Let the poor man get the value of his labour. If the rich would not give it, Providence, in his wisdom, has thought fit to do so. Let them make good use of it, and let them act on the great principles – morality, justice, and truth. They talk of the morality of Mr La Trobe in private life, but I unhesitatingly assert that Mr La Trobe is an immoral man, in every sense of the word. Like the man who strained at the gnat and swallowed the camel, he lay the tax upon the people that were compelled to shear, sow, and reap, until he drove them to agitate. He finds his conduct deprecated, and that destruction must follow. He says we must let it pass; the people will endure it no longer, and thus he plays with their feelings. Now, my friends, make up your minds; if you find a man who does pay £3 for his license, although he obtain 50 lbs. of gold per day, surround his hole, and prevent him working . . . *(Long and continued cheering, accompanied with – We will, we will!)*

'Let us, my friends, unite as one people *(great cheering)* without respect to creed or country, and victory will crown our efforts.' *(It was some minutes before the next speaker could be heard above the cheering)*

And the motion – 'that this meeting deprecates as unjust, illegal, and impolitic, the attempt to increase the license fee from 30s to £3' – is carried, seemingly unanimously.[59]

The meeting finishes with one more cheer for *The Argus* and three groans for *The Herald*, which had referred to them as 'cut-throats and scoundrels', and after a vote of thanks to the chairman, one of the brass bands that accompanies the marching men strikes up a merry tune, and – after agreeing to an ideal that each digger will contribute a shilling a month to Captain Harrison representing their interests in Melbourne – the crowd begins to disperse.

Christmas Eve, 1851, Ballarat rejoices

Have ye heard? Joe La Trobe! He has caved in like a rotten mine-shaft. *Joe!*

He has decided not to double the license fee after all! The rumour races around the diggings like a deranged dog, even if it is far more joyously received. And though there are one or two doubters, it is in fact true. For though it has taken well over a week for the news to reach the goldfields, it is soon confirmed that the *Victorian Government Gazette* made the announcement in its 17 December 1851 issue that there is a change of plan, that the doubling of the tax *won't* be invoked, even though there is a warning that there are new regulations being considered to replace the existing license fee, as soon as circumstances permit, based on the 'principle of a Royalty leviable upon the amount actually raised'.[60]

And that idea, to place a levy only on the gold that is raised and not trying to apply it to all diggers, irrespective of whether or not they have found gold, clearly makes a lot of sense. Certainly, the mighty *Argus* thinks so, noting, 'We entirely approve of the principle of exacting a direct tax upon the gold, whether under the appellation of Royalty, or otherwise, rather than the continuance of the present most impracticable, and really inequitable license system. The charge ought to be proportioned to the amount of success, and not a mere poll-tax leviable on successful and unsuccessful alike. The new mode of impost is surrounded with serious difficulties, and we are quite prepared to expect that any fresh system may break down as pitiably as this last attempt. But the principle involved is an improvement upon the last, and with due caution there is no absolute need of failure. The rate of the charge should be a moderate one, and it should be payable in town, not upon the gold field itself . . .'

CHAPTER FOUR

EXODUS

Thank God there is some prospect of a cessation of the cursed gold seeking for some time owing to the creeks becoming dry. The rascals can't wash [gold] without water . . . It is really ludicrous to see the feeling of indifference (not to say contempt) with which everything appertaining to squatters or squatting is now treated in Melbourne . . . They will not always remain under a cloud. The profits of labor will be equalized in time while we have a monopoly of the land which with the help of God we will keep in spite of the Melbourne gold worshippers. Our time will come yet, land will tell in the long run. No one can blame us using any powers circumstances may place within our reach. We are the victims at present, let us hope we shall be the sacrificers by & bye.[1]

Squatter William Forlonge to C. Barnes, in late 1851

[Outsiders] cannot imagine the state of things here. Men who have been servants all their lives are now, after a few weeks work at the diggings, independent.[2]

Victorian squatter Alfred Burchett, January 1852

Early 1852, London, a ship sets sail on the Thames

In London, as the ships make ready to leave on their journey down the Thames and then into the English Channel leading to the open ocean, a colonial office clerk, John Capper, who seeks to be published in Charles Dickens's magazine *Household Words*, wanders among them, carefully formulating his lines for a forthcoming article: 'Mid-summer of the present year is sending quite as many, and more, of our countrymen away from London, to say nothing of Liverpool and other places as fast as sailing ships and steam-vessels can carry them, to join in the Golden Fair in Australia; the great South Land . . .

'What a sight there was upon the jetty! I would have fancied the whole export trade of this country had gone stark staring mad with the gold fever.'[3]

As it happens, Dickens's David Copperfield had already visited one of these ships when he had gone to farewell the Micawbers on their way to Australia.

'It was such a strange scene to me,' young David had recounted, 'and so confined and dark that, at first, I could make out hardly anything; but, by degrees, it cleared, as my eyes became more accustomed to the gloom . . .

'Among the great beams, bulks, and ringbolts of the ship, and the emigrant-berths, and chests, and bundles, and barrels, and heaps of miscellaneous baggage – lighted up, here and there, by dangling lanterns; and elsewhere by the yellow daylight straying, down a windsail or a hatchway – were crowded groups of people, making new friendships, taking leave of one another, talking, laughing, crying, eating and drinking; some, already settled down into the possession of their few feet of space.'[4]

Many of those who are leaving Great Britain for Australia carry books by Dickens to help to occupy them on the long journey, but they also carry works of non-fiction, often about Australia, giving them a guide for what to expect. One is indeed written by John Capper, under the title *Philips' Emigrants' Guide to Australia: containing the fullest particulars relating to the recently-discovered gold-fields, the government regulations for gold seeking, etc,* and includes 'a new map of the goldfields, comprising the recent discoveries of Mr Hargraves, Mr Hunter, Rev. W. Clark and others'.[5]

First up, the guide advises that the emigrant must expect to find the continent itself composed of 'unprofitable . . . barren soil or rocky hills' while its animals are 'few and of little value' and its fruit 'very few and scarcely worth mention'.[6]

The good news is that there is plenty of work there, even for those with little to offer bar the sweat of their brow, for they will be knocked over in the rush to secure their services as labourers and domestic servants.

'Should the intending emigrant be married,' Capper writes, 'so much the better, provided the wife be frugal and industrious: such a helper will not only be no expense, but she will actually often earn nearly as much as the husband.'[7]

But here perhaps in another guide – *The Gold Colonies of Australia and Gold Seeker's Manual* – is the most important thing of all that the emigrants must understand about this strange land that they are heading to: 'To the poorer of the aristocracy of this country, Australia offers an enticing field; but they must be careful to leave their aristocracy at home. Rank and title have no charms at the antipodes; and the most that they could affect for the bearers, would be an occasional lionization at snob dinners in the town in which the aristocrat may be wasting his time and his money. Great family connections in ancestry would only provoke, to any who should parade them, the remark that 'he was like a potato: all that was good belonging to him was underground.'[8]

Let us give the last word on the subject, however, to the opening words of Samuel Sidney, who in his book *The Three Colonies of Australia*, which has also come out this year, assures his readers that the discovery of gold will – yes, my friends – transform Australia from a mere 'sheepwalk tended by nomadic burglars to the wealthiest offset of the British Crown – a land of promise for the adventurous – a home of peace and independence for the industrious – an El Dorado and an Arcadia combined, where the hardest and the easiest best-paid employments are to be found; where every striving man who rears a race of industrious children may sit under the shadow of his own vine and his own fig-tree not without work, but with little care living on his own land, looking down the valleys to his herds, and towards the hills to his flocks, amid the humming of bees which know no winter'.[9]

18 March 1852, Forrest Creek receives a military 'force'

It has taken a great deal of time, admittedly, but after Charles La Trobe's desperate plea three months earlier to the Lieutenant-Governor of Van Diemen's Land, this is the morning, at 7 am, that from out of the thick mist suddenly appears at the Forrest Creek diggings the old army pensioners – the 99th Regiment! And, look, maybe they feel they are marching onto the diggings, but that is not the way it looks to the diggers. Shuffling, more like it. There are a little over a hundred of these ghostly figures in their blue cloth coats and forage caps, with bushy white whiskers, limping along the best they can.

One digger, Oliver Ragless, and his mates are having their usual morning repast of lightly burnt damper washed down by gallons of black billy tea when they see these extraordinary figures slowly emerge. When finally the diggers do make the arrivals out, the reaction is swift: they burst out laughing. This little posse is going to control the whole 25,000 of them? That is a *riot*. And it very well might result in one . . .

For all the pensioners' drunken ways, however – and Police Commissioner Sturt would say of them, '[They] appear to me to be the most drunken set of men I have ever met with'[10] – the view of the authorities is that they are better than nothing. This very month the local foot police have gone on strike for higher wages, and it is now doubly important to have *some* men in uniform on the diggings. And the way things are turning out, it is becoming ever more apparent that in a choice between military and police, it is better to have military men because not only do you only have to pay them a shilling a day – 'taking the Queen's shilling', as it is referred to – but, far more importantly, they can also be shot for desertion.

Late May 1852, on the Eureka, a man does not look a gift-horse in the mouth . . .

Strange, how things work out.

Sometimes, when the horse has bolted it brings great good fortune instead of calamity. On this particular day a Ballarat storekeeper by the name of Paul Gooch sends out a blackfella to look for his animal, and it this man who, as Gooch would later explain to the *Geelong Advertiser*, 'picked up a nugget on the surface. Afterwards I sent out a party to explore, who proved that gold was really to be found in abundance.'[11] This place, just a mile north-east of Golden Point, comes to be known as 'Eureka', and within days hordes of diggers – with the Irish heavily represented – are streaming there.

And in equally classic fashion, from the central part of the goldfields, the diggers 'follow the lead', branching out as they try to follow the course of the ancient creek beds far below, where the jewellers' shops may be found – always praying to find a junction of such creek beds, where the treasures would be guaranteed to make Aladdin himself blush.

In the case of the Eureka lead, it soon becomes apparent that it is heading to a junction with both the Canadian Lead and the Gravel Pits Lead – the latter of which lies right beneath the Government Camp. As noted by one of the first of the roughly contemporary writers to do the story justice, W. B. Withers, those three leads make up 'the Golden Trinity that made Ballarat famous throughout the civilised world'.[12]

16 June 1852, Gravesend, Kent, 27 miles east of London, on the south bank of the Thames[13]

She is the good ship *Scindian,* a three-masted barque of 650 tons, and on this sparkling English summer's day she is shipshape and at last ready to go. For not only are her passengers all aboard and below decks, but the wind is finally blowing from the west.

Thrilled to be leaving many of their woes in their wake, the bulk of the passengers are in fact assisted emigrants courtesy of Caroline Chisholm's Family Colonization Loan Society program, an organisation that receives strong support from the great Charles Dickens, among others. The system is that those emigrants (or their relatives in Australia) first put their life savings with the Society, which then lends the passenger whatever else they need to pay their fare. Then, once they land in the colony, agents of Caroline Chisholm welcome them, help them to find employment and arrange to have the debt repaid by convenient instalments.

With the weather-worn visage of one who has spent a lifetime at sea, and the grin of one who knows the moment he has been waiting for is at hand, Captain James Cammell gives the order: 'Weigh the anchors!' Like an echo, that order bizarrely grows louder as it is repeated down the chain of command from the First Mate to the Second Mate and the Second Mate to the sailors, who then begin the hard haul on the ropes, then the whole ship is suddenly alive with the booming command . . . 'Weigh the anchor . . !' *'Weigh the anchor . . !'* 'WEIGH THE ANCHOR . . !'

The crew weigh the anchor, singing a ditty as they go, so as to keep in the same rhythm, even as the next order issues forth. And all haul now, lads, as we sing . . . and *haul* . . . and . . . HAUL!

The cry goes up: 'Raise tacks and sheets . . !' *'Raise tacks and sheets!'* 'RAISE TACKS AND SHEETS!'

And sing as we haul, lads!

Oh, I'm bound for Australia, the land of the free
Where there'll be a welcome for me . . .
When I've worked in Australia for twenty long years
One day will I head homeward bound
With a nice little fortune tucked under me wing
By a steamship I'll travel, I'm bound.
So, 'tis goodbye to Sally and goodbye to Sue
When I'm leavin' Australia so free
Where the gals are so kind, but the one left behind
Is the one that will one day splice me.[14]

The songs go on, even as dozens of sailors are now shinnying up the masts and the rigging like demented monkeys, and only seconds later the first of the sails is unfurled, catching that precious westerly wind.

Of course, with all the shouting the realisation hits all aboard that they are underway, and the ship suddenly disgorges onto its deck most of its 192 adult passengers with their 77 children, all eager to get a last look at England as it slowly, almost imperceptibly, begins to drift away.

Three of those adults are from the family of the late, great Fintan Lalor, who had given his life to the cause of liberating Ireland from seven centuries of British occupation. One of Fintan's sisters, Margarett, who is in her early 40s, and his younger brothers – the 29-year-old Richard and 25-year-old Peter – have come to the heart-wrenching decision that the best thing is to leave all the troubles of Ireland behind and start anew in a distant land. And, of course, there are many on the ship just like them, members of the one family leaving behind everything they know to pay £26 for a steerage ticket – giving them the right to a rough sleeping berth and just 20 cubic feet of baggage space.

Standing on deck with the others are two young Scots from the small town of Lanarkshire, the 19-year-old Samuel Craig and his

18-year-old brother, William, both of them printers. Together they gaze more towards the open water ahead than the stifling, tight land behind. It had been William who had first read in *The Illustrated London News* the staggering account of the nuggets scattered around the Australian bush just *waiting* for those bold enough to travel to those remote parts to claim them, and he had finally convinced his brother: that is *us*, Samuel, don't ye see?

What Samuel sees now, just before dusk falls, is the English Channel stretching before them, and an hour after that the wind has picked up in company with the waves slapping hard against the bows of *Scindian*. All of her sails are now completely filled with bounteous winds from the north, and her three oak masts creak happily under the joyous strain of it all. As the ship arrows south, the moonbeams sparkle in her wake, and their journey proper of four gruelling months has truly begun. You'd better be right, young William.

8 July 1852, La Trobe writes to the Colonial Secretary, Earl Grey:

'A new working, called the "Eureka," . . . as well as two or three others, were discovered in the month of May . . .

'On all hands it must be considered that the population at the workings, taken as a whole, are as orderly and well-disposed as can be met with in any part of the colony. The comparative rarity of instances of grave outrage or of capital crime is a subject of great gratitude to God.'[15]

Late August 1852, Philadelphia, USA, worries for Her Majesty's servant

The British consul, William Peters, is not happy. A recent arrival from Australia has told him that, in part courtesy of work done by Americans, a Republican form of Government is in the offing, and things are moving so fast that 'a speedy declaration of Independence of the Mother Country is expected'.[16]

The idea of Americans in Australia – guests of Her Majesty Queen Victoria in a lately coveted part of the British Empire – working to promote such an insidious form of government as republicanism is anathema to Consul Peters. As a point of honour, thus, he feels obliged to give fair warning to the man who is effectively his counterpart in Melbourne – the nearest big city to where most of the Americans are centred on the diggings – and that is His Excellency Charles La Trobe. Taking quill in hand, he writes the letter.

For La Trobe must know that most of 'that class of [Americans] now on their way to Australia . . . are bent on "extending the area of Freedom" and aiding their fellow men in the pursuit of "Liberty and Republicanism". Indeed, an Order, entitled "The Order of the Lone Star", has been established here within this last twelvemonth, and for this avowed purpose. "Believing" (say its founders) "that Liberty and Republicanism are essential to the happiness of Man, and to the full development of his virtues and intelligence, and that it is the duty of all men to aid others, to the extent of their ability in the pursuit of happiness; – regarding it as one of the first duties of American Republicans to endeavour, by all lawful and proper means, to diffuse throughout the world the principles of Liberty and Republicanism."'

The important thing, Peters concludes, is for La Trobe to inform 'our Authorities in that part of the world to be on their guard'.[17]

Mid-September 1852, aboard *Scindian*, out on the Southern Ocean, heading towards Australia

How does one pass the time aboard a relatively small ship on a journey lasting at least a third of a year? The short answer is . . . with some difficulty. Certainly, playing the likes of chess and backgammon allows some of the sand to slip easily through the hourglass, as does endlessly reading and swapping finished books with other passengers. Too, when there is a lull in the wind it is possible to lower a boat and go for a row around the ship, always being careful to stay close, the way a baby chick does around a mother hen for fear she will up and bolt away.

For most of the ship's company not used to sea travel, though, it all seems so unchanging, so endlessly *endless,* that the sand moves only grain by grain. Day after day, on and on and on, each minute drags its weary way forward until enough of them are assembled for another hour to slowly drop away . . . Seemingly, nothing ever changes 'neath the stark blue sky. *Nothing.*

And of course in such circumstances, fresh conversations with your fellow passengers are highly prized, especially with the more interesting of those passengers.

One fellow on this voyage particularly stands out, however, and excites the curiosity of the others. It is the handsome, curly-haired Irishman Peter Lalor, who is a great favourite of many of the ladies on board, none more so than a young Irish female by the name of Alicia Dunne, who appears to be quite smitten.

All up, this highly educated man, from a highly educated family, appears to the others to be 'a picture of robust manhood'[18] and, in the words of one of his fellow passengers, William Craig, 'From his demeanour I surmised he was a man who thought for himself, and that something would be heard of him later on. After a time a friendly feeling became established between us, and I discovered in him a man of high intelligence and of sterling worth, yet one who might be led into unwise courses by sheer impulsiveness. Still, he possessed important qualifications for a successful career – ambition, energy, and courage.'[19]

In talking extensively to Lalor on the journey and becoming

close, Craig understands that he comes from 'a family of high social status and political influence in Ireland, [and that] his leading characteristics are patriotic ardour and a warm attachment to the land of his birth'.[20]

Lalor's favourite topic of conversation appears to be all the wrongs visited upon Ireland by iniquitous British rule and, though he is careful not to say too much, it is obvious that he had either been personally involved in the Irish uprising of '48 or some of his family had been. It had obviously been his disgust at the total and ignominious collapse of that movement that put him on this ship in the first place. For while just about everybody else on board is hustling to Australia with all speed, desperate to get to the goldfields to try to acquire instant wealth, Lalor evinces no interest in that at all. Rather, what seems to attract him to Australia is more the relatively clean political slate, the chance to play a part in the creation of the kind of self-government on Australian shores that the British had crushed in Ireland. And this portion of his views he is not remotely shy about expressing.

One hot afternoon as Craig and Lalor are chatting on the deck, in the vain hope of cooling themselves with an all-too-rare sea breeze from the shimmering ocean as they approach Australian climes, they are discussing – as ever – the state of affairs in Ireland. Lalor comments that, ultimately, the only way to redress the ills in his native land will be by recourse to 'physical force'.[21]

Craig demurs. Any effort in that direction, he says, against the immense power and wealth of Britain would be futile, as they would simply crush any revolution as they always had. Surely the only true solution could be 'the establishment of a peasant proprietary on the land.'

'Well,' Lalor replies, 'we shall see if a better state of things cannot be worked out in Australia. I intend to have a voice in its government before two years are over. The Lalors have always had a weakness for politics. My father sat in the British Parliament for Queen's County, and I intend to sit in the Victorian Parliament after I find out where improvements are needed.'[22]

September 1852, taxing times at 'The Chalet' in Jolimont, Melbourne

Improvements are needed.

Most particularly in the manner of revenue collection for the government coffers. In his increasingly desperate effort to balance his budget and find a way to match his revenue to his ever greater expenses in maintaining law and order on the goldfields, Lieutenant-Governor La Trobe peremptorily announces – right after receiving word from the Colonial Office that the matter of how the colonies raise their tax is a local matter – that he intends to place a duty of just over two shillings and sixpence on every ounce of gold exported from Victorian shores. To him, this makes a lot more sense than taxing men who frequently haven't yet found gold – if tax were blood, stones would be tax free – and it would be a lot easier to collect besides. Against that, he does *not* announce an intent to eliminate the license fee, just to impose the export fee in addition to it. Once again, there is an enormous backlash. The diggers insist it should *replace* the license tax. Gold traders say it will 'encourage smuggling'[23] because merchants will try to move their goods out through Sydney and Adelaide instead. And the Chamber of Commerce is vociferously opposed to all new taxes placed on the business community, just on principle. So great is the outcry, most particularly from those powerful enough to cry out loudest, that the proposal soon loses traction, the Lieutenant-Governor backs down, and the system with the license fees stays exactly as it is – unjust!

As to Charles La Trobe, once the most highly respected man in the colony, his stocks have now fallen so low that a mock advertisement has started to regularly appear in the advertising columns of *The Argus*:

WANTED, a governor.
     Apply to the People of Victoria[24]

It does not make for pleasant reading over his morning cup of tea at *Jolimont*. He has been doing this for a long time. Perhaps too long? No matter that the advertisement appears in that notoriously republican rag that is always attacking him, it is tiring all the same, and he is not as strong as he once was.

It is now well over a decade since he came here from Europe, and he misses his homeland. True, not as much as he and his wife, Sophie, miss their daughter, Agnes, who they sent back to Switzerland seven years earlier to be educated in the care of Sophie's lovely sister, Rose, but still a lot . . .

Sunday afternoon, 11 October 1852, aboard *Scindian*, approaching Melbourne

At last they near journey's end. On this sparkling day, finally, *Scindian* closes with the coast. There before them, the passengers can see the heads of Port Phillip Bay. Shortly afterwards, a pilot comes aboard and those who can crowd around hear the latest news of the colony they are about to land on.

And it is good news! At least insofar as gold is concerned, if not everything else . . . Alternating his ruminations with puffs on his pipe, the old salt informs them that every day in Melbourne Town comes news of more discoveries of gold to the near north and north-west, and the gold fever has so taken hold of the town that the civil servants – including police officers, hospital staff and prison guards – have resigned practically en masse, and things are so tight now that the government has had to get soldiers to do the work of the police while the whole service is being reorganised. (Even then, the pilot advises, a fortnight ago 15 of the soldiers had scarpered. What's worse, the Corporal's guard sent out after them had still not returned.)

But it isn't just in Melbourne – *puff, puff* – oh no. For practically all of the able-bodied men of Victoria, South Australia and Van Diemen's Land had also tossed in their previous work and gone in search of gold, while the men of New South Wales tend to be pursuing their fortunes at Bathurst. In Adelaide, which has a population just on 14,000, nearly 10,000 men have left for the Victorian diggings. As a matter of fact, the entire economy of Adelaide has ground to a miserable halt. Customs revenue, which had been up to £3000 a week, is now not too far north of nothing, and those still left in town are agog that a property that had sold the year before for £1500 has just sold for £43.

Everywhere bar the goldfields, ruin stalks close. There is insufficient manpower now to harvest the crops; shops close their doors; ships are abandoned in the harbour as sailors jump. Houses are going for a quarter of their previous price and are sometimes exchanged just for the horse and dray that would comfortably allow the previous owners to get their supplies to the goldfield to get started. Against that, the pilot also has to report that there is barely a bed to be had in all of Melbourne for under a pound a night, and the passengers will find everything very expensive. Against that again – *puff, puff* – there is so much money around and so much work with so few to do it that anyone with even the most basic skills should be able to make between £10 and £20 a week!

But, really, while small fortunes can be made doing such work, and large fortunes made in supplying the diggers, the most spectacular fortunes are made by those who *find* the gold, and – *puff, puff, puff* – it is the new arrivals who have the gold fever the worst of all.

This last point, he says, they will be able to see for themselves when they arrive at Hobson's Bay, right by the Port of Melbourne, as there are now no fewer than 50 ships there – everything from American clippers and towering East Indiamen to whalers, steamers, traders and foreign vessels of indeterminate type, unable to return to their ports of origin for the moment. Their crews have deserted and their captains are unable to get replacements, even on the offer of £50 for the return run.

All up, every morsel of news from the old pilot is devoured, first by the ship's company within immediate earshot as they wait for the breeze to take them towards Williamstown, and shortly afterwards by everyone else in the ship as the good tidings are spread. Gold! There really is gold in those distant hills, apparently so plentiful that fortunes are being made overnight. The problem being, of course, that the fortunes made on this very night – and the next night and the night after that – would be made by others! They have to get to the diggings as soon as possible.

In the words of William Craig, the pilot's story 'created a profound longing on the part of almost all on board, the sailors included, to find the shortest way to Ballarat'.[25]

As the ship has taken a pounding in high seas as it came around the Cape of Good Hope, there is a lot of maintenance work to be done now that *Scindian* is in a safe harbour. The captain orders four men to take the quarter boat from where it was stored on the foredeck, lower it to the water and begin to clean and paint the ship.

Aye-aye, Cap'n.

But now here's a funny thing. William Craig notes that as the quarter boat is being prepared for service, one of the four men appears to be in deep conversation with a ship's apprentice. What is going on? Whatever they are talking about seems conspiratorial in nature, and only a few seconds after they have finished, the apprentice shinnies up the main rigging and looks to be scanning the nearest land around Port Phillip Heads. He quickly descends all the way to the quarter boat, which now bears his four companions and is rising and falling on the gentle swell. And then they start rowing! Not around the boat to get a better look at where they might start on the cleaning and painting, but after a farewell cheer of triumph and joy, they steer away from the ship, towards the shore, and no doubt soon to the goldfields!

Alerted by the commotion, Captain James Cammell soon charges up on deck and instantly appraises the situation. His first question: where the blazes is his Second Officer, the man he has left on watch to prevent precisely this kind of thing happening?

Oh. Oh dear. It is not by coincidence that the extra time it takes between searching for the Second Officer and him appearing before the skipper is exactly the same amount of time it takes for a man to hastily get dressed and walk the short distance from his cabin. For if the ship has been rocking a little more easily here at anchor, it is because the Second Officer has been entertaining in the traditional manner a comely female passenger in steerage and has had more important, alluring things on his mind than watching out for escapees.

The Captain is, justifiably, furious and immediately announces that the cost of the lost boat will be coming directly from the Second Officer's wages. Unflinching, the Second Officer looks the skipper right in the eye and responds coolly that the Captain may charge for half a dozen such boats, for all he cares . . . so long as he is prepared to accept an IOU.

The ship's company takes pause. For though the Second Officer is not insolent, per se, nor is he deferential, recognising the authority of the skipper. It marks the moment where the skipper's lawful authority on *Scindian* has come to an end, where instead of the crew all finding themselves part of a strict hierarchy, they are all . . . equal. A staggering turn of events. It is William Craig who sums it up best. The pilot, he will later recount, 'had given us to understand that, under existing conditions in Victoria, "Jack was as good as his master, and in many cases better".'[26]

The following morning, shortly after sunrise, the bulk of the crew gathers on the forecastle deck, an assembly that the passengers cannot even get close to if they wanted for, contrary to custom, two burly sailors are blocking the passage. Whatever these fellows are discussing, they intend to do it in private. It is obvious to all that something else is afoot.

And, sure enough . . .

Suddenly the meeting breaks up and within minutes the remaining quarter boat is the repository of several cases of spirits, some provisions, as well as oars and a sail! Where is the Second Officer this time? Why, if you please, right among them – and this time supervising the whole operation! The penultimate part of their plan is to grease the blocks so that the boat can be lowered to the water on the ropes without making too much noise. This accomplished, the entire remaining crew, less the Captain, the Chief Officer and just one sailor, climb aboard and cast off.

This time there is no cheer – the Captain is asleep and his crew prefer to get away without arousing him – but that good man has been awoken anyway by the last loyal sailor. He charges up onto the deck, again trying to take it all in at once.

It does not take long, for there, down in the departing boat, is the Second Officer with nearly all the remaining crew, pulling away on the oars.

'We hope to see you soon on the diggings!' his second-in-command calls out cheerily.[27]

The time for talk is past. Without a word, the Captain races back to his cabin to retrieve the firearms he loaded the previous evening and returns on deck. At this point, the boat is just 50 yards from the ship and, amazingly, the men have ceased to row!

The Captain raises the most powerful of his guns to his shoulder and calls out that they must return at once to their duties, or he will fire upon them!

One of the crew, a real scallywag if ever there was one, calls to the Captain that he is the one who has lead them to do this, and therefore he is the one who should be the first victim shot. No, no, no, call out the others – their mate is being far too self-sacrificing. They all must be shot together, or none at all!

Extremely reluctant to fire on his crew, the Captain calls that he will give them five minutes to decide.

No need, Cap'n. 'Fire away!' they roar. Another scallywag stands up, bends over and offers the captain his rump as a fair old target.

What is going on?

And then the Cap'n realises: his weapons have been got at. That morning, the Second Officer poured water down the barrels of his guns and removed the percussion caps from the firing mechanism, rendering them useless. Apoplectic with rage, the Captain bursts forth with fearful combinations of every swear word he has ever heard on the seven seas in a manner both shocking and new to the passengers. His last two loyal crew members listen, perhaps impressed at the range and depth of the Captain's vulgar vocabulary, but certainly not unduly frightened by it. For in this country they are as good a man as him, and perhaps even better! Suddenly, however, like a volcano that is finally spent, the Captain runs out of swear words, and with that most of his anger seems to be exhausted, too. He can even see the funny side of it, a glimmer of humour returning to his eyes.

One of the departing crew calls out, 'Look here, old man, if you were like us chaps, working for 40 shillings a month, would you go back in that old hooker, and gold lying about in every direction, waiting to be picked up? We'll see yourself on the diggings a week after the ship arrives.'[28]

On this point the captain is noncommittal, but at least he does not bother arguing the point. Instead, with a deep sigh of resignation, he lights a cigar and returns to his cabin.

Down in the quarter boat the crew opens a case of brandy, toasts 'health and happiness' to all those left aboard, and then the Second Officer asks in jocular fashion that when the Captain surfaces once more, could they remind the worthy gentlemen to debit him for the value of both the boat of yesterday and today, along with this case of spirits?

'Then,' as William Craig will recount, 'with three hearty cheers they took to their oars, and went up the bay, all joining in a song that had become familiar to us when pumping during the voyage:

Oh, fare you well, my own Mary Ann,
Fare you well for awhile . . .'[29]

A small parenthesis here: there is of course ample precedent for such scarpering seamen to do well for themselves on the goldfields. In Sydney, a celebrated story circulated that when one of the desperate captains had searched through the bars and brothels for either his men or anyone who he could employ to get his vessel back to England, a simple sailor had pulled out an enormous wad of notes and 'offered to buy the ship and the captain'.[30] Close parenthesis.

———————

For those aboard *Scindian*, the biggest problem for now is that with nigh on a couple of dozen sailors scarpered, there remains only the skipper, the Chief Officer, one sailor and the cook to do the work of 25 men, all while a dead calm keeps the ship stuck exactly where they are. This requires many of the passengers to fulfil the duties of the recently departed, meaning that the wind that blows up the following morning is more than ever welcome, as they are moving once more in the direction of Williamstown, and many a passenger who has 'learnt the ropes' on the way over hauls on the lines.

Scindian anchors off Williamstown and some of the ship's passengers are shuttled to shore. Now shakily disembarking at what passes for a pier – rocking enough to make a sea-dog feel at home and 'an inlander sea-sick'[31] – the weary voyagers are confronted by 'a leviathan eatinghouse', superscribed with the notification 'Dinners always ready from morning till night' and the postscript 'Hot soups always on hand'[32] – a place more interesting to those freshly arrived, who have been without fresh meat for so long. And next to it again, a blacksmith operating out of a tent, the chief wonder of which is that it has not burnt down long before as an unending stream of sparks flies upwards from the smithy's forge to the canvas roof.

Their task is neither an easy nor cheap one, organising travel from Williamstown into the heart of Melbourne. Getting freight from London to Port Phillip Bay – a distance of almost 13,000 miles – comes at a cost of £3 (60 shillings) per ton. And yet to get themselves and their luggage onto one of the small, dilapidated boats that passengers are able to take to ferry their possessions the eight miles to Cole's Wharf costs five shillings.

Little by little, this bustling city that was no more than virgin bush less than two decades earlier heaves into view.

If this El Dorado be, then a strange looking one it is. For while, yes, the spires and the many chimneys with the lazy curls of smoke in the distance really, clearly, are those of an established town of bricks and mortar, just as the many wooden cottages bespeak a civilised if not wealthy people, what can one make of the hundreds of acres of canvas that mark the approaches to this town? As with an army besieging a city – and that is what they are, an army of immigrants – on every landed horizon surrounding Melbourne there are tents set up.

But it is just the beginning for those like Ellen Clacy, an Englishwoman who has come to Australia with her brother and some friends to try to make their fortune.

For as they at last set foot on dry land at Sandridge Wharf, in Hobson's Bay, staggering slightly in the classic manner of people with 'sea legs', who for many months have been used to standing on heaving decks, these new arrivals are confronted by a group of 'watermen' and find 'the whole cost of transferring your effects overland to your lodgings in the town is actually more than bringing them the previous 13,000 miles, including the cost of conveying them from your house to the London Docks'.[33] They have little choice but to agree, and the surly watermen – mostly absconded sailors who have decided that certain daylight robbery of this kind will be more lucrative than chancing their arms on the dark diggings anyway – sulkily load their belongings onto one of their hideous carts, even as they look longingly towards Liardet's public house, just over the road from where their targets have landed, a place they are clearly desperate to return to.

With the cart loaded high with carpetbags, baskets, parcels, portmanteaux, seachests and the like, the only place left to sit for the dozen or so passengers on the side are the narrow planks of the cart for this purpose. With a curse from the waterman and a touch of his whip, his weary nags whinny plaintively and the cart starts off with an exhausted lurch. In short order the new arrivals pass a massive open-air market, where many of the vendors are people just like them – except six months on. That is, they are immigrants who have tried their luck on the diggings, found nothing and now must sell everything they have, for whatever they can get, in the hope they can raise enough money to get back to the civilisation of their homelands. Others are clearly more recent arrivals – they're not nearly so battered or weathered – who are about to head to the diggings and realise that much of what they have brought from their homelands is superfluous to their needs and they'd be much better to have money instead . . .

And speaking of Jack being as good as his master, it also appears that many of the structures the new chums can see beside these small businesses are houses that Jack built. For the most part they are rickety, lopsided affairs that have clearly been put together with whatever materials have come to hand – and the result is that the houses rather resemble their sullen owners, who are lounging out on their verandahs, watching the newcomers balefully as the carts trundle by loaded with their luggage.

The various paths from the wharves to Melbourne Town that the Lalors, the Craigs and the Clacys are following are, of course, already very well travelled. Many of those who take them – past, present and in the coming days, weeks and months – though unknown to them at the time, are of significance.

A Frenchman, Antoine Fauchery, who, coming from Gravesend, has arrived in Victoria aboard *Emily* just a week before those on *Scindian*, has come *pour suivre la fortune*, to try his luck on the goldfields. From Toronto, Canada, aboard *Magnolia*, comes Charles Ross, in the company of his great friend and old school chum Thomas Budden, while from ever-green County Kilkenny in Ireland arrives Timothy Hayes and his wife, the beautiful and heavily pregnant Anastasia – she with such fiery red hair that it very nearly matches her temper when things displease her – together with their first five children. Having survived both the potato famine and their involvement with the uprising of the Young Ireland movement, the Hayes, like pretty much everyone else in Melbourne, have decided to come to Australia to make a new start.

For his part, Raffaello Carboni, the similarly red-headed revolutionary from the Young Italy movement, who had been wounded three times while fighting for Garibaldi to throw the Austrians out of Italy, is similarly motivated.

Eager to discover new worlds, and having read about the goldfields with growing excitement, Carboni has journeyed all the way to Australia in the hope of starting a new, rich life, free from the oppression he has known. In his pocket, as one raised on the Catholic duty to always have alms for the poor, he has a few copper coins, ready to hand to whichever beggars he might see. So far, there have been none!

All he can see, instead, are either manifestations of great wealth or, more pertinently, another whole strand of people who are after his coins and more for an entirely different reason. They are, as he will later describe them, 'a shoal of land-sharks, who swarmed at that time the Yarra Yarra wharfs'.[34] They take £5 from him, merely for landing his luggage!

19 October 1852, *Vulcan* arrives, bearing the 40th Regiment

A lot less welcome than *Scindian*, and even *Araminta*, is the state-of-the-art iron steamship *Vulcan*, which on this day passes through the heads of Port Phillip Bay bearing 800 Redcoats of the 40th (2nd Somersetshire) Foot Regiment. Yes, they are a relatively famous military unit, known as 'The Excellers' – with a proud history going all the way back to 1717, and a renown renewed in the previous decade through their fearful work with the bayonet in the battle of Maharajapore in the Gwalior Campaign in Madhya Pradesh, India – but in many ways that is the whole point of the colony's revulsion. For what is a crack military unit doing in this peaceful part of the world in the first place?

It is, not untypically, *The Argus* that is most forward in expressing its disgust: 'The soldiers are come at last. The *Vulcan* steamer anchored yesterday in Hobson's Bay, freighted with a cargo of two kindred evils – two malignant diseases which have perhaps about equally desolated the world – the red-jacket and the small-pox.

'True to their nature, while shut out from inflicting their woes upon mankind, they have waged war upon each other, and for the present, we are to be precluded from the satisfaction of actual contact with either of them . . .

'The red coat has ever been the foe of all true liberty. In precise proportion as it has in any country advanced, has constitutional freedom stood still or gone back.' [35]

But here they are, and here they will stay for some time. On board, two particular officers gaze to the shore – just as soldiers have done since time immemorial when first sighting a new land where they are to serve – wondering what it holds for them.

Yes, yes, of course these newly arrived Englishmen have been quick to hear the stories of others deserting their posts as soon they get close enough to the goldfields to do so, but neither are they remotely the type to do so. Both Captain John Wellesley Thomas and Lieutenant Joseph Henry Wise are career British Army men – men of honour, men of duty, men who know to pass the port to the left and love nothing better than raising a glass, gentlemen, to Her Majesty . . . the Queen!

The Queen . . . *The Queen* . . . *The Queen* . . .

Ah, but their part in our story is truly yet to come.

October–November 1852, on the track winding back to Melbourne

While the soldiers and officers from *Vulcan* must stay in wretched and frustrating quarantine for the next fortnight, other recent arrivals are initially free to traipse where they will. And so it is that after landing, all of the many new arrivals set off on the well-worn and meandering path around the contours of the bay for the next eight miles, the shores of which are strewn at the high-water mark with 'a debris of drift spars, broken oars, ship-blocks, dead-eyes, used-up passengers' beds and pillows, dilapidated hencoops, empty brandy cases, broken bottles, and kegs with a ballast of salt water.'[36]

It is not something to gladden the newcomer's heart.

'"And is this the beautiful scenery of Australia?" was my first melancholy reflection,' Ellen Clacy will record of her impressions. 'Mud and swamp – swamp and mud – relieved here and there by some few trees which looked as starved and miserable as ourselves. The cattle we passed appeared in a wretched condition, and the human beings on the road seemed all to belong to one family, so truly Vandemonian was the cast of their countenances. On we went towards Melbourne.'[37]

As the newcomers cross the Yarra on an admittedly new-looking bridge, the dismal sight comes of many wooden huts on its banks, said to be boiling-down works – to boil down the fat from sheep and cattle to make tallow for candles and soap – and the stench emanating from them would seem to bear that out. Beside the huts are huge, white pyramids of bones, extending up to 40 feet high. Behind those stinking huts are slightly undulating slopes on which, Antoine Fauchery records, 'grows grass that is neither green nor yellow, and on which here and there a few thin oxen are grazing. Plains, and then more plains stretching out *ad infinitum*, like the boredom that comes over you at the sight of them.'[38]

And now here is Melbourne proper before them and . . .

And what is this? Of course, they should have known: before they can properly enter the town all must pay an entrance tax according to the amount of luggage they bear. (The economic times are apparently tough and, after being previously fleeced by both the boatmen and the watermen, the new arrivals now find themselves fleeced by the authorities as well!) For most of them this is a matter of eight to ten shillings.

As they head up Swanston Street, it is apparent the buildings are far more solid in nature than the wooden ones on the outskirts and are built of mostly brick, sometimes even sandstone. Most are small, though among them are dotted 14 much larger stone constructions, each of them churches.

While those churches are at least solace to those who have feared they have come to a city beyond the bounds of civilisation, the truth is that for most of the newcomers, had bad first impressions been a ticket home, there are few who would have made it to the downtown area.

Still, as to the city itself, it proves to be surprisingly well designed and is done in the manner of the Americans – laid out in a grid pattern, like a chessboard. Six main roads running north and south come straight up from the river, with four major arteries crossed by six streets running at right angles in turn, making 24 blocks. While this is quite unlike the layout of London, where streets have grown organically, one thing a little similar is the frequent 'fog' that comes from the whirligigs of dust that descend from the hinterland.

A typical first night for newcomers is extremely uncomfortable. Simply finding a bed in a town that does not have enough of them and can therefore charge exorbitant rates for those they do have is a challenge. Most people have to trek over the hill that lies just beyond the town where, as far as the eye can see, fields are covered in tiny little hovels thrown together with mostly scrapwood, 'the upper portion being called Collingwood and the lower Richmond. These suburbs contain a population equal to that of Melbourne itself; and they have flung up from the vast influx of population, chiefly since the gold discovery.'[39]

Another place, for the truly poor – situated in the rough plain on the south side of the Yarra – is called 'Canvas Town'.[40] And it is, as it sounds, a place where any family with any canvas may 'install itself as it likes, either in the north or the south; providing, none the less, that it pays in advance a fee of five shillings a week levied by the very paternal government of the colony'.[41]

Having secured lodging *somewhere*, the new arrival's next challenge is to get to sleep in a place that does not rock the way their ship had rocked, where infernal dogs keep barking all night long and, for whatever frightening reason, there seems to be a discharge of pistols going off both near and far until dawn. (In England they at least have the decency to only begin their rare pistol duels at dawn.)

There are many ways to identify the new arrivals to Melbourne. The first and most obvious is that they look lost, but there are many clues beyond that.

Sometimes, if they were born and raised in the upper classes, they have unusually fine clothes that they have clearly bought in Europe only months before. Other times, there is a sheer English-ness about them, a certain superior and disdainful way they have of walking around – at least until they come to the realisation that no-one cares in these parts and they are only making themselves look ridiculous. But the surest way, the catch-all for all classes and nationalities, is the obvious open-mouthed wonder with which these fresh arrivals survey the scenes of the city.

For Melbourne at this time is like no other city on earth. A large part of it is the sheer *wild energy* – the exuberance, the recklessness and roughness – and the feeling that, here on the very edge of the known world, everything, but everything, is different to the way it is in other cities.

Look-ee there!

William Craig observes an open carriage roaring down the street, 'drawn by a superb pair of horses, driven at breakneck pace through the main streets by a sailor dressed in an orthodox man-of-war suit, his hat and sleeves decorated with ribbons. A number of his mates, similarly attired, accompanied by coarse-looking specimens of feminine frailty – the latter attired in the most costly and garish hued clothing – occupied seats in the body of the vehicle. The gold ornaments on the women would have been sufficient to start a jeweller's shop with.'[42]

And here now is a man, obviously a goldminer who has struck it rich. Despite being very drunk he still has the wherewithal to be handing out glasses of champagne to whichever passers-by on the street might like to join him, drawing from a number of cases of champagne bottles that lie beside him.

'Men appeared to vie with each other,' Craig records, 'as to who should get quit of their easily acquired wealth with the greatest celerity.'[43]

This includes smoking £5 and £10 banknotes as tobacco paper and, for high hilarity, even eating sandwiches using money as the filler! One digger is seen to be rifling through a huge wad of notes, furiously pulling out and tearing up every dirty one he finds, swearing at the wretched gold brokers for 'giving him dirty paper money for pure Alexander gold; he wouldn't carry dirt in his pocket; not he; thank God! He'd plenty to tear up and spend too.'[44]

The 'law', such as it is, does not work the way it does in places like London. For in the English capital the law is the law and everyone understands that the police are on the right side of it while the criminals are on the wrong side. Here, the matter is sometimes up for debate, and not for nothing would the Colonial Secretary, John Foster – a man of ever-severe expression, with nearly as much starch as his high collar – go on to describe the Victorian police in 1852 as 'convicts, drunkards, open to bribery and wholly untrustworthy'.[45]

That is certainly the experience of many of the new arrivals . . .

While walking up Elizabeth Street in the middle of the day, Ellen Clacy hears the roar of an approaching mob behind her and ducks into a spare patch of ground in front of St Francis Church so as to keep out of their way and let them pass. It turns out that a man had been arrested by two policemen for horse-stealing, and 'a rare ruffianly set of both sexes were following the prisoner',[46] doing everything they could to free him, and the crowd is following close to see what happens. It is rare sport. And then it happens, right in front of her.

'If but six of ye were of my mind,' shouts one of the ruffians, 'it's this moment you'd release him.'[47]

And this is even better sport! For all but instantaneously the crowd closes on the policemen and begins yelling at them, swearing viciously enough to peel paint and pushing them with terrible violence. As Ellen Clacy observed, 'The owner of the stolen horse got up a counter demonstration, and every few yards, the procession was delayed by a trial of strength between the two parties. Ultimately the police conquered; but this is not always the case, and often lives are lost and limbs broken in the struggle, so weak is the force maintained by the colonial government for the preservation of order.'[48]

In another, much later episode, when a robber is arrested and a constable takes him in hand, a mob bearing pistols, bludgeons and axe handles gathers to free him. At the end of the wild melee, after the prisoner is rescued, a dead man is left on the ground. What to do? The obvious – the body is carried into the nearest public house where an inquest is immediately held.

'The deceased,' Clacy recounts, 'is recognized as a drunkard, the jury is assured that a post-mortem examination is quite unnecessary; and the man is buried, after a verdict is brought in of "Died by the visitation of God;" the said visitation of God having, in this instance, assumed the somewhat peculiar form of a fractured skull!'[49]

It is only the newcomers, however, who stare in open-mouthed wonder at such antics – everyone else has seen it all before. Besides which, the old hands are simply too busy either spending the fruits of their labours on the goldfields to worry about it, or they are preparing to get to the fields themselves with all possible haste.

Most other cities in the world are populated by predominantly people of just the one race . . .

Not Melbourne. Here, if you spit over your shoulder you're just as likely to hit a haughty Englishman in the eye as an escaped American slave; a Chinaman with a pigtail as an Aborigine with a lone blanket protecting what is left of his modesty; a beady-eyed Vandemonian pickpocket as an obviously successful digger dressed in his regulation blue serge shirt and newly purchased 'wide-awake hat', the green veil still hanging from its lid to protect him from the flies.

Strangely, there are far more women than men. They range from the obviously well-born English ladies dressed in the latest fashions to low-brow, up-skirt harlots; from old ladies with bonnets and parasols protecting their skin from the harsh Australian sun to young Aboriginal women who appear to have fallen on hard times. Far and away the most common, however, and this is where the great numbers come from – despite men in the colonies outnumbering women four to one overall – are the so-called 'grass widows'. These are the myriad middle-aged married women who have been left behind to run the house and raise the children while their men have simply upped sticks and left for the goldfields. If their husbands do find gold, the women may be well-turned out and carrying large bundles of shopping on one of the only three streets that are paved – Bourke, Collins and Elizabeth streets. If not, they are more likely to have a hard-pinched, poverty-stricken look about them and are more frequently seen on the muddy streets, holding out nothing but the hope that their husbands will soon make a breakthrough. But life is far tougher for them now than just a year ago, before gold was discovered. Then you could buy a four-pound loaf of bread for five pence – now it costs a shilling and sixpence. And they say that on the Ballarat goldfields it now costs four shillings.

Here in Melbourne, meat is twice as expensive and bacon four times as dear. Rents have gone up at least 50 per cent, if not more. Everything has soared in price by simple dint of the fact that with all the newcomers there is much more demand and, with all the men gone to the goldfields, far fewer to provide goods and services.

As to those newcomers, they are not only bemused by the strange ways the colonials born and bred in this country speak – for reasons best known to themselves they have trodden upon and squashed every syllable in their armoury – but also by their curious colonial ways. For again, look here now! Here is a colonial couple heading down Great Bourke Street. The 'Australian' man has a letter in his hand to put in the mailbox but, as there is a lot of mud between him and the box, without a word he hands the letter to his wife and nods casually towards the box. That good woman understands and leaves the shelter of their common umbrella to pick her way through the mud and post the letter before returning, wet through, all without a *word* of complaint.

'Colonial politeness,'[50] the staggered English arrivals call it.

And over there is a very common-looking digger, asking the driver of a cab what the fare would be to have his services for a whole day.

'Perhaps more than you'd like,' says the driver, eyeing the digger's poor dress and obvious poverty.

'What is it?' asks the digger.

'Seven pounds for the day.'

'There is ten,' says the digger, peeling off just one note from the whole roll he has in his pocket. 'You can light your pipe with the difference.'[51]

They are a weird mob, and the English writer William Howitt, a Quaker, aptly describes Victoria at this time as being in the grip of a 'hairystocracy',[52] filled as it is with huge, hairy men with untamed whiskers and wild hair, galloping through the streets and brawling their way through the bars and brothels with equal abandon, unceasing in their endeavours to drink the town dry. And the shopkeepers, of course, love them for their exuberantly free-spending ways, even outright advertising for their customers by referring to them as, well, as this:

TO THE NEW ARISTOCRACY.

If you want the best article of any description to be had in the city, you can be supplied by De Carle and Co., Gold Diggers' General Provision Stores, Little Bourke Street.[53]

Such appeals to their vanity *work*, and to many a genuine aristocrat visiting these shores it seems that the diggers have no sense of their . . . *place* in the world. These hairy brutes simply don't care that an English gentlemen is due deference from the lower orders as a matter of basic principle. In this place, everything is turvy-topsy, front-to-back and the polloi hoi really do have the attitude that Jack is as good as his master, and in many cases better . . .

Signs of the city's obsession with gold are everywhere, including in every shopfront window, up to and including baby linen warehouses and milliners. Often on a white placard there is a drawing of a pile of gold on one side, while on the other is a pile of sovereigns or a wad of banknotes. This indicates that the shopkeeper is happy to pay cash for whatever gold you have, and all of them will have carefully calibrated scales for the purpose. The most striking advertisement of all is in the window of a shop in Collins Street because – far from being a drawing – it is a real human skull, perforated by a bullet. That bullet lies a foot or so away to the left, 'as if coolly examining or speculating on the mischief it had done',[54] while on one side is a revolver and on the other a seeming pile of nuggets. Above all is a large sign blaring the words: 'Beware in time.'

For, you see, clearly this skull was once upon the shoulders of a digger who did not have the brains to sell his nuggets to this shopkeeper, preferring to keep his gold in his pockets and so make himself a target of violent robbers!

What do the conservative denizens of Victoria think of this turn of events? Very, very little . . .

Chief Justice Sir William à Beckett, for starters, is deeply disturbed. As he makes clear in a pamphlet entitled *Does the Discovery of Gold in Victoria, Viewed in Relation to its Moral and Social Effects, As Hitherto Developed, Deserve to be Considered a National Blessing or a National Curse,* it is a toss-up as to whether it is the way the diggers look or the way they live that is more appalling.

'The general contempt of dress and personal appearance, the crowding together of numbers in places where decent accommodation can hardly be provided for one – the smoking and drinking and swearing . . . all this might have a tendency to weaken that regard for external decencies, and to impair that sense of self-respect, which lies at the foundation of the manners, not to say the morals, of civilized and domestic life. Certainly these are not the substantials of existence; but they are most valuable accessories, and without them we should speedily relapse into a state of barbarism.'[55]

It has no effect. For *still* they keep coming.

CHAPTER FIVE

TO THE DIGGINGS

All aristocratic feelings and associations of the old
country are at once annihilated . . . It is not what you
were, but what you are that is the criterion.[1]
John Sherer, an English digger

It is every man's business to take care of himself here. They are just as
independent in their speech as in their actions. It is a wonderful place to
take the conceit out of men who expect much deference. The Governor
was yesterday riding along among this crew, attended by one soldier; but
not the slightest notice was taken of him, not even by a touch of the hat.
They are just as free in helping themselves to your property.
William Howitt, on his first impressions of Melbourne in 1852[2]

December 1852, launching from Melbourne

All up, this town is as wondrous as it is crazy, as rich in some pockets
as it is poor in others, and as quintessentially *Australian* in some
sections as it is merely 'England transplanted' in other parts.

Of course, for most of the fresh arrivals Melbourne itself is no
more than a staging post for where they truly want to get to, which
is the goldfields. Pushed along by the fact that the city is too crip-
plingly expensive to stay in long, most are not long in leaving.

An early exception to the exodus is civil engineer Peter Lalor who,
along with his brother Richard and another Irishman, sets up as a
liquor merchant in Melbourne before finding work planning the

railway between Melbourne and Geelong. He has decided to follow his first instincts and seek rather more stable work than the diggings. For one thing, he is now courting his fellow passenger on the ship, Alicia Dunne, and given that she settles first in Melbourne and then in Geelong – where her uncle is a priest and can give her work at his Catholic school – he does not want to be too far from her.

For most of the rest of the new arrivals, just as in Europe all roads lead to Rome, in mainland Australia all roads lead to the goldfields. And it is along these roads in the latter months of 1852 – particularly those leading out of Melbourne – that a stream of people flows, originating from not only all parts of settled Australia, but indeed all corners of the earth.

Here are the native-born Australians, distinctive with their broad accents, rough dress with no hint of Europe about them and usually very weathered visages. Many of them look less born than quarried, and their skin tends to be darker than the Europeans' from long exposure under the hot sun in these parts.

And yet they are not the toughest looking. That distinction belongs to the often limping, narrow-eyed freed convicts and ticket-of-leave men, who are desperate to restore their lives and gain their fortunes with one lucky strike – perhaps to the head of a newly wealthy digger they can steal from.

Then there are the '49ers', usually, but not always, Americans who have been on the diggings in California, know what they are doing and are now trying their luck here after the easy pickings of the goldfields there have already been plucked. You can tell them by the fact that they habitually have beards, sombreros, coloured flannel shirts and, most fabulously, are 'girthed in above the hips with a red sash, that was stuck round with knives'.[3] The knives are described by prominent Legislative Council member John Pascoe Fawkner as the 'murderous bowie',[4] and they usually are only part of the 'bandit accoutrements'[5] these men wear, as they also have other daggers and revolvers on their persons. These are men to be a little wary of. It is not that they are bad men, necessarily, but they do, after all, come from that most dangerous of things: a *republic*. Having lived free of swearing eternal fealty to Her Majesty the Queen, they are known to be sometimes dangerously independent in their political views, just as, having been in a very wild and oft violent place in the California diggings, there is no doubt that a lot of that wildness and tendency to violence has rubbed off on them.

On the strength of that reputation, a strong editorial in the *Empire* has even demanded that 'no door be opened to receive the blood stained wretches'.[6] But they keep coming anyway, often on specially chartered steamships that, for a $60 fare, promise, 'a most favourable opportunity for those who are desirous of reaching the gold regions without delay, as it is fully expected that the passage will be made in 30 days'.[7] The Americans seem not at all troubled by such wariness at their presence, with one of their supporters noting cheerfully that, 'The worst scoundrels that ever infested California were from these Colonies',[8] so it must now be all even on the card. And he is right. In August of 1850, as one writer to *The Sydney Morning Herald* recalls, 'out of sixteen awaiting trial for serious crime in San Francisco, twelve were from Sydney. At much the same time, while out of seventy in custody for thieving, forty-eight were from Sydney. Yours very truly, A Citizen of The States.'[9] The reputation of the Australians is so bad that by now incoming ships to San Francisco Bay are searched to make sure none is on board.

And getting back to the streets of Melbourne, there too, usually entirely separate from the rest of the press of humanity, are the tiny and oft barefooted Chinamen, usually moving in groups of 100, with huge bamboo poles stretched long across their shoulders, each end bearing their belongings and bouncing up and down in rhythm as they half-trot with their oh-so-curious wide-legged, short-stepped gait. An inscrutable invasion – at least that is the way it feels to most other nationalities, who eye them with cool disdain – the sense of their 'otherness' is heightened by the fact that beneath their strange wide, peaked straw hats their hair is shaved across the temples at the front, while at the back it extends into a long, braided ponytail tied up with a ribbon, just like an English girl!

And what of the continental Europeans, who are also here in force? Well, to start with, the southern Europeans tend to have slightly olive skin, while the northern Europeans are more often red – the hot Australian sun burns them quickly. True, that skin is not quite as red as the red pants the Dutch always wear for reasons unknown, but it runs them close. Too, with the Europeans there is a certain hardness to their eyes – they have suffered under repressive regimes at home – mixed with an odd sparkle, for they are here to begin again.

The Irish are the easiest to spot, usually gaunt and with that hollow-eyed look of people escaping from a land of recent starvation. They have a curious mix of general good humour, tempered by an innate anger for what they have been through at the hands of the English occupiers.

Even the Scots are heading there in force, with one lot marching to the diggings in draughty kilts behind other Scots who at first glance appear to be slowly strangling large, colourful cats, but who are in fact playing bagpipes. Tight behind are their oft stony-faced wives with the wee bairns all on drays. Perhaps what is worrying them and other people on the road is the contemplation of just what they are letting themselves in for in this strange country. For at least an inkling of what awaits them is to be found in the names of some of their destinations: Murdering Flat, Dead Man's Gully, Dead Horse Gully, One-eye Gully, Rotten Gully, Poverty Gully, Terrible Gully, Grumble-Gut Gully . . .

Still they push on, trying to think of places they've heard of with much happier names, like Golden Gully, so called because its riches were discovered by a fellow who was taking a rest by lying down and passing the time pulling up grass by the roots – and with one set of roots came 'a nest of golden nuggets'.[10]

And it won't be long before they will hear about 'White Horse Gully', which earned its name when an enraged beast of that description was snorting and cavorting all about, plunging its front and back hooves into the dirt, only to have yet more nuggets appear!

Dingley Dell? That place, newcomers are told, is a grassy tract by the water, beloved by bullock drivers who camp there at the end of a long day's haul, listening to the 'dingle' made by the bullock's bells.

Speaking of which – *crack!* – push on!

Descending Great Bourke Street, many of the cavalcade make their last stop opposite the general post office to check if the last ship in to Port Phillip might have included a long-awaited letter from home, then head up past the Horse Bazaar. From there they turn into Queen Street and continue through a veritable forest of huge red gums, white gums and stringybark trees towards the small village of Flemington – which boasts some 40 small houses, an inn and a blacksmith's shop – all of which lie some three-and-half-miles north-west of the post office.

Then the exodus continues overland, to Buninyong, Ballarat, Creswick Creek, Forrest Creek, Bendigo and all the rest.

After passing through Flemington and then by the Benevolent Asylum, some of the former criminals among this cavalcade look nervously at the road to their right, which leads to the recently constructed Pentridge Stockade – *those cells, those lashes, that gruel!* – before setting their eyes once more resolutely north-west. Not for them anymore, that infernal institution – they are heading to El Dorado itself!

Pushing on into the deep bush, however, the light dims as it strains through the heavy canopy, and their heavy sense of foreboding rises as all signs of human habitation vanish, when suddenly they hear the most unlikely of sounds.

'Without the slightest warning,' as William Craig would recount, 'our whole surroundings appeared to be alive with human revelry.

Simultaneously peal after peal of what appeared like mockery of our dispirited frame of mind broke from the throats of a flock of laughing jackasses in the tree against which we were reclining. It was the first time we had heard that most remarkable of all Australian birds, and the human-like way in which they enjoyed their scrimmage for what appeared to be a large iguana was irresistible.'[11]

And now they know why kookaburras are called the 'settler's alarm clock'. They also see an extraordinary, small, bear-like creature that climbs high into the trees and benignly blinks down upon them as they pass.

The further you get from Melbourne the more the countryside is crisscrossed by as many tracks as creeks, the tracks guided less by anything so prosaic as a compass and more by paths of least resistance through bush and swamps and around hills and other obstacles.

Yet it is not the physical rigours of passing through such rough country that presents the greatest danger. No, travellers both to and from the goldfields must be wary of bushrangers, most particularly in the areas around Black Forest, the Jim Crow Ranges and Bullarook Forest. Often working in gangs of up to half a dozen, these common criminals on horseback – frequently prison escapees and ticket-of-leave men turned to highway robbery – congregate in the thickest parts of the bush and frequently fall upon whatever isolated wayfarers they can find. Those heading 'up' to the diggings are usually relieved of whatever of their life savings they have left after buying their supplies, while those going 'down' to Melbourne are fallen upon and robbed of nuggets, money, cheques and gold receipts. In the case of those receipts, a frequent occurrence is for the bearer to be taken deeper into the bush and tied to a tree while one of the bushrangers gallops off to Melbourne and exchanges the slip of paper for the gold that the said receipt entitles the bearer to.

And so . . . what of the police?

What police?

Oh yes, there is still some kind of police force *per se*, but the truth of it is that just about every able-bodied man who was in the police when the gold rush began has long ago departed for the goldfields, leaving behind only a curious combination of the absolutely most loyal . . . and the dregs. And not all the men who had been recruited to replace those deserters are really *police*, as heavily represented among them are many drunkards, wastrels and ne'er-do-wells merely wearing police uniforms. This is the only certain job they can get, when even having the wherewithal to get themselves to the diggings like everyone else is beyond them.

Still, that bad patch on Mt Alexander Road? That is the result of gold fever run amok when some small nuggets had no sooner been discovered along the track than hopeful miners started tearing it apart. (The nuggets had actually fallen off a bullion wagon but, as there is little public money available, the road has remained in poor condition.)

The cavalcade pushes on with little respite, though those heading to Ballarat can at least take brief pause in the wilderness of Warrenheip, which lies at the base of a small pyramidal mountain just under three miles from the diggings, and refresh themselves with cool, fresh water at a well-frequented spring. And then they must push on again.

15 December 1852, Melbourne receives amazing news

There is always an excitement among the clerks when official communiqués come from Whitehall. For these are not like regular letters, simply unloaded from the ships at much the same time as the other things. These missives are given directly *by* the captain *to* a high official of the Lieutenant-Governor's staff and, under guard, that official takes them directly to His Excellency in Government House. Then, and only then, are the seals on the waterproof wrapping around the parchment broken, always by His Excellency, and he is ever and always the first to read Whitehall's ruminations, news and instructions.

This time the news is extraordinary. On a tightly rolled piece of official parchment, Lieutenant-Governor La Trobe, along with the heads of all the other colonies, is informed by Britain's Secretary of State, Sir John Pakington – in his last despatch before this role is assumed by the Duke of Newcastle – that because 'the extraordinary discoveries of Gold' had created 'new and unforseen features to the political and social conditions' things must radically change for the colonies, and it is now a matter of urgency that the colonies of South Australia, Victoria and New South Wales move towards independence. It is the decision of Her Majesty's Government 'to place full powers of self-government in the hands of a people so advanced in wealth and prosperity'.[12]

While New South Wales rather than Victoria has been the originator of the proposal for self-government, Pakington writes that there is 'no hesitation in offering to the colony of Victoria the same concessions on the same terms'.[13]

It is true! Only eighteen months earlier, when the Separation[14] Act came into effect, Victoria had broken away from New South Wales to be a separate entity under the rule of its own Lieutenant-Governor. Now the Secretary of State is writing to each colony encouraging it to draft a constitutional act, suggesting this include the creation of a bicameral legislature with an elected Lower House and a Legislative Council nominated by the Crown, and legislation that includes allowance for payment of the principal officers of government and control over their colonial wastelands. Revenue raised from the goldfields, such as license fees, will now be in the hands of the Legislature. (Previously this was controlled by the Executive Council branch.) Van Diemen's Land will be granted its wish to end the transportation of convicts.

In effect, the colonies will control all their own local affairs, raise their own revenue and no longer be as tightly tied to the legal framework and purse strings of Mother England.

And so it begins . . .

In short order, across all those colonies, the issue among the good and the great becomes exactly what kind of Constitution they should have, what kind of set-up for their bicameral parliaments, who should be allowed to vote, who to serve in those parliaments and what their structure should be.

In New South Wales, no less than the famously irascible explorer/ journalist/politician/ squatter William Charles Wentworth – a long-time passionate advocate of self-rule of the colonies – is installed as the head of the committee to draft the New South Wales Constitution, in the company of Colonial Secretary Edward Deas Thomson and that scion of the squatting class, James Macarthur.

In Victoria, Wentworth's equivalent on the issue of heading the committee to come up with a draft Constitution is the man with surely the greatest mutton-chop whiskers in all of Victoria, Colonial Secretary John Foster, and he is quick to place at his right hand his cousin and the colony's first Attorney-General, William Foster Stawell. (This legal luminary has many points of distinction beyond his prowess administering Her Majesty's law, though perhaps the greatest has been his passionate advocacy – within the confines of the Anti-Transportation League – of stopping the flow of British convicts into the colony. He is not, however, a believer in changing the current limits of those who may stand for the Legislative Council: those over 30 owning freehold property worth more than £5000, or in possession of an annual valuation of at least £500. That means power remains with squatters and men such as himself and John Foster – for though their primary profession is based in Melbourne, the two share title to leases on a large property, *Rathscar,* on the Avoca River, as well as a 43,000-acre property *Natte Yallock,* with 18 miles of frontage of that same river. It is for the same reason that he has no desire to change the limits on those who may vote for the Legislative Council: persons over 21 years of age, owning property worth in excess of £1000 or being from an appropriate professional background or the armed services.)

The cousins are joined by the Auditor-General, Hugh Culling Eardley Childers, who is shortly to become the first Vice-Chancellor of the University of Melbourne. All three are members nominated by the Lieutenant-Governor to sit on the Legislative Council – making them rolled gold members of the Victorian establishment – and they form the nucleus of the twelve-man committee that sets out to draft the Victorian Constitution.[15]

Christmas, December 1852, Ballarat, *ti amo*

At long last, Raffaello Carboni has arrived in Ballarat, to find it amazingly sparsely populated. Though there had been many thousands here only a few months before, by this time many diggers have abandoned these goldfields to pursue what are said to be much richer fields around Mt Alexander.

But what cares the Italian? He is just glad to have arrived after the difficult and exhausting journey. He has joined up with a party of other hopefuls, and they soon set up their tent at a place called Canadian Flat before going to wait in a line at the Government Camp, where for the not inconsiderable sum of £1 and ten shillings per person in their group, they are able to purchase a license entitling each to 'dig, search for, and remove gold' on a 64-square-foot area for the next month.

Thus equipped, they head off to get their bearings on the goldfields, which is not easy – everywhere they look, there appears to be a whole slew of massive rabbit burrows. While some go as deep as 50 feet, many others are just small holes in the ground, measuring some three feet in diameter and about the height of a man or a bit over in depth, the most a man could safely dig on his own without risking the walls collapsing in on him. But the best thing of all is that the vast majority of these holes have been abandoned. Certainly whatever has been easy pickings here has long gone, but that does not mean that there is not still gold – GOLD! – there.

Carboni jumps down into one hole with his shovel and pick, and no more than five minutes later spots something that is gleaming back at him. It is gold, and he can barely breathe.

The Italian stops, holds it up in the sunshine where it sparkles even more, almost as much as his own eyes are sparkling to see it. He turns it over and over, and he feels a sensation identical to one he had first felt many years before. It is love.

Yes, he feels *exactly* the way he did the first time he fervently told someone in his hometown of Urbino, *Ti amo*, I love you, and he knows instinctively that this new affair will last considerably longer than the first one did.

True, this first particular pellet of gold is tiny – no bigger than the head of a bull ant – but it is valuable for all that. Back in London, working as an interpreter to whichever foreigner needed his services, Carboni had to take his hat off at least half a dozen times by way of introduction and go from one side of the city to the other to earn just a pound. And here he is, fossicking for no more than five minutes in a spot abandoned by other diggers as unworthy of their attention, and he has something worth *twice* that amount! All 'without crouching or crawling to Jew or Christian'.[16]

His small hazel eyes simply won't stop twinkling. It is *intoxicating*.

But why continue pursuing this abandoned hole when, clearly, those who had dug it felt there were even richer, easier pickings elsewhere? And is there not still plenty of virgin land left for Carboni and his companions to try on their own account? There is. Returning to their camp at Canadian Gully, they choose a bit of ground on the right-hand slope and begin digging. Gold. *More* gold! *Still* more gold.

They are in luck – going no deeper than ten feet they manage to pounce on no less than 17 and a half ounces of the glorious metal.

They are off to a wonderful start . . .

31 December 1852 – 1 January 1853, The Chalet provides no rest

His Excellency the Lieutenant-Governor Charles Joseph La Trobe is tired. And worried . . .

When he had first ventured to Victorian shores fifteen years earlier, his energy for the task at hand – essentially founding or lending support to the establishment[17] of institutions for a colony from the ground up – had been indefatigable. These include the Melbourne Hospital, the University of Melbourne and the Melbourne Public Library (co-founder along with the leading judicial figure and prominent man about town Judge Redmond Barry), the Melbourne Benevolent Asylum, the Melbourne Mechanics' Institute[18] and the Royal Melbourne Philharmonic.[19] Additionally, he pushed through the plans and oversaw the building of the Royal Botanic Gardens, as well as turning the first sod for the artificial lake, Yan Yean Reservoir, that was to become the centrepiece of the nascent city's growing water supply. For all this and more, including twice refusing to allow convicts to land at Port Phillip, he has mostly enjoyed the respect of the people he has overseen and generally enjoyed his role.

But now, all that has changed. Not only is he older and less able to cope, but the pressures placed upon him by this infernal gold rush are getting worse by the month and even by the *week*. The exploding population is now making demands of his administration – both unstated and shrilly expressed – that either because of lack of resources, lack of authority from his masters in England or simply his own inexperience in such a responsible role he is unable to meet. Between the goldfields and the Colonial Office in Whitehall, he is caught between the devil and the deep blue sea, and an inevitable result is that in recent years he has lost the respect of the people and the press.

On top of it all, his beloved wife and mother of his now four children, Sophie, has been ailing for several years, and he is insisting she and the remaining three children precede him in returning to Europe. The lot of his beloved, a 43-year-old aristocrat, has not been easy. She was from a fine Swiss family, the eighth of 13 children in a tight and very well-heeled family, and she had, she thought, married well to a fast-rising Englishman, only to spend 14 of her 18 years of married life here on the edge of the unknown. Her recent illness has compounded her general dissatisfaction, and she, too, has had *enough*. Neither of them has seen their beloved daughter Agnes for seven years, since they sent her back to Switzerland for her education, and the family continues to miss her desperately.

All put together, after long consideration, La Trobe puts pen to paper and writes with some feeling. It is his resignation letter. He no longer wants this post and wishes for the Colonial Office to send a replacement as soon as possible.

Letter to Sir John Pakington, Secretary of State for the Colonies, 31st of December 1852

. . . 'I must at length acknowledge that I feel the necessity of seeking to secure, as soon as may be, some breathing time and some degree of complete relaxation from that constant strain upon the mind more than the body, which the weight and character of my public duty, particularly of late, have brought with them.

But beyond this, I think that the time has now arrived when a change in the head of the Executive Government of the colony would be no disadvantage to the community.[20]

Certainly, it will take some time for the Colonial Office to receive his letter and get back to him as to whether or not they have been able to find a suitable replacement and accept his resignation, but he immediately feels relieved for having written it. It is a start. He hopes the New Year will bring better things.

The next day his wife writes to their daughter:

Dear Agnes,

I begin the new [year] by . . . praying that if it is His will we may meet and see each other before many months are over. I need not tell you dear child that the joy to see you will be great – the prospect of having to leave your dear papa, on this side of the world, is a very sorrowful and grievous one to me – and if I had been allowed to choose, I would have much preferred waiting for him that we might all meet again together – but it [is] not to be . . . What will [Charley] and his two sisters say when they know that they are to leave this country to go to Europe and see their dear sister Agnes? I think they will only be half pleased at first – as they always say they would not like to leave their dear Jolimont and their native country . . .[21]

Early January 1853, Magpie Gully, learning the lingo on the Ballarat goldfields

With his companions, Raffaello Carboni is now getting into the swing of it all and has been not long in understanding, and embracing, the ways of the place. Just as the diggings are a world unto themselves, so too does this world have a language unto itself – or at least phrases and words peculiar to it – and the newcomer, or the 'new chums' as we call you lot still wet behind the ears, must quickly learn it. So . . . 'spell ho!' . . . take a break, and I'll explain.

Firstly, and most importantly, as you already know, we miners are known as 'diggers', but rather than a merely descriptive term of what we do, it is an honourable sobriquet for what and who we are. To be a 'digger' is to be an independent man capable of having come here from great distances. If you're a digger, thus, you are in all likelihood a good bloke, unless of course you are a 'Vandemonian', likely an ex-convict from Van Diemen's Land who is going to try to 'jump' our claim, that is, steal all or part of it from us. We don't like Vandemonians in these parts. If the difference in weight between them and violent drunks was in gold and you sold it . . . you couldn't buy a cup of tea.

True, it is not only Vandemonians who try the jumping, and there is a lesser sin of 'shepherding' – squatting on a claim for some-one else without genuinely trying to work on it. For once a patch is not worked on, it is presumed to be abandoned and reverts to the Crown, meaning it is available for another group to work on. The inevitable result of shepherding are vicious disputes as to whether the ground is being properly worked on or is, in fact, available to be claimed by others.

In that case, we might strip to the waist and have a 'donnybrook' – a fight – at which point the cry will go up on the goldfields, 'A ring! A ring!', as the other diggers form a circle around us while we hurl haymakers. But even then, once it is all settled, we're just as likely when the sun goes down to have a 'nobbler', local parlance for a drink of spirits – you with a black eye and me with a swollen lip – and forget all about it. (Say, care for a nobbler of 'blow my skull off'[22] from the sly grog seller? A mixture of 'cocculus indicus, spirits of wine, Turkey opium, cayenne pepper and rum, diluted with five times the quantity of water',[23] it sells for 2 shillings and sixpence a glass. A couple of those and you'll forget the black eye, I promise!)

Whatever happens, though, make sure you don't get in the ring with one of the 'New Zealand Aborigines'. Huge Maori men with olive skin, they are heavily covered with tattoos, even over their faces, and most of them would sooner a fight than a feed. And when they do fight, they're not too keen on any of these London Prize Ring Rules either, none of this stuff about just using your fists – they come at you with everything they can get their hands on, including picks and shovels. They're fair-minded and don't try to steal others' claims, but God help you if you try to steal theirs.

One who certainly agrees with this estimation is William Craig, who has also now arrived on the diggings. His later recorded views of the New Zealand Aborigines would be clear, for they have, he says, no 'conception of the legal aspect of the question; possession with them was nine points of the law; so when the rowdy *pakehas* attempted to peg them off, they resorted to hostilities, and their savage instincts being roused by the sight of blood, they chased the "pugs" off the field with what offensive weapons could be laid hold of. The general impression at that time was that all Maoris were cannibals . . . However that may be, the New Zealanders were allowed undisputed possession of the ground.'[24]

But then back to the digging. Always back to the digging. As we do so, our chief hope is to find that we are 'on the lead' – that is, that we 'bottom out' right on the remains of the ancient creek bed, the 'gutter', where large nuggets of alluvial gold are to be found in such abundance we call it a 'jeweller's shop'. If we're 'off the lead', though, there'll probably be just about nothing there and our hole will be called a 'shicer', from the vulgar German word *Scheisse,* which is the same as our vulgar word sh– well, never mind. There are ladies present.

Each time we hear the cry of 'RUSH HO!' our ears prick up, for that is the call that a new lot of jeweller's shops has been found in a particular area and plenty of us diggers abandon the claims we're on and rush to the new one. Yes, a lot of luck is involved, and there will be many who miss out, but against that there is many a digger who, as Ellen Clacy would note, says he would 'rather spend his last farthing digging fifty holes, even if he found nothing in them, than "tamely" earn an ounce a day by washing the surface soil; on the same principle, I suppose, that a gambler would throw up a small but certain income to be earned by his own industry, for the uncertain profits of the cue or dice.'[25]

But remember: whatever happens, we all stick together.

Your 'mates' – those who are working your claim with you – are probably good blokes too, as are my mates, and as a matter of fact there are so many mates in these parts that we may as well all be mates together and even address each other as 'mate'.

We know how to work, alright, even while recognising it is hard and brutal, and frequently attended by disappointment, disaster and deepening debt.

But, you know what? There is also a rough kind of prestige and a great sense of community in being a 'digger', a sense of belonging to an earthy fraternity that is the talk of all the colonies. Let others work for wages in the cities or on the farms, keeping regular hours, endlessly doffing their cap to their bosses, but that life is not for us. Here on the goldfields, a digger is his own boss and answers to no-one other than his 'mates' – the men he is specifically digging with – just as they are answerable to him.

And because there are so many like us, living just like this, there is an immediate affinity between us all from the start. As one, we have left our other places of work, even our other countries, to get here and live this life, and we understand each other. Back in the city they divide themselves up into 'Emancipists', 'Natives' and 'Emigrants', but not here. Here we are all just 'diggers'; we are all 'mates'. Strike it rich or not, we understand each other and broadly like each other. A lot.

One thing that unites us is that we have common enemies: the 'Toorac spiders', the government officials who no doubt spend all day engaged in 'yabber yabber', useless talk, and wouldn't know a real day's work if it bit them on the bum.

Raffaello Carboni's own education in these troublesome matters takes a large leap forward on a particular morning in late January, when he is hard at work on his claim and suddenly hears some movement in the nearby bush, followed shortly thereafter by wild barking from his dog, Bonaparte. A few seconds later, a shadow falls upon him, much as a shadow falls on his soul once he sees who it is.

It is a 'trap', a big brute of a man in his blue uniform, with the hardened face of a ruffian, all of six foot and armed with a rifle at the end of which a bayonet is clearly capable of making any cruel point that it so desires.

'What's up?' asks the Italian.

'Your license, mate,'[26] replies the trap in a manner that brooks no argument. There is an arrogance about him, an insolence, a manner of demand that is so overbearing that, even though the Italian does in fact have the required license and is able to retrieve it and show it to the trap's rough satisfaction, he is not able to do another lick of work. For he is deeply troubled.

Has he really journeyed 16,000 miles to the other side of the world to get away from the iniquitous 'law of the sword'[27] only to find it here, too?

Will he really have to suffer the ongoing indignity of bowing and scraping to men such as this? For the truth of it is, it is not just this man, but practically every man in authority on the goldfields that troubles him.

This country really is, it is clear now, a penal settlement populated by a huge proportion of criminals where the ruling triumvirate – at least here on the goldfields – consists of 'inveterate murderers, audacious burglars and bloodthirsty bushrangers'.[28] Far from finding Nirvana, as he had hoped, Carboni is in this bullock drivers' land at the mercy of uniformed thugs with guns.

Late January 1853, fare thee well, from the shores of Victoria

The forlorn figure standing high in the lighthouse at Shortlands

Bluff, Queenscliff, just inside Port Phillip Bay, straining his eyes for more than an hour as he stares after a disappearing ship, is most particular. For it is, in fact, none other than His Excellency Lieutenant-Governor Charles La Trobe, and the ship he is staring at is bearing his wife and three young children back to Europe.

A devoted husband and father, he has been on ship with them for all of the previous week, ensuring that they are comfortable and settled in, and then accompanied them all the way to the heads as they started off, before he had had to say an all-too-hurried goodbye before jumping into a government vessel that has accompanied the ship for the purpose.

That vessel has dropped him on the shore so he can better watch their ship gradually recede, grieving at his separation from his family and particularly his still ailing wife, even as he prays to 'our merciful Father, with full confidence that He will be with them, & watch over them by day & night; & in His own good time bring them to their desired Haven'.[29]

Finally satisfied that they are on their way, and that he can no longer see a speck of them on the far horizon, he re-embarks and heads back to Melbourne to what he describes in a letter to his daughter Agnes that night as, 'Poor deserted Jolimont! And all there so reminds me at each step of Mamma & the children – that I could almost begin to avoid the sight of it. However I have so much to do, & such weighty duties on my hands, that I have no time to sit & mope & grieve'.[30]

31 January 1853, Ballarat diggings, a breakthrough at Canadian Gully

What will the diggings bring this day? No-one ever knows. All they can do is keep going the best they can and hope that down there in the hole Lady Luck will guide their picks as they work away in the near stygian darkness. On this particular late afternoon, four Englishmen – cousins Daniel and Jack Evans, John Lees and William Green – are working away on a difficult hole they've established at Canadian Gully, East Ballarat. Only 20 feet down they met the watertable, but, nonetheless, sensing that Lady Luck might come with them if they go deeper, they procured timber to case the shaft, put clay and bark in the cracks, bucketed out the water and kept going. On this day, they are at 66 feet when they hit bedrock, and so start a horizontal shaft of some 30 inches high for 36 inches wide. The Evans boys go on rotation digging, while the other two cart away the dirt. When Daniel finds some handsome nuggets, he is thrilled and climbs to the surface to boast to the others.

'This is the way to get gold,' he tells Jack. 'You don't know how to get it.'[31]

We'll see about that. At 5 pm Jack climbs back down to take his turn. Only a short time later, those up above hear a strange commotion. Cave-in? *Catastrophe?*

No, wait. Laughing. Jack is laughing! And calling out his cousin's name, 'Daniel! Daniel! Daniel!'

Daniel looks down to see his cousin looking up at him, but Jack can hardly speak.

'What is it, Jack?' Daniel repeats.

'I've found it!' says Jack. 'And it's a big'un.'

'Softly, for God's sake, keep quiet,' Daniel hisses back, terrified that if other miners hear, there will be a stampede to their hole.

'How big is it?'

'Three or four hundred weight,'[32] Jack replies before laughing again, a gurgling eruption of joy he simply cannot control.

And this time it is Daniel who can barely speak, and nor can his two companions. And yet, Jack is not far off!

It is only with extraordinary effort that the four of them are able to haul the nugget to the surface. The Frenchman, Antoine Fauchery, is there and records that the man who has found the nugget, which looks like a leg of mutton, is 'speaking very softly, like a man who had just committed a crime'.[33]

Putting the nugget in a bag, they sling it between a pole and then, with great difficulty manage to get it back to their tent while they decide what to do. Eventually, they get a policeman to come to escort themselves and the nugget back to the government station, where it is weighed.

It comes in at a mighty 134 pounds 8 ounces, meaning the 'Canadian Nugget', as it will become known, is worth – *dot three, carry one, subtract two* – nearly £9000.[34] And that's these Victoria diggings for you. In California they measure their gold by ounces – here, we do it by the *pound*. No Americans have even heard of such a nugget ever being discovered in their own country.

Immediately taking the goldfield Commissioner's advice, the four lucky souls head off to Melbourne and, together with their sizeable booty, set sail for ye merry old England, very rich men indeed.

Behind them, they leave the goldfields transformed – their find has changed the whole way of thinking. In May of the previous year, it had been first discovered that gold could be found by digging shafts rather than mere surface holes, but now it is obvious that the treasures to be found deeper and deeper still are extraordinary.

To this point, it had been felt that the hard, rocky crust struck generally 50 feet down was the true bottom, beyond which there was no point in trying to go further. The sailors, however, have chanced on the truth: that is a false bottom. The true jeweller's shop is just as likely to lie beneath. The aim is to try to get to the ancient creek bed that lies far below, and these men have helped to show their compatriots the way.

On the instant, there is as great a rush to start once more in previously abandoned diggings as there is for those who have drifted away from Ballarat to get back there immediately. It becomes a gold rush within the gold rush, with the returnees joining those who are now rushing to the gold city to beat them all for the first time – many of them to sink shafts as deep as 150 feet.

But how to get down that deep, and overcome the fact that you are nearly always digging well below the watertable and have to frequently dig through entirely unstable mud?

The first thing is to work with a lot of mates. Instead of working solo or with one or two others on a round hole dug in an eight by eight foot square, when working in a co-operative of up to 12 men, that shaft could expand to 24 by 24 feet. And no more circles . . . We're talking square shafts, usually just big enough to get a man with a leather or wooden bucket down comfortably.

With the collective of many mates on high, some would haul up buckets of dirt and rock as the others dig deeper, carting the tailings away by wheelbarrow – sometimes known as an 'Irish baby buggy' – or in sacks, to where the cradle is set up by the creek, just in case any gold has been missed. And here is the key. To prevent the walls of the shaft from caving in as you get below the watertable, it needs to be reinforced with split slabs of eucalyptus timber to hold back the mud – sometimes with sheets of bark laid perpendicularly against the slabs – as well as the gaps being packed with thick clay. Even then the water at the bottom of the shaft must be removed by pulling up endless buckets, though there is talk that some fellows on the Gravel Pits have started using a very noisy engine to pump it out.

When the diggers do get this deep, the danger is that water from an adjoining shaft will burst in so one precaution is that – together with the rope from the windlass on the surface used to haul up buckets of mud, clay, rock and *gold* – there is always another rope dangling 'so that on any sudden emergency the man below may climb a distance up until there is time to lower the rope from the windlass'.[35] Another problem at these depths is the foul and dangerous air, and a system of ventilation needs to be set up using calico sails on the surface to catch the wind and send it down below.

And, of course, the deeper the shafts go the bigger and tighter the population becomes – Ballarat will boast 19,000 residents by the end of the year – both in terms of physical proximity to each other and in the bonds of their mateship. And with the deep digging, since it can take as long as six months for diggers to work out if they have struck paydirt, the population also becomes more stable. By year's end, Ballarat will boast 19,000 residents.

'No diggings that I have seen,' William Howitt would record, 'and I have seen all of any importance – lie so compact as those of Ballarat.'[36]

But as ever, the skill in deep digging lies in picking just which way those creek beds far below twist and turn as the diggers try to 'follow the lead', no matter how deep it goes.

And if it all gets too hard? Too bad. You must keep going. Once we get down deep, all of us diggers are depending on each other. If your shaft, just next to our shaft, fills with water, then ours risks doing so, too, through seepage or even wall collapse. We are all bound together. You may not be my mate on my particular shaft, but you are still my mate on these diggings. (And even the shopkeepers are mates, as many of them agree to provide the supplies we need to keep going for as long as six months, on the proviso they get a share of the proceeds. And, of course, to write down and administer such agreements come a slew of serious lawyers, not to mention medicos to tend to this increasingly sophisticated township.)

Soon enough, the more experienced of the diggers know roughly-as-gutsly what to expect as they get ever lower: After the relatively easy shovel digging through the rich, black surface soil, they come to the harder red clay about nine feet down, and this stratum can be up to 50 feet deep until they hit a flinty hard crust that is neither dirt nor rock, but so close to the latter you can barely tell the difference. This stratum is known to the diggers as 'burnt stuff',[37] and is on the one hand hated because it quickly blunts the points of the pick that the blacksmith will soon charge another two shillings and sixpence to sharpen . . . but, on the other hand, looked forward to, because it means that easy digging is ahead. For after that comes a thin stratum, the yellow and blue clay of the men's most vivid dreams.

It is here, *here,* dear friends, once down to the level of the ancient creek bed, that our golden dreams are to be found, sometimes in small particles, sometimes in large nuggets and sometimes in smaller nuggets gathered together like bunches of grapes. If that is the case, what joy is ours! What riches are now in our possession!

And there is still more to come as, at this level, we expand our small shaft out into a large chamber – the size we have been allotted on the surface – which requires a great deal more slabs and technical ingenuity to hold back the mud. Then we can gather the gold, the gold, and still more gold.

And what was that line in the Reverend Dr John Dunmore Lang's *Australian Emigrant's Manual,* again? Ah, yes, here it is: 'Are we not told in the word of God that *the Earth is the Lord's and the fullness thereof? The silver and the gold* it contains are *His,* for *He made it,* that is the earth, and deposited these precious metals in it, as in a bank deposit, thousands and perhaps tens of thousands of years ago that they be searched for and found, and drawn forth, and turned to account by intelligent, enterprising and energetic men.'[38]

Well, we have now accessed God's account, Heaven is ours, and what a life we can now lead! For the wise, it will be a wonderful life for many years to come. For the foolhardy, just a few weeks in Melbourne, but it is all equally exciting.

Failing to find gold, however, all the diggers can do is to keep digging until they hit solid rock, meaning they have 'bottomed out' and are without luck. Whichever way the ancient creek ran, it did not gurgle here. It is time to move on, to try to follow the lead of the creek elsewhere. If only that ancient brook had gone straighter it would have been easier to predict, but at least as it is, it means that even late arrivals have a chance of striking it lucky.

All up, deep-shaft mining is gut-wrenching, dangerous work, taking an average of six months to reach paydirt – if it is there at all

– and fatalities from collapsing mines are as frequent as the rewards are stupendous.

But what is clear, as Carboni expresses it, is that Canadian Gully is 'as rich in lumps as other goldfields are in dust. Diggers, whom the gold fever had rendered stark blind, so as to desert Ballarat for Mount Alexander and Bendigo, now returned as ravens to the old spot; and towards the end of February, '53, Canadian Gully was in its full glory'.[39]

And of course – *of course!* – where there are diggers there are troopers not far behind, always in pursuit.

As described by Carboni, 'The troopers were despatched like bloodhounds, in all directions, to beat the bush; and the traps who had a more confined scent, creeped and crawled among the holes, and sneaked into the sly-grog tents round about, in search of the swarming unlicensed game. In a word, it was a regular hunt. Anyone who in Old England went fox-hunting, can understand pretty well, the detestable sport we had then on the goldfields of Victoria.'[40]

And look here, there is no point in saying you have bought your license, but you just don't have it on you. *It must be on you at all times.*

Of course this is a real problem if you have the paper license in your pants when you're engaged in often muddy mining, at the bottom of wet shafts or knee deep in the creek, but that is not our problem. It is the *law*, so show us your license or face the consequences. Those consequences are severe and include first being chained to trees and logs like wild dogs before you're marched off to the Camp lock-up – a very rough wooden cell somehow as capable of keeping the prisoners in as it is incapable of keeping the weather out – where the only way free is to pay the license fee, plus a fine.

What do you do, thus, when the cries of 'Joe!' go up, when you don't have your license on you?

Run, Ron! Like rabbits who have caught the scent of a fox in the wind, diggers disappear down their holes as if they are burrows, and then often head off into the labyrinthine tunnels that lie beneath. It is a brave trooper indeed who will venture down there, and for the most part diggers can safely remain underground until the 'All clear!' is sounded by their licensed mates above.

Even then, however, the troopers have their ruses to effectively smoke their prey out. On one occasion, they dress a couple of troopers as dirty diggers and then have them put on a blue in a dispute over a claim. Of course, the inevitable cry goes up, 'A ring! A ring!',[41] bringing real diggers from far and wide, including up from their holes. Then, just as the two 'diggers' are shaping up to strike their first blows, suddenly the traps with fixed bayonets appear on all sides, backed by troopers on horseback.

'Present your licenses!'

As if the traps had cast a fishing net where the shoal is at its thickest, on this occasion no fewer than 60 diggers without licenses are handcuffed to each other like common criminals and marched off to the lock-up, cursing all the while.

It is all so appallingly unfair. Nearly all new arrivals have a starting point of very little or no capital at all, having spent everything on the materials to do the digging, their passage to the goldfields and then food and housing when they are there. That means, after scraping together the money to pay the initial license, they are dependent thereafter on finding enough gold to afford the next month's instalment. Those who can't have no choice but to try to proceed without a license, with many ending up in a cell for their trouble – not for being criminal, but for being merely *unlucky*. It is an infamy!

And where does the license money of those who do manage to pay go? Certainly not towards providing any government facilities, schools or hospitals on the goldfields, for of these there is nothing – with the exception of the large Government Camp that houses their oppressors. No, it goes back to Melbourne, most of it, and pays the wages of the administration that is running this whole iniquitous system. Now, in another place, at another time, perhaps the people could mount a political action to change that system, but here, now, the diggers do not have the vote, and, apart from John Pascoe Fawkner, there is no consistent voice raised on their behalf in the Legislative Council.

The Americans, of course, fought their War of Independence on precisely this issue – 'no taxation without representation' – and there are enough Americans on the goldfields conversant with the idea, not to mention British and Irish Chartists, that organised anger at this situation begins to bubble and spread.

In the meantime, however, the hunts go on, day after day, week after week, on and on and on.

On one occasion a digger by the name of Robert Serjeant returns with his mate to their hut to find the whole gully surrounded by troopers on a license-hunt. Serjeant and his mate are not worried for themselves as they both have their papers, but what about their other mate, the always unlicensed Joe – and for once, that is his real name – who they have left back at the hut?

Aghast, they look to their hut where they can see smoke curling from the chimney into the chilly air. The door – an old flour sack stretched across a frame of wattle saplings – is wide open, and two Joes are heading towards their Joe!

Hurrying forward to see if they can help, or talk the Joes out of it, they are just yards away from the entrance when the two troopers suddenly reel back from the open doorway.

To Serjeant's stunned amazement, and the troopers' great surprise, they have been confronted by a rather bulky but certainly smart-looking female, who asks them their business. Before they can even reply, however, she looks over their shoulders to see Serjeant and says, 'Perhaps my brother can answer your enquiries, gentlemen!'[42]

The Joes, however, have completely lost interest, beg the lady's pardon and quickly head off. Clearly no lady such as this would ever be harbouring men without licenses.

It is only when the troopers are safely out of earshot that Serjeant's newly found 'sister' allows herself to throw up her heels and cut 'most unladylike capers round the dining table',[43] as Serjeant would later describe it.

What a lark! For the sister is, of course, Joe himself. Chortling all the while, he tells his mates he never has taken out a license, never will take out a license, and from this moment forth he is not to be addressed as Joe, but by his new name . . . Josephine!

8 February 1853, Sofala, the Turon, New South Wales, coming to the 'pinch' . . .

The diggers in New South Wales are not happy. By now most of them are concentrated around the Turon River, first prospected with minimal success by John Lister and James Tom two years earlier, and in certain places blessed with rich pickings.

On this fine, hot morning, though, no fewer than 1000 of the diggers head off on 'shank's nag' – digger parlance for walking – to cover the five miles into the township of Sofala, where they intend to make their views known about the *Goldfields Management Act of 1853*, which has been championed by the hero of the squatters, William Charles Wentworth. The central thrust of the Act is that henceforth the diggers' license fee is not only doubled on aliens – defined as any non-British foreigners – to 60 shillings, but it would also apply to all people on the goldfields over the age of fourteen, *whether engaged in mining or not* – of course, 'except in connection with pastoral or agricultural pursuits',[44] whose practicants get off scot-free.

The diggers know precisely what that is about. Wentworth, on behalf of the squatters, is trying to make things ever more difficult for those on the goldfields and force them back to work on the squatters' properties. As a matter of fact, in the diggers' view, this is what the whole license fee has been about from the beginning.

And the diggers on the Turon River have had a gutful of it.

Pausing only, as recorded by *The Sydney Morning Herald* journalist on the spot, to '[break] the cradles of those who had taken out licenses and were working,'[45] they continue streaming towards the meeting place. Among them are some thinly scattered Aboriginal miners, who have a strong history of protesting against the license fee. A few months earlier, one miner had overheard an Aboriginal miner 'chaffing a sergeant of the mounted police . . . asking him what business had he or any other white fellow to come and take *his* land, and rob him of *his* gold? What would [the sergeant] say, if a black fellow went to England and "turn 'em Queen out"?'[46] This was very much in the vein of a group of Aboriginal diggers the year before who, when asked to show their licenses at Forrest Creek, replied to the mounted police that 'the gold and land [are ours] by right so why should [we] pay money to the Queen?'[47]

Another digger, James Bonwick, had met a party of natives at Bullock Creek, 'well clothed, with a good supply of food, new cooking utensils and money in their pockets. One remarked with a becoming expression of dignity "me no poor blackfellow now, me plenty rich blackfellow".'[48]

Sadly, however, the rich blackfellows remain a rarity and, on this day, it is mostly fairly poor whitefellows on the march. Astute observers note that many of them have bulky, odd shapes showing up beneath their shirts at belt level – obviously guns – and their broad view is expressed in a large sign painted on canvas that adorns the podium in Sofala, where they now assemble:

'AUSTRALIA EXPECTS THAT EVERY MAN THIS DAY WILL DO HIS DUTY.' [49]

And that duty is to fight, to protest, to make themselves heard! The best way to do that, in the view of the Chair of the meeting, a Mr Maxwell, is to not pay the license fee – a view that is all but unanimously acclaimed, with speaker after speaker lining up to agree.

At first the idea is for all the men to march on the Commissioner at his headquarters and *tell* him they will no longer pay their license fees, but when it is decided that this is too provocative, the meeting agrees to send just four men instead, as a delegation.

When those four men take their leave to do exactly that, crossing the Turon River to present themselves, the situation becomes rather odd. Once they advise the Commissioner and his police of their intent, they are treated with great courtesy.

'Do you have licenses?'

'No.'

'Do you intend taking licenses?'

'No, not while this law remains in force.'

'Very well, we are sorry you have involved us in the disagreeable necessity of taking you, but other than to do our duty we have no alternative!'[50]

And the four are indeed arrested.

Apprised of this news, the masses on the other side of the river react savagely.

'To the rescue!'[51] comes the cry. Some diggers take out their pistols, while others wildly flourish clubs, and all set off to do exactly that when the local Wesleyan minister, the Very Reverend Mr Piddington, rushes to the platform and implores the mob to at least wait a while, stay their anger and see if there might be a peaceful solution.

Sure enough, a second delegation of miners is soon advised that the first delegation will be released upon paying a fine of £1 each, which they do. Further, the Commissioner politely informs them that there will be no more pursuits for license fees until further instructions are received from Sydney, and a universal bonhomie replaces the anger. 'At parting they gave the Commissioners three cheers, and the latter acknowledged the salutes.'[52]

As the satisfied diggers return to their huts and tents, a happy calm descends on the Turon River goldfields once more. Violent disaster has been averted by wise counsel, a decent Commissioner and goodwill on all sides.

The correspondent for the *Empire* is among those impressed, noting the great forbearance of the officials from making a difficult situation worse. 'They have, I say, done their duty, and to their coolness, firmness and prudence, must be attributed the shedding of no blood, this day, upon the Turon.'[53]

He is under no illusion, however, as to who is to blame for what could have been a catastrophic situation. For it is neither the diggers, nor the Commissioners and their men, 'but evil be to them who have framed laws to bring friends into deadly collision'.[54]

May 1853, Ballarat continues to grow

Ballarat is not only growing wider as ever more people flood in and dig deeper, but it is also growing up. By now the streets that the government surveyor, Mr Urquhart, had first drawn on a piece of paper only eighteen months earlier are actually taking shape. Though habitations of canvas still predominate, here and there they are giving way to stone and wood as more and more diggers – particularly those with a missus and kids – are choosing to live in solid constructions.

You can often tell where the Americans are living because they tend to build log cabins and display their curious flag of stars and stripes, while the English and most other Europeans favour habitations composed of bullock hides and sheep skins nailed to vertical slabs of wood for walls under tin roofs. As to the Irish . . . well, the only symmetry to their huts is that individually they tend to have no symmetry at all. As described by William Howitt, 'They seem to be tossed up, rather than built.'[55]

And, of course, now that the town is more established, some of the new constructions are businesses, like banks and stores.

In a community with as much sudden wealth as Ballarat, there prove to be many ways of making money that do not involve digging for gold. Selling supplies to the diggers, for example, can reap enormous profits for a canny operator. Many of the stores springing up in town are as extraordinary for the diversity of their contents as for their expense. Inside the doors are to be found everything from sugar-candy to potted anchovies; from East India pickles to Bass's pale ale; from ankle jackboots to a pair of stays; from a baby's cap to a cradle; and every apparatus for mining, from a pick to a needle . . . Here lies a pair of herrings dripping into a bag of sugar, or a box of raisins; there a gay-looking bundle of ribbons beneath two tumblers, and a half-finished bottle of ale. Cheese and butter, bread and yellow soap, pork and currants, saddles and frocks, wide-awakes and blue serge shirts, green veils and shovels, baby linen and tallow candles, are all heaped indiscriminately together.[56]

One can pay for this with pounds, but the shopkeepers' preference, of course, is for the currency of all of their dreams: gold. And yet in these exchanges, as the veteran diggers know, they must be more than careful. As elucidated by Ellen Clacy, who has spent many months on the goldfields by this time, there are many ruses. One is to weigh the gold in separate lots, on the reckoning that scales could not cope with the whole, and then, in the quick calculations adding it all up, make a mistake in the shopkeeper's favour. Another method is to fix the scales themselves so they always weigh light, and still another is to have the gold dust weighed in a zinc pan with slightly raised sides. Clacy is one who notes that these pans are then 'well rubbed over with grease; and under the plea of a careful examination, the purchaser shakes and rubs the dust, and a considerable quantity adheres to the sides. A commoner practice still is for examiners of gold-dust to cultivate long finger-nails, and, in drawing the fingers about it, gather some up.'[57]

But perhaps the surest way of making money is to sell the thing that nearly all the diggers want: alcohol.

For at this very time, in this month of May, 1853, a further sign that Ballarat is no longer the remote outpost it once was is the first hotel going up, on Lydiard Street, courtesy of one of the first diggers to Golden Point, Thomas Bath, who has now decided to become a publican. Real walls of flat wooden planks! A real iron roof! A real bar! Its own *clock-tower*!

And they say that within a month it will actually be licensed, making it the only hotel between Buninyong and Lexton. As a legal drinking establishment, Bath's Hotel will be something that Ballarat has not seen to this point – though there has never been any lack of sly grog tents – and there is a great deal of excitement as it takes form. Soon enough, the word will spread that there are more hotels coming, that former convict James Bentley, the big Vandemonian, is actually – if you can believe it – wanting to build his own hotel over on the Eureka.

The only people desperately *unhappy* about the advent of hotels are the sly-grog sellers, who have been making a fortune over the last couple of years, all but entirely untroubled by the Joes, many of whom are happy to take bribes to let those grog sellers ply their trade. (At £50 for a first offence of selling sly grog, it had been a wonderful windfall for the constables taking half the fine, though as the second offence brought six months hard labour and no fine, it had meant that the usual practice was for the constables just to take an ongoing £5 a pop to simply continue looking the other way week after week. Police Sergeant Major Robert Milne is particularly notorious for this and other corrupt practices, not to mention his high-handed haughtiness and lowdown ways.) While that grog is harmlessly enjoyed by many – if you've found a nugget on the day, it helps you to celebrate; if you've found nothing, it helps you to forget – there are others for whom it is more problematic . . .

For while there are those who are immeasurably enriched by the diggings, there are those destroyed on the diggings . . . and there are those hit by both fates. By this time William Craig is well established on the diggings, and things for him and his mates are going moderately well – apart from having been robbed the week before – without yet having struck the jeweller's shop that would allow them all to retire. All they can do is keep going, and on this June day in 1853, 20 miles north-east of Ballarat, Craig is interested when three new arrivals announce themselves as deserting sailors from a ship at Port Phillip. Craig likes the cut of their jib and finds them friendly, well behaved and so hard-working that soon enough the creek they are digging becomes known as 'Sailors Creek' on the strength of it.

Before long they are on paying ground and earning well. The fellow that Craig notices most is one George Brentford, who had been an officer on the ship and carried himself as such. Though without arrogance, Brentford is clearly just a cut above – well spoken, of sunny disposition, quick to laugh and make friends with all around. All is going well and the three sailors are soon on their way to a small fortune when . . . one of the Bullarook sly grog carts arrives.

The sailors are doing so well by now that they buy a case of liquor with the wonderful label upon it, claiming it to be 'Martell's Pure Cognac'. Whether or not Mr Martell has had anything to do with its production is uncertain, but what is sure is that it has nothing whatsoever to do with cognac, for instead of a sparkling and transparent copper colour, this is a fiery red. And yet it is alcohol and Brentford helps himself to some more. And some more and some more . . . to the point that he can no longer speak, let alone stand. This is not an uncommon occurrence on the goldfields, as diggers who are doing well frequently go on benders. The difference on this occasion is that when Brentford wakes from his drunken slumber, his first desire is for still more drink. He soon insists on his fair share of the case, which by this time is calculated at three bottles, and he quickly starts imbibing. Gone now is his happy nature, replaced by a surly presence who is interested only in drinking more. And so he does.

The more his companions on the diggings try to sober him up over the next few days, the more he drinks. True, twice he tries himself to stay away from the grog, but just as soon returns to it – the more so when the grog cart returns. As later recounted by William Craig, 'After consuming some half-dozen bottles of the liquor he appeared to have lost every human instinct beyond the knowledge that he had a mouth and a stomach.'[58]

All his mates can do is leave him in the tent while they get on with working their claim, a little under half a mile away, and it is on emerging from this claim one morning that they look back to see smoke coming from where their tent is situated. They race back with other diggers to find that in his drunken insanity George Brentford has ignited the dry kangaroo grass that abounds in these parts and – all but nude – then walked through the flames! They can see him burning within the tent, smell his flesh, hear his screams, but they just cannot get to him until the flames have diminished. 'What was only a week previously a perfect specimen of manhood,' Craig would report, 'had become a spectacle divested of human semblance.'[59] And that, dear friends, was the end of George Brentford.

Another case in point comes to Craig's notice while he is visiting Bendigo.

Heading down the main thoroughfare one day, he looks up to see a wild-eyed man divested of most of his clothing and on a horse, galloping towards him at full pace. It is a miracle that he does not fall down one of the many holes that there abound, but somehow he manages and Craig thinks no more about it until that evening when, passing the same way, he sees the man's dead body in the back of a cart with a crowd of miners all around.

Turns out that, not long after passing Craig, both the horse and the rider had a'tumbled, a'tumbled, a'tumbled down a very deep shaft and been killed on impact. So just what had possessed the rider to take such risks? A temporary bout of insanity it seems. And what has brought this on?

Therein lies the story. Just two days earlier – working as a 'hatter', which is to say on his own, the young Englishman who had arrived in the colonies a few months earlier had discovered a 27-pound nugget! Somehow, by hook or by crook, by heaving and straining, he had managed to get the nugget to the surface and, once gazing upon it, his mind had become unhinged. He talked to it, shouted at it, embraced it. He loved it to the point of such distraction that it soon became apparent to other kindly diggers that he and the nugget had to be taken in hand to the Government Camp, where they had ensured that both were safely looked after.

'Reason,' Craig recounted, 'was to some extent restored when he realised that his treasure was in safe keeping; but later on he was induced to visit a sly-grog shanty, and was there plied with drink – burning, adulterated drink – and became the maniac I had seen in the morning.'[60]

It is, of course, a very sad case, and while the goldfield authorities do the best they can to get to the bottom of what happened, so as to try to prevent it happening again, the truth is that there are far too many sly-grog sellers and diggers, and far too few officials on the ground to really have much effect on the welfare of those who fall by the wayside.

One official who manages to stand out at this time, however, for his generally efficient manner and proficiency is none other than the one-time 'little doctor' of the Bendigo diggings, Robert William Rede, who in October of '52 had thrown down his tools and taken up a roving commission on the staff of Mr. J. A. Panton, the Resident Commissioner on Bendigo, as Assistant-Commissioner of Crown Lands for the Gold District. The position sees Rede constantly shift camp according to the ebb and flow of the goldfields to the east and north of Bendigo.

Late May 1853, the Ovens goldfields, 230 miles north-east of Ballarat, the word spreads

Roll up! Roll up! For Row's Circus is in town. Of the many circuses that circulate around the towns and goldfields, allowing the diggers and sometimes their families respite from the endless tedium of their tough lives, this particular circus has a great attraction. Yes, it has a horse trained to lie on its back and 'flourish his heels in the air'.[61] What is more, though his shoes are of gilded iron, to the audience it looks like they are forged of gold, and the word soon spreads uphill, down dale and even further along the diggings. Have you heard? A horse with shoes of gold! At a local election, the owner of the circus rents out the horse so that it can lead the procession that takes the candidate to the polls, and as thousands pour into the streets to see those marvellous shoes glinting in the sunlight, the word spreads still further! A gold-shod horse! 'Shoes of gold at the Ovens!'[62] run the headlines. There is something so pleasing about the yarn that it travels on to Melbourne, Sydney, London and beyond! It is nonsense, of course, but it is too good a tale not to repeat, and in short order crowds of diggers head to the Ovens. Just as people in far off countries eschew their visions of finding a land of milk and honey – no, they want to go to a place where the horses are shod with gold!

1 June 1853, at 'The Chalet', it's about the Americans . . .

It has been a very grim, very lonely few months for Charles La Trobe since his family left. In their absence, his time has been spent doing two principal things: waiting for news that his resignation has not only been accepted but that a suitable replacement has been found; and engaging in the endless business of running the colony. On this evening he addresses himself to writing to the Duke of Newcastle

– the new Secretary of State – to keep his superior up to date. Though there have been no more recent large-scale protest meetings, which is a relief, there is no doubt that the problems with the licensing system, the question of its adequate policing and general unrest have not disappeared.

One issue that he is particularly concerned about is the Americans and the danger they might present, as republicans, to the security of the colony remaining a part of Her Majesty's domain.

For this fear is not just in Victoria itself. In Washington, before long, the British Ambassador to the US would be frank in an official report to his masters at the Colonial Office: 'There can be no doubt that a revolution in Australia by which its connections with Great Britain should be severed would be an event highly acceptable to the great mass of the American people.'[63]

La Trobe does not see it quite like that.

While acknowledging that 'some danger might be apprehended'[64] from the Americans, his strong view is that they are not the primary danger.

No, the real problem in these parts is the newspapers, most particularly *The Argus*, which is committed to promoting 'the idea of a substitution of republican institutions for the present monarchical form of Government'.[65]

What makes this doubly dangerous is that *The Argus* is so cheap to purchase, at just threepence, that it means even a 'day labourer' can buy a copy. Worse still, as it is 'diligently and widely distributed through agencies established at the several goldfields', those ideas are in danger of spreading.[66] And it really is a danger that must be watched very carefully indeed. 'I would neither deceive myself or others,' La Trobe writes, 'as to the power which republican and democratic tendencies . . . possess when fairly roused and found to be supported by the masses within, and by sympathy if not by actual aid from without'.[67]

Yes, it is not the Americans that worry him, but those people who most support *The Argus*, the 'chartists, socialists, and others . . . who have recently come amongst us, [all of them influenced by] the growing sense of importance and independence arising from unexampled prosperity, emancipation from old ties and obligations, and powers of self-support, and self-government, which should not influence the multitude'.[68]

All up, heading into this southern winter, La Trobe feels a growing foreboding, and he is more glad than ever that he has tendered his resignation and should be heading home before another year has passed. The only thing he is looking forward to now, more than news that his family has arrived safely in Europe, is news that his replacement, whoever he is, has been selected and is on his way . . .

CHAPTER SIX

TROUBLE BREWS

Hardly a man is to be found contented to remain where he is . . . You hear endless stories of ladies who have been used to large establishments and giving parties, now obliged to give up all thoughts of appearance, and open the doors even themselves . . . No servants are to be had, and many of the best and pleasant families [are] literally driven out of the country by it . . . Almost all the best families there . . . are going home to England, and taking this opportunity of getting out of the country; most of them hoping to return when things have returned into something like better order.[1]

Charlotte Godley, wife of John Robert Godley, the founder of Christchurch, New Zealand, was most unimpressed when she arrived in Sydney in 1853 to discover the only available domestic servant was the 'unsuccessful digger, whose health has suffered, or who has no luck at all'.

It was a digger's life. Hard work by day, blazing fire in the evening, and sound sleep by night at the music of drunken quarrels all around, far and near.[2]

Raffaello Carboni

Although our property has nearly doubled in value since the discovery of gold, I would myself rather have back the olden times when labour was plentiful and everything went on regularly and steady. We were then at least tranquil and easy in our minds, whereas we are now nearly worried to death with cares for the present and anxiety for the future.[3]

Alfred Joyce, a squatter who had a run west of Castlemaine, writing in 1853

Winter 1853, into the swing on the Victorian gold diggings

Across all the diggings of Victoria, the sun rises, the sun falls, the gold comes up from the ground and is soon on its way to Melbourne under escort, followed closely by the diggers who found it. They cannot wait to spend the proceeds – usually like mad things – and return a few weeks or months later with the glazed look in their eyes of men who have lived and loved hard and fast, and want to do some more of it, if only they can strike another vein.

Ballarat itself is continuing to grow to the point that the Government Camp now moves from a bushy outpost to a mound situated on a small rise about a mile to the west of Ballarat Flat, on the edge of the township – exactly where Government Surveyor Urquhart designated its proper position. It is bound by Camp, Sturt and Field streets, with the large gully that contains Yarrowee Creek providing the other boundary. Yes, this Camp will remain rustic in the extreme, based as it is around rough wooden barracks for the soldiers and police, some storerooms, doctor's quarters, the officers' mess house, the Camp hospital, the Commissioner's residence, together with a few administrative buildings. The whole thing is enclosed by a high picket fence, with the Police Magistrates' Court just outside. But it is at least a vast improvement on the previous tent outpost, and it also has an extremely primitive wooden cell for a lockup, which is certainly better than chaining offenders to a log, like a dog.[4] From the point of view of those down in the gully on the wet diggings, the Camp is always up on high, removed and infuriatingly aloof.

Meanwhile, things have also consolidated to the point that by now some 15 of the 40 original land lots marked out by the surveyor and his men have been sold, mostly to businesses and shop owners. True, there remains some agitation from diggers who want to buy property outside the township, perhaps for farming and homestead purposes, but the administration of Charles La Trobe has for the most part resisted to this point. The government's hope, however, that such agitation on this and other issues – like the license fees – will remain within manageable bounds proves misplaced.

The ongoing slew of new gold discoveries in the first half of the year in Ballarat and elsewhere caused such a daily rush of frantic diggers to newly popular hills and gullies that there was little time for organised protest – and they were all flush with cash anyway – but now the situation changes.

The autumn had been particularly dry and many of the small creeks had ceased to run, meaning that 'in every quarter of the goldfields thousands of cartloads of the auriferous soil are seen heaped up at the edges of the workings awaiting the change of the season and the ready means of washing the ore'.[5] With the coming of the wintry rains and the sudden availability of water, the population swells again with the creeks as thousands of men return from the cities to work the waiting heaps of soil. And yet, as most of them arrive with entirely unrealistic expectations of what they might earn, so does agitation increase for the total abolition of the gold license fee, which many of them now struggle to pay. And if the New South Wales Legislative Council is considering it, why not Victoria?

It is worth reflecting upon.

La Trobe himself describes the unifying effect of resistance to the license across the Victorian goldfields in a despatch to the Secretary of State, the grand old Duke of Newcastle: 'It was one [subject] which touched every man's private interest and feelings, through his pocket; it at once furnished a main thread with which all other minor subjects of discontent or agitation, or grievance, real or supposed, could be linked; and engaged the co-operation to a greater or lesser extent, of a large mass of the population of all classes, otherwise little disposed to complain and hitherto unaffected by the ordinary subjects of agitation. As usual in such cases, it brought into immediate notoriety, and to the aid of the agents, fresh force in the persons of certain individuals hitherto unheard of; but, however worthless, evidently adepts in the science of popular agitation. Public meetings were held in all quarters.'[6]

But is any one of these 'certain individuals' made of the right stuff to lead the diggers in a sustained struggle for justice?

Since the monster meeting by the Old Shepherd's Hut seven months earlier, Captain Harrison has been in Melbourne, acting as the gold diggers' delegate and making regular appeals through the pages of *The Argus* for the diggers to contribute their promised one shilling per man, per month, so that he may continue his agitation with the authorities on their behalf – not that it is obvious exactly what he does or what progress he is making.

For, really, as one contemporary writer notes in the pages of *The Sydney Morning Herald*, Captain Harrison was 'forgotten the moment he left the stage'. The correspondent goes on: 'It is surprising that, with such a cause as the gold digger boasts with his means – with the large bodies of men of one calling unanimous on many points as to their grievances – that not one man has turned up having the least pretension to the talent of a leader.'[7]

Despite the absence of that one truly charismatic leader to galvanise the diggers, at least the agitation persists, and on this occasion it takes an oddly lyrical turn . . .

The net result of, to use La Trobe's term, 'co-operation' on the diggings in Victoria is the formation of an 'Anti-Gold License Association', and in early June it is decided that all the diggers should sign a petition to be presented to His Excellency. But this, my friends, is not just any petition. *This*, the Bendigo Petition, is bound with green silk, runs to over 30 feet long and bears, it is claimed, 23,000 signatures[8] gathered from the diggers all over Bendigo, Castlemaine, Ballarat, Stawell and Forrest Creek.

Would that all of man's angst could always turn into such a thing of physical and moral beauty as this. For the diggers not only affirm their view that 'in the present impoverished condition of the Goldfields, the impost of Thirty Shillings a Month is more than

Your Petitioners can pay',[9] but it also records their grievances on more temporal matters, specifically decrying 'the Squatter Land Monopoly,'[10] and that 'armed men (many of whom are of notorious bad character)'[11] are sent to collect the diggers' license fees.

The diggers maintain to His Excellency that the way they are treated for non-payment – being chained to trees and logs – is 'contrary to the spirit of the British law which does not recognise the principle of the subject being a criminal because he is indebted to the state'.[12]

Because the current across-the-board 30 shilling license fee makes no distinction between the successful and unsuccessful digger, and, regardless, the average digger is currently only making £3 15 shillings per month, the petitioners earnestly request His Excellency to reduce it to ten shillings per month and allow 15 fee-free days to registered newcomers, as well as ceasing to send armed men to collect the fee.

In conclusion, the document reads: 'Your petitioners would remind Your Excellency that a Petition is the only mode by which they can submit their wants to your Excellency's consideration, as although they contribute more to the Exchequer than half the Revenue of the Colony they are the largest class of Her Majesty's Subjects in the Colony unrepresented.'[13]

It is with high hopes that the petition is carefully secured and sent off to the Lieutenant-Governor in Melbourne, escorted by a delegation of three diggers from Bendigo, who personally hand it to His Excellency on 1 August.

13–27 August 1853, Bendigo and surrounds

And so, on Saturday 13 August, the diggers come from everywhere: up from every gully, up from every shaft, down from every hill and across from many other goldfields. This is not just a gathering, it is nothing less than a festival![14] For the opportunity to have a break in the tedium from eternal digging, digging, digging by attending the gathering to hear His Excellency's reply, via the men who have just returned from Melbourne, is one embraced by many. Huge swathes of the diggings community meet at Golden Square, Fourth White Hill, and march in two files to the meeting at View Point (an elevated location adjacent to 'the Camp'[15]) as part of a grand parade behind their own national flags, frequently accompanied by bands playing some of their favourite tunes.

First are the Irish, 'with their green banner . . . with the harp and shamrock on it, accompanied by the pick and shovel'.[16] And then come the Scots. But what's this? As described by digger William Howitt, 'As if only third, instead of first in rank, the Union Jack of Great Britain. Close to it came crowding up the revolutionary flags of France and Germany accompanied by the stars and stripes of America, with some other minor flags.'[17]

And yet the flag that garners most attention is the one that actually purports to represent them all. It is called the Diggers' Banner and shows, 'the pick, the shovel, and the cradle – that represented labour. There were the scales – that meant justice. There was the Roman bundle of sticks – that meant union. There were the kangaroo and emu – that meant Australia, &c. &c'.[18]

Something new under the sun, this banner is not only symbolic of the growing feeling that these men are more than just a gathering of different nationalities but actually a band of brothers. It encourages those bonds, and there is great excitement at the idea of having a flag of their own.

As to the downgrading in prominence of the Union Jack, that does not trouble an Englishman by the name of William Dexter, an avowed republican who had designed the Diggers' Banner. He is forthright in saying, 'Wherever any people had risen against their tyrants, that flag had waved in the van of Englishmen who had gone to put the people down again.'[19]

But to tintacks, to brass buckles, and to the wretched matter of the gold licenses . . .

The main speakers on the day will now address this gathering of 10,000 men pressed tightly in front of the gaily coloured tent that houses the speakers' podium.

George Thompson, one of the three delegates sent to Melbourne, gives the account of what happened at their meeting with the Lieutenant-Governor on 1 August, and the crowd leans forward as one to catch every word. They are immediately on edge, for amongst the many of La Trobe's unsatisfactory, informal responses to their claims – a written reply is due in a week – is his response to reducing the license fee. 'The law is the law,' he has told the delegation. 'You ask me to do what is impossible, I cannot destroy the law . . . While the license tax is a law it must be obeyed . . . I must do my duty regardless of the consequences *(Boo, hiss)* . . . Besides, there are other and more important interests to be considered than the gold-diggers.'[20] *(How dare he! Even more booing and hissing)*[21] However, it is perhaps the reading of La Trobe's reported closing statement to the delegation that now particularly galls the foreign diggers in the audience: 'If I find this petition signed by Germans and aliens, it will militate against its force with me.'[22]

In essence, both the petition and the delegation's trip to Melbourne has so far come to naught. La Trobe clearly does not intend to change anything. (In fact, quietly and privately, La Trobe agrees that the license fee started life as a temporary measure but has now become unworkable, and he would like to replace it with an export tax, but to acknowledge such a thing to his interlocutors would entirely destroy the authority of the tax as it stands. He dare not.) The diggers are incandescent with fury. Won't listen to them? Doesn't care about their legitimate grievances? Treating them as if they have no voice, no *rights*? More important interests? Well, perhaps we need to make the point.

After the meeting breaks up, some of the more hot-headed men begin to gather arms and collect whatever ammunition they can get their hands on. The latter is so scarce that some break down tea-chests so they can strip off the lead fittings, melt them down and make musket balls. Some of the Germans and Americans even try to form armed companies, though one Polish digger, Seweryn Korzelinski – who had unsuccessfully fought for Polish independence against the Russians – is unimpressed. As an old soldier he knows only too well the likely result of civilians, no matter how engaged and enraged, taking on the trained and armed government soldiers. In his view, it can only lead to disaster.

The feeling against La Trobe becomes all the stronger a week later at Bendigo when his written reply is circulated. True, La Trobe does make some positive, if hazy, noises in his long-winded dissertation, and they do include allowing some digger representation on the Legislative Council, releasing some land for purchase and disarming the goldfields constabulary, not to mention reducing the license fee and even coming up with a different 'arrangement' to extract the tax. But it is all so vague and wafty, like smoke from a distant fire that has no actual form, and the diggers know they can set no store by it.

What they do focus on is the fact that La Trobe rejects outright any notion that the license fee could in any way be seen as an unjust tax. Far from it! According to him, 'It is a charge made upon the individual for the liberty of seeking and appropriating to his own use that which, according to Law, is the property of the public, Property from which it is but reasonable and just, that the community at large . . . should reap some advantage for the common good.'[23]

His Excellency also does not want to hear any more of the outrageous allegations made against the police: 'I can only repeat . . . that I have been from first to last anxious that the administration of the law, and the necessary control over the gold field for the public security, should be carried on without undue severity . . . With regard to the broad assertion that unlicensed miners have been chained to trees, and condemned to hard labour, I am satisfied by the result of the enquiry I have made, that the statement will not stand the test of investigation . . . I am assured that no such illegal sentence as that of condemning the non-possessors of licenses to hard labour on the public roads has been passed, still less carried out.'[24]

In short, he totally rejects everything the diggers have written to him about police brutality, in effect calling them liars. It is, in the view of the diggers, outrageous.

As it happens, it is not just in Victoria, and not just on the diggings, that feelings are running high . . .

The afternoon of 15 August 1853, Pitt St, Sydney speaks

Enough is enough is *enough*. This packed meeting in the Royal Victoria Theatre,[25] on Sydney's Pitt Street – known for its graciousness and the fact that it is the first theatre in Sydney to have ultra-modern gas-lighting instead of candles – is not merely about the very serious issue of just what the Constitution of this colony should consist of, and therefore what kind of parliament we should have. It is also to kill stone-dead the draft legislation – the New Constitution Bill – put forward by William Charles Wentworth and his minions. Clearly it is an issue concerning many people, as witness the fact that not only is the floor of this late Georgian theatre full, but also the Regency-style boxes, both upper and lower, where it is standing room only. On stage are assembled no less than the good and great of the day, the Sydney establishment.

It is the opening words of the Secretary of the New South Wales Constitution Committee, Mr William R. Piddington, reading the terms of the advertisement that have brought them together, and the crowd's response, echoing from the gods, also reported by the *Herald*, that best captures the tone of the meeting:

'COLONISTS! Will you submit to be robbed of your rights?' *(Shouts of 'No')*

'A Committee of the Legislative Council has passed a New Constitution, for the colony, by which it is proposed . . . One! To create a colonial nobility, with hereditary privileges.' *(Tremendous groans)*

'Two! To construct an Upper House of Legislature, in which the people will have no voice.' *(Great disapprobation)*

'Three! To add 18 new seats to the Lower House, only one of which is to be allotted to Sydney, while the other 17 are to be distributed among the country and squatting districts.' *(Disapprobation)*

'Four! To squander the public revenue by pensioning off the officers of the government at their full salaries, thus implanting in our institutions a principle of endless jobbery and corruption.' *(Groans)*

'Five! To fix this oligarchy, in the name of free institutions, on the people irrevocably, so that no future Legislature can reform it, even by an absolute majority.' *(Groans)*

'The Legislative Council have had the hardihood to propose passing this unconstitutional and anti-British measure with only a few days' notice, and before it can possibly be considered by the colonists at large.' *(Great disapprobation)*

'Colonists! Speak now, or forever hold your peace.' *(Loud cheering)*[26]

And speak they most certainly do, one after the other, each man outdoing the previous speaker in the outrage expressed at the notion of having the whole political process controlled by the squatting class. And to hell with Wentworth's publicly expressed notion that power should reside with those who create the wealth. The effect of the shimmering gaslight as it bounces back and forth from the pale salmon and blue of the walls to the heavy crimson material covering the boxes and seats is to create a sense that they are in another world. For all they know, the rest of Sydney, and indeed the country, has entirely stopped. *This* is all that matters now.

Henry Parkes himself, the well-known political activist and proprietor of the *Empire* newspaper – a strong man with rugged features – is received with tumultuous acclaim and is equally strong and rugged in his forthright remarks, saying flatly, 'I deny the right of the present Legislative Council of this colony to frame a new Constitution. *(Renewed applause)* A body delegated by the people themselves should be entrusted with this duty!' *(Hear, hear)*[27]

And so it goes. The highlight of the meeting, however, is yet to come. It is that tiny fellow, that 'perfect little dandy',[28] Dan Deniehy, the lawyer son of Irish convict parents and one of the beloved orators in the colony. In his soft Irish lilt, 'the boy orator' is as entertaining in general as he is critical of William Charles Wentworth in particular.

For Wentworth's plan, Deniehy says, 'would treat the people at large as if they are cattle to be bought and sold in the market' *(loud cheers)* 'or as they indeed are in American slave States, and now in Australian markets' *(tremendous cheering)* 'where we might find bamboozled coolies and kidnapped Chinamen' *(immense applause).*

And being in a figurative humour, he might endeavour to make some of the proposed nobility pass before the stage of our imagination, as the ghost of Banquo walked along in the vision of Macbeth, so that we might have a fair view of these 'harlequin aristocrats' *(laughter),* 'these Botany Bay magníficos' *(laughter),* 'these Australian mandarins' *(roars of laughter).*

'Let them walk across the stage in all the pomp and circumstances of hereditary titles . . . In fact, I am puzzled how to classify them. They could not aspire to the miserable and effete dignity of the grandees of Spain. *(Laughter)* They have antiquity of birth, but I would defy any naturalist properly to classify them. But perhaps it is only a specimen of the remarkable contrariety that exists at the Antipodes. We all know the common water mole was transferred into the duck-billed platypus, and in some distant emulation of this degeneration, I supposed we are to be favoured with a bunyip aristocracy . . .' *(Great laughter)*[29]

Did you hear that? Did you *hear* that? A 'bunyip aristocracy'! It is perfect! It is wonderful! It is *exactly* the right phrase to sum up the Wentworth proposal, and the explosive audience laughter is a wave, carrying all before it as it sweeps out of the theatre to those hovering outside, and through the streets of Sydney – seemingly the whole colony rocks with merriment. It is, in fact, a wave of laughter so powerful that it sweeps away Wentworth's proposed legislation for members of a hereditary peerage to sit in the Upper House for life. And it will be in vain for Wentworth to subsequently defend his idea of an Upper House formed in this manner by saying, 'We want a British, not a Yankee Constitution.'[30]

And yet there is one more significant speaker to be heard before the meeting is closed, a formidable figure who is visiting Sydney all the way from Melbourne, if you can believe it. He is a Member of the Legislative Council of Victoria by the name of John Pascoe Fawkner, one of the first settlers in those parts, who made a fortune of £20,000 in just his first four years there, through farming, hotel-keeping, bookselling and becoming a newspaper proprietor, before pursuing his true passion: politics. With his learned long face, aquiline nose and remarkably high forehead, he certainly looks the part of a distinguished gentleman – even if one of his contemporaries has described the former convict as 'half-froth, half-venom'.

Now, after some preliminary remarks thanking the men of Sydney for allowing him to address them, Fawkner gets to the point. He wishes to give a few statistics to 'show the absolute necessity of a reform in the electoral system and Government of the colony'.[31]

No matter that one critic would say he gave the same speech for fifteen years – it is for that reason that he now knows how to deliver it so well. His special bugbear is the issue of land and the outrage of the squatters having claimed so much of it that they deny others the right to claim any for themselves – and they give so little in return. In Victoria, just 700 squatters have control of the bulk of the colony, and they exert so much influence through this that they grind 'the bulk of the people to the very dust'.[32] Their obvious principle concern is not to lose control of the Legislative Council as, with their licenses to squat being annually renewed, the danger is that a truly democratic government would deny them their land.

'After all,' Fawkner now roars in the distinctly broad and sunburnt vowels of one who has been raised in this country, 'you must know the squatters hold 250 millions of acres of land, which they pay only a nominal rent for, and which they have the power to buy at any time, at their own price. Yet the value of the land could not be calculated at less than a thousand million of pounds sterling, being at the rate of something like half-a-million of money to each of the squatters.

'Now, should men that rich not be able to swamp the King or the Queen or any government upon earth with taxes well-paid? In the face of this, what have we made the poor digger pay for licenses to dig on Crown lands! Why, we make them pay £60,000 for a few acres in one year, while the squatters who have 250 millions of acres between them pay a mere trifle; and this was imposed upon them only because they belong to the class to which I belong – the industrious labouring class.'[33]

Hooray! Cheers ring out around the theatre. Fawkner is a new kind of 'Australian'. He has not the slightest hint of apology about him for his rough experience, for not having been raised in England, even though he had been born there. He is not an aristocrat. He is of the people, and for the people.

And he goes on, in full flight now: 'A single squatter pays but £10 a year for the occupation of hundreds of thousands of acres, whilst the poor gold digger was made to pay £13 for two or three feet of ground on which to pitch his tent. And to effect these iniquitous robberies the squatters and the Government were combined in one vile conspiracy.' *(Loud cheers)*

The meeting goes for four hours and is in the vanguard of many subsequent gatherings that see men from across the land pushing for the formation of a true democracy, as opposed to a government formed only to advance the interests of the wealthy squatters. It is, broadly, exactly the same argument that had been occurring in Europe for over 20 years. The forces for true democracy had met with defeat there, with the most telling points raised against them being the sharp ends of a mass of bayonets. The question remains how the situation will be resolved in Australia.

Whatever else, however, Wentworth would be some time – specifically, never – in living down his proposal for a 'bunyip aristocracy'. Ah, how they laugh and laugh at the very suggestion of it. Whatever else, those in New South Wales would not be accepting a bunyip aristocracy.

And nor would the people in Victoria. Few are more appalled than the lead writer at *The Argus*, who notes that this 'most impudent document' from New South Wales 'really does constitute a new Hereditary Peerage for that colony'. The paper reminds its readers, 'The parents of this unexpected proposition are necessarily the very persons who, from the accident of their position are most likely to benefit by its adoption.'[34]

As to Victoria's new Constitution, when its Legislative Council recommences just three weeks after this Sydney meeting, Colonial Secretary John Leslie Fitzgerald Vesey Foster is heard to speak with great 'liberality, soundness and openness to conviction',[35] as on behalf of the Executive he announces that, in agreement with public sentiment, the new Constitution will provide for an elected second chamber, not the colonial peerage many had been fearing. True, those men able to vote for both the Upper and Lower Houses would be severely restricted to those of the propertied and professional classes, but it is a start.[36]

In response, *The Argus* is quite overcome: '. . . we have no hesitation in saying that the proceedings of yesterday constitute a great epoch in the history of Australia. The time is going past, and will shortly be almost forgotten, when it seemed a sort of settled thing that the Government should be in a condition of continuous antagonism with the people.'[37]

18 August 1853, agitation rises a little on Ballarat

The movement across the goldfields to resist the license fee is strengthening. Leading moral-force Chartist Captain Browne – one of the Bendigo Petition delegates to Melbourne – has travelled to Ballarat drumming up support for the association and does well from the first. A series of well-attended and ever more passionate meetings is held over several days to express solidarity with the diggers of Bendigo, while also being careful to stress that the principle of 'moral force' is the only way to achieve their objectives. Nothing should be done to 'unsettle the minds of the population'.[38]

Another speaker at one of the meetings is none other than Raffaello Carboni. Always interested in the politics of the day, he has come more to keep in touch than with any deep-seated grievance. 'For the fun of the thing',[39] he mounts the podium to say a few eloquent words in support of the proposal.

Still, he is impressive enough in his words – and the gathering strong enough – that when he descends from the podium one of the storekeepers from Ballarat Flat that he knows, a Mr Hetherington, who happens to speak French, is more than positive in his assessment, saying, *'Nous allons bientôt avoir la Republique Australienne, Signore!'* We are going to have an Australian republic before long, sir.

'*Quelle farce!*'[40]

For at least on this day there is not remotely enough heat in the air to move the republic idea forward by much, and after just a couple of hours of collective grumbling, the meeting disperses and the men return to their work, albeit with a few pausing to down a nobbler or two.

Despite the thrill of having spoken from the podium, Raffaello Carboni has nevertheless had enough of life on the goldfields. Just as he had fallen in love with fossicking for gold during his first try at it, he has now firmly fallen out of love with it. Climbing from his all-but-barren pit one hot day in early December, he discovers that his washing cradle has been stolen, and it proves to be the last straw, coming as it does on the back of a terrible case of dysentery – always more than problematic when a man is at the bottom of a shaft. There are swarms of flies moving all over him wherever he goes, and this last hole is marginally less satisfactory than the partner he has been digging with. In sum, *basta!* Enough! It is time to try something new, and he soon enough finds a job working for a squatter as a shepherd looking after large flocks of sheep, going from grassy paddock to grassy paddock.

Those 50,000-odd men who remain on the Victorian goldfields, however, are becoming increasingly more outraged, as August in Bendigo sees the birth of the 'Red Ribbon Rebellion', whereby all those diggers wishing to show their solidarity with each other and the whole movement start wearing red ribbons in their hats. And they mean it, too. For they are united in their view: if His Excellency won't reduce the license fee from 30 to 10 shillings, then the diggers, in turn, will refuse to pay, bringing on a crisis for the government coffers, which currently have over £50,000 per month in license fees pouring into them.

While the view of most of the squatters about this turn of events is unprintable, one expression of outrage does make it into the public domain, black on white. According to *The Argus*, some squatters in the Legislative Council – certainly not aligned with John Pascoe Fawkner – advocate that the best solution is 'to arm the young men of Melbourne and send them on horseback to make the diggers pay!'[41]

For his part, the correspondent for the *Geelong Advertiser*, Samuel Irwin, expresses a common view well: 'Oh, that we had but one good man and true to bring our claims before the council, not as lucky taxable vagabonds but as hardworking taxed unrepresented members of the body politic, who are hampered by regulations so absurd that we are compelled to believe that the framers of them wished merely to tolerate such a class.'[42]

'Tolerating' the diggers, however, is at this point far from the mind of Charles La Trobe. In the face of this general refusal by a large mass of armed men to pay the current 30 shillings license fee, he feels he has no choice.

Fifty Redcoats of the 40th regiment are immediately despatched from Melbourne to Bendigo, and an officer and 30 troops are transferred over from Forrest Creek.

By the beginning of September, La Trobe's worries deepen that the diggers' protests will escalate. They have now placed an embargo on those storekeepers who pay the license fee, meaning there is another source of revenue that is drying up. Contrary to Chief Gold Commissioner William Henry Wright's conviction that 'the current force at present on these Goldfields is sufficient',[43] La Trobe orders the 'whole of the effective military force remaining at his command'[44] – four officers and 145 men of all ranks of the 40th – to proceed to Bendigo. The total number of army men on the ground in Bendigo is now a staggering 274, in addition to the 171 police. It is obviously an unsustainable situation, and the inability of the Bench to effectively fine potentially thousands of miners across all the Victorian goldfields who refuse to pay the license fee is obvious to all. Clearly, La Trobe must look for another solution.

Chief Commissioner Wright agrees and is nothing if not frank in the report he has already submitted on 28 August: 'We are compelled to report that the reduction of the license-fee, if not its abolition altogether is inevitable . . . If blood should once be shed it is impossible to foresee the consequences, but it would very possibly throw serious obstacles in the way of establishing regulations to be enforced on the goldfields.'[45]

It is with this in mind that the Lieutenant-Governor proposes to the Legislative Council that the whole license fee system be done away with and replaced by a tax imposed on all exported gold, thus ensuring it would only be those who actually had the riches who would have to pay. But the Legislative Council – composed, after all, of merchants, officials and pastoralists from the pre-gold era – won't hear a *word* of it and continues to insist that a direct tax on the diggers is the only way.

Unsurprisingly, this majority of the Legislative Council has received the full support of the Melbourne Chamber of Commerce, which had earlier passed a sanctimonious resolution: 'Any restraint on exportation is contrary to established principle of the commercial system, as tending to trammel and retard the free operation of trade.'[46]

One of the only members of the Legislative Council who does speak up for the diggers during the second reading of the Goldfields Management Bill is John Pascoe Fawkner, who proposes that the license fee be cut to five shillings a month, pointing out that the amount exacted in license fees from the diggers is 'more than half as much as the whole annual value of wool derived from flocks depastured nearly gratuitously on millions of acres'.[47] Why should the squatters pay far less for the lease of their land, from which is derived such vast guaranteed annual profits, while the diggers are left paying such a vast sum for a relatively tiny claim with practically no guarantees at all?

But come, come, come, Fawkner. The member for the Loddon, John Goodman, takes the long handle to what he perceives to be Fawkner's deprecation of the value of the wool industry, pointing out that with the increased price of wool and mutton, pastoral revenues had gone up four-fold from the year before to now be £4 million!

. . .

In short . . . though the squatters are now rolling in it as never before, they're *still* paying barely any tax at all?

. . .

Er, yes.

The most obvious loser on the day is the government of Charles La Trobe. Seen 'to fall in with the wish of the majority',[48] it caves in and withdraws support for the very gold export duty it has proposed. In the end, amendments are made to the new gold license fees it has sought to abolish, which become law in November: £1(20s) for one month, £2 for three months, £4 for six months and £8 for a year. Alas, for the diggers, there would still be license-hunts to ensure that all diggers were fully paid up, and the licenses would only be issued for specific goldfields, meaning they were not transferable.

The whole thing is a mess, and all who follow the issue closely know it.

Captain John Dane MLC is commendably curt in recording what he thinks of the latest change of direction, claiming of the La Trobe government that he 'would not put it to govern a colony of cats'.[49]

———

As to those in London keeping a weather eye on events in the colonies, they despair at the direction things are taking, with no less than *The Times* harrumphing unpleasantly, 'The Government of Victoria is humbled in the dust before a lawless mob; the reign of order and the supremacy of the law are at an end.'[50]

There is, however, one particular reason for at least a little optimism. Charles La Trobe's letter of resignation has been received and the individual charged with finding his replacement, the Secretary of State, the Duke of Newcastle, feels he has just the kind of man they need to replace the vacillating La Trobe: a military man, a man of stern character with a ramrod spine and devotion to duty, a man with a proven record of using a small military force to take on a rebellious mob. At one point in his naval career, with just over 300 men at his command, Sir Charles Hotham – for it is he – successfully routed 3500 Argentinians trying to enforce a blockade on the Paraná River, and it was for this feat that he was knighted. Hotham *does* have fight in him, and it is the firm view of the Duke that that is what Victoria needs at this moment.

The Duke of Newcastle is pleased with the appointment, as he writes to Charles La Trobe in a note apologising for having taken so long to find his replacement: 'I have felt so strongly the vast importance . . . of selecting a first rate man, that I could not conscientiously appoint anyone of whose qualifications I was not thoroughly assured.'[51]

It is true that there is some kerfuffle when the Crimean War breaks out, as Sir Charles tries to get out of the appointment in the hope of receiving a senior posting to command a ship in the Black Sea theatre of that war. For, as Sir Charles would later recount, 'My previous habits had in no way qualified me for such employment . . . I endeavoured to convince both his Grace and the Prime Minister that a better selection might without any difficulty be made.'[52]

But neither man will hear of it, and it falls to the Duke to tell Sir Charles that, in the service of Her Majesty, this is his only option.

'Notwithstanding my entire conviction that the Government were mistaken, I had either to decline serving the public or comply with their wishes,' Hotham writes to his sponsor, the Earl of Malmesbury. 'Thus placed, I accepted the latter alternative, and with a sorrowful heart go to Victoria.'[53]

Still, one more thing, sir, before you depart . . .

Taking a sheaf of papers that contain the financial estimates of the colony of Victoria, the Duke of Newcastle hands them to the incoming Lieutenant-Governor and says, 'This, Sir Charles . . . is the difficulty you have got to face. There is an enormously extravagant expenditure going on in that colony which, if not arrested, will cause its ruin.'[54]

It is for Sir Charles to fix that problem, and he is not long in looking at all options, including getting the license money by force of arms. But what arms? It is with this in mind that he has written to the Colonial Office before departure, querying, 'On what am I to depend if a struggle arises? Can I call a regiment from Sydney, Van Diemen's Land or New Zealand?'[55]

4 March 1854, Ballarat, 'Read all about it!'

And here now is something new. For on this day in a building in Mair Street, right opposite the Market Square, a massive printing press that was moved in just the week before, starts to roll. The press is substantially composed of an enormous cylinder upon which each letter of every article has been individually set. With a turn of the cylinder, each one of the newspaper's four pages is printed and . . . out comes the first edition of the weekly *The Ballarat Times: Buninyong & Creswick's Creek Advertiser*. It is a fresh triumph for its proprietor and editor, 25-year-old Englishman Henry Seekamp, who has invested his life savings in the venture.

From the beginning, Seekamp – closely supported by his common-law wife ten years his senior, the Irishwoman Clara, who had first come to the goldfields as a star beauty actress of her own theatrical troupe – intends his newspaper to pursue a civic-minded and radical agenda. Seekamp is a 'short, thick, rare sort of man, of quick and precise movements, sardonic countenance; and one look from his sharp, round set of eyes tells you at once that you must not trifle with him',[56] for he is one who frequently struggles to keep his temper under control. He has no truck with the authorities, detests the amount charged for licenses and is firmly on the side of his readers – the diggers – in all things. He wants them to have the vote, to begin with, and their own representatives in parliament. He wants hospitals and schools paid for by the government and thinks it an outrage, an OUTRAGE, sir, that these things have been so long denied.

True, it would be said that he writes 'occasionally under inspiration from the source whence tradition tells us Dutchmen have drawn their courage',[57] but there is no doubt he writes a compelling editorial, much more given to confrontation than consultation.

Not that *The Ballarat Times* is without competition, for all that. Also read widely on the goldfields, firstly, is the sporadically issued *The Gold Diggers' Advocate & Commercial Advertiser*, with its notable masthead motto, 'Labour found empires; knowledge and virtue exalt and perpetuate them'. It is an openly political paper re-started just a little earlier in the year with the abundantly red-haired and heavily bewhiskered George Black, as editor and proprietor. Many of those involved with *The Diggers' Advocate*, including Henry Holyoake, were heavily involved in pushing the cause of Chartism in Great Britain – and they are eagerly doing the same here now. With a strong republican slant, *The Diggers' Advocate* is composed and printed in Melbourne – with the enthusiastic assistance of an intensely Christian journalist and recent arrival from Scotland, Ebenezer Syme – and rushed to the selling posts around the goldfields from there. Syme's youngest brother, David, is on these Ballarat goldfields, and he feels the issues every bit as strongly as Seekamp, Holyoake and Black, and they are consumed with passion for their cause.

All put together, Ballarat just happens to be awash with men such as this: articulate and dedicated journalists and editors who have long ago eschewed the notion that the proper job of journalism is to merely chronicle history. For they want to help *make* it.

Early April, 1854, Ballarat has a strange exchange

It is only a small exchange, but as it is more than passing curious.

For while there are certainly rough Vandemonians, there are rougher Vandemonians, and James Bentley, a local storekeeper of noted cunning, is very likely the roughest of them all. He is a former convict from Surrey, and his piercingly blue eyes glare from a face that bears the scars of dozens of fights every bit as much as his back bears the marks of many well-deserved lashes. And he walks with a severe limp, his ankles having spent 12 months in manacles on Norfolk Island before he was transferred to Van Diemen's Land, before being granted a ticket-of-leave on 18 March 1850, before receiving a conditional pardon the following year.

To see the 35-year-old standing on the verandah of the Police Magistrates' Court is not a surprise. What is a surprise is that he is not in manacles, being led away to the lockup. And what is even more surprising is the 'business' he is on.

'Where is Mr Dewes?'[58] he asks casually of a bystander, John Dewes being the most powerful judicial official at the Ballarat diggings – a blue-blood Englishman who had attended Rugby School and only arrived from Melbourne the month before.

Even more interesting is that when Bentley is advised that His Honour is 'in the magistrate's room', Bentley simply heads off with the confident swagger of a man who knows these buildings well, even beyond the cells. And, sure enough, Bentley soon reappears with Dewes by his side and, as friendly as you please, the two cross the road to the large tent opposite the court, where His Honour lives.

Oh, yes, it is noted alright – they make a curious pair. Bentley is to the legal system what a furious welt is to a branding iron – the ugly result of its mismanagement – and Dewes *is* the legal system in these parts. Bentley had learned his discipline in gaol before being transported to Australia; Dewes learned his in the British Army for many a year before he made his way to Australia and wandered into the judicial system. And yet here the two are, clearly thick as thieves.

Oh, yes, it is noted alright.

Just as it is noted when, not long afterwards, Dewes, as Police

Magistrate, finds fault with police evidence that links Bentley's general store to sly-grog selling. He even goes so far as to recommend the dismissal of the police who have charged Mr Bentley – and their prosecution – for perjury. All this from a man who believes that 'the prevailing failing of the colony [is] "nobblerizing".'[59]

And it is *certainly* noted when Bentley is indeed granted by Magistrate Dewes a highly coveted license to build a huge hotel on the diggings, with weatherboard walls, sash windows and a shingled roof. If you can believe it, this place is going to have no fewer than three bars, 80 rooms, a billiard room, a couple of Waterford crystal chandeliers in its bagatelle room, where they play a kind of billiards, and an actual bowling alley on the side run by an American – and it is all going to cost £30,000!

Where would a bloke with a background like Bentley's have been able to put together that kind of money? Well, they reckon that, despite his lack of education and refinement, he is ruthless in business. After his release from gaol he earned a fortune in Hobart, making and flogging lemonade and ginger beer, before doing much the same with confectionery and gold-trading in Elizabeth Street, Melbourne, which is where they say he met Dewes. Last year, Bentley came to Ballarat to start up that general store, and now – *now* – he wants to have the biggest hotel in all Ballarat!

Mid-April 1854, Ballarat receives significant new arrivals

The only thing worse than living on the gold diggings, scratching dirt for a living? It has taken Raffaello Carboni some time to come up with the answer: *not* living on the goldfields, scratching dirt for a living. For at least on the goldfields, as opposed to wandering after infernal sheep all day long and into the night, there is a chance – a *chance, capisci?* – that you will strike it big. It is this hope that keeps you going day after day. And at least there is companionship and camaraderie and occasional revelry in the night, as opposed to being lost and forgotten on an even more lost and forgotten sheep run. So it is that, having spent a few months as a shepherd and a few weeks living with an Aboriginal tribe just for a complete change of scenery, the Italian now makes his way back to Ballarat. On much the same road as Carboni, and at much the same time, comes Peter Lalor.

Lalor's path, like that of many diggers, has been a winding one since his arrival in Australia in October of '52. After establishing a moderately successful liquor merchant business with his brother Richard, and then working as a civil engineer on the proposed Melbourne–Geelong railway, he wandered a little, including making as many trips as possible to Geelong where Alicia, the woman he fell in love with on *Scindian*, is now assistant teacher at St Mary's School. Lalor had then tried his luck first at the Ovens diggings before spending a short time at Buninyong. But he has yet to make a big find or discover the place where his soul could settle . . . perhaps a place where he and Alicia could make their home, if he could just gather the necessary capital?

And so he has kept going, now heading to the newly popular Ballarat, where in recent weeks the word is that the finds have been fabulous but deep underground. More men are needed to dig that deep, and more men want to come dig in for the winter.

Lalor is eager to see the place that he, like everyone in Victoria – if not the world – has heard so much about. As he gets close, the track starts to gently fall away, even as the trees grow taller and thicker before the road bottoms out to a valley. Then he begins to see tents peeking through the trees . . . until suddenly the trees stop marching with him and he is in the open once more, with the vista of the Ballarat goldfields lying before him.

Across the muddy flat he can make out what he knows must be the curiously elongated form of Black Hill in the near distance, with Yarrowee Creek running immediately in front of it, lined with cradles being worked by what appears to be a whole army of workers, an army fed by the hundreds of workers trekking back and forth from the myriad mine-shafts, which are marked in turn by the huge piles of dirt that lie beside them. This, this before him now, dear friends, is the famous diggings of Ballarat that so many visitors to these shores had started dreaming of after seeing it in the likes of *The Illustrated London News*.

A short climb up one rise, down into a small valley, and up and over another rise, and there is the staggering sight. What had once been a pristine creek running through the wilderness is now no more. All that is left of the trees that used to line it are hundreds of bleeding stumps; all that had been undergrowth is now only dirt. And that sound? The one like 'distant thunder'?[60] It is the sound of hundreds of cradles, rhythmically rocking, endlessly, back and forth, forth and back . . .

And everywhere there are diggers! Diggers working, swearing, scolding, carrying dirt, carrying on – the occasional cry of exultation when something is found sounds out against a background of low rumbling and grumbling that the yield is not what had been hoped for. There appears to be not one bit of ground that has not been torn asunder, squatted upon or despoiled. Everywhere there are tents, many of which have brightly coloured flags gaily flying from their peaks. And yes, too, there is a strong smell, a kind of *eau de unwashed bodies, piled rubbish and human waste*, but he will get used to that soon enough.

Along both sides of the banks of the creek, the men are so furiously working their tubs and cradles that the once-green water now runs yellow as the paydirt is sluiced through and the muddy water flows away. All over the banks are small piles of red, yellow and white dirt showing the remains of that paydirt, while the freshly shorn slopes 'where the prospectors found the gold of Golden Point, changed from their aboriginal condition to the appearance of a fresh and rudely made burial ground'.[61]

Of course, with so much mud in the creek, the water is now undrinkable. This means that the diggers must either make a major trek upstream when they want fresh water, or drink from stagnant pools that they need to boil to purify – frequently adding brandy beforehand to give it that extra bite. If they're lucky, they can get water from other pools that are not so stagnant, with 'the surest sign that the water is ok is if frogs are swimming in it'.[62] And if no pools are apparent, then the old hands know that the best chance is to dig beneath tea-trees, as they only grow where fresh water is near the surface. (Failing all that, just drink grog, because for all its sins you can at least be sure you won't get dysentery.)

After some exploring across the diggings, Lalor decides to stake his claim on the Eureka, not far from a spot where a hotel is soon to be built, next to a Scot by the name of James Scobie.

This proves to be fortunate, as Scobie is greatly liked by those on the goldfields. Very quietly spoken and unassuming – at least when he doesn't have grog in him, at which point he can be very merry indeed – he's a young man in his mid-20s who had only been allowed by his parents to leave Scotland on the reckoning that he would stick close to his older brother by several years, George. As well as the diggings, where the brothers are regarded as 'pioneers' in an environment two or three years in development, George and James Scobie run something of a carting business between Geelong and Ballarat, meaning that despite that parental promise they are often separated, as one or the other is on the road.

Lalor likes James a great deal from the first and always keeps an almost fraternal eye on him when George is away. Another digger that Lalor falls in with shortly afterwards is none other than the jovial and portly Timothy Hayes – once an activist in the Young Ireland movement, father of five children and husband of the heavily pregnant Anastasia. Hayes had arrived in Melbourne at much the same time as Lalor and comes from the adjoining county to his in Ireland. But this is the first time they have met.[63]

They quickly become 'mates' with some other diggers and work on their claim together under the traditional arrangement: all gold is to be divided equally and accounts settled every Saturday night. (The usual way is to store the gold in a carefully secreted German matchbox, which are notable for their four-by-three-by-one inch size and the fact that they hold an average of eight ounces of gold.)

A contemporary would say of Hayes, 'His outward appearance is that of a noble fellow – a tall, stout, healthy-looking man, giving himself the airs of a high-born gentleman, fit to rule, direct, super-intend, not to work; that's quite another thing. Of a liberal mind, however, and, above all, of a kind heart, and that covers a multitude of sins.'[64]

As to Hayes's wife, the fiery Anastasia, she quickly realises that getting her children educated in these parts will not be easy, but solves the problem by taking a job teaching at the local Catholic school conducted in the rough chapel in the area of Bakery Hill, the low bump that lies just to the south-east of Government Camp. That way she can not only teach her own children but also others, and draw a steady wage. (No small thing, when your husband is a digger and there are no guarantees.) While she teaches the girls, a bald-headed, 30-year-old Irishman by the name of John Manning teaches the boys. And to further ensure an income for the family beyond the uncertain finding of gold, Timothy Hayes leavens the hard physical work of digging for gold by penning elegant articles for *The Ballarat Times,* for which Seekamp pays him a small sum. That is alright with Lalor as he, too, regularly takes time off to walk the 100 miles there and 100 miles back to see Alicia in Geelong, becoming a familiar figure on those roads.

Raffaello Carboni, meantime, has arrived in town and is 'delighted to see the old spot once more'.[65] He runs into one of his old mates from these very diggings, and the two soon agree to work together once more. In short order, Carboni pitches his tent in the bush, prophesying that from his tent flap he will see 'the golden hole in the gully below'.[66]

And yet, the two need to decide where to stake their claim. They are both reluctant to try the Gravel Pits, where many of the English, German and Scottish are now thickly congregated, 'famous for its strong muster of golden holes and blasting shicers',[67] as it now requires shafts way too deep for them to contemplate. (Besides which, as the spot on the diggings closest to Government Camp, it tends to have more license-hunts than anywhere else.) Perhaps then, Canadian Gully, so-called as it was started by a Canadian named Swift, is still going well, with plenty of 'jeweller's shops' being the talk of the day. But, no, it is Eureka that most excites the Italian's interest. Notwithstanding that it is here where Young Ireland clearly holds sway, it is also the place where there seems to be the most discoveries of serious gold, and Carboni and his partner decide to plant their claim here.

By now all of the easy surface nuggets have long gone across all of the Ballarat area surrounding that first spot discovered by Dunlop and Regan. Still, there are no fewer than 25,000 diggers across the local goldfields, all busily trying to reach the magical, ancient creek beds that lie far beneath the surface, twisting and turning in unpredictable fashion.

Sometimes the call goes up that 'the gutter has gammoned', meaning the bottom of the lead has been reached and there is no gold there, while at other times a roar of joy from the bowels of the earth means that there is a wild rush to plant claims right next to it. This inevitably leads to disputes as to who was there first, resulting in cries of 'Ring! Ring! Ring!'

Raffaello would later recount, 'By this time, two covies – one of them generally an Irishman – had stripped to their middle, and were "shaping" for a round or two. A broken nose, with the desired accomplishment of a pair of black eyes, and in all cases, when manageable, a good smash in the regions either of the teeth, or of the ribs – both, if possible, preferred – was supposed to improve the transaction so much, that, what with the tooth dropping, or the rib cracking, or both, as aforesaid, it was considered "settled". Thus originated the special title of "rowdy mob," or Tipperary [mob], in reference to the Irish.'[68]

Sometimes of a night, if you're lucky, an Irishman might pull out his harp to pluck or an American his fiddle to play, and if you're unlucky a Scotsman might bring out his bagpipes, but somehow there is usually some kind of music to be heard.

The Frenchman Antoine Fauchery is there one evening when a band of wandering musicians performs, and among those who gather is a group of Aborigines – men, women and children all – 'laughing, foaming, twisting in a general fit of epilepsy'.[69]

Fauchery would report that just one old man, a little removed from the rest, kept his dignity with all of his attention focused on just one thing: the trombone. He is fascinated as this 'yellow, shining creature'[70] goes back and forth from being four feet long to just two feet, and then back out again. On and on: 'A mystery! The full extension of the instrument did not over-astonish the black man; but when he saw it, drawn back by the instrumentalist's hand, go up again, diminish and reduce itself to its simplest proportions, he completely lost his head; he touched the brass with his black quivering hands then he came back to the Alsatian, on whose person he devoted himself to the most minute researches, opening his coat, his waistcoat, feeling in his pockets, pulling aside the pleats of his shirt, thrusting his hands everywhere, but finding nothing, nothing at all that might tell him where half of the instrument disappeared. Suddenly he stopped, enveloped in a fiery gaze the musician and the trombone now all of one piece, then struck his forehead and cried, "He is swallowing it." And he ran away, waving his arms in the air, and showing signs of the most dreadful despair.'[71]

Music is part of the gold digger's life, its scenes played out across the Victorian goldfields. For look there now at the four black men from America! Likely, they are former slaves from the Deep South – who have made good their escape and have got clear out of the whole country – and, oh Lord, how they can *sing!* See now as the saddest looking one of the lot starts singing the saddest of all dirges about slave life, even as he 'is accompanying himself on a banjo'.[72] The haunting quality of his singing brings all of us in close, as he wails of his girl from faraway and long ago . . .

> *O poor Lucy Neal! O dear Lucy Neal!*
> *If I had you by my side how happy I would feel!*
> As all the other black Americans join in, the beat lifts . . .
> *Come, gals, let us sing,*
> *Don't you hear the banjo ring, ring, ring?*

And now, as William Craig describes it, 'banjo, bones, and tambourine assist in the amusement, the clouds that hung over the lamentable position of Lucy Neal are dispelled; the springs of hilarity are loosened; the quartette yell, and laugh, and romp with an abandon that can be only badly imitated by other races'.[73]

Finally, though, the music stops, and there is a return to the usual sounds of the diggings at night, as described by Ellen Clacy: 'Revolvers cracking – blunderbusses bombing – rifles going off – balls whistling – one man groaning with a broken leg – another shouting because he couldn't find the way to his hole, and a third equally vociferous because he has tumbled into one – this man swearing – another praying – a party of bacchanals chanting various ditties to different time and tune, or rather minus both. Here is one man grumbling because he has brought his wife with him, another ditto because he has left his behind, or sold her for an ounce of gold or a bottle of rum. Donny-brook Fair is not to be compared to an evening [on the diggings].'[74]

But you must be careful. For if ever things get too out of hand, you risk being arrested by the Joes, to be dragged off to the lockup in the Government Camp.

It is from here that the newly promoted Resident Gold Commissioner, Robert Rede – who arrives on the Ballarat goldfields just a few weeks after Carboni and Lalor – rules his domain. With a backing of 100 or so police, who are in turn supported by a military garrison of equal number, they are a little like an occupying army. And a well-heeled army they are, at that. A new official who had arrived before Rede to become one of the Gold Commissioner's staff was frank in his subsequent description: 'Everything was upon the grandest scale: commissioners, inspectors, captains, sub-inspectors, lieutenants, cadets in silver-lace and embroidery, capering about on splendid horses, and new diggings continually being discovered in the vicinity.'[75]

Though living grandly himself, Rede is not without sympathy for the gold-diggers, having originally come to Australia himself for that very purpose. Despite his position in officialdom, even Raffaello Carboni has some regard for him, in part because he is one of the few officials who can speak a European language, in his case, French. A quite cosmopolitan fellow, Rede had also lived in Greece, where, replete with the symbol of a silver greyhound on his dress, he had worked as a 'Queen's Messenger', a courier engaged by the British Foreign Office.

6 May 1854, Port Phillip Bay, outbound on *Golden Age*

Farewell to Australia forever.

Charles La Trobe knows he will be unlikely to miss it. As he sails out of Port Phillip Bay on this suddenly wintry day, the outgoing Lieutenant-Governor of Victoria is beset by sadness, mixed with heavy nostalgia for some good times gone.

The source of his devastating sadness is that just a week earlier he had picked up a London paper and seen his wife's death notice. His beloved wife of 18 years, Sophie de Montmollin, had died at her mother's house in Neuchâtel, Switzerland, on 30 January 1854. (The only good news was that, before she died, she had succeeded in being reunited with their now 17-year-old daughter, Agnes.)

Despite his melancholy, gazing back at Melbourne, it is impossible for La Trobe not to compare the bustling, thrusting city before his eyes with the rustic outpost he had encountered when he arrived almost 15 years earlier. Back then, muddy Melbourne had just one street worthy of the name, Collins Street – penned in on each side by higgledy-piggledy, single-storey houses made from the wood of wattle trees plastered with mud, known as 'wattle and daub'. Then, there had been just 3000 free settlers, most of them struggling. Now, there were myriad streets stretching to the far horizons and beyond, with many stylish double-storey brick houses that would do London proud, and the colony of Victoria itself had tripled in population in the last three years to boast around 250,000 people, many of them wealthy beyond their wildest dreams. The population of Melbourne itself is approaching 80,000.

Clearly La Trobe must have been doing *some* things well to have presided over such a stunning transformation.

As to the diggers, he feels he has done what he can, including a plea that the franchise be extended to them.

'I would briefly explain,' he writes to the Duke of Newcastle, in a letter accompanying the proposed Bill to establish a Constitution for Victoria, 'that, under the existing Constitutional Act, individuals occupying waste lands of the Crown for the purpose of mining, are not entitled to exercise the elective franchise. As persons of this class now form so large a proportion of our population, and contribute so much to our revenue, the propriety and necessity of their being fairly represented in the Legislature has been fully recognised.'[76]

(For, against the wishes of La Trobe, the Victorian Constitution that has been presented has an Upper House elected by a small elite of the propertied classes, making it even more conservative than its New South Wales counterpart, where the Upper House is exclusively nominated by the Governor.) But it is equally true, and La Trobe knows it, that the city of Melbourne and the colony have now grown beyond his capacity to control them. Like a baby tiger cub that was once so much fun to play with, and even train, Victoria is now grown to the point where that control cannot endure. At least not under his stewardship. It will be for the next Lieutenant-Governor to try to sort it out, when he arrives in a month's time . . .

CHAPTER SEVEN
ENTER HOTHAM

Went to Geelong in right good times, everything going on first rate until the news of the discovery of the gold. Then everything was upside down, men would not work at any price, contracts broke, men and masters going to the diggings. Jack was as good as his master.[1]

John Brooksbank, a hardworking Yorkshireman from Bradford

Thursday, 23 June 1854,[2] by Port Phillip Bay, on Sandridge Pier, an auspicious arrival

Positions, everyone, for the great man is nearly here! Yes, His Excellency Sir Charles Hotham, Knight Commander of the Most Honourable Order of the Bath, former Royal Navy Commodore and the man personally selected by the Fifth Duke of Newcastle, Secretary of State for War and the Colonies, to replace Charles Joseph La Trobe, is, as we speak, upon his ship, the mighty *Queen of the South*, and about to land on Australian shores for the first time. A public holiday has been declared in Victoria to mark the occasion!

True, we Victorians don't know a great deal about this fellow, other than that he is a 48-year-old knight of the realm who has recently married no less than Jane Sarah, daughter of Samuel Hood, Second Baron Bridport and grand-niece of Horatio Nelson on her mother's side. The main thing is that Hotham is *not* Charles La Trobe, who departed for home four months ago, and we have high hopes that the new man can put many things to rights that La Trobe was incapable of.

Gaily hanging across every street that the procession is to make its way down are colourfully decorated banners bearing mottos of loyalty to the crown in general, and welcome to the new Lieutenant-Governor specifically. At every window and house front there is exhibited either a Union Jack or a decoration composed of the wild-flowers and evergreens of Victoria.

Out on *Queen of the South*, Sir Charles Hotham, his wife, Lady Hotham, and his tight entourage of officials are making their own preparations to alight. Having entered Port Phillip Bay the previous afternoon, they had awoken this morning to see a thick mist covering everything. As the sun has shone the mist has burnt off, revealing a thick forest of masts in that little nook of Port Phillip Bay known as Hobson's Bay, indicating that, whatever else, they are entering a port of great commercial importance. Sir Charles himself, of course, knows that already, having been fully briefed in London before departing and having studied his papers on the journey to this distant shore. But he equally knows that while the colony's financial numbers are impressively high in terms of commerce, they are unsustainably high in terms of expenditure. His principal job in Victoria will be to balance the books, no matter what it takes. He is so intent on this mission that he has been heard to remark as the ship was leaving England, 'A little blood-letting would not do the unruly gold-miners any harm.'[3] He is determined to make the most of this new position, to demonstrate his capacities before this new challenge and . . .

And from the shores, all the way across Port Phillip Bay, the explosion of the much-awaited signal rocket is heard, followed by the sight of its red flare high in the sky above them. It is the signal that all is now ready on the shore to properly receive them.

———

At Sandridge Pier, just fifteen minutes later, the signal rocket receives its reply as the sound of booming cannon fire from Her Majesty's ships *Electra* and *Fantome* comes rolling across the water, telling those ashore that His Excellency has disembarked onto the barge of *Electra* and is now on his way towards them. Then comes the strangest sound of all. It starts as a low murmur and builds in intensity until it is rather like distant thunder. What can it be? Why it is, as *The Argus* subsequently reports, 'The resounding cheers of British tars belonging to the shipping in the Bay, greeting the arrival of a Governor of their own profession.'[4]

And just a few minutes later, there he is! As the barge comes gliding towards the pier, propelled by the powerful arms of ten good men and true, a slim, uniformed figure, wearing around his neck a broad scarlet riband supporting the jewels of the Order of the Bath, is seen standing on its bow, a beautifully attired young woman beside him. That must be *him*. And Lady Hotham.

Positions, everyone.

In only a minute more the barge is alongside the pier platform, where the Right Worshipful, newly installed Mayor of Melbourne, John Thomas Smith, stands with his head uncovered to greet the Vice-Regal party, at the head of the City Council and Town Clerk, other government officers, Members of the Executive Council – the four-member advisory body placed at the service of the Lieutenant-Governor – military officers and foreign consuls. There is rapturous applause and cheering as His Excellency steps forward to shake hands with them all. All lean forward to get a better look at this grand personage.

Slightly taller than average, this knight is rather slight in aspect, slightly bald and, frankly, a little ordinary looking for one so grand. Nor does he seem to have much of the sailor about him for one with such a naval record.

'He has not,' *The Argus* correspondent feels bound to report, 'we fancy, the inventive faculty, so useful in suggesting ingenious expedients for untried circumstances; or the political faculty, fitting him for the higher walks of statesmanship; but he has the administrative faculty, which constitutes a thorough man of business . . . His mind is sharp, but probably deficient in breadth. Upon the whole, his appearance is in his favour; his head is well balanced, and admirably adapted for practical life.'[5]

His good lady wife, who is clearly much younger than her second husband, Sir Charles – perhaps by as much as a decade, for a lady never tells – makes a stronger first-up impression. With a fair complexion and piercing blue eyes, she has the air of being that most wonderful personage, the unaffected aristocrat.

'Nothing,' *The Argus* reports, 'could be more gratifying than the joyous expression of her ladyship's countenance upon ascending the platform, indicating the delight she experienced from the reception given to her gallant husband.'[6]

And now as the honour guard of the 40th Regiment, under the approving eye of commanding officer Captain John Wellesley Thomas, 'pre-*sents* . . . arms', the band strikes up the national anthem, 'God Save the Queen', before the whole party slowly forms up and heads off beneath a triumphal arch with the motto **'Welcome to Sandridge, Sir Charles Hotham'** brightly emblazoned upon it. They make their way off the pier to yet more wild cheering as they proceed between all those groups who are to take part in the cavalcade. Met by the Mayor and ascending through the guard of honour, Lady Hotham is put in a horse-drawn carriage with the Lieutenant-Governor's private secretary, Captain J. H. Kay, whilst His Excellency is accompanied by the officer administering the government and his large staff on horseback, as they ride along the path formed by the two roaring lines of people, the whole three miles to the city.

Finally, the procession is ready to head off with Sir Charles and his entourage in the lead. Together they all make their way towards the city of Melbourne and then Government House in Toorac – a mansion especially chosen for the incoming Lieutenant-Governor by

Charles La Trobe before he had departed for home. And of course the streets are lined with people, dozens deep, cheering them all to the echo. Upon every balcony, and from every window, there are yet more people cheering, waving flags.

As the correspondent for *The Argus* comments, 'It was more like the ovation of a conquering hero, and reminded us of Shakespeare's description of the triumphs of ancient Rome,

Many a time and oft have ye climb'd up
To towers and battlements – yea, to chimney tops,
Your children in your arms, and thereto have sat
The livelong day to see

Not "great Pompey pass the streets of Rome", but gallant Hotham pass the streets of Melbourne; not in triumph over seas of blood, but amid a hearty welcome from loyal British hearts, over whom he is destined to exercise the functions of loyalty for a time.'[7]

And yet, surely not even one of Pompey's wives (for that great Roman leader was blessed with no fewer than five such delights) was treated in the manner that Hotham later describes to Newcastle. Witness Sir Charles's own words to his superior: 'Nor can I omit mentioning a trifling circumstance which will give your Grace an idea of the feelings of this hardy and energetic people, the leaders of Lady Hotham's carriage proving restive, it was resolved to take them off, and the populace with difficulty dissuaded from yoking themselves and dragging the carriage the whole distance from Sandridge to Melbourne.'[8]

Lead on, Sir Charles, followed by, in strict order of importance – an order that has been hotly negotiated – the pillars of Melbourne society upon whom the new Lieutenant-Governor's authority will be principally relying.

First up come the members of the Town Council, together with the Chief Magistrate, and, as *The Argus* would report, this 'gave an imprimatur of authority and publicity to the demonstration'.[9] Next are the Magistrates in their full legal robes, not only 'the upholders of law and order', but also 'the link between the Crown and the people'. Following them are 'the clergy, the inculcators of religion, morality, and loyalty'.[10] Then come the Legislative Council, Judges, Consuls, the heads of the government's administrative departments, closely followed by the Chamber of Commerce in the form of some of Melbourne's leading merchants, proudly taking their place as the people cheer them on.

And look, ye! Here now are the Societies and Lodges of Freemasonry, Odd Fellowship, Ancient Foresters and the Sons of St Patrick, each group dressed and adorned with their own costumes and regalia, holding up banners bearing loyal mottos and accompanied by bands of music. Among them we see an extraordinary figure adorned with 'the pure white robes of an ancient bard or harper, with grey locks and flowing beard, crowned with laurel and playing on his harp, the emblem of the Emerald Isle.'[11] Not to be outdone, the other national groups like the Welsh Colonists, the Germans, Frenchmen, Poles, Hungarians and Italians are also gaily adorned.

Few are more impressive or numerous, however, than the Americans, who are doing what Americans always do so well – turning out in force. Their contingent includes the American Consul, James Tarleton, in his official uniform, riding in a gilded carriage drawn by six splendid horses, the carriage magnificently decorated with national emblems, arms and colours, followed by many fine Americans on horseback wearing military caps and sashes.

And still the procession goes on! After the foreigners come the jolly, ruddy-faced farmers, 'with ears of wheat or other cereal produce in their hats, bound with ribands of red, white, and blue', then the Licensed Victuallers' Association, and then yet one more delight. 'Next . . . came Typo, the great intelligencer of the age, with his Press at work on a four wheeled wagon, throwing off a brief history of the colony up to the arrival of Sir Charles Hotham, in an ornamental form of typography. The senior pressman of the trade, dressed in masonic orders, and wearing the cap of liberty, presided at this locomotive Press, and a large muster of the profession were present in the procession.'[12]

Hard behind are the carpenters, builders and plumbers, the Total Abstinence Society, the company and handsome horses of Row's Circus and the excited children of the colony, 'with their tiny voices joining in the general hurrah',[13] bringing up the rear.

Borne along by the unending cheering, the procession winds its way along the road from the beach towards Melbourne proper, with the crowd getting ever thicker as it moves along.

Governor Hotham finally crosses the Yarra River to enter the city beneath a huge banner embossed with a large gilt crown beneath which, in blue letters upon a white background, are the words, **'VICTORIA WELCOMES VICTORIA'S CHOICE'.**[14]

Hotham, even with his ample experience of such public occasions, is quite overcome by the magnitude and opulence of his reception by no fewer than 60,000 people: 'Politics were forgotten, loyalty prevailed – men, women and children gave way to recollections of the old country and devotion to their Sovereign.'[15]

There is much more to come as the procession makes its way towards Government House in Toorac. The shouts become more deafening as the convoy continues. It passes the Criterion Hotel, where, at great expense, an immense crown of gold and crimson, trimmed with green boughs and measuring not less than sixteen feet in diameter and about ten feet in height, has been erected on the façade.

'Around the crown was a wreath of green leaves, and on a blue ground and in golden letters the following inscription was emblazoned: **"A QUEEN'S CHOICE, A PEOPLE'S PRIDE, WELCOME!"**'[16]

Turning at William Street, the procession passes government

offices, then St James Cathedral, and finally arrives at the gates of Government House, where it is estimated a crowd of some eight to 10,000 people have gathered.

As Sir Charles enters his new gates and confidently alights from the carriage to walk the last 50 yards, the people cheer and wave their hats and handkerchiefs. The glorious Vice-Regal standard is run up the flagpole to show His Excellency is in residence, just as the cannon from the barracks roars its own notification that Her Majesty's representative is now on site at Government House.

At the door to the magnificent building await immaculately attired ladies and gentlemen of Victoria's high society, while a company of 100 men of the mighty 40th Regiment forms up a fine guard of honour. They stand silent and straight-backed sentinel as the Vice-Regal party enters the green grass-plot formed by their obeisance, all of it joyously observed by the people crowded on the roofs opposite.

Presently, all the major players gather in a square of power formed by the ranks of the 40th Regiment as Mr Rusden, the Clerk of the Executive Council, reads the proclamation from the official scroll, and graced with the great seal of England, signed by the Duke of Newcastle, appointing Sir Charles Augustus Hotham, KCB, to be Lieutenant-Governor of the colony of Victoria . . .

'The following oaths were then administered to Sir Charles *seriatim* [in order], the oath of allegiance, the oath of abjuration, the oath of supremacy, the oath of office, the oath to preserve the laws of trade, and the declaration of Protestantism.'[17]

Sir Charles solemnly takes all the oaths, signs documents to that effect and, now that he is officially the Lieutenant-Governor, he is greeted with enormous cheering, quite equal to the cheering extended to Lady Hotham!

His Excellency then enters Government House, and it looks as thought it is all over bar the shouting – and cheering. And yet, feeling it his duty to address the masses, he breaks with protocol, soon re-emerging on the small upper window balcony on the top of the porch. In a clear, loud, 'quarter-deck' voice, he addresses the throng:

'Gentlemen, I know not whether it be according to custom, that I should address you on the present occasion, but this I do know, that it would be most unbecoming in me, to allow you to separate without expressing my hearty thanks for the very cordial welcome which you have this day given me.

'I come among you, an entire stranger – your welcome is not therefore for me, but for the representative of the Queen, and in Her Majesty's name I thank you. I shall officially and in my public despatches make this known to Her Majesty's Government and I have also other means privately to bring the same before Her Majesty.

'I shall govern you as an honest man; I shall look neither to the right nor the left – I shall do my duty and try to please you – again, I thank you.'[18]

Again, he is cheered to the echo.

Did you hear him? This is a man who personally communicates with the Queen! And we practically *know* him.

His Excellency is off to a wonderful start.

'It was essentially a popular demonstration of the most enthusiastic kind,' *The Argus* reports the following day, 'and as a means of building up a kindly sympathy between the ruler and the ruled, its effects cannot but be largely beneficial.'[19]

Hear, hear!

Hear, HEAR!

Sunday, 25 June 1854, Ballarat takes an alternative view, not for the last time

This is not quite the way we see it on the diggings. Up here, Melbourne is a faraway place, and the arrival of such a personage as Sir Charles does not occasion enormous excitement, most particularly when there are things of more moment happening on the goldfields. On this day, digger Thomas Pierson carefully writes in his diary:

This morning as is our Sundays wont to do we got the weekly Argus Newspaper price 3/4 we learn from it that our new governor Sir Charles Hotham has arrived — our old Governor La Trobe left here for England in the Golden age on 5th of May after filling the office 15 years — before the Gold diggings the Governor salary was £4000. It now is £15,000 annually and £5,000 for travel expenses. I see from the papers they are giving him a grand reception at Sandridge of Melbourne — with Arches flags, songs etc etc — last week a hole caved in on a man and broke his shin — when they brought him up out of the hole his shin bone protruded 2 inches through his stocking.[20]

12 July 1854, on the Eureka, there are wild celebrations

It is a big day on the diggings. For it is the day that, amid much fanfare, James and Catherine Bentley's Eureka Hotel is opened for business. And what a wonder to behold it is! The whole thing, standing proud on Eureka Street, covers an entire half-acre. Over the front door it has a beautiful lamp to light the way for all who would cross its portals and tread its boards. You can certainly see where the rumoured £30,000 to build it went, though there remains speculation on how Bentley raised such an amount.

One rumour, and there is a fair bit to back it, is that local Magistrate John Dewes, the one who has signed off on the license for Bentley to have this bar, is a silent partner, though in what manner is not obvious. What *is* certain around the diggings is that Dewes is notorious — though nothing has ever been proved — for demanding bribes from sly-grog sellers, hoteliers and victuallers in return for looking the other way while they break the law. And it is in this way, it is presumed, that Dewes may have earned the capital he needs to invest. The most intriguing, and therefore the most popular, rumour is that because of the license he has granted, the money he has put in and the favours he is expected to do, Bentley has given Dewes a quarter share in the Eureka Hotel.

From the beginning the bar is a great favourite of all the Joes, with police, troopers and magistrates all seen to drink there regularly. One constant customer is Magistrate Dewes himself, and he is personally involved enough to later exult in the fact that '£350 were received over the bar counter in payment for liquors on the first day of its opening'.[21] Oh, yes, it is noted alright – it is all so out of the ordinary. For the most part, those who are based in the Government Camp up on the hill, well above those of us on the lowly diggings, live in a world unto themselves. They live well, dine well, socialise with each other, receive distinguished visitors such as squatters and government officials, and allow no free access to *their* Camp for such as us. And yet, here *they* are now, frequently venturing out and spending time on the diggings in Bentley's Eureka Hotel. It is all very strange. And we don't like it . . .

17 July 1854, Ballarat, teaching's loss is journalism's gain

John Manning has just about had enough. For the last six months he has been teaching at the makeshift Catholic school in the chapel that lies at the foot of Bakery Hill, in the company of Anastasia Hayes, who teaches the girls, and in all that time they have had next to no support from the government. When he had taken over in April, there had been just 15 students, and he and the worthy Anastasia now have 89 between them.

It is with all this in mind that the small but ever-feisty Irishman writes to the Secretary of the Denominational Schools Board, pointing out just how dire things are: 'One very ungainly table of about twelve feet long serves as a writing desk for as many as can crowd around it – all who cannot must kneel on the wet floor along the seats and write thereon. But description is almost impossible – in one word, sir, the school I have the honour of conducting is emphatically more like the [churlish] seminary of a hedge schoolmaster than anything I can compare it to.'[22]

Not only that, but in all the time he has been here, he has had not the slightest correspondence with the Board – not even a school inspector has visited. The result is that many of the students are leaving to go to the National School, and while he would be inclined to try to stop them, that would be 'tantamount to an assassination of the scholars' time.'[23]

A nice turn of phrase? Manning rather thinks so himself.

Perhaps he should try another line of work, start writing for one of the many papers now flourishing on the diggings? It is not a bad idea, and Manning does indeed leave shortly afterwards to take up a position with Henry Seekamp's *Ballarat Times*.

26 July 1854, Government House, Toorac, the spectre of penury looms

It has been something of a long haul, but after carefully going through all the accounts left by his predecessor, Lieutenant-Governor Hotham and his senior staff are getting a clearer idea of the financial situation faced by the newly established colony of Victoria. And it is grim.

As extraordinary as it seems, the deficit is just over £1,000,000, and the colony is teetering on the edge of outright bankruptcy. The police bills alone are staggering, even for such poor police as they have. In 1851, policing had cost Victoria just £25,000. But with the explosion of the goldfields it had blown out to £300,000 in just two years and, with the rising goldfields population and continued agitations, it is ever on the increase.

Of all the problems Lieutenant-Governor Hotham faces, this draining of the government coffers is the most severe as his mandate from London to *balance the budget* has always been paramount.

After examining the many reports he has requested over the past few months on comparative annual payment of license fees, the most obvious problem Sir Charles can see is that only half the diggers (and storekeepers) are actually paying the tax.

The quarter ending 30 June had shown 43,700 licenses issued and £87,800 raised, representing a decrease of 78,000 licenses on the preceding year and £100,000 in revenue, despite the fact that the goldfields' male adult population had increased by over 20,000. The preceding quarter, ending 31 March 1853, appeared as bad if not worse. Although the male adult population had increased by over 10,000 on 1853 figures, it was down 88,800 licenses and showed a decrease of £104,000. No matter which way Hotham looks at it, the extremely frustrating truth is that goldfields license revenue has fallen away by nearly half even though the goldfields' population has gone up every month and has never been higher.[24]

Of course, Hotham's first response is to hold his underlings accountable, and he begins by haranguing his Chief Gold Commissioner endlessly and often over these appalling figures. Despite Wright's protestations that the license fee is 'being paid as well as at any other time', [25] the new Lieutenant-Governor is convinced 'that the evasion of the license was from right to left throughout the goldfields', and it could be explained by nothing other than 'laxity on the part of the commissioners'.[26]

Well, they would just have to see about that. For Sir Charles, the law is the law is the law, and it must be administered by the authorities whether they like it or not and obeyed by the people – double the ditto and the diggers be damned.

Meantime, in an effort to work out just how bad the situation is, on this day he makes a snap decision and charges the Auditor-General to further scrutinise all of the colony's finances and submit a report.

6 August 1854, Melbourne, the Redcoats gather with intent

It is a move that delights the Melbourne establishment, every bit as much as it horrifies Sydney. Steaming through the heads of Port Phillip Bay comes the Commander-in-Chief of the military forces of the colonies, Sir Robert Nickle, a highly decorated and gloriously bewhiskered 67-year-old career army officer of enormous distinction, who has served his Sovereigns for the last 55 years in uprisings and wars everywhere from the Irish Rebellion to the Peninsular War, from South America to America, the West Indies, the Canadian Rebellion and, since July 1853, here in Australia.

Given the growing unrest in Victoria and the increasing demand for soldiers on Victoria's goldfields, the decision had been taken in London that the proper place for Her Majesty's military headquarters in the colonies is Melbourne, not Sydney – and today Sir Robert arrives with 20 of his senior officers, ready to join the 611 soldiers of the 40th Regiment who are already here in Victoria.

'We denounce it as unjust,' *The Sydney Morning Herald* had growled, 'because it is not only giving to Melbourne what she has no claim to, but taking from Sydney that which is her own inherent right.'[27]

Yes, there are those who think the reasons are justified, but in reality those reasons 'are of little weight, and derive what shallow plausibility they possess from bugbears which exist only in ignorant minds or distempered imaginations'.[28] In short, those living in Melbourne . . .

For where might it end? There had even been talk in *The Sydney Morning Herald* that Victoria's Lieutenant-General, Sir Charles Hotham, would replace New South Wales's Sir Charles FitzRoy as Governor-General, 'a step which there is every reason to believe has been for some time contemplated'.[29]

And it really has. Shortly after Sir Charles FitzRoy had arrived in Australia with his wife, Lady Mary, and one of their two adult sons, she was killed when a carriage the Governor was driving overturned in the grounds of Government House at Parramatta. As a widower, he seemed to have lost his way soon thereafter. For Sir Charles's problems had grown in tandem with the belly of the young woman he had lain with in Berrima one night in early 1849, and his illegitimate son was born later in the year.[30] Not that Sir Charles was alone at Government House in his wild ways, for all that. When the young Berrima woman's outraged father had presented himself to the Governor's secretary – who was also one of His Excellency's sons – that gentleman had begun his reply by saying, 'How can you be sure it was the Governor, for we all . . .'[31] That son is even more active than his father with ladies of the night and, among people in the know, Government House is oft referred to as the 'FitzRoy stud'.

It is a *disgrace*, I tell you. But also useful fodder for those who want a republic.

The People's Advocate even goes so far as to print an assertion from the Provisional Committee of the Australian League, claiming of the particularly riotous son, George FitzRoy, that no-one could help bring about faster a republic than he. For after he and his friends, along with prostitutes, had been thrown out of the Windsor Inn, he needs to be thanked for 'bringing the whole system of British Government in the Colonies into utter contempt, and proving to the satisfaction of all reputable and candid persons, that it ought to be put an end to, with all convenient speed, as being thoroughly unprincipled, discreditable, and intolerable'.[32]

All that aside, Sir Charles Hotham is extremely heartened to now have crack military leadership and troops on call in Victoria. These men are not clapped-out military pensioners from Van Diemen's Land – men who had proven to be drunken nightmares on the diggings. These are serious, well-trained troops – Redcoats, come to bolster his all-too-meagre force. Melbourne now has no fewer than 700 soldiers in the Victoria Barracks in St Kilda Road. With two companies of the 12th Regiment from England also due to land in Melbourne in three months, and a force of English police due to arrive shortly after that, Victoria will at last have a substantial armed force to preserve the Queen's peace.

Mid-August 1854, Ballarat, trouble brews

One morning in his tent, just before dawn, Raffaello Carboni is suddenly awoken by the sound of thundering hooves just outside, as are all his companions in nearby tents. *What on earth is going on?*

Popping his head through the flaps, he instantly has his answer. Just up from where they are situated there is a sly-grog seller at the top of the hill, and just next to his store – nominally to sell other things – is a tent crammed as full as a goog with brandy and other spirits, newly arrived from Melbourne. The goldfields are overrun with spies – operatives from Government Camp who look like diggers, dress like diggers and sound like diggers but who are in fact no more than scurvy rats whose real job in life is to report to their bosses on whatever 'illegal' activities they can spot. Obviously, one of these spies has caught wind of this brandy and reported it, and now the mounted troopers, closely followed by their lesser species, the plodding government traps, go straight to the store.

'Whose tent is that?' asks the Commissioner to the storekeeper, pointing to the small tent in question.

'I don't know,' comes the nervous reply.

'Who lives in it? Who owns it?' demands the Commissioner,

bristling. 'Is anybody in?'[33]

'An old man owns it, but he is gone to town on business and left it to the care of his mate who is on the night shift,' replies the storekeeper miserably, surely knowing what is coming.

'I won't peck up that chaff of yours, sir,' roars the Commissioner. 'Halloo! Who is in? Open the tent!'[34]

Still there is no answer, and so comes the order that was always going to come.

'I say,' says the Commissioner to two rough and swarthy troopers, 'cut down this tent, and we'll see who is in.'[35]

These two ruffians in uniform instantly step forward and, just as a duck alights naturally on a pond and paddles happily, so too do they do what comes entirely natural to them. That is, after taking their swords and lifting them on high, they thrash about with savage joy and total disregard for private property, cutting the tent to ribbons. And there, just as the spy had told them, are the boxes of brandy and other assorted spirits.

But look there – wouldn't you know it – the troopers just happen to have a horse and cart handy! That cart is brought forward and in no more than five minutes flat all of the precious, high-priced alcohol is loaded and taken off to the Camp.

There are few things that could have aroused the diggers to greater indignation. The infamy of it! The gross unfairness! The high-handed manner in which the whole exercise is carried out!

It is with this in mind that the diggers now gather around the triumphant troopers, roaring, 'Shame! Shame!'[36]

And maybe they would have taken it further and physically intervened, but two things stop them. Firstly, this particular sly-grog seller is a bit of a brute and many of the onlookers are not sorry to see his noisy establishment taken apart. And secondly, as Carboni characterises it, 'The plunderers were such Vandemonian-looking traps and troopers, that we were not encouraged to say much, because it would have been of no use.'[37]

So, for the moment, all the diggers are left with is their festering discontent, a feeling that grows as the day progresses and they reflect on what has occurred. The Government Camp has not made this raid to prevent sly-grog selling. That is impossible and everyone knows it. The demand on the goldfields for grog at the end of both bitter and joyous days is so strong that the profits are huge for those who can provide it, even at outrageous prices marked up by as much as 150 per cent. And, yes, the diggers could go if necessary to the government-licensed, official establishments that stand by the main roads just a mile or two away, but why bother when there is a shop near-handy right here at the diggings?

So who really profits by closing down the sly-grog sellers? Why, the official grog sellers, of course, who have their competitors eliminated. What's in it for the government officials to close down the sly ones, beyond nominal enforcement of the law? The fact that many of them – particularly, it is said, Police Magistrate John Dewes – are in cahoots with the official establishments' owners.

For the difference between the sly-grog sellers and the official grog sellers is certainly not one of class or education. Take James and Catherine Bentley's Eureka Hotel, for example. She's alright, I guess, but there isn't a badder bastard on the entire goldfields than him, nor a rougher man. And yet their hotel is where many of the Joes and the Commissioners gather to drink every night. Many of the diggers know the hotel as the 'Slaughterhouse' because in the lesser bars, well away from where the Joes drink, all kinds of assaults, atrocities and acts of ill-repute are notoriously common. One Ballarat pioneer, William Carroll, would later say of it, 'It was generally remarked it was a wonder Bentley did not lose his license; the house was of infamous repute. As one of the oldest residents in the Colony, I can say I never knew so shamefully conducted a house. The worst characters lived about his place; midnight robberies were frequent, and life and property were not safe.'[38]

19 August 1854, the Victorian goldfields tense and tighten

Things are tightening on the goldfields, particularly at Ballarat. In days of yore – which is to say mere weeks ago – there would be the regular cries of exultation as one group or another would find a nugget or a jeweller's shop. Lately, though, the shafts are more likely to be shicers as the last of the easy finds seem gone. All that is left is hard, hard work to mine down deeper in the hope that the gold will come again. So tight have things been on the Eureka that Carboni notes it as a 'Nugety Eldorado for a few, a ruinous Field of hard labour for many, a profound ditch of perdition for Body and Soul to all'.[39]

While March to April of this year produced 135,000 ounces of gold under escort, and May to June 121,000 ounces, July to August is now on track to produce just 88,000 ounces – less than two-thirds of what it had been just five months earlier.

And, of course, with that tightening of the gold supply, many diggers are finding it harder to come up with the license fee month by month, and the resistance to it grows – all the more so since La Trobe had mooted its possible abolition. And the diggers certainly have the local press behind them, with one lead writer for *The Diggers' Advocate* putting it particularly well.

'Here we think is a good parallel for the digger,' he posits. 'The fisherman takes fish out of the sea and digger takes gold out of the earth. The latter uses the earth only in the same sense as the former uses the sea. Is the former ever taxed for the use of the sea? Does he pay rent for it? Legislation never stumbled into such an absurdity. On the contrary, it has generally encouraged the development of this branch of industry by offering a bounty.

'If it were wise, it would carry out the same spirit in the case of the digger. The interest should be encouraged, not by a bounty, but negatively by the removal of whatever tends to repress it . . .

Down with the [Gold] Commission! Down with the license-fee! Let the colony begin to learn that its prosperity, under present circumstances, hangs upon the working of the gold-field.[40]

Saturday and Sunday, 26–27 August 1854, the great man and his good lady wife arrive in Ballarat

Quickly, now! Have you heard? The new Lieutenant-Governor himself is here! With his good Lady wife! And indeed it is true. At around half-past five in the afternoon, just after the heavy rain has ceased, His Excellency – who has come to the diggings in an effort to better understand the domain over which he rules – arrives from Bacchus Marsh, accompanied by his small entourage, which includes the delightful Lady Hotham in a carriage.

'Is that the Governor, mate, with the four-and-nine [low-priced hat] and the white cravat?' asks a digger.

'No, you fool, that's a Methodist preacher, that's the Governor,' his mate replies, pointing out the sinewy Sir Charles.[41]

His Nibs! Lord Muck! He is here, among us. And he's said to be a good cove, too. Just a few days earlier it had been reported that while in Geelong, on his way here, he had told a roaring gathering, 'All power proceeds from the people. It is on that principle that I intend to conduct my administration.'[42]

Hooray! That's our kind of language, and this is the man who will see to our problems, most particularly on the subject of the license fees. He is the one who is going to put things to rights!

Once word gets out that it really is him, the diggers stream in from everywhere, eager just to catch sight of the man who embodies the power of the British Empire in these distant parts, a representative of Her Majesty, Queen Victoria herself. It is exciting, thrilling, to see his graceful form in the flesh, and though there is a sole cry of 'Joe!', no-one else joins in as full Vice-Regal reverence takes hold.

And the good Lieutenant-Governor and his lady are liked even more when, after taking the Sabbath off to rest and recuperate – for, of course, nothing ever happens on the diggings on the Sabbath – on this windy, cloudy Monday he makes his way around the diggings in his tweeds and mud-splattered shoes, frequently unrecognised and engaging many diggers in conversation. He seems so surprisingly *humble* for such a distinguished man. But there are issues that need to be addressed, and now is the time to address them.

While inspecting the process of puddling the rich paydirt coming out of Canadian Gully, Sir Charles is stunned by both the strength of the gold yield and the warmth with which the diggers welcome him and his wife. As to the first, the nuggets, by one account, 'are as thick and perceptible as currants in a pudding, yielding as much as one pound weight of gold to a tub',[43] and he can scarcely believe the wealth these common men are generating before his very eyes.

Moved by the diggers' welcome, Sir Charles asks at one point, 'What can I do for you, my friends, in return for your kindness?'

'Abolish the license tax,'[44] comes one frank reply, at which point all the diggers break out cheering.

The diggers again address this theme a short time later when, at a shaft situated just behind the Ballarat Dining Rooms, Sir Charles must pause to politely take receipt of a petition from a crowd of diggers, whereby they express their dissatisfaction with the licensing system.

His Excellency hands it to an underling and then steps forward to speak. The men gather close – in their thousands by now – and hang on his every word.

'Diggers,' he says in his plummy English tones, 'I feel delighted with your reception – I shall not neglect your interests and welfare – again, I thank you.'[45]

At the conclusion of His Excellency's remarks, their acclaim is strong.

Hip-hip . . .

'HURRAH!'

Hip-hip . . .

'HURRAH!'

Hip-hip . . .

'HURRAH!'

For now the diggers go well beyond being merely reverential and are positively adulatory. As the Lieutenant-Governor and lady Hotham make their way back to the Government Camp, the men outdo themselves in laying down massive slabs of wood – normally used to hold back the walls in their mine-shafts – upon the rough road to make it easier for the party to proceed. And, of course, all of the men have respectfully removed their caps and hats.

When the Vice-Regal party comes to a hole in the road that her Ladyship pauses before, a massive Irish digger, known to one and all as 'Big Larry', steps forward and – in a manner that Sir Walter Raleigh might have done, had he been three times the size, far from the civilised world *and* an illiterate stowaway – grabs Lady Hotham by the waist and steps across in one massive stride. 'Hearty peals of laughter'[46] break out all around, including from the Lady herself. Still not content, Big Larry then walks in front of the Vice-Regal couple, playfully but forcefully brandishing a switch all around him so that no digger may come too close to them.

For her part, Lady Hotham, a large watch on a gold chain hanging carelessly from her neck her only adornment, and at a momentary distance from her husband, turns to one rough digger and says, 'Well, I declare, these diggers are, after all, fine hearty fellows: I shall speak to Charles to be kind to the poor fellows, when we get back to town.'[47]

It remains all in good fun, and for the next mile or so, even as they make their way towards the hated Government Camp – the place where too many of the diggers have had to proceed in chains – the party is met with cheers for the 'Diggers' Charlie'.[48]

After this, the diggers return to either their work or the hotels, where they raise a glass to Sir Charles's health and success. He looks and sounds like a man with fresh ideas, who will be able to sort out their grievances.

'V-e-r-y correct, that's the style,' writes a newly devoted digger to *The Ballarat Times*, 'just like a leading man in a party who consults all his mates how the work is to be done, and then sets his head to work and plans the whole. Sir Charles is no shicer. Dear me! How he chats and talks to the men like one of ourselves; why if Mr Evans was here he'd draw his sword and order the rabble to "stand back".'[49]

And even the paper itself is impressed, as it would note in its next edition: 'A bold vigorous and farseeing man has been amongst us, and the many grievances and useless restrictions by which a digger's success is impeded will be swept away.'[50]

Inside the Government Camp, meanwhile, Hotham holds a more formal meeting with Commissioner Robert Rede, who, if he does say so himself, has come a long way from the poor man who had only arrived in Australia two years earlier to try his luck on the diggings.

And now look at him! Honoured to be in a meeting with no less than a knight of the realm, the Lieutenant-Governor of Victoria. This representative of the Sovereign wishes to discuss many things, including the system of collecting the license fees and penalties for those who do not have licenses, and Rede tells him everything he can. It is Sir Charles's particular desire that Rede turn his mind to how collection may be better conducted to maximise revenue before putting it all in a written report, and Rede assures him he will do just that. After all, Sir Charles reasons, with the kind of staggering wealth he has seen coming up from the ground, he is now convinced that the license fees are fair and says so to Rede. He then retires to join his wife for the evening, in the house designated to them, one originally built for the inspector of police, into which is now crammed 'almost every piece of furniture to be found in the camp.'[51]

Eight days later, Lieutenant-Governor Hotham and his entourage visit Bendigo, where, if anything, his welcome is even greater.

'No less than 25,000 men assembled a league from the town to greet me,' he reports to the new Secretary of State in London, Sir George Grey. 'By force they took the horses from my carriage and yoked themselves instead, dragging it into town.'[52]

Here, too, it is true, they present Sir Charles with a petition protesting against the license fees, a petition that he promises to examine upon his return to Government House, though he is careful to note that as Her Majesty's loyal subjects they must pay for 'liberty and order'.[53]

The cheers from the diggers are perhaps a little more muted at this remark, but at the least it may be said that the diggers remain upbeat and heartily cheer the Lieutenant-Governor at his conclusion.

While the diggers are impressed with Her Majesty's representative, so too is Sir Charles impressed with them, reporting shortly afterwards to Sir George Grey, 'I found an orderly well-conducted people, particular in their observance of the Sunday, living generally in tents, having amongst them a large proportion of women and children; schools of every denomination, and people of every nation are on the diggings, and there was an appearance of tranquillity and confidence, which would reflect honour on any community . . . The mass of the diggers here, as on all the other goldfields, are true-hearted and loyal, and men who, if well treated, may be thoroughly depended upon . . . and are all interested in upholding authority and the law.'[54]

As to their ability to pay the license fees, His Excellency, in his report, has little doubt: 'The miner of Ballarat must be a man of capital, able to wait the result of five or six months toil before he wins his prize.'[55] And if the men could wait that long before a return, then it is Sir Charles's view that, almost by definition, they are also men who would be untroubled by a small monthly impost of a 'trifling'[56] amount. Some say the squatters should be the ones who pay most of the massive debt inherited from the La Trobe government, but Sir Charles does not agree. The squatters form the rich elite of this society – part of Hotham's own class – and it is obvious they would simply not accept being imposed upon in that way, either personally or in the realm of the Legislative Council, where they hold sway.

The merchants then?

Yes, Sir Charles wishes to revisit making up that difference by raising the import tariff, and once again considers imposing an export duty on gold – but those two measures are mere possibilities. What remains certain is that since only half the diggers are getting licenses, the obvious solution is to increase the license-hunts to ensure that *all* diggers are paying their dues to Her Majesty. He estimates that that will raise an additional £400,000-plus per annum.

The only reservation Sir Charles has about unleashing his forces, however, is that his military eye has noticed something significant while on this visit it the goldfields.

If the worst does come to the worst and some kind of punitive military action is necessary, then, as he makes clear to the Secretary of State, 'I deem it my duty to state my conviction, that no amount of military force at the disposal of Her Majesty's Government, can coerce the diggers, as the goldfields may be likened to a network of rabbit burrows. For miles, the holes adjoin each other, each is a fortification . . . Nowhere can four men move abreast, so that the soldier is powerless against the digger, who is well armed, and sheltering himself by the earth thrown up around him, can easily pick off his opponent. By tact and management must these men be governed; amenable to reason, they are deaf to force.'[57]

But surely force will not be necessary? After leaving Ballarat, His Excellency and his entourage move on to Castlemaine and Mount Alexander, where their reception is even stronger and they are near 'deafened by the shouts of loyalty'.[58]

13 September 1854, tension rises at Toorac

Victoria's most senior administrative officer, Colonial Secretary John Foster, is just not sure about this new man. Whereas Charles La Trobe had always been of a consultative nature and journeyed each day to work out of the government offices, Sir Charles lives more in the manner of a prince in his palace, only leaving Government House a couple of times a week, and for the rest requiring all the government papers requiring action to be sent to him. He would read them and then write quick peremptory notes in the margin, giving terse instructions as to what should be done – 'put aside', as in ignore, is a particular favourite – and that would be it. For Sir Charles Hotham is a man who rose to a position of great eminence in the navy, where his orders were obeyed without question, in part because of his ability to follow orders without question. Consultation with people below him in the hierarchy is neither in his nature nor his background. The four-man Executive Council of which John Foster and his cousin, William Stawell, are a part is there only to advise the Lieutenant-Governor – they have no authority over him – so His Excellency is free to ignore them when he likes, and frequently does so.

'I do not consider that he intended any personal slight to myself, by not consulting me,' Foster would later state in evidence, 'he seldom consulted any of his officers at all.'[59] But it nevertheless grates on Foster. No matter, for Sir Charles does not much like Foster either. Just a week after arriving at Toorac House to such fanfare, the Lieutenant-Governor had been presented with a bill for £600, the amount it had cost to put in elaborate furnishings and stock its cellars. Though he had paid it – by selling the furniture he had brought from England for a great loss – it had strained his relationship with his Colonial Secretary along with his finances. Hotham felt it to be a deliberate snub.

Of course, it is to be expected that the diggers will not be happy about the Lieutenant-Governor's plans. But against that, Sir Charles really does have broad instructions from the Colonial Office that there is to be no more 'yielding to intimidation',[60] and such an instruction came with the full understanding that 'the question was not very likely to be settled without a fight'.[61]

And if that fight be bloody, then so be it. In his long military career, Hotham has seen his fair share of blood and is not averse to it. Hotham speaks with Chief Gold Commissioner Wright and gives the order that the license hunts be stepped up on the diggings to at least *twice weekly.*

Accordingly on this day, a circular – later described by Foster as 'most injudicious',[62] though at the time it happens entirely without his knowledge – is issued on behalf of Wright to his Goldfields Department, instructing all supervisors on the diggings 'that they are to go out not less than twice a week in search of unlicensed miners, and that their weekly diaries are to specify the number of persons found unprovided with licenses and how disposed of . . . Should anything prevent this being done, an explanation of the cause of hindrance must be given in the diary'.[63]

This is serious. The Gold Commissioners are to send their men out after the diggers and enforce the law, come what may, or their superiors would want to know the reason why.

Sympathy is simply not in Sir Charles's nature. For it is not long after this that a petition comes across his desk, organised by the wife of one James Grant, a Ballarat digger who had been caught with a fully paid-up license but was *still* given a two-month sentence. Grant had bought it from a digger who was leaving Ballarat, and it had that person's name on it. The petition, humbly enclosed for His Excellency's favourable consideration, is signed by another 110 of Her Majesty's loyal subjects of Ballarat. It is also pointed out that James Grant had not found gold for six months, that Mrs Grant is confined with child and their other children are 'looking to her for the means of subsistence'.[64] Surely His Excellency could take the case into his 'merciful consideration' and free James Grant? His Excellency could not. He writes across the petition, '*Never interfere with sentences – culprit knew the law and risked being found out.*'[65]

21–22 September 1854, the reading is grim in Government House

For a man about to make the most important speech of his public career, in the first meeting of the Legislative Council that he will attend, the morning's newspaper makes most uncomfortable reading for Lieutenant-Governor Hotham . . . On the occasion of the Legislative Council meeting to pass the bill to send the draft Constitution to Britain for ratification, *The Argus* does not mince words: 'Considerable interest is attachable to the present occasion, in consequence of the presence of a new Governor, of whom high hopes are entertained; and people will look with a good deal of anxiety for the enunciation of the measures with which he will commence the legislative campaign, and proceed to reduce to reality the favourable expectations which his various addresses have excited . . .'[66]

The problem with the Legislative Council, *The Argus* maintains, is that 'a properly-constructed representative assembly . . . embodies public opinion, and really represents the people, and our Victorian Parliament does nothing of the kind.'[67]

If the morning's reading is difficult for Sir Charles, the next day proves more ominous when he reads the reviews of his speech. To say the press is underwhelmed is not to do justice to their crushing sense of disappointment that Sir Charles has not even *mentioned* the most pressing issue of the day – the instability wrought by the gold rush and, more particularly, the recent protests against the gold licenses. He has given no real leadership.

The Argus is most forthright, noting that the general expectation of his speech was high and hopes were that 'it would contain a candid, if not an elaborate, exposition of his general policy.'

'But, unfortunately,' the article continues, 'Sir Charles has, in this instance, abandoned the straightforward, outspoken line of policy which he has hitherto exhibited. In this speech he has sunk the man in the Governor; and either distrusting himself, his audience, or his assistants, he has veiled his intentions upon great principles of Government, amidst a dry enunciation of a few of the measures which it is his intention to initiate.'[68]

The *Geelong Advertiser* is rather more to the point, commenting dryly, 'The much abused La Trobe might have delivered Sir Charles Hotham's speech.'[69]

Now that *is* a low blow.

And the paper also takes direct aim at Sir Charles's ramblings on one issue that is foremost in the public mind, the fact that the colony's best land has long ago been settled by the very people who are his most outspoken supporters, the ones in firm control of the political process – the squatters – thus denying others the chance to buy it. Worse, the laws framed by those squatting interests are such that most of the best land available can usually only be bought in large, expensive lots, cutting out the common man. The limited number of small parcels that are put on the market are sold by auction and fetch ludicrously inflated prices, thus thwarting 'the strong desire of immigrants to locate themselves on the lands of the colony'.[70]

30 September 1854, Ballarat brews

Ballarat is starting to take an equally dim view of the new Lieutenant-Governor, who had promised everything and delivered not too far north of nothing. Writing in the mighty *Ballarat Times*, Seekamp is strong in his condemnation of the government of Sir Charles Hotham. For despite the Englishman's protestations that he wishes to give the diggers a fair go and look after their interests, the truth is that Sir Charles has secretly ordered the police to 'prosecute the obnoxious inquisition for the license fees'.[71]

And it is certainly true that something is going on. To this point, license searches have only been conducted on the goldfields once a month, if that. But somewhere, someone must have given an order to increase the frequency, for suddenly such searches have increased eight-fold. At least twice every week the troopers are swoopers. Inevitably they catch many men who are without the requisite piece of paper, who are marched off to the cell like common criminals. And the diggers' bitter protestations have no effect!

As recorded by Raffaello Carboni, 'The more the diggers felt annoyed at it, the more our Camp officials persisted in goading us, to render our yoke palatable by habit.'[72]

And the diggers are indeed outraged. One law-abiding digger, Thomas Pierson, writes in his diary with great feeling, if not necessarily great spelling:

'When the New Governor was here he made firm promises to the miners that he was going to study their interests – but since he has gone his orders do not correspond with his promises . . . – he does not allow the miners to be represented in the Legislation, and ordered the traps, or constables and Comissioners to scour all over the diggers 5 days in each week to make every one show them their Lycense and if they find any one without a Lycense they take them up make them pay a fine of £5 or one months Labour on the roads taken no excuse. It is most disgusting to see the Governors emisarys vomit themselves forth from their camp five days in a week to hunt down the diggers & others for their Lycense in front of is 16 Bullys on horseback with muskets Loaded & a sword – and about fifty on foot each with a loaded club and soon as they find any one without a Lycense he has either to follow those with the club – or the horsemen whitchever happened to catch them – I have seen poor fellows who were unable to buy a Lycense compelled to follow after a horse half a day wherever they went exposed to all on the diggings – it is a criminal offence here to be poor, sutch a sample of liberty speaks for itself, needs no comment and yet they will tell you they are the finest people in the world.

'Rule Britton Rule the slave

Till Liberty points you out a grave.'[73]

Friday, 6 October 1854, that's the way to serve those sweeps

From the top of the valley, the effect of seeing so many scattered campfires blazing makes the scene look like a thousand candles in the night. The darkness takes away the scunge, the mess, the rubble and leaves only those cheery points of light. It's another night at the diggings . . .

The day's work is done, and for most of the workers, once they have finished their dinner of damper and meat washed down by tea, they can enjoy their one moment of leisure, the time they have been looking forward to all day. On this chilly, moonlit night, some simply relax by the fires, while others riotously celebrate their luck at one of the hotels, while still others drink away their rising desperation that they have found nothing for days.

From just down towards the Gravel Pits a ways comes the noise of several drunken diggers laughing uproariously at some joke unknown. Up on the hill there is a fight going on, with grunts and groans and the sounds of fists on flesh, all of it punctuated by the barking of dogs and the odd shrill scream of encouragement – presumably the wife of one of the men involved in the fight. Or maybe it is one of the women having a donnybrook with another woman. Or a man . . .

Who knows? On it goes, just like any other evening, with nothing to mark it as special. By midnight, though, things have mostly fallen quiet – most of the fires have blinked out, most of the diggers retired to their tents, and even the dogs have stopped barking.

Softly, softly now the whole site is about to fall completely quiet when suddenly more drunken shouting breaks out: Who? Where?

Why, it sounds like that cheery young fellow James Scobie, and I think he must be up at the grog shop of that scoundrel, Bentley – still the worst Vandemonian in the valley, though many have pushed him close – the Eureka Hotel. There is more shouting, and it includes someone divesting himself of the view that Mrs Bentley is 'a whore'.[74] After that there is silence for a time, followed by the sound of a door opening . . . many feet running . . . a scuffle and swearing . . . a long, low expiratory *grooooaaaaan* . . . followed by a heavy thud and then silence, broken only for the people in some tents by the sound of one man – but not two – running away.

What is going on? That very question is one that will be the subject of much speculation in days, weeks and even many decades to come.

What is definitely known on the night, as some men take their lanterns to investigate, is that earlier this evening Scobie had run into a friend from Scotland, Peter Martin, and the two countrymen had been beside themselves with joy to be so met. To celebrate, they had shared a wee drink in Scobie's tent, and then another wee one, and why not a wee one more?

'For Auld Lang Syne, my friendsssss, for Auld Lang Syne . . . We'll take a cup of kindness yet . . . for the sake of Auld Lang Syne . . .'

And then more and more . . .

At midnight, when the drink starts to run out, Scobie has another idea. Spying the light on the hill through his tent flaps, he says, 'Let us have some more to drink.'[75]

And so, staggering, they make their way beneath a moon shining 'as light as day'[76] to the grandest establishment on all the diggings, the still-lit Eureka Hotel for – why not? – one lasht wee drinkie. As a matter of fact, Scobie has been there that very afternoon, to sell some gold to a gold buyer at the public bar – which is one of the reasons he is so flush with cash – but now he wants to return to satisfy a thirst for alcohol that just won't quit.

Not put off by the fact that the doors have just been locked and the establishment is closed for business, Scobie starts to pound on the door and is refused admittance by the publican, Bentley, who appears to take a very dim view of this young pup's carry-on, as does his wife. Scobie appears not to care and shtill wants a little drink. After a further exchange of insults and the sound of breaking glass, a female voice is heard to cry, 'How dare you break my window?'[77] From the sounds of it, Scobie is thrown into the street for his trouble.

And then?

And then the facts are in dispute. What is immediately thought to have happened, however, is that after Scobie and Martin head back towards Scobie's tent, they have only proceeded some 150 yards when Bentley and his wife emerge from the hotel, accompanied by no fewer than four of their employees, Thomas Farrell, William Hance, William Duncan and Thomas Mooney, who all set off in hot pursuit. As he runs, Bentley is seen to pick up a shovel from outside Mrs Welch's tent and lead the charge.

Mrs Bentley is heard to say, 'That's the man that broke the window.'[78]

Then come the sounds of a serious beating taking place – sickening thuds, groans, bodies hitting the ground – before there is a cry and one man, at least, is heard running away in the darkness. Shortly afterwards, the pursuing party walks back towards the hotel, and a female voice says, 'That's the way to serve those sweeps.'[79]

The sound of a spade being thrown to the ground is heard. When all is quiet and Martin comes back to check on his friend, it is to find the badly bloodied and unmoving Scobie still lying there. Martin shakes him by the shoulder, but there is no response. Panicking, he puts his hand on Scobie's chest and though relieved to feel the heart beating – just – he now notices blood pouring from his fellow Scot's mouth and nose. Martin immediately seeks help from the only medical man within coo-ee he knows of: Dr Alfred Carr, a middle-aged English medico of somewhat damaged reputation for the fact that two years earlier he had arrived on a catastrophic ship, *Araminta,* and was found medically responsible for the deaths of many people.

Hurrying to Scobie, Dr Carr finds that there no longer seems to be a pulse. What is most urgently needed is light, and as the only place available is the Eureka Hotel, where all this started, that is where Scobie is carried. (In fact, it is a very familiar place to Dr Carr, who is a friend of Bentley's. He is so constant a patron – he had been at the bar that very day – that he is very close to being part of the furniture.)

Now it is one thing to hit a man on the head with a shovel in a blind fury, and quite another to gaze upon your handiwork a short time later when, with a terrible bruise on his head from where the shovel struck, that man appears to be *dead*. After the door to the hotel is opened and light falls upon Scobie for the first time, Dr Carr could swing a dead cat around him and not hit anybody, so reluctant are Bentley and his brethren to be anywhere near. At least one of Bentley's men, however, Farrell – the one-time Chief Constable and Prosecutor at Castlemaine – is prevailed upon to help when, in the fashion of the day, the doctor cuts Scobie on his arm in the hope that bleeding will bring him back to consciousness. But there is nothing. Nor is there any response when Dr Carr vigorously rubs the Scot's skin with cloths to warm him, and not even the tiniest cough is heard when the doctor pours strong alcohol down the supine man's open throat.[80] Certainly there is a wound left by the knife, but just like the gash in his head, not an ounce of blood seeps forth. There is no escaping the conclusion: Scobie is dead.

7 October 1854, out of the mouths of babes

The appalling news spreads rapidly. Scobie is dead. Killed by that bastard Bentley and his evil thugs. Uproar! Scobie had been a popular figure and his *murder* – for that is what it was, whatever the courts might say – must be avenged!

Few diggers are more appalled than Peter Lalor, who had been a friend of the young Scotsman and had come to know him well as they worked adjoining claims over the previous months. Beyond feeling sick at heart for the fate of James Scobie, he is devastated for Scobie's brother, George, and their parents in Scotland, as he knows of George's promise to them. Thus, Lalor follows closely the workings of the law thereafter, in the hope that justice will prevail and punish the people who have done this terrible thing.

Indeed, this very afternoon the inquest is held across the gully and up the hill at the Government Camp, with local doctor David John Williamson acting as coroner and – hopefully – a dozen plus one good men and true sworn in to determine 'when, where, how and by what means'[81] Scobie died.

James Bentley's evidence is firm: he had not even left the hotel the night before, and, as a matter of fact, had not even known of the death until the body was brought to the hotel, at which point, of course, he and his staff had done all possible to save the young man's life.

'You did not leave your room when first disturbed?' the Coroner follows up.

'No, not until aroused by Dr Carr,' Bentley says flatly.

'Did you hear any noise,' a member of the jury asks, 'between hearing the first disturbance and when Dr Carr came?'

'No.'[82]

He is supported in this contention by his rather nervous night-watchman, Thomas Mooney, who seems unaccountably pale.

'I was on duty last night,' he says falteringly, his eyes flickering.

'I heard some men knocking at the door and heard Duncan the Barman speak and one of the men answered "all right". The men then went away. There were two of them. Some time afterwards Dr Carr came with the deceased and asked to bring him into the house. I heard no noise between the time when the men made the first noise to when Dr Carr came. No one left the house after the men made the disturbance.'[83]

The 'Manager at the Bar' of the bowling alley next door, Everand Gad, states emphatically, 'I can positively swear that Mr and Mrs Bentley did not leave their bed-room, from the time I heard the first noise, until Dr Carr came at the front door to say that a man had been killed outside.'[84]

Neither he nor the Bentleys ever left the hotel, and he knows *nothing* of who might have killed Scobie.

It is then, however, that a ten-year-old lad, Barnard Welch, is called to testify.

Young Barnard's intelligent account, delivered with a respect for the courts beyond his years, is graphic and – in its way – devastating: 'I live within about thirty yards from where Deceased was found dead. Mr Bentley, Mrs Bentley and three or four other men came last night between one and two o'clock and stood by the corner of our tent for about three minutes and then went on after picking something up which I thought was a spade, I do not know which of the party picked it up. They went a little way on when I heard a scuffle and a blow.'[85]

Most outraged and uncomfortable at this testimony is Bentley himself, but there is a bigger outrage to come. For, against all legal precedent and over the protest of the jurors, the coroner allows Bentley to effectively cross-examine the young lad.

'Will you swear positively that you saw me last night at your tent?'

'No, I will not swear positively, but I believe it was Mr and Mrs Bentley I saw and heard. I do not know who the other parties were.'[86]

The legal outrages continue. While Dr Carr gives his own testimony, Bentley sits right among the jurors and whispers to one of them. That man is Henry Green, a thoroughly disreputable character who is well known to prop up the bar at the Eureka Hotel every night.

Watching it all closely, his fury rising every minute, is none other than Peter Lalor, who had felt so protective of young Scobie, only to have this happen. All he can hope for now is justice and yet, from the looks of what is happening right before his eyes, there will be no justice for the dead Scot.

That opinion is confirmed when, as the jury retires, Lalor sees the Coroner speaking to Bentley 'in a distant part of the room'[87] and doubly confirmed when the jury gives its verdict. It has failed to achieve unanimity in the view held by most of them – that Scobie had been murdered by Bentley and his accomplices – and without that unanimity, must return an open finding. Yes, Scobie had died 'by a blow, but by whom it was given is at present unknown'.[88]

The Coroner is clearly pleased and announces, rather pompously, 'Gentlemen of the jury, you could find no other verdict.'[89]

The gallery, however, is not pleased, and nor are the rest of the those on the diggings when they find out. Unknown? *Unknown?* Every bastard knows it was that bastard Bentley and his thugs what done it! How could the jury have come up with such a result?

By the next day a public committee is formed, which most particularly includes the furious Peter Lalor, and together with no fewer than nine jurors from the coronial inquiry, he is one of the signatories to a letter to the editor that soon appears in the columns of *The Ballarat Times*, bitterly criticising the conduct of the coroner, who had so clearly ignored 'any evidence that might serve to incriminate any members of Mr Bentley's establishment'.[90] They demand that the case be properly heard in a court of law.

So enormous is the outcry – for it is so disgustingly typical of the lack of justice with which the government always treats the diggers – that, in the end, the Attorney-General William Stawell feels he has no choice but to cede to the demands. To Bentley's amazement, on 9 October, he, his wife, and two of his staff are arrested and remanded to appear before a properly constituted judicial inquiry on 12 October. Lieutenant-Governor Hotham, in fact, when he later hears of the case, will go further and orders that a reward be posted for those who can provide evidence that will lead to the conviction of Scobie's killers.

But it is also on this ninth day of October that an alarmed Hotham gives a key instruction to Commissioner Rede – from now on, all political meetings of the diggers on Ballarat must have a magistrate and a shorthand writer present, who can document exactly what is said by those on the podium. 'It will be the duty of such Magistrate and of persons accompanying him,' the instruction runs, 'carefully to watch the proceedings noting any seditious or inflammatory language if made use of or any attempt to incite persons to a breach of the peace or other infraction of the law.'[91]

10–11 October 1854, Ballarat, a servant of a servant of God falls foul

With tensions on the goldfield such as they are, there could be no worse time for continual waves of license hunts to sweep across the goldfields, but such is the result of the order given by Governor Hotham a fortnight earlier. On this hot Ballarat morning, the police are launching yet one more hunt when they happen upon the tent of a sick digger at a time when he is being visited by Johannes Gregorius, the gentle young Armenian servant of a favourite of the diggings, Father Patricius Smyth, who had arrived at Ballarat just a few weeks earlier.

With precisely the kind of on-high insolence the diggers most detest, this particular trap, a big brute of a man by the rank and name of Trooper James Lord, comes galloping up to the tent and shouts, 'Come out here, you damned wretches! There's a good many like you on the diggings.'[92]

Now the young servant emerges, limping, for he is practically a cripple himself. Blinking because of the strong sunlight, or perhaps out of sheer astonishment at being so addressed – though his grasp of English is not the equivalent of the way the diggers hold on to a nugget, he certainly understands the outraged tone – the trooper roars at him, 'Have you got a license?'[93]

Stuttering, Johannes, a rather withered, kind of broken man, replies in equally broken English that, no, he does not have a license as he is not a digger; he is simply a lowly servant to the priest.

'Damn you and the priest!'[94] Trooper Lord roars back, before dismounting so he can arrest the unfortunate young man and take him to be charged. Now properly terrified, the servant replies with the truth that he is a cripple and can only walk a short distance with great difficulty, let alone traipse behind the trooper as he visits other camps looking for unlicensed miners. But, he says tremulously in his thickly accented English, he would be h-h-h-happy to go direct to the Government Camp if that w-w-w-would be alright with you, s-s-s-sir?

Enraged at this damn impertinence, the trooper now smites the young man with a mighty blow, knocking him down before dragging the whimpering one about in such a fashion that his shirt is torn. Johannes is further hurt when, remounting, the trooper has the horse trample upon him.[95]

It is appalling behaviour and the diggers who witness it are united in their call: 'Shame! *Shame!*'[96] To treat a humble servant of an esteemed servant of God in this fashion! To think that Johannes could possibly afford £1 a month, simply for looking after the good Father. Why, it is an outrage, and all the more so because, as everyone but the trooper knows, the law actually excludes religious ministers and their servants from having to pay the license fee.

The situation is ugly and in danger of getting out of hand – quick, run for Father Smyth! – and it is likely a mercy for the suddenly surrounded trooper that at this point Assistant-Commissioner James Johnstone[97] gallops up and says sharply to the crowd that they must not interfere with the trooper doing his 'dooty'.[98] And then Father Smyth himself hurries up, a man of peace. The 35-year-old Irishman with the tousled hair, a native of Mayo, is horrified at this turn of events. He was only ordained two years before, and arrived on Ballarat a few weeks earlier, so he does not have an enormous reservoir of experience to call upon, but at least manages to calm things by giving Johnstone a £5 note, by way of bail. He assures the Assistant-Commissioner that he will bring his servant in the next day to the office of the police.

And, sure enough, as good as his word, the priest does indeed bring his servant before Magistrate John Dewes, where he is first charged with being without a license and then – when it is pointed out that the law says a servant of a minister of religion does not need a license – Assistant-Commissioner Johnstone again comes to the 'rescue': Johannes Gregorius, still bearing the wounds of yesterday's trampling, is charged with striking the trooper instead! The trooper is called to give evidence and, under oath, confirms what Assistant-Commissioner Johnstone has said, that the day before he had only been trying to execute his 'dooty' and the servant had struck him.

Monstrous lies! About a man of a man of God!

No matter that an obviously respectable digger immediately takes the stand and swears under oath the truth of the matter, testifying to the trooper's aggression. Magistrate Dewes – a curious combination of being both rough and officious in manner – is unmoved. He takes up his gavel and, with a dismissive wave of the easily bored, peremptorily beats out the tune of the times in Ballarat: 'Fined £5; take him away.'[99] The unfortunate servant is indeed taken away to the lockup until such time as his fine is paid.

It is yet one more story of injustice and the gross abuse of the diggers by the authorities, and it travels all over the diggings in nothing flat, heightening the tension still further. In this sense of outrage, Henry Seekamp's *Ballarat Times* takes the lead, describing the trooper in question as 'savage and cowardly' and a 'monster'.[100] These prove to be merely his opening remarks.

12 October 1853, at the Police Magistrates' Court, Ballarat, justice is outraged

It is a busy time of it these days for Police Magistrate John Dewes. No sooner is the Gregorius case satisfactorily resolved than the even more troublesome case of Bentley comes before him.

Presiding with him on this case at the Ballarat Police Magistrates' Court in this exercise of British rolled-gold justice is Gold Commissioner Robert Rede and Assistant-Commissioner James Johnstone, who has gone from sitting atop a horse in one legal case to sitting on the bench for this one.

At Dewes's appearance in this role, there is an immediate stirring in the large crowd assembled for the occasion. For the question is asked: how can Dewes, who is known to be very friendly with Bentley and who, it is rumoured, is a secret partner with him in the Eureka Hotel possibly be impartial?

Word spreads among the gallery that during one adjournment Dewes had even been seen to allow Bentley in to chat with him in his private chambers for ten minutes. From the bench, however, he so relentlessly badgers all the hostile witnesses that the solicitor engaged by Scobie's supporters, Adam Loftus Lynn, threatens to withdraw from proceedings. But nothing restrains the magistrate.

Dewes ignores such clear depositions as those tendered by the likes of Peter Martin, who states, '[Scobie] went up to one of the windows and asked to get in and a blow was struck at the head of the Deceased through the window as if by a man's hand. I was knocked down . . . before I could distinguish who struck me . . . my eyes were attracted towards [Bentley] because he was the only person I saw with a weapon in his hand.'[101]

Here is the key witness to the terrible event, a man with no reason to lie, positively identifying Bentley as the man with the weapon in his hand!

None of it seems to impress Magistrate Dewes. Sure enough, after hearing from other witnesses who swear that Bentley never left his premises, he very quickly brings down his gavel on his majority verdict, with only Johnstone dissenting, that Bentley, his wife and associates have no case to answer and are free to go. The stunned spectators respond with groans and hisses, not believing that Dewes can really be pretending that he is administering justice.

But the Magistrate is not done and goes even further to publicly state, 'Not the shadow of an imputation can remain on Mr Bentley's character.'[102] More groans and hisses. The only solace is the surprising integrity shown by Assistant-Commissioner Johnstone – he feels so strongly about Bentley's guilt that he will soon write a formal letter to Attorney-General William Stawell on the subject, including with it a copy of the depositions. This gives hope . . .

As reported by *The Ballarat Times*, 'It is thought that the decision (which gave unmistakeable offence to all who heard it) will not be final.'[103]

One appalled spectator through the whole proceedings is once again Peter Lalor. The outrage over the decision is so widespread, again led by Lalor, that the same committee that had pushed for this judicial hearing now calls for a public meeting to be held outside Bentley's Eureka Hotel on the afternoon of 17 October, to discuss what further steps should be taken . . .

Mid-October 1854, Ballarat, are diggers dogs, to be hunted so?

The license-hunts go on. And the anger rises.

What makes matters even worse for some of the diggers is that, as the goldfields at Ballarat have now become so large, there are now four Commissioners, nominally overseeing four sectors of the goldfields, but it is anyone's guess as to where the precise boundaries between those sectors lie. This means that at the behest of different Commissioners, different groups of troopers frequently go on license hunts over the same ground, harassing the same diggers. It is intolerable.

And the only consistent thing in this turvy-topsy, strange world is how in these pursuits everything is the reverse of the way it is in Europe. Over there, a similar situation of armed men pursuing law-breakers would see fine, upstanding men pursuing common criminals who have offended against the moral standards of society. But not here.

For who are these traps, anyway? Very few of them have been with the police for long.

The truth of it is that most decent men with any ability have come to the goldfields to try their luck. It is only those without any ability, without any pluck, and perhaps without even the barest bones of capital necessary to buy such things as picks and shovels who have been left behind – and it is from this resentful bunch of lazy ne'er-do-wells, blackguards and braggarts that the police have had to be recruited. Lacking the energy to wield a pick or a shovel, these men only truly come to life when it comes to ruthlessly chasing down those who do and putting them in manacles.

Frequently thus, the situation arises where men whose natural home is in the slums or gaols are hunting down well-educated gentlemen of good breeding, and – after heartily abusing them in a vicious manner – throwing them into the lockup. It is just not right, and the resentment builds daily.

One digger, William Howitt, would leave a particularly eloquent account of his and his fellow diggers' feelings on this matter: 'The men employed by the police to hunt over licenses were too often excessively ignorant and vulgar persons, who, never having before enjoyed the slightest shadow of power, [now do so] with a coarse brutality which was intolerable to generous minds. Men who were found without licenses on their persons, but who had them in their tents, were dragged off to the Government Camp, and fined. [If] they remonstrated with the police, they would probably be instantly clamped into handcuffs.'[104]

Soon, however, the situation is brought to the attention of the outside world. One Ballarat digger writes a considered though scathing letter to the *Geelong Advertiser*, where he is quick in coming to the point: 'Since the visit of Sir Charles Hotham an unusual degree of severity has been exercised towards the more unfortunate of the mining population . . . We are ignorant and "wandering tribes", not much acquainted with civilised life up here. Does a military police parade your public ways, and ask you if you have paid your taxes?'[105]

It is true that not all the police behave badly towards the diggers, and some of them are decent. But all of them are in the invidious position of having to enforce a bitterly resented law upon a population that is beginning to rise against it. Far from the law providing the structure for the proper behaviour of all in society towards each other, in this case it is causing society to fracture.

This sense of rising fury and frustration on the goldfields at the waves of license-hunts is confirmed by the *Geelong Advertiser*'s Ballarat correspondent, when he informs his readers:

There are breakers ahead. If Sir Charles manages to avoid the reefs by which he is surrounded, he will prove himself a pilot of no mean ability. For the last week or so the spirit of disaffection has been rapidly increasing and, unless a change for the better be speedily brought about, Ballarat, I fear me, may soon cease to be worthy of praise from the lips of the Governor in matters of loyalty.[106]

CHAPTER EIGHT

FIRE'S BURNING, FIRE'S BURNING, DRAW NEARER

It is not fines, imprisonment, taxation and bayonets that is required to keep a people tranquil and content. It is attention to their wants and their just rights alone that will make the miners content.[1]

The Ballarat Times, 28 October 1854

Canadian Gully was as rich in lumps as other goldfields are in dust.

Raffaello Carboni[2]

The European gold hunter [in Victoria] had no more voice than the naked aborigine he saw prowling about the bush. At the root of all the troubles that led to the Eureka Stockade, lay the old tyranny of taxation without representation. Before he could legally put pick or shovel into the ground, the digger had to pay a heavy monthly tax, levied upon him by a Government and Parliament in which he was not represented.

W. B. Withers in *History of Ballarat*[3]

Afternoon, 14 October 1854, outrage on the Eureka . . .

Have you heard? Bentley and his missus, and that other bloke? They have got off! The case against them has been dismissed by Magistrate Dewes, the very bastard Bentley is in cahoots with!

The news spreads around the diggings like a bushfire with a hot, howling westerly behind it – it is, after all, a scorching, blustery day, perfect for such fires – passing from pit to pit, tent to tent, man to man, burning ear to burning ear. Scobie had been as popular with the diggers as Bentley has been unpopular, though the notoriously corrupt Dewes, who had personally fined many of them, many times, certainly runs Bentley close. It is a communal anger that starts to boil and bubble with the sun. That evening, eyewitness Thomas Pierson writes in his diary:

The jury's verdict whitch I heard given was that there was not a particle of evidence against him – it gave general dissatisfaction and is supposed Bentley Bribed his servants & others . . .[4]

The Ballarat Times is stronger in its promise to its readers: 'We intend to cleanse the Augean stable of the Ballarat Camp and purify its fetid atmosphere of those putrescent particles which offend the senses, by a rigid but wholesome exposure before the bar of public opinion.'[5]

Early afternoon, 16 October 1854, on Ballarat, the heat starts to rise

The posters – organised by Peter Lalor and his cohorts – are now all over the goldfields, calling on those concerned with the lack of justice for Scobie to gather at noon on Sunday, 17 October, on the spot where he died, for a meeting.

Again, the word spreads quickly. *We're gathering at the spot where Scobie got done in. Pass it on.*

A worried Bentley quickly dashes off a note to tell Dewes what is afoot:

Sir,

Inflammatory placards have been posted about the Diggings, to get up a meeting, on the ground were James Scobie was murdered, near to my House, to enquire into the best method of convicting the murderer of the said James Scobie, and to demonstrate public feeling as to the manner in which the case has hitherto been conducted.

I have been informed that the meeting alluded to, is to be got up for the purpose of Riot and violence upon my person and House . . .

I therefore request that a strong force of protection may be present at 12 o'clock Tomorrow to see that the Law is in no way violated.[6]

Dewes, while a little alarmed, cannot be there himself as he already has a legal commitment in Buninyong to preside over – a case of armed robbery – but he is quick to consult with Commissioner Rede, showing him the letter.

Rede moves promptly, giving orders to Police Inspector Gordon Evans to ensure his officers will be in attendance. Evans feels that five police should be sufficient.

Rede himself, as he would explain afterwards, decides not to attend: 'There was some irritation against me in consequence of having sat on the Bench when Bentley was dismissed.'[7] Instead, he goes to the Eureka Station, the spot where Assistant-Commissioner Amos has his digs, from where he can observe the meeting while also sending a magistrate along 'furnished . . . with the Riot Act to use in case of necessity'.[8]

Meanwhile, as insurance, Dewes also talks to Lieutenant Broadhurst of the 40th Regiment to have some of his own men on stand-by. Satisfied that the matter is now covered, he prepares for his trip to Buninyong.

Still, Bentley is not the only one sensing trouble on the morrow, as digger Thomas Pierson writes in his diary:

> *[Bentley] is a ritch man and what they call here an old lag – he was sent out here some years ago for life for some crime committed in England – the Inhabitants of Ballarat call a General meeting tomorrow to consider the whole of the Circumstances and from symtoms whitch exhibit themselves I should not wonder if the whole house was raided to the ground tomorrow.*[9]

Noon, 17 October 1854, Ballarat boils

And yet . . . perhaps five police might not be enough. So many diggers are streaming towards the meeting, such is the evident excitement on the diggings, that well before it begins Sub-Inspector Maurice Ximenes puts his police, armed with nothing but staves, *inside* the Eureka Hotel as insurance that it will be protected and to conceal any display of force that might aggravate the diggers.

And still from everywhere the diggers come, even as an intolerable dust storm is blowing hard. There is menace in the air, with this swirling, dirty heat just made for trouble. When the sun is near its highest in the sky, there are at least 3000 diggers milling around the spot where Scobie was murdered – joined soon by so many that they spill to 'far, far off, on every hill round about'.[10] Though there is a broad mood of mayhem abroad, there is no specific plan, no particular malice aforethought and, like the police, the diggers carry no firearms – at least no obvious ones. All they know is that they are collectively angry and intent on expressing that anger in some manner. And they are also, come to think of it, thirsty in the pressing heat. Having taken the opportunity of a day off work, they drink heavily as the sly-grog sellers move freely among them.[11]

But to the business at hand!

The man who is to chair the gathering, Hugh Meikle, had been a juror at the coroner's inquest and was horrified and bewildered in equal measure at the verdict given and how it was received by the onlookers with such great and appropriate hissing.

William Cockhill who, like Peter Lalor and the other jurors and witnesses, had signed the letter to the editor that appeared in *The Ballarat Times* critical of the judicial inquest is not long in putting the first of four motions: 'This meeting, not being satisfied with the manner in which the proceedings connected with the death of the late James Scobie have been conducted, either by the magistrates or by the coroner, pledges itself to use every lawful means to have the case brought before other and more competent authorities.' The motion is quickly seconded by the man who had been the foreman of that jury, James Russell Thompson.[12]

Having seen all the evidence firsthand, the jurors are united in their horror at the verdict as it stands and in their passion for seeing justice done. The motion is carried unanimously.

The next motion is also passed, attacking those many storekeepers and business owners who still stand by Bentley – including an American by the name of John W. Emery, who owns the bowling alley adjoining the hotel – and who have published a letter to that effect in *The Ballarat Times*. And then a new speaker steps up.

He is an imposing albeit squat Glaswegian shoemaker, head bald and bold, who stands on an upturned barrel to address the diggers, and in response they jostle a little forward to hear him better. For it is not just that their huge numbers mean that many men have to stand a long way away. It is that Tom Kennedy's heavily lined face and jutting jaw somehow suggest that despite having known many anxieties in his life, he has borne them all with strength. He is obviously worth listening to.

Carboni describes him as 'the lion of the day . . . [full] of the Chartist slang; hence his cleverness in spinning a yarn . . . blathered with long phrases and bubbling with cant'.[13] The 35-year-old Kennedy is a handsome, strong, bewhiskered father of four, a veteran of many Chartist meetings and a fiery Baptist preacher besides. It all means he is nothing if not comfortable upon such a podium, speaking to such a throng, as he introduces the third motion: 'That this meeting deems it necessary to collect subscriptions for the purpose of offering a reward for the conviction of the murderer or murderers, and defraying all other expenses connected with prosecution of the case.'[14]

And here's cheers to that! On this hot day, gathered for this purpose, the sly-grog sellers continue to do a roaring trade and the mood of the mass of men starts to become headier. The third motion is carried without one dissenting voice. And yet, as far as Kennedy is concerned, while speeches and resolutions are fine as far they go, it is simply not enough. He has contempt for the advocates of moral force, only exceeded by the contempt he has for the authorities, and he doesn't mind saying so. For they have a *duty*, here, and that duty is clear!

For, do you not see, the spirit of the murdered Scobie is hovering over us right here, right now? Do you not know that justice – yes, my friends, justice – demands that he be avenged?

The diggers certainly do know, and roar their savage acclaim!

A final motion is put, appointing a seven-man Committee for the Prosecution of the Investigation into the Death of James Scobie – including Peter Lalor as secretary – responsible for seeing to all the resolutions that have been carried and getting a petition to His Excellency in Melbourne. And the hat is also passed around, with no less than £200 quickly raised as a reward for anyone who can come forward and provide evidence that will help convict Scobie's murderers.

But is that enough? No, it is bloody well not enough. Why not march on the Eureka Hotel?

It is at this point that the authorities decide to make what *The Ballarat Times* calls 'a very injudicious display of strength'[15] as mounted troopers suddenly make their way from the gully through the crowd and towards the hotel. They are not charging; they have neither swords drawn nor bayonets fixed – and in fact are armed only with staves – but it is done at a time when the diggers are feeling particularly aggrieved at the authorities and powerful in their own collective. Some of them begin to shout abuse. The diggers are many. The shocked troopers and police are few – perhaps no more than 80 men against a mob of thousands. And so when the troopers on horseback start to ride through the miners, breaking them up, trying to assert their authority, the diggers aren't intimidated.[16]

Instead they are furious at such high-handedness from those on their high horses. And they are not going to cop this any longer!

'The people are not to be terrified like children,' writes *The Ballarat Times*, 'especially the men who have stood the working of a Canadian or Gravel Pit shicer. They have seen the earth, when at a depth of one hundred and fifty feet below the surface, move and tumble in; they have stood the risk of being buried alive underneath, and will such men tremble at a cap trimmed with silver or gold lace? Not they. They *shall not* as long as we can wield a pen to show them their majesty when united.'[17]

More diggers begin to shout as the mood turns uglier and the surge starts towards the Eureka Hotel . . .

In the hotel, a worried Bentley can hear the approaching shouts but is soon soothed when one of his men, whom he has sent to observe proceedings, returns to tell him that most of the meeting was calm. In fact, the man says, the likelihood is that if the mob does turn up, they will probably 'groan' and then pass on, 'as is usual with English crowds'.[18]

'They were "joeyed" most perseveringly,' records *The Ballarat Times*.[19] Those police who had ventured out to survey the meeting now retreat to the sparkling hotel – its last features had been finished off by five carpenters that very morning – as the mob closes in. And the shouting begins: 'Murderer!' . . . 'Justice!'

And, most alarmingly, 'We'll hang you from the lamp post!'[20]

Caught up in the fun and fury of it all, a lad throws a well-aimed stone, which shatters the exquisite lamp positioned just above the hotel's front door. And then someone else throws a rock and a window is broken. And then another digger does the same.

'The sound of the falling glass,' Carboni would recount, 'appeared to act like magic on the multitude; and bottles, stones, sticks, and other missiles, were speedily put in requisition to demolish the windows, until not a single pane was left entire, while every one that was broken drew a cheer from the crowd.'[21]

Outside the fun is building. Inside the tension is rising.

Seriously worried, Sub-Inspector Ximenes suggests to Bentley that the best way is for Bentley to take Ximenes's own horse and gallop away to the Camp, hopefully diffusing the focus of the mob . . .

And there he is! Suddenly, from the back of the hotel, Bentley appears without his hat and coat, and some would even swear afterwards that he was in women's clothes! *He was, I tell ya!* Complete with bonnet, bodice and bloomers . . .

Whatever he is wearing, Bentley quickly jumps on a fine horse and gallops away to the Camp – leaving his heavily pregnant wife, Catherine, behind in the threatened hotel – with the jeers and shouts of the mob ringing in his ears.

'He rushed past me in his flight,' the 19-year-old auctioneer and digger Samuel Lazarus would record in his diary, 'and I think I never saw such a look of terror on a man's face.'[22]

Far from placating the mob, Bentley's move further fans their ire. The sound of the galloping horse is still in the wind when one of the diggers – a 40-ish, fattish fellow with barely a hair on his bonce, known to one and all as 'Yorkey' – steps forward, starts pounding the weatherboard sides of the hotel and, still imbued with the spirit of the meeting, yells, 'I propose that this house belongs to the diggers!'[23] Then he proceeds to rip off one board after another, demonstrating how easy it is!

And now, suddenly more troopers on horseback turn up, some 30 of them.[24]

Under normal conditions the sight of this many troopers and traps would encourage some circumspection. But not on this occasion – the diggers' grievance is large. And Scobie's ghost is watching his mates, demanding revenge.

There is more shouting and yelling at the police, even as some speakers, as digger Thomas Pierson records it, are 'preaching Republican principals urging all the people to drive off all the government officers, send the Governor home and to declare their Independence'.[25] Why, one speaker later says, 'Instead of being oppressed on all hands and hunted down like game for taxes . . . each of you might stand here as Proud as any of the sons of America!'[26]

Then, suddenly, here is Commissioner Rede in his dark blue uniform trimmed with sparkling gold braid, after having raced here from Assistant-Commissioner Gilbert Amos's camp on the Eureka, with Amos himself in tow.

Now, instead of doing what many of his officers think he should do, which is to read the Riot Act and allow the police and troopers to shoot if necessary – entirely legally – Robert Rede does what he can to calm the mob. He even climbs onto one of the shattered windowsills and tries to restore order with his words alone.

'I have been a digger myself,' he says, 'and I will see justice done for you.'[27]

But he is like one man trying to stop a stampede of cattle.

It is not long before another digger, a Scot by the name of Andrew McIntyre, climbs onto the sill beside Rede to speak on the outrage of the Bentley trial. Then an egg is hurled and sails near the Commissioner's head, splattering on the wall beside him.

Infuriated, the Commissioner believes he can identify who threw it and orders his men to take the man in hand. Not one trooper moves. Ride into that mob and arrest the offender? It would be easier to pluck out the eye of the devil in hell. In the midst of it all, Commissioner Rede can't help but notice that he is receiving precious little in the way of support from the man commanding those soldiers, Captain Hans T. Fell White, who . . .

Splat! Another egg again narrowly misses the noggin of the outraged Commissioner.

Now who is intimidated? Certainly not the miners. For the first time it is the police who are showing fear, and all the troopers can do is take their horses and fall back, riding around in an effort to protect the hotel.

Thus encouraged – what joy to have the police in fear of *them* for a change – the miners surge forward, close enough to take sticks and start beating on the side of the hotel.

At this point Andrew McIntyre says to Assistant-Commissioner Gilbert Amos, 'You will not give us justice. We will take the law in our own hands and see if we cannot do better.'[28] Not long afterwards he is seen pulling weatherboards off the side of the building.

As the madness of the mob takes hold, it is not long before the first of the diggers, including 'Yorkey', storm through the front and back doors. To even more cheering, they begin to throw furniture, curtains – anything they can get their hands on – out the windows. For many of the troopers on horseback below, it is all they can do to keep their saddles, let alone stop the crowd. As diggers swarm forward and start to rip more planking from the side of the hotel, one of the Californians inside takes it up another notch by throwing crockery out the windows, which smashes satisfyingly.

Soon enough, it becomes apparent that the diggers really are intent on the total destruction of the hotel, tearing down the Waterford chandeliers. The sound of the shattering of glass is only drowned out by the throaty roar of yet more malcontents pouring in to join the fun.

Should the armed troopers shoot at the diggers . . . ?

'FIRE!'

Inside the hotel, one of the diggers has thrown a match onto some shattered bottles of spirits, and though this time some police rush in to successfully extinguish the flames, both the mathematics and the mood tell against them. What can several dozen terrified troopers and traps do against thousands of angry miners? The truth is soon more than apparent: they can do very little. Two men who try to put the fire out are Commissioner Rede and Andrew McIntyre, the latter of whom would also claim he even burnt himself in the process.

McIntyre expresses his fear to Commissioner Rede that some might think he has been trying to add to the flames, rather than put them out. The Commissioner replies, as McIntyre would later swear under oath, 'There's no danger, I can swear you have done your duty like a man.'[29]

Though some of the troopers are able to put the first fire out and establish a partial cordon around the building, they are not quick enough. Even more of the mob swarm into the hotel, while others stave in the water cart to make sure it can't be used to put the fire out.

And then the shout goes up: 'The 40th are coming!'[30]

'Where's the Redcoats?'

'There they come, yonder up the hill!'

'Hurrah! Three cheers.'[31]

Again, there is no fear at the sight of the mounted British forces. Even when the foot soldiers arrive and form up in front of the hotel and draw their swords, the diggers do not back off.

'Hurrah, boys!'

'No use waiting any longer.'

'Down she comes.'[32]

'She', as it turns out, is the bowling alley at the side of the hotel, which is not only made of highly valuable and flammable canvas but, more importantly, is owned by the American who had been so public in his support of Bentley.

Not long after, a digger is seen running into the back of the bowling alley holding a whole pile of paper. It, too, is seen to be properly roaring, its canvas sides falling away in blazing strips.

The police again move to quell the flames, but this time it is as if God Himself has come down on the side of the diggers. The flames catch on to the back corner of the hotel and take hold, to universal cheering, and sudden gusts of wind spring up to fan the flames further.

Hurrah! Hurrah! Hurrah!

Amid all the cheering, billowing smoke and sounds of what remains of the windows cracking and breaking in the heat, Raffaello Carboni takes pause to consider what a curious thing it is 'that a characteristic of the British race is to make fun of the calamity of fire'.[33] He noticed this first while living in London, and now here it is again. The destruction of this hotel is a positively joyous thing, and the diggers are enjoying it hugely.

'Burn the bloody murderer's house down,'[34] an American by the name of Albert Hurd shouts, even as he pauses while ripping palings off the back wall to throw burning rags through the shattered windows. 'Come on my boy and we will have plenty wood – let us tear it down!' he is heard to cry.[35] And yet he is only one of many others who start to tear the side of the house down to feed the flames. It is even possible that some of the men supposed to be stopping this destruction are actually loving it, as *The Ballarat Times* would report: 'The police all this time were riding round and round the hotel, but did not take any vigorous measures to deter the people from the sport they appeared to enjoy so much.'[36]

Not that some care isn't taken, for all that. Before the stables are burnt down, the horses are ushered out and the sheep and pigs are taken from the yard.[37] Many of the servants are allowed to save their own property, just as the musicians save their instruments. After a dray is run into the flames, on the reckoning it is Bentley's, a sudden cry goes up – maybe it is *not* Bentley's!

'[The dray] was at some risk rescued; but on further enquiry it was ascertained to be his property, and immediately run into the burning mass and totally consumed.'[38]

When a maid then cries out that her dowry box is inside and will be burnt, one valiant young digger charges in and retrieves it for her. (This proves doubly useful, as he would later marry her.)[39]

And now, as if the gods themselves are angry, and complicit in fuelling the fury, those first gusts of wind have now turned into a full-blown gale, coming from exactly the right direction to stoke the flames higher. Soon the entire hotel is ablaze, something that would surely please the departed spirit of the murdered miner, James Scobie. Yes, there is a sudden burst of rain from the heavens, accompanied by booming thunder that rolls like a dirty ball across the goldfields, but neither lasts long.

As the roof of the main building catches alight, it is the shingles, being very thin and flammable, that roar into flame first, 'leaving the joists and ridge-pole glowing vividly in the sky. To the onlookers at a distance it seemed for a few moments like ribs of fire supporting a fiery keel.'[40]

In the face of the inferno, the order is given and the forces of law and order suddenly make their move. They perform an about-face and march back to their Camp. And though they try to arrest Andrew McIntyre, such is the weight of numbers that when other diggers move to free him they are powerless to resist, happy just to get away from the mob.

As it happens, the backs of them are still in sight when the roof at the back of the hotel falls in with a thunderous roar, followed by flames shooting ever higher . . .

And now some of the rioters have got their hands on the bottles in the bar stores of the hotel not yet burnt down. No matter that the bottles are burning hot, it is still grog. In short order they are handed out, their necks clashed together to knock the tops off, and the liquid swigged directly from there – a uniquely colonial way of doing it.

And look out! Even as the mass of diggers drink deeply, the rest of the hotel is collapsing as the roof and sides fall in upon themselves. More flames, more billowing smoke, more trails of sparks roaring high into the smoke-filled sky. Oh, it was grand, I tell you. Within minutes, what had been the Eureka Hotel is well on its way to what it will be – an enormous, twisted mess of a bonfire, the memory of which will warm everyone's souls.

———

Back at the Camp, things are starkly different. There is no animated conversation, no-one doing drills, no clip-clop of horses, no clipped orders to underlings, not even a hint of the usual chaff and laughter between the men.

Instead, as recorded by Commissioner Rede's Canadian chief clerk, Samuel Huyghue, there is 'a strange silence. There was none of the usual loitering about, and what of speech was heard in the tents was reserved and low. The general feeling amongst us was one of angry humiliation, for it was believed that instead of making conciliatory speeches to an infuriated crowd, had those in command made prompt use of the force at hand, the hotel might have been saved.'[41]

The humiliation is compounded shortly afterwards when word spreads at teatime that the diggers are about to attack the Camp en masse in order to get their dirty hands on Bentley. It takes only minutes and the whole garrison is under arms, with no fewer than '1000 rounds of ball cartridge . . . issued to the police'[42] and double guards posted on several approaches. No-one is allowed to enter or leave the Camp without a password. A dispatch is sent to Melbourne at all speed, asking for reinforcements, while the wives and children of those serving in the Camp – of whom there is a good sprinkling

– are asked to leave. It is no longer considered safe.

Mercifully, no attack proves forthcoming. Smoke continues to fill the air as the remains of the Eureka Hotel burn into the night, little flickers of flame in the darkness around which the drunken diggers are still cavorting. (Nothing better than a good public fire!)

Later that evening, Magistrate Dewes is returning from Buninyong, where he has been presiding over a legal matter, when he suddenly looks up to see one of his servants, Edward, rushing towards him, holding a pair of his finest pistols. Advising his master what has happened, it is his earnest advice that the Magistrate should make a detour on his way home, so as to avoid going past the Eureka.

Dewes will have none of it and – outraged almost in the manner of a man who has lost a hotel in which he is a part-owner – gallops towards it. He arrives in time to see the last of the timber framework of the once fine hotel crash into no more than flaming embers, the whole thing totally uninsured, and . . .

And there he is! The Magistrate is well known to many diggers, particularly the ill-behaved ones who have appeared before him so many times, and it is no coincidence that a fair measure of these last are still there, enjoying the flames of redemption. And yet, such is their joy that they greet him cheerily in the manner of men who have changed shoes to their other foot – how does the magistrate like it *now*? Some of them are even so bold as to quietly point to the smoking ruins and say openly to him that, given the law had not dealt justly with the murder of Scobie, they had been obliged to take the law into their own hands.

For his part, Dewes is so apoplectic with rage (and perhaps grief at the loss of such an asset) that all he can do is snarl back, 'Some of you will have no reason to congratulate yourself on today's work.'[43]

And then he gallops off, still fuming. It is his strong view that,

'If the inspector of police and chief magistrates on the spot had behaved with firmness and judgement, this catastrophe would never have ensued . . . but nothing of this sort was done, and merely useless remonstrance used, which only gave the rioters an additional consciouness of their power.'[44]

As it is, not even wild horses could drag the remaining diggers away from the carnage. It is the most fun they've had in months.

'The entire diggings, in a state of extreme excitement,'[45] Carboni would recount. 'The diggers are lords and masters of Ballarat; and the prestige of the Camp is gone for ever.'[46]

This exultation does not last long, however. On receipt of the news concerning this open revolt against the law, Sir Charles Hotham is also enraged and insistent that the law immediately strike back hard.

On the instant, he sends every trooper and policeman the colony can muster to Ballarat, and within four days the roads leading into those diggings begin to fill with the first detachments of what will eventually amount to a local force of no fewer than 450. Sir Charles's instructions to Commissioner Rede could not be more clear: 'Use force whenever legally called upon to do so, without regard to the consequences which might ensue.'[47] This instruction fits Rede's mood. He and his forces have been humiliated by the burning down of the Eureka Hotel, and now the diggers must be held to account.

Though clearly intent on demonstrating that the writ of law runs over Ballarat, the authorities do not seem too particular as to which diggers it arrests – it seems that anyone will do.

Early hours, Saturday, 21 October 1854, on Ballarat, a digger's dilemma

Andrew McIntyre is restless. Late the night before, one of the officers in the police whom he knows, a detective, quietly came to give him fair warning that he is to be arrested this day. Sure enough, even though it is still only two in the morning, he can hear men marching outside, quietly grunting, cursing. Perhaps in the darkness they're not sure which is his tent. But he has no doubt, from the clink of stirrups, the snorting of horses and the guttural commands, that there is a substantial armed force not far away. What to do? Surrender? Flee?

McIntyre feels himself to be innocent and has no desire to flee. Instead, he leaves the searchers waiting for two hours until the first light of dawn, then goes out and pleasantly asks if they would like to come in for a nobbler or two.

No, they would not. The ten detectives and the sergeant major of police would like to arrest him. And just to be sure that there will be no trouble, they are backed by a file of mounted police.

McIntyre is manacled and marched away to the lockup.

Another fellow, a printer by the name of Thomas Fletcher, is also quickly taken, and it is not long before both are brought before the presiding magistrate, Commissioner Johnstone, to defend the charge that they did on 'the 17th day of October last, at Ballarat, unlawfully, riotously, and tumultuously assemble together to the disturbance of the public peace, and being then so unlawfully, riotously, and tumultuously assembled together, as aforesaid, did then feloniously, unlawfully, and with force, demolish and pull down the dwelling-house of one James Francis Bentley, there situated, in contempt of our lady the Queen and her laws, to the evil example of all others in the like case offending . . .'[48]

Eight policemen give eye-witness evidence against McIntyre before the case is opened against Fletcher. One young rebel who is there, Samuel Lazarus – he came to Australia at the same time as Tim and Anastasia Hayes and their children – records in his diary that the second witness, 'a thin cadaverous sickly looking wretch (useful only for such vile purposes) . . . went on as fluently as though he was reading from a book, charging him with destroying property, arson and even inciting to murder. Poor Fletcher grew pale as death as the wretch proceeded in his diabolical evidence and seemed as though he could hardly support himself at the bar.'[49]

Bail refused. (And this, after Bentley, accused of murdering a man, had been bailed. The sheer injustice of it is staggering.) The two men are ordered to stand trial the following Thursday, whereby, whereb . . . whe . . . *What is that noise?*

It is the sound of shouting.

Word has spread and by now some 7000 outraged diggers have gathered outside, demanding that McIntyre and Fletcher be released on bail or they will storm the Government Camp.

Of *all* people to have arrested. Throughout the madness on that night, it had been McIntyre who had been actively trying to calm things down, while many of the diggers seem to feel – mistakenly – that Fletcher had not even been there at all!

So volatile is the situation that anything might happen, and it is all that some of the more moderate diggers can do to restrain the others from storming the premises.

In the end, the mob agrees to stay well back while a delegation of 12 men go inside to negotiate. Even then it is a close-run thing.

In extremis, Magistrate Sturt, after consulting with Acting-Commissioner of the Victoria Police Charles MacMahon – both men have arrived together in Ballarat that very afternoon – reach an agreement with the delegates inside the Police Magistrates' Court. Arthur Akehurst, the young 'Clerk of the Peace' and leading legal functionary in the court, carefully notes that each man is to be released with bail of £500 and sureties of £250. (Which, again, is staggering considering that the presumed murderer, Bentley, only had bail of £200 and £100 surety.)

Still, when Sturt tells them he is only interested in 'investigating the matter'[50] and is remarkably conciliatory in his approach regarding bail, the diggers feel that the authorities have tacitly promised that there will be no more arrests. The delegation also meets MacMahon, who quietly and privately feels a little less conciliatory than the Magistrate he has advised. He reports to Colonial Secretary Foster that he actually thinks the diggers are 'exhibiting a bullying spirit' and are lacking any 'proper respect for authority'.[51] But given that he had been quietly told by a couple of men in whom he has implicit confidence that unless he gives bail to the men, the Camp would likely be attacked in order to force their release, he feels he had no choice but to grant bail. It is with this threat in mind that he orders that there are indeed to be no more arrests . . . until a detachment of the 12th Regiment arrives on Ballarat in a few days' time.

Meanwhile, the situation outside remains volatile. The 7000 diggers who have promised to stay back from the Camp first get to the gully below it, then cross the Yarrowee upon the newly constructed bridge and approach the entrance of the Camp itself, where they are confronted by armed police and troopers.

'Nothing could exceed the wild frenzy, the commotion, and even the terrible determination that prevailed of proceeding to violence at once,' *The Ballarat Times* would report, 'notwithstanding the previous arrangement of sending a deputation. In this manner the people were agitated like a troubled ocean for upwards of an hour on the precincts of the Camp. During the whole time the Camp was panic-stricken, dismayed and terrified.'[52]

Anything could happen at this point, most particularly after one rough-looking bear of a man cries out, 'Come on, I'll be your Bloody Captain!'[53] and starts to lead them forward. Just when it seems that a violent clash is inevitable, just after five o'clock on this Saturday afternoon . . . *there they are!*

McIntyre and Fletcher, surrounded by the diggers' delegation, triumphantly appear from the Camp entrance and walk towards the bridge. The sum of £1000 for their release has been raised by the committee for their defence.

They are quickly engulfed by the masses and head back down

the road, away from the Government Camp. Catastrophe is avoided, though many in the crowd can't resist firing their pistols in the air as they go, a gesture of both celebratory defiance and warning. 'One Irish man,' McIntyre would later write to his brother, 'had 6 six-barreled revolvers in his hand, in all 36 shots.'[54] The crowd wants to carry McIntyre away on their shoulders and have a German band ready to lead them, but the Scot, 'got them advised to desist such a demonstration'.[55]

At this point it is Tom Kennedy's considered advice that McIntyre should flee from Ballarat, a point vigorously objected to by one of the committee who has put up a fair portion of his bail. In any case, McIntyre will have none of it. He says he has done nothing wrong and refuses to hide for so much as an hour. He is happy to have his day in court.

Commissioner Rede, for one, is very glad to see the back of the lot of them, as all of the goldfields now seem to be in revolt. Apart from the burning of the Eureka Hotel, the issue of the maltreatment of Father Smyth's servant has continued to bubble and boil, to trouble and toil. There is to be a meeting of the diggers in the chapel after Mass on Bakery Hill the next day, to look at ways of seeking justice.

On the direct orders of His Excellency, Rede has to call on Father Smyth and officially tell him that Sir Charles 'sees no reason for being dissatisfied with Mr Johnstone's conduct, [and] say that [Sir Charles] relies upon the Priest using that influence he possesses over his flock to maintain the peace and stop excitement'.[56] Against that, Sir Charles has also taken the precaution of removing James Lord from Ballarat.

Not to worry, the priest tells him. As Rede would later recount in a report to his superiors, 'He said he did not wish to press the charge, and promised he would keep the people so late at Chapel that they would not have time to assemble.'[57]

Evening, 21 October 1854, Star Hotel, Main Road Ballarat East, a committee is formed

Yes, the Eureka Hotel is gone, but few of the diggers ever drank there anyway, so no-one misses it. For many of the most distinguished diggers, their preferred place to drink is the Star Hotel on Main Road, and it is here in the days after the arrests that a gathering of diggers and other interested parties votes to form a committee – composed of Friedrich Vern, John Basson Humffray and, of course, Thomas Kennedy – to organise the defence of the arrested men.

Of these men, perhaps the most impressive 'gentleman' – for that is his whole persona – is the good-looking, eloquent and softly spoken 30-year-old Welshman and moral-force Chartist, Humffray.

Eighteen months earlier, Humffray had been living and working in Cardiff, doing his articles to become a solicitor when, like so many, he had chanced to read some articles about the riches to be found on the Australian goldfields. Shortly thereafter, he threw it all in to try his luck.

After arriving on Victorian shores aboard *Star of the East* on 19 September 1853, he quickly made his way to the goldfields and soon recognised that precisely the same issues that the Chartists were concerned with were also present here. It was natural that he should also become involved in the reform movement in Australia. He had always made the case, however, that the people should make their fight via the legal routes of petitions and resolutions, and never by attempting to take the law into their own hands. The moment you step outside the law, you lose all moral authority to make your case for legal redress.

In fact, his approach to the matter at hand has been neatly summed up in a letter to *The Ballarat Times*, where he describes the charred rafters of the Eureka Hotel as a 'bundle of crayons with which to write the black history of crime and colonial misrule . . .'

'The diggers know their rights,' he continues. 'They know also they have the power to enforce them, but they are also willing to hail them under the banner of peace, law and order . . . The people ask for justice not bullets! . . . The land question, the license question, and the representative question are all questions of moment and must be satisfactorily answered.'[58]

Carboni, always a hard marker in such matters, likes Humffray from the first and later describes him thus: 'He had an honest and benevolent heart, directed by a liberal mind . . . possessing . . . a fine forehead, denoting astuteness . . . a pair of eyes that mark the spell . . . a Grecian nose; of a mouth remarkable for the elasticity of the lips, that make him a model of pronunciation of English language.'[59]

Humffray is a well-educated, natural leader of men, with a melodic way of speaking. There is no violence in him, no hint of menace. If the time has now come to parley with the Lieutenant-Governor is now, he is the obvious one among them to speak to His Excellency on his own level.

For his own part, Carboni is typically caustic in his summation of Vern, the Hanoverian, who is nevertheless liked by others, 'With the eyes of an opossum, a common nose, healthy looking cheeks, not very small mouth, no beard . . . broad shoulders . . . splendid chest, long arms – the whole of your appearance makes you a lion amongst the fair sex, in spite of your bad English, worse German, abominable French . . . You have not a dishonest heart, but you believe in nothing except the gratification of your silly vanity, or ambition, as you call it.'[60]

In the meantime, all over the diggings, placards are now posted, declaring:

FIVE HUNDRED POUNDS REWARD

WHEREAS James Scobie was, early on the morning of the 7th instant, found murdered near the Eureka Hotel, Ballarat.

Notice is hereby given that a reward of Five hundred pounds will be paid to any person...[61]

And at least, in this case, the government has done the right thing, putting up the money for the reward and allowing those diggers who had previously raised the £200 for their own reward to be reimbursed.

One who takes particular notice of the Scobie poster is the man who used to be the nightwatchman at the Eureka Hotel when it was still standing, Thomas Mooney. As one who is now without a job and without prospects, he decides to confess everything about the murder in the hope of claiming the reward. He was there on the night; he saw it all. It is with this in mind that the next day he quietly, oh so quietly, presents himself to the authorities and asks to speak to someone on the matter of the death of James Scobie...

Not long afterwards, there is yet one more fellow who, after flitting through the long shadows of dusk, suddenly emerges to whisper that he would also like to have a quiet chat with the constabulary at Government Camp, Ballarat. And so it is that the important deposition of one Michael Welsh – a waiter who lived at the Eureka Hotel, was there on that fateful, fatal night and saw it all – is also taken down and added to the weight of evidence for the prosecution. By that night, Welsh is on his way under armed guard to Geelong, where he will be secured for his own safety.

One bit of positive news for the diggers amid all the drama is that Peter Lalor and his committee composed their petition to His Excellency – '. . . *your petitioners [are] dissatisfied with the manner in which justice has been administered in regard to the death of one James Scobie . . .*'[62] – and received a positive response.

In the face of the uprising and the petition, in receipt of the dissenting view from Assistant-Commissioner Johnstone – and with the news that two of Bentley's staff have come forward and offered to give evidence against their employer – the judicial authorities under Sir Charles, led by Attorney-General Stawell, feel they have no choice but to act. Stawell feels so strongly that, once he is convinced 'the authorities had taken the wrong course',[63] he immediately journeys out to Toorac House and exhorts His Excellency to have Bentley and his companions arrested once more and again brought to trial, something Sir Charles readily agrees to.

As it turns out, the Bentleys have already done half the work for the authorities: when they cannot be found on Ballarat, they are soon enough found in Melbourne. A warrant is ordered for their apprehension and the two are arrested by Detective Senior Sergeant Cummings – who has travelled from Ballarat to track down the dastardly duo – and thrown into prison to await trial.

Meantime, Sir Charles also begins to wrestle with the problem of what to do about the growing allegations of corruption coming from Ballarat, most particularly those concerning Magistrate Dewes . . .

22 October 1854, Bakery Hill, on the Ballarat diggings, the diggers speak truth to power

In truth, the 'chapel' on Bakery Hill is little more than a rough construction of upright slabs of wood upon which a canvas roof has been attached to keep the rain out, but at 85 feet long by 27 feet wide it is the largest construction on the goldfields and serves a variety of purposes beyond allowing Father Smyth to hold Mass for the 1100 Catholics of all nations on the Ballarat goldfields. It also serves as a meeting place and a school for the Catholic children – though John Manning left a few weeks earlier to take up a post as a writer with *The Ballarat Times*, Anastasia Hayes is still a teacher there.

This particular Sunday, however, such are the tensions on the goldfields, so high are the passions over the conduct of the troopers towards the diggers, that after Mass – which seems to last an extraordinarily long time as Father Smyth unaccountably goes on and on – a meeting is held to discuss what can be done to help the 'helpless Armenian'.[64]

After much discussion, two motions are passed:

> *That this meeting is of the opinion that their respected pastor has been insulted by the disgraceful maltreatment endured by his servant at the hands of a government officer.*

> *That this meeting is of the opinion that the Magistrates of Ballarat have been premature in the decision to which they have arrived on the matter, and that we . . . therefore call for a revision of the case, and if the evidence adduced demand a reversion of the sentence that such be promptly and publicly done.*[65]

Another step the meeting settles on is to immediately send a delegation to 'wait upon the Bench'[66] at Ballarat and demand the case be revisited . . .

At meeting's end the diggers are asked to make donations to the defence fund, at which point, sadly, there is hardly a flurry of pound notes. While it is one thing to put your hand in the air to vote for a motion, it is quite another thing to put that same hand in your purse – particularly when many of them have already given generously for McIntyre and Fletcher's bail and defence fund.

Early afternoon, 23 October 1854, on Bakery Hill, anger unites

And yet so troubled are the Ballarat goldfields at this point that the following day, just 150 yards away atop Bakery Hill, a stunning 9000 diggers turn up to protest against the arrests of McIntyre and Fletcher and pass their own angry motions in their support. Donations are again called for, though the biggest cheer of the day comes when Sarah Hanmer, the American owner of the newly established Adelphi Theatre – 'a vast tent, with plain benches and a rough stage'[67] – announces that she will put on a benefit show the following night, with all proceeds going to the defence fund. *Hurrah!* The formation of a 'Diggers' Rights Society' is discussed, and a committee is chosen, *The Argus* observes, 'to tickle the Camp when it acted unconstitutionally'.[68] Many note that it is Friedrich Vern who readily puts £100 of his own money into the fund. There is something about Vern that is quite compelling. In the later words of digger John Lynch, 'Brave words came bubbling from his lips, and he spoke with the air of one having authority.'[69]

The meeting concludes with three groans for the turncoat *Argus* – which has been unaccustomedly critical of the diggers of late – and three cheers and one more for the kindness of Mrs Hanmer.[70] As Bakery Hill is clearly visible to all those in the Government Camp, the massive gathering is regarded with some alarm. This alarm becomes all the greater when the report of the magistrate and shorthand writer is submitted as – following Sir Charles's instructions – they were present and recorded all of the speeches.

For Commissioner Rede, there are so many meetings going on, so many motions passed, so many petitions circulating, it is hard to keep track. What he does know is that the goldfields are now in a dangerous state of agitation.

Not that he is afraid of the diggers by any means, or at all inclined to bow down to their demands. As a matter of fact, when the Catholic deputation comprising Timothy Hayes, Thomas Kennedy and the

Irish firebrand John Manning – now the editor and reporter on *The Ballarat Times* – arrive for their first meeting with the Commissioner to express their concerns, the man with the gold lace on his uniform keeps them waiting so long they are insulted. Manning reports in the pages of his own newspaper, with the full approval of the owner and publisher, Henry Seekamp, 'Mr Commissioner Rede, after detaining the deputation for an unreasonable time, at length made his appearance, and whether influenced by a sense of his own importance, or actuated with contempt for the deputation and its object, there appeared to be a certain haughtiness in his manner which offended the deputation.'[71]

Finally, however, Rede grants the delegation their audience with the Bench, which comprises Police Magistrate Sturt, Acting Chief Commissioner of Police Captain Charles MacMahon and his goodly self.

And he does give them one bit of good news: 'The trooper who has so abused the priest's man, and so insulted the priest himself, is now under arrest.'[72]

Beyond that, however, the best the Bench can advise is that the only way to get the Lieutenant-Governor to reopen the case on the priest's servant Gregorius is to get up yet another petition with thousands of signatures upon it – *Maybe this one will actually make a difference?* – and send it to His Excellency. Though Manning, for one, is growing fatigued with petitions and resolutions, the delegation tells him that they will organise just that and take their leave.

Fine, Commissioner Rede for one is glad to see them go. For the truth of it is that he remains so horrified by the burning of the Eureka Hotel and is so little in the mood for conciliation on any front – let alone the matter of the priest's servant – that the previous evening he wrote to the Colonial Secretary in Melbourne, offering his formal advice that the best way forward was to toughen the government's stance, not soften it. 'I would strongly advise . . . to arrest all implicated [in the burning of the Eureka Hotel] as far as possible and if anything like a serious resistance is made or an attempt at rescue, a lesson should be given them which should prove that the Government could insist . . .

'I feel convinced that if the License Fee is to be continued it must be by coercion and the sooner the miners are shewn that coercion can be used successfully the better.'[73]

In fact, with the arrival of the reinforcements, Commissioner Rede – who has long been caught between what he sees as his duty to impose the *law*, come what may, and his instinct to at least try to understand the grievances of the diggers and act accordingly – is feeling more aggressive by the day. It is his growing view that the essence of the problem is neither his administration nor the laws, but the fact that he is dealing with 'the Tipperary Mob'[74] – or 'Young Ireland', as Carboni terms the group – with headquarters on the Eureka lead near the Catholic church, and Irishmen looking for trouble where no trouble truly exists.

Tuesday, 24 October 1854, the Legislative Council receives good news

St Patrick's Hall is an imposing building, standing proudly at 85 Bourke Street West. Constructed in classic Victorian style, in a manner reminiscent of a Renaissance palace, it has high ceilings, arched windows and classical Ionic columns. Dedicated to the 'memory of Ireland', the hall opened five years earlier and was so highly esteemed by both the people and the body politic that it is here that the Legislative Council has met since its first days of existence on 11 November of 1851. Despite this, rarely has that council discussed more grave issues than it has lately, with report after report coming in from the goldfields. Today, however, the news is good.

Rising to speak, the Colonial Secretary, John Foster, is pleased to report that after the recent riot in Ballarat, 'Captain Sturt, the

Melbourne superintendent of police, with all the spare police, horse and foot, have been dispatched to Ballarat by the Government, together with a company or more of soldiers'.[75] Altogether 450 soldiers and police, all armed, are now on Ballarat, meaning 'that, no matter what the result might be, the law will be upheld, and it will be shown to the misguided men that the laws of the country are not to be broken with impunity'.[76] Cheering breaks out around the chamber at this bit of news. The Government appears to at last have the situation regarding the men Foster considers as 'lucky vaga-bonds'[77] in hand.

26–27 October 1854, on Ballarat, fortifications are strengthened

The bastards! Despite the promises that there would be no more arrests made over the burning of the Eureka Hotel, over two days the authorities have put eight more diggers in manacles, includ-ing Henry 'Yorkey' Westerby and the American Albert Hurd. Yes, Yorkey and Hurd were involved, but they certainly were not the key instigators any more than the other six men. Who knew who did what in all that madness? It really does look like the authorities don't care so long as they can be seen to be punishing a few of the diggers.

Do they not understand?

It seems not. Even when over subsequent days the charges against all bar McIntyre, Fletcher and Westerby are dismissed – mostly for want of evidence, and in the case of Hurd, perhaps because he was an American – the anger does not abate. It is enough that the authorities intend to put three of their mates on trial, and likely in gaol, for engaging in what the diggers feel was a hugely justifiable act in the first place.

(For his part, Attorney-General William Stawell is equally intran-sigent. Appalled at this first case of 'lynch law'[78] in the colonies, he is determined to make the charges stick and see the diggers held accountable for the unconscionable destruction.)

Meanwhile at the Government Camp, as tensions on the goldfields continue to rise so does Rede's fear that the digger discontent will turn into armed insurrection. The mood has become so dark in recent days, the stance of the mass of diggers so threatening, that Commissioner Rede is not at all confident that he has the military wherewithal on hand to defeat them.

The first thing he decides to do is take measures to improve security and gives carriage of it to the finest military man on site, Captain John Wellesley Thomas, who arrived in command of a detachment of mounted men of the 40th Regiment just two days earlier in response to the urgent despatch requesting reinforcements after the burning of the Eureka Hotel. The highly decorated 32-year-old son of a gun of a famous British admiral has been with the 40th Regiment for the last 15 years, having graduated from the prestigious military college Sandhurst in southern England and served in front-line positions in Afghanistan and India. He arrived in Australia on his latest posting aboard *Vulcan* in late 1852.

Sah!

A slim, neat man with a slim, neat manner, Thomas is nevertheless extremely energetic and has no sooner arrived in Ballarat than he begins a detailed study of the Government Camp, going from building to building and – only occasionally pausing to stroke his slim, neat moustache – works out exactly how the compound might be better fortified for defence. He determines just how many soldiers and police are needed to guard each building, which unit they should come from, how many should be in reserve and where a cavalry of 26 sabres of the mounted 40th Regiment and 50 mounted police should position themselves, ready to counterattack should any major offensive be launched. Still not content, he instructs carpenters on where to bore holes in the wall for defenders to fire through. Water barrels are to be immediately filled and placed strategically throughout the camp, in case the rebels try to set fire to the buildings.

'Responsible persons are to be appointed to take charge of, and arrange the issue of Ammunition'[79] and all officers and 'gentlemen' not attached to any unit are to be held in reserve. If an attack beckons, all women and children are to be sent to the commissariat store building. Utmost silence is to be maintained, with no talking above a whisper, and all orders by officers and NCOs are to be given in a low voice.

It is a comprehensive effort, and Commissioner Rede is highly impressed at Captain Thomas's military acumen. He regrets it when Thomas is called back to Melbourne only shortly after compiling the plan.

28 October 1854, Ballarat, the temper of the times starts to boil over

Henry Seekamp is in his element.

He is at his best when there is something to be upset about, and now there are more reasons upsetting him than he has fingers and toes, but he sums it up in a 28 October editorial in *The Ballarat Times*: 'Everyone who has been a reflective spectator of the partial, oppressive, domineering and unjust line of conduct pursued of late by the authorities at Ballarat, must have considered the people less than men and worse than brutes to endure it much longer; must have considered the authorities more than men, and not less than gods to be able to continue their course of corrupt injustice without a serious interruption – without some popular and terrible demonstration of terrible disfavour . . .

'The corruption of every department connected with the government in Ballaarat is become so notorious and barefaced that public indignation is thoroughly aroused; and though the expression of public feeling be for a time in abeyance on account of the numerous armed mercenaries lately sent up from town, the fire of indignation is not extinguished; it still smoulders, only to burn forth again with unabated and unbeatable vigour.

'The Government deceive themselves most egregiously if they suppose that the present display of armed force is sufficient to over-awe the miners into passive submission to any measure they please to bring forward, to any law they please to enact, or to protect its corrupt officials from the just indignation of an oppressed people.'[80]

1 November 1854, Ballarat, the diggers gather at Bakery Hill in force

And so it has come to this.

On this afternoon a meeting to protest against the actions of the Ballarat authorities is attended by no fewer than 5000 diggers at Bakery Hill, where a few boards placed upon some tree stumps form a podium, allowing the meeting to begin at 2 pm.

As Commissioner Rede and his staff watch nervously from the Government Camp, tension rises at the vision of such a large mass of men gathered in the one spot at the one time, talking about their unhappiness with the authorities. In response, Commissioner Rede gives orders that all his soldiers are to keep their weaponry close, while the sentry guard is doubled.

'Every precaution is taken,' one correspondent would note, 'as if the authorities were in a real enemy's country.'[81]

The atmosphere, to begin with, is festive. In attendance is a German band – composed of diggers who have brought their musical instruments all the way from that nation – who play several popular airs. Around the speakers' platform are placed the gaily coloured English, Scottish and Irish national flags, as well as those of France and the United States.

There are many speakers, but the most powerful of them are, as ever, the organisers of this meeting: John Basson Humffray, Thomas Kennedy, George Black and Henry Holyoake. All of them had been heavily involved with the Chartist movement in England – Henry's brother is no less than the great George Jacob Holyoake, England's most famed Chartist and atheist – and all meet regularly at the Star Hotel on Main Road in Ballarat East, with people such as Sam Irwin, the regular contributor to the *Geelong Advertiser*, John Manning of *The Ballarat Times*, and, of course, Timothy Hayes, to discuss the issues of the day.[82]

The first pressing issue is the need to have all the charges dropped against Fletcher, McIntyre and Westerby. Having journeyed to Geelong – where superior judicial authorities reside – in an effort to do exactly that, Henry Holyoake and a 27-year-old Canadian digger by the name of Charles Ross report back that there is no sign that their release from gaol is imminent, though everyone at Bakery Hill appreciates Holyoake and Ross's efforts.

An even larger issue is the continued attempts by officials from the Government Camp to make even more arrests for the burning down of the hotel, despite officials having intimated eight days earlier to the digger delegation that such arrests would cease.

A strong resolution is passed condemning this outrage, and then the assembly begins to grapple with the issue of what they can do to stop these offenses.

Now, as moral-force Chartists, those on the podium believe that the best method of change is by exactly that – the moral force of their arguments – calmly and consistently expressing the legitimate will of the people. Ideally, that view could also have been expressed via the ballot box. Yet, sadly, as diggers they have not been invited to contribute to the electoral process and are in fact barred from it as they do not satisfy the electors' (let alone Members') property qualifications. And they are not alone.

The only people allowed to vote in the colony of Victoria for the 20 non-appointed members of the Legislative Council are those in possession of a freehold estate of the value of £100, those who have been resident in a dwelling house with a value of £10 per annum for at least six months, those holders of a lease with an annual value of £10 with three years to run, and those holding a depasturing license. This means that only 4000 men out of a total Victorian population of some quarter million can vote at this time.

And so the likes of Humffray and Holyoake warm to the theme that they must unite in their political actions, not only with each other but also with the diggers at other goldfields, who are all facing the same issues. After debate and discussion lasting no less than three hours, they reach a resolution: 'That the diggers of Ballarat do enter into a communication with the men of the other goldfields, with a view to the immediate formation of a general league, having for its object the attainment of the moral and social rights of the diggers.'[83]

For those here at these diggings, the idea of this 'reform league' is to have a body that can express their united views and allow their voice to be heard by a Government that has allowed them no voice in its Legislative Council, apart from that coming from sympathisers like John Pascoe Fawkner. (Fawkner had, after all, recently published a pamphlet entitled, 'Squatting Orders . . . Orders in Council . . . Locking Up the Lands of the Colony in the Hands of a Small Minority, Giving Them, Without Any Real Reason, the Right to Buy the Whole or Any Part of the Sixty Million Acres of This Fine Colony, at Their Own Price.')

Meanwhile at the meeting, one of the speakers, as recorded by Thomas Pierson, said, 'If all the people would only just assert their rights that they [would be] able to maintain a Republican Government!'[84]

As is ever his way, Thomas Kennedy goes further: 'The press has called us demagogues, who must be put down,' he thunders. 'But I for one will die a free man, though I drink the poison as Socrates of yore. We have come 15,000 miles, and left the enlightenment of the age and of the press, not to suffer insult, but to obtain greater liberty.

We want *men* to rule over us [not such as we have]. Most of all, we have to think of our children, who will grow up in this great colony, and all of us must never forget *their* own dearest interests.'[85]

And yet, he asks, is *this* the way to proceed? Constantly signing petitions and passing resolutions, all for no result?

'Moral persuasion,' Thomas Kennedy says, with everyone leaning forward as before, to catch every word, 'is all humbug. Nothing convinces like a lick in the lug!'[86]

Hurrah! Exactly!

Though not yet sure which lug, particularly, should be licked, a growing body of diggers are becoming ever more conscious that, together, they are strong. As the *Geelong Advertiser* astutely reports, 'It is evident that the agitation is about to assume a new shape . . .'[87]

2 November 1854, on the Ballarat Diggings, a breakthrough

The news breaks on this very day: Sir Charles Hotham has buckled! No longer able to ignore the growing outcry coming from Ballarat – the editorials, the two petitions – asking for the release of the diggers arrested for burning the Eureka Hotel and complaining of the treatment of the priest's servant – he has at last done something.

'Notice is hereby given,' the announcement runs, 'that a board has been appointed by His Excellency to investigate all circumstances in connexion with the murder of Scobie and the burning down of the Eureka Hotel . . .'[88]

As he explains in a despatch to London, Sir Charles – on the strong advice of Attorney-General William Stawell – has decided that after all the outcry it behoves him 'to investigate the charges which poured in from all quarters, of general corruption on the part of the authorities of the Ballarat gold field'.[89] And that Board of Inquiry into the circumstances surrounding the burning of the Eureka Hotel is due to get underway this very day at the mercifully still standing Bath's Hotel. It will be led by Sturt, who used to be Melbourne's Superintendent of Police but has now returned to his old job as Melbourne's Police Magistrate. He will be assisted by Ballarat Police Magistrate Charles Prendergast Hackett and the Chief Health Officer of the colony, William McCrea, who had previously served as a naval officer under the command of Sir Charles Hotham.

Now, *now* the diggers feel they are starting to get somewhere.

One of the witnesses to the inquiry at Bath's Hotel proves to be Peter Lalor, who gives his evidence on 4 November with some difficulty, his voice straining to keep calm under the anger he so evidently feels.

Speaking to the lack of justice delivered at the Coroner's inquest into the death of Scobie, which has directly led to the burning of the hotel, his testimony is devastating. 'While the jury were retired to consult on the verdict,' he begins, 'I saw the Coroner speaking to Bentley in a distant part of the room. Bentley had left the room before the jury returned. When they gave their verdict, he was sent for and the verdict read to him. The Coroner then said, "Gentlemen of the jury, you could find no other verdict." Mr Bentley asked whether the jury did not exonerate himself and the character of his house from all suspicion. The Coroner replied, without appealing to the jury, that with the two witnesses in his favour, there could be no suspicion against him.'[90]

This is only one of the many allegations of endemic corruption that the Board of Inquiry will hear or receive. One significant letter that is tendered claims the entire Government Camp at Ballarat is 'a kind of legal store where justice [is] bought and sold, bribery being the governing element of success, and perjury the base instrument of baser minds to victimize honest and honorable men, thus defeating the ends of justice'.[91]

And the principal problem remains unchanged.

'Honest men,' the letter further asserts, 'are hunted by the police like kangaroos, and if they do not possess a license (too often from want of means of paying for one, as poverty is the lot of many a digger) are paraded through the diggings by the commissioners and police up to the camp, and if unable to pay, are rudely locked up with any thief or thieves who happen to be in the camp cells at the time – in short, treated in every way as like a felon.'

It is signed 'On Behalf of the Ballarat Reform League'[92] by John Basson Humffray, George Black, Friedrich Vern, Charles Ross and the noted journalist for *The Ballarat Times* and *Geelong Advertiser*, Samuel Irwin. Another who is *very* strong in his personal criticism of both Commisioner Rede and Assistant-Commisioner Johnstone is the editor of *The Ballarat Times*, Henry Seekamp, something that Commisioner Rede takes a very dim view of when he finds out about it. Seekamp is not just a problem, he is an ever more troubling one – and therefore a problem that must be resolved.

4 o'clock on the afternoon of 3 November 1854, Port Phillip Bay, Sir Charles Hotham's ship comes in

The cavalry has arrived! Well, perhaps not the cavalry, but certainly Sir Charles Hotham feels some sense of relief that on this day the good ship *Empress Eugenie* drops anchor in Hobson's Bay and shortly thereafter begins unloading eight officers, ten sergeants and 167 rank and file Redcoats from the second division of the first battalion of Her Majesty's 12th Regiment to join the 321 Redcoats from the first division who arrived a fortnight earlier. Sir Charles's military complement is now complete, with as many troops on the ground as he could have reasonably hoped for.

'The troops are very healthy,' the *Empire* reports, 'and the vessel presents an appearance of cleanliness and order unequalled by any troop ship that has entered Hobson's Bay, and reflects the greatest credit on the commanding officer, and Dr Rogers, medical officer in charge.'[93] This credit is doubled when the band of the 12th division occupies the orchestra at the Melbourne Exhibition over three nights and provides an entertaining program that included the 'Polka Waterloo' and 'Polka Downshire'.

7 November 1854, Government Camp, Ballarat, Commissioner Rede ponders an alternative way

Well, the truth of it is obvious, is it not? The licensing system does not work, and it was never going to work.

None other than Gold Commissioner Robert Rede feels so strongly on this point that, in response to Sir Charles's private circular, he has been examining other ways of raising revenue. On this day, he commits his thoughts, black on white, in an elegantly penned letter, reporting that, alas, the alternative methods – including imposing a tax on the number of men employed on each claim or the number of people in each tent – won't work either.

'After giving the subject the most attentive consideration,' he writes, 'and talking it over with others who are capable of giving an opinion on such matters I must state that . . . the levying of a tax upon the inmates of a Tent could not be put into effect without a severe system of espionage which would be excessively obnoxious.'[94]

He regrets the current system, noting that he could get by with a quarter of the force he now has, 'had it not to act as a Tax gatherer. The miners have no personal ill feeling towards the Police but they detest the system, that is they detest the enforcings'.[95]

In place of the odious license fee, might Commissioner Rede make several suggestions to His Excellency? He decides to do so and details his considered views that the best way to proceed is to have an export duty on gold, sufficiently low that it will not encourage smuggling; a stamp duty on the sale of lands, houses, horses and cattle; a duty on imports with the exception of staples; licenses for the sale of wine and spirits to be doubled; and a tax imposed on the largest of the goldfields' 'refreshment tents', to all intents public houses.

Whatever His Excellency decides, Rede affirms, in signing off, that he will remain Sir Charles's 'most obedient servant'.[96]

Saturday afternoon, 11 November 1854, atop Bakery Hill,[97] the dogs of war are heard to bark

Roll up! Roll up!

For though the gathering on Bakery Hill ten days before had been far from the mother of all meetings, it had at least been the mother of this monster. Bands play and flags of many nationalities are raised as, again, 10,000 diggers turn up to express their displeasure with the Government and solidarity with those who are trying to do something about it.

Only minutes after the formalities begin, Timothy Hayes, with his 'pleasing deportment, suave manners and good address',[98] is unanimously voted to the chair, while John Basson Humffray – the secretary to the committee established to raise funds for the trial of McIntyre, Fletcher and Westerby – rises to his feet and clears his throat. As soon as he notes how low the funds are for their defence, the hat is immediately passed round and £45 6 pence is immediately collected.

As the sun beats down, the oratory heats up as speaker after speaker denounces the authorities and a veritable sea of hands is raised in total support of four proposed resolutions.

The first calls for the removal of a corrupt member of the police, Sergeant Major Milne, a move entirely endorsed by *The Ballarat Times*, while it also notes that Milne is 'but the tool – the machine in the hands of the government that employs him'.[99] (Milne is hated nearly as much as Assistant-Commissioner David Armstrong, of brass riding crop infamy, who last year had left the goldfields boasting of the £15,000 he made in bribes and extortion.)

The second resolution condemns the insolent language used by the authorities for 'their unwarrantable assertions regarding the veracity of the diggers and the respectability of the representatives of the public press on the goldfields and their *sneering* contempt at an appeal for an investigation into the malpractices of the corrupt camp at Ballarat'.[100]

As eloquent as ever, John Humffray introduces the third resolution, regarding formation of the Ballarat Reform League, explaining to his audience in his melodic voice the principles, articles and doctrines of this League, 'which if approved, means we could act in concurrence with, and hold out the right hand of fellowship to all on the goldfields'.[101]

Thus, this most important resolution is proposed by Humffray:[102] 'That this meeting having heard . . . the draft prospectus of the Ballarat Reform League approve of and adopt the same, and hereby pledge themselves to support the Committee in carrying out its principles and attaining its objects – which are the full political rights of the people.'[103]

George Black, the strapping six-foot editor of *The Diggers' Advocate*, takes up the torch of justice in seconding Humffray's motion, telling the assembled throng that 'our business is now to proceed to the shortest way to our rights . . . The authorities are now afraid of the diggers . . . Humanity has been insulted, now is the time to rise and act; to demand our rights; and the Governor if pressed, will yield'.[104]

He is every bit as eloquent as Humffray and when the motion is put and passed unanimously, the declaration is made that the Ballarat Reform League is formed, whereupon it is christened with three cheers for Mr Humffray and one cheer more for the League, which goes on for a great deal of time.

The fourth resolution expresses the meeting's total lack of confidence in the honesty of the Legislative Council, and pledges 'to use every constitutional means to have them removed from the offices they disgrace'.[105]

In seconding this resolution with typical ardour, Thomas Kennedy is once again in full cry: 'The day is come when we must speak of eternal brotherhood, and he who will not fall in with us, let him go away over the ocean.' *(Cheers)* 'Go to the Queen of England, a simple-minded mother far away from these her children and ask if the child sucks too long it will not injure both one and the other . . .

'When next we meet we must have *done* something – we must have the lands opened, the franchise and representation and our license fee abolished, and the diggers must all look upon each other as brothers.'[106] *(Cheers)*

And now another digger addresses the meeting, taking direct aim at the Lieutenant-Governor, noting, as reported by *The Argus,* that 'Sir Charles was a sailor, so was he, but he was not on board his frigate now. The diggers had made Victoria what it was, and were not to be put down. The ice was broken now. Sir Charles's motto was "Lead on", let theirs be "No surrender".'[107] *(Loud cheers)*

Delighting in it all, notes the correspondent for *The Argus,* is the newly installed Chairman of the Ballarat Reform League, Timothy Hayes – watched proudly from the front row by his wife, Anastasia, with her babe in arms – who steps forward: 'If their rights were not granted he would then say "To your Tents, O Israel" and he would if forced even go so far as to invoke the God of Battle.'[108]

The stage is set.

Prepare the bass drums for thunder.

None of this, of course, is secret and all of the proceedings are closely watched by mounted troopers on the fringes of the crowd. Notes are taken and everything is reported carefully back to Commissioner Rede, including the highly troubling 'principles and objects' of this newly formed Ballarat Reform League:

That it is the inalienable right of every citizen to have a

voice in making the laws he is called upon to obey – that taxation without representation is tyranny.

That, being as the people have been hitherto unrepresented in the Legislative Council of the Colony of Victoria, they have been tyrannised over, and it becomes their duty as well as interest to resist, and if necessary to remove the irresponsible power which so tyrannises over them.

It is the object of the 'League' to place the power in the hands of responsible representatives of the people to frame wholesome laws and carry on an honest Government.

That it is not the wish of the 'League' to effect an immediate separation of this Colony from the parent country, if equal laws and equal rights are dealt out to the whole free community. But that if Queen Victoria continues to act upon the ill advice of the dishonest ministers and insists upon indirectly dictating obnoxious laws for the Colony under the assumed authority of the Royal Prerogative the Reform League will endeavour to supersede such Royal Prerogative by asserting that of the People which is the most Royal of all Prerogatives, as the people are the only legitimate source of all political power.

Political changes contemplated by the Reform League:

1. A full and fair representation

2. Manhood suffrage

3. No property qualification of Members for the Legislative Council

4. Payment of Members

5. Short duration of Parliament

Immediate objects of the Reform League – An immediate change in the management of the Goldfields, by disbanding the Commissioners.

The total abolition of the Diggers' and Storekeepers' license tax, and a thorough and organised agitation of the Goldfields and the Towns.[109]

There is no disguising the fact that there is barely the thinness of a cigarette paper's difference between the resolutions of the Ballarat Reform League in 1854 and the Chartists of England in 1848 – and the previous two decades. The Chartists had been ruthlessly crushed back home, but now those aims have flowered in Australia and are being publicly expressed once more. This time, however, it is being expressed by a hardy group of men who swear that they won't back down.

'The agitators,' Thomas Pierson confides in his diary, 'seem determined to make Australia free.'[110]

For all that, one who is not impressed is Raffaello Carboni: 'What was the freight per ton, of this sort of worn-out twaddle imported from old England?'[111]

Although the majority of the men at the meeting have voted to support the executive of the Ballarat Reform League, there remains a growing feeling among some of them, of whom Carboni is but one, that while the aims of the League are admirable, the chances that the Government will actually care about something so benign as speeches and resolutions are lower than the red belly of a black snake. Against that, there is no doubt that the League has the full support of *The Ballarat Times* behind it, as Henry Seekamp soars to the heights of his prose when writing about it:

There is something strange, and to the government of this country, something not quite comprehensible, in this League. For the first time in the southern hemisphere, a Reform League is to be inaugurated. There is something ominous in this; the word 'League,' in a time of such feverish excitement as the present, is big

> with immense purport. Indeed, it would ill become the Times to mince in matter of such weighty importance. This League is not more or less than the germ of Australian independence. The die is cast, and fate has stamped upon the movement its indelible signature. No power on earth can restrain the united might and headlong strides for freedom of the people of this country, and we are lost in amazement while contemplating the dazzling panorama of the Australian future. We salute the League and tender our hopes and prayers for its prosperity. The League has undertaken a mighty task, fit only for a great people – that of changing the dynasty of the country.[112]

Not surprisingly, those who lead that dynasty are far from impressed at such advocacy, and Commissioner Rede has no sooner read it than he encloses the article with another, even more outrageous article in the same edition – one asserting the people are 'the only legitimate source of all political power' – in a satchel of official papers to be sent to Lieutenant-Governor Hotham in Melbourne, recommending that Henry Seekamp be charged with sedition. After all, the *Treason Felony Act 1848*, which had been brought in after the clash with the Chartists in Great Britain that year, makes it a serious offence to 'imagine, invent, devise, or intend to deprive or depose our most Gracious Lady the Queen, Her Heirs or Successors, from the Style, Honour, or Royal Name of the Imperial Crown of the United Kingdom . . . by publishing any Printing or Writing'[113] and, in Rede's view, Seekamp has at least done that.

While these men of the goldfields may be rebels, they are a very particular kind of rebel, as attested to by the correspondent of *The Argus*:

> These Ballarat diggers are most extraordinary rebels. It struck me to remark particularly, and to enquire as to their conduct and observance of the Sabbath. Truly they have few advantages, precious little of the gospel offered to them, little either of

> education given; no wonder, indeed, if they were
> vagabonds. But, as far as I could hear or see, the
> greatest possible order and sobriety, the utmost
> observance possible, I may say, of the Sabbath, has
> characterised their proceedings. Clean and neat in
> their diggers' best costume, they promenade over
> these vast goldfields, their wives and children in their
> best frocks too; but anything more calm or becoming
> or regardful of the day could hardly be witnessed
> in the best towns of even Christian Britain. How
> delightful would it not be to rule such men well![114]

At this point, however, Lieutenant-Governor Hotham and his leading officials, such as Commissioner Rede, are not finding it delightful at all. Notwithstanding His Excellency's previous blandishments in Geelong that 'all power proceeds from the people', he had never meant it like this!

The notion proposed by the Ballarat Reform League, that authority for power could come *up* from the people and not *down* from Her Majesty the Queen – and that it is therefore the people's right to remove whatever authority they don't agree with – is truly dangerous, bordering on revolutionary. That much is highlighted by the threat to 'effect an immediate separation of this Colony from the parent country'[115] if their demands are not met.

Simply ignoring such demands and trusting that as moral-force Chartists the men will not take violent action is not enough. The movement itself must be stopped, and yet, for the moment, Robert Rede is not sure how to do it. It is obvious that the Camp urgently needs more troops than the 450 it already has, but after that? Rede's mood changes by the hour, vacillating between wanting to send the troops in to crush the rebels and coming up with something to placate them.

Another week, another devastating financial report. This one received by Lieutenant-Governor Hotham details that the projected deficit for 1854 is – *dot three, carry one, subtract two* – £2,226,616, 5s.[116] To run the colony (including vast expenditure on new public works), the Government is already spending money it simply doesn't have and, more than ever, the urgent need is to get the miners to make up the difference. Sir Charles has tried other methods, like imposing a levy of £10 on every Chinese male who arrived at Port Phillip – no-one is more foreign than them, and it doesn't matter if they don't like it – but it came to nothing. The canny Chinese had simply gone on to Adelaide and walked overland from there. Which leaves Sir Charles where he started.

This movement against paying license fees must be *crushed*.

For Governor Hotham, mere military might is not enough. He also wants a well-oiled intelligence system to gather as much information as possible about what the 'enemy' is up to at all times. This is one of the many reasons that in the second week of November he summons Commissioner Rede to Melbourne to ensure that everything possible is being done to place their own men among the diggers – in the very garb of the diggers, pretending to *be* diggers. Rede has already been instructed to have observers and magistrates at every public meeting to write shorthand reports on everything that is said, but he also must ensure that things outside of public meetings are being recorded as well. What is happening? What are the diggers saying? What is their likely next move?

Obviously these men will have to be operating in conditions of strictest secrecy, lest they be exposed, and on the subject of secrecy Hotham is also insistent that he and Rede have a means of communicating with each other in code, so that he can send Rede 'orders in cypher'.[117] The Commissioner can then send coded messages back without the risk of sensitive information falling into the wrong hands. So clandestine is this method that not even Sir Charles's most high-powered official, Colonial Secretary John Foster, will be aware of it.

For his part, Commissioner Rede reports that the key trouble-makers are principally the non-English-speaking foreigners, who have as their ultimate goal the overthrow of the colonial government. These wretched 'democrats' will stop at nothing and must be held accountable by the law. Sir Charles finds it hard to believe that it is quite as bad as Rede makes out, but does agree that the law must be enforced, come what may . . .

CHAPTER NINE

ALL RISE

An unnatural separation was, so to speak, created by the law between the majority of the people and the Crown; and to give intensity to the danger, the people here were for the most part superior in mental and bodily capacities to the average capacities of their fellow countrymen whom they had left in their fatherlands. The courage and adventure which had made them emigrants, and the physical strength which had enabled them to weather the rude elements of early goldfields life, were qualities which made them valuable as freemen, but dangerous as slaves.

W. B. Withers in *History of Ballarat*[1]

[Robert Rede] was so puffed up with a sense of his own social importance that he made no attempt to conceal his contempt for the diggers. He was fond of using the language members of an elite use when discussing those placed under them. He was always talking of giving the diggers 'a fearful lesson . . .' It was the language of the English public school . . . Chance had placed him in authority over men who were likely to boil over when treated as inferiors.

Manning Clark in *A History of Australia*[2]

Saturday, 18 November 1854, a day of reckoning in the Melbourne Supreme Court

All rise.

Judge Redmond Barry presiding . . .

On this hot morning of late spring in the recently constructed

321

Supreme Court on the north-west corner of La Trobe and Russell streets – with sandstone walls and shining mahogany interior – the case of *Queen v. James Francis Bentley, Catherine Bentley, William Henry Hance and Thomas Farrell* on the matter of the murder of the miner from Ballarat, James Scobie, may finally get under way.

And this time it is serious. Judge Barry is a carefully coiffed, good-looking 40-year-old Anglican Irishman of legendary learnedness, who is revered in Melbourne for the fact that his Old-World courtesy extends even to criminals – apart from his sentences, of course, which can sometimes be most *discourteous.* He is – with Chief Justice Sir William à Beckett – one of the two most respected judicial figures in the colony, not to mention one of the founding fathers of both the Melbourne Public Library[3] and Melbourne University. There is a strong feeling that if he can't provide justice, no-one can. (True, there had been a slight kerfuffle many years before when on his trip to Australia in 1839 the ship's captain had been obliged to confine the young tearaway lawyer to his cabin to thwart the raging and very public love affair he was conducting with a female passenger – a woman every bit as beautiful as she was married – but it takes more than that to do a man down in these parts. As a matter of fact, even in the here and now, Judge Barry is not married to the woman who has already borne him two children – the small, dark-haired and strong-willed Louisa Barrow – but not even that is a problem.) He is also known to be a mostly kindly man, even if he is too kindly for some. It is known that, when a barrister, he frequently represented the natives, for free, if you can believe it.

As they take their place prior to the proceedings proper, the four accused prisoners sit glowering, none more than Bentley himself. His wife, Catherine, sits beside him, looking pale and unwell, though this admittedly may be because she is clearly not far away from confinement – perhaps in both senses of the word. Through the course of the day she is frequently seen to sob.

And why wouldn't she?

To begin the case, the Crown Prosecutor, Attorney-General Stawell, offers a new witness who did not testify at the previous hearing. He is the waiter from the Eureka Hotel, Michael Welsh, who tells the court that on the night in question he had personally seen Scobie arguing through the broken window with one of the accused, William Hance, entirely destroying the notion that the victim had no interaction with anyone in the hotel before he was carried there. This evidence is corroborated by Tom Mooney's crucial testimony. The hotel's nightwatchman not only gives details of the subsequent assault, but also swears that his boss, Bentley, had told him to lie!

'He told me not to say anything about it except that two men were in the front of the house and he was in bed himself and that the two men went away . . . When Bentley returned from the Camp with the police he called me in again and again told me not to say anything more than he previously directed . . .

'I did not tell what I knew at the inquest, nor did any of the witnesses there. I said nothing, because Bentley told me to keep it quiet, and it would all go off like a bottle of smoke. I denied all I knew, because Bentley told me to do so, and to keep it all very secret.'[4]

It is devastating testimony, demonstrating from an obviously sincere man that Bentley, Farrell and Hance have been lying through their teeth, making all of their denials worthless. The only saving grace for the three men is that when the Attorney-General asks nightwatchman Mooney to identify the accused, he falters.

Going up to Hance, he confirms his identity, but then before Farrell he says, 'This man I don't know, he was not one.' The gallery gasps. Standing right in front of the glaring Bentley, he stares at him for some time and again says, 'I do not know this man, he is not one of them.'[5]

This time the gallery bursts into uproarious laughter, prompting Judge Barry to sternly admonish, 'This Court is not to be constantly made the scene for levity and outbursts of laughter. I will the very next time order the Court to be cleared. This is the most solemn enquiry that can take place anywhere.'[6]

Mooney defends himself. 'Bentley is altered or else my eyesight is. I am not a madman. I have not been in a lunatic asylum.'[7]

It is a curious episode, but it has not swayed the court's view that Bentley had indeed told him to lie. And yet can it be established that the actions of the defendants actually *killed* Scobie?

It is here that the evidence of Dr Alfred Carr is crucial. After being sworn in, the remarkably diffident doctor gets to the thrust of his testimony.

'He was quite dead when I first saw him,' he says of Scobie. 'There was no trace of life. He was warm. I had him removed to the hotel, and sent for the police. I made a post mortem examination next day. There was a bruise on the left collarbone, a severe bruise over the lips, especially the upper lip. The right cheek very much bruised and grazed. The right eyebrow, the lower part of the upper lid was slightly bruised and grazed. Also near the nose. There were two slight bruises on the head. I detected no wound from which blood could flow except from the nose . . .

'I think it highly improbable that a spade would have caused these wounds, unless it was that one on the side of the head. The witness Martin was very tipsy, tumbling about the hotel. In about half an hour after, he gave an account of how the occurrence happened. In the state of Scobie's stomach a very slight blow would have occasioned death.'[8]

It is those last words that are the most staggering, as noted by the correspondent for *The Argus*. 'According to his statement, no wound had been inflicted by the spade; nor were any of the wounds apparently of a serious nature. Indeed, he seemed to treat the cause of death as a very light affair, and was disposed to think that it might have resulted from a fall, or from some trifling blow.'[9]

Finally, however, at the end of the long day, the prosecution is finished, the defence rests, the jury retires to begin its deliberations and . . .

And, *hulloa!*, the jury is already back

They have taken just 15 minutes to make their deliberations.

Has the jury reached a decision?

We have, Your Honour.

'We find James Francis Bentley, William Henry Hance and Thomas Farrell all guilty of manslaughter. We find Catherine Bentley innocent of all charges.'

Their sentencing is to be in two days' time, on the Monday morning, at which point Judge Barry will then preside on his next case: the three men charged over the burning of the Eureka Hotel.

Monday, 20 November 1854, Melbourne feels denuded

Colonial Secretary John Foster is worried. It has been one thing to have 450 armed men on the ground in the highly troublesome area of Ballarat, and they still have some more in reserve, but what if Ballarat should flare again and they have to send reinforcements? Who, then, would be able to guard Melbourne? Already there are rumours of armed diggers marching on the city, and there is also the matter of the Russians, who are at war with Britain in the Crimea, and might also be disposed to attack elsewhere. It is for this reason that Foster writes on behalf of the Lieutenant-Governor to the Assistant Military Secretary, William F. A. Wallace, to enable one of the volunteer corps of riflemen to be put on stand-by. (Under an Act just passed by the Legislative Council, loyal subjects are enabled to enrol in one of these volunteer corps, which could be called upon to serve in times of crisis, side by side with Her Majesty's forces, with their officers to be appointed by His Excellency.) The Melbourne Volunteer Rifle Regiment was the first formed, and joined shortly thereafter by the Richmond Rifles, the Victorian Yeomanry Corps, the Geelong Volunteer Rifle Corps, the East Collingwood Rifles and the FitzRoy Volunteer Rifles, commanded by none other than

Judge-cum-Captain Redmond Barry – a dab shot, if he does say so himself.

For Foster, the point now is to formally notify the colony's military authorities: 'Recent events have pointed out to [His Excellency] the uncertain temper of the vast population of the Goldfields; no-one from day to day can tell when an outbreak may arise, and therefore . . . it is upon these Volunteer Corps that the [Lieutenant-Governor] depends to guard the Cities if the 40th Regiment should suddenly be required elsewhere.'[10]

Yes, the 12th is on its way to the goldfields, and if something happens that the 40th must go too, the volunteers have to be ready. Their best hope is that nothing else will greatly upset the diggers, no provocation that might act as a catalyst for another uprising . . .

Wednesday evening, 22 November 1854, Ballarat makes a demand

The goldfields remain aflame. A serious injustice has been done and it must be put right. On this evening the executive committee of the Ballarat Reform League meets at the usual watering hole of the moral-force Chartists, the Star Hotel. There, in a back room clutching their nobblers, they resolve that the best way forward is for a delegation from the diggers, composed of Black and Kennedy, to return to Melbourne (along with Humffray, they had just been there to formally observe the trial and sentencing of Fletcher, McIntyre and Westerby on behalf of the League) and wait upon His Excellency, the Lieutenant-Governor. If they put their case in reasonable terms to a reasonable man, surely they will be rewarded with a reasonable result. Surely these iniquitous sentences will be overturned by the representative of Her Majesty's law and order, her *justice*, in this colony. The key sticking point at the meeting – and it does become very heated – is whether to use the word 'demand' or 'petition' in their statement to the Lieutenant-Governor. By a bare majority they finally settle on 'demand'[11] because the committee sees 'the stronger, but less politic, word as honestly expressive of their own and the public opinion in reference to the matter'.[12]

Obvious to most diggers is that, just as by their combined and vigorous might they have been able to alter the course of justice in the Scobie case, so too must they do the same when it comes to the three innocent men in prison. They don't want to merely beg for justice, they *demand* it! There is a monster meeting of the Ballarat Reform League coming up the following Wednesday. That will be the obvious time for Black and Kennedy to report back to them what the Lieutenant-Governor has said to them in Melbourne. From there they can determine their course of action, and that upcoming monster meeting is already arousing a great deal of interest.

Saturday, 25 November 1854, Ballarat receives good news

Gather round lads and look at this!

From everywhere they come – from every digging, from the bottom of every hole, from every tent – for the front page of *The Ballarat Times* has the news they've all been waiting to hear:

TRIAL OF
MR AND MRS BENTLEY
Hanse, and Farrel,
FOR THE MURDER OF
JAMES SCOBIE.
Supreme Court, Melbourne.
GUILTY! of Manslaughter.
Mrs Bentley scot-free.
His Honour considered their conduct

was wanton and reckless. He should
mark his sense of the outrage of which
they have been found guilty, by passing on each of them a sentence of
THREE (!) YEARS' IMPRISON-
MENT WITH HARD LABOUR
ON THE ROADS.[13]

No, it is not the murder conviction the diggers wanted, but it is something alright. Sentenced for manslaughter to three years' hard labour on the roads is a whole lot better for that bastard – and he probably *is* a bastard – than getting off scot-free. And it is vindication for the destructive action that the diggers took against the Eureka Hotel.

If the people had not reacted to the situation en masse and with outrage, justice would not have prevailed. United, they have shifted the course of the government and its judiciary!

And yet there is a rather troubling article in the edition of *The Ballarat Times*:

TRIAL OF

FLETCHER, MCINTYRE AND WESTERBY
for
BURNING THE EUREKA HOTEL
Supreme Court, Melbourne.
CRIMINAL SITTINGS.

GUILTY, WITH A RECOMMENDATION TO MERCY![14]

'The Foreman of the jury appended the following rider to the verdict: "The jury feel, in giving their verdict against the prisoners at the bar, that in all probability [the jury] should never have had that painful duty to perform if those entrusted with the government offices at Ballaarat had done theirs properly. His Honour said: "The sentence of the Court is that you, McIntyre, be confined in H. M. Gaol at Melbourne for three months, but I shall not subject you to labour. You, Fletcher, to four months and you, Westerby, to six months confinement . . .".'[15]

The diggers' reaction is pure outrage. When a thousand of them had participated in meting out true justice to a real murderer that the judiciary had let off, these brave men had to spend time in gaol? When even one of the authorities, Commissioner Gilbert Amos himself, had wonderfully testified that McIntyre, for one, was not guilty of what he had been charged with? *Still,* the judge found them guilty?

So heated is the feeling among the diggers that it would be the later testimony of Commissioner Robert Rede that on the very afternoon that news of the ongoing imprisonment of the three diggers breaks, he receives a credible threat that if they are not immediately released and have their convictions for arson overturned, the Government Camp would be burned down.

Clearly, the situation is getting out of hand.

All over the goldfields, posters printed by Henry Seekamp's presses are nailed to every solid vertical surface available:

DOWN WITH the LICENSE FEE

DOWN WITH DESPOTISM

WEDNESDAY NEXT
ON BAKERY HILL[16]

As to the views of Henry Seekamp, he leaves little doubt as his prose in his newspapers reaches for the full revolutionary heights and sets the tone. Not for nothing would admiring digger John Lynch say of *The Ballarat Times*, 'When hard hitting had to be done, it could deal blows like the hammer of Thor.'[17]

It is not for us to say how much we have been instrumental in rousing up the people to a sense of their wrongs, we leave that to the public and the world. The coming Christmas is pregnant of change, for on next Wednesday will be held such a meeting for a fixed determinate purposes as was never before held in Australia. The Australian flag shall triumphantly wave in the sunshine of its own blue and peerless sky over thousands of Australia's adopted sons. And when the loud paean of

NOW'S THE DAY AND NOW'S THE HOUR,

SEE THE FRONT OF BATTLE LOUR,

shall have pierced the blue vaults of Australia's matchless sky, from the brave men of Ballarat on next Wednesday at Bakery Hill, there will not be one discordant voice in the sublime and heroic chorus. Go forth indomitable people! Gain your rights, and may the God of creation smile down propitiously upon your glorious cause! **FORWARD PEOPLE, FORWARD!**'[18]

What makes the whole issue of Fletcher, McIntyre and Westerby even more galling is that only four days earlier the Board of Inquiry, which interviewed 58 witnesses at Bath's Hotel in the first weeks of November, released a public report heavily covered in the newspapers that went a long way towards acknowledging that the diggers' outrage over both the collection of license fees and the Scobie case were justified! In the case of the Bentley trial, it said, 'the Bench's decision was opposed to the facts and evidence elicited', the effect of which created 'a unanimity in the popular feeling' among the rioters.[19]

But look what the Board said about the man in charge of that whole case!

'A subject of deep regret', it noted, is how Police Magistrate John Dewes 'laid himself under obligation to a class of person whose conduct in their capacity of licensed victuallers brought them under the supervision and scrutiny of the Bench of which he was Chairman, thereby subjecting himself to influences unbecoming to his position as police magistrate and public officer'.[20]

Exactly!

Among the report's final conclusions is the observation that 'hunting sly grog sellers and taking up unlicensed miners' have made the police 'very obnoxious to the diggers, and it had a most pernicious effect on the morals of the police force . . .

'With regard to the employment of Police in arresting unlicensed miners, your Board believe that no duty in which the police are employed is so calculated as to render them hateful to the population as this . . . Your Board are therefore of the opinion that, were the license fee abolished, and the police released from the false position in which they are placed by being made collectors of revenue, their efficiency would be greatly increased, their moral influence with the community would be raised, and, as a consequence, the extent of the force which is now hardly adequate to the duties required would no longer be necessary.'[21]

For the trouble Dewes has caused them, for the way he has conducted recent judicial proceedings in a manner that has subverted 'public confidence in the integrity and impartiality of the the Bench',[22] His Excellency has already directed that 'the name of Mr Dewes be erased from the Commission of the Peace, and that he be informed that the Lieutenant-Governor has no further occasion for his services'.[23] The government had even gone one better and announced the week earlier that another, more powerful Goldfields Commission of Enquiry would soon be set up to investigate the whole administration of the law at the goldfields.

Despite this tacit recognition that the administration of law was lacking and the official acknowledgement that Dewes had been corrupt – which had, after all, been the primary cause for the Eureka Hotel being burnt down – the government had *still* gaoled McIntyre, Fletcher and Westerby. Hopefully, the diggers' delegation will be able to sort this out in person with Sir Charles Hotham.

Some on the goldfields, however, do not wish to wait and would prefer a more violent means of liberating the diggers. That evening Commissioner Rede is visited, as he immediately informs his superiors, 'by a person in whose veracity I believe I can rely, but who does not wish his name to appear', that in the event of His Excellency the Lieutenant-Governor refusing to liberate the prisoners McIntyre, Fletcher and Westby [Westerby], a large number of persons have pledged themselves to attack the Camp and drive the officials off this Gold Field.'[24] With every passing day, the mood at Ballarat is blackening.

Monday morning, 27 November 1854, Sir Charles receives some visitors

This way please, er . . . gentlemen.

The truth of it is that the three men who have just arrived at the government offices in William Street are of a breed not usually sighted within this heart of colonial power. For though they are well-educated men, nothing can disguise the fact that George Black, Tom Kennedy and John Basson Humffray – who has joined the delegation, uninvited, in Melbourne – are . . . miners . . . from the diggings. Large, weathered men with ruddy faces and rough hands, there is the look of unease about them, though whether it is because they are in such august surroundings or because they have the unpleasant duty of talking to him and his leading officials, Hotham is yet to determine.

For not only are they ushered into the presence of His Excellency himself, but also that of his two key executive officers in the persons of Colonial Secretary John Foster and Attorney-General William Stawell.

Gentlemen, please state your business and why you have requested this audience . . .

It is the startlingly blue-eyed George Black who takes the lead, addressing the Lieutenant-Governor directly, and from the first it is obvious that he is not shy.

'We are here, Your Excellency,' he states simply, 'at the request of the diggers of Ballarat. We are requested to demand the release of Fletcher, McIntyre and Westerby, who are now in gaol under sentence for having been concerned in the burning of the Eureka Hotel –'[25]

Sir Charles interrupts Black even before he is properly launched.

'You have made use,' he says with insistent iciness, 'of one word which I think it my duty at once to allude to; and that is the word "demand". You "demand", you say, the release of men who have been convicted for burning the Eureka Hotel. Was that not what you said?'[26]

'That is the message,' Black replies, 'which we have been requested to deliver to Your Excellency. The word "demand" we were requested to use on behalf of the diggers of Ballarat to Your Excellency. They, from frequent disappointments, or from former disappointments, object to the use of the word "petition" now. It is not that there is any wish to hold out threats to Your Excellency . . .'[27]

Sir Charles is not moved. Even if he might want to, he says, he cannot take the law into his own hands. The fact that the verdict was reached by 12 good men and true of a properly constituted jury, and the sentence imposed by a lawfully appointed judge, means he has no capacity to change either the verdict or the sentence arrived at.

If he were to intervene, he says, 'I should inflict the greatest blow that could possibly be inflicted upon the welfare of the colony.'[28]

(Besides which, as one who feels his true calling at this time would have been leading his men to naval battle on the Baltic Sea as part of the Crimea War, he is highly indisposed to be seen backing down to a bunch of rich, disgruntled diggers.)

No matter, the delegates continue to make their case. Together, they had spent the better part of the day before discussing the situation on the goldfields with Ebenezer Syme, the nearly 30-year-old Scottish journalist who is now working on *The Argus*, and, together, they now push the points they had agreed would most likely resonate with Sir Charles.

Their point now is that even if the men in question had broken Her Majesty's law, they had broken no moral law, and it is only right that this be recognised. Alas, the Lieutenant-Governor, backed by his Colonial Secretary and Attorney-General, reiterates that in good faith the results of the case in question cannot be altered, no matter what.

But now it is the miners' turn to be insistent.

'I solemnly implore you,' says Kennedy to the Lieutenant-Governor, 'to consider the position in which you are placed, and if it were no other reason than that of keeping back the spilling of blood, which must be the case with infuriated men, let us have peace, even if thought inconsistent with the dignity of the British Crown.'[29]

But the man who represents that dignity is not inclined to cede, and does not hesitate in saying so. His Attorney-General is equally imitative of a stone wall when Black raises the subject of the Constitution Bill and the fact that 'no digger can be elected to a seat in the Assembly unless he is worth one or two thousand pounds of freehold property. They object to this'.[30]

William Stawell is nothing if not frank, saying flatly to Sir Charles, 'The power does not exist, either in Your Excellency or in the Legislative Council to alter it.'[31]

But Black will not back off.

'I think you scarcely understand what I mean; it is this. The

Legislative Council in framing that bill for the new Constitution could have enfranchised the diggers and could have given to them universal suffrage. Instead of having inserted a clause in the bill requiring the diggers to take out a twelve months' license, they could have inserted a clause giving them the franchise without that qualification. That is what I mean. That was not done, and because it was not done, that is why they feel an injustice has been done to them.'[32]

The Colonial Secretary, John Foster, is unmoved, saying, 'The Legislature did not see any reason why the diggers should have universal suffrage more than any other class of the community.'[33]

Then Black raises another issue that has the diggers worked up. 'I am desired by the married men of Ballarat to make a request of Your Excellency. It is this, that every possible facility may be afforded by Your Excellency to enable them to settle and have their wives and families there. They are all anxious to settle upon the land, but at present the difficulties of their so doing are too great, and I am requested to bring that subject especially before Your Excellency's notice.'

'That is a point which presses very much,' Sir Charles acknowledges, 'but it is of such a very serious character that . . . I can give no answer at present further than agreeing with you in the necessity of some provision being made.'

'I find by looking over the land that has been selected for sale,' Black comes back, 'and the sales that have taken place, that the very best land, or rather the land of the very best quality, is put up in the largest allotments, so that only men of capital can purchase the good land and the poorer land is cut up into small slices for the diggers.'

'That shall be looked to,' says Sir Charles, even as he looks at the clock, 'and considered certainly.'

There is really nowhere further to go on the matter.

And yet Kennedy simply cannot help himself from having one more pointed go, telling His Excellency with some force, 'Sir Robert Peel did not think it beneath him to change his mind, and we hope you will grant the diggers their wishes on this point of the release of these men.'[34]

Yes, Sir Robert Peel had famously changed his mind on the matter of the Corn Laws and repealed the protection of homegrown grain, but that was in another time and another place, and even then Sir Robert had authority to do so. Even if Lieutenant-Governor Hotham had the authority to make the diggers' changes, frankly, he would not be so inclined.

Other matters beckon.

'Passing from that subject,' Black says, 'we would wish to know from Your Excellency what the government intend to do with regard to giving the diggers full and equal representation . . .'

'You know that a despatch has gone home asking for the franchise,' His Excellency replies. 'This event took place before my coming into the colony and therefore I cannot speak with confidence upon it. You know also that I have no power to deal with the question, and could not do so if I would. You know also, as I have said before, that if the diggers will elect a nominee I will at once put him in and shall only be too glad to do it . . .'

'I am quite sure,' Black replies rather archly, 'that only one seat in the Council would not satisfy the diggers.'

It is an obviously reasonable point, but Sir Charles is not moved.

'I have not the means of doing more,' he says. 'You are asking me to do that which is impossible, and an impossibility cannot be got over.'

He does, however, draw their attention to the fact that 'a commission has been appointed composed of gentlemen almost all of whom are in opposition to the government, and almost all of whom are representative members of the Legislature, selected with very great care purposely to enquire into the state of the goldfields, and it will be for you to come forward and state fairly and frankly to them what you require.'

George Black, for one, is not impressed, noting that the diggers would have been 'better satisfied with that board had [we] been allowed to appoint or elect one half of that board'.

Certainly they are happy with John Pascoe Fawkner, and no doubt with other members of the board, but that is not the point. The point is, once again, people have been put into a position of power by appointment, not by election! As a significant body, the Ballarat Reform League should have been consulted. Instead, it is being *told* from on high.

'I can only conclude by saying this,' Sir Charles says. 'You have placed me in a position which renders the release of these men impossible . . . As it has been observed, we have all of us to give an account to those above us, and it cannot be. I am sorry for it. Tell the diggers from me, and tell them carefully, that this commission will enquire into everything and everybody, high and low, rich and poor, and you have only to come forward and state your grievances, and, in what relates to me, they shall be redressed. I can say no more; we are all in a false position altogether. I can say no more than that.'[35]

The three delegates leave the government offices with nothing less than a blank refusal to cede on any front.

What is clear to Sir Charles is that things are now getting out of hand and he is thankful that that very morning – even before the deputation had arrived – he had issued orders for 70 rank and file men of the 12th Regiment under the command of Captain Richard Atkinson and 50 Redcoats of the 40th Regiment under Captain Henry Wise to be dispatched by steamer to Geelong, with instructions to proceed at all speed to Ballarat. Captain Wise, for one, is chafing at the bit to go. Though from a fine family in England with the capacity to give him a very comfortable life without ever having to put himself in danger, he had always been one hungering for adventure, for action, and this certainly looks to be both.

A body of mounted police troopers is also placed under orders to proceed to the scene of the action, taking with them two pieces of artillery. *The Argus* reports they are to be followed by 'large drafts from the City and District police . . . their places being supplied by special constables, who are to be sworn in forthwith'.[36]

Monday evening, 27 November 1854, Government Camp receives a man in black

It is a very difficult meeting to participate in, but Father Smyth feels he has no choice. Deeply troubled by the direction things are heading, on this night he slips towards the Government Camp under cover of darkness and is soon taken to see Commissioner Rede. On the strict understanding that the Commissioner must never make use of Smyth's name in any public forum, the priest tells him that things are taking a very dangerous turn. He fears that the emotions are so high among the diggers that there will soon be a 'general assault on the Camp'.[37]

Speaking urgently but quietly, a man torn between his commitment to civic peace and his loyalty to his flock – a flock he does not wish to see shot to pieces – he tells the Commissioner that the diggers are far better organised than anyone in the Government Camp can conceive and that no fewer than '1000 rifles can be brought to one spot'.[38] It is on the strength of this warning that Commissioner Rede calls in the Sub-Inspector of Police, Samuel Furnell, an honest man who has been with Victoria Police since the crisis of filling the ranks hit in December 1852 and has risen quickly from there. Father Smyth says that he would 'tell much more but feared to do so, that things [are] in a dreadful state . . . The only people not mixed up in it are the English. Amongst the agitators are men of most determined character and they are resolved to put down the Government at all costs'.[39]

Deeply concerned at all this information, Commissioner Rede thanks the holy man, who takes his leave, the darkness soon swallowing his black-frocked figure whole.

Yet his words have had an effect on the Englishman, for no sooner has the priest departed than the Commissioner writes a frank missive to Colonial Secretary John Foster.

'If law and order are to exert on the Goldfields, and I still believe that nothing but crushing the agitators' movement can do it – should such a measure be intended a large force would be required . . . Whatever His Excellency may decide as to reinforcements I have one urgent request to make which is that Captain Thomas or some officer of known capability be sent up without delay as I do not place confidence in the present Officer.'[40]

It is an astute choice. Captain John Wellesley Thomas is the softly spoken career officer who has already done great work improving the security at the Camp when he was on Ballarat a month earlier, and that is precisely what Rede feels he needs more of at this moment, as the situation deteriorates. It is one thing to have many men under arms, but having them properly organised militarily is quite another, and as that is not something within Rede's field of training, Thomas would be a good fit.

As it turns out, Thomas is already on his way.

Tuesday morning, 28 November 1854, Ballarat boils

There is revolution in the air. It is not open rebellion, yet, but that heady sense that the diggers are rising against an iniquitous regime is everywhere, touching everything. All over the diggings, notices have been placed on posts, on walls, on anything standing still, advising of a meeting to be held on the morrow, mates:

DOWN WITH the LICENSE FEE

DOWN WITH DESPOTISM!

'WHO SO BASE AS BE A SLAVE?'

ON

WEDNESDAY NEXT

The 29th Instant, at Two o'clock

A MEETING

Of all the DIGGERS; STOREKEEPERS, and Inhabitants
of Ballarat generally, will be held

ON BAKERY HILL

For the immediate Abolition of the License Fee, and the speedy attainment of the other objects of the Ballarat Reform League. The report of the Deputations which have gone to the Lieutenant-Governor to demand the release of the prisoners lately convicted, and to Creswick and Forest Creeks, Bendigo, &c., will also be submitted at the same time.

All who claim the right to a voice in the framing of the Laws under which they should live, are solemnly bound to attend the Meeting and further its objects to the utmost extent of their power.

N.B. Bring your Licenses, they may be wanted.[41]

PRINTED AT THE TIMES OFFICE, BAKERY HILL, BALLARAT

It is with great interest that the increasingly alarmed authorities note that the posters have been printed in the office of Henry Seekamp's *Ballarat Times*.

Tuesday morning, 28 November 1854, Melbourne looks north-west with anxiety

The good people of Melbourne are watching events in Ballarat with a growing, fearful fascination. On this day *The Argus* reports, in an article entitled 'GOVERNMENT BY ARTILLERY', 'Intelligence reached town yesterday that the diggers at Ballarat were in open revolt and had seized upon Commissioner Rede and Inspector Evans, as hostages, till the release of the three men now in the Eureka riot. How this is true, we are unable positively to state but it is certain that troops, police, and artillery, have again been ordered up to the scene of action. This looks serious; and we fear that we may shortly have to report very sorrowful news indeed . . .

'But threatening as appearances may be, the Government is now but receiving the due reward of its deeds. It sowed the wind, and it is reaping the whirlwind . . .

'If blood be shed, the results will probably be very serious indeed . . . To fire rashly or inconsiderately upon such a mob would be to throw down the gauntlet of battle, and plunge the colony in the calamities of civil war.

'But on the other hand we must warn the diggers that it is no slight affair upon which they are entering. They have a gentleman to deal with who will not bear to be trifled with. Sir Charles Hotham is, as he himself expresses it, 'a man of war', and as one who has smelt gunpowder, he is not likely to mince matters . . .'[42]

Tuesday afternoon, 28 November 1854, an English officer arrives at the Government Camp in Ballarat

As opposed to many of the military men now in Ballarat, the newest arrival to the troubled town, Captain Charles Pasley, is not here because he has been commanded to be so. The 30-year-old Englishman is a high-ranking army officer with the Royal Engineers and of impeccable pedigree. His father is Sir Charles Pasley, founder of the Royal Military School of Engineering in 1812 and the current Colonel Commandant of the Royal Engineers. Charles Jnr is now the Colonial Engineer of Victoria and recently appointed by Lieutenant-Governor Hotham to the Legislative Council, so there are few who can actually give him orders.

Militarily, he is second-in-command to Captain Wellesley Thomas, who arrived again just the day before, but politically he reigns supreme on these goldfields. He has come from Melbourne at his own request, because, as he would explain in a letter to his father, he is fully cognisant of the political implications of the unrest should it start to grow in amplitude and spread to other diggings.

'I thought the consequences would be very serious, and at the same time, if [we soldiers] resisted and were beaten in fights by the insurgents I had no doubt that a general rebellion would ensue. Feeling as I did upon the subject I thought it was my duty to offer my services at once, as I could not tell whether the authorities at Ballarat were as much impressed as I was with the importance of the events which must occur in a very few days.'[43]

True, the reason he had been nominated to the Legislative Council in the first place had been to mollify him after the Lieutenant-Governor, without consulting the Executive Council or anyone else as far as Pasley could see, had appointed a rival as Director of Public Works. A pity, because Charles Pasley, too, really prefers building things to tearing them down. But now he is on the ground, in the middle of the greatest issue of the day, and determined to prove himself in this sphere.

He is appalled by what he observes upon his arrival at the Government Camp:

'I . . . found a small force . . . in an exposed and defenceless camp, consisting of tents and light wooden buildings, by no means musket proof, surrounded on three sides by hills and houses, pressing close upon it.'[44]

The one positive thing that he can see is the presence of Captain Thomas, whom, though they have never met before, he likes a great deal and immediately respects for his 'steady, resolute, business-like, and at the same time quiet manner'.[45]

The two soldiers immediately get to work on how they can make the Camp more secure, and it is Pasley who comes up with the first serious idea, which Thomas immediately embraces. Noting how many habitations there are that practically surround the Camp, it becomes obvious that the buildings have to be neutralised as a staging point from which any attack could be launched. So Thomas and Pasley immediately call all the householders of the township together and tell them, frankly, that if that does happen their houses will be burnt to the ground. It is their duty to maintain the Camp's position at any cost, including lost life and property, but they feel equally obliged to give fair warning to that effect so the residents and shop-owners can make their arrangements accordingly.

'I believe this had a very good effect,' Pasley tells his father, 'because it brought their pecuniary interests on the side of order. This was not however a mere threat – it was fully intended to be carried out, and I had prepared fire balls to throw on the houses if necessary.'[46]

It is something, anyway. Both men feel relieved that military reinforcements are not far off, as they had been due to leave Melbourne just behind them.

Tuesday evening, 28 November 1854, cries in the night on the Ballarat diggings

In that strong twilight hour of dusk, when the battle between day and night is at its most evenly balanced, when the air is thick with the delicious smoke of burning eucalyptus from the newly lit evening fires around the diggings, there is many a digger who has finished his day's work and is just getting ready to rustle up some grub when he suddenly cocks his ear to the softly-softly wind. Say, mate, what is that . . .? Horses? Yes, horses. Many of them. And that jingle-jangle of the stirrups, the occasional guttural command from far off and the odd screech of, yes, metal on rock, says it is most likely military horsemen, mounted troopers leading horse-drawn carts in which many foot soldiers and supplies are being transported. And sure enough, within minutes, 106 Redcoats of the 40th Regiment appear. Having arrived in Geelong aboard the steamer *Shandon* from Melbourne just before midnight the previous evening, they immediately embark on the approximately 60-mile journey to Ballarat,[47] and they are accompanied by a party of mounted police from Geelong.

From the beginning, and despite their obvious exhaustion at the end of such a long journey, the Redcoats have the manner about them of British men who are just *spoiling* for a battle – let the diggers make just one wrong move. This feeling is further exacerbated when their commanding officer, Captain Henry Wise, has his men load their muskets even as they unlatch the cartridge boxes that they have on their right hips attached to a shoulder belt, and *fix bayonets,* even as they march through the diggings. It is an aggressive move, calculated to demonstrate that a serious military force is now on the ground.

And so, of course, the diggers greet the arrivals in the now traditional manner . . . and the cry goes up.

'Joe!' *'Joe!'* 'JOE!'

Like a strange breed of rabbit, digger after digger pops his head up from his hole, or from behind a pile of earth beside it, or from out the flap of his tent, and spies the new arrivals and echoes: 'Joe!' *'Joe!'* 'JOE!'

Such calls arouse other diggers to take a look, and soon it has gone from the odd cry to an outcry: 'JOE!' 'JOE!' 'JOE!'[48]

Yes, the calls come in nigh on as many accents as there are diggers, but the common feature is taunting insolence. For it is not yelled by way of cheery greeting, but spat out with venom – a release of disgust that it has come to this, that the government is sending whole armed regiments to quell their legitimate plaints.

For their part, the troopers stare balefully back at these uncouth, rude and positively insolent mud-men from the mining shafts. The tension between the mounted and the miners is indeed so great that it is the opinion of *The Ballarat Times* that had the diggers themselves been armed at the time, 'nothing could have saved a collision'.[49]

Just as it is truly falling dark, the unmistakable sound of men approaching on horseback is heard once more . . .

―――――

Only a couple of miles away at this time, Ballarat is being visited by the Melbourne-based Consul of the United States, James Tarleton, a personal friend of no less than US President Franklin Pierce, who had taken up his posting some six months earlier. As Tarleton is representative of a nation whose birth was marked by the throwing off of British shackles under the cry of 'No taxation without representation', there is more interest than usual in his presence at such a tense time, by both the diggers in general and the authorities, not to mention the roughly 600 American diggers on the Ballarat goldfields.[50]

That evening there is a reception in honour of Thanksgiving Day to be held at the Victoria Saloon,[51] and both Commissioner Rede and Acting Police Magistrate Charles Prendergast Hackett – who had earnt his law degree from the prestigious Trinity College in Dublin – are sure to attend in their finery, together with other officials, the leading burghers of Ballarat and representatives from the *Geelong Advertiser*, *The Ballarat Times* and *The Melbourne Morning Herald*. Despite the fine clothes and wine, and the best silver on the goldfields set on the table, the tensions in the outside world, including the world far beyond Ballarat, do not abate.

Given that Great Britain is at war with Russia in the Crimea at this time, the former is more keen than usual to have close relations with its former adversary and increasingly important trading partner, the United States of America. The British fear that the Russians will invade Port Phillip Bay is so great that fortifications at the head of the bay are already being built on that contingency – just as they are in Sydney Harbour – while an armed steam sloop, *Victoria*, is being constructed. It is time for English-speaking countries to strengthen their ties, not loosen them.

So the delicate task at hand then is to persuade the Americans to cease and desist beating the republican drum while in Australia without antagonising them. At least, it appears that Tarleton is aware of his diplomatic responsibilities as he notes to the gathered Americans in the audience how important it is 'to obey the laws and instructions of this country'[52] and how sure he is that his country-men will 'abstain from interference in the present agitation'.[53] It is heartening that both such sentiments are greeted with great applause from the Americans present.

Against that, quietly, Commissioner Rede has his suspicions, as he would subsequently report to his superiors 'that the Americans are playing a deep game' and 'without appearing to take any part in the [protest] meetings . . . they are in a most insidious manner urging on the mob without showing themselves, and I can only sup-pose it is with the view of Americanising this Colony'.[54]

Even as James Tarleton is making his speech, there is the sound of shots being fired in the distance. Tarleton soldiers on, but then one of Rede's underlings whispers something in the Commissioner's ear, something that visibly upsets him. He rises to respond to Tarleton when the time is right – congratulating the Consul on dispensing such wise advice to his countrymen – but excuses himself shortly thereafter as he must away on urgent business un-named, height-ening the sense that not far 'neath the seeming normality a crisis is building to its climax. The likelihood that this crisis involves a person or people breaking the law is apparent in that Magistrate Charles Hackett, who has been seated just to the right of the Consul, is in close attendance on Rede as he leaves.

The sound of more gunshots in the distance does nothing to dispel this sense. Conversation invariably ceases for seconds at a time . . . All strain to hear if there are any follow-up shots. No? Then it is only an isolated act of anger, and perhaps not worth worrying about for the moment.

The evening's proceedings continue with a very well-cut and obviously intelligent young American digger by the name of James McGill, who claims to have been trained at the United States Military Academy at West Point, rising to graciously respond to a toast that has been made to the US Army, in which he says he has had the great honour to serve. And yet, soon afterwards, when another aide comes in and whispers into the ear of James Tarleton, the Consul, too, presents his excuses and heads away to troubles unknown.

But enough of that for now . . .

It is time for the chairman, the venerable and impressively named Dr William Beauclerk Otway – an Englishman who served in the US Army before becoming a digger – who now stands for a toast.

'Gentlemen,' he says, lifting his glass, 'to Her Majesty, the Queen.'
. . .

There is no response!

Protocol would have deemed it proper for Commissioner Rede to respond to the toast to Her Majesty Queen Victoria. In his absence, alas, not one of the Queen's loyal subjects steps forward to do the honours and an exceedingly awkward silence falls upon the room.

For Otway is joined by . . . no-one? Yes, no-one.

Unable to bear it a second longer, Otway, appalled at this affront to Her Majesty, says if no British subject will volunteer, then he will toast her alone.

Not to be outdone, at this point the chief correspondent for *The*

Ballarat Times, Samuel Irwin, leaving behind all notions that a journalist should be a chronicler of events and not a participant therein – he is, after all, a fully paid-up member of the Ballarat Reform League – jumps to his feet. 'While I and my fellow Colonists claim to be, and are thoroughly loyal to our sovereign lady the Queen, we do not, and will not respect her men servants, her oxen, or her asses.'[55]

With these last words he gestures towards the recently vacated chairs of Rede and Hackett and is rewarded by 'tumultuous applause'[56] from seemingly all present, including, of course, many of the American diggers.

The Americans have been in quite a sensitive position on the diggings as the situation has become more and more unstable. They have always been regarded with a gimlet eye by the colonial authorities for their revolutionary leanings, and for that reason have been careful not to push themselves to the fore in the protests.

'But the time had now come,' American digger Charles Ferguson would later recount, 'when we were compelled to act or stand neutral. Others complained that we were doing nothing . . . and began to accuse us of cowardice . . . [though we] were in full and hearty sympathy with the miners . . . We told them that if they went on they would have our sympathy, and if they made a stand they would not find us wanting, but we were not going to have it thrown upon our shoulders that we were the instigators of the outbreak, which it would be if it failed, and which, I ventured to add, it would; for which remark I was called a coward.'[57]

The time is indeed coming fast, bearing down upon them, when every man will have to choose between standing neutral and acting.

———

Back out on the goldfields, no-one challenges the capricious rule of cruel chaos in the moonlight. The latest arrival has been a company from the 12th Regiment, which is the 40th's brother regiment. And while there are ways to get to the Government Camp that do not involve marching right by the diggings, the soldiers do not take that sensible option and are soon in the thick of diggers who suddenly feel invaded. This provocative move proves to be even more unwise because this time the soldiers march without muskets loaded or bayonets bared, making themselves easy targets. And to make matters worse, they then get lost in the thin light.

It is an opportunity too good to miss. The diggers around Eureka – where the more hot-headed of the Irish are thicker than fleas on a stray dog – perhaps regretting that they had let the 40th through relatively unscathed, are even more aggressive in their hooted derision. This time they press in even closer, demanding to know if the drays bear any weapons to be used on the diggers in coming days?

The commanding officer of the 12th, Captain Richard Atkinson, who is appalled at their presumption, draws himself high on his remarkably high horse, and says he wishes to hold 'no communication with rebels'.[58]

It is not just his haughty words, however, but the manner in which the Englishman delivers them that infuriates the mob, and what little remains of their self-control suddenly evaporates in an outpouring of heated emotion.

Of an instant, they suddenly rush the Captain, crying 'JOE! JOE!', whereupon, as reported by *The Ballarat Times*, 'The gallant officer galloped away as fast as possible across the ranges leaving his men to do the best they could in his absence!'[59] That best, alas, was not very good at all.

To the cries of 'JOE!' is soon added a flurry of bottles, rocks, sticks – anything the diggers can get their hands on to demonstrate their complete contempt – all of which trace perfect arcs in the dusky twilight to land on and around the soldiers and startled horses in a rain of rebellion.

In the face of it, many a Redcoat are visibly shaken, and some of the soldiers respond by firing wild shots in the direction that the missiles are coming from. Just what kind of a place is this? What have they let themselves in for? *What are they facing?*

As it happens, this last question is still being decided, but the outcry is not quite as spontaneous as it seems. In fact, there have been rumours all over the goldfields just in recent hours that the three representatives they have sent to Melbourne have been arrested and the government, intent on massacre, is now sending cannon to the goldfields to train upon the meeting the following day. So neither the question, nor the diggers' response to the government's answer, is particularly surprising.

The diggers fall upon the last two carts they fear might contain cannon. In the melee, groups of soldiers become separated from each other and therefore vulnerable. Some have been shot at, and a handful savagely beaten, while a drummer boy, John Egan, a 'favourite with the men',[60] is shot in the thigh. Two officers, Police Sub-Inspector Samuel Furnell and his boss, Senior Sub-Inspector Thomas Langley, are shaken as bullets have passed so close to their heads they have heard them. (The diggers, too, have sustained damage. Brenden Hassell, a co-owner of the London Hotel, was standing in the doorway of his establishment shortly after giving an officer of the 12th Regiment directions to the Government Camp when the first shots were fired. One bullet came from out of the dark and shattered his shin.)

Not all the diggers are pleased with the affair. Watching the whole thing, Samuel Lazarus would shortly record in his diary:

It was a lovely moonlight night and the soft placid beauty of the sky was strangely at variance with the scene below where hootings groans curses the clatter of horses feet and the rattle of swords made up a horrible din which it would be difficult to describe. It is some relief to the feelings of Englishmen to know that the row was commenced and principally carried on by the worst portion of the digging community – old Convicts and Tipperary men, for no man however well disposed towards the diggers interests can disguise the fact from himself that it was a cowardly affair.[61]

Back at the Camp, Captain Wise of the 40th bursts through the main entrance, caught between outrage at what has just occurred and joy at being back on the premises. The previous year he had spent time stationed here in charge of the pensioner force, and the beaming young officer is soon awash in handshakes from old friends and acquaintances who are equally delighted to see him. Wise and his regiment were overdue and those at the Camp were worried. And yet there is little time for such hail-fellow-well-met, under the circumstances. Suddenly, coming from the far distance, everyone is startled to hear the distinctive notes of a bugle from the distant realms of the Melbourne Road.

In this man's army, every bugle call has a different meaning, and this is one of alarm. Their troops – probably the follow-up 12th Regiment – are under attack! This is confirmed an instant later by the sound of gunfire, followed by a police officer bursting into the Camp a few minutes later in nearly as much of a lather as his horse, babbling something of what has happened. It is time for a bugle call of their own in the Camp, and when that call goes out the result is instantaneous as the mounted troopers quickly assemble and gallop away – the cavalry to the rescue.

After they depart, Commissioner Rede's very timid and artistic Chief Clerk, Samuel Douglas Smyth Huyghue – since arriving here, he has felt 'a forlorn sense of exile under strange stars, and failed to recognize in the hard face of Australian nature, the face of a mother'[62] – goes to the lip of the escarpment of the Government Camp looking out on the diggings, and would later compose an evocative account of what it was like, what he saw and heard:

By this time it was intensely dark; one of those cloudless nights when the blackness under the stars seems palpable – but the entire area of the gold workings became transfigured into a sea of palpitating flame. First, far away on the Eureka line the illumination began through the lighting of innumerable fires and the incessant flashes from guns and revolvers discharged before each tent on the crowded slopes. It then spread gradually to Bakery Hill, the Gravel Pits, Red Streak and Golden Point – the most famous of the workings – until it lit up the whole valley beyond the Yarrowee and seemed to break into intenser surges of fire in the track of the approaching troops. I never witnessed such a sight before and probably never shall again. It was accompanied too by an ever-increasing roar from the throats of what might have been the entire mining population, which, fury-urged, rolled towards us as the voice of doom. Had a legion of gnomes burst raging from the 'swamped out' sinkings, with a chorus other than that of the frogs of Aristophanes, they could not have added much to the din of the infernal discord.[63]

Every now and then a galloping horseman returns, seeking fresh squadrons of reinforcements, which are in turn dispatched.

Meanwhile, out on the diggings, Raffaello Carboni is with some other miners on Bakery Hill discussing the news of the attack when a fresh detachment of Redcoats and mounted police arrives from the Camp, led by an officer of the 40th Regiment who is apoplectic with rage. His sword drawn, almost as if he would smite them all with a single blow, the officer accuses them of having launched the attack, 'pack of scoundrels'[64] that they are. It is with some difficulty that the officer is persuaded that they are not the instigators, in part because the miners sincerely offer to help find the soldiers still missing from the fracas. One is discovered in an abandoned tent, another in a hole down Warrenheip Gully way, and so forth until they are all collected.

As Carboni would note, that is not the end of the tension. Sporadic gunfire from sources unknown heightens the atmosphere of lawlessness, danger, revolution . . . coming fast.

Courtesy of the cavalry, the bulk of the 12th Regiment are able to gather themselves and fight their way back to the bridge over the Yarrowee. Hotly pursued by the angry diggers, they make their hurried way to the Camp and are more than relieved when the mob does not follow them over the bridge.

'Up to this point the mob stuck like hungry wolves close to the heels of the soldiers,' Samuel Huyghue would recount, 'only kept back by the bristling sabres of the cavalry. There however the troops charged; the insurgents were driven back, one being cut down and several wounded. Then they slowly retired with a roar of baffled rage, while the soldiers affected a passage and made good their entrance within the lines.'[65]

It is now 11 o'clock and Huyghue wanders among the battered and bewildered young soldiers who have only just made it to safety – six of whom have to be rushed to the infirmary – stunned at how youthful they appear.

'They were stripplings, mostly – half-weaned cubs of the Lion Mother, and had only just landed from the transport that brought them out from the Depot in sober England to receive their first lesson in "colonial experience" from the [diggers] of the Goldfields.'[66]

When apprised of the full details of what has happened, the outraged Commissioner Rede wastes little time in reporting the events to the Chief Commissioner of the Goldfields, Wright, and setting out his plans for the immediate future, most particularly pertaining to the meeting of the diggers that is scheduled to take place on the morrow. 'I have decided on the following mode of action. A magistrate accompanied by persons on whom I can depend will attend. They will report to one immediately if anything seditious is said or if any advice should be given to the miners to commit an illegal act. Immediately on receiving such report I shall proceed accompanied by the whole of the force I can take without endangering the safety of the Camp and shall call on the people to disperse, should they refuse I will read the riot act and then order the police to disperse the meeting. Should a shot be fired or the police roughly handled, I will call on the military to act, I will arrest the speakers on the spot if possible or if not as soon as they can be found. I am so convinced that active measures must be employed to maintain order and give confidence to the well disposed that I am determining to act in the most energetic manner. I will endeavour in every respect to act in strict conformity to the law but I hope that under the very peculiar and pressing circumstances in which I now find myself placed that should I overstep the exact line I may confidently look for the support of His Excellency the Lieutenant-Governor.'[67]

The Commissioner also feels strongly enough on another matter – the lack of formal guidance he has received – to add a small reproach:

It would have been a great assistance to me had I received some instructions or the opinion of the law offices of the Crown on the exact extent to which I am legally empowered to go in a case of sedition. I cannot too strongly urge that the editor of the Ballarat Times should be arrested and sent to Melbourne

354

for his seditious article in the copy I sent down. The soldiers
& police I am happy to state show the very best dispositions.
I have the honour to be, Sir,
Your most obedient servant,
ROBERT REDE, Resident Commissioner.[68]

The Commissioner puts down his quill and breathes heavily. There is no way around the fact that he is responsible for a part of Her Majesty's empire that is now getting totally out of hand. He knows, more than ever, that he must act strongly and decisively to bring it back under control.

From all across the diggings comes the constant flash and roar of guns fired into the air. Not that the sound of gunfire is rare on the goldfield – it is, in fact, a common practice for the diggers to discharge their guns into the air at the end of the day to ensure that they remain in working order. But it has never been like this.

These are not scattered shots. This is a constant roar. This is a warning from the diggers that they, too, are heavily armed, and no occupying army is going to be able to easily quell them.

11 pm, Tuesday, 28 November 1854, on the Eureka, they flag the future

And, yes, it is difficult to concentrate, and even to talk with such constant gunfire going on nearby, but talk they must. The subject being discussed by Peter Lalor, Tom Kennedy, John Basson Humffray, Charles Ross and another digger by the name of John Wilson[69] in a tent out the back of Cameron's store is the need to have a flag of their own, a unifying symbol to signify that they are no longer loyal to the Union Jack and do not recognise the authority of those who bear arms under it. But just what should their own flag look like?

As it happens, although Wilson is perhaps the one who has said the least to this point, it is while he chances to gaze at the night sky that the gentle muse of inspiration alights on his shoulder. The Southern Cross.[70]

It is the most recognisable constellation in this wonderful, strange country they've come to, and they all know it.

'I've got it,' he would ever after remember calling to the others. 'Here's the idea . . . There. The Southern Cross, five white stars on a blue field.'[71]

Most importantly, when Wilson puts the suggestion to the others, the idea is instantly embraced – and by no-one more eagerly than Charles Ross, a third-generation military man from Canada, of fine and distinguished features, regarded by his mates as a man of 'force and spirit',[72] who has just the right idea of how it should look.

Taking up his quill, he draws upon a scrap of paper, modifies it, and then modifies it some more. Drawing and re-drawing, he comes up with a design that he thinks is more than satisfactory – a flag that perhaps has echoes of the NSW Ensign of 1832, which boasts a cross of St George with the stars of the Southern Cross, and, more recently, the flag of the Australasian Anti-Transportation League, which also features the Southern Cross.

Who then can he enlist to make this flag for them? There are some diggers' wives around, of whom a few have been intimately involved in the agitation of previous weeks, and none more so than Anastasia, wife of the Chairman of the Ballarat Reform League, Tim Hayes. As beautiful as she is tough, Anastasia was involved in the Young Ireland movement of Fintan Lalor, made it through the potato famine, managed to give birth to five children in Ireland and transport them to the other side of the world, and then gave birth to her latest right here in a tent on the goldfields.

Of course Anastasia is only too pleased to take Charles Ross's rough drawing and, with the help of her friends Anastasia Withers and Anne Duke, gather up blue wool and cotton cloth of the type used to make the diggers' shirts for the base material, twill and cotton material for the cross and 100 per cent cream wool for the stars. They set to with a will as all falls quiet . . .[73]

CHAPTER TEN

READING THE RIOT ACT

*Yentlemens. Go vere you vill, you meet mit der tyrann. Ze only
way to meet tyrann ish mit der pistole in der handt!* [1]

Friedrich Vern, to his fellow diggers

Commissioner Rede to John Basson Humffray in the midst of
the Gravel Pits riot: *'See now the consequences of your agitation!'*
Humffray replies: *'No, but see the consequences of impolitic coercion.'* [2]

Wednesday morning, 29 November 1854, the standard is raised atop Bakery Hill

Of course the sound of sawing and hammers pounding on wood
is not unusual on the diggings at this time, because the process of
sinking the shafts 150 feet deep requires a great deal of carpentry,
as the miners constantly shore up the collapsing sides with wooden
walls. But on this bright, searingly hot morning, all the activity is
put to a different purpose. In preparation for the meeting that is to
be held this afternoon to hear personally what the response was to
the demands Black and Kennedy made to the Lieutenant-Governor
on their behalf, several miners particularly handy with hammers,
saws and hard yakka are putting their energy towards building a
stage. It comes complete with an impressive flagpole from a tree cut
down from Byle's[3] Swamp in the Bullarook Forest, soaring no less

358

than 60 feet. With its base in an abandoned shaft, the flagpole now stands straight and true, and the fact that it is situated atop Bakery Hill means it is visible from all over the diggings.

Once the whole thing is completed in the late morning, the moment comes when 'bridegroom' Charles Ross comes forward with the new flag that the Anastasias – Withers and Hayes – together with Anne Duke, have been working on. For it is now ready to be displayed, and there will never be a better time than right now as this group of armed men reach for a new symbol of their unity, a symbol entirely separate from that which the Union Jack represents.

At first the flag hangs loosely as it is hoisted up the mast, and it is not easy for the gathering of grimy men of the diggings to focus on its form. But once at the top, it catches the light breeze of liberty and, sure enough, there it is! Now the massed men can for the first time appreciate the simple beauty of the massive standard – measuring roughly three yards high and four-and-a-half yards wide.

Charles Ross stands at the base of the flagpole, sword in hand, as if he is ready to fight to defend it. And yet, in this company, with these assembled men gazing up at it intently and proudly, there is clearly no need.

As reported by the impressed correspondent for *The Ballarat Times*: 'Its maiden appearance was a fascinating object to behold. There is no flag in Europe, or in the civilised world, half so beautiful and Bakery Hill, as being the first place where the Australian ensign was first hoisted, will be recorded in the deathless and indelible pages of history.'[4]

And beautiful the wool and cotton flag indeed is, displaying as its primary feature a white cross upon a dark blue background, upon which four stars represent the Southern Cross constellation. 'No device or arms, but all exceedingly chaste and natural.'[5]

Thomas Pierson is among those impressed by the sight, and would later make a drawing of the flag in his diary, beneath the inscription:

I should have stated that the diggers hoisted at the meetings their flag whitch they called the flag of the southern Hemisphere, I will try to sketch it – it was made of silk + quite neat.[6]

And indeed it is. There it gracefully flies and acts as a beacon for the next three hours or so as, in their thousands, the diggers start to emerge from their holes, humpies, huts and tents, and stream towards it for the meeting due to start at 2 pm.

In the meantime, however, all is not happy on the goldfields. A meeting of the committee of the Ballarat Reform League at the Star Hotel breaks up in near carnage as the passions between those who believe in 'moral force' – continuing with petitions and resolutions – and those who believe in 'physical force' – taking up arms against the British brutes who so goad them – becomes ever more inflamed. The leader of the moral-force men is John Basson Humffray, and he is doing precisely what he does best, making a speech, when one of the physical-force men pulls out a gun and points it at his head. Yes, the gun is quickly wrestled away from the aggressor by another committee member, but it is as good an indication as any of just how fiery the feeling is now as the schism in the Ballarat Reform League grows. In any case, while the meeting finishes in an uproar, there is little time to reflect on it – the big meeting is about to begin.

In the searing sunshine – the afternoon is now hotter even than the morning – they come in force, some 12,000 diggers strong, in front of the newly constructed podium and wait for their leaders to speak. It is the biggest meeting yet held on these goldfields, which now boast a total population of some 32,000.

Also in attendance, sitting on rough benches upon the podium, are Melbourne's founding Roman Catholic Bishop – now Archbishop – the Right Reverend Alipius Goold, together with Ballarat's former priest, Reverend Father Downing, and his successor, the popular Father Smyth. Both Archbishop Goold and Father Downing look exhausted, and for good reason – it is said they have both travelled through the night to get here. It is also said they are here at the earnest instigation of the government to try to calm things down, though that is not sure. (And even the government is represented, though not openly, as Lieutenant-Governor Hotham has personally ordered a magistrate and two witnesses to attend, so His Excellency may gain a full and reliable report of the situation.)

Up on stage, Father Smyth looks worried, knowing far better than his superiors just how hot the mood on the diggings is and what risks happening from here and . . .

And hark! The first of the delegates is about to speak and give us news of the Governor's response to our demands.

It's shortly after three o'clock and at the invitation of the Chairman of the League, Timothy Hayes, the man of the moment, George Black, takes the stage, having only arrived back on the goldfields an hour earlier. His very appearance is greeted with three hearty cheers from the diggers, for there have been rumours that he and his two companions were arrested in Melbourne. Black is easily recognisable by both his height and long, flowing red locks, and the cheers build and roll across the diggings with such clamour that yet more diggers are brought to the surface. They soon wipe themselves down and make their way to join the assembly.

First up, Black informs the crowd that the delegation was

courteously received by Lieutenant-Governor Hotham. He is, however, sorry to report that His Excellency strongly resented their use of the word 'demand' and was quick to note a general lack of courtesy in the wording of the statement.

Black's words are measured and far from inflammatory – in fact, as a strong advocate of moral force, he is rather like a wet blanket on a field of dry grass that is just beginning to catch flame. In the estimation of that keen observer Carboni, the lean Black looks more like the deeply religious Methodist lay preacher he is by passion than the miner he has become by pursuit: 'Conscious of having received an education, and being born a gentleman, he never prostitutes his tongue to colonial phraseology . . . From the paleness of his cheeks, and the dryness of his lips, you might see that the spirit was indeed willing, though the flesh was weak. The clearness of his eyes, the sharpness of his nose, the liveliness of his forehead, lend to his countenance a decided expression of his belief in the resurrection of life.'[7]

But this crowd is only interested in the resurrection of their demands. Sensing, perhaps, that their delegates have not been as strong with the Lieutenant-Governor as they had wished them to be, they stir restlessly as a field of wheat before the coming storm, while Black goes on. He does not wish to speak ill of Sir Charles Hotham, he makes clear again and again. As a matter of fact, he offers the view that, as far as he can personally tell, Sir Charles is in their favour. The problem is most likely that he is surrounded by many injudicious advisers, rendering him entirely impotent in matters of state.

Perhaps then the answer is to modify and moderate their manner of addressing the Lieutenant-Governor? That, at least, is the motion put to the gathering, one that is soon howled down on the grounds that it would be humiliating for the League if passed. One day they are 'demanding' and two days later they are 'praying leave'? Absolutely not!

As frustration rises, the mood of the gathering starts to become more aggressive and strong-willed than the mood projected by those on the podium. The mass of diggers begin to overflow with emotion – it is outrageous that His Nibs has dismissed their demands in this high-handed manner. They want nothing more than justice, and he is now denying them that.

They must *rise*.

But no. Next up is Secretary John Basson Humffray, who also asserts that the Lieutenant-Governor is truly on their side and eager to resolve their grievances, even if he won't overturn the convictions and the sentences of the innocent miners. That is why His Excellency has appointed a Commission of Inquiry, and Humffray himself is sure that once that Commission has made its report, the Lieutenant-Governor will 'act accordingly'. Sir Charles told them that he'll abolish the license fee if advised to do so by the Commission he has set up, and the Commission will surely advise exactly that. Hopefully they will be rid of the whole license system before long.

In his entire manner, Humffray stands out in this environment. A well-mannered gentleman from a good family, he is extremely well read and even better spoken, a deep thinker who – despite failing to make it rich on the Gravel Pit diggings – is actually far more concerned with the welfare of his fellow man. There is something of an air of vulnerability about him, a sense that he is a man who has given his best to making the world a better place and, despite being continually disappointed, persists regardless. Just like George Black, he does not use emotional language, just gives a clear account of what has occurred. He seeks not to inflame, only to inform.

But as the sun beats down and the temperature rises, not only do his carefully chosen words not match the growing outrage of the diggers, they are not long in telling him about it.

When Humffray acknowledges that he had, without authorisation from the Ballarat Reform League, a private meeting with Sir Charles prior to them being received as an official delegation, there are shouts from the diggers and dark looks from Kennedy and

Black. They had not agreed with this meeting, either.

Together the diggers, as reported by *The Ballarat Times*, 'denounced the conduct of Humffray as arising in this manner . . . unwarrantable, without its instructions and diametrically opposed to the . . . sentiments of the committee'.[8]

As a mass, the diggers' anger grows at the realisation that their representatives simply have not pressed their case hard enough. These blokes just aren't up to it! Humffray is so aggrieved by this reaction that he gives notice, then and there, that he intends to resign his office as Secretary of the Ballarat Reform League. No-one tries to dissuade him.

Standing down among the crowd, near the front, is Peter Lalor, struggling with his own rising emotions. He, too, is deeply frustrated by what he has been hearing from the podium. But should he get more involved than he already is?

Having grown up around his older brother, Fintan, he is familiar with high political passions, with taking the fight to the oppressors, with pursuing strong actions to change things. Yet, to this point, he has never been involved himself, at least not to the extent of standing on a podium to address the throng.

Perhaps he should do so now! That is certainly the view of one of Lalor's Irish mates, James Brown, who is standing beside him in the crowd, now urging him to get up, get going, to say what needs to be said.

Take t'*lead*, Peter.

Should he . . .? Or should he stay in the background, keep his peace and let others act on his behalf? It is a decision he wrestles with. What he *is* certain of is that Brown is right: *someone* needs to step up to the podium to better express the mood of the masses, a mood that is in entire accordance with his own.

He stands there contemplating this very thing while another man is speaking, at least more aggressively, about the 'daring calumny of his honour the Acting Chief Justice', who had dared to stigmatise 'as riots, the persevering and indomitable struggles for freedom of the brave people of England and Ireland for the last eighty years'.[9] Should he join him? Get up and say his piece? Or keep his peace?

———

And now there is a new speaker, one who the broad mass of miners have not seen or heard much from before, though his name seems to be bandied around a little lately. I think it must be that Lalor fellow, Scobie's mate, the one who first organised that meeting to try to get justice for the Scotsman.

'Here,' Lalor begins in his soft Irish lilt, 'is tyranny as bad as that in old Ireland.'[10]

What they are about here, he says, his tone rising, is democracy against tyranny.

The diggers hang on every precious word. The sun continues to beat down, the bottles and flasks of grog are passed back and forth and the speaker goes on. It is a heady day.

Not only do the people need to install democracy on the diggings and in the colony of Victoria, Lalor says, but the whole structure of the Ballarat Reform League needs to be both democratised and streamlined to become a more effective opponent of the government. And it is with this in mind that he now proposes his motion: 'That a meeting of the members of the Reform League be called at the Adelphi Theatre next Sunday, at 2 pm, to elect a central committee, and that each fifty members of the League have power to elect one member for the central committee.'[11]

All those in favour say 'Aye' . . .

Aye! *Si! Oui! Jawohl!* Yaah! *SI!*

'Lalor's speech,' John Lynch would later note, 'had the merit of brevity, but went to the point at once.'[12] The diggers liked the look of this new man a great deal. 'For tall-talk and bluster he substituted moderation and common sense.'[13]

In the general acclamation of Lalor's proposal, the Irishman's eyes lock with those of Carboni, who has been positively wild in his applause for both Lalor's speech and in support of his motion. He reaches his hand down from the platform and grips that of the Italian, pulling him up onto the platform to more properly talk amid the tumult.

The two know each other a little, and that morning Lalor noticed Carboni's tent was a regular riot of representatives from seemingly every nationality on the diggings. All those with no great grasp of the English language crowded around to hear his translations of *The Ballarat Times* and *Geelong Advertiser* and tried to work out exactly what was going on. As Carboni has command of English, Italian, Spanish, French and German, this is an easy matter, and he is an obvious candidate to be an effective leader of those foreigners. Lalor invites him to speak, and Carboni does not have to be asked twice.

'I came from old Europe, 16,000 miles across two oceans, and I thought it a respectable distance from the hated Austrian rule . . .' he begins in his thick accent, adding a melody to words that English-speaking tongues say flatly. 'I hate the oppressor, let him wear a red, blue, white, or black coat. [And so I call on you,] all my fellow-diggers, irrespective of nationality, religion, and colour, to salute the "Southern Cross" as the refuge of all the oppressed from all countries on earth.'[14]

His stirring words are greeted with thunderous applause as the meeting moves further and further away from the moderate tones of the first speakers and more towards armed insurrection. Indeed, his words are so impassioned that even Tom Kennedy – who had done so much to stir up the passions of the men after the murder of Scobie – thinks Carboni has gone too far and steps forward to usher him away from the front of the stage. It is only with great reluctance that the fiery Italian is pulled away.

But if Carboni can speak, then other foreigners want to speak, too, none more than Friedrich Vern, who roars that the diggers must take their licenses out and burn them, rather than giving in to this outrageous government.

'Yentlemens,' he says, his accent thick and only just comprehensible. 'Go vere you vill, you meet mit der tyrann. Ze only way to meet tyrann ish mit der pistole in der handt!'[15, 16] To provide a slew of exclamation marks to this observation, he takes two fully loaded pepperbox revolvers from his belt and fires off all twelve shots in the air.

'To Arms! To Arms!'[17] come the shouts from hundreds in the crowd. He has their complete attention. And Vern's formal motion results in much subsequent discussion:

'That this meeting, being convinced that the obnoxious license-fee is an imposition and an unjustifiable tax on free labour, pledges itself to make immediate steps to abolish the same, by at once burning all their licenses. That in the event of any party being arrested for having no licenses, the united people will, under all circumstances, defend and protect them.'[18, 19]

Father Downing, truly alarmed at the rising anger of the meeting, speaks strongly against Vern's motion and proposes a moderate amendment to the effect that the licenses specifically should *not* be burned. Even though the diggers hear him out with barely restrained silence, he cannot get even a single one to second the motion. Another digger proposes that instead of burning the licenses, the men should simply refuse to show them, meaning they would have to go en masse to the Camp lockup, overwhelming the government's legal processes. This, too, is howled down as being nowhere near aggressive and forthright enough.

The fierce debate goes on under the blazing hot sun, and Carboni notes 'a peculiar colonial habit'[20] taking place as a sly-grogger plies his trade, selling swigs from his black bottle to all present – even to those on the podium.

Father Downing could be forgiven for swigging deeply, so alarmed is he by what is being said. After the clergyman has finished, a person by the name of Fraser is granted leave to speak by Chairman Timothy Hayes. Alas, when this fellow also waxes moderation and the virtues of British law – unprotected by the clerical collar as Father Downing is – the mob reacts with a rage so strong that *The Ballarat Times* notes, 'Were it not for the influence of the chairman and his numerous supporters, the man would have been torn limb from limb by the infuriated people.'[21]

The diggers have had enough and now they really do want to give the government a 'lick in the lug', and Fraser the same in the short term, but he is hurried away for his own safety. It is time for Chairman Hayes, thus, to put Vern's original motion to the vote, and he chooses his words carefully, a man who has slowly come to the conclusion that it really is time to move beyond mere speeches.

'Gentlemen,' he says in stentorian tones, 'many a time I have seen large public meetings pass resolutions with as much earnestness and unanimity as you show this day; and yet, when the time came to test the sincerity, and prove the determination necessary for carrying out those resolutions, it was found then that "the spirit, indeed, is willing, but the flesh is weak".

'Now, then, before I put this resolution from the chair, let me point out to you the responsibility of it will lay upon you. And so I feel bound to ask you, gentlemen, to speak out your mind. Should any member of the League be dragged to the lockup for not having the license, will a thousand of you volunteer to liberate the man?'

'Yes! Yes!' the diggers roar.

'Will two thousand of you come forward?'

'Yes! Yes! Yes!'

'Will four thousand of you volunteer to march up to the Camp and open the lock-up to liberate the man?'

'Yes! Yes!' they roar even louder, some firing their pistols into the air to signal their wild approval.

'Are you ready to die?' he shouts, stretching forth his clenched right fist.

'Yes, yes! Hurrah!'[22]

Dozens more take their guns and revolvers, point them skywards and fire deafening volleys of joyous shots. Others start two bonfires, into which they hurl their licenses, even as – in classic Chartist fashion – they pay two shillings and sixpence apiece and take proffered membership tickets for the Ballarat Reform League.

And so it goes. The mood of the miners is now one of sheer, eyeballs-rolling fury. As noted by Thomas Pierson, they are so upset that 'formal declaration for Independence in consequence was made and nearly all determined to pay no more License'.[23]

But some of the men are contemplating taking even sterner action. Combined action. *Armed* action, if necessary. All of it is noted carefully by the journalists present, and even more carefully by those whose job in life it is to report back to the Government Camp just what the diggers are up to so it can be passed along to Sir Charles Hotham from there. Commissioner Rede will have the report within the hour.

But in the meantime, oh, how those licenses blaze, as the symbol of the diggers' subservience to this government is now no more . . . no more . . . it is now *no more* . . .

Watching it all from the podium with giddy satisfaction, Hayes is moved – as he is often wont to be – to shout out some lines from one of his favourite poems:

> On to the field, our doom is sealed,
> To conquer or be slaves;
> The sun shall see our country free,
> Or set upon our graves.[24]

There is revolution in the air, an intoxicating headiness. Together they are going to overturn an unjust regime, or at least the writ of that regime, in this part of that world. Had there been a bastille handy, the crowd might well have stormed it; a harbour nearby, and throwing crates of tea into it would have been a definite possibility. Oh, yes, many of the men on the field had been part of such rallies before, with the Chartists in Europe, replete with equally high-blown rhetoric. But then the Chartist movement had come to nothing. Then, in the face of government troops with glistening bayonets thrust forward, people had all backed down. But now it is different! In this land, far away from their homelands, the men are gathered once more to fight against the same injustice as before . . . but this time they're not going to back down.

In their dozens now, they push to the bonfires and throw their licenses in. In typical fashion, it is not enough for Tom Kennedy to simply follow suit – he must do it in the most dramatic fashion possible. Opening his shirt to expose his chest, he dramatically cries, 'Here's my breast, ready for the bullets',[25] and then and only then, he throws his piece of paper into the flames.

The fires roar and so do the diggers. The bonfire smoke billows into the otherwise clear, blue sky.

'It was at this time or thereabouts,' digger John Lynch later astutely observed, 'that the [moral-force Chartist and physical-force Chartist] chiefs separated. Mr Humffray wanted to still further try the efficacy of soft flattery and hard words in alternate doses. Mr Lalor, finding that there had been too much talk already and that more of it would only bring ridicule, resolved to try conclusions by the only means left when all others had failed.'[26]

And indeed, throwing their licenses into those bonfires was one of the only means left.

From the Camp, an arrival to the diggings just the afternoon before, Captain Charles Pasley watches closely. From his vantage point high above Bakery Hill three-quarters of a mile away, he can see everything. Should the diggers leave the meeting and attempt to storm the Camp, or behave in any threatening manner, he has troops positioned in the gully below, ready and waiting to advance on his signal. All about him at the Camp, the men are under arms. Pasley has no doubt that in the event he gives the order to attack, the Camp is secure and the diggers atop Bakery Hill are 'in a position convenient for military operations'.[27] So important does he judge this precaution that he has no hesitation in rejecting the diggers' request, passed on by Father Smyth and Tom Kennedy at the request of the committee, that 'the military be withdrawn from the sight of the meeting, as there was no real use for the display, and that many felt irritated at such an open parade of power'.[28] Pasley wants precisely such a display, to demonstrate to the diggers just what they are facing if things get out of hand, and to move quickly if that happens.

But there is no need.

Not long after three more resolutions are passed, a wild man comes onto the stage wielding a double-barrelled shotgun and interrupts John Basson Humffray, who happens to be in full flight. Hayes announces, amid all the shouting and continued small-arms fire from the crowd, that he hereby dissolves the meeting.

Amazingly, despite such an irregular and potentially violent ending, the miners quietly head back to their diggings and their tents. As John Manning reports for the next edition of *The Ballarat Times*, 'Nothing could exceed the order and regularity with which the people, some 15,000 in number, retired.'[29] (Not that Manning truly pretends to be a neutral observer, for all that. Like his boss, Henry Seekamp, he is involved. He is a *believer*. 'Of all the men who took part in the struggle of those times,' John Lynch would say of him, 'not one surpassed John Manning in earnestness of feeling or singleness of purpose.'[30])

This order and calm is not matched in the Government Camp, however, where Commissioner Rede is soon in earnest discussions with captains John Wellesley Thomas and Charles Pasley about the military situation and, most particularly, how the Camp could be better protected against a full-blown attack. One thing they all agree on is that further reinforcements from Melbourne are essential.

Pasley has no doubts: steps must be taken to bring the matter to a head.[31]

In this way, Pasley reasons,[32] by having justification to crush the rebels and doing that in such a resounding manner as to demonstrate the futility of resistance, the authorities would be quickly able to bring the other diggers – the majority of them, who have had no part in the rebellion – to their side.

And what better way to bring on a crisis than by instituting the very thing that the diggers are complaining most strongly about? That is, conduct another license-hunt, but this one on a massive scale? It makes a certain amount of sense, and Commissioner Rede, who is infuriated by the burning of licenses and the defiant firing of pistols, pushes this strategy particularly strongly.

Before retiring for the evening, Rede and Pasley take time to write reports to their superiors in Melbourne to keep them fully informed. Ballarat is now balanced on a razor's edge, with two opposing forces, two bodies of armed men, both calling for more men with more guns to come to their assistance. All voices of moderation have been either howled down or cowed from speaking up.

10 o'clock, Thursday morning, 30 November 1854, mayhem on the diggings

Let a man but sleep for a few hours and he will frequently look upon the decision reached the night before as so much madness that could only live by the light of the moon, and he will immediately alter course once the sun shines upon it. At other times, of course, the rising sun only illuminates the conviction that the decision was well made and will be followed through.

In this instance, it is the latter case that applies.

Charles Joseph La Trobe, Superintendent of the Port Phillip District (1839–51), first Lieutenant-Governor of Victoria (1851–54). (STATE LIBRARY OF VICTORIA)

Jolimont, La Trobe's modest prefabricated residence in Melbourne, is referred to by locals as 'The Chalet' because of its Continental form. (GEORGE ALEXANDER GILBERT/ STATE LIBRARY OF VICTORIA)

Edward Hammond Hargraves, rewarded as the first discoverer of payable gold at Ophir, New South Wales, in 1851. (STATE LIBRARY OF NEW SOUTH WALES)

Panning for gold. (SAMUEL THOMAS GILL/REX NAN KIVELL COLLECTION/ NATIONAL LIBRARY OF AUSTRALIA)

New South Wales's first gold digging at FitzRoy Bar, Ophir, is soon in full swing after the newspapers announce Hargraves's discovery in May 1851. (FROM *SKETCHES IN AUSTRALIA* BY GEORGE FRENCH ANGAS/STATE LIBRARY OF NEW SOUTH WALES)

Optimistic diggers making their way to Ballarat in 1854. (SAMUEL THOMAS GILL/
NATIONAL LIBRARY OF AUSTRALIA)

Goldmining techniques: panning, puddling (where clayey dirt is broken down
with water in a tub) and cradling. (EDWIN STOCQUELER/REX NAN KIVELL COLLECTION/
NATIONAL LIBRARY OF AUSTRALIA)

Cradling at Forrest Creek, the fabulously auriferous goldfield that opened up in September 1851. (SAMUEL THOMAS GILL/REX NAN KIVELL COLLECTION/NATIONAL LIBRARY OF AUSTRALIA)

Deep sinking, digging in teams to depths of 150 feet, can mean toiling for up to six months before any prize is won. (SAMUEL THOMAS GILL/NATIONAL LIBRARY OF AUSTRALIA)

'Shepherding' can result in disputes as to whether the ground is being properly worked on or is, in fact, available to be claimed by others. (SAMUEL THOMAS GILL/REX NAN KIVELL COLLECTION/NATIONAL LIBRARY OF AUSTRALIA)

Sir Charles Hotham,
Lieutenant-Governor of
Victoria (1854–55), and first
Governor of Victoria (1855).
(State Library of Victoria)

Ballarat diggings in the summer of 1853–54, looking south from Black Hill towards
Buninyong. Row's Circus tent can be seen on the flat. (Eugene von Guérard /
Art Gallery of Ballarat)

Assistant-Commissioner Amos's camp located on the Eureka. (Thomas Ham/
Rex Nan Kivell Collection/National Library of Australia)

Castlemaine diggers line up to pay their license fees. (Samuel Thomas Gill/La Trobe
Picture Collection/State Library of Victoria)

A mass meeting typically concludes with diggers giving three cheers or groans for those newspapers that either support or oppose the diggers (in this case, *The Argus* and *The Herald* respectively). (Rex Nan Kivell Collection/National Library of Australia)

Sunday outdoor service at Forrest Creek. (Samuel Thomas Gill/Rex Nan Kivell Collection/National Library of Australia)

'I propose that this house belongs to the diggers!' The burning down of the Eureka Hotel, 17 October 1854. (*Eureka Riot* by Charles Doudiet/Art Gallery of Ballarat)

'Bridegroom' of the Southern Cross flag, Canadian digger Charles Ross.
(Art Gallery of Ballarat)

Robert Rede, Resident
Commissioner of Crown Lands for
the Goldfields at Ballarat (1854–55).

John Leslie Fitzgerald Vesey Foster,
Colonial Secretary of Victoria (1853–54).
(T. F. Chuck/State Library of Victoria)

Secretary of the Ballarat Reform League,
moral-force Chartist and Welshman,
John Basson Humffray. (La Trobe
Picture Collection/State Library of
Victoria)

Italian man of letters, Raffaello Carboni,
friend of Peter Lalor and author of *The
Eureka Stockade*.

'We swear by the Southern Cross . . .' Digger swearing-in ceremony, 30 November 1854, at Bakery Hill. (F. A. SLEAP/STATE LIBRARY OF VICTORIA)

Swearing Allegiance to the 'Southern Cross' by Charles Doudiet. (ART GALLERY OF BALLARAT)

Members of the 12th Foot (*left*) and 40th Foot Gold Escort (*right*). (Lindsay Cox)

Eureka Slaughter by Charles Doudiet. (Art Gallery of Ballarat)

The military attack on the Eureka Stockade, 3 December 1854. (*The Eureka Stockade* by Beryl Ireland/La Trobe Picture Collection/State Library of Victoria)

The Stockade wall is breached by foot soldiers of the 12th and 40th Regiments. (*Eureka Stockade Riot* by J. B. Henderson/La Trobe Picture Collection/State Library of Victoria)

Members of the Independent California Rangers' Revolver Brigade standing their ground during the attack on the Stockade. (GREGORY BLAKE)

Pikeman Hafele's terrier is never far from his side, even at the height of the attack on the Stockade. (GREGORY BLAKE)

Father Smyth's Catholic chapel, Bakery Hill, Ballarat. (Eugene von Guérard/
La Trobe Picture Library/State Library of Victoria)

Purportedly one of the three women who sewed the Southern Cross flag, the redoubtable Anastasia Hayes. (Public Record Office Victoria, © State of Victoria)

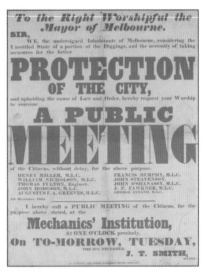

Concerned citizens of Melbourne organise a public meeting on 5 December 1854, ostensibly to discuss the protection of the city following the rebellion. (John Ferres/ State Library of Victoria)

The crowd celebrates the acquittal of a Ballarat rioter accused of High Treason. (STATE LIBRARY OF VICTORIA)

Prominent Melburnian Judge Redmond Barry, who presided over the Scobie murder trial and the Eureka Stockade treason trials. (LA TROBE PICTURE COLLECTION/STATE LIBRARY OF VICTORIA)

One of the 'Tipperary Mob', Irishman Peter Lalor, Eureka Stockade leader and later long-serving Victorian State politician. (La Trobe Picture Collection/ State Library of Victoria)

The Eureka Stockade Monument (erected in 1884), located within the Eureka Stockade Gardens, Ballarat. The inscription tablet (added in 1923) reads: 'Sacred to the Memory of Those who fell on the memorable 3rd Dec, 1854, In resisting The Unconstitutional Proceedings of the Victorian Government.' (State Library of Victoria)

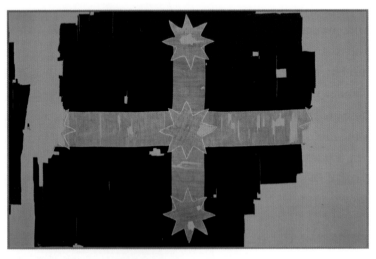

The original Southern Cross flag (also known as 'The Eureka flag') on display at the Ballarat Art Gallery. (Ballarat Art Gallery)

In the wake of the monster meeting of diggers upon Bakery Hill, a more cautious man than Commissioner Rede might have chosen upon reflection to let things settle a little, to do nothing that would unnecessarily provoke men who are clearly spoiling for a fight.

But no. Notwithstanding that in the silent watch of night Rede has enduring misgivings about the lack of fairness of the whole licensing system, he has come to the conclusion that the law has to be upheld. This issue must be settled, once and for all – and it is his job to settle it. It is no small achievement to have risen to be the highest civil authority in an important town, able to call on assistance from a force of 500 armed men, with more on the way. If only they could see him now, back in old England, as he gives the order for the men – *his* men – to move out and for yet one more license-hunt to begin.

———

In the Star Hotel, meanwhile, on this same morning, Timothy Hayes is convening a meeting with several other committee members of the Ballarat Reform League, and they decide they need to send emissaries immediately to their fellow diggers on other goldfields. None other than Tom Kennedy and George Black must head off, within the hour, to the closest major goldfield, which is at Creswick, around 11 miles north. Henry Holyoake has already left for Bendigo. On those goldfields they can detail to the other diggers the resolution of the meeting on this day and tell them they need help. They need men, *armed* men, to come to their aid, immediately. Even as they speak, however, they become aware of a commotion outside. Men, many men, are rushing past. Something is going on out there.

———

And so it is that at 11 o'clock on this hot, blustery day, where the wind itself has both menace and malice, the Commissioner – following 'instructions from the highest authority to this effect'[33] – is intent on demonstrating that it is he and his men who are in charge of these goldfields, and their authority will be respected. It is with this in mind that he has sent out Commissioner Johnstone and a party of police to conduct a license-hunt on the Gravel Pits diggings, which lie nearby to the Government Camp.

'Let there be no addition to your force,' Rede tells Johnstone, eager to make the point to the diggers that they are not *expecting* a confrontation. 'Go out in exactly the same manner, and with the same number of police you have been in the habit of going out with.'[34]

Johnstone follows orders and heads off towards the Gravel Pits with a body of 30 police on foot carrying batons, accompanied by mounted troopers, carefully watched from on high by Commissioner Rede.

———

'Joe! *Joe!* JOE!'

Again the cry goes up at the very sight of the hated Johnstone – the perfidious wretch who was so arrogant and inflammatory in his treatment of Father Smyth's servant – and his force of mounted troopers and foot police with drawn swords, fixed bayonets and threatening glares drive the diggers to distraction. And Johnstone is infuriated in turn and even less inclined to forbearance than usual, for these cries of 'Joe!' are nothing less than damned insolence.

The calls have no sooner begun than Johnstone orders his men to surround the party of diggers cajoling them in the vicinity of the Gravel Pits. The response is a flurry of stones and curses so jointly powerful – injuring his men physically and outraging them morally – that the shocked Johnstone immediately withdraws the troops just far enough away to be safe and sends a messenger on the gallop to inform Commissioner Rede, who sends down mounted troops as reinforcements. Similarly treated, it is not long before Rede himself appears on the Gravel Pits while Captain Thomas is left in charge of the Camp's defence.

Upon arrival, Rede – his gold lace shining brightly, the very personification of government authority on these goldfields – strains to keep things under control.

'Nothing would grieve me more than to have to recourse to violence,' he tells the diggers. 'But as long as the license fee is the law it is my duty to maintain it, and I will do so.'[35]

When the diggers argue, he returns doggedly to his theme: 'I must do my duty . . . and do it I will.'[36] He asks them to disperse, to return to their diggings and their tents and not to engage in this riotous assembly.

Need he remind them, he goes on, that on the reckoning of their own delegation – as they were informed just yesterday – the Lieutenant-Governor himself had told them that if they properly petitioned him they would get their rights! Furthermore, as they know, one of their most public supporters, Mr Fawkner himself, had been selected as 'one of the number to inquire into the grievances of the goldfields'.[37]

At this point, three cheers ring out at the mention of Fawkner's name. But the goodwill does not last for long. When the Commissioner calls – no fewer than three times – for the law-abiding among them to retire and disperse, they do not. Worse, by way of emphasis that they are not backing down, some of the diggers even throw stones at the Commissioner, one large chunk of quartz only narrowly missing his head. (At this point, he could be forgiven for viewing with fond nostalgia the days when they only threw eggs at his head.) The situation is now truly out of hand.

He must take action, and so he does, crying out, 'My lads, I must read the riot act.'[38]

'Read it! Read it!'[39] the diggers roar back.

Again, standing in the saddle, Rede now reads out the Riot

Act from the large piece of paper he holds in his right hand: 'Our Sovereign Lady the Queen chargeth and commandeth all persons, being assembled, immediately to disperse themselves, and peaceably to depart to their habitations, or to their lawful business, upon the pains contained in the act made in the first year of King George, for preventing tumults and riotous assemblies. God Save the Queen!'[40]

At this point, many of the diggers do indeed disperse, knowing that Rede has now set up a legal situation whereby, because there are 12 or more of them gathered in 'riots and tumults', he and his men have the right to fire upon them if they don't follow instructions. But many stand their ground.

As described by digger John Lynch, Rede's whole license-hunt and reading of the Riot Act 'was meant for a challenge, and as such was accepted. The gauntlet was thrown down with the recklessness of malice; it was taken up with solemn decision, amidst cheers, every wave of which reverberated defiance'.[41]

Shocked that so many diggers have indeed picked up the said gauntlet thrown down, Rede plays for time and attempts to ride away from the confrontation. But he is immediately stopped by one enormous digger, who simply stands there, roaring abuse at him. With this, Commissioner Rede can tolerate no more and decides to personally make an example of him.

'Have you got your license?'

'No,' says the bear of a man.

'Then,' says Rede, 'I will arrest you . . .'[42]

And Rede would have done exactly that. Alas, as soon as he and the troopers take the man in hand, other diggers rush them and free the recalcitrant digger, running off with him.

'Very well,' says Rede, 'since you have resisted me in the execution of my duty, both as a Commissioner and a Magistrate, if you do not disperse I will clear you off with the military.'[43]

With great reluctance, Rede sends for armed troops, and he is not long in hearing that the diggers have sent their own runners to alert the Tipperary mob on the Eureka what is happening and relay their need for support. Fortunately for Rede, his own troops arrive first. Captain Thomas, who has also been watching closely, has immediately sent the same infantry of the 40th Regiment under the command of Captain Pasley that had been ready to break up the meeting the day before had it got out of hand.

Again, the sight of these heavily armed men inflames the diggers even more, and now they call out, 'We will not have drawn swords or fixed bayonets.' 'Where is the Governor?' 'Send up Sir Charles Hotham.' 'We want justice, and we will have it.'[44]

Upon such cries, Commissioner Rede declares he is determined to check licenses whether anyone likes it or not, which sets the diggers off once more:

'We haven't got them; we can't give them,' the grubby diggers cry at the familiar figure in the always impeccable blue uniform. 'We have burnt them.'[45]

Despite the tall forest of long bayonets glinting in the sunlight above the heads of the massed infantry behind Rede, many of the diggers still stand their ground. Having gone this far, the intoxicating whiff of rebellion momentarily in their nostrils, after whole months of suffering in rough silence, they decide to go still further and unleash another volley of rocks on Rede and his men. In for a penny, in for a pound . . . To be hanged for a sheep as for a lamb . . . Let the devil take the hindmost and prudence be damned . . .

Now, as the mob thickens, rather in the manner of the filthy dust storm that is rolling in with a sudden violence from the north, the cry goes up: 'To the Camp, boys, to the Camp!'[46]

To the alarm of Rede and his forces, it really looks as though the diggers are going to storm the Government Camp. Some of the foot soldiers and police instantly fall back to protect it, helped by the fact that soldiers of the 40th and 12th Regiment have now formed up at the bridge, ready to shoot any digger who tries to cross it, in exactly the same manner as the Houses of Parliament had been protected in 1848 from the Chartists who would cross the Thames. However, a new cry rings out: 'Not to the Camp, boys, not to the Camp. Back to our own ground on Bakery Hill!'[47]

Confusion reigns supreme with carnage riding shotgun, ready to fire at just one more provocation.

What to do now? There has been a partial dispersion of the mob, giving Commissioner Rede enough time to consult with his commanding officers. Between them, they decide that the important thing now is to do what they came to do: conduct a license-hunt on the Gravel Pits!

Rede, infuriated by this affront to the Crown, by this appalling treatment of his men, stands in his saddle and gives his men instructions. 'The licenses must be shown. We must apprehend all who have not their licenses.'[48]

And what do we do, Assistant-Commissioner Johnstone asks, if the diggers show violence to us?

The order from the officer in specific command of the police is clear: 'If a man raises his hand to strike, or throws a stone, shoot him on the spot.'[49]

And so it begins.

The sweaty police begin the chase, both on foot and on horseback, and all those diggers who are without licenses – which is the better part of them – race madly for their holes. Safety lies underground, where the infernal soldiers cannot get at them. But not all of the diggers scurry. Some of them are so enraged or emboldened or tired of running away that they continue to throw stones, bottles, chunks of hard clay, pieces of wood and, generally, anything other than nuggets at the troopers. A whole rain of debris pelts down upon the men in uniform, the bottles sometimes exploding in cruel shards, even as the general insurrection spreads.

The universal cry is heard: 'We will not pay the license. We WILL have our rights!'[50]

Some of the diggers who had been running stop and join in the furious fracas instead. This is too good an opportunity to miss.

Shouts of anger from troopers now mingle with shouts of anger from the diggers, interspersed with the odd *thunk* as rock meets skull or body and the increasingly loud neighing of frightened, bucking horses which are sometimes throwing their riders to the ground. The first violent digger caught is put under the guard of two troopers, who are harshly ordered to take him back to the Camp lockup. And if he makes any attempt to escape, 'blow his brains out'.[51]

For his part Commissioner Johnstone gives direct orders to his men: 'In the event of any outbreak the whole of the tents and stores on the flat are to be burnt to the ground.'[52]

In short order, in a separate movement, the Redcoats form up in a tightly packed line, bayonets fixed, with some mounted troopers in the prow of the attack while the remainder form up on both flanks.

And . . . forward!

They march ahead in the military formation called 'line abreast' – with their skirmishers forward and their bayonets levelled – clearing the Gravel Pits as they go.

Serious and sustained resistance is obviously out of the question. At least for now. Those diggers who are above ground and without a license run every which way, trying to escape. The diggers below ground stay there or head off into the tunnels, daring the troopers to try to follow them. It is one thing to have bravely burned their licenses the day before and quite another to face the painful consequences now. Much better to scarper, Arthur.

The troops continue their advance, with Captain Pasley riding tightly behind, back and forth between the several detachments as he keeps them all co-ordinated. 'I had consequently an opportunity of observing the feeling of those assembled in the neighbourhood,' he would subsequently report, 'which did not appear to be very much in our favour.'[53]

And there is one not in their favour now. Seemingly from out of nowhere, 'a swarthy ruffian sprang out of the crowd and struck a policeman a ruthless blow across the face with an axe handle, which felled him.'[54]

The policeman behind brings his musket to his shoulder and fires, missing the miscreant and wounding another digger nearby, which draws another outraged digger from his tent, who fires at the second policeman and . . . mercifully misses. Bullets fly, stones are hurled. So many, from so many angles and places, it is impossible to determine just who has done what. But the result is the same – shouts of anger and pain fill the air from both sides.

Amid all of the chaos, Commissioner Rede at one point recognises the figure of John Basson Humffray, and shouts at him, 'See now the consequences of your agitation!'

Humffray, however, is equal to the occasion and replies with dignity, 'No, but see the consequences of impolitic coercion.'[55]

The madness goes on.

Those few diggers who have not only paid for their licenses but still have them on their person, present them to whichever soldiers ask. Most of the soldiers' attention, however, is focused on the openly rebellious diggers. When one digger without a license decides to make a run for it, instead of pursuing him on foot or horseback, the soldiers are given the clear order: 'Fire on him . . . shoot him down.'[56]

The fact that the first flurry of shots misses the quickly retreating figure causes a very ill wind to blow upon Her Majesty's peace. For just as man has ever been prone to fight fire with fire, so too is gunfire in one direction prone to be met with gunfire from the other direction, and so it proves on this occasion.

On this occasion, the fleeing digger is mercifully able to dive down a shaft and escape into the dark, labyrinthine netherworld. While the soldiers are restrained, the musket fire both from the troopers and diggers has now started, and it goes on as the sound of shot after shot rolls across the goldfields of Ballarat, arousing many miners deep in their shafts who had not previously been aware that the Joes are here.

One of those miners is Peter Lalor, working at a depth of 140 feet in a shaft at the Eureka, while Timothy Hayes stays above working the windlass. Lalor is just using his pick to break up the muddy clay beneath his boots before he shovels it into a bucket when he hears wisps of the first shots rolling over the open shaft above him..

He quickly surfaces just as the first of the retreating diggers runs past, shouting the news: 'The Joes . . . They're *shooting* us over at the Gravel Pits!'[57]

Their rage is as incandescent as it is infectious, spreading right throughout the diggings. The government has abandoned all restraint and is openly attacking us!

At this moment, Raffaello Carboni is in his tent, writing a letter to a friend, and now quickly finishes it.

Just on my preparing to go and post this letter, we are worried by the usual Irish cry, to run to Gravel-pits. The traps are out for licenses, and playing hell with the diggers. If that be the case, I am not inclined to give half-a-crown for the whole fixtures at the Camp.

I must go and see what's up.

Always your affectionate,

CARBONI RAFFAELLO.[58]

Elsewhere on the diggings, the men do not take time to finish their letters or the equivalent, for the general reaction is fury all around. Actually shooting us! *Has it come to this?* It has. And there can only be one response. They must fire back.

'To arms!'[59] is the cry.

In Lalor's later words, 'All that could muster arms moved forward in great confusion towards the Gravel Pits.'[60]

As to Samuel Lazarus, who had been so critical of the diggers in the way they had attacked the 12th Regiment two nights earlier, he is in no doubt now where the blame lies, as he writes in his diary: 'A little forbearance on the part of the authorities and I believe all would have been well, but this morning's disastrous policy has [raised] feelings of bitter animosity in the breasts of many who a little while ago were eager that the difficulties should be settled by moral means.'[61]

Anyway, it is now obvious to most diggers that the time for moral persuasion has gone. From all over they grab whatever weaponry comes to hand and race towards the Gravel Pits in support of their brother diggers.

There are not enough men on either side for this to turn into a true pitched battle, but the diggers' resistance is fierce. It is through good fortune alone that when the shooting stops and the skirmish is over, the casualties are mercifully light. One of the troopers' horses has taken a bullet to its neck and is in a bad way, while a policeman has sustained a serious, but not life-threatening, wound to his head. (An axe handle will do that to you.) As for the miners, no fewer than seven of them have been arrested and taken prisoner for resisting the lawful authorities, and one of them has taken a bullet through his hand. Those criminals are now led away in chains. Beyond arresting the worst of the rioters, however, the authorities have gained some idea of just what they are up against, should it come to a major military confrontation.

Rede and his men return to the Camp to find it barricaded with sandbags and trusses of hay all around, manned by parties of armed soldiers and police. Captain Thomas has astutely given the order that no digger – no *person* – from the diggings may approach the Camp. Even those who attempt to pass by close on the main road are told to move on.

And move on they quickly do. For as it happens, it seems an impromptu meeting is shortly to begin on Bakery Hill.

CHAPTER ELEVEN

'WE SWEAR BY THE SOUTHERN CROSS...'

*[They] despatched emissaries to the other diggings to excite the miners,
and held a meeting whereat the Australian flag of independence
was solemnly consecrated and vows proffered for its defence...*[1]

Sir Charles Hotham, to Secretary of State Sir George Grey in London

Two o'clock, Thursday afternoon, 30 November 1854, atop Bakery Hill, the second 'monster meeting' warms up

To Bakery Hill, men. And to our flag! Again the standard is raised, once more with the man described as its 'bridegroom', Charles Ross, standing at the base of the flagpole, gazing proudly up at it.

Bakery Hill, the small nob of land within sight of the Government Camp, has become the gathering point for discontent – and as a mob the diggers passed mere discontent days ago. They are now boiling with rage like a billy atop a roaring fire at what has occurred, and they gravitate quickly to the new-found symbol of their unity.

The leaders and speakers from the day before – the moral-force Chartists – well, all of them seem to have disappeared. For they are speakers of moderation and compromise, and the time for moderation and compromise has passed. No-one wants to hear from Humffray, for example, telling them the Governor and his men are 'reasonable' and that their grievances will sort themselves out – even if he had shown himself, it is unlikely the diggers would have let him speak.

The speaker they do want to hear from, though, is Peter Lalor, and after waiting in vain for one of the leaders to show up, the Irishman decides he has no choice but to respond to the urgings of his fellow diggers, mount the podium and take the lead. Appalled by the government's calculated and uncaring aggression, and more impassioned by the cause than ever before, the last of his reservations disappear.

And yet, before speaking, Lalor takes pause, savouring the moment.

'I looked around me,' he would later recount. 'I saw brave and honest men, who had come thousands of miles to labour for independence. I knew that hundreds were in great poverty, who would possess wealth and happiness if allowed to cultivate the wilderness that surrounded us. The grievances under which we had long suffered, and the brutal attack of the day, flashed across my mind; and with the burning feelings of an injured man, I mounted the stump and proclaimed "Liberty".'[2]

It is the moment when the moral-force Chartists finally fade entirely from view, and those who – even if reluctantly – have come to believe in physical force take over.

Led by Peter Lalor.

Standing on a stump before the pole that bears their new flag, the Irishman holds the muzzle of his rifle with his left hand, its butt resting on his foot, and is suddenly an imposing figure as he clears his throat to address them.

The men, *his men*, hang on his every word as in eloquent language that would have done his brother Fintan and his father, Patrick, proud, Peter Lalor makes his rallying cry. This fight for liberty is serious, and if the men who stand here really are ready to honour the promise of the day before to rescue by force any here who should be arrested, then they must understand that the result can only be a clash with the armed might of the government. For seven of their number have been arrested this very morning! If they are not ready to resist that, then they should leave now.

The resolute expressions of the men before him and their murmurings of approval tell him that he has their support. He goes on, calling for volunteers to come forward and enrol themselves in the militia that he is then and there forming, to do what needs to be done.

Companies are put together on the spot through a combination of natural affiliations and common weaponry. Pistols go with pistols, swords with swords and rifles with rifles. Here are the diggers with shotguns, there the French and Italians forming a troop, there the sailors, and over there those who have no firearms but fancy their chances with pikes . . . and so on.

Lalor's insists they choose 'the best men amongst you, those you can most depend upon'[3] to lead them.

A large group of Americans who possess many rifles and, of course, their ubiquitous Colt revolvers are present. In short order they have formed themselves into the 'California Rifles', commanded by one 'Captain' Nelson – the honorific being instantly accorded to all those elected to lead their companies.

Because language is clearly going to be a problem, given the number of nationalities present, Lalor is again eager that Raffaello Carboni be involved as much as possible. Not only is Carboni deeply experienced in insurrection – he is quick to boast that he was taught the art of guerrilla warfare under the eye of Garibaldi himself – but he is also a firm believer in the cause at hand and speaks all the major European languages.

'I want you, Signore,' Lalor says, gripping the hand of Raffaello Carboni warmly before pointing to a group of French and Italians who are without weaponry. 'Tell these gentlemen, that, if they cannot provide themselves with fire-arms, let each of them procure a piece of steel, five or six inches long, attached to a pole, and that will pierce the tyrants' hearts.'[4]

It is a strong line – and totally treasonous, of course – and is overheard by one who takes careful mental note of it to report in full later. To Carboni, it is as music to his ears. Though Lalor can speak a few words of French tolerably well, he knows few more Italian, German or Spanish words than 'Rome', 'Munich' and 'Madrid'. The chance to be his interpreter and thus, effectively, his aide-de-camp is thrilling.

Hundreds of men step forward to affirm their willingness to do so, as the brother of George Black, Alfred Black – who Lalor names as his 'Secretary of War' – notes down the names of each of the companies, together with those whom they have elected to be their 'captains'.

Not surprisingly, Carboni is captain of the French and Italians, while none other than that well-known figure on the goldfields, the quietly spoken but resolute James Esmond, the discoverer of gold at Clunes, commands the Second Rangers. A young German–Jewish man by the name of Edward Thonen emerges as the leader of a company of riflemen; Charles Ross, a group with rifles and muskets; and two Irishmen, Patrick Curtain and Michael Hanrahan,[5] form up their countrymen and a scattering of other nationalities, including a native-born Australian, Monty Miller, with the Irish weapon of choice throughout the ages: the pike.

With a modicum of organisation thus imposed on the throng, the men in their six companies, with their captains in front, now form up before the podium. And now Lalor raises his right hand towards the Southern Cross, palm facing outwards, and indicates that he wishes them to do the same – an order instantly complied with.

'It is my duty now to swear you in,' he begins, his words rolling over this international sea of hard men, 'and to take with you the oath to be faithful to the Southern Cross. Hear me with attention. The man who, after this solemn oath, does not stand by our standard, is a coward in heart. I order all persons who do not intend to take the oath, to leave the meeting at once. Let all [companies] under arms "fall in" in their order round the flag-staff . . .'[6]

Not one man leaves the meeting. They are staying. They are committed to the cause. By way of emphasis, that all their men are present and accounted for, the captains fire off a rough military salute to their leader, their open hands to their foreheads and quickly back down to their sides.

All is ready.

Again indicating he wishes them to follow his lead, Lalor removes his hat, kneels and raises his right palm outwards to the flag, *their* flag, and says in a forceful tone with measured pace, 'We swear by the Southern Cross to stand truly by each other, and fight to defend our rights and liberties.'[7]

The sea of men, their heads bowed, their hands raised, repeat the words with an earthy, throaty rumble, 'WE SWEAR BY THE SOUTHERN CROSS . . .'[8] which is followed by a unanimous 'AMEN'.[9]

Raffaello Carboni would also record the wondrous look of the men at this moment: 'The earnestness of so many faces of all kinds of shape and colour; the motley heads of all sorts of size and hair; the shagginess of so many beards of all lengths and thicknesses; the vividness of double the number of eyes electrified by the magnetism of the southern cross; was one of those grand sights, such as are recorded only in the history of "the Crusaders in Palestine".'[10]

It is done. For the first time since the colonisation of this land began seven decades earlier, the fealty of a large body of colonists has been sworn to an entity other than the British crown. Instead, these men have sworn loyalty to each other, to their rights and liberties, and to this land beneath the Southern Cross. True, from a purely legal point of view, this could be construed as treason, but it does not feel like this.

For indeed this really is a land where Jack is every bit as good as his master, and if his master does not accept that and insists on treating Jack as a mere vassal, then, reluctantly but forcefully, Jack will have to teach him some respect.

———————

To arms, brothers! It is time for a show of strength. The men need to do something to demonstrate to all on the goldfields just how strong and united they are – something to help galvanise those who might like to join them but are wavering.

Why not a march? Yes, a march, a real 'military' one.

Or at least as military as they can make it. After Captain Ross retrieves the Southern Cross from the flagpole and fastens it atop a staff long enough to keep it from the dirt, he personally leads their procession. The rest of the diggers fall in behind him in their companies, marching two abreast the half mile or so. from Bakery Hill to the Eureka.

Of course, when leading such a procession, it is a good look to be carrying something slightly different from everyone else, so Patrick Curtain, who is the leader of the worthy pikeman, asks Raffaello Carboni if they can swap weapons. He will take Carboni's sword, brought all the way from Italy, and give him his pike to carry. Alright . . . ?

Va bene.

All up, as they march behind Peter Lalor, who is proudly bearing his own family sword, more and more diggers join the happy, angry, determined throng, and no fewer than 1000 of them are under arms in some fashion, be it gun, pike, knife or sword – even shovel and pick. They make an impressive sight. The procession is so long that when the flag of the Southern Cross is visible on the road that reaches the Eureka on one hill, the tail end is visible by the Catholic church on the opposite hill, at least half a mile away across the gully.

This is a show of force, a statement that the arguments the diggers have on the issues before them are not mere words. They have muscle, too. Armed muscle. So much muscle, it seems, that none of the Redcoats, traps and troopers are visible, having chosen this very time to have a bit of a spell back at the Government Camp. How very, very convenient . . .

For the diggers, it feels good to be part of the movement, parading thus. But there is also an ugly edge to it. When that bastard Dr Alfred Carr is spotted – the very one whose testimony tried to get that even bigger bastard Bentley off, the one who is thought to be a spy for the government – he is grabbed by the collar by one enormous digger, who puts a cocked revolver to his head. There is a general rush upon Carr by other diggers, and it is only by the considerable efforts of Timothy Hayes that the doctor is saved and told to stay well clear of the scene. Carr does not have to be told twice.

And now Lalor gives an order. If they are going to make a stand – and by God they *are* – then they are going to need a central and defendable stronghold. And there it is, lads. Just a hundred yards from where they have finished their parade is a small hillock that – in his first major act as their leader – Lalor designates as the spot where they will make that stand. It is on the Eureka part of the goldfield, in the heart of where the Tipperary mob holds sway.

Around its lower reaches, Lalor orders his men to build a defined enclosure with clear boundaries where they can muster, go through drills and, if necessary, find armed refuge from the next license-hunt. It is with this in mind that the diggers begin to busy themselves constructing a kind of 'stockade' – a rough, higgledy-piggledy rectangular barricade composed of slabs of wood from their shafts placed broadly upright but sloped a little away from the vertical facing outwards,[11] together with upturned old carts and anything else that comes to hand. To make the whole thing more secure, huge mounds of earth are shovelled up against its base. The roughly four-foot-high barricade surrounds a broad four acres of land measuring about 100 by 200 yards.[12] After all, if the government can have their enclosed Camp, which lies on the other side of the large gully from Eureka, then the diggers can have their own defensive enclosure.

Yes, the whole thing encompasses the tents of a number of miners, including Lalor's, but most of it is open ground on a slope overlooked by the Free Trade Hotel on high. It is situated little more than 200 yards from the shattered, blackened ruins of Bentley's hotel, and Lalor has especially selected it for its commanding view of the Camp, which lies on its own rise a little under a mile to the west. If there is any attack coming, the diggers should be able to see it and have plenty of warning. A bonus is the number of 'shepherds' holes' at the site – shallow pits left by the half-hearted diggers who were minding the spot for other diggers – that lie on the north-westernmost part of the Stockade, which are ideally suited to hold men with rifles in comparative shelter. Most of these holes come complete with a small framework of logs around them to hold the windlass, with dirt packed up around their sides, making them superb defensive positions. Those inside can poke their guns through the small gaps in the logs, which are further protected by large slabs of bark nailed horizontally.

The outward tilted angle of those slabs of split logs is designed to make it difficult for men on horseback or foot to easily charge over the barricade, even in lower parts. Between and around those slabs are overturned carts, bags of sand, felled trees, branches and anything else that comes to hand.

In other places, higher up, small 'portholes' have also been left in the barricades for the same purpose, so that defenders can fire on attackers while either staying relatively safe or positioning themselves over the top of the barricade. Against that, a defensive weakness of the Stockade is that, because it is built on a slope, there is higher ground overlooking it, from which a fair portion of those inside would be exposed.

In this matter Vern proves himself useful, and with his tremendous sword giving him an appropriately martial air, issues quite expert directions as to how the whole thing should be constructed most quickly and efficiently, giving the Stockade maximum defensive advantage.[13] In the words of digger John Lynch, who has just been elected a captain himself, '[Vern's] military learning comprehended the whole system of warfare, every mode of attack and defence. He could dilate on them for hours, and with eclectic nicety describe their strong and weak points. But fortification was his strong point. . . .'[14]

True, with only four hours put to its construction, the Eureka Stockade is a long way from being an impregnable fortress, but it will provide some relief from both flying bullets and galloping horsemen if the time comes and, whatever else, it gives the diggers a recognised gathering point.

Keeping the men together is clearly going to be important – their unity is their strength. If they are separated from each other, the Joes could easily pick them off one by one. And yet, as Lalor makes clear to his men, the place is more like their secure barracks than a sure citadel. They need to be ready to move at a moment's notice, to attack their foes from outside, should the need arise.

They have scouts placed throughout the diggings, looking out for the traps and troopers, and Lalor and his men intend to be ready to race wherever they might be needed most urgently. And hopefully, they might soon be receiving reinforcements from other diggings . . .

Mid-afternoon, Thursday, 30 November 1854, the Creswick Creek diggers rally . . .

In full cry, Thomas Kennedy is an impassioned and impressive speaker, and rarely has he been in fuller cry than now.[15] An hour before the atrocities of the morning in Ballarat, he had, in the company of George Black, commenced to race the 11 miles to Creswick on horseback and is now nearing the climax of his speech. In something between a howl and a harangue, he is making clear to the 2000 Creswick diggers that their brothers on the Eureka *need* them – their muscle and might – and the Creswickians must quickly march to Ballarat before the Redcoats attack. Then a messenger from Eureka suddenly appears, bearing a letter written by Samuel Irwin of the *Geelong Advertiser*, addressed to George Black and Tom Kennedy or '*any MAN on Creswick*'.[16]

It is passed to George Black, who is on the podium with Kennedy, and so Black now steps forward to read it. The letter communicates the shocking license-hunt of the morning with the subsequent arrests, the resultant meeting on Bakery Hill and that an attack really is imminent. They need help *now*. Not tomorrow morning, not the next day, not when the Creswick men can manage to get away. NOW! A similar message has been sent to Bendigo, where Henry Holyoake is attempting the same task as Thomas Kennedy.

Here at Creswick, the letter provides the perfect fuel for Kennedy, who once again soars to the heights of oratory, inspiring, imploring, *insisting* that all brave men immediately start the march to Ballarat. If they will but just come, they will find plenty of space for them – plenty of food, arms and ammunition – and all they must do is get themselves there, NOW.

To arms, brothers! The diggers of Creswick begin to prepare for the journey this very evening! And they will also need everything they can get from the local storekeepers in terms of guns and ammunition.

While Kennedy stays behind to rally them, George Black gallops back to the Stockade.

Late Thursday afternoon, 30 November 1854, drills at the Stockade

For the rest of the day the various companies go through a variety of drills. Some of the squads have pikes, others rifles.

Here, now, one old miner with military experience draws himself up and says . . .

'Shoulder . . . poles!' *(The men bring their poles up to their shoulders)*

'Order . . . poles!' *(They bring their poles back down to their sides)*

'Ground arms.' *(They place their poles on the ground before them)*

'Stand at ease.' *(They slump back to something approaching their normal form)*

'Pick up pole . . .'

'Shoulder pole . . .'

'Right face . . .'

'Quick march . . .'

'Right countermarch . . .'[17]

And so it goes as they march back and forth for over two hours as the sun beats down, and they go from being totally shambolic to something a little less than shambolic. At this point Lieutenant Michael Hanrahan, the fiery Irishman,[18] who is Patrick Curtain's second-in-command, has his men line up in ranks three deep in front of him and orders them to, 'Prepare to receive cavalry!'[19]

To what? 'Prepare to receive cavalry!'[20]

This, it turns out, means preparing themselves to face men charging at them on horseback, and Hanrahan gives it to them straight. They must charge at the horses with their weapons first and foremost. 'Poke your pike into the guts of the horse, and draw it out from under their tail . . .'[21]

All up, there is general enthusiasm for what they are embarked on, but none appears more passionate for the cause than the digger who charges back and forth, shouting wildly in a manner that shows he is badly drunken.

'We'll fight!' roars he. 'We'll take them on! We'll fight for our rights and liberties and we'll burn the Government Camp so it blazes like the Eureka Hotel!'[22]

Perhaps it amuses some diggers, but certainly not all. Of course Vandemonians are known to shout and drink and carry on like that, but, as far anyone knows, Henry Goodenough – a rather pompous Englishman with mutton-chop whiskers – has never even been to Van Diemen's Land, so it doesn't quite fit.

For his part, Carboni puts up with it for as long as he can – which is not very long at all – and then loses his temper. Framing his right foot to an all-but-exact replica of the country he is proud to hail from, he skips forward, swings and plants one of his precious new watertight boots right in Goodenough's ample posterior.

Basta! BASTA! Enough. Enough. Enough.

For all that, Carboni must get back to drilling his own company, though he is not impressed with what he has seen thus far, all this 'marching, counter-marching, orders given by everybody, attended to by nobody'.[23]

Another who is highly uncomfortable with the whole scene is John Basson Humffray. Throughout he has been a man for moral force, for constitutional agitation, for the rule of law . . . and now that the physical-force men have taken over, now that it really looks as if there will be serious violence, he knows firmly that he wants no part of it.

When the drilling started a little earlier, one man approached the moral Chartist and threatened him: '[If you do] not form a company, and join the diggers, I will despatch you'.[24] Again, the situation was defused by others intervening, but there had been no relief. Only a short time after that, a red-faced, pepperbox-revolver-wielding, cussing Yankee similarly threatened to take his life.

'I am unarmed,' Humffray replied with dignity. 'If you choose to be a murderer, fire away.'[25] And with that, he walks away from the affray and reaches his tent unharmed.

Back inside the Stockade the captains decide that that is enough drilling for one day.

As the sun begins to fall towards the western horizon on this last day of November, Carboni must hurry off to attend a hastily convened meeting of all the captains of the divisions with Lalor.

Thursday, 30 November 1854, late afternoon, the Government Camp receives, and writes, troubling reports

It has been a long, troubling day. But at least the troopers have managed to make those seven arrests. Commissioner Rede is just in the process of forming up a report to his superiors, addressed to Colonial Secretary John Foster with a penmanship as thin and elegant as his hand – *Our object was gained: we maintained the law . .* .[26] – when he is interrupted by a rather breathless spy from the diggings who has news that cannot wait. This spy, who seems to be slurring his words a little as if he might be drunk, reports that the Government Camp will come under attack at four o'clock the following morning! The diggers will be armed and determined to release the prisoners.

In light of this news, the Commissioner is not panicked, feeling that the authorities will have the means of defending themselves, but he does finish his report with a rather more urgent tone: 'We shall be on the alert. The absolute necessity of putting down all meetings, public and private, I think must now be apparent for the abolition of the license-fee is merely a watchword. The whole affair is a strong democratic agitation by an armed mob. If the Government will hold this and the other goldfields it must at once crush this movement, and I would advise again that this gold field be put under Martial Law, and artillery and a strong force sent up to enforce it. I would also suggest a proclamation from His Excellency that it is his determination to stop it. I must also earnestly request some instruction for my further guidance. I have &c. (Signed) Robt. Rede. Resdt. Commissioner.'[27]

———

Captain Pasley, meanwhile, is dashing off his own quick report to the Colonial Secretary, to ensure the government is fully informed: 'From what I have seen today, I am convinced more than ever that very strong measures are necessary on this Gold Field, and that sedition must be put down by force. I feel sure that conciliatory measures will only do harm at such a late period in the disturbances, and that the disaffected must be coerced. Although I have no doubt of our holding the camp against any force that the diggers can bring into the field, I think it is very desirable that we should be reinforced by the whole disposable troops in Melbourne, and by Artillery.'[28]

A rider is soon dispatched to Melbourne bearing both of their communiqués, the hooves of his galloping horse throwing up little spurts of dust behind.

Early evening, Thursday, 30 November 1854, a meeting of minds inside the Stockade

After the excitement of the monster meeting and the drilling and the marching, relative quiet has once again descended on the diggings as the men make their way back to their tents and hovels to either throw together some tucker for themselves or – if they are so blessed – have their missus do the same. (On the menu tonight, the same thing as every night – chops, sausages, damper and 'black murphies', otherwise known as potatoes, all of it washed down with billy tea.)

Not all of them are so engaged.

Within the confines of the canvas-walled general store of a just-married young couple, Martin[29] and Anne Diamond, Peter Lalor has convened a meeting of all the captains of the divisions formed that afternoon. Joining them are those influential leaders of the Ballarat Reform League who believe the time has come for physical force to be ranged against the Ballarat authorities. Effectively the BRL, such as it was originally constituted, is now no more – in Hotham's later estimation, this day has marked the time 'the professional agitator gave place to the man of physical force'.[30]

The meeting is held in a room only half again as big as an eight-by-eight-foot claim, meaning the dozen men are sitting around a small table packed shoulder to shoulder – fitting for the tight, tense atmosphere. It is one thing to have gathered all the diggers together, to have made fine speeches, to have saluted their new flag, and to have given their solemn oath of allegiance to each other and that flag. But now that the sheer excitement and exultation has passed, these men are left with the serious business of actually leading this mass of men in an armed rebellion against a serious force of troopers and soldiers. Against the possibility that they might be burst in upon by some of the spies they feel sure are amongst them, the experienced Raffaello Carboni places on the table some black bottles of rum and gives everyone a tumbler, so that it might look as if they are doing no more than having a nobbler or two together.

And then to business. There is Lalor at the head of the table, his eyes glittering and intense, his expression resolute. For the first time he understands the passions that so gripped his brother Fintan all those years ago when he rose to the fore of the Free Ireland movement.

There is, of course, Raffaello Carboni, like a frenetic cat, bursting with energy and only just managing to sit still. There is the grave-looking Irishman Timothy Hayes. As he has a wife and children, the stakes for him are higher than most. In good conscience he cannot be anywhere but here in the group that is leading the movement, while still not being comfortable at the increasingly militant turn it is taking. George Black feels much the same. For his part, however, John Manning has no such reservations, and he doesn't mind saying so.

Also present is the exceedingly slight and short 23-year-old, Edward Thonen, the Jewish man from 'Prussia', which is situated somewhere between Prague and Russia, as far as the other diggers can work out. He has always stood out on the goldfields for the 'lemonade' he sells to thirsty miners and his shrewd chess playing, and now stands out for the intensity of his gaze. All blazing eyes burning through a bushy beard and whiskers, he exudes determination to see this thing through, *komme was wolle* – come what may. Thonen is from the town in Germany where Karl Marx's great compadre Friedrich Engels spent a great deal of time – Elberfeld – and was involved in the very uprising that Engels had participated in, which caused Thonen to effectively be expelled from Prussia.

Carboni describes him, ever-colourfully, as, 'Shrewd, yet honest; benevolent, but scorning the knave; of deep thought, though prompt in action; Thonen possessed the head belonging to that cast of men whose word is their bond.'[31]

The affection that Carboni has for Thonen, as a matter of fact, is only matched by the extreme dislike he has for Thonen's rough compatriot, Friedrich Vern, who is also at the meeting and clearly itching to *'meet zer Tyrann mit der Pistole in der Handt!'*[32]

The oldest among them, at 40, is the Irishman Patrick Curtain, who, like Timothy Hayes and Tom Kennedy, is a family man and father of four. That afternoon, Curtain was impressive in the way he handled his newly formed pikemen division and is clearly a man of some military experience.

It is time to get to grips. As a result of a previous quick meeting in Carboni's tent, John Manning now hands over to Lalor a proposed motion – seconded by Carboni – to properly get the meeting underway, calling on Peter Lalor to be formally elevated to the position of 'Commander-in-Chief, by the majority of votes'.[33] (No, they do not live in a democracy in Victoria, as none of them has the right to vote for those in the Legislative Council, but there is, by God, a democracy in the Stockade.)

Now, being careful about such things – after the bitter experience of his family in Ireland – Lalor is careful to tear up the piece of paper after reading the motion for fear that it will fall into the wrong hands. Not that he is remotely nervous or lacking in confidence.

It is at this point that Lalor rises and proceeds to choose his words carefully.

'Gentlemen,' he begins in his rich Irish brogue, 'I find myself in the responsible position I now occupy, for this reason. The diggers, outraged at the unaccountable conduct of the Camp officials in such a wicked license-hunt at the point of the bayonet, as the one of this morning, took it as an insult to their manhood, and a challenge to the determination come to at the monster meeting of yesterday. The diggers rushed to their tents for arms, and crowded on Bakery Hill. They wanted a leader. No-one came forward, and confusion was the consequence. I mounted the stump, where you saw me, and called on the people to "fall in" into divisions, according to the fire-arms they had got, and to choose their own captains out of the best men they had among themselves. My call was answered with unanimous acclamation, and complied to with willing obedience. The result is that I have been able to bring about that order, without which it would be folly to face the pending struggle like men.

'I make no pretensions to military knowledge. I have not the presumption to assume the chief command, no more than any other man who means well in the cause of the diggers. I shall be glad to see the best among us take the lead.

'In fact, gentlemen, I expected someone who is really well known,' he says, referring to the notably absent John Basson Humffray, 'to come forward and direct our movement! However, if you appoint me your commander-in-chief, I shall not shrink; I mean to do my duty as a man. I tell you, gentlemen, if once I pledge my hand to the diggers, I will neither defile it with treachery, nor render it contemptible by cowardice.'[34]

It is an impressive speech, with John Lynch recording, 'The delivery, pregnant with manly sentiment, and modest withal, depicts the man — for sincerity and courage, worthy of a place in the rank of heroes.'[35]

Still, one man does not obviously agree.

For his part, Friedrich Vern also feels qualified to lead and steps up to actively campaign for the position. In an accent so thick it's like wading through springtime mud on the diggings, Vern unburdens himself of every ounce of military knowledge he has in him. At least that is what those at the meeting suppose he is talking about, through the few bits and pieces of phrases the listeners can decipher.

There is no doubt Vern really is a man with military nous and has overseen the efficient construction of the Stockade with that keen eye. He writes clear, concise instructions in the military manner that are well thought out and easy to follow, the lack of grammatical English notwithstanding. He is totally committed to the diggers' cause and generous — all remember his £100 contribution to get the legal defence campaign started for the three diggers accused of burning down the Eureka Hotel. And yet, having a foreigner as their formal leader would make it very difficult to get many of the Irish and British diggers to follow them, just on principle.

One thing the meeting can make out, however, is that he claims to have a rifle brigade of 500 German diggers ready to roll at his command, a welcome piece of news, if any of them could bring themselves to believe it. Where is this mysterious brigade? Certainly there are quite a few Germans among the diggers — but hardly 500 of them.

And even Lalor's personal questioning on the subject does not prompt the German to reveal the tiniest clue as to where these men might actually be. In short, while Vern's martial ardour is never in doubt, it is obvious to them all – with the exception of Vern himself – that he is not the man to lead them overall. (None is more opposed than Carboni, who actively dislikes Vern from the beginning and records his own view that nothing the German says is ever anything more than a particular English-like word he has invented for the occasion: 'blabberdom'.)[36] After Vern has finished his speech, Carboni speaks up and promptly and formally proposes that Lalor should be elected Commander-in-Chief.

The motion is quickly seconded by Edward Thonen, and the vote in the Irishman's favour is carried by the crushing majority of 11 to one, with only Vern voting against,[37] and there is immediately warm acclaim from the other members of the Council.

A grave and committed Lalor now stands to thank the Council for the honour of leading them and to state once more that he will do his utmost to lead the diggers so they can successfully resist the force of the authorities with their own, superior force. And he is also gracious to Vern, quickly installing him as his second-in-command to be, effectively, in charge of all things military.

When the Council adjourns – as the sun begins to sink on the eve of the first day of summer, shining strongly through a few scattered clouds with golden fringes above, while on the northern horizon some dark clouds have suddenly appeared – everyone understands that under Lalor's leadership they are committed. The authorities can do their worst, but they will be met by armed resistance, so long as the diggers can get the weaponry and ammunition they need. Their grim course is set.

Early evening, 30 November 1854, on the diggings, put up your arms

And now in the deep shade thrown by the quartz-strewn ranges across the diggings, the fires are being lit and the billies boiled as the men prepare to have an evening pot of tea. Outside one of these tents, Henry Nicholls is sitting with his brother Charles and others, including the exhausted editor of *The Diggers' Advocate*, George Black, waiting for their brew. They look up to see a man familiar to Henry – the very good-looking and ardent Canadian, Charles Ross. With his piercing blue eyes, tousled hair, fine features and barrel chest, Ross is known as a firm favourite with the ladies on the diggings, but now he looks *commanding*. He has with him nothing less than a file of men, lined up in rough military formation. What is going on?

Could Ross have a quick word with Henry and Charles?

Certainly. Come into the tent.

Now, 'Captain Ross', as the men outside refer to him, is very gentlemanly about it and practically statesmanlike – even if he does refuse their offer of a cup of tea – but is also clear and determined. He wants their guns. Because Ross has been friendly with the Nicholls brothers, he happens to know that they possess two very valuable double-barrelled guns made in London.

'We have embarked on a perilous enterprise,' he says of the afternoon's events, 'and must protect ourselves the best we can, and as we are acting for the general good, if you do not choose to join us, it is at least fair that you contribute your arms.'[38]

At first blush Henry Nicholls thinks this a very fair argument. And even if it isn't, it is fairly obvious that Captain Ross does not have to ask – the men outside are the best argument of all that the Canadian can just take their guns if he so chooses. And yet, those guns are particularly valuable, together worth in excess of £30, and Nicholls is reluctant to just hand them over. But he has an idea . . .

'How do you know we will not join you?' he asks Ross reasonably.

'That's all I ask,' Ross replies. 'I'd sooner have you with the guns, than the guns without you.'

'I can't promise to join you until I see what you're doing,' Henry Nicholls says, 'but perhaps I can come and have a look tomorrow, and if I approve, my brother and I will join, not to mention others.'[39]

A reasonably happy Ross agrees to this – at least more happy than his men are when he emerges from the tent sans guns – and they all take their leave. The Nicholls brothers are happy to see them go. While they are both sympathetic to the aims of the diggers to abolish the license fee – Henry has, after all, written as much many times in *The Diggers' Advocate* – neither is convinced that taking up arms against the Redcoats is wise. The main thing, for the moment, is that they still have their precious guns.

7 pm, 30 November 1854, inside Diamond's Store at the Stockade, the priest presses for peace

The Council for the Defence is being quickly reconvened, this time with a non-Council member in attendance – Father Smyth. Upon consideration, it has been decided to attempt, one more time, to avoid the bloodshed that now seems inevitable.

George Black puts forward to the meeting a proposal, which is instantly seconded by John Manning, that they should this very evening send a deputation to the Camp, to demand the immediate release of the diggers who had been dragged to the lockup that morning, and to also demand that Commissioner Rede make a pledge to stop the license-hunting.

In return, the diggers would agree to disarm, disperse and get back to work, allowing the time necessary to see if this could be sorted out peacefully. Ideally, they would again petition the Lieutenant-Governor and this time he would see reason.

All those in favour, say 'Aye'.

Aye! *Aye!* AYE! *Si! Jawohl!*

Father Smyth proposes – speaking up a little now, as a sudden rainstorm on the roof has begun to make a din – that George Black himself should go, while Peter Lalor insists that Raffaello Carboni be the second man of the delegation. For one thing, the fact that the Italian has a slight personal acquaintance with the Commissioner cannot hurt. This, too, is agreed to unanimously. Father Smyth promises to accompany both gentlemen into the Camp that evening to provide safe passage.

7.30 pm, 30 November 1854, the Government Camp girds its considerable loins

Fie, fie, the battle is nigh. Rumours swirl, tension rises. The strong feeling among the officers, soldiers and police inside the Camp is that an attack is imminent, perhaps within hours. After all, they reason, the armed diggers are outside in their thousands, while inside the walls of the Camp they are in their mere hundreds, waiting for reinforcements. Strategically, it would make a lot of sense for the diggers to attack immediately.

Around the perimeter of the Government Camp all the sentries have their guns loaded and capped – putting a percussion cap atop the weapon's nipple, thus requiring only the hammer to drop for it to fire – and all are on full alert. Inside, the soldiers and police keep their guns by them at all times and speak in that roaring whisper in order to be heard above the heavy rain that has suddenly broken upon them. They are in near darkness, the order having been given to douse all lights to make everyone less visible targets should there be an attack. Because some soldiers, in the British military tradition, have their families living with them in the barracks, all of those women and children have been placed inside one secure storeroom with walls so thick they will be safe from bullets and musket balls alike. Other buildings within the compound have everything from bags of corn to piles of firewood stacked around to enable them to better withstand whatever is fired at them. The troopers' horses have saddles on, ready to be ridden out at a moment's notice. The soldiers and police sleep in their uniforms, guns by their side, ready to move.

8 pm, 30 November 1854, on the Ballarat diggings

Music in the distance. Rough, raucous music. These are not songs to soothe the savage breast, but to rally it, whatever the mood. It is coming from the blaring band of Row's Circus, playing up a storm in the cold moonlight now that the rain has stopped and the clouds have cleared, and yet it would require far more than the musical abilities of the ragtag musicians within the tent to lift the mood of the three men on a mission, who now make their way past and barely glance in their direction. For from the diggings, George Black, Raffaello Carboni and Father Smyth are on their way to the Government Camp to meet Commissioner Rede in an attempt to avert disaster.

As they pass the circus, they hear the drunken cursing and shouting of the revellers, and an old meditation pops into Carboni's head, *'Unde bella et pugna infer vos?'*[40] 'Whence come wars and fights among you?' Proceeding, they come across various groups of men anxiously discussing the day's events. Some, of course, are aware of just where the Father and two men are going. Those who aren't are duly informed.

As the men reach the bridge that leads to the Camp, they find it heavily guarded by stern police who block their free passage. No matter, it is for this precise purpose that Father Smyth has come. No man on earth, no matter the rank, has the authority to stop a man of God, and the Father is allowed in to arrange the meeting with Commissioner Rede.

Shortly thereafter, the good Father returns with Rede's second-in-command, Sub-Inspector Taylor, complete with 'his silver-lace cap, blue frock, and jingling sword, so precise in his movement, so

Frenchman-like in his manners, such a puss-in-boots',[41] as Carboni would later describe him. Yet Taylor is remarkably friendly, shaking the Italian's hand as soon as he has recognised him, saying in a forthright manner, 'We have been always on good terms with the diggers, and I hope we may keep friends still . . .'[42]

Taylor ushers them into the presence of 'King Rede', as Carboni thinks of him.

In the shadow of the moonlight, beneath a massive gum tree in front of the Police Magistrates' Court just outside the Camp – for the Commissioner does not want the diggers' delegation to see up close the fortifications that are being readied for the Camp's defence – Rede momentarily looks like an antipodean Napoleon Bonaparte, with such a bearing does he stand, complete with his right hand buried deep within his military jacket. This imperial effect is exacerbated by the two men immediately behind Rede – Taylor standing silent sentinel off his right shoulder; Police Magistrate Charles Henry Hackett, who is suddenly not so friendly while in the presence of Rede, off his left shoulder. Hackett, at least, gives Carboni some sense of confidence. 'His amiable countenance is of the cast that commands respect, not fear,' he would record.[43]

Speaking of whom . . .

The Commissioner begins by explaining that he could not take them to his own residence within the Camp, as his men are preparing for an attack from men looking just like them – diggers – and it would therefore not be safe. And then, after rather officiously asking their names, he advises that everything they say will be reported to his superiors in Melbourne. Black quickly makes clear, while Father Smyth hovers anxiously, that their business is firstly to express digger exasperation over that morning's license-hunt.

'To say the least,' says Black pointedly, 'it was very imprudent of you, Mr Rede, to challenge the diggers at the point of the bayonet. Englishmen will not put up with your shooting down any of our mates, because he has not got a license.'[44]

'Daddy Rede', as Carboni now has him, is affronted. 'Now Mr Black, how can you say that I ever gave such an order as to shoot down any digger for his not having a license?'[45]

Black does not back down. Does the Commissioner not understand that the diggers were only responding to the insults of the soldiery; that, good men that they are, they simply refused to be bullied in such a fashion over their licenses, and that is how the whole thing has come to this pass?

Which brings Black to the point of their visit: 'We demand the immediate release of those diggers who had been dragged to the lock-up in the morning hunt, for want of the license.'[46]

'*Demand?*' the Commissioner bursts back in a manner that would have made Lieutenant-Governor Hotham proud. 'First of all, I object to the word, because, myself, I am only responsible to government, and must obey them only: and secondly, were those men taken prisoners because they had not licenses? Not at all. This is the way in which the honest among the diggers are misled. Any bad character gets up a false report: it soon finds its way in certain newspapers, and the Camp officials are held up as the cause of all the mischief. Now, Mr Black, look at the case how it really stands. Those men are charged with rioting; they will be brought before the magistrate, and it is out of my power to interfere with the course of justice.'[47]

It is at this point that Hackett utters his first words, noting in his judicial capacity that the approach of the Commissioner has his full support.

With the chance of a full release thus disappeared, Black tries a new approach. 'Will you,' he asks, 'accept bail for them to any amount you please to mention?'[48]

After a brief consultation, Rede and Hackett agree that would be acceptable. Father Smyth would bring the money on the morrow and bail would be accepted for two of the prisoners – which is at least one concession. This leads Black to his second demand.

'We demand that you, as Commissioner, make a pledge not to come out any more for license-hunting.'[49]

Again, the Commissioner is nonplussed and not shy about expressing it. 'What do you think, gentlemen, Sir Charles Hotham would say to me if I were to give such a pledge? Why Sir Charles Hotham would have at once to appoint another Resident Commissioner in my place! I have a *dooty* to perform, I know my duty, I must *nolens volens* (willing or not) adhere to it.'[50]

Yes, Black acknowledges, the Commissioner does have a duty and many responsibilities, but a key part of those responsibilities is to act in a manner that will prevent bloodshed.

Again, Commissioner Rede is more than firm in his reply: 'It is all nonsense to make me believe that the present agitation is intended solely to abolish the license. Do you really wish to make me believe that the diggers of Ballarat won't pay any longer £2 for three months? The license is a mere cloak to cover a democratic revolution!'[51]

It is true, Black acknowledges carefully, that the license fee is not all of it.

'You yourselves very well know,' says the Commissioner, 'that if the license fee was abolished tomorrow you would have some other agitation.'[52]

'Well,' Black replies, 'we should agitate immediately for the franchise.'

'Yes,' says Rede, 'and after the franchise what next?'[53]

Funny he should ask. Does the catchcry 'unlock the lands'[54] – so the diggers can own and work their own properties nearby the diggings – ring any bell in the good ear of the Commissioner? But, for the moment, no issue is so important as stopping the license-hunts and the ongoing brutalisation of the diggers.

Raffaello Carboni now speaks his first words: 'Mr Rede, I beg you would allow me to state, that the immediate object of the diggers taking up arms was to resist any further license-hunting. I speak for the foreign diggers whom I here represent. We object to the Austrian rule under the British flag. If you would pledge yourself not to come out any more for the license, until you have communicated with *Son Excellence*, I would give you my pledge–'[55]

'Give no pledge, sir,' Father Smyth interrupts. 'You have no power to do so.'[56]

Rede, noting this curious stifling of the Italian, puts his hands together as in prayer, tapping together his forefingers, and says to Carboni, 'My dear fellow, the license is a mere watchword of the day, and they make a cat's-paw of you.' Smyth then chips in to Rede, 'You must also release the prisoners.'[57]

'I shall not do anything of the kind,' replies Commissioner Rede with a sense of outraged dignity at the Father's presumption.[58] 'As for giving any pledges or assurances, in the face of an armed mob, that is the last thing I will do. But if the people go quietly back to their work at once . . . I will not do anything further until I have received instructions from Melbourne.'[59]

Meeting concluded, the three visitors are escorted back to the bridge by Sub-Inspector Taylor, where the password is given and they are allowed to leave. As the disappointed group heads back, threading their way past the circus once again – now more raucous than ever – the road is busy and they are frequently stopped by groups of anxious men wanting to know the news. Will the authorities cede to their demands, or will the diggers have to fight for their cause?

Not an inflammatory man by nature, Black tells the inquirers as calmly as possible that while it appears to be out of the question that the seven men will be released, the Commissioner has at least promised to cease the license-hunts, so it is possible they are making some progress. This is wonderful news! No more license-hunts means no more confrontations, means it is highly unlikely that the government will be attacking them any time soon.

Alas, Carboni begs to differ, and says so. While he allows that the Commissioner might indeed consider holding off on the hunts, his own impression remains that 'the Camp, choked with Redcoats, would quash Mr Rede's "good judgment", get the better of his sense, if he had any of either, and that he would come out license-hunting in an improved style.'60

As the three continue to make their way back, Carboni is distracted by the fact that the good Father and Black keep whispering to each other, just as they have done on the way to the Camp, though what they are saying, he knows not. It just seems very rude.

Returning to the Stockade, where they quickly report their lack of progress to Lalor, each man heads off in search of some grub. And yet if the others are of heavy heart as they make for their tents, Lalor's is surely heavier still. He did not ask for this. He did not seek leadership of this affair just as, back in Ireland, he stood back from the fulminations of his father and brother about the rule of Britain. There, they were more passionate and better equipped to take the lead, and he was happy to let them do so.

But here? Here the leadership had been thrust upon him, and he had simply not resiled from it. For how could he?

He'd be damned if he would leave the iniquities of British rule in Ireland to make a new home in a new land, only to have the same oppressors follow him here. At some point a man has to make a stand, and that point has now come. And yet, he also knew what he was risking. All this and more he now tries to explain to the love of his life, Alicia Dunne, who awaits news in Geelong, where the 22-year-old is living with her uncle, Father Patrick Dunne, and continues to work as a schoolteacher:

Ballarat, November 30, 1854

My Dear,
Since my last, a most unfortunate state of things has arisen here. J mentioned that great excitement prevailed here, owing to the attempt of the magistrates to screen the murderer of a digger.

That excitement has been still further increased by wicked license-hunting. The authorities have gone so far as to have had the diggers fired upon this morning, who, in self-defence, have taken up arms and are resolved to use them. In fact, my dear, to confess the truth, I am one amongst them. You must not be unhappy on this account. I would be unworthy of being called a man, I would be unworthy of myself, and, above all, I would be unworthy of you and of your love, were I base enough to desert my companions in danger. Should I fall, I beseech you by your love for me – that love which has increased in proportion to my misfortunes – to shed but a single tear on the grave of one who has died in the cause of honour and liberty, and then forget me until we meet in heaven.

Farewell, and believe me, my dear—,
Yours until death,
PETER LALOR [61]

At this time, unbeknownst to any of those inside the Stockade, a distraught Father Smyth has returned alone to the Government Camp in the dead of night to see if he can help avoid the bloodshed that he believes is now otherwise guaranteed because, as he explains to Rede, 'There is no doubt the Camp will be attacked.'[62] It is the good Father's plea once more for the Commissioner to release the prisoners and call off the license-hunts while he, as a man of the cloth, will do everything he can to get the diggers to back down, disperse and return to their diggings.

The Commissioner is tired of all the talk: as long as the diggers remain armed, he will hear none of it. He is set on his course and knows what he wants – to crush this armed mob. Good luck, good night and may your God go with you, Father.

'I should not mention this,' Rede later writes of the night's meetings to his superior, 'but I think it shews they are frightened & from the fact of Humffray & other delegates having withdrawn themselves they begin to find it is a dangerous game they are playing.'[63]

Late evening, 30 November 1854, leaving Creswick for Ballarat

There is just something about Tom Kennedy – a man who knows how to move the masses. On this occasion he really has got them moving, marching, on the way to Ballarat, this very night! And, of course, he is at their head, wildly waving a sword as he leads the way. Not by the windy, circuitous roads – no, that would take too long – but as the kookaburra flies: through the bushes, down the gullies, up the hills, o'er the ranges.

And did someone say, '*Allons, mes amis,* let *nous* storm *la Bastille?*'

Not quite, but in a final bit of inspiration on what has already been an inspiring day, as the armed diggers march out of Creswick, the German band that is accompanying them strikes up the tune of the wonderful French national anthem and battle hymn, *La Marseillaise,* the most famous revolutionary song of them all. And so they go, some humming, the French among them singing, *'Allons enfants de la Patrie, le jour de gloire est arrivé.'*

Perhaps the day of glory really has arrived – perhaps it has not – but the binding force upon these antipodean marching men is a little further along in the song:

'Contre nous, de la tyrannie, l'étendard sanglant est levé, l'étendard sanglant est levé!' Against us tyranny's bloody flag is raised, the bloody flag is raised.

'MARCHONS! MARCHONS! Qu'un sangue impur, abreuve nos sillons.' March, march, so that their impure blood should water our fields.

On the one hand, an extraordinarily romantic scene. On the other, one that might make the heavens weep for fear of the way things are heading for all of God's children. And, in fact . . .

Just after 10 o'clock, deep in the bush, a sudden breath of cool, moaning wind wafts over the marching diggers even as, from somewhere to their far north, they hear a menacing boom. The trees themselves shudder and sway; dark clouds suddenly obscure the moon and stars; then the wind gets colder and stronger. The boom grows louder. And then lightning! And then furious thunder all but instantly afterwards! And then the lightning and thunder coming together, cracking like a dozen drovers' whips above their poor benighted heads.

And then comes the rain . . . torrents of it. *Torrents* of it, soaking them to the skin and through their belongings. It is more rain than most of the men have ever experienced in their lives – a thunderstorm for the ages with enough rain to make Noah start calling the animals in.

It dampens their ardour somewhat, as deep within the wilderness, without shelter, the sheer madness of what they are doing hits them. Some men turn back for good, some turn back to try again on the morrow, some find shelter where they can stop for the night.

Late evening, 30 November 1854, Government Camp

As soon as Father Smyth has left, once more the alarm goes up that the diggers will shortly attack the Camp. Even more quickly now, as they have practised, every man in the enclosure either takes his own weapon or is given one, along with ammunition, and goes to his appointed post. Key buildings within the Camp – the officers' mess, the hospital, the Commissioner's quarters and the barracks – are further fortified. They have further stacks of firewood, trusses of hay, bags of oats and bran put against them to better protect those inside from flying bullets.

Alas, no sooner have the fatigue parties finished this exhausting work than the violent storm that had so recently broken over the poor, sorry heads of the Creswick diggers now hits them. Certainly, some of the men can take shelter, but not the police troopers and their still saddled horses, as they must remain at their posts, exposed to the downpour, ready to move at a moment's notice. All the troopers can do through the sodden night is lie on the ground, wrapped in their cloaks, using their horses for what shelter they can.

Late evening, 30 November 1854, in Father Smyth's presbytery, Victoria St, Ballarat

Now back in his own quarters, a completely distraught Father Smyth, certain that catastrophe is now inevitable, writes a letter of last resort in his elegant hand:

To His Excellency Sir Charles Hotham HCB and Governor General of Victoria

Sir,

I have the honour to address Your Excellency, and most respectfully beg here to state what, in the opinion of many, is best calculated to allay our present excitement. The present emergency is a pressing one, and requires all the consideration and indulgence Your Excellency can extend us. Should Your Excellency so far favour us as to suspend the operation of the License Law here for some definite period – say till the coming Commission close their enquiries – I, at least, would feel certain of our being more than partially restored to law and order. May I assure Your Excellency that my only motive for being so bold, is my concern for those who are entrusted to my care.

I have the honour to be
Your Excellency's Very humble and obedient servant
Patrick Smyth
Catholic Priest [64]

Hotham, when he receives the letter, writes upon it 'Put away', and so a clerk does.

CHAPTER TWELVE

'AUX ARMES, CITOYENS!'

I am convinced that the future of this Colony depends on the
crushing of this movement in such a manner that it may act
as a warning . . . I should be sorry to see them return to their
work . . . We may be able to crush the democratic agitation at
one blow, which can only be done if we find them with arms
in their hands and acting in direct opposition to the laws.[1]

Commissioner Robert Rede writes to the Chief Commissioner of
the Goldfields on Saturday afternoon, 2 December 1854

The government of the day, schooled in the highways of
Imperial tradition, when aroused from repose on the sudden
discovery of gold, proved unequal to the emergency.[2]

Samuel Douglas Smyth Huyghue, Chief Clerk to
Commissioner Robert Rede, in his diary

Friday morning, 1 December, on the Eureka, the word is out

In a community as tight as that of the goldfields, it does not take long for news to travel – from digger to digger, tent to tent, diggings to diggings – particularly when the news is so alarming. That bastard Rede has refused to budge an inch, and the seven diggers arrested yesterday will be feeling the full weight of the law. He wouldn't even guarantee to our blokes that there'll be no further license-hunts! Such news galvanises the men not yet fully committed to the cause, and by mid-morning all of them have downed tools and upped arms. This is not through any command from Lalor's Council for the Defence, but from the pure desire of the broad mass of men – there will be no digging done this day and few businesses open.

In the Stockade, Lalor gives the order for the military drills to recommence in earnest, and the 1000 men now inside the fortifications set to with a will, engaging in exercises that lift in intensity when word arrives that heavily armed Redcoats are heading this way!

No matter that this proves to be a false alarm. Even if the troopers are not attacking now, it is obvious to all present that it is only a matter of time. Fortunately, more and more diggers keep pouring into their Stockade, particularly those who have been able to lay their hands on firearms and the homemade pikes that they now set to sharpening with great enthusiasm. The new arrivals form new divisions, the ranks of the pikemen becoming particularly strong. Drilling proceeds apace.

Even if the Redcoats haven't come yet, it can't be long before they do come – perhaps as soon as the first day after the Sabbath – and it is important to be ready for them. The orders ring out once more.

'Present . . . arms!'

'Shoulder . . . arms!'

'Right . . . face!'

'Quick . . . march!

Yes, in some ways they are like an army, but in one key way they are different. This nascent army has men from all over the world, most particularly Europe, the Americas and Australia itself – men of entirely different cultures and levels of education. As later described by Carboni, 'We were of all nations and colours.'[3] One of them, in fact, in Carboni's own company, is John Joseph, a black man from America who some say is an escaped slave. With large intelligent eyes, he is as passionate as any of the diggers-cum-soldiers in his troop, and Carboni is glad to have him.

The men are also of a wide variety of ages, with everyone from such young'uns as the 15-year-old Monty Miller from Van Diemen's Land and William Atherden, a 16-year-old English lad who deserted his ship at Geelong the year before, to 54-year-old John O'Neil from Cork, Ireland. Their points of unity, however, far outweigh their points of difference. Together, they are diggers; they are mates. They have worked together, suffered together, rejoiced together, and now they are united in their common disgust with an iniquitous government and a corrupt police force that have attempted to crush them. They want democracy. They want the right to buy land. They want a *fair go*, mate. And they will simply no longer be denied. This far and no further . . .

Only for lunch, as the heat of the day starts to gain a real grip, do the men in the Stockade finally take a breather. One man who has no time to stop, however, is swarthy German blacksmith, John Hafele. With his bulging biceps and glistening brow, he keeps working feverishly before his roaring furnace, pounding his hammer, making vicious-looking pikes – sharpened metal spikes secured to eight-foot poles – which he promises will most definitely 'fix red-toads and blue pissants especially'.[4] And he is serious in this claim. Some of the pikes are especially designed and constructed with a kind of razor-sharp, cruel hook on the end, potentially fulfilling three functions. Firstly, once stabbed into an abdomen it will pull half of the contents out again. Secondly, it is perfect to cut the bridle and saddle girth of any charging cavalry. Thirdly and even better, it can simply be used to hook a trooper out of the saddle.

Carboni is personally not convinced. As a veteran of real battles, he feels that the pikes will struggle to dispatch an opossum, let alone a man, if it comes to that. In fact, the diggers are so desperate for anything that even looks like real weaponry that they gratefully accept the offer of Sarah Hanmer, the American owner of Ballarat's

Adelphi Theatre, to take over her entire stock of swords from the props department.

What is needed, of course, is real weaponry and real ammunition.

One solution, as pushed by Captain Ross in recent days, is to simply take what is needed from those stores that have them. Lalor is pressed to give the order but for the moment refuses, even going so far as to issue a warning: 'Any man, who is found stealing, or in any way interfering with private property, may look to himself, for as sure as death my gun shall find him out.'[5]

For the moment, the redoubtable Vern, perhaps the most visibly active man in the Stockade – his long, flowing hair and jangling sword in motion as he strides back and forth, shouting guttural commands at whomever will listen – tells them not to worry, for he is certain that his fully armed and provisioned German Rifle Brigade will be arriving shortly. And yet the troop that turns up is not what he is expecting at all . . .

———————

Far and near and low and louder . . . On the roads of earth go by. Dear to friends and food for powder, Soldiers marching, all to die . . .[6]

On this occasion, the soldiers in question are actually the foot-slogging diggers from Creswick Creek, some 300 to 400 strong. Exhausted perhaps as much by Kennedy's rhetoric as by the storm-interrupted journey, they arrive in Ballarat from their diggings some 10 miles to the north, expecting to be provided with the 'arms, ammunitions, forage, and provisions'[7] that had been promised.

Alas, this is not the case. The rebels of Ballarat have neither arms to spare, nor alms for the poor, which these men clearly are. It is one thing to have reinforcements, but the truth of it is – as quickly becomes apparent – it is also a great inconvenience when the new arrivals bring so little with them. Nevertheless, arrangements are quickly made, with Edward Thonen organising for the local butcher to provide meat, the stores to provide bread and the men to gather wood. In short order a large fire is burning right in the middle of the Stockade and the Creswick men are fed.

This is good enough to get them through one meal, but it is now obvious that what was promised them is non-existent. While some remain and are quartered with friends both inside and more often outside the Stockade, most of them are soon dispersed across the Eureka.

Tim Hayes, for that matter, is also nowhere to be seen within the Stockade, and John Basson Humffray, whose 'moral force' philosophy has now been so completely run over by events and men of violent disposition, has also entirely disappeared. Raffaello Carboni hears from John Manning that the moral Chartists are continuing with their 'hallucinated yabber-yabber'[8] at the Star Hotel, and he is only glad that he is not present.

There are plenty of new arrivals, too. Among them are the Nicholls brothers, who have honoured their commitment of the evening before to Captain Ross and now turn up with their guns, while still being far from convinced that they want to join the cause. The first thing they see is Captain Nelson, the likeable, energetic American carpenter, drilling his men – all of them armed with guns – and getting them into some kind of military structure the best he can.[9] Many of these men are carrying powder flasks, some are making cartridges by 'rolling powder with shot in paper'[10] – which they can later empty down the barrel of their gun before ramming it and firing – and still others are having to make do with swords and even *sticks*. Clearly, however, they are deadly serious as they go through their drills and, with no real choice, the Nicholls brothers nominally join this company.

And there, of course, in the middle of the Stockade, is Peter Lalor.

'I was keenly observant to discover what kind of man he was,' Nicholls would later recount, 'and I quickly reached the conclusion that he hardly knew what he was doing. He seemed to me to be letting things take their own course. It did not appear to have occurred to him that he was taking a step which meant loss of life or liberty to many and that he had embarked on an enterprise from which there was hardly the possibility of retreat.'[11]

A brief conversation with Lalor confirms for Henry Nicholls that the Irishman does not even contemplate the possibility of retreat. For when Nicholls asks him what he wants from this rebellion, Lalor's words are explicit and exact: 'Independence!'[12] Nothing less than independence and a complete break with all things British, just as his father and brother had been actively agitating for in Ireland. And there is something about the way he says it that can make a man believe.

'Then I am with you,' promptly answers one of Nicholls's friends who is with him, before picking up a pike and proceeding to 'manifest warlike symptoms at once'.[13]

And he is not the only one. John Manning himself is heard to say 'We have ten against one of them. It will be very easy for us to take the Camp.'[14]

But neither Henry Nicholls nor his brother Charles are truly consumed with the same passion, though neither wishes to say so, as they both want to hold on to their guns. (In Henry Nicholls's words, 'I was not for independence . . . I was for the abolition of the licenses, as was everybody else, angry, ready to do almost anything to get rid of the degradation of being hunted, but not for independence in the fashion proposed.'[15])

For the moment, though, they bide their time and continue with the drills under Captain Nelson. They have no trouble seeing why their guns are so urgently required. By now the issue of the lack of supplies and munitions is becoming so critical that on the strength of it Lalor comes to a decision. Scribed by his newly installed Minister of War, Alfred Black, he issues the first of his 'Orders of War' – handed over to a trusted posse of armed men under the direct command of Lalor – for merchants to hand over the arms, ammunition and victuals needed for the Stockade. Lalor is insistent that the storekeepers be given receipts for everything, along with the assurance that they will be repaid.

The problem, of course, is how to differentiate between the 'authorised' Lalor men and roaming bands of armed thugs taking whatever they want from storekeepers 'in the name of the republic'?[16]

It is not easy.

Lalor's men do, indeed, hand over such receipts:

Received from the Ballarat Store 1 Pistol, for the Comtee X. Hugh M'Carty – Hurra for the people.[17]

The Reform Lege Comete – 4 Drenks, fower chillings; 4 Pies for fower of thee neight watch patriots. – X. P.[18]

But there is equally no doubt that many men, mostly Vandemonians, simply take advantage of the crisis to help themselves to whatever they like at gunpoint. All over the diggings, roving bands of men are descending on stores and 'in the name of the committee of the Eureka Stockade'[19] forcibly helping themselves first to munitions and then whatever else takes their fancy, from plump Yorkshire hams and coffee to wash them down with, right up to the cash-box containing the £20 of the day's takings. Yes, Lalor has, as he would describe it, 'promised to shoot the first man who took any property from another, except arms and ammunition, and what was necessary for the volunteers to use in their defence',[20] but neither he nor his men can be everywhere at once.

In such a situation, what Lalor most needs are good men whom he can count on, and one of them proves to be none other than James Esmond. As the acknowledged discoverer of gold in Victoria, Esmond has a certain prestige about him and, being the captain of his own company of men, proves to be very assiduous in doing everything he can to prevent looting. At one point when a particularly violent digger by the name of Moran points a gun at a shopkeeper, telling him to 'hand over quick',[21] it is Esmond who steps in. The shopkeeper would later say, 'I have very little doubt my life would have been taken that night only for Esmond.'[22]

As a matter of fact, Esmond becomes known among the shopkeepers as one who pays for powder and shot from *his own pocket*, so reluctant is he to take supplies in the name of a committee that actually has no funds to speak of. And yet, with Esmond's attitude so rare, there continue to be many cases of outright theft by those inside the Stockade.

Upon finding that one of his valuable horses has been stolen, a digger by the name of James McDowall marches to the Stockade to protest and is soon presented to Friedrich Vern, who introduces himself – wrongly – as 'the Commander-in-Chief' (he is still having a little trouble accepting the ascension of Peter Lalor). Vern makes no apology, saying that he and his men need horses and that is that. But at least McDowall is able to get a written guarantee that if the animal is hurt in any way he will be compensated. The document is signed:

A. A. Black, Secretary of War.
By order of the Commander in Chief, Friedrich Vern.[23]

This wildness coming from the Stockade is now threatening to run completely out of control. In the early evening, a digger rushes to John Basson Humffray's tent and tells him that the Council of War had sentenced Humffray 'to be hanged on the gum tree' outside his tent.[24]

The digger urges him to run for his life, but Humffray firmly refuses. It is true that he has been publicly denouncing the physical-force movement, knowing it to be 'unnecessary, ill-advised, and ill-timed',[25] but he cannot resile from that, and nor does he actually believe that the Council of War would have handed down any such punishment. He stands his ground.

Nearby, Henry Nicholls has just been summoned by Lalor's Secretary of War, Alfred Black, whom he knows well from sharing a tent together. Black has something to show him. It is nothing less than a Declaration of Independence that he has been working on, a document he hopes might be like the American Declaration of Independence that three-quarters of a century earlier had provided the framework by which America had severed its links with Great Britain. As Black regards Nicholls as a 'literary character'[26], he asks if Nicholls would mind having a look at it?

Without waiting for an answer, but with a great deal of pride, Alfred Black begins reading it, and, as Nicholls would recall, 'rounded out his words with unction, rolling them over his tongue as if he enjoyed their flavour'.[27]

Nicholls, however does not. While the Americans had held in their precious document that 'we hold these truths to be self-evident', whatever truths are in this Australian version are rather less inclined to immediately present themselves.

'It was long, very long, very flowery and decidedly verbose,' Nicholls would later recall of it. 'It was spicy, high-flavored, and I fancy that in it tyrants in general had a bad time of it.'[28] (Another witness would report it as rather 'bombastic and incoherent'.)[29]

When asked his opinion by Alfred Black on this occasion, however, Nicholls declines to criticise as he sees that Black really only wants an opinion if it is a positive one. It would be unwise to say what he truly thinks. Whatever he says is just noncommittal enough that Alfred Black is more convinced than ever that he has a masterpiece on his hands, one that Nicholls could probably not improve upon anyway. Before long, just as the sun is falling, Black stands on a stump – always the prop of first choice for diggers with something to say – and reads it out to the assembled armed diggers. Sure enough, he is cheered loudly at the whole idea of separating from Great Britain, if not necessarily at the words that he has chosen to express this view.

In the later words of Henry Nicholls, 'Those who were in the Stockade at the time, and there were many . . . committed themselves to a fight for independence . . . as if they could carry the whole colony with them.'[30]

Personally, Nicholls does not believe that for a moment, and nothing he has seen since he has entered the Stockade has changed his mind. It is total folly and he says so to his brother in the strongest terms as they return to their tent that night, there being no problem at this time with either entering or leaving the Stockade. They are expecting Alfred Black to return to the tent that evening, but he does not appear. They turn in, knowing that they must also turn up at the Stockade on the morrow or risk having their guns taken.

Early evening, Friday, 1 December 1854, Melbourne, time to move out

The situation in Ballarat now is judged to be so urgent that even on ten hours' notice Major-General Sir Robert Nickle has been able to marshal his troops, and they now set off for the diggings. They include, *The Argus* reports, 'twenty-four men-of-war's men, and about twenty marines from H.M. ship *Electra*',[31] and those remaining companies of the 12th and 40th Regiments who had not yet been committed, together with 50 mounted troopers and the same number of foot police – a body totalling 800 men to bolster the 450 men already on site. They take with them no fewer than 57 baggage and ammunition wagons in a column a mile long with two six-pounder field guns and two twelve-pounder howitzers. And they are carrying specially selected 'shrapnel shell ammunition' to cause maximum damage. A single shot from one of the twelve-pounders would be capable of killing a dozen diggers at a time, not to mention grievously wounding many more – along with completely demolishing a section of the wall of the Stockade, should it come to that. It is not possible for such a huge body of men and munitions to move quickly, and it is for this reason that Sir Robert Nickle and his adjutant general, Colonel Macartney, plan to delay their own departure until three o'clock on the Sunday morning. Even that far behind, by travelling fast and light, they will still be able to catch their heavily laden men up in time to get to Ballarat sometime on Tuesday afternoon.

While some of the loyal burghers of Melbourne are pleased to see this major military force head out to put these wretched rebels down, it is not as if they don't have qualms, also. There is no doubt that it also leaves Melbourne itself rather exposed, should trouble arise here . . . or, say, 25,000 armed diggers decide to march upon the city.

In fact, it is for this very reason that no sooner have those troops marched out – all of them desperately uncomfortable in their uniforms made to survive an English winter, replete with stiff leather shakos,[32] red woollen coats, dark blue trousers and black leather boots – than 300 loyal civilians are quickly sworn in as 'special constables' to keep law and order in Melbourne, and more particularly, to protect it.

Early evening, Friday, 1 December 1854, on the Eureka it's time to move out

After a report comes in that a large troop of reinforcement Redcoats is on the way from Melbourne and will soon be on Ballarat, the War Council inside the Stockade convenes. It is decided that Captain Ross and Captain Nelson will take a total of nearly 200 of their best men from their respective companies out to intercept the Redcoats. They are to set up an ambush near Warrenheip, some four miles away, at a spot where the 'road', such as it is, must skirt a hill, meaning the troops would be nicely concentrated for those attacking from the heights of that hill or from the nearby bush. Ideally, the attackers could launch a mounted raid on the wagons, and, if not stop them entirely, at least throw all the government's plans askew and seize the weaponry and ammunition those in the Stockade need.

In his diary that evening, Samuel Lazarus sums up the mood on the diggings: 'The crisis seems now hourly approaching, and all are waiting with a good deal of dread for the result.'[33] True, Lazarus is aware that he is himself prone to an 'attack of the glooms',[34] but he has never been more gloomy than now.

Friday night, 1 December 1854, Government Camp, the Council of War resolves

It is time for the authorities to have their own Council of War, and on this evening Commissioner Rede is again in conference with his two top military officers, discussing what must be done. Personally, Rede has little doubt: they must move against the Stockade. Precisely *how* they should move against it is not a matter for him – it is a matter for these officers – but he has no doubt that it is the right course of action.

Rumours are still sweeping the goldfields that the diggers will attack the Camp first, and Rede is convinced that the ramifications of the success of such an offensive would be devastating. It is unthinkable what would happen if the men inside the Camp were overwhelmed and had to surrender. He is in no doubt that if the authorities lose this battle, they risk losing the entire colony – the stakes are that high.

But the same fear is felt by those within the Stockade. If the rebels lose control of the Stockade, they lose the diggings and the fight – and the rule of Her Majesty's law will be re-established across the entire Colony of Victoria, not excepting one fly-blown bit of dirt at its heart.

It is a matter of who can, and will, move first. And when.

Rede feels strongly that it should be sooner rather than later. The Camp knows from its spies that the diggers seem to be getting stronger with each passing day. A meeting is also planned for this Sunday at the Adelphi Theatre, where the violent faction that seems to have gained control of the so-called Ballarat Reform League risks consolidating its power. So that means the military should make a move sometime within the next thirty-six hours.

How? When, precisely? It is a delicate matter. One key factor is the potential consequences if the troops sally out, as Captain Pasley would later recount: 'We did not know but they might have a force ready to assault the camp when we left it, and to risk the camp was to risk the Colony.'[35]

This is where Captain Thomas puts forward his own considered thoughts, as he has been working on a plan. Both Commissioner Rede and Captain Pasley like the plan, but it does not necessarily matter whether they do or don't. Thomas is the senior military man – if an attack goes ahead, it will proceed under his direction. The three men finally finish their Council of War near midnight with no firm decision taken and head for their cold bunks. Before turning in, however, Captain Pasley does one last quick check on the Camp's defences. He does not find a camp any more at ease in the curious Australian night air than a horse that hears thunder approaching.

For every man, following orders, has 'to sleep as well as he could', as Pasley would describe it in a subsequent letter to his father, 'with his musket in his hand in the very place where he would have to fire in case of attack'.[36] That means just about none of the men is in bed, and none has been able to wash for days. Rather, the smelly bulk of them sleep around the perimeter at their posts.

Pasley's advice to the men is firm: if an attack comes, they must not immediately charge out at the attackers. Their success will be to keep themselves secreted and sheltered as best they can, so as not to allow the rebels to draw a bead on them. Then, once engaged, 'stick to their posts to the last – unless they receive Captain Thomas's orders to move'.[37]

Most uncomfortable of all is the chain of mounted men secreted in pockets about half a mile out from the Camp in every direction, posted there to provide early warning of any approaching mob. No matter that some of these men are already shaken as, out of the darkness a couple of hours earlier, shots appear to have been fired just over their heads. They must stay by their horses, ready to react quickly. All such men, thus, must sleep on the ground with their bridles in their hands, 'and if the disturbances had lasted another week, the mounted police and soldiers would have been *hors de combat*'.[38]

Another unit of armed troopers remains on call inside the Camp through the night, occupying 'the position that a bastion does in a fortress, ready to sweep any front that might be attacked'.[39]

This cannot go on – his men will soon be too exhausted to fight – and having seen their hollow-eyed gaze up close, Pasley is more glad than ever that it is they who are intending to move against the diggers first.

And soon.

Friday night, 1 December 1854, Government House, Toorac, it has come to this

Truly, Sir Charles Hotham has never wanted it to come to this. Yes, he was firm from the beginning that the diggers would have to pay their license fee come what may, and yes, even on his first visit to Ballarat he cast his experienced military eye over the layout against the day that military action might have to be taken against the locals. It is also true he failed to immediately act on every overture by the diggers to find a peaceful solution, so perhaps it was always going to come to this.

But now that it has reached this impasse, now that there seems no recourse but to take harsh military action, all Hotham can do is give instructions to the Ballarat authorities to keep that action in check. He reminds them, in written instructions, to 'enforce the existing laws with temper, moderation and firmness'.[40]

Wee hours, early Saturday morning, 2 December 1854, Ballarat, phantoms in the night

Again and again and again and *AGAIN!*

All through the night in *both* camps the alarm goes up that they are about to be attacked. Inside the Stockade, seemingly every hour, the cry, 'The military are coming!'[41] is heard, only to be proved false each time.

Inside the Government Camp, at 4 o'clock in the tortured morning, the soldiers become *so* convinced that 400 rebels are about to set upon them that a company of soldiers bursts forth ready to beat the attackers back, only to find . . . it is only the phantoms of their imagination. Them and the moon gazing down benignly. In the far, far distance, a kookaburra, getting ready to catch a worm, is heard to laugh – possibly at them – but it, too, is all alone.

Though they all remain on duty, and on edge, no attack eventuates.

From dawn to midday, Saturday, 2 December 1854

This morning could have been made by the Lord for the Garden of Eden . . .

Though the night before has been exceedingly cold, wet and

stormy, now the sun is shining brightly, all the birds are singing and the butterflies of summer are swarming to the warming. And yet, look at what the rest of God's creatures, the two-legged variety frequently seen to be smoking pipes, are up to on this day.

The sun has risen on what is no fewer than two armed camps, separated by a large gully, flying different flags – one standing for the establishment, the other proclaiming a new power in the land and separation from the old order. The men in each camp glower across the gully at the other, wondering just who will make the first move.

'The portents of battle could be read in the distraction around,' John Lynch would record. 'The air seemed charged with strife. Ordinary business was paralysed, the coming struggle engrossing all thoughts.'[42]

All work on the diggings has ceased. Rede has ordered the public houses and post office closed, and no civilians are permitted in the township. When a mounted trooper from Melbourne arrives with dispatches, he is fired upon from somewhere near the Eureka line and arrives at the Camp shaken and furious.

At that Camp, the soldiers are nothing if not busy. That raspy sound? It is many of the soldiers taking their special files to sharpen their bayonets – back and forth, back and forth, up and down, up and down, round and round. They are not sure precisely when they will be using these bayonets; they can only feel a growing certainty that it will likely be sometime soon.

Outside the Camp, pickets are being posted to ensure that no-one approaches within 100 yards.

———

Elsewhere on the diggings, while those inside the Stockade enjoy broad support for what they are doing, many diggers have qualms. One of them is Samuel Lazarus, who has barely been able to sleep for two nights, such is his anxiety.

'One topic of conversation engrosses the attention of diggers & storekeepers,' he records in his diary. 'Those whose means enable them are sending their families away while others whose poverty compels them to keep their wives & families amidst the scene of threatened dangers are awaiting the approach of events.'[43]

Similarly, the correspondent for *The Melbourne Morning Herald* contemplates what might occur if the diggers actually attacked the Camp, as is rumoured: 'A large majority were with the diggers, but were also in favour of moral force only being used, as they dreaded that should the diggers obtain possession of the Camp, a state of confusion and insecurity as to property would ensue.'[44] For if the forces of law and order really are destroyed, then who can protect those who have the best gold-claims by virtue of that law?

———————

On the Eureka they are either getting ready for an onslaught of soldiers or getting ready to launch their own attack – no-one is yet sure. Up and about from well before dawn, with their night-time lookouts now relieved and fresh lookouts posted so the rebels will not be taken by surprise, many of the men are going through their drills, marching back and forth, shouldering arms, while others are sorting out whatever ammunition they have. Those who have previously served their own country's military are trying to awaken long-forgotten skills; those who are new to such practices are trying to pick up the basics. In one corner of the Stockade, Friedrich Vern is holding court, giving all and sundry his copious views on exactly the kind of tactics that should be used when the soldiers come. And it is he who has made the decision to expand the Stockade a little so that it now goes right across the road from Melbourne. Any reinforcements, any supply columns coming up that road, will now have to pass through them. *Und . . . zey . . . von't!*

Just as the last soft light of dawn gives way to the fullness of the day, a stream of diggers who slept in their own tents the night before begins to return to the Stockade. A few hours later, the divisions of Captain Ross and Captain Nelson, who have been out to Warrenheip, waiting to ambush whatever reinforcements are on their way from Melbourne, also return. The renewed presence of these two companies of armed men gives ever more energy and confidence to the rebels. With this surge, as Carboni recalled, 'the scene became soon animated, and the usual drilling was pushed on with more ardour than ever'.[45]

Around 10.30 in the morning, an extremely worried Father Smyth, dressed in his clerical garb, makes his way into the Stockade. He immediately begs Lalor to be allowed to address those of his flock who are in the Stockade.

The Father is no fool: he knows that the whole situation is a powder keg where just one spark is capable of setting the whole thing off. An editorial in today's edition of *The Ballarat Times*, written by Henry Seekamp, sets the tone and is being passed from hand to hand by those diggers who can read English:

> Those men who have the power and can exercise it will take the law into their own hands and enforce their principles where the Government now little expect. Instead, therefore, of the diggers looking for remedies where none can be found let them strike deep at the root of rottenness and reform the chief government . . . If they are not satisfied the gathering clouds of popular indignation will burst like a whirlwind over guilty and suspecting heads and sweep the length and breadth of the land.[46]

Yes, the good Father knows, despite Commissioner Rede's ongoing refusal to bend even a little bit, he must personally do everything he can to stop this madness – now.

Lalor, a Catholic to his core, cannot deny the priest's request to speak to his men. The opportunity to listen to the soothing words of a priest is embraced by the large contingent of devout Catholics among the rebels.

And yet most of the Father's words are not so much sayings of solace as words of warning. Smyth wishes to tell them, as a man free to move between opposing camps, that they must understand the forces they are up against. The Government Camp is awash with men under arms, 'some seven or eight hundred strong'[47] with another squadron of mounted police just arrived from Castlemaine a few hours earlier – and they still have more men on their way from Melbourne at this very time!

Bravery is one thing, he says, but bloodshed without gain is quite another, and they must understand exactly just how hopeless their position is. In short, as good Catholics he does hope that they are men of peace and he desires to see as many of them as possible at Mass on the morrow in that rickety wooden building up at the Gravel Pits that he is pleased to call his 'chapel'. And he hopes that in the meantime they will reflect on his words and the duty they bear to their families to keep themselves safe.[48]

Yes, Father. Thank you, Father, and God bless you, too, Father. The priest is known to be a good man and is listened to respect-fully, but precious few choose to lay down their arms because of his admonitions. What most of them are fighting for is justice, and a democracy too long denied them. First in Europe, and now here. They have had enough. In this fight, there are more important things than personal wellbeing.

In fact, it is only a short time after this that some of the diggers ask the question: Why wait to be attacked? Why not attack the gov-ernment forces ourselves, before their reinforcements arrive?

It is a view put most forcefully by the journalist John Manning, who with every passing day is less a believer that the pen is mightier than the sword – the musket and pike, in the hands of a band of committed men, is mightier than both of them. The diggers number in their *thousands*, and the troops are still only in their hundreds.

With one enormous attack, the diggers would surely overwhelm them![49]

Lalor is not convinced, and though he is firm in his order that, 'If the soldiers attack you, resist them,' he does not want to take the step of attacking first.

Others – most particularly George Black and Tom Kennedy – agree with Lalor and feel it is more important to stay on the defensive and let the Redcoats come to them. Though Kennedy, at least for the moment, is with Lalor and Black on the winning side of this argument, he shortly afterwards makes himself scarce, returning to his tent to be with his wife and four children.

———

Once the newly formed companies are properly organised, it is Friedrich Vern who gives quick instructions as to which ones must defend which part of the Stockade. At 11 o'clock a yell goes up: a report has just come in that the Redcoats have been spotted emerging from the Camp. Quickly each company races to its appointed part of the perimeter, even as hurried improvements to the bulwark are made – more slabs added, more earth heaped to its side as a protection against flying musket balls, more nooks filled with spare bits of wood.

Unbeknownst to the diggers at the Stockade, the Redcoats are merely making a preliminary sortie to deal with other groups of angry diggers who have started to gather, in particularly large numbers about Bath's Hotel. No, it is not yet a riotous assembly, but it has the potential to become so and the Camp is not taking any chances.

Strangely, however, when these diggers are told to disperse, they reply very pleasantly, 'We've only come here to get out of the way of the mob, and would be very willing to be sworn as special constables.'[50]

Told of this, Commissioner Rede is astonished that this could really be the case, and frankly doubtful. Nevertheless, he decides to give them the benefit of the doubt and sends over two magistrates to swear them in.

And, sure enough . . .

The magistrates have no sooner arrived than the cry goes up, 'Joe!' 'Joe!' 'JOE!'[51] The diggers break out into derisive, hooting laughter. Under such trying circumstances Rede has no hesitation in sending out Civil Commissary George Webster to read the now rather familiar Riot Act, at which point the mounted police move in to enforce the order to disperse and clear the diggers from the township and away from the hotel. It is noticed that many of them are insolently carrying poorly secreted revolvers inside their shirts, but at least they obey – even if two more diggers are arrested in the process. They are dragged away to the lockup, where they can see firsthand how their mates imprisoned the day before are faring.

And then another report comes in

'A body of armed men [is] marching in order around the Black Hill,' the breathless messenger gets out, 'as if to take the Camp in the rear.'[52]

They are reporterly around 300 strong, while there are 1200 on Bakery Hill and 400 collected about the township – some 2000 diggers all up. Doing what, exactly?

Exactly. Rede reports to his superiors, '[The diggers] were in hopes that we would go out to disperse the armed men on Bakery Hill, in which case those on the township were to take the Camp in the rear and burn it, and the Black Hill people were to have made a diversion also.'[53]

Saturday morning, 2 December 1854, Government Camp, lockdown

Just inside the picket fence that marks the extended boundary of the expanding Government Camp, all along Lydiard Street, myriad horses are munching on the fodder that has been fed to them by their exhausted masters. All around, fresh tents have been pitched on every spare bit of space to squeeze in the latest arrivals from the 12th and 40th Regiments. Everywhere there is hustling, bustling movement as troops drill, bugles sound, supplies are handed out. Extra security measures are taken on every building and, indeed, the palisade itself.

Yes, a part of the influx of people into the Camp are those flitting figures with nervous, darting eyes, never sure who is watching their entry – the government spies who have just come from the Eureka to report on the doings of the diggers. So it is on this morning that Captain Thomas receives a full briefing from one of his spies who has managed to inveigle himself right into the heart of the rebels.

The news is that the situation is now well out of hand. Not only have the diggers continued to build up their Stockade, not only have they been joined by yet more rebels coming from Creswick, but the previous evening they had even sent out a force to intercept and attack the government troops en route from Melbourne. They may very well do the same tonight.

Thomas, a softly spoken man not given to flights of great emotion one way or t'other but always considered and crisply professional, thanks his informer and orders him to keep in close touch. He then begins to make his detailed plans.

Noon, 2 December 1854, on Ballarat, if you are not with us you are agin us

Around and about Ballarat, as Samuel Huyghue records it, 'an ominous and oppressive silence [broods] over the deserted workings, and no one [is] now to be seen in the neighbouring streets'.[54]

That is not the case inside the Stockade, however, where the intense military drilling goes on.

Thomas Allen, an old fellow who runs a coffee house on the Eureka and is known as 'Old Waterloo' because he had been in that very battle, cannot help but compare this ragged brigade with the highly disciplined troops he once fought with. Back then, fighting the French under the leadership of the Duke of Wellington, they had shiny uniforms with bright buttons and boots almost as polished as their manoeuvres. But this lot, with their pikes, blundberbusses and pretend drills? It is a joke!

It is, perhaps, a measure of both the violence in the air and the edge of desperation that for some it is not enough to see Thomas Allen just standing there watching. Some want this aged man to participate.

'Come, Old Waterloo,'[55] says one company officer, trying to put a pike into his withered hand. But Old Waterloo declines to take it, whereupon he is marched to his quarters with three pikes in his back and two sentries to guard him. The feeling is getting stronger: if you are not with us, you are against us.

Some men, however, really do manage a middle course. One who decides to follow Father Smyth's advice is the fiercely religious father of six, Timothy Hayes. Over these last few days the whole movement has got away from him, and he knows it. All his life he has been an advocate of reform, but up until the last few days the BRL's actions had always been within the realms of legal and constitutional reform. Yes, he had briefly waxed violent lately, calling on the men to free by force any of them who were arrested, but on this afternoon he realises it just isn't in him. When it comes to bearing arms and causing bloodshed, his own blood runs cold – he has no passion for it, no feeling, and he now quietly slips away.

And even for those who do remain resolute, as the heat of the day rises, it is time to cease drilling. As there has been no license-hunt all morning it seems unlikely that there will be one this afternoon. In their entire time on the diggings, no-one can ever recall there being such a hunt on a Saturday afternoon. As for Sunday, well, not even Rede has ever sent out troopers on the Sabbath, and it is inconceivable that he will do so tomorrow.

That certainty takes a lot of the tension and emotion from the day. Instead, the focus begins to switch to the next meeting of the Ballarat Reform League leadership, at the Adelphi Theatre on the morrow at 2 pm, when, as proposed by Peter Lalor, they will elect a new executive.

Besides which, as the sun climbs and the temperature rises, there is one thing even more imperative than fomenting revolution: finding shade. There is little inside the Stockade to speak of, apart from the 30 or 40 tents that cannot possibly accommodate everyone there. So, one by one, after carefully reciting the password, the diggers simply drift away.

Most go back to their own tents, where at least they can be comfortable. Some go as far as the bottom of their diggings where, whatever else, it is cooler. In this high point of the sweltering day, there is no sense of impending doom. The mood is more hopeful that 'Charley'[56], as the diggers are wont to refer to His Excellency, Sir Charles Augustus Hotham, KCB, Lieutenant-Governor of the colony of Victoria, will soon dismiss the mostly hated Goldfield Commissioners – only Amos is respected as being basically decent and honest – and restore a just system to the goldfields. Rede's recent assurance that he will refer the issue of the manner of the license-hunts to Melbourne before conducting another contributes to this current easing of tension . . .

———

A notice is posted in the afternoon on buildings and the few remaining trees all over the diggings by order of Captain Thomas of the 40th Regiment:

NOTICE.

No light will be allowed to be kept burning in any tent within musket-shot of the line of sentries after 1 o'clock p.m. No discharge of firearms in the neighbourhood of the Camp will be permitted for any purpose whatever.

The sentries have orders to fire upon any person offending against these rules.

(By order),   **T. BAILEY RICHARDS**
                                         Lieut. 40th Regt., Garrison Adjutant.[57]

Midafternoon, Saturday, 2 December 1854, Melbourne, news travels fast

While it is the nature of mere rumours to rumble, panic pursues a much faster course. And this is a panic. Word's out, racing from customer to shopkeeper to pedestrians to passers-by and back again . . . diggers are on the march! Five hundred of them! Armed and heading to Melbourne!

The best informed of the rumour-mongers knows that on the track between Ballarat and Melbourne there is a particularly narrow pass and, apparently, the rebels' plan is to wait for the soldiers going towards Ballarat and, at that strategic point, do them in. That pass, if properly defended, is almost impregnable. If the soldiers, fatigued by the long, rapid marches and with a long column of drays behind, really are ambushed, they would be easily overcome and have all their arms and munitions confiscated.

Once the diggers have done this, they are going to be joined by a mass of diggers from other fields, and together they will march on

Melbourne, where they hope that the dregs of the population will join them in the uprising. They're going to sack the Treasury and the banks, pillage the city and take the Governor – it's looking like revolution, I tells ya!

4 pm, 2 December 1854, Eureka Stockade, here they come!

Here they come.

On yonder hill, marching double time towards them with a few mounted officers, comes what is clearly an armed group of men.

On the instant, Vern, still needled by the fact that he was not elected as Commander-in-Chief, cries out for all the world as if he had been so elected after all: 'Here zey are coming, boys: now I vill lead you to death or wictory!'[58]

The chill of the battle knell instantly falls upon those in the Stockade, a shadow across the souls of all men as they suddenly contemplate their own mortality. From performing impotent training exercises, they about to be in the fight of their lives, *for* their very lives? As one, the men reach for their rifles, their pistols, their ammunition, their pikes, their wooden swords, even as they look closer . . .

Which is when they realise: it is not the Redcoats at all.

Instead of 200 lackeys of the British government trying to impose their iniquitous rule, it proves to be 200 men of the mighty 'Independent Californian Rangers' Revolver Brigade'[59] as they have titled themselves, composed of mostly Californian 49ers from more distant parts of the diggings and under the command of the apparently West-Point-trained American[60] James McGill. He has no sooner dismounted from his horse with easy grace than he asks the assembled diggers, 'What's up?'[61]

Not a lot.

But the fact that the Californians – who have come complete with huge Colt revolvers tucked into their belts and sashes, Bowie knives and a pleasingly insolent swagger – are now here in force lifts morale and confidence.

Yes, they might be in for the battle of their lives, *for* their lives, but they are not alone.

A large part of the upswing in mood is the confidence projected by the very attractive character of McGill himself. But why wouldn't he be confident? In his belt he has a .44-calibre six-shot Colt Walker revolver, known as the most powerful black-powder repeating hand-gun yet made – capable of firing six bullets twice the size of the ones in the normal Colt. McGill looks like a natural leader of men from the first.

'His complexion,' as Carboni would describe it, 'bears the stamp of one born of a good family, but you can read in the white of his eyes, in the colouring of his cheeks, in the paleness of his lips, that his heart is for violence. When he gets a pair of solid whiskers, he may pass for a Scotchman, for he has already a nose as if moulded in Scotland. He speaks the English language correctly, and when not prompted by the audacity of his heart, shows good sense, delicate feelings, a pleasing way of conversation.'[62]

Lalor himself is so pleased to see McGill and impressed by the force that he commands that he installs the American on the spot as his second-in-command, replacing Vern, something that enrages the German, who has cherished the post.

For all the rest, however, it seems that McGill and his men have arrived in the nick of time.

For have you heard?

Once again, they say that the whole of the Melbourne Road is swarming with Redcoats. Hundreds of them, coming this way. The word spreads. The situation is changing. An attack really might be imminent. The response is not one of panic – certainly not from Vern, who tells anyone who will listen to just let the Redcoats attack – he and his riflemen, the very ones who are still expected any time, will make short work of them. But certainly many a man does become anxious.

In the face of such rumours, Carboni leaves the Stockade to see for himself the state of the Melbourne Road, and he does indeed sight a mass of 200 Redcoats stationed at Black Hill, under arms and clearly spoiling for some kind of action. Worse, he hears that they are intent on massacring the lot of them! (In truth, it later came out that the Redcoats marching up from Melbourne had indeed been overheard while camping at Ballan, making jokes about 'ripping'[63] the rebels on the points of their bayonets and how they would shoot even their own brothers should they find them amongst the 'revolters'.)[64]

Of course, Carboni must get this information to Lalor as quickly as possible, but therein lies a real problem. With the arrival of the Californians, the Council room has been placed under the strict security imposed by Captain McGill – for fear of spies, which would be the worst possible thing. Since the Italian does not know the password that has been instituted that afternoon, they won't let him in. And no, the newly installed Californian sentries have no idea who Captain Raffaello Carboni is and don't care to discuss it. Move on.

It is in vain for the aggrieved Italian to *protesta* that – Madonna! – he is part of this Council. The Americans, as Americans are wont to do, refuse to bend, insisting that the formula is simple: no password = no access.

Move on, fella.

He moves on.

And yet even in the short time he has been away it is obvious that the word of the approaching Redcoats has spread and unleashed a kind of manic energy about the place – the first wisps of wind from the coming storm, causing men to charge to and fro, back and forth, getting ready for come-what-may. All round and about, the Stockade old-fellows, with the weather-beaten visages and squinty eyes of men who have lived long in a land of glaring sun, are carrying guns and boxes of ammunition, canisters of gunpowder and bags of shot. Others are doing what they can to strengthen the Stockade against any full-on charges that might be coming.

Look there, for example, as a sly-grog seller with no less than a small keg of brandy hanging around his neck is moving among the diggers, offering them a nobbler in return for just a few coins. Many diggers are availing themselves of it, some knocking it back like water. Appalled, Lalor gives an order to kick the sly-grog seller out – the last thing they need in this situation is drunkenness.

And now two diggers on horseback are seen crossing the gully that, crisscrossed by small streams, lies below.

At one glance, Secretary of War Alfred Black decides the opportunity is too good to miss to purloin the steeds for the war effort and immediately orders Raffaello Carboni to take some men and confiscate the horses. In the urgency of the moment, the mood abroad to simply take whatever is needed in the name of the uprising is strengthening.

But Carboni is appalled. While it is one thing to take munitions and the like from the government, it is quite something else again to take from fellow diggers, and he has no hesitation in telling this upstart Black – who to this point has not even been in the Stockade, let alone the committee room – exactly that.

'I won't do the bushranger yet,' says he, flatly refusing.[65]

Others from within the Stockade are not so reluctant, however, and in short order men entirely unknown to Carboni rush upon the horsemen, draw their revolvers and order them to bring their fine steeds within the Stockade. The Italian is even more appalled, and there are other things amiss.

When Carboni spies Vern shortly afterwards and asks, '*Wie lautet das Passwort?*' – 'What is the password?' – Vern is quick with his accented reply: 'Winegar Hill.'[66]

'*Ne,*' Carboni says to himself, appalled. '*Nein . . . eine solch' eklige Wirtschaft hab' ich noch nie geseh'n.*'[67] No . . . I have *never* seen such a disgusting thing before.

Such a password is *madness*. This has been an uprising of diggers from all nations, united in their desire for justice. Yes, about a third of those diggers are Irish, but it has not been an *Irish* uprising, so why – *nome di Dio*, in the name of God – have a password that recalls the most famous Irish uprisings in both Ireland and Australia? No matter that the Australian uprising had been crushed like the previous battle of Vinegar Hill in Ireland 56 years before that . . . Among the Irish it is still revered, the first time the people of their race had truly asserted themselves in this new land. Yes, Lalor and other Irish might find it inspiring, but for the men of other nationalities it is exclusionary. And Carboni is not the only one who feels it.

In the words of Lalor's friend, William Craig, who would write his own account of the reaction of the non-Irish rebels, 'They concluded that Lalor's object was more to strike a blow for Ireland than at official despotism . . .

'Bendigo, Forrest Creek, and Creswick contributed contingents to assist in the struggle. From the latter place alone a thousand men were on the march to Ballarat; but when the news circulated that Irish independence had crept into the movement, almost all turned back.'[68]

Even allowing for a likely exaggeration here – the figure is probably closer to 500 – there is no doubt that the Stockade is denied many strong-armed men because of the feeling that the Irish have taken over.

While it is one thing to be ready to die for a cause, it needs to be *our* cause. Die for an Irish cause, under Irish leadership? *Nein, non* and be *damned*, sir! The lower the sun falls, the more the ranks within the Stockade thin.

What Carboni most needs right now is a stiff nobbler, and he heads off to the Prince Albert Hotel, near Bakery Hill, to meet up

with a couple of friends. When he arrives he is appalled at the looting that has gone on, as roaming gangs of diggers have claimed the
authorisation of the 'Council of War'[69] for taking what they like
from the stores and fearfully beating all storekeepers brave enough
to resist. It is a drink he certainly needs.

Late-afternoon, 2 December 1854, Commissioner's outpost on the Eureka, Assistant Amos amiss

It is an outrage. One moment the distinguished graduate of the
Royal Military College of Sandhurst, Assistant-Commissioner
Gilbert Amos, is attending to paperwork in his large tent, and the
next he looks up through the flaps to see 100 rebel diggers storming
his camp. Their leader is a startlingly good-looking, well-armed man
who introduces himself as Captain Ross – indeed, the most unlikely
looking brigand Amos has ever seen – who explains in his rather
fetching Canadian accent that they have come for his fine horse.
And while they're at it, they decide to take his two double-barrelled
pistols, his dray, his dignity and his good self as prisoner. Many of
the rebels are menacing as they even cock and uncock their pistols
in Amos's face – he is terrified that one of them might go off by
mistake – and though Captain Ross manages to keep them in check,
it is not as if the Canadian wants him to go free.

In fact, Captain Ross decides to lead Commissioner Amos back
to the Stockade. As he is led away, Amos must suffer the humiliation
of a man who in his august person represents the authority of Her
Majesty the Queen – *the QUEEN! the Queen* . . . *the Queen* . . . – his
silver braid shining in the sun, no match for Ross's musket at his
back. He is taken right to the portals of the Stockade, where the
Captain and his men are greeted with shouts of joy by the rebels
when they arrive with the horse and new supplies.

Commissioner Amos is staggered to see, up close, just how

formidable a defence the barricades of the Stockade present. He realises, for the first time, what the Redcoats will be up against if they try to storm it.[70]

And other things worry him. As an afternoon drizzle begins – it looks very much like a big storm is on its way – almost as one, the insurgents 'secure arms', protecting the firelocks of their guns from getting wet with their hands, sleeves and hats. Amos is amazed. As a man who has spent some years in the army as an officer, he knows this manoeuvre to keep gunpowder dry is one that drill sergeants do not typically teach new recruits. Whoever these particular men are, they are not without experience. There is something about the calm, controlled manner in which they perform this act that bespeaks a real military force, not just the mob of ruffians he imagined them to be.

Amos is about to be ushered through the portals proper of the Stockade, swallowed whole, when a man who is not a mere 'Captain' but is referred to by the others as 'Colonel' – and is, in fact, the just-arrived James McGill – stops them and says to Captain Ross, 'We do not wish to have any prisoners.'[71]

And with that, Amos, whom the diggers like and respect as an honest man, especially after he gave evidence in defence of McIntyre – is set free and soon reporting the whole affair to his outraged superior, Commissioner Rede.

———

But let's all gather in now, for McGill has been busily working out the strengths and weaknesses of the Stockade, and he is ready to institute some changes. From now on, the 'night-watch patriots',[72] those on duty as night sentries, need to be properly organised to ensure that they are there around the clock and positioned so that all angles of approach are covered. And they must be on the lookout for spies.

After consultation with Lalor, McGill also has Secretary of War Alfred Black draw up a 'general order for the night',[73] which is read out to the diggers. Part of this order is for McGill and Nelson to take their men out once more onto the Melbourne Road, well after dark, and then 'march to intercept reinforcements'[74] to see if they can stop the troops that are now known to be on their way. Apparently, the Lieutenant-Governor himself, Sir Charles Hotham, is commanding them, and they are bringing artillery!

As the sun sets on this long, exhausting day, there is no sudden flurry of cheery lanterns and fires to illuminate the Ballarat night – orders have been put up earlier banning such lights. All is quiet. From the Government Camp, the troopers are seen bringing long lines of troop horses down to the watering place on Yarrowee Creek, where they can have their thirsty fill in the cool of the evening. (The general cessation of business in Ballarat has even affected the Camp's own delivery of water and other much needed supplies.)

At this time, Commissioner Rede is in his relatively well-appointed private quarters right in the heart of the Government Camp – in one of the buildings that actually has solid walls – writing a letter to the Chief Commissioner of the Goldfields, where he makes clear that he is under no illusions as to just what is at stake:

I am convinced that the future of this Colony depends on the crushing of this movement in such a manner that it may act as a warning . . . I should be sorry to see them return to their work . . . We may be able to crush the democratic agitation at one blow, which can only be done if we find them with arms in their hands and acting in direct opposition to the laws.[75]

It is for this reason that Rede now convenes his own, very intimate 'Council of War', consisting of himself, Captain Thomas and Captain Pasley, together with Assistant-Commissioner Gilbert Amos, since the latter knows the district in which the Stockade is situated very well and has seen up close the Stockade itself, albeit only from the outside. The meeting is held in strictest secrecy, because in Rede's view they have 'every reason to suppose the enemy had spies'[76] in the Camp, and their voices remain hushed as they review what they know of the situation. Of greatest and most immediate concern is the fact that the rebels have, according to Thomas, the 'avowed intention of intercepting the force under the Major General's command en route from Melbourne'.[77]

The diggers have no more fear, no respect whatsoever for authority.

With the meeting of the Reform League due to be held on the morrow at 2 pm, with well over 10,000 disaffected diggers expected to turn up, anything might happen. If the diggers are brazen enough to raid Assistant-Commissioner Amos's camp, take him prisoner and take his horse, then they are surely brazen enough to do anything. If those 10,000 men and more decided to storm, *en masse,* the Camp, there would be nothing that could stop them. Even failing that, if the Ballarat Reform League falls fully into the hands of those who have raised the rebel army beneath the Southern Cross, the whole thing could turn into the very revolution the authorities fear, one that could sweep the entire colony.

Captain Thomas has been receiving reports for most of the day and all of them are troubling. 'Complaints were coming in from all directions stating that the stores were being stuck up – that people were afraid for their lives – that men were being pressed into a stockade and armed against their inclination.'[78] He also knows that a significant number of armed American diggers has just arrived.

And Rede is equally troubled. As he would subsequently report, they concluded that, 'To put an end to this state of anarchy and confusion it would be absolutely necessary to turn the rebels, or rioters, or whatever you call them, out of the stockade, and that the stockade must be pulled down, and we were determined to use all means in our power to that end.'[79]

But when?

According to intelligence, with the setting of the sun on this hot Saturday, the diggers are apparently beginning to relax, convinced that nothing would ever happen on tomorrow's Sabbath. Many of them are either starting to return to their own tents outside the Stockade to be more comfortable or marauding out on the fields. However, Captain Thomas, as he would later report, does 'not consider it prudent to attack them [at this time], as they were not collected in any one spot; and the safety of the Camp would have been risked had a large portion of the force been withdrawn'.[80]

What better time to strike? Surely, it must be 'at dawn the following morning'[81] when, crucially, the heavily armed Americans are expected to be absent once again, attempting to intercept the military force marching north from Melbourne.

Yes, moving into position at night would be difficult, but attacking at dawn on Sunday would be when the diggers least expect it, when their forces would be depleted and yet most of the ringleaders and their hard-core followers would be in the one place at the one time, relatively unprotected by a mass of armed men.

So the troops *have* to move – tonight! With that decided, it is Captain Thomas who takes the lead. He is, after all, the only true military man with experience.

The first thing he insists on is that the men from the Camp do not move against the Stockade via the Melbourne Road – even though that would be far and away the easiest approach. No, just as they are moving against the rebels at the least expected time, so too must they appear from the least expected direction.

The War Council goes over endless details and even when completed the plan is kept secret amongst the four of them, until the moment for action shall arrive.

Late Saturday evening, 2 December 1854, Ballarat, anarchy abounds

There is madness in the air. A high, frenetic energy all over, with men rushing hither and thither, shots ringing out, yells, imprecations. For out and about on the diggings an ugly mood is abroad. Yes, those within the Stockade have embraced the prospect of challenging the law for the higher virtue of justice, but there are many others who love lawlessness for its own sake, as it allows their baser instincts full rein.

Late Saturday evening, 2 December 1854, on the Eureka, on the grog

Again the word is passed that the government troops from Melbourne are on their way, and again it is the judgement of the Committee for the Defence that the best thing is for McGill and Nelson to take about 200 of the best-armed insurgents – most on foot and some on horseback – and position themselves four miles away at Warrenheip, so as to ambush them.

In the meantime, pickets have been posted at a distance from the Stockade to ensure that those inside will receive plenty of warning should any attack emerge. On this night the job falls to the Nicholls brothers, Henry and Charles, to check on several of them. It is not easy. In fact, the pickets are not at their appointed positions and instead are found in a sly-grog tent, according to Henry, 'playing cribbage and drinking, and, apparently, in the best of humours with themselves'.[82]

Both brothers remonstrate with the pickets heavily, persuading them to return to their posts, but once the nightwatchmen are gone they can't help but notice the 'young lady, decidedly good-looking who presided over the grog', and decide to stay for a few drinks themselves. Indeed, there is a good deal of drinking going on this night, both inside and outside the Stockade.

By the time the two brothers return to the Stockade, it is nearing midnight on this unseasonably freezing night. They find two enormous Irishmen with gigantic pikes taking great pleasure guarding the place of exit, while of the 120 or so men who are present within the Stockade, those few who are awake are gathered closely to a large fire, trying to warm themselves in the chill night air.

Nearing midnight, 2 December, inside the Stockade, Carboni is on a mission

Appalled by the widespread looting that is going on all over the diggings, Carboni heads back to the Stockade in the hope of telling Lalor that something must be done.

'Vinegar Hill', the Italian says to the American sentries, the very words grating once more, and he is soon inside the Stockade. It is just before midnight and, here at least, all is relatively quiet.

And there is Thonen. Speaking in German, he briefly tells Carboni the situation. The ranks inside the Stockade have dwindled rapidly, and what is left is little more than a skeleton force of what had been there in the afternoon.

But to the point.

'*Kann ich Lalor sehen?* – Can I see Lalor?'[83] Carboni asks.

'*Nein,*' Thonen says flatly.

Lalor is severely exhausted and snatching a couple of hours sleep for fear of dropping. He cannot be woken until the morrow. He will need all his strength for whatever that day will bring, including the important meeting at the Adelphi.

It is on that same reckoning that Carboni bids *gute Nacht* to Thonen, the one member of the Council for the Defence on duty through the night. Thonen gives the nod to the Californian sentries that the Italian should be allowed to leave, and Carboni returns to the place where he can get the best night's rest for himself: his own tent outside the Stcokade. He leaves Thonen gazing out from his position halfway down on the western perimeter of the Stockade.

All is quiet on the western front . . .

———

Nearing two in the morning, Henry and Charles Nicholls also start to leave – after Henry persuades his brother that it is too dangerous to stay in the Stockade – though, this time, their way is barred by two big Irishmen with pikes, who also refuse the right of exit without the password.

'Vinegar Hill,' says Henry – the pikes are lowered and they are out. Still anxious about the feeling of menace in the air, Henry also convinces his brother to take a circuitous route back to their tent, which lies by the main road near Red Hill, not far from the Government Camp. On the off-chance the troops launch an attack tonight, it would not be wise to be between them and the Stockade.

'It was a true Australian night,' Nicholls would later recount, 'not a breath of wind stirred the leaves of the stringy-bark trees, which then grew thickly on the ranges, or of the gums whose white stems gleamed ghostly on the flats as we passed . . . The most profound silence prevailed; no lights were to be seen, the whole visible world was at rest . . . the very tents seemed to be asleep.

'The whole air was full of that fine haze which is seen on such nights once or twice in the year, a haze which slightly veils but does not conceal, lending a ghostly, yet beautiful appearance to all around.' [84]

It feels good to be alive.

CHAPTER THIRTEEN

THE QUEEN'S PEACE IS DISTURBED

Riot was rapidly growing into a revolution.[1]
Lieutenant-Governor Hotham on the events of the morning of
3 December 1854 to the Colonial Secretary in London

Although in a military point of view the thing is trifling enough – in
a political sense the fate of the Colony hinged upon it, and if any
mistake had been made, the results would have been fearful . . .[2]
Captain Charles Pasley in a subsequent letter to his father, 27 June 1855

Rule Britton, rule the slave
Till Liberty points you out a grave . . .[3]
Digger Thomas Pierson in his diary on 10 October 1854

6 pm, 2 December 1854, Windsor Castle, England and the valley of death

Despite her relative youth at 35, Queen Victoria has already been on her throne 17 years and has seen the respect – even adoration – of her people grow over her reign. She has been happily married to Prince Albert for most of that time and loves to entertain, most particularly here at Windsor Castle.

On this very evening, as a matter of fact, she is sitting at the end of the dining table in the glorious State Dining Room, which has frescoes of food painted over the ceiling, while the walls are covered with red damask upon which hang portraits of kings and queens, forever staring glumly at each other across the festive tables they once knew. Many of the solid surfaces are gilt-edged, perhaps the tiniest of reminders to the reigning Queen of her prospering goldfields in faraway colonies.

Prince Albert sits at the other end of the table, while ranged down each side are such luminaries of the regal world as the Queen Mother, Her Royal Highness the Duchess of Kent; His Serene Highness Prince Ernest of Leiningen; the Lord Chancellor and Lady Cranworth; the Ladies Augusta and Frances Bruce; the Right Hon. William Gladstone, Chancellor of the Exchequer, and Mrs Gladstone; Sir George Cooper and Lieutenant-Colonel Dennis, commanding officer of the 94th Regiment. As ever, Queen Victoria displays her strong appetite as she tucks into each course with gusto. The other guests try hard to keep pace – they know from experience that as Her Majesty finishes each plate, they must finish too.

It is a reasonably happy gathering, though tempered by the news that has only arrived a few days earlier that in the suicidal charge of the Light Brigade in the Crimean War – *'Forward, the Light Brigade!/ Charge for the guns, he said:/ Into the valley of Death/ Rode the six hundred'*[4] – nearly half of her brave military servants there had been killed or wounded.

Entirely unbeknownst to Queen Victoria, of course, at this very time, in a far-flung outpost of her Empire, some more of her loyal subjects are about to make their own charges against some of her *disloyal* subjects. At least that is the way the loyal ones see it.

Pre-dawn, Sunday, 3 December 1854, a girding of loins at the Government Camp

Startled grunts fill the night. It is just after 2.30 am. One by one, very quietly, 182 men of the 12th and 40th Regiments and 94 police, together with their officers, are being silently woken inside the Government Camp. Stay quiet. It's on. We're moving against the rebels – *now*. Leaving from the back of the camp to shield their move from possible observers outside the main gates, they are told to form up in the gully just to the east of that small rise in the ground known as 'Soldiers Hill', a little under one mile north of the Camp.

Usually such an exercise would be accompanied by any number of shouted orders or bugle calls. But not on this occasion. The men know what to do. All their training, all their drills, have led to them this moment, to be able to form up quickly and move with stealth.

Once his men are gathered on the eastern flank of Soldiers Hill in the chill damp air, Captain Thomas, his epaulettes still lustrous in the thin moonlight, the rest of his body seemingly covered in a cloak of shadows, steps forward, while an aide de camp holds the bridle of his horse. Now each man, carefully holding his regula-tion smooth-bore, single-shot musket by his side, leans in close as the officer whispers instructions, even as they are served a tot of rum to warm their bellies.[5] (The police have already had a nobbler of the same before formal assembly.) Captain Wise hovers closely, ensuring that no man overindulges, that all is as it should be, that every man is ready.

Captain Thomas's words are crisp and precise: they are about to launch an attack on the rebels' Stockade up on the Eureka, and they will go in just before dawn. Now, listen carefully. The soldiers of the 12th and 40th Regiments – 65 mostly youthful soldiers under Captain William Queade and 87 rather more grizzled veterans led by Captain Wise, with Thomas personally in overall command – are to move on foot from the north-west, up the gully that lies just to the west of Stockyard Hill, against the Stockade at the point where the defences are at their thinnest.

As to the 30 mounted men of the 40th Regiment under Hall and the dozen mounted police under Kossack, they are to move to the high ground of Stockyard Hill, where the Free Trade Hotel lies. From there they will not only be able to watch proceedings, but Kossack's men (armed with rifled carbines) will be able to fire down into the Stockade if necessary. All of them can hold there until ordered to move down the east side of the Stockade. The foot police under Sub-Inspector Charles Carter are to advance alongside the infantry. Meanwhile, Samuel Furnell's 55 mounted police will move out to the right of the infantry and down along the western face of the Stockade towards the south-west corner. Once Kossack and Hall have led the Mounted 40th and police down along the eastern side, the Stockade will effectively be encircled.

Meanwhile, 175 soldiers are to remain in the Government Camp under Captain Atkinson, should the diggers attack while well over half the garrison is away. This splitting of the available force does not sit easily with Pasley, but he reluctantly accepts that it has to be done. For those moving against the Stockade, they are not to fire upon the diggers until so ordered. Those insurgents who 'cease to resist'[6] are to be spared. And a last point: the soldiers are to do everything possible to remain silent – it is extremely important to get as close as possible to the Stockade without being detected.

All good? All understood? All content?

No, not entirely. Two soldiers, knowing they will be expected to fire on men whom they regard as innocent, promptly fall out of the ranks and resolutely announce that they will not march – only to be immediately arrested for their trouble.[7]

No matter. Better off without cowards in our ranks. Now we can go. *Company, advance.*

'We marched off in the dark,' Captain Pasley would later tell his father, 'in such perfect silence that you could almost have heard a pin drop.'[8] Soft whinnying in the moonlight. The light grunts of horses suddenly bearing the weight of big men. And all of it at an unaccustomed hour.

No fewer than 100 are on horseback, while 176 – composed of foot police and men from the 12th and 40th Regiments – are on foot. The soldiers with their muskets are in the middle, the police with their pistols, carbines and shotguns on the flanks, with the mounted men at the rear – a military spear. Unsure if they may be ambushed as soon as they move beyond the protective embrace of the Camp, the formation is framed to react quickly to any such possibility.

They are a formidable force with ferocious firepower. And they have *legal* firepower, to boot, with Police Magistrate Charles Prendergast Hackett and Civil Commissary George Webster accompanying them. The presence of these officials is intended to make the difference between this being a brutal military exercise to crush rebels who do not recognise Her Majesty's authority – which would not do at all – and a far more sophisticated judicial and civil action to restore order among those who refuse to obey Her Majesty's laws. Though for reasons of security Captain Thomas has not confided it to the man in question, his plan is for Hackett to loudly read the Riot Act to the rebels, commanding them to disperse, whereupon, once they refuse, the military would be permitted by law to respond with firepower. Ideally, the diggers would see the formidable military array surrounding them, hear the Riot Act and lose all will to fight – as had happened at the great armed Chartist demonstrations in Great Britain, bar one.

As to Assistant-Commissioner Gilbert Amos, he is coming along as something of a guide, since he knows the area well, particularly the route they are taking to the Stockade. (Neither Commissioner Rede nor Assistant-Commissioner Johnstone, however, will go. It is Rede's opinion, as expressed to the Chief Commissioner of the Goldfields, that the rebels would have but to see Mr Johnstone and himself, and the two would be 'doomed . . . [as] in their instructions in drilling they especially point out the necessity of first shooting the officers'.[9] Far better to not give them such a target and remain in the barracks, ready to give authority to the group of armed men staying back to defend the Camp.)

Pre-dawn, Sunday, 3 December 1854, many cloaks of shadows stalk the Eureka

All is quiet in the Stockade. True, there had been great excitement a couple of hours earlier when the defenders received two reports in fairly quick succession from the Californian pickets that a large body of Redcoats was on its way towards them, but things had settled quickly after both proved to be false alarms. The rebels seek the comfort of their own tents, while others adhere to Father Smyth's admonition and try to stay clear of the trouble that is clearly brewing. It has been one thing to march drills back and forth and talk of revolt, but as the pressure has started to boil like a billy . . . it's quite another matter to actually stay there and bear arms.

There are sentries on duty at the Stockade, of course, and a few men are awake, keeping the large fire in the middle of the Stockade stoked. The vast majority, however, are sleeping the sleep of the dead, the dead-drunk and the dead-exhausted. All up, of the more than 500 men who were in the Stockade the previous afternoon, maybe just 120 remain now, if you count a few of the shadows too.

———————

At least the way she would tell it ever afterwards, alone in her bed in a small house in Geelong at the time, Alicia Dunne wakes with a start. Something is not right. And from the first she knows it is Peter. She worries about him constantly – she knows how dangerous the goldfields can be – but now her worry focuses. There! In this 'vision of the night' she sees her Peter 'wounded and bleeding'.[10] A cold, gripping horror possesses her, and she cannot shake it. Somewhere in the distance a dog is barking.

Pre-dawn, Sunday, 3 December, the Redcoats close in

Carefully now in that early pre-dawn where they are less men than ghostly spectres – their red jackets making little impact on the all-enveloping blackness that is just starting to lift – Thomas keeps his forces moving down into the gully and eastwards for some fifteen minutes along the northern banks of Yarrowee Creek. Then, on Amos's signal, at a point a little less than one mile north-west of the Stockade, they cross the creek and head due south. The going is not easy, particularly for the foot soldiers carrying their heavy muskets over their shoulders and watching every step carefully in the dark, but . . . *theirs is not to reason why.* In the thin, frozen moonlight, every breath from the horses' nostrils and mouths instantly condenses into a smoky mist.

They navigate their way by moonlight through a landscape shorn of all landmarks, past endless mullock heaps, cruel shafts, shepherds' holes, fallen logs, piles of slabs, muddy pools, pits full of trash and broken bottles, huts and tents held up by innumerable ropes as long as they are taut. It's all but impossible to see in this light – made even more so since Thomas's own edict that no lights are to be shown after dark has been obeyed everywhere but inside the Stockade, and all the tents and huts remain dark.

Still, with the tail obliged to follow the body, as the body must follow the head, the main thing is that the head is Commissioner Amos, and he knows the route well. Carefully, quietly, he now turns the column due east parallel to the north bank of Specimen Gully as the men keep moving in their 'muffled tramp'.[11]

A shot rings out in the night, coming from somewhere up on the curiously elongated mound of Black Hill. Mercifully, it has come from a great distance away. The crack of the gun has not faded before, among the advancing troops, Captain Thomas cocks his ear towards where the shot originated and whispers, 'We are seen. Forward, and steady men! Don't fire; let the insurgents fire first. You wait for the sound of the bugle.'[12]

They push on a little faster than before, and there is no further gunfire.

After 50 careful minutes, the men and horses arrive at their appointed position, just 300 yards to the north of the Stockade, hidden from whatever rebels might be on the lookout by the small rise of Stockyard Hill. The moon has now set, leaving only the most determined stars behind. On the eastern horizon, the first flush of dawn is starting to creep into the night sky above Warrenheip.

It is just after 4.20 am.

'The Infantry,' Captain Pasley would recount to his father, 'were then formed in skirmishing order, with supports, and the Cavalry sent round to turn the left flank of the entrenchment. By Thomas's desire I kept in the Centre of the skirmishers whilst he went to the right flank to be able to communicate with the Cavalry.'[13]

Indeed, as Sub-Inspector Samuel Furnell takes his mounted police out onto that right flank to come at the Stockade from the south-west, the mounted infantry of the 40th Regiment, under the command of Lieutenant Hall, and the mounted police under Sub-Inspector Ladislaus Kossak, move up to the Free Trade Hotel on Stockyard Hill, to initially cover the north-east face of the Stockade – effectively its rear – about 250 yards away. Captain Thomas, meanwhile, whispers more instructions to his soldiers and they arrange themselves in battle order. And so, just as they have been trained to do, drilling for many months and even years, the government's real soldiers arrange themselves into formation to advance. As they do so, officers on horseback – distinguishable from other mounted troopers by their golden braid and epaulets – wheel their mounts back and forth behind their men to be certain that all is just so.

Meanwhile, the rest of the infantry, waiting to the rear in close-packed ranks, are to remain in reserve and called up as required.

Once all is in place, near silence again reigns supreme as the men await the order to advance.

Among those readying to move closer to action, the more experienced of the soldiers take half a dozen rounds from their cartridge boxes and stuff them under their waist belts or into the waistband of their trousers. This tactic makes the ammunition easily accessible when the battle begins – when bullets are whizzing past your ears, the last thing you want is to be fumbling for cartridges in a box on your hip. Heard, too, are whispered prayers and the click of rosary beads.

All up, it is a great satisfaction to captains Thomas, Pasley and Wise that so far they have been able to manoeuvre this close to the Stockade without alerting the diggers inside. And yet, as quiet as the soldiers have been, it has not been possible to move such a large body of armed men so close to the Stockade, some of them on horseback, without having now been noticed outside its walls.

One man who has been aroused, who heard the approaching corps and reacted instantly, is Canadian digger Thomas Budden, camped just a couple of hundred yards from the Stockade. Realising that the worst is about to happen, Budden, who went to school in Toronto with Captain Charles Ross, now takes a courageous risk by racing to the Stockade, dodging the mounds of tailings and gaping mine-shafts as he goes, to warn Ross that the soldiers are coming. Running as silently as he can, he tells the sentries what is about to befall them and is allowed to pass, whereupon he immediately makes his way to rouse Ross. Speaking feverishly, Budden urges his old friend to get out *now,* while he still can. If he stays he risks losing his life. Come NOW, Charles!

Ross thanks his old friend but calmly refuses. If the Redcoats are about to attack, then his place is right here. What sort of a man would he be to turn tail at the first sight of the armed foe? He is staying and it is all that Budden can do now to safely get away.

At least Budden has given some warning that the troopers are indeed on their way, and the sentries now gaze down the hill. In the tepid and tragic light, there is suddenly an enormous sense of menace in the air as the realisation hits those in the Stockade: it really has come to this; they will shortly be under attack.

With all men now in position and the Stockade effectively surrounded, the word is quietly passed from rank to rank, soldier to soldier: 'Advance.'

And now the main body of soldiers under Captain Thomas, with Pasley leading the forward elements, marches up and over the small rise they have been sheltering behind, while the mounted soldiers and police on the fringes go around it. As one they strain their eyes to the east, looking for some sign of the rebels, something to help them get their bearings. It is nigh on impossible, though some think as they begin their ascent of the small gully in front of them that they can see the barest silhouette of the enemy flag against the lightening sky way up to their east, fluttering just above the tree line. But if the soldiers can see the Stockade, that must mean that those in the Stockade can . . .

Suddenly the blare of a bugle coming from the Stockade shatters the pre-dawn silence, As the soldiers continue to gaze upwards at the rebel stronghold, a shiver moves through them, almost as one. Some fancy they can see dim figures scurrying hither and thither, but the light is still so poor and the Stockade so distant at 300 yards that it might equally be the phantoms of their imagination.

As to the rebels, one of the men with the Independent California Rangers' Revolver Brigade, John Lynch, would record 'a terrible effervescence of hurry-skurry' around him as his fellow rebels rush from their bunks and tents and take up their posts, their guns and pikes in hand. But it is an effervescence that throws little light, for he would also report that he 'could hardly discern the military force at first'.[14]

Soon enough, though, there they are. Up in the Stockade, the diggers really can now just make out the long line of Redcoats some 150 yards down the slope, moving into the open and advancing.

The first of the sentries runs back, shouting a warning to the others: 'To Arms! To Arms!'[15] This is not just another false alarm such as those they have already had twice on this night and many times over previous nights. This is real. With the bugle, and now the shouting, it is enough to wake even the most profoundly asleep, including Peter Lalor. He is instantly up and moving, realising that the Redcoats have clearly come and, while more of a moral leader than a military one, at the very least he must quickly be seen to be present, doing whatever he can to get the defences of the Stockade organised.

And yet, *where are his men?* Emerging from his tent, his form throwing thin shadows from the flickering light of the fire in the middle of the Stockade, it is immediately apparent in this last gasp of night before Sunday morning that the ranks are alarmingly thin. The one clear order that does ring out, however, is at least a significant one, for it brings immediate results: 'California Rangers, to the front!'[16]

The Americans, many of them veterans of the Mexican War, leap to action and they are soon joined by other diggers.

At this point, the forces at Lalor's rough command are just 70 men holding shotguns and rifles, 30 or so with pistols and 20 men with pikes, many of which have been fashioned by the German blacksmith John Hafele, who is now worthily holding one himself.[17]

Even as the soldiers advance on the face of the Stockade, where the diggers least expect it because the going is so difficult, Captain Thomas tells the young bugle boy by his side to blow a key call, one recognised by all the men under his command. The lad does so, standing bravely and emptying his lungs into his brass instrument.

Just outside the Stockade, Tom Green, a veteran ex-rifleman who had fought under Lord Gough in India, instantly recognises the bugle. 'That call,' he roars to his mate, now also awake beside him, 'means extend into skirmishing order, the military are here!'[18]

And indeed it does. 'Extend to skirmishing order' means that instead of advancing in tightly packed formal ranks, a thin line of foot soldiers of the 12th and 40th Regiments commanded by Captain Wise go forward in a methodical manner. Working in groups of four – 'a chain', in military parlance – the men now ready themselves so that, once the battle proper begins, they can alternately step forward and kneel to fire before stepping back and reloading. This will ensure that there is a constant stream of gunfire coming from each group, rather than spasmodic volleys, and present a moving and broken line to those trying to draw a bead upon them. Yes, it is difficult to move up the slope over broken ground, but it is because of that very slope that Captain Thomas has chosen to attack from there. He knows that an idiosyncrasy of the smooth bore weapons the diggers will be using is that when they are fired downwards the bullets tend to follow a trajectory higher than intended – hopefully over the soldiers' heads. (It was for this reason that, at the Battle of Waterloo, the Duke of Wellington ordered his men to aim for the groins of the Frenchmen, on the reckoning that the bullets would likely hit them in the chest.) The men start moving, slowly, methodically, towards the north-western face of the Stockade.

Their officers stay just behind them, and a tighter formation of soldiers continues to advance 50 paces behind them all, ready to react to whatever happens with that front line – to plug gaps or follow up hard on any breakthroughs. To the right of the skirmishers are the foot police.

———

At the Stockade, by the time the bulk of the diggers have taken up their positions at the barricades, the situation is becoming just a little clearer. By now the Redcoats and some of the foot police who are accompanying them are close enough – coming up the slight gully that starts just next to Stockyard Hill and goes right to the wall of the Stockade – that the diggers can clearly distinguish features.

It is time.

The diggers' own Robert Burnette, a tiny but game-as-all-get-out fighting force of the California Rangers,[19] steps forward, smoothly raises his rifle to his shoulder, takes aim in the rough direction of the advancing Redcoats and pulls the trigger.

Down in the advancing line, a lead ball sears from the shadows and hits Private Michael Roney of the 40th Regiment directly in the head.

RIP. Michael Roney. Born in Belfast 1833, died on the Eureka, in Australia, 3 December 1854.[20]

The true significance of the shot, however, would be accurately described by digger John Lynch when he would later write that the 'shot from our encampment was taken for a declaration of war.'[21] Captain Thomas, who is on horseback on the right of the infantry line, takes just a split second to determine that the shot has not come from beside or behind him, but from the Stockade.

This established, he is free to give the command for the bugle to sound the 'Commence Firing' order.[22] The soldiers do not need to be told twice and, almost as one, swing their muskets to their shoulders, kneel and, with a terrible belch of white smoke and a tremendous roar, unleash an enormous volley of shots. True, at this distance the musket fire is wildly inaccurate, but at least some of the three-quarter-inch-calibre soft lead balls hit their mark and raise splinters from the bulwarks of the Stockade. No fewer than nine of the diggers fall.

The diggers are not long in making reply and the next flurry of shots hurtles down into the gully, one of them bearing an irretrievable fate.

An instant later, not far from where Roney fell, another soldier, Felix Boyle, is hit in the head through his nose and goes down with a cry of anguish. He is quickly dragged back by two comrades before they rejoin the skirmishing line. But this veteran of the Sikh Wars in India is hurt badly alright, with the bullet clearly lodged in his head. And then another scream as Private William Juniper is taken down by a musket ball to the thigh, resulting in a compound fracture of the femur.

Whatever else, the Redcoats and police know they are now in a real *battle*. (Under the circumstances, it is not surprising that Magistrate Hackett has no time to read the Riot Act – though he had made a preliminary sortie forward with Captain Thomas to see if it might be possible.)

'I had no opportunity of calling upon the people to disperse as the first certainty we had of their exact position was by a volley of musketry being poured in upon us,' Hackett would later report.[23]

———————

Back in the Camp, a small knot of men has gathered at a high spot, gazing earnestly towards the gloomy Eureka – still fully immersed in the black background of Mount Warrenheip. They try in vain to work out just what the flashes in the semi-darkness, the booms of gunfire rolling up to them a few seconds later, can possibly mean. *Just what is happening down there?* All they know for certain from the constant rattling gunfire is that the battle proper has begun.

———————

The soldiers keep coming, Captain Pasley on horseback still right in their midst, urging them forward. Highly trained, they are generally capable of getting off three volleys in a minute, though the best of them can fire five shots in that time, their hands a blur of movement as they *load-cap-cock-kneel-and-fire. Load-cap-cock-kneel-and-fire. Load-cap-cock-kneel-and-fire.*

All over the diggings the sound of shots, screams and yelling has awoken many. In his own tent, some 150 yards from the Stockade, Raffaello Carboni comes to with a start as the bullets begin to fly past. Then he hears the 'discharge of musketry – then a round from a bugle – the command "forward!"', followed by another discharge of musketry.[24] His first reaction is to take shelter by putting the chimney at the end of his tent between himself and the direction of the shooting, but soon enough his passion gets the better of him. At least by his later account – though others would dispute it – he races towards the men and the flag he has sworn to defend.

In their store, Mrs Bridget Shanahan is also awoken by the firing and immediately jostles her husband, yelling, 'Take out your gun.'[25] Shanahan does just that and heads out.

Though they are still firing furiously, the soldiers' advance remains militarily precise. As the skirmishers slowly advance up the hill, the growing light reveals to them the rough contours of the Stockade only – here an upright slab, there the top of the wheel of an upturned dray, beside it a broken Californian cradle – and from its base comes the heavy flashing and powerful roar of shotguns, rifles and pistols. But beyond that there is little detail. However, while the first flush of the still faraway dawn behind the trees at the back of the Stockade to the east keeps the rebels in strong shadows, it places the soldiers in fairly strong light and makes them good targets. And there is firing aplenty, particularly from the 20 or so remaining brave Americans of the Independent California Rangers' Revolver Brigade, secreted in their shepherds' holes. They have not flinched at the attack and are proving that the words of Charles Ferguson – 'If you make a stand, you will not find us wanting'[26] – were not uttered in vain.

For now these Americans, together with the men of Ross and Thonen particularly, train down fire so 'sharp and sustained'[27] that Pasley's advance is momentarily checked and appears to 'swerve from its ground'.[28]

The British soldiers, trained from their first days in the army for precisely this situation, give at least as good as they receive, notwithstanding that some of the rebels' fire – including shots that come from the tents outside the Stockade – are hitting their marks and there is the frequent groan or scream from falling soldiers as they advance.

'The fire had terrible effect, but we returned it with like effect, as deadly as theirs,' Ferguson of the Rangers would later write.[29]

Both sides are taking punishment and yet, at this point, it is those in the Stockade who momentarily have the advantage as at least they have partial shelter. The Redcoats and the police on the flanks are exposed, coming up a slope in very good light. And the closer the skirmishers get to the Stockade – now just 50 yards away ten minutes after the battle has begun – the easier they are to hit.

What makes matters even worse for the Redcoats is that they are also taking fire from their flanks, as diggers in tents outside the Stockade draw a bead on them. In fact, to the joy of the diggers, it now becomes apparent that the soldiers' relentless advance is *not* as relentless as they had feared. Their line is seen to falter and, finally, is 'arrested for a moment'.[30]

It is the troops of the 40th Regiment who have taken the most punishment, and Captain Henry Wise realises that their situation has become perilous. It is obvious that the longer they take to reach the top of the slope, the more men they will lose. The urgency now is to breach the barricades of the Stockade as soon as possible and fight the rebels at close quarters. Yet his men have wavered and even begun to *back up* as the barrage of bullets start to take its toll, prompting him to cry: 'Fortieth! Are you going to retreat?'[31]

The gnarled and experienced Sergeant Edward Harris[32] is certainly with Wise and has in fact preceded him in his call of 'Forward!'[33] And the youngest of them all, the boy bugler by Wise's side, 'took up boldly his stand to the left of the gully',[34] awaiting further commands. And now even the overall leader of the attack, Captain Thomas, has dismounted and joined Wise's men – a jolt for the soldiers, as a commanding officer would only so expose himself if the battle hangs in the balance, and even then it is rare. Under those circumstances, how could the veterans of the 40th not form up and rally once more? And rally they do, with Wise taking the lead. Crying out 'Charge!',[35] he foregoes firing and with his sword forward – for gentlemen officers do not carry dirty muskets – starts to run straight up the slope, the men under his command following hard.

Behind the Americans in the Stockade, other diggers have now gathered themselves to come forward and fire down the hill, adding to the barrage, before . . .

Before suddenly some of them cry out and fall with splotches of red on their *backs*. In an instant the survivors are aware that shots are now coming from *behind* them! It proves to be Sub-Inspector Samuel Furnell's mounted police troopers attacking the thinly defended southern end of the Stockade's western wall, at the spot where Commissioner Amos has led them to, and doing it at a time when they are most needed by the troops who are hopefully about to breach the diggers' defences. Suddenly some of the fire trained down the gully has to divert to deal with this new threat, allowing Wise and his men a proper chance to attack without being cut to pieces. It is also the moment when many of soldiers who have been held back in reserve now rush forward to replace the fallen. In fact, it is a half dozen of those eager reserves who end up leading the charge towards the Stockade walls, running 'pell-mell'[36] into hell.

The air is now filled with the acrid smoke from the muskets, the endless thunder of so many guns firing at once, the whine of outgoing lead balls and the hiss of incoming bullets, the screams of dying and fearfully wounded men, shouts of aggression and fear, and the unearthly shriek of terrified horses.

And there is the wall! Up and over, the half-dozen reserves are the first to breach the defences and enter the Stockade while the diggers under the command of Captain Ross and Captain Thonen are mostly distracted with Furnell's mounted police attacking their flank.

Alas, once the reserves do get inside the Stockade, they are confronted by diggers only too eager to get at them. What to do now? The obvious . . .

For there is the wall! Up and over, the half-dozen reserves are also the first to now smartly get back over it. By this time, however, the main body of the soldiers has arrived, under the leadership of Captain Wise. These men, too, scramble over the barricade en masse. While some diggers begin to flee for their lives, it is here that the Californians truly come into their own, rushing forward with their Colt revolvers in hand, sometimes firing from the hip, sometimes firing with their arm and hand stretched horizontally before them. True, this daring prevents 'the riflemen and other comrades from supporting them',[37] but they do it anyway.

Whatever else, they know they must get close to the soldiers to be any chance of hitting them with these guns, even if it means they take a terrible toll in turn as the soldiers fire their muskets at near point-blank range.

Carnage and confusion now join the battle, sometimes side by side, sometimes clashing fiercely – no-one quite knows. Each blast of the muskets and revolvers from both sides creates so much smoke that a fog of spent ordnance has now enveloped the Stockade.

In the thick of it all, Captain Wise is just shaping to climb up and over the Stockade wall, choosing which spoke of a dray wheel to put his right foot on and . . .

And it is a strange thing to be shot. Not nearly as agonising as one might imagine in the first instance, particularly when, like this bullet, it does not take Wise in one of his vital organs. Rather, a bullet fired from an unknown rebel hits Wise high in the right thigh and is more like a very hard kick that brings him down than anything else. Still, it is not enough to stop him outright and, after quaveringly quipping that forevermore 'my dancing is spoiled',[38] he is soon enough up and staggering forward once more. Now that his men are on the rebel wall, with an entirely different kind of battle beckoning, it is obvious what needs to be done. Captain Wise is quick to give the order: 'Fix bayonets!'[39]

The Redcoats continue to move with superbly trained precision and, with a whip from their hip, take the 22-inch pieces of cruel steel from their scabbards and fit them to the muzzles of their muskets. And then they renew their scramble up and over the Stockade wall.

It is at close quarters that the soldiers are at their most devastating. Having been exposed in the open as they made their way to the Stockade, they are now ready to even accounts. After marching here expecting an easy victory, the infamy of their own men being shot by the rebels – 12 men of the 12th and four of the 40th have fallen in the opening exchanges – fuels the soldiers' rage. They are intent on revenge from the first.

Suddenly, Private John Sullivan of the 12th Regiment sees a flitting figure ahead – a digger running from tent to tent, trying to keep under cover. Even though the fellow does not appear to be carrying a weapon, Sullivan brings his musket to his shoulder and fires . . . only to hear a throaty cry of agony from beside him.

It is Captain Wise! One of the diggers has just shot him!

Wise had just brought himself to a head-on confrontation with the California Rifle Brigade's Robert Burnette, who remained right in the thick of it, but the digger had managed to fire first at his opposite number with his Colt revolver. Or was it, in fact, the black American rebel John Joseph with a double-barrelled shotgun? Amidst the chaos, Sullivan is far from sure. Whoever it is, his aim is good, for now a second bullet hits Captain Wise, this one passing through both his legs around the knees. The English officer goes down, crippled.

Beside Wise, two other Redcoats fall grievously wounded as the rebels' vicious volley hits them, while another two also suffer bloody wounds. Charles Hackett, who is right in the thick of the action despite not bearing a weapon, races to Wise's aid but is roughly pushed aside by Sergeant Daniel Hegarty of the 40th, who drags Wise to some cover, where he tries in vain to stem the good Captain's copious bleeding.

If the soldiers hesitate momentarily at this point after taking such punishment, that hesitation is soon dispelled as Captain Thomas again shows daring in the midst of doubt. With his yell of 'Come on 40th!',[40] the men sally forth with at least this part of the battle in the balance, for the diggers are at their best in hand-to-hand fighting and using their pistols at close quarters. The pikemen are also holding their own, their weapons far outreaching the soldiers' bayonets.

Overall, however, the number of firearms levelled against the diggers is devastating. As described by Lynch, 'Our left being unprotected, the troopers seized the advantage, wheeled round, and took us in the rear. We were then placed between two fires, and further resistance was useless.'[41]

That is certainly the view of many a digger who, in the face of flying bullets and flashing bayonets, finds that his bravado of the last week has completely deserted him. Dropping their weapons, they surge over the south-eastern barricades themselves in the rough direction of Warrenheip Gully. With the enemy coming at them from all angles, it is time to get out and save their lives at least.

From a distance, Raffaello Carboni sees the vision of 'long-legged Vern'[42] – he who seemed to talk with such knowledge about military tactics and stratagems – floundering 'across the stockade eastward'.[43] It seems the German has decided that the best tactic on this occasion is to head for the hills just as fast as those legs can carry him, also in the direction of Warrenheip.

When Californian Charles Ferguson calls out after the Hanoverian for him to stop and fight, Vern yells back over his shoulder that he is running 'to stop the others'.[44] Ferguson is not convinced.

Captain John Lynch would write of Vern's action at this point: 'How he escaped from the enclosure is indeed a mystery; but not so his action outside. Those who saw him run averred that his performance was such as to suggest a past-mastership in the art of desertion.'[45]

So much for the man who wanted to be the Commander-in-Chief. Carboni and Ferguson are not the only ones appalled, as one Patrick Curtain orders a rebel rifleman to shoot him, but on the instant it is too late – Vern has disappeared and the battle is soon raging all around. Those who don't flee at least have plenty of fight left in them. (To be fair to Vern, at least he had been present and done his best. The same could not be said of Tom Kennedy. Despite his magnificent oratory, the lugs of the Redcoats will go entirely unlicked by him, and again it is John Lynch who would later assert, 'When the time came to put his principles into action he was absent from his post; and the story ran that he prudently withdrew from the scene of danger to seek safety in the seclusion of a pipe-clay cross-drive in a blind shaft.')[46]

One man who has been present from the beginning and stands his ground magnificently is Captain Charles Ross. Four days earlier, he, like all of the rebels, had sworn 'by the Southern Cross to stand truly by each other and to fight to defend our rights and liberties'. He is now living that sacred oath and, if necessary, dying by it, as he stands by the flagpole upon which the Southern Cross is flying proud, sword in one hand and pistol in the other. Standing shoulder to shoulder with the Canadian is an American rebel with the California Rangers who has also taken the oath seriously and is seen to be '[fighting] like a tiger'.[47] His name is currently lost to history.

Alas, their defence cannot last long. Captain Thomas, realising that the battle has swung his way, needs only one more major effort to finish off the rebels, and he immediately calls up the rest of his reserve troops to surge forward. A new wave of Redcoats is soon crashing over the Stockade walls.

In the face of the fresh swarm, Peter Lalor is standing and delivering from atop a large miner's mound, totally exposed beside an open mine-shaft, pistol in hand and fighting with everything he has in him. The crack of his gunfire meets with the rather heavier boom of the soldiers' muskets.

With each shot fired by Lalor, the flash at the muzzle of his pistol briefly illuminates the grim determination of his face. *Who strikes the first blow for Ireland? Who draws first blood for Ireland? Who wins a wreath that will be green forever?* Of course this is not Ireland, but the sentiment – throwing off iniquitous British rule with violence, when all else has failed – is much the same.

Lalor roars to Patrick Curtain and his company, 'Pikemen, advance! Now, for God's sake do your duty.'[48]

By God, and so they do. No matter that the battle is all but gone, that the Redcoats are surging, backed by dozens of police. Lalor has given the order and the pikemen are willing. All this time they have been frustrated by their inability to get at the attackers from afar, but that is put to rights now that the Redcoats are among them so thickly. They set to with a will, swinging out viciously at these first arrivals. In an instant, Private Joseph Wall of the 40th takes a pike right through the stomach and instantly falls to the ground, his hands clawing to prevent his intestines from spilling onto the black dirt – in vain. His mortal coil is loosening by the minute.

Yet despite the courage of the pikemen – in fact, because of it – they present relatively easy targets for the now enraged Redcoats. A volley of shots rings out and half a dozen fall. And now with the Redcoats right upon them, it gets bloodier still, as the pikemen are cut to pieces by their bayonets. In these exchanges the soldiers are without mercy. They have been trained, again and again, when using the bayonet not to 'give them the false touch, but push it home to the muzzle',[49] and so they now do – again and again.

On the fallen diggers the first of the bayonet thrusts brings a quick fountain of blood, while the last of them usually brings nothing as the heart no longer beats. However, it is the brave resistance of these pikemen, standing their ground in the face of such carnage, that allows crucial time for the diggers behind them to either mount their own attacks or – for so many – to continue to flee.

Peter Lalor is not among the deserters. In the middle of the maelstrom, the rebel leader also stands his ground, even as one from the group of Redcoats he has been firing into takes better aim with his musket . . . and shoots.

On the instant, Lalor suddenly drops his gun from his right hand and grasps his left shoulder where he has been hit by a round called a 'buck and ball' – a large bullet (ball) packed into the barrel along with two smaller bullets. It is a round beloved by the military when firing smooth bore muskets and carbines, as it increases the lethality of the weapon at short range. The troopers rush forward. Lalor is hurt, bleeding profusely from his shattered arm.

Clearly, the battle is lost. His first thought, however, is not for himself, but for the others who have been fighting alongside him, who may still be able to save themselves. Running towards a group of fellow rebels, nursing his injured arm, Lalor shouts, 'Get away, boys, as quickly as you can; the Stockade is taken.'[50]

'You come with us,' one of the rebels exhorts, while another, an American by the name of Jim Hull, removes his neckerchief and fastens it tightly around Lalor's arm to stem the gushing flow.

'No, I can't go,' Lalor replies, now unsteady on his feet and white as the ghost he may soon become. 'Get away and save yourselves.'[51]

These last words seem to exhaust what little oomph he has left as the firing continues to ring out, punctuated by the odd scream and agonised death rattle as the bullets and bayonets continue to hit their marks. Lalor slumps back and lands heavily, sitting just upright on a pile of slabs.

Again, Hull has quick command of the situation: 'Drop in there, and we'll cover you up.'[52]

Beside the pile of wood is a 'shallow slab hutch'[53] large enough to secrete a man, and the diggers quickly place the faint but groaning Lalor inside and replace the slabs.

The battle goes on.

Near the flagpole, first the tigerish American is brought low by a bullet to his right thigh, and then Captain Ross – with Charles Ferguson standing right beside him – says to him in one breath, 'Charlie, it is no use, the men have all left us', before exclaiming, 'My God, I am shot.'[54] He has been felled by a vicious musket ball to his groin. Ferguson attempts an escape, during which a soldier's fired ball passes through his hat but, ultimately, finding himself alone among the military, he is forced to make a formal surrender to Captain Carter of the foot police, with 'only one thought for self congratulation, and that was that the soldiers did not take me'.[55] To further save himself, he is also careful to dump his Colt revolver and bowie knife down the leg of his pants and onto the ground, so he won't be captured with arms in hand.

Only moments later the first of the soldiers are at the foot of the flagpole and policeman John King now delights in shinnying up the pole, his arms and legs pumping like those of a crazed monkey. He is only a short way up, however, when the slender pole, which had already been hit by heavy fire, splinters and breaks, bringing the flag to the ground.[56] A mighty cheer goes up from the soldiers, who grab it, toss it from man to man, and, as if the standard is a living, breathing thing, throw it to the ground where they first kick and then continually stab it with their bayonets. When their passion has played out, King joyously claims the flag again and secures it beneath his tunic – there is still more killing to be done as yet more diggers turn and run for their lives.

Quickly now, lads, away, for the Redcoats are all around!

Another shot and brave Edward Thonen goes down with several bullets at once 'exactly in the mouth'[57] – his boots on, gun in his hand, still firing – but he is dead before he hits the ground.

Although the Redcoats are now well on top, still the pikemen fight on, even after losing many of their number and the first of the mounted troopers having passed through. One Irishman, Thomas O'Neill, has a musket ball in his chest, both legs broken and can no longer stand, but it takes more than that to stop a man from Kilkenny when his blood is fairly up. Though in agony and sitting in a fresh pool of blood, he still manages to furiously swing his pike around above his head, a whirling dervish who manages to wound several flat-footed troopers until they wreak their terrible revenge with many musket balls.

And nor are any braver than the German blacksmith Hafele, who has worked so hard to forge all those pikes. Right in the thick of it, he is flailing his own pike at every soldier who comes within range – and even those who don't[58] – before he, too, is struck down, his corpse run through with frenzied and repeated bayonet thrusts.

Just ten yards away from the freshly fallen Hafele, the black American John Joseph fights on, no more intimidated by such bloody violence than John Manning, who is right beside him with rifle in hand, standing his ground.

When trooper William Revell of the Mounted 40th goes after one pike-bearing digger, Thomas Dignum – born and bred in *Sydney* – who to this point had also 'fought like a tiger [and] repented not of having put on stretchers a couple of Redcoats',[59] the Australian suddenly turns on Revell and thrusts his pike at him. Though it misses, the pike strikes home into a Redcoat mate beside him, whereupon the enraged Revell instantly strikes the Australian on the head with his sword. Dignum goes down with a heavy wound to his skull.

Some 20 minutes after the first shots, however, as more diggers fall and others flee, the worst of the fighting is over. And yet, even after it is clear that the resistance of the diggers has ceased, that the government forces have won the day, still the killing does not stop. A terrible kind of madness appears to have overtaken some of the uniformed men and they continue their murdering and maiming, hunting down every digger they can see, whether or not he has even been involved in any of the hostilities. The worst of the murderers, for that is what they have become, are the police, who now wreak cruel revenge for the humiliations they have suffered in recent times.

By now, many of those diggers not killed in the initial assault or its aftermath have taken refuge back in their tents, but this presents no problem for the conquering forces. As it happens, Martin and Anne Diamond have not been remotely involved in the uprising beyond having had their place sequestered for some crucial meetings of the Council for the Defence. Their whole presence within the Stockade is no more than a geographical quirk, as the boundaries of the Stockade left their store half-in and half-out of it. None of this registers on the soldiers and troopers. As the couple run out of their tent to try and get to the relative safety of the bush, Martin stumbles and falls flat on his face. He attempts to rise when the first soldier reaches him and triumphantly impales him in the back with his bayonet, and that soldier is soon joined by police, who slash at him with their swords. Diamond is dead within a minute, all of it in front of his screaming wife.

There must be a lot of others in those tents? Well then, says Sub-Inspector Carter, 'Set the tents on fire!'[60]

The order is instantly obeyed as Carter's foot police take the cool ends of some burning logs and sticks from one of the fires in the middle of the Stockade and run from tent to tent, setting them alight. (Oh so very strange, these British, how they love to put the torch to anything that will burn.)

One of the first tents to go down is Diamond's store, which blazes in an instant after a 'Vandemonian-looking trooper' – though this frankly describes most of them – sets fire to the northern end and lets the rising wind from that very direction take care of the rest. In short order, dozens of tents are ablaze, along with the wounded, who are burnt alive. As Carboni would recall, 'The howling and yelling was horrible.'[61]

That will bring them out once more.

And so it does, as the fires soon illuminate screaming, coughing figures rushing out into the open air. Who knows if they have been involved in the rebellion or not? It doesn't matter anymore. The butchering goes on.

———

Up on the courthouse verandah back at the Camp, Samuel Huyghue and other officials see the flames and smoke billowing from the Stockade with some relief. The soldiers have clearly made it inside and are now destroying whatever it is they have found.

———

As other diggers and their families rush from their tents, the troopers inevitably knock the men down and let the screaming women and children go where they will. If the men resist and try to fight back, their end comes quickly. If they submit, they are immediately arrested and dragged away. When one group of diggers falls back to some tents near the blacksmith's workshop, those tents are quickly torched, smoking the rebels out, and another furious outbreak of violence takes place – hand to hand, pike to bayonet, dirty rebel to loyal servant of Her Majesty Queen Victoria. This group of diggers fights well, but the weight of numbers against them is so strong that it is not long before they are quelled.

'When we were in that helpless state, an unconditional surrender ought to have been proposed to us,' digger John Lynch would later recall. 'It would have been accepted, and the future spared many bitter memories. But the spirit of revenge was uppermost, and revelled in a fierce saturnalia of carnage. More than half the loss of life took place after resistance had ceased. A few, who surrendered on challenge – and very few got the chance – were placed under guard; but as the wantonness of destruction on the one side grew with hopelessness of resistance on the other, the guards had enough to do to save their charges from being shot or hacked to pieces'.[62]

Still not content that they have wrought enough destruction, many of the Redcoats now decide to spread the inferno to other tents well outside the Stockade walls. After all, they took fire from some treasonous diggers in those canvas caves. They must be put to the torch also.

In all the madness, atrocities abound. One 23-year-old digger, Henry Powell, has had nothing to do with anything – he had come over the day before from Creswick to visit a friend. Curious about the shots and screams, he has just ventured from his friend's tent and is in the open when soldiers on horseback come roaring over the rise. At the first sight of them, Powell realises the danger he is in and starts to run, something that automatically makes the police – the scent of victory in their nostrils – pursue him hard and bring him down. All is chaos and quick-fire, but at least Powell recognises one of the horsemen, a young fellow called Arthur Akehurst – a Clerk of the Peace, usually seen in the Ballarat courthouse inside the Camp – notable for his fair complexion and reddish hair.

Not only is this no time for pleasantries, but Akehurst, who has been sworn in as a special constable just that morning, is violently aggressive from the first.

'Stand up in the Queen's name, you bastard,' he says.

'Very good, sir,' the frightened Powell replies, now with as many as 30 troopers surrounding him. 'Very well, gentlemen, don't be alarmed, there are plenty of you.'[63]

There is no fight in him at all – just fear and the earnest hope that he will not be hurt. Alas, with nary another word, Akehurst takes his three-and-a-half-foot sword and strikes him a fearful blow on the head.

Powell first falls down, then gets up, bleeding, only to have one of the troopers now fire into him and shout, 'There, you bugger, that shows you!'[64]

Even as the young man screams for help, the other troopers take their horses back and forth over him, their hooves inflicting cruel damage. When he again tries to rise, they first fire pistols and then slash viciously at him with their swords, and again he falls. Thomas Pierson would write of such acts in his diary, 'It was a most cowardly disgraceful Butchery, worthy only off sutch scamps as those who instigated it.'[65]

In their own tent inside the Stockade, Matthew Faulds and his heavily pregnant wife, Mary, cower in terror. Mary is due to give birth at any moment, fleeing is out of the question, and all Matthew can do is have her lie on her back, roll two logs either side of her for protection and put a blanket over her as they pray for a miracle. A mounted trooper suddenly slashes open the tent, the flooding light revealing the situation. He turns and leaves them be. Their daughter, Adeliza, is born not long afterwards.

Ah, but there are many more atrocities to come, as recorded by Samuel Lazarus: 'Another man, a considerable distance from the Stockade . . . went out of his tent in his shirt and drawers and seeing the savage butchery going on cried out in terror to a trooper galloping by, "For God's sake don't kill my wife and children," his prayer may as well have been addressed to a devil. He was shot dead on his own threshold.'[66] Not far away and only shortly afterwards, former *Ballarat Times* and *Melbourne Morning Herald* correspondent Frank Hasleham turned digger and part-time reporter (he provides information to the current *Geelong Advertiser* correspondent) is trying to find a safe place away from the danger of the Stockade. He happens upon a quiet gully when he looks up to see three horsemen heading his way.

'One of them,' he would later recount, 'who rode considerably ahead of the other two arrived within hailing distance, [and] he hailed me as a friend.'[67]

The trooper now addresses him, asking pleasantly, 'Do you wish to join our force?'

'No,' Hasleham replies a little uncertainly, surprised by the question. 'I am unarmed, and in a weak state of health. I hope this madness with the diggers will soon be over.'

Ah, but there is some madness yet to go: at a distance of just four paces, the trooper raises his pistol, points at Hasleham's breast and shoots.

Hasleham falls hard, bleeding heavily. The trooper isn't done, however. Dismounting, he handcuffs the innocent man, who lies there for the next 'two hours, bleeding from a wound in his breast, until his friends send for a blacksmith who forces off the handcuffs with a hammer and cold chisel'.[68]

———————

In their humble abode some two miles from Eureka, Henry Seekamp and his wife, Clara, are woken by a furious pounding on the door and before they can even open it, a friend by the name of Underwood bursts in.

'I'm as glad as if I'd got a thousand pounds to find you in bed,' says he. 'The military have gone down and fired upon the diggers.'[69]

No sooner have the Seekamps tried to absorb this appalling news than a young boy comes and says to their servant girl, 'Your brother's been shot dead.'[70] The distressed young girl falls away into a dead faint.

———————

Meanwhile outside the Stockade, Raffaello Carboni, seeing that the tent next to his own is in flames and that his own is likely next, rushes to retrieve some important papers. Once they are secured, he has just emerged again when he comes face to face with the commander of the foot police, Sub-Inspector Carter, pointing his pistol and giving him the sharp order to fall in with the other prisoners.

With no other choice, Carboni obeys. Then, in the middle of the gully, he spies Captain Thomas, whom he knows a little. Thomas asks the Italian whether he had indeed been made a prisoner within the Stockade.

'No, sir,'[71] Carboni replies frankly, before adding a brief explanation of where he had been. There is something in the way the Italian speaks, in the way he is happy to look the officer in the eyes, that connotes honesty – and the thoroughly decent Captain Thomas reacts in kind.

'If you really are an honest digger,' the English officer says with a gentle stroke of his sword, 'I do not want you, sir; you may return to your tent.'[72]

Still, the fiery Italian is not out of danger. Upon deciding to return to his tent, he is crossing the gully once more when a trooper who has spied him in the distance smoothly holds out his gun and fires! The bullet flies 'with such a tolerable precision'[73] that it blows off his cabbage-tree hat, and he is only narrowly able to escape.

At this point, a lesser man than Carboni would have done anything rather than continue to expose himself in the open but, as a man who has fought with Garibaldi, he is made of stronger stuff. In short order, when he hears himself called by name by Doctor Carr and Father Smyth, who are making their way to the Stockade to help with the wounded – and seeking his assistance – he instantly responds.

Meanwhile, many weeping, shrieking women have now emerged to throw themselves over the bleeding forms of their husbands to protect them from further bayonets and bullets, even as others collapse in anguish upon the bodies of their freshly slaughtered husbands, their frequently very young children 'frightened into quietness'.[74] Mercifully, some women whose husbands have survived also appear, and soon bring handkerchiefs to cover the faces of the dead, and matting to cover their bodies.

But the slaughter is still not over, as there remain many other targets for the soldiers to go after. The soldiers, as recorded by Captain Pasley, 'hated the insurgents . . . for having wounded a drummer boy, and dangerously wounded Captain Wise, [and] were very anxious to kill the prisoners and it was with great difficulty, that they were restrained by the officers from doing so'.[75]

When Pasley comes across a party of prisoners who are about to be bayoneted by their guard, he takes out his revolver and declares, 'I will shoot the first man who injures a digger who has surrendered.'

'This had the desired effect,' he would later write to his father, 'although I do not believe the prisoners themselves cared much, because they fully believed . . . that they would be hanged directly they got to the Camp.'[76] Nevertheless, beyond Thomas and Pasley, there remain other pockets of decency among the police and military forces.

Both the black American John Joseph and the Irishman John Manning have just emerged from a burning tent and are likely about to be shot when, with great force, Sub-Inspector Carter yells to the officer in charge to order his men to lower their guns.

Elsewhere, just as one digger, John Tye, is being marched away in manacles, his wife runs up in her nightdress and sobbingly pleads for his release, only for that good woman to be laughed at and pushed around roughly by the soldiers. This is witnessed by an outraged officer, who thunders up on horseback and furiously upbraids the soldiers, ordering the woman to be let alone *and* her husband to be released.

At much the same time, Mrs Shanahan is all alone in her tent, worried for the safety of her husband, when there is a knock on the door. She opens it to find a trooper and a soldier.

'Shoot that woman,' says the trooper without preamble.

'Spare the woman,' the shocked foot soldier replies.

'Well, get out,' says the trooper, 'the place is going to be burnt down.'[77]

And the intent of the other soldiers outside is clearly to do exactly that, because in shorter order the tent is set ablaze and the men gallop away. Mercifully, Mrs Shanahan manages to extinguish her tent.

Finally some equilibrium is achieved as the last of the fight goes out of the diggers and the worst of the bloodlust fades from the police and soldiers. Both the shooting and screaming at last, mercifully, stops. The red mist lifts, leaving behind the sickly sweet stench of burnt human flesh mixed with the acrid whiff of gunpowder smoke.

With each passing minute, now well after six o'clock, the growing light illuminates an ever more ghastly scene. 'Pikes, spent balls, and pools of blood, showed where the contest had been most deadly.'[78] Some diggers have gushing, gaping wounds in their abdomens and the haunted eyes of men who know they are about to die. Others, who just an hour ago were living and breathing and talking, are now no more than grotesque corpses, their hideous grimaces a testament to the agony with which they met their deaths.

A distressing number of diggers from other parts of the goldfields, who have not been involved at all, have simply come to gawk with open-mouthed wonder at this tragic spectacle. Carboni, for one, is 'amazed at the apathy shown by the diggers . . . None would stir a finger.'[79] Henry Seekamp and his wife are there, but not as gawkers. They are there as journalists – *witnesses* – and wander about, furiously taking notes for the next edition of *The Ballarat Times*. One man also there is the auctioneer and storekeeper Samuel Lazarus, who was asleep in his tent when the attack began.

'A ghastly scene lay before me,' he would shortly after confide to his diary, 'which it is vain to attempt to describe. My blood crept as I looked upon it. Stretched on the ground in all the horror of a bloody death lay 18 or twenty lifeless and mutilated bodies. Some shot in the face, others literally riddled with wounds – one with a ghastly wound in the temples and one side of his body roasted by the flames of his tent – another, the most horrible of these appalling spectacles with a frightful gaping wound in his head through which the brains protruded, lay with his chest feebly heaving in the last agony of death.'[80]

In one particular tent lies 'the bodies of two men, their clothes ignited and their flesh partly consumed. They had been shot in their sleep probably, or were too drunk to escape from their burning tent and so perished. The sight caused even the rude soldiers to turn sickening away.'[81]

Poor, brave John Hafele lies in grotesque pose, his intestines spilling onto the black dirt and still worse wounds apparent. 'He had three contusions in the head, three strokes across the brow, a bayonet wound in the throat under the ear – I counted fifteen wounds in that carcass,' a *Geelong Advertiser* correspondent and immediate eyewitness to the aftermath of the carnage would later report. 'O! God, Sir, it was a sight for a sabbath morn that I humbly implore Heaven may never be seen again.'[82] Strangely and most movingly of all, in the face of all the devastation around and about Hafele, his dog – a tiny Irish terrier – won't stop howling and trying to lick his master awake. Time and again, the dog is removed, for decency's sake, but time and again the dog comes back and, 'lying again on his master's breast [begins] howling again.'[83]

Not far away is the broke-legged Irishman Thomas O'Neill, who had fought so valiantly, pike in hand, also with grievous wounds all over his torso and head. Though still alive, just, he is no more than a mass of pain, and as it is obvious that his situation is hopeless, he is quickly 'despatched'.[84]

And, of course, there is Edward Thonen, the popular 'lemonade man', 'his mouth literally choked with bullets',[85] the bottom part of his face and jawline shot away.

Yet another of the severely wounded not long for this world is poor James Brown, the Irishman who had first encouraged his mate Peter Lalor to take to the podium and the lead all at once. He is now all shot to pieces.

Many of the freshly wounded have blood spurting from the 'round blue holes in their flesh, already swollen, where a bullet or bayonet entered',[86] pulsing in rough rhythm to every agonised rising and falling of their chests. Sometimes the blood forms bubbles as the air finds a different way out and runs in dreadful rivulets onto the parched earth below. Flies have started to buzz in from everywhere and are now crawling over unattended wounds, already laying their eggs.

One of the most terribly wounded and flyblown is Henry Powell, who, though entirely innocent, has been knocked down by horses, trampled, shot three times and then slashed with sabres. He is hanging on to life by a thread. Many such men who still have life in them are now being visited by Father Smyth, who is caught between deep grief at what he is seeing and cold fury that it has come to this. He now moves from dying man to dying man, administering the last rites to those who would receive him and to even the insensible ones when he knows they are Catholic. That Father Smyth is discouraged in this, shouted at by the troopers to move away, troubles him not at all. He continues to try to ease the diggers' passage to the next world.

All around him are scenes that no man who believes in a just God should ever have to witness – much of it powered by the devil in the dynamic between victor and vanquished. And just as many of the police have enjoyed boosting their income by purloining a good chunk of the fines levied on the diggers when they were alive, so now do many of them loot the bodies of the dead. And not just the police, for the Redcoats, too, rifle through the corpses and the prisoners, taking everything they can get as they 'search'[87] for hidden weaponry – from pound notes to watches to small collections of gold. One wounded rebel even has two Redcoats kneeling on his chest, holding him down, while another goes through his pockets.

Finally, however, one of the officers has had enough and gives a sharp command to his soldiers, who instantly obey. Taking their pistols from their holsters, they clear the Stockade – under pain of being shot on the spot – of everyone bar the prisoners, the dead and the dying. And this includes a fiercely defiant and even more furious Father Smyth, who is 'threatened with his life, and *forced* . . . at last to desist'.[88]

It is now that Doctor Carr and Raffaello Carboni come to the fore, and it is at their direction that the severely wounded are at least separated from the rest, put on makeshift stretchers and carried up the Melbourne Road to the London Hotel, which is being converted into an even more makeshift hospital.

(And if several diggers are staring at Carboni with wonder on their faces, it is for very good reason. 'Old fellow, I am glad to see you alive!' a digger by the name of Binney says to Carboni, gripping him with one hand while pointing at a dead digger with flowing red hair and bushy red beard with the other. 'Everyone thinks that's [you]!')[89] Another case of a mistaken identity, mercifully, proves to be the tragic report about the brother of the servant girl of the Seekamps. Yes, he has been shot and has lost an arm, but he will live.

An officer gallops into the Camp at full cry. He has come from the Stockade and reports to all the soldiers, officers and officials now gathered around that it is all over. They have won the day, and now he needs horses and carts to bring in the dead and wounded.

What is left of the Stockade is already being pulled down or simply burnt. By the end of the day it will be no more than a black scar on the earth, much like the Eureka Hotel had been. Terrified

groups of prisoners who have been rounded up and put in manacles are now vainly trying to come to terms with their fate. Yes, the
prospect of the battle had been so exciting yesterday that it stiffened
the sinews, flared the nostrils and had them breathing fire, but now
they are left with a truly horrifying reality. The danger of fighting
for your freedom is that you are not only in danger of losing the
freedom you do enjoy but the spectre of an even worse possibility
dances before you.

'What will become of us?' many of the prisoners want to know.

Their jeering guards are quick with their response: 'Why, hung
of course!'[90]

It is a matter of curiosity to Charles Ferguson that, in regards to
the prisoners, 'Some who were the most frightened were the bravest
only a few hours before; others were sullen and said nothing.'[91]

A shattering bugle call rings out across the Stockade . . . and
there is an instant reaction from the soldiers – 'general assembly'. It
is time for the victorious forces to gather the dead, the wounded and
their prisoners and head back to the Camp. One of those prisoners
is a digger, Samuel Perry, and though he has just been arrested after
being caught in the thick of the fight, his chief hope is that the gold
nugget he has managed to secrete in flour in a baker's trough will
remain undetected until he can get free once more.

In a curious resemblance to the Stockade itself, the prisoners are
put in the rough formation of a 'hollow square',[92] wedged between
the three carts in front and three carts behind, bearing the government force's wounded and dead – and, more particularly, the digger
dead. And there are many of them.

On a rough count by Captain Thomas, 'not less than thirty [were]
killed on the spot',[93] while others have clearly not got long to live.

A little over half are identifiable, while the rest will have to go to
their graves anonymously. At least ten of the latter group are likely
Americans, perhaps because, given the political sensitivities of the
day, it is better not to have it recorded that these men of a famous

and newly important republic have taken part.

The thing now is to get everyone back to the Camp.

Alas, when the body of John Hafele is lifted into the dray, his little terrier reaches new depths of misery and jumps up to sit on his master's chest, where he once more tries to lick him awake as the cart crunches and sways its leaden way towards the Government Camp.

'No human being,' Christopher Cook would later write, 'could have lamented more at the loss of their dearest relative or friend than that affectionate and faithful dog bewailed the loss of his master.'[94]

Those judged able are marched to the Government Camp. No matter that some of the rebels can barely walk, they must limp along the best they can, sooled from behind by military bayonet. Those unconscious are piled on top of each other in the drays like sacks of potatoes, in the same manner as the digger dead.

It does not matter that there appears to be little fight left in this defeated group, just to be sure, the troopers guard them closely on each side, their swords up and ready to strike, their pistols and carbines cocked and primed to fire.

The order comes – *move out* – and the first mass of 40 prisoners heads off with some mounted troopers in front and beside. The joyous foot soldiers fall in behind, pricking the stragglers with the points of their bayonets, even as many of the other soldiers joyously throw around the captured 'Australian flag'[95] between them, waving it around in the air and then throwing it in the dust to trample upon it. Eventually, it is hilariously tied to a horse's tail and dragged to the Camp.

And the indignities do not stop there. As they continue on their way towards the Camp, there are many troopers jumping around, flourishing their swords in victory and mockingly shouting in the face of their prisoners, 'We have waked up Joe!' to which other troopers reply uproariously, 'And sent Joe to sleep again!'[96]

Ah, the fun of it. The sergeant of the detachment jeers, 'I think we roused 'em up early enough this morning. Joe's dead now.'[97]

And yet this is not merely a trail of triumph, for on one dray, behind the victorious soldiers, come their own dead. Privates Michael Roney and Denis Brien of the 40th Regiment, the latter of whom was killed shortly after the former, are far more respectfully laid out in their bloodied uniforms with their eyes closed and arms crossed in the manner of readiness for Christian burial. It is a shocking sight, 'the dead soldiers stretched stiff and silent in carts, their showy uniforms a mockery now'.[98]

In another dray close behind are the 13 men classified as 'dangerously wounded', including Captain Henry Wise, whose blue military trousers are drenched to the bottom of his boots with his own blood. (And, not that it matters, but he is also missing his watch, as it was stolen by one of the soldiers who carried him away.) They must get him back to the Camp quickly to try to save his life and the lives of at least two others thought to be mortally wounded – but they'll do their best.

For one of the prisoners being marched, however, it is already too late. He stumbles out of the line, faint from blood loss. John Lynch and another man are ordered to assist him and, though they do their best, 'as he was fast dying we had to lay him down'.[99]

———

Even now, however, as this catastrophic cavalcade heads back down to the gully before crossing Yarrowee Creek and climbing to the Government Camp, the atrocities do not cease. When a few prisoners try to make a break for it, they are furiously pursued just at a time when an anonymous Welsh digger – who has had no involvement with either the battle or the Stockade in general – has come on the scene. He just happens to be talking to the father of young Barnard Welch, Benjamin Welch, sitting on a hill just below the late Eureka

Hotel discussing the whole affair, when the two of them spy some of the prisoners making a run for it do.

'Oh, here's a lark,' says the fellow upon spying the prisoners running down the opposite hill by the Catholic Chapel, 'I will go and see what is the matter.'

'Do not run,' warns Mr Welch. 'If you run you may be mistaken for one of them.'[100]

But the Welsh digger does not listen and immediately takes off on this bit of fun when to his horror he sees two mounted troopers, one apparently a sergeant, galloping towards him with intent. 'Stop!' the sergeant calls out. Panicking, the Welshman about-faces and quickly squeezes under the flap of a nearby tent. 'Surrender!' orders the trooper in pursuit.

'No,' replies the digger. 'I'm going home. I had nothing to do with the fight. I've just come from my work.'[101]

Once more, the trooper calls on him to surrender. Once more, the terrified Welshman refuses.

'Fire!' the sergeant shouts at a distance. The trooper mechanically dismounts, removes his pistol from its holster, points its muzzle at the digger's chest and pulls the trigger. When the troopers have left, Mr Welch rushes to the fallen man where he lies, and finds him 'totally dead'. The bullet appears to have pierced his heart and passed clean out the other side.

It is with a quivering hand that he removes the poor fellow's wallet from his pocket and opens it. Within, he finds a fully paid up, fully registered license from which he learns this poor soul's name.

Llewellyn Rowlands.

Another good man, gone to God.

And for what?

———

As the tragic train of drays squeaks and scrapes into the Government

Camp, bearing its catastrophic cargo, those untouched by the morning's battle lust gaze upon the bodies with horror.

'The dead rebels,' records Commissioner Rede's Chief Clerk, Samuel Huyghue, 'presented an example of humanity in its worst guise, their faces ghastly and passion-distorted and their eyes staring with stony fixedness, and in some instances, with their arms upraised, and fingers bent as though grasping a weapon in the death struggle.'[102]

As the prisoners are crammed into the log lockup, chaos reigns, a chaos that worsens when shortly afterwards another, larger, body of prisoners arrives under guard. As they are all crammed together the authorities quickly lose track of who had been arrested under arms and who had simply been picked up in the general area. In the miserable madness of it all, there is one question that all those under guard want answered.

What, pray God, is going to happen now? Are they really going to be hanged?

CHAPTER FOURTEEN

AFTER THE TEMPEST

But the light of the morning was deadened an'
smoke drifted far o'er the town.
An' the clay o' Eureka was reddened ere the flag o' the diggers came down.[1]

Henry Lawson, *The Fight at Eureka Stockade*, 1890

Seven o'clock, Sunday morning, 3 December 1854, 'The tumult and the shouting dies / the captains and the kings depart'

With the vast bulk of the Redcoats and police gone, those who had secreted Peter Lalor beneath the slabs decide to risk returning to see if he is still alive. There is so much blood apparent on the earth beside those slabs that the first man there – Lalor's former shipmate and now fellow digger and rebel, James Ashburner – fears the worst. And yet, when he whispers to Lalor that most of the Redcoats have headed back to the Camp, a whispered response comes back. In a moaning muttering, Lalor asks him to go get Father Smyth.

Ashburner is outside the Stockade in the company of Timothy Hayes, tending to some of the wounded when he finds the priest, and the three men quickly make their way back towards where Lalor lies. They are spotted by someone in the crowd, who immediately calls out to Police Sub-Inspector Thomas Langley.

'There goes Hayes. He is one of the ringleaders,' the informant blabbers. 'He deserves more than those poor fellows.'[2] Moving quickly, Langley immediately claims the prize arrest of the Irishman Hayes, together with Ashburner. But there is a problem once the trooper takes Hayes in hand. Though shocked – he had not been in the Stockade at the time of the battle and had taken no part in the clash – Hayes is by nature a gentle man and simply does not have it in him to lash out verbally or physically. This, however, is not the case with his wife, the worthy Anastasia, who had a part in sewing the flag that has been so worthily fought for.

Sub-Inspector Langley is just leading the manacled Hayes and Ashburner away to join the line of prisoners when the red-headed Anastasia, her blue eyes flashing with anger, rushes up from where she has been tending some wounded diggers. After a withering look at her husband, she approaches Lieutenant Richards, Adjutant Commander of the 40th, as he marches with the wounded and prisoners back to Government Camp. Through clenched teeth, she says, 'If I had been a man, I would not have allowed myself to be taken by the likes of you.'[3]

One look in her eyes and Lieutenant Richards does not doubt it. More pointedly, she follows up directly to the English officer: 'Why didn't you attack the Stockade yesterday, when we were prepared to receive you?'[4] It is less a question than a statement of real regret. She clearly would have loved to have seen the soldiers take on the diggers when the latter had been present in force and capable of delivering far greater firepower to their rebellion.

And she is not the only one disappointed in her husband. After all that has happened, Mrs Shanahan found her husband hiding in the small outhouse.

———

With only his grey horse for company, Father Smyth heads off to the pile of slabs, where, after establishing that Lalor is still alive, he furiously waves his arms to signal to some passing men that he needs help. One of the men who answers the call is still in his nightshirt, under-drawers and slippers. A group of them have all just assembled before the slabs when a stray trooper, coming from parts unknown, thunders up on horseback and, ignoring the Father while all the others quickly shrink away, aggressively addresses himself to the half-dressed man.

'Oh!' he roars, his sword raised above his head, as if ready to smite him dead. 'You bloody bastard, you was one of them. Come along with me, and if you look back I will cut you down.'[5]

With no choice but to follow the tragic line of prisoners, off the unfortunate man goes in his nightclothes, careful not to look back, the trooper close behind.

At last, at last, the mournful bugle calls the last of the police and troopers away from the Stockade. Only then do the other diggers rejoin Father Smyth before the pile of slabs. It is now judged safe and they can even speak openly to the still-buried Lalor, who now weakly whispers back up to them, 'For God's sake, boys, go and leave me.'[6]

A Scottish digger by the name of Robert Lorimer, however, will not hear of it. He talks urgently but quietly to Lalor, his words tumbling over each other like a small waterfall. 'If you wish to escape, now is your time. The soldiers are gone, and the troopers have cleared away also.'[7] Not waiting for a reply this time, Lorimer urges, 'Down with the pile of slabs, boys,'[8] and many willing hands set to.

Lifting the slabs from his hiding place, they soon have the exceedingly pale and groaning Lalor in the open air, where the severity of his wounds are reflected in his ashen face. His left arm is still well-attached to his shoulder, but he has no control of it. Now that he is standing, the blood comes from the wound in spurts.

Lorimer had completed some medical studies at Edinburgh

University before coming to Australia, and he now takes Lalor's own coloured neckerchief and ties it tightly over the worst of his wounds, attempting to stem the continuing blood loss.

Then, after getting Lalor onto Father Smyth's horse, they put him in the charge of a trustworthy digger by the name of Billy Smythe, who rides beside him and practically holds him on the saddle. The two head off for Warrenheip, and they arrive not long after Independent California Rangers' Revolver Brigade Commander James McGill has left for Melbourne in a Cobb coach. The 21-year-old is disguised in women's clothes provided by – who else? – Sarah Hanmer of the Adelphi Theatre. (She did such a good job that a story would circulate afterwards that a male passenger on the coach proposed to McGill.)

Another who manages to get away, in his case to Geelong, is James Esmond. He was in the thick of the action throughout and fought with the best of them as captain of one of the companies. Once resistance ceased, he was able to make his way out of the Stockade unmolested. The fact that he is far and away Victoria's best known and most prestigious goldminer – credited and rewarded by the government as one of the discoverers of gold in the state – cannot have hurt him in this endeavour. Should it be known that a man of Esmond's pedigree was in the thick of the fight against government forces, it would be an embarrassment to both that government and those forces.

———

Many of the wounded diggers who have escaped being marched off to the lockup – it is considered they will likely die anyway – are being tended by Doctor Carr and his helpers in the nearby London Hotel, where the Englishman's surgical skills have never been on such call as now. Many of the bayonet gashes are not mere flesh wounds or slashes to the skin; they have penetrated deep into vital organs. There is little that can be done, bar make the injured as comfortable as possible as their life ebbs.

In the bar, just after 8.30 am, Raffaello Carboni is engaged in bandaging the wounds of a brave American digger, a man who stood his ground throughout the entire battle despite taking six wounds – all on the front of his body – and had only finally fallen when he fainted through loss of blood. For such a man, there is not a lot that a person as limited in medical experience as Carboni can do beyond cleaning and dressing those wounds the best he can and offering soothing words.

Yet, just as he is assisting in the dressing of the man's thigh, he looks up to see a digger he never liked, Henry Goodenough, enter the salon with wild eyes and gasping breath, holding a cocked pistol. The same fellow who was always exhorting them to attack the Camp, without ever wanting to get involved himself. *Che cosa? What on earth is going on?* Does Goodenough think the battle continues? And why is he poking the muzzle of the pistol right in Carboni's face?

'I want you!' he roars at the Italian.

'What for?'

'None of your damned nonsense, or I will shoot you down like a rat.'

'My good fellow, don't you see? I am assisting Dr Carr to dress the wounds of my friends!'[9]

Goodenough has no interest in any explanation that Carboni has to offer, and it is only now that the Italian understands. Far from being a rebel, the Englishman reveals he has been working for the troopers all along. Goodenough is a traitor, in the pay of those who have visited this terrible injustice upon them and then slaughtered them for daring to protest. Carboni is speechless with rage, but he's also surprised that Dr Carr does not speak up for him, does not step forward and demand that trooper Goodenough unhand the Italian immediately. Despite Carboni now begging him to intervene, Dr Carr speaks not a word and stands silently as the fiery Italian is roughly dragged outside and manacled to a dozen other straggling rebels who have also been taken prisoner inside the Stockade and are in all states of exhaustion, trauma and injury. Bound to each other, some weeping, they are marched to the Camp, where, at this very time, there is a sudden outcry . . .

Him! That's HIM!

Seeing a black man among the prisoners – none other than John Joseph – a soldier is convinced that he is the one who shot the now grievously wounded Captain Wise. The man is quite prepared to shoot Joseph on the spot, and this is exactly what would have occurred, 'had it not been for the officers'[10] who restrain the soldier. It has been one thing for summary executions to take place in and around the Stockade, but it is quite another here.

―――――――

At the Star Hotel, the worthy Captain Ross of Canada, the bridegroom of the Eureka flag, is even now rattling out his last agonising breaths. He was carried there as soon as the battle was over and lain on a sofa, but though two doctors work feverishly, his wounds are simply too grave.

As desperate as the situation is, the licensee, William McCrae, is so panicked by having a rebel on his premises that he sends out a Camp runner to inform them of the situation. It is not long before a trooper arrives, pistol loaded. After telling McCrae that his license would not be renewed for harbouring a rebel, he searches the hotel and finds Ross, dead on the sofa in a pool of his own blood.

―――――――

Of course, it is not just the diggers that misfortune and tragedy have descended upon. Within the confines of the Camp's rough hospital, the medical staff are doing what they can for Captain

Wise and the other wounded soldiers, but it is little enough.

The wounds to Wise's legs are deep, he has lost a lot of blood, and he is now breathing with some difficulty on a cot. It is touch and go whether he will survive – only amputation might save him. Around and about, many of the other soldiers who have been seriously wounded are also having those wounds and slashes attended to. The lucky ones only have bits of lead dug out of their bodies. In both cases, the blood flows freely and the scene is terribly grisly and sad. Outside the hospital, however, among the soldiers in the Camp courtyard, the mood is entirely different.

Upon the smoke and dust of the dispersing battle, there is a human dynamic that sees the misery of the shattered and scattered rebels more than matched by the joy of the victors coming together to toast each other three times over and once more for luck.

The soldiers, some of them still smeared with blood, are laughing, chiacking and joyfully jostling each other as they dip their pannikins into a bucket full of brandy and gulp it down deeply. Rodomontade abounds: did you see the corporal and how his bayonet went right *through* that rebel?

More laughter, more drinking and more jeering at the swell of prisoners who continue to dribble in.

These last now include the dirty dozen with the dazed Raffaello Carboni, who is struggling to grasp what is happening and how, despite not even having been inside the Stockade when the attack came, he is under arrest. In short order he joins over 100 prisoners in the poisonously overcrowded log gaol.

Two hours later, police inspector Henry Foster commands all the prisoners to strip down to their bare shirts and line up so that their details can be taken.

One by one they step forward.

'Timothy Hayes.'

'John Joseph.'

'William Atherden.'

'John Manning.'

'Raffaello Carboni.'

Raffy Carbi-what? asks the trooper, not a little confused at such a bizarre and entirely unpatriotic name.

He finally masters it, however, and writes down 'Charles Raffaello'. In order to help him spell it, the Italian pulls out the small bag he has with him, which contains both his mining license and some of the gold he has gathered over previous days. Mr Foster takes the bag while the trooper takes the license, whereupon the next lot of prisoners arrives and he is again called outside the room. At this point Carboni is ordered to strip, when a trooper suddenly steps up and identifies Carboni as the very man he has seen whipping up the miners at the monster meeting, making him guilty of sedition.

'It was easy to see,' Lynch would record, 'that the enmity of the police was particularly directed against a few, whom they blamed for instigating the others to insurrection. Hayes, Raffaello . . . Manning (non-combatants) were particularly disliked. So was a coloured gentleman, who was arrested in the thick of the fight, and who bore himself throughout the whole ordeal with a degree of dignity.'[11]

In the confusion of it all, Carboni tries to keep his waistcoat with him, since it contains both money and papers. This request is not only refused but his clothes are now physically torn from him. Carboni is then kicked to the ground, knocked out and thrown – clothed only in his undershirt – into a cell with the other moaning men who used to be proud diggers but are now rather pathetic prisoners.

True, those cells had only been intended to cope with a bare handful of prisoners, but that is just too bad. Just like bellowing cattle, the rest of the prisoners are herded, poked and prodded into the wooden enclosure, each one forced to press up hard against the other, with not even room enough to change their mind.

Since each man is manacled to another, the only way they can cope is to take it in turns to stand or lie, but always in tandem. When they do rest, they have to 'lie on the floor in rows, with narrow lanes between'.[12] There is no straw on the floor, and they don't even have their boots to use as pillows.

With a rumour circulating that the mass of diggers outside is going to attempt a rescue, the soldiers are taking no chances. So seriously do they guard their prisoners that, as Lynch would record, they 'were . . . separated from us by a rampart formed of hay-trusses, sand-bags, and such materials; behind this stood the guards with levelled muskets all night.'[13] At least in all the madness Lynch is able to remove the small powder flask hanging around his neck and drop it between the cracks in the floorboards.

Not far away in the main administrative building, just before half past one in the afternoon, Captain Thomas has no sooner finished writing a report of the battle and its result – they have recorded a decisive victory and those inside the Stockade have been crushed – than a despatch rider puts it in his satchel and gallops past the heavily armed sentries on his way towards Melbourne.

In the meantime, Commissioner Rede is now having notices printed that will shortly be placed prominently all over the diggings:

V. R. NOTICE.

Government Camp, Ballarat, Dec. 3rd, 1854.

Her Majesty's forces were this morning fired upon by a large body of evil-disposed persons of various nations, who had entrenched themselves in a Stockade on the Eureka, and some officers and men were killed or wounded.

Several of the rioters have paid the penalty of their crime, and a large number are in custody.

All well-disposed persons are earnestly requested to return to their ordinary occupations, and to abstain from assembling in groups, and every protection will be afforded to them.

Robt. Rede,
'Resident Commissioner'[14]

And now, out and about in Ballarat, hammering is heard again. This time it is not to construct a podium, but rather to quickly knock together some coffins. There is no need for inquests – there is no mystery as to how any of them died – so the dead can be buried immediately.

At lunchtime, a digger by the name of Charles Rich had received sudden notice from the government contractor, Mr Watkins, asking him to join a young Welshman to make a large excavation in Ballarat's makeshift cemetery. In truth it is less a cemetery than a relatively flat piece of ground that, rarely for Ballarat, is judged to be better for putting bodies into than getting gold out of.

The two immediately set to and late that afternoon, just as the sun is beginning to fade, this final resting place is only just ready before the 'mournful cavalcade'[15] arrives. It is a procession of diggers some 200 strong, bearing the bodies of seven diggers who had been slain just that morning. The cortege passes right by the Government Camp – a camp under arms at this moment, ready for a fresh outbreak of violence – and creates a great deal of tension that somehow remains in check.

The seven coffins arrive before the freshly dug hole and are placed in two tiers – four on the bottom and three on top – reaching to within a foot of the surface. So makeshift are the coffins that the bodies and faces of the dead are plainly discernible through the joints in the lids, and it somehow doesn't seem quite right, as they throw shovelfuls of earth into the grave, that some of that dirt goes straight into their dead faces.

The gravediggers are just finishing when another procession arrives, this one bearing an equally rough coffin that holds the cadaver of the poor Welshman Llewellyn Rowlands. All those bodies that are identified and claimed are accorded individual funerals, though many are unclaimed, meaning that over the next two days – just like this first funeral – three batches of unidentified rebels are collectively interred.[16] When the time comes to bury the poor German pike-man Hafele, the huge procession is accompanied closely by the same faithful terrier who hovered by the morgue all night long, and now follows his 'dead master to the grave, perhaps the deepest mourner in the procession'.[17]

Hafele is buried just a short distance from James Scobie, the Scot's grave marked by a broken column – the symbol of a life cut short. While the biggest of the many funeral processions that occurs over the next two days is 300 strong – for brave Captain Ross – the most devastated group is the rather small one behind a coffin trimmed with white, as recorded by Samuel Lazarus, '[Inside] was the body of a woman who was mercilessly butchered by a mounted trooper while she was pleading for the life of her husband. The mind recoils with horror & disgust from the thought that an Englishman can be found capable of an act so monstrous & inhuman.'[18]

Privates Roney and Wall are also buried with full military hon-ours on this day, the previous joy of their fellow soldiers now entirely gone as they face the bitter reality that they are putting two of their own beneath the sod.

Sunday evening, 3 December 1854, a mysterious figure arrives on Ballarat

A priest? He certainly has the garb of one, with the black shirt, white collar and heavy black coat, but there is something about this lone figure traipsing through the goldfields that just doesn't look quite right. Real priests in these parts rarely just go about their business – they insert themselves into other people's business and stop along the way to chat to diggers, make visits, comfort the ill and soothe the troubled. After what has happened on this day, one would have expected a priest to be talking to everyone. But this priest does no such thing. With eyes down and one arm clearly across his belly in a manner reminiscent of Napoleon, he shuffles along – stumbling a little – and talks to no-one, heading to parts unknown.

Watching him closely, digger Stephen Cummins realises that something is badly amiss, that the man is only just staying upright. He engages him in conversation and quickly realises just what is wrong. The man has been shot and has lost a lot of blood. Why, it is Peter Lalor!

At this point, if there is not quite fear in Lalor's eyes then there is at least enormous wariness. Will Cummins turn him in? Having spent the better part of the day in a tent in the bush near Warrenheip, Lalor knows he needs help and is now at the mercy of this first man he has come across.

But not a bit of it. Cummins admires Lalor, has been present at the monster meetings that he has addressed and now quickly ushers the critically wounded Irishman back to his tent, where he feeds and waters him, and tries to tend to his terrible wounds.

As Lalor slips in and out of consciousness, it is soon going to be a matter of life and death if he doesn't get serious medical help. Rousing him and helping him to his feet, Cummins gathers Lalor's big coat back around him and the two make their way to Father Smyth's presbytery in the soft light of the evening. There, Lalor is immediately bustled inside and taken into the care of not only the Father himself, but also Anastasia Hayes. She has taken refuge there with her six children after the Hayes tent and everything inside it was burnt to the ground. Now, by the light of a lamp, it is Anastasia who slowly, carefully, tries to clean the terrible wounds on the groaning Lalor's shattered and bloody left shoulder.

Late Sunday night/early Monday morning, 3–4 December 1854, on Ballarat, in the lockup

The piteous darkness presses, the misery rises. Inside the stinking lockup there is no respite as too many men in too little space compete for too little foetid, filthy air.

Even in hell, however, there proves to be humanity. Long after the main troop of guards has gone to bed, the 40th Regiment's Sergeant Edward Harris – he had been at the forefront of the fight against these same men less than 24 hours earlier – makes repeated visits to offer words of comfort, water and even 'ease [manacles] or replace them with others more easily fitting'.[19]

Finally the moans, groans and outright howling from the lockup reaches the ears of Commissioner Rede, and at two o'clock in the morning he arrives to make an inspection. He is clearly troubled by how desperate the prisoners' situation is and immediately orders their transfer from the lockup. They are taken to a 'new and more commodious building, lined with zinc and intended for a commissariat store which was nearer the entrance of the Camp'[20] – a place where they can at least spread out from one another, and are able to move and breathe fresh air.

Seeing the Commissioner, Raffaello Carboni, who is by now delirious, gathers himself and addresses Rede in French, knowing that the man is proud of how well he can speak the language. After Carboni conveys just how unjust and appalling his situation is – given that Dr Carr could affirm that he was not even in the Stockade at the time it was all happening – he implores him to *do* something.

'I will be sure to speak to Doctor Carr,' Commissioner Rede replies, 'and if what you say is true, I will get involved in looking after you.'

'You are very kind, *Monsieur le Commissionaire*. But what cruel enemies I must have in the Camp! Are they thirsty for my blood, or are they mercenaries? This is a real secret, and I'd give my life to know it. God may pardon them, but I never will be able to.'[21]

Rede leaves and goes back to bed. Around and about the storehouse, however, the Camp remains under arms, 'as it was reported that a number of insurgents, including a corps of eighty riflemen, were assembled among the ranges'.[22] Who knew but that the vengeful diggers might be about to launch on them? In the night, every footstep sounds like thunder, every night-noise a harbinger of doom.

Early Monday morning, 4 December 1854, Melbourne, thundering hooves are heard

The sound of thundering hooves on city streets is unnerving enough in daylight, let alone at three o'clock in the morning in the streets of Melbourne. *What is going on?* The people of this bustling metropolis are about to find out as the exhausted despatch rider, now on his fourth fresh horse, finally arrives with news of the battle.

Sir Charles is woken in his Toorac residence to receive the devastating news: two privates killed, with Captain Wise of the 40th Regiment dangerously wounded, Lieutenant Paul of the 12th Regiment severely wounded, and 11 privates of the 12th and 40th Regiments wounded. As to the insurgents, Captain Thomas confesses in his report that, while it is not easy to determine, he has reason to believe that 'not less than thirty [were] killed on the spot, and I know that many have since died of their wounds'.[23]

Sir Charles knows from the first that he needs to move quickly, for the situation is precarious. Certainly his soldiers have recorded a rousing victory at this point, but what now? How will the diggers on other goldfields react when they hear the news? What about the people of Melbourne? Among other things, he is keenly aware from the first that, apart from those 'special constables' that have been sworn in, Melbourne stands essentially unprotected, denuded of troops, for they are now all in Ballarat. Messengers are quickly dispatched and the sun is not long risen before the Lieutenant-Governor's Executive Council is on its way to Government House to decide what course of action to take.

Once so gathered, the first and most obvious thing to do, the council decides, is for Hotham to proclaim martial law for the district around Ballarat. Sir Charles is careful, however, to also include in the proclamation that no-one be executed without his 'express consent'.[24]

Another key question to be resolved is whether, with all the soldiers gone, the Council members would be prepared to bear arms themselves and do everything in their power to encourage the other men in their circles to defend the city.

As to just *how* they will defend the city, that, too, is discussed. A first step, they agree, will be to call for more volunteers to enrol as special constables, while also calling for reinforcements. Each man then takes his leave, many of them wondering about the safety of their families.

His Excellency now takes time to dash off a quick letter to Lieutenant-Governor Denison in Van Diemen's Land, advising him that the insurgents are 'principally foreigners, well drilled, and said to be well commanded'.[25] On the one hand Denison is not to worry, as Sir Charles assures him, 'They have been . . . completely routed, and may I hope now be discouraged from assembling again in force'.[26]

On the other hand, as there are so many goldfields and so many disaffected people, 'it is impossible to say from hour to hour, whether disaffection may not show itself in some other quarter. And I am therefore obliged to request that you will allow as many companies of the 99th Regiment as can be spared to proceed to Melbourne forthwith, bringing with them any available field pieces.'[27]

Sir Charles needs men and he needs artillery. As he would later put in a letter to Sir George Grey, he needs a battery of 32-pounder artillery rockets from Britain 'to dissuade the disaffected.'[28] It is a matter of urgency.

He further directs Colonial Secretary Foster to write to Commissioner Rede, complimenting his 'sound and wise discretion in attacking the insurgents' and thanking 'all the officers and men, civil and military . . . for their zeal and ability, and especially to Captain Thomas.'[29] While Hotham seeks a concerted effort in arresting all those who spoke at the license-burning meeting – if they have not been already – he also calls for 'the exercise of moderation and forbearance.'[30]

Monday morning, 4 December 1854, in offices of *The Ballarat Times*, the fourth estate is escorted to a fifth estate

Henry Seekamp is incandescent with rage: infuriated that good men have been needlessly massacred, that innocent men have been taken prisoner, that the authorities have acted with such callous disregard for both the law and common decency.

The outlet for his outrage is of course the editorial for the special edition of the paper he is then and there preparing to put out. The words for his editorial pour out of him as never before, each one a literary bullet aimed directly at the breasts of the beasts – for he will not call them 'men' – who have done this.

'Surely the massacre of these human beings call from their fellow country-men – from all who call themselves miners – from nature? – from even Heaven itself – a vengeance deep and terrible and that vengeance is as sure to follow as death succeeds life . . . May the God of Liberty and Justice defend the right!'[31]

And yet in the early afternoon, just as he is putting the finishing touches to the typesetting of this very editorial, there is a sudden commotion outside, some angry shouts, then police under the command of Sub-Inspector Charles Jeffries Carter burst into the offices and arrest Seekamp 'in consequence of certain articles which have appeared in his paper and which [are] seditious and calculated to excite disturbances on the diggings'.[32]

The outrage! The infamy! The *injustice!*

In lock-step protest, Henry Seekamp, that good and noble man, moustache bristling, is dragged away to the cells at Government Camp. Upon his arrival, troopers gather round and gawk at their latest prize scalp, gleefully braying '*The Times! The Times!*'[33]

Still, in the grand traditions of the free press, the paper must come out regardless. Stepping into the breach, his wife, Clara, oversees getting the edition out, adding only beneath her husband's thundering editorial the words:

**THE EDITOR of the BALLARAT
TIMES has been arrested since
the above was written!**[34]

Oh, but she is proud of him, alright, and would later say, 'If Lalor was the sword of the movement, my husband was the pen.'[35]

In the cells, Seekamp is chained to Charles Ferguson. The American feels sorry for this poor, sick fellow, who is clearly taking the whole thing very badly and seems without any resilience left to rise up.

'What do you think they will do with us?' Ferguson asks.

'The government has shown no mercy before,' Seekamp replies bleakly, 'and there is none to be expected now. At least I expect none.'[36]

Monday morning, 4 December 1854, panic in the lockup

In the Camp cells, things remain grim, and all the more so because a rumour is circulating among the prisoners, passed on by a guard, that a gang of Redcoats have been sighted digging a very large hole just a few hundred yards away, within the boundaries of the Camp.

Could it be . . .?

Is it possible . . .?

Are these troops digging a *mass grave*?

From the windows of their new quarters in the storeroom, the prisoners can certainly hear the sound of digging going on not far away. The cold grip of panic begins to tighten their chests and even loosen their bowels.

'Are they going to bury us alive without any flogging?' Carboni asks the Irishman next to him. 'That's not half so merciful as Haynau's rule in Austria.'[37]

Ah yes, Carboni knows Julius Jacob von Haynau's rule, alright. The notoriously brutal Austrian General whose army had occupied Italy and then moved into Hungary had not been known as 'the Hyena of Brescia' or 'the Hangman of Arad' for nothing.

'Where did you read in history,' the Irishman sorrowfully replies, 'that the British Lion was ever merciful to a fallen foe?'[38]

Horrifyingly, this makes a certain amount of sense. The rebels have dared to mount an armed resistance to British rule, and the punishment for that offence is clear. Perhaps if such a place as Norfolk Island was not being wound down they could retain hope of a death sentence being commuted to serve out their life sentences in such a place, but in recent times all such reminders of the colonies' convict past, bar Western Australia, are in the process of being shut down on principle. These men are left with little doubt that if the British can make the charges against them stick – whatever they prove to be – then death will be their fate. After all, three months earlier, Hotham had infamously refused to show mercy to the father of starving children by locking the man up for two months because he could not afford to pay for his license – what chance he would show greater forgiveness this time?

Monday afternoon, 4 December 1854, courage in Father Smyth's residence

Easy. Easy. Steady. Steady. Big breaths. For there at Bakery Hill, on Father Smyth's table, lies Peter Lalor. Peering down above him is Dr Doyle, assisted by the American surgeon Dr Kinsworthy, as they prepare to amputate what is left of the rebel leader's left arm, with none other than Anastasia Hayes acting as nurse. But the heavy breathing is not coming from Lalor alone – Dr Doyle is also feeling ill at all the gore and wondering if he is up to removing an arm in such circumstances. Peter Lalor's upper arm and shoulder is now no more than a twisted mess of putrescent flesh and shattered bone, with the humerus completely torn asunder, as is the artery beside it. One of the musket balls that hit him has carried pieces of Lalor's shirt into the jagged wound from which shards of bone are visible, and the whole thing emits a stench that is truly nauseating.[39]

Legend would have it that, sensing this, Lalor opens his eyes, looks at Dr Doyle and says rather impatiently, 'Courage, courage, take it off.'[40]

They take it off, using just as much chloroform as they dare, since a heavy dose would be too dangerous for a man in his condition. Pulling his arm right out of the shoulder joint,[41] they also manage to remove two of the three bullets that hit him. They then tie off the largest spurting blood vessels with thread before using a hot iron to seal the smaller ones.[42] Rightly or wrongly – it could never be proven – the story circulates afterwards that Anastasia Hayes disposed of the severed limb down a deep, abandoned mine shaft.

Monday afternoon, 4 December 1854, the panic grows in Melbourne

In small graveyard groups all over Melbourne, they huddle together, reading this first of scattered reports from Ballarat in a special edition of *The Argus*.

BY EXPRESS
FATAL COLLISION AT BALLAARAT

At four a.m. this morning (Sunday) the troopers advanced on the right of the Warraneep Gulley, and another division on the left of the Eureka line, encompassing the camp of the diggers. A shout was raised, and after a sharp firing of about twenty minutes the troopers called to the soldiers, who were advancing, that it was all over . . .

The London Hotel is the chief repository for the dead and wounded. The troopers swept the diggings, and are making several captures now at the moment of writing.

The most harrowing and heartrending scenes amongst the women and children I have witnessed through this dreadful morning. Many innocent persons have suffered . . .[43]

It is a report that gives credence to the rumours that have been circulating throughout the day, fuelling the worst rumour of all: the vengeful diggers now really *are* marching on Melbourne! No more mere red ribbons in their hats, they now have red sashes across their chest and pistols in both hands! And they're not just coming from Ballarat, but from all over the diggings. They will sack the city. Whole sections of the road between here and Ballarat have been taken over by guerrilla parties, ready to fall upon any isolated group of troops or police! The horror! Oh, the *horror*. A dark mood begins to fall on Melbourne, as all wonder what will happen next.

Monday evening, 4 December 1854, more shots on Ballarat

Tension is the father of aggression, and all too frequently the bastard brother of catastrophic error. On this dark, cloudy evening the soldiers in the Camp have no sooner seen a flitting figure 'running out of the Camp and down the hill',[44] keeping close to the picket fence, than in a split second a dozen muskets are brought to shoulders as they draw a bead.

Yet, right at the moment they are about to fire, a single ray of moonlight breaks through the clouds and illuminates the figure. It is a woman! Anastasia Hayes – who has been visiting her husband and, for reasons unknown, is now running away – will never know how close she has come to losing her life in a hail of bullets and musket balls. Upon investigation, it appears that via one of the guards, she has been in secret communication with her husband.

Catastrophe still stalks close, however. The two armed and glowering camps of a couple of days before have now turned into one destroyed camp with its furious survivors scattered and the other camp victorious but still angrily grieving for the good men it has lost. Trigger fingers on both sides have never been itchier. As Samuel Lazarus records in his diary at eight o'clock that night, 'A shot had been fired into the [Government] camp & for this solitary misdemeanour 50 or 60 musket shots had been fired indiscriminately among the tents.'[45] Among those who are in the way of the bullets is a mother with a babe in arms. 'The same ball which murdered the Mother (for that is the term for it) passed through the child as it lay sleeping in her arms.'[46] And there is yet more devastation to come as the barrage of bullets is heavy.

'A gentleman on horseback was wounded in the leg,' the *Geelong Advertiser* would report. 'Another gentleman informs us that three children were killed by the discharge.'[47]

The fury of the diggers is overwhelming.

'Tomorrow morning,' Lazarus says, 'will show the result of this wanton & tyrannical use of power. I hear many disastrous reports tonight but hope there is the foundation for them. After the blood stained lesson which was offered on Sunday morning (not a very fit day for such teaching,) the people will bear a great deal before they will risk a repetition but there are some deeds which will grace men beyond the power of endurance and this seems very like one of them.'[48]

The fury of the diggers is manifested by many shots being fired into the diggers' camp that night, all of it without retribution, and those inside, rightly, feel themselves to be under siege.

Tuesday, 5 December 1854, Melbourne, the outrage rises

And with those first reports the previous day come many more detailed, harrowing accounts. Most poignant is the correspondent of *The Melbourne Herald*: 'I was attracted by the smoke of the tents burnt by the soldiers, and there a most appalling sight presented itself. Many more are said to have been killed and wounded, but I myself saw eleven dead bodies of diggers lying within a very small space of ground, and the earth was besprinkled with blood, and covered with the smoking mass of tents recently occupied. Could the government but have seen the awful sight presented at Ballarat on this Sabbath morning – the women in tears, mourning over their dead relations, and the blood-bespattered countenances of many men in the diggers' camp.'[49]

It is through the reading of this, and many such accounts, that the popular mood of the people of Melbourne starts rapidly to swing from fear of the diggers to outright anger at what the government has done to those diggers.

For already, *The Age* has done its sums and now sums up neatly: 'Let the Government be undeceived. There are not a dozen respectable citizens in Melbourne who do not entertain an indignant feeling against it for its weakness, its folly and its last crowning error . . . They do not sympathize with injustice and coercion.'[50]

The public mood towards the government is dark and only getting darker.

In answer to the request of eight members of the Legislative Council and self-interested Melbourne businessmen keen to see law and order restored, Mayor Smith calls a public meeting at one o'clock that afternoon in the Mechanics' Institute Hall on Collins Street. However, so many unexpectedly attend – around 5000, as estimated by *The Age* – that it requires a full contingent of police and troopers to keep order, even after the meeting moves to the front of the City Court House in Swanston Street. And they are not long in dividing up between those who seek a return to law and order and those seeking justice for the diggers . . .

After the Mayor, as Chair, exhorts the boisterous outdoor gathering to remain controlled, it is a barely audible John Pascoe Fawkner MLC who, just above the din, proposes the first resolution: 'That this meeting deeply deplore that any sense of wrong doing should have induced a portion of our fellow colonists at Ballaarat to resort to the use of arms in resistance to lawful authority.'[51] Fawkner also argues, however, that the government should pardon the diggers – 'let bygones be bygones'[52] – and 'give the diggers what they demand'. *(Cheers)* Fawkner goes on to exhort the diggers to show patience in temporarily paying the license fee and obeying the law until the forthcoming Inquiry (in which he will take part) can try to get to the bottom of their grievances and propose solutions.

'It was not the Governor's fault,' he continues. 'He wished to act honestly by them. It was the fault of the Colonial Secretary Foster. *(Groans)* Let the reasonable demands of the diggers be conceded, but let them no longer continue their present unlawful opposition.' *(Cheers)* [53]

When the seconder of Fawkner's resolution, however, returns to the issue of law and order and asks the crowd to support the government, the pro-digger lobby erupts: 'They are wholesale butchers!' *(Repeated groans)* 'The diggers were driven to it.' 'It was in self defence.' [54]

Rather than address the actual plight of the digger, the next three speakers prattle on about maintaining law and order (the original purpose of the meeting) and the need to act like Englishmen in order that business as usual may continue. After Henry Miller MLC asks the crowd to make a choice between 'the flag of England' and 'the new flag of the Southern Cross', more chaotic calls break out – and so much groaning it drowns out all else. It is obvious that he is not getting the response he wants. Outraged at the current tenor of the meeting, a digger in the crowd shouts out a motion from the crowd, 'The only way to restore order . . . is to get rid of those who caused the disorder.' The government. [55]

Despite the protestations of the Chair, who has by now lost control of the meeting, the next speaker, a Mr Hibberd, starts to call once again for the immediate head of Foster, and asserts that Foster's 'memory would be execrated by the widows and orphans of the poor men who had fallen at Ballarat'. [56]

As the crowd continues to cheer a series of speakers who support the diggers and denounce the actions of the Executive Council (though somehow Hotham escapes the worst of it), the harried

Chair hurriedly declares the meeting closed. But no, the people do not want it closed, and cry out in protest.

Dr Embling replaces the Mayor as Chair and now another digger, with a moustache so curly the tips nearly come back to meet his nose, steps forward. Henry Frencham is well known for being one of the earliest after Esmond to have found payable gold in Victoria – in his case, around Bendigo – and he now roars to the appreciative crowd that the people 'must go forth with their brother diggers to conquer or die!'[57]

Previously interrupted, Mr Hibbard now completes his resolution calling for the immediate dismissal of the Colonial Secretary, and it is carried 'amidst the most tumultuous cheering, every hand being uplifted in its favour'.[58] Three deep groans are then given for Mr Foster, followed by three cheers for the replacement chairman, and with some loud cheers for the diggers in general, the gathering disperses.

Now, as the meeting's proceedings have been duly noted by both the journalists and Sir Charles's men, the anxious Lieutenant-Governor and Colonial Secretary Foster are shortly afterwards presented with a full report occasioning ever more anxiety, particularly from Foster, at the way things are turning.

However, out on those same streets an extraordinary edition of *The Government Gazette* is issued, calling on 'all true subjects of the Queen, and all strangers who have received hospitality and protection under Her flag . . . to enrol themselves [as special constables]'.[59]

Three o'clock, Tuesday afternoon, 5 December 1854, on Ballarat, the Camp is saved

Men on horseback. *Many* men on horseback. After a journey lasting four gruelling days, on this hot afternoon Major-General Sir Robert Nickle and his force of 800 armed men with squadrons of cavalry sent out in support arrive at last at the head of a seemingly endless train of supply wagons, which also boasts two 600-pounder field guns and two 12-pounder howitzers. Those at the diggings watch them with enormous trepidation and outright fear, for, just as rumours have swirled through Melbourne that an army of diggers was on the march, ready to kill them all, so too has Ballarat been beset by rumours that they are soon to be slaughtered by a vengeful army of Redcoats. And now here they are.

It is for this reason that one of the first things Sir Robert and his men see as they reach Ballarat is diggers and their families running for the hills. It takes some time before those who have departed with such haste feel confident enough to make their way back.

By contrast, for those in the Government Camp, the vision of Sir Robert and his men is greeted with unbridled joy. 'We now felt like Red Indians after a siege,' Samuel Huyghue would recall, 'who, discarding weapons and war paint, smoke the [peace pipe] with a pleasing assurance of the preservation of their scalps, preparatory to the luxury of a big sleep.'[60]

From the first, Sir Robert is a different sort of man. Instead of staying in the heavily defended Government Camp or being aggressive, the day after arriving he heads out on foot, without even a mounted escort, something that greatly impresses the diggers under the circumstances. He asks questions as he proceeds and even – and this is the most astonishing thing – *listens* to the diggers and their plaints. When something of a crowd gathers round him, however, Sir Robert is equally quick to make his own remarks. He is not talking down to them, however, but *to* them, man to men.

To begin with, do they not realise that these laws they are fighting against are works in progress, experimental only? Do they really want to give their lives against something that would likely not last long anyway?

And you English and Scots, he says, you are from the land where they respect law and order the most. How can *you* be lining up on the side of the foreign anarchists? It is *they* who have caused this terrible loss of life and we British who must restore order. *All* of us British. Yes, those foreign anarchists who have abused the hospitality this country has extended them might choose to go on with their fight, but Sir Robert is here to tell them that if they do, he will round them up and have them deported to some uninhabited South Sea island.

But now to the Irish. What to say to the men who had clearly been at the forefront of the fight? He chooses his words carefully. Do they not realise that it is because they are such fine fighting men that the foreign agitators want to stir them up? They must know that if those agitators are 'not kept under vigilant control, they would ultimately not only have the principal voice in the government of the colony, but would draw thither hordes of aliens, who would take complete possession of their rich goldfields'.[61]

At this point, a cry of 'Hear! Hear!' from somewhere deep within the throng clearly encourages Sir Robert, for he concludes his remarks with a little oratory that is as inspired in choice as it is inspiring to his audience. Referring to the current war Great Britain is having with Russia, he finishes, 'I wish, that instead of you fellows making targets of yourselves for the bullets of your countrymen, I had you enrolled and trained as a troop of the Connaught Rangers, and that I was leading you in a tussle with the Russians at Sebastopol.'[62]

Beyond mere oratory, however, Sir Robert is not long in restoring a sense of stability to the goldfields by sheer force of arms. With so many men and supplies, there can be no further doubt as to who is in control, a point underlined by the fact that Sir Robert immediately enforces Lieutenant-Governor Hotham's declaration of martial law, meaning that the entire administration of the law moves from civil to military jurisdiction. Major-General Nickle immediately supersedes Commissioner Rede as the most important authority on the diggings.

Sir Robert's first command under this new regime is that all those who possess firearms must bring them to the Camp and turn them in or face the consequences. But there is more – much more. No firearms or munitions are to be brought into the area, and anyone found with the same on their premises or engaging in violence or insult to a soldier or policeman 'would be subject to a General Court Martial'.[63] And be told, you diggers – if a shot is fired at the Camp, then any tent in the 'neighbourhood' of the shot will be burned down unless the owners can prove they were not involved. There is to be a continuation of the policy of 'no lights within gunshot of the camp after 8 pm', which had been initiated prior to the Stockade – effectively a curfew in that limited area.

This last measure troubles most particularly the diggers doing deep-shaft mining, as the only way they can operate is around the clock, pulling out the water at the bottom of the shaft that continues to flow in. When the plaint is put to Sir Robert, however, he immediately softens that part of martial law, and allows them to use lanterns so long as they are well sheltered.

Though it is clear that Sir Robert is in firm control, it is not as if the diggers themselves are eager to throw in their lot with the authorities. When, for example, the Major-General puts out a call for interested diggers to present themselves at the tent on the lawn just to the south of the Camp to be sworn in as special constables, seconded to keep the peace, not a single volunteer actually signs up. Rather, the small crowd listens to his patriotic speech politely then moves off quietly.

Nevertheless, bit by bit, tension dissipates as the reign of Sir Robert on the goldfields continues. He has obviously given instructions to his men to be restrained in their actions. There are no more license-hunts, and suddenly the soldiers and police are even *polite*.

The Melbourne Morning Herald's correspondent, for one, is impressed: 'Had Sir Robert Nickle arrived here a few days before, the bloodshed of last Sunday would have been avoided.'[64]

Not that all dissent has been extinguished, for all that. One such dissenter is Commissioner Amos, a decent man who has always had the respect of the diggers. He was so shocked by what occurred on Sunday morning, that 'owing to some expressions which had lately fallen from him'[65] he was placed under arrest. While he is released within days, he quickly resigns and heads to Melbourne, and his departure is just one more sign that the previously united façade of the government and its minions is crumbling.

Another man instantly placed under arrest shortly after appearing at a public meeting is John Basson Humffray. His time of incarceration is even shorter, as he is released within minutes of pointing out that he resigned from the Ballarat Reform League the previous Wednesday and played no part in the Stockade. (In fact, at that public meeting he had been outspoken once more as 'the strenuous advocate of constitutional agitation, as opposed to armed resistance',[66] which sentiment had been cheered to the echo.)

Wednesday, 6 December 1854, Melbourne, Foster falls on his sword

All across town there remains only one topic of conversation, as even more horrifying details emerge from Ballarat. On this day it is *The Argus* that sets the tone, with its headline 'Massacre at Eureka . . . cowardly massacre' above one more Samuel Irwin story.

In Government House, Sir Charles receives first a formal delegation of squatters, who affirm that they support him entirely and wish to help him maintain law and order, then members of the Legislative Council, who also want to personally express their loyalty. Sir Charles, with his high officials, receives both delegations dressed in the full regalia of the highest servants of Her Majesty, Queen Victoria, and in gracious language thanks them for their patriotic support. This is a time when all Englishmen must remain true to each other and to Her Majesty.

Hear, hear. Hear, *hear!*

Despite such fine words, the truth is that in the face of the enormous public outcry, the whole edifice of the previously rock-solid government continues to crumble. In the Legislative Council in the early afternoon, an ashen-faced Colonial Secretary John Foster asks for the indulgence of the House while he refers to a matter personal to himself.

'I am aware,' he says, 'as the House doubtless is also, that a great personal dislike is entertained towards me in certain quarters, and from the public expression of this feeling, I have been induced to . . . resign.'[67]

Before formally leaving, however, he is happy to record his views to the Council that in reference to what happened at Eureka, he is 'truly happy to say that the majority of the prisoners, as well as those killed, were foreigners'.[68]

The mood of the meeting is heavy – sorry, in some measure, to see Foster resign, while also understanding that his departure may help salve some of the growing public outrage. The main thing now is to rally to Sir Charles, and John Pascoe Fawkner goes so far as to support a resolution of sympathy for the Lieutenant-Governor.

The one serious voice raised in opposition to any suggested motion vindicating the government, however, is Councillor John Myles, who defends the course pursued by the diggers, and denounces the recent engagement as 'a shooting down of the people for refusing to comply with a mere fiscal regulation'.[69]

'After all,' Myles thunders, 'they were only banding together to save themselves from being hunted down like wild animals. In the meantime, every step taken by the authorities had been on the spur of the moment, and without thought, clearly showing that the men at the head of affairs are totally incompetent for the government of the colony.'[70]

This last sentiment is certainly one shared by the broad mass of people.

After the debacle of the meeting the day before, on this late afternoon another meeting has been called on the large grassed area outside St Paul's Church, 'for the assertion of order and the protection of constitutional liberty'.[71] This time no fewer than 7000 people turn up. And there are a few more besides – they, however, are not participants in the normal sense.

Sir Charles Hotham was disturbed to hear how that meeting the day before had 'been borne down by a turbulent section, and adverse resolutions carried'.[72] And yet, even in that short time the level of public alarm has risen still more, and there have been further reports of diggers on the march from the disturbed districts, heading their way and determined to seek revenge on the government forces.

Immediately after the news of Ballarat had hit, the call Sir Charles put out for special constables was answered, and the first of a flood of what will be 1500 men have already been sworn in. But for this job he is taking no chances with amateurs and orders 300 armed police and 100 warders from Pentridge and Melbourne gaols to surround the meeting, while the last available seamen and marines of HMS *Electra* and *Fantome* guard the powder magazine and Treasury.

No matter. Entirely untroubled by their presence, the crowd is quick to vent its anger, particularly once the rumour spreads that Colonial Secretary John Foster has resigned. Far from placating them, the effect is the reverse – like a lion that has the whiff of blood, it now wants to go in for the kill.

'Bring him to justice!'[73] the cry rings out.

But to the business at hand. Again with the likes of Fawkner, Embling and Frencham taking the lead, three resolutions – most of them drafted earlier by the passionate Scottish journalist Ebenezer Syme – are passed. They blame the tragedy at Ballarat squarely on 'the coercion of a military force . . . [and] the harsh and imprudent recommencement of digger hunting during a period of excitement,' and seek a guarantee that steps will be taken such 'that a military despotism will no longer be required'.[74] They demand that a

Commission be established to work out the differences between the government and the diggers, but also call for the immediate 'withdrawal of the military from the diggings'.[75]

As to John Pascoe Fawkner, he is strong and getting stronger . . .

'I will tell you why you are being misgoverned,' he says. 'It is because you are governed by the squatters, who have held 60,000,000 acres of the land for thirteen years, for which they had only paid to the government a quarter of a million of pounds! There are in the Council not less than a dozen of squatters so that their interests are always well represented whether the interest of the colonists at large are so or not!'[76]

But one thing he does wish to make clear is that while he and one or two others will represent the interests of the people in Council, he would not take up a musket – Fawkner is a proponent of moral force and moral force alone. 'If you support your members,' he insists, 'you will get your rights. Petition the Council and you will soon get all you want and . . .'[77]

'We want the troops out of Ballarat!' a voice rings out. They should have it. For now, however, Fawkner is obliged to leave them for the purpose of attending to their interests in another place. The tone for the rest of the meeting is less angry than united – a terrible thing has occurred, and they are unanimous in the view that the government must change its whole approach. And perhaps it has an effect: that same afternoon a Victoria *Government Gazette* is issued announcing the revocation of martial law on Ballarat.

Thursday, 7 December – Saturday, 9 December 1854, Government Camp, charges are laid

Of all the prisoners, the one in the worst shape is a fellow by the name of James Powell, known to the diggers as 'New Zealand Jamie'. He had been cut to pieces by sabres and stabbed with bayonets, and it is amazing he is alive at all. This once-vibrant man is now little more than a breeding site for the 'hundreds of maggots . . . crawling in and out of the festering sores, which were disgusting to behold'.[78]

There is no help for him and, though the others do what they can, it is obvious he does not have long.

On this morning, however, there is at least some respite for the others as – sweet mercy – they are to be let out of the cell. This is not through any sense of mercy, but simply because it is time for the legal process of the committal hearings to begin. The short shuffle from the lockup to the courthouse in fetters is awkward and, once inside, the prisoners stand in line and make their way towards the bench. After magistrates Evelyn Sturt and George Webster read the statements already made about the accused by the Redcoats and the police, they then question the prisoners about their actions on the day, what they saw and what they were doing in the Stockade in the first place, to try to determine whether each man has a case to answer and whether he should be formally charged. In a process that will go on for the next three days, the prisoners are particularly encouraged to make statements about what they witnessed other diggers do in the Stockade so that all the statements can be cross-referenced to determine the most guilty. In building a case against the accused, various troopers, soldiers and other government witnesses are there to give their own account of the events, and the entire proceeding is observed by two journalists from *The Melbourne Morning Herald* and two from *The Argus*.

First up are those men against whom only trifling charges are recorded, for which there is little hard evidence. One of these is John Lynch. Charged with sedition – encouraging one's fellow subjects to rebel against royal authority – he pleads not guilty. In response, there is a stirring among the posse of witnesses, some whispering, but no-one offers to step forward to the witness box. Lynch is just taking this as a good omen when a trooper of sneeringly superior mien and sparkling epaulettes struts forth and offers to give testimony, almost as if he would like to do the Bench a favour.

Upon questioning, however – Lynch and many other prisoners are defended by Ballarat barrister Joseph Henry Dunne, whose pro bono offer has been gratefully accepted by all – the trooper proves to have scant recollection of what he had seen Lynch doing, beyond the fact that he had been responsible for mischief.

'The more they tried to get something definite out of him,' Lynch would later recount, 'the less he yielded. At last he became quite confused, and was ordered out of the box: no other appeared. Then that terrible record, the police charge-sheet, was appealed to. No entry appearing there against my name, solemnly the magical word "discharged" was pronounced, and in a couple of seconds I found myself outside in the midst of a congratulating crowd.'[79]

For Raffaello Carboni, it is perhaps a measure of how eager the authorities are to indict him that in going through this process he finds himself chained to the one man who seems universally reviled by all the authorities: the so-called 'nigger-rebel' from America, John Joseph.

The only good thing is that the whole process does not take long. As Carboni and Joseph stand manacled before the bench, the Italian is staggered to find that several government witnesses – none of whom he recognises – do hereby solemnly swear that he was inside the Stockade on the morning in question, that he had attacked them with pikes and that he had been captured *in* the Stockade.

The outraged Italian swears in vain that none of these things is true, and that he can prove that they are not true. However, when he insists that both Dr Carr and Captain Charles Carter of the foot police, the officer who had first arrested him *outside* the Stockade, could definitively establish that the charges are false, neither man can be found. The only witnesses are for the prosecution, who take the sacred oath on the Bible and testify with 'savage eagerness'.[80]

Most devastating is the evidence of Henry Goodenough, who testifies that the Italian 'Charles Rafaello' was not only the captain of a company of 25 men armed with swords and knives, but that he had publically exhorted those men – and all other men – to *use* their weapons. Why, on Thursday, 30 November, Goodenough had personally heard the prisoner urge from the platform, 'Gentlemen soldiers, those that cannot provide themselves with firearms, let them provide themselves with a piece of steel, if it is only six inches long, attached to a pole, and that will pierce the tyrant's heart.'[81] And he had seen Carboni marching them back and forth, drilling them. Other witnesses back him up.

Carboni is shocked and appalled. 'I shall not prostitute my intelligence and comment on the "evidence" against me,' he would later recount, 'from a gang of bloodthirsty mercenary spies'.[82]

He doesn't need to.

For the evidence, such as it is presented, is overwhelming, and at the end the verdict comes down hard as the magistrates commit Raffaello Carboni to stand trial. John Joseph is, of course, similarly charged, as is John Manning shortly afterwards. When the lawyer for the Australian rebel Thomas Dignum tries to deny that he was the one with pike in hand who had struck a Redcoat, Trooper William Revell steps forward and says, 'I cannot be mistaken in the identity of prisoner Thomas Dignum, for I cut him on the head. He has a cut on his head now.'[83] All look to the prisoner's head, and there is no doubting the still-angry wound. Dignum declines to make a statement in his own defence, and the verdict comes down against him, also.

Oddly, of the 125 diggers who had been rounded up on the Sunday, after three days of such court processes there are just 13 left who are committed for trial – perhaps because, under Hotham's express instruction, 'the magistrates were instructed to limit the commitments to those against whom the proof of participation was of the clearest kind'.[84] They are all to stand trial for High Treason under the legislation introduced in Great Britain following the Chartist uprising six years earlier – the *Treason Felony Act 1848*. These charges are laid despite the fact that Sir Charles Hotham's own high legal counsel has tendered the view that it will be very difficult to make the charge stick, as it was no more than 'the expression of seditious opinions in which a considerable portion of the public coincide'.[85]

Sir Charles decides to ignore that and does not interfere with the Attorney-General's determination to prosecute, come what may. Given the number of deaths and the outcry against his government, he feels it is important that the men who have instigated this bloodshed are found guilty of a major crime and punished accordingly. Yes, before the week is out he will announce the establishment of a Goldfields Commission of Enquiry to investigate the events on the Eureka and the management of the Victorian goldfields in general, and he will also gladly accept the resignation of John Foster as Colonial Secretary, but he is never in any doubt – at least not publicly – where the blame lies. It lies with the diggers, most particularly the 'foreigners . . . found amongst the most active'.[86]

As to the authorities at Ballarat, it has not taken them long to realise that, while they have most of the ringleaders and troublemakers, there are three key ones who are missing: Vern, Lalor and Black. (The authorities don't appear to know there are two Blacks who have been heavily involved, including Lalor's Secretary of War, but George Black is the one they are after.) At least there is some good news: it is soon reported that, 'Lawler the chief is dead',[87] though this is as yet unconfirmed.

On this afternoon, Assistant Military Secretary William Wallace of the Grenadier Guards writes to the Colonial Secretary in Melbourne, informing him, 'The man Vern is said to be the mainspring of this discontent; and Sir Robert Nickle having received information that he was located near Buninyong with three hundred men, his company of picked Riflemen, sent a mounted force yesterday; but he had left that, the day before.'[88]

Inspector Gordon Evans, meanwhile, writes to the Chief Commissioner of Police, Charles MacMahon, on the same day, saying, 'Lawler and Black who are known to be two of the principal ringleaders are not yet arrested. I have sent out men in disguise to all parts of the District and I hope soon to be able to arrest them.'[89]

It is no time to be a one-armed bandit in Ballarat, and Lalor continues to lie low. As to George Black, he has long ago made good his escape and is now heading for Melbourne, while Alfred Black seems to have disappeared.

Saturday, 9 December, Castlemaine agitates

It has been going on all week. Word spreads all over the diggings: a *massacre* at Eureka. The Redcoats killed dozens of them and threw the rest into the lockup! Meetings were held and resolutions passed as the diggers expressed their solidarity with their brothers on Ballarat and their anger at the authorities who did this.

And yet there is also something beyond the anger and solidarity – there is a desire to continue the political fight that the diggers of Eureka died for, a desire to show that the government might have won the week before with bullets and bayonets, but the fight for tomorrow goes on. And on this day at Castlemaine it has all come together. No fewer than 20,000 diggers gather to hear the likes of prominent Chartist William Dixon Campbell Denovan give a horrific account of the 'massacre' and exhort that, in regard to those who died, 'Might their names descend to posterity among the heroes of Australia!'[90]

Together, the diggers roar their unanimous endorsement for this and other motions that had been passed at Bendigo the week before, including: 'That, as all men are born free and equal, this meeting demands the right to a voice in the framing and making of the laws which they are called upon to obey, [and] . . . will not accept as a gift that which is their inherent right . . . will have nothing short of their full and fair share in the representation of the country.'[91]

Indeed, all the resolutions are received with enormous cheering – most particularly including the one which states 'that the present pernicious land system should, without delay, be abrogated'[92] – until they get to the last one, for which the diggers remove their hats and bow their heads.

'That this meeting from their very souls sympathise with the true men of the people who are unjustly imprisoned for taking part in the late outbreak and also desire to publicly express their esteem for the memory of the brave men who have fallen in battle, and that to [show] their respect every digger and their friends do wear tomorrow (Sunday) a band of black crepe on his hat and in their public and private devotions remember the widows and orphans of the dead warriors.'[93]

Sunday afternoon, 10–11 December 1854, down in the dumps in the Camp lockup

In the cells, Timothy Hayes is struggling. He is a man of rather aristocratic bearing, with clothes well above the cut of the average digger, so the comedown of being in the lockup with common criminals – for the usual run-of-the mill murderers and the like are also in there with the Eureka prisoners – has been a far greater fall for him than for others. He misses his wife and children terribly, and his discomfort has been compounded by the fact that his plump body is now covered in maddening lice.

Has Hayes been brought low enough?

One of the guards thinks not and decides that it is henceforth to be the job of Hayes to daily empty the slops bucket in which the men void themselves. Hayes agrees to do it once, but that is enough. Yes, he has been brought low, but decidedly not *that* low. The guard is infuriated, but given that Hayes is already in gaol, there is not a whole lot more that he can do, so the prisoner is allowed to record a rare win.

What is certain, though, is that he is a man with a great deal to live for.

The sun is just beginning to mercifully sink below the brown hills that lie beside Ballarat on this stiflingly hot Sunday afternoon that has sapped the energy from all and sundry when Sergeant Harris informs the Chairman of the so-called 'Ballarat Reform League' that he has visitors. It proves to be Hayes's wife, Anastasia – a vision of fresh loveliness and unbowed strength – and his six children, one of whom is presently suckling at his mother's breast as she holds him in the crook of her arm. There is a warmth to her, a care for her husband and children, that deeply moves the other prisoners.

Like men dying of thirst in the desert suddenly hit by the remembrance of things past, both the prisoners and many of the guards now gaze mutely and longingly on this splendid portrait of a family, a real *family*.

Anastasia has brought a pile of freshly laundered clothes, neatly bundled together with a small basket of supplies so he can look like what he is – an innocent gentlemen – as he heads off to trial in Melbourne in a matter of days. She assures him that she will be there for him, now and always, and he is seen to straighten his back and even muster a wan smile. And now his children crowd around him. He gathers up one toddler daughter to embrace her, and she immediately tries to climb up on his shoulders. The eldest, a 12-year-old lad, valiantly holds back his tears – his father would want him to be strong – but soon he gives up the struggle. After kissing his father's left hand, he proceeds to cover it in tears. It is all Timothy Hayes can do not to cover his son in the same – never has he been brought so low.

At least Hayes remains relatively robust. The same, alas, cannot be said for poor Henry Powell out on the diggings, who has been suffering terribly since that horrifying Sunday morning. His deep wounds simply have not healed, and he grows worse by the day.

Apart from getting well, what he most wants is justice, so he sends a friend to the Camp, begging that a magistrate take down his statement of what occurred. But this magistrate must come quickly, he insists, because Powell is 'in immediate danger'.[94]

Police Inspector Gordon Evans is quickly dispatched with some colleagues, and the scene they find is a troubling one. Poor Henry Powell is seriously ill and lying on a filthy bunk in the tent of the same Mr Cox who he had originally come to visit. Drifting in and out of lucidity – he is sometimes coherent for as long as 90 seconds at a time – his agonised statement is carefully taken down: the attempted arrest, the blow to the head, the trampling and beating, and how 'the troopers rode over me, the blow was struck with something like a knife about three and a half inches long'.[95]

Only a short time later, at ten o'clock, Henry Powell dies.

While those who know and love Henry well are, of course, grief-stricken, the one bit of solace is that at the inquest the following day – a well-run, proper inquest, far removed from the debacle surrounding poor James Scobie – 'Arthur Purcell Akehurst' is found to have a case to answer and is committed to trial for the 'willful murder'[96] of the late Henry Powell, buried this very day. The jury even notes, '[We] view with extreme horror, the brutal conduct of the mounted police, in firing and cutting down the unarmed and innocent persons of both sexes, at a distance from the scene of the disturbance . . .'[97]

The deeply stunned Akehurst is immediately arrested, placed under guard and sent to Melbourne to await trial.

Elsewhere, most of the legal focus remains on capturing those ringleaders at the Stockade who have so far escaped justice, and it is on this 11th day of December that the government announces a reward of no less than £500 for anyone who can capture the man described as the mastermind – none other than Friedrich Vern! Capturing the Hanoverian is particularly urgent, as one of the rumours circulating is that Vern is 'erecting another Stockade in the Warrenheip forest'.[98] The word goes out: the Commander-in-Chief of the 'forces of the Republic of Victoria'[99] must be captured, and quickly, for he is nothing less than 'their generalissimo . . . a man of considerable talent, daring and impetuous'.[100]

Somewhere, Vern is surely blushing with pleasure.

Four o'clock in the morning, Tuesday, 12 December 1854, in the Camp cells, bound up and Melbourne bound

Moving the manacled prisoners is far easier said than done for men who have been inadequately fed and cared for over the last nine days, some of whom are still grievously wounded. But presently it is done and they all stand as respectfully as they can – many of them still chained together – so that Captain Thomas, all spick and span in his sparkling uniform, can address them and give them the 'Order of the Day'.[101]

That order is very simple: they are to be transferred for trial in Melbourne, where the juries will be less inclined to be sympathetic. But the good captain needs them to understand one thing. If any of them raises a finger against this transfer or, worse still, raises his voice as they cross the diggings, they will be summarily shot.

On receipt of this piece of information, Raffaello Carboni, as downtrodden and depressed as he is, simply cannot contain himself. So reminiscent is this arrangement of the Austrian rule he long suffered under that he bursts out with, 'God save the Queen!'[102]

His reward is to have one of the policemen, Inspector Foster, instantly spring to him and unbearably tighten the ropes that bind him to Joseph. Then, when he is taken outside and put into one of the carts, the Italian and the American are positioned right in front with Inspector Foster, with the trooper in command given specific instructions: if they so much as turn their his heads, the two of them are to be shot.

And so, even before the sun is up, the convoy makes ready to move off. Thomas is taking no chances of a rescue attempt. At the front of the 13 prisoners on three horse-drawn carts, he has a dozen dragoons on superb horses. The soldiers are armed, dangerous and well-trained, with orders to shoot to kill at the first sign of trouble. Pressed in tightly around the carts on their own horses are no fewer than a score of the more familiar troopers of the Ballarat stamp, their swords resting on their laps, carbines cocked, ready for anything. A sharp command from Captain Thomas and – altogether now – they move off at a canter, the prisoners bouncing in the carts like rocks in a shaking bucket.

Now, despite the threat to shoot him if he so much as turns his head, Carboni does risk a quick glance at the tent he had left just over a week earlier, a snug little place where he had passed so many happy hours. There it lies, deserted and uncared for, and he simply cannot help himself – he begins to weep, and the tears will not stop.

In the first few miles they see only one digger on the main road, and some three hours later the convoy stops in Ballan to change horses and have food and refreshments. At least the horsemen and Captain Thomas have biscuits and cheese washed down with ale, served on the stump of a tree outside the public house, while the prisoners beg for water. Arriving in Bacchus Marsh, the prisoners spend the night in a dark lockup and, upon the orders of Captain Thomas, in the morning they are served plenty of damper and a gallon of porter to share. And then they are on the move again.

Finally, after a second day of no fewer than 16 hours on the track, with only the odd stop along the way, the prisoners arrive at their

Melbourne gaol in Russell Street at eight o'clock on the Wednesday evening. They are exhausted, covered in dust and so thirsty it feels as though they have been licking the Lieutenant-Governor's boots for hours. The troopers hand them over to turnkeys, and a whole new phase of their lives as prisoners begins.

After some bread and cheese, they are ordered by the prison governor to strip down to their shirts and directed to their shared cells – all stone walls and iron bars – where they see a bare board for a bed and a single blanket for protection against the night's cold. Then the heavy metal door is shut and bolted upon them.

And then?

As Raffaello Carboni would later recount, 'Within the darkness of our cell, we now gave vent to our grief, each in his own way.'[103]

14 December 1854, Melbourne, let the Commission of Enquiry commence

All sit.

And so they do. It is on this day, for the first time, that the Goldfields Commission of Enquiry meets in a chamber of the Legislative Council under the chairmanship of William Westgarth – he who was the first member of the Legislative Council to visit the goldfields in 1851 – and including John Pascoe Fawkner, and Chief Commissioner of Goldfields, William H. Wright, to 'enquire into the Laws and Regulations now in force affecting the mining population',[104] and to work out if they might be more fairly framed.

After that first day's sitting in Melbourne, the Commission proceeds to visit Ballarat, Creswick, Castlemaine and Bendigo, meeting with interested parties including diggers, traders and officials. Finally, the administration is actively listening, instead of simply telling.

18 December 1854, the ante is upped on Ballarat

Posters go up all over Ballarat:

Colonial Secretary's Office,
Melobourne 18ᵗʰ December, 1854

£400

REWARD

Whereas two persons of the names of

Lawlor & Black,

LATE OF BALLARAT,

**Did on or about the 13th day of November
last, at that place, use certain TREASONABLE
AND SEDITIOUS LANGUAGE,
And incite Men to take up Arms, with a view
to make war against
Our Sovereign Lady the QUEEN!**

NOTICE IS HERBY GIVEN

That a Reward of £200 will be paid to any person or persons giving such information as may lead to the apprehension of either of the above named parties.

DESCRIPTIONS.

LAWLOR.—Height 5 feet 11 inches, age 35, hair dark brown, whiskers dark brown and shaved under the chin, no moustache, long face, rather good looking, and is a well made man.

BLACK.—Height over 6 feet, straight figure, slight build, bright red hair worn in general rather long and brushed backwards, red and large whiskers meeting under the chin, blue eyes, large thin nose, ruddy complexion and rather small mouth.

By His Excellency's Command,

WILLIAM C. HAINES.

Late December, 1854, Melbourne Gaol, hominy and hope

With five prisoners pressed into each tiny cell, life settles down to a dull, dark routine, interrupted only by the occasional strip-search. Breakfast at dreary dawn is not much more than slops, a dish of 'hominy' – boiled corn meal from which every ounce of nutrition has been removed, though it is admittedly often fattened with whatever grubs are ruling in the prison kitchen at that time.

Lunch consists of boiling water in which the turnkeys have dropped a few grains of rice, allowing them to call it 'soup', together with small piece of dried bullock's flesh, a piece of sour bread and a couple of black potatoes. Dinner is anything the prisoners like on the menu, which means more hominy. The Eureka men's companions are bushrangers, horse-thieves and common criminals.

On Sundays, at least, Carboni is let out of his cell with the other Catholics to hear Mass, such as it is. The priest is always in a hurry and on two occasions does not turn up at all. He never once comes to visit the prisoners in their cells to offer Christian consolation.

O Father, why hast thou forsaken us?

And then it happens. One bright morning, Carboni is visited in his cell by an extraordinarily distinguished-looking gentleman with a high forehead and kindly eyes. Despite looking entirely out of place among the poorly dressed prisoners and shabby uniformed officers, he still evinces an air of complete comfort and confidence.

'My name,' he says in the unmistakable accent of a man who is as Scottish as haggis, even as he proffers his hand to the Italian, 'is James Grant and I am a solicitor who would like to represent you in the coming trial.'[105]

There is a God.

After the Italian quickly agrees that he would be delighted if Mr Grant would represent him, the two engage in a detailed discussion of just what Carboni did and said at the Stockade – and when he did it and said it – all of it carefully noted down by the Scotsman's clerk.

The older man is not long in pronouncing his conclusion: 'You need not fear. You will soon be out, all of you.'[106]

And God is good, yea, verily, He is great!

Dusk, 21 December 1854, in the Government Camp, a Wise last word

Easy. Easy. Steady. Steady. Big breaths. Big, rattling breaths. And now more rattle than breath. And now nothing. Nothing at all. Blackness, eternal.

Captain Wise has survived for over two weeks after the fearful wounds he suffered during the attack, but now, as the sun goes down on this 21st day of December, it takes with it the last, tortured gasps of his life.

The next day, in the shimmering heat that is now blasting the Ballarat goldfields, a large cortege of mourners, 260 strong, is seen making its way toward Ballarat Cemetery. With full military honours, which includes volleys of shots fired into the air by a guard of honour, the display of the regimental colours and the regimental chaplain delivering a eulogy recording him as 'one of the best loved men of those who fell',[107] the brave English officer is laid beneath the sod. Samuel Huyghue is one who notes the occasion with great sadness.

'He was,' the functionary records, 'a gentleman of good prospect, being heir to a large fortune, and had left home with his regiment contrary to the wishes of his relatives, little supposing that he was fated to fall in the civil fray so far from all he held dear.'[108]

Around the diggings, many flags, led by the flag in the Government Camp, are lowered to half-mast in respect.

CHAPTER FIFTEEN

TRIALS AND TRIBULATIONS

A mongrel crew of German, Italian and Negro rebels . . .[1]
The Sydney Morning Herald defines those about to go on
trial for their lives, on Monday, 1 January 1855

Early January 1855, on another track winding back, between Ballarat and Geelong

It is a common thing for wagons travelling on the track between Geelong and Ballarat to have hidden contraband – usually vast quantities of grog secreted between the other supplies of flour, shovels, clothes, etc. The differences on this occasion are twofold. Firstly, this particular contraband is heading *from* Ballarat *to* Geelong and, secondly, the forbidden thing in the wagon is not grog at all, but a man – none other than Peter Lalor.

Recovered just enough to make such an arduous journey, he lies in the back of the dray of a carrier by the name of Patrick Carroll, covered by tarpaulins and feeling every bump in the track through his excruciatingly painful shoulder. Accompanying Carroll is an old Cornish digger, Thomas Marks, who acts as Lalor's nurse, confirming from time to time that the rebel leader is still conscious.

For his part, Lalor can only wish that he were unconscious – no matter how much he wants to cry out, he knows he cannot. Any such outburst would not only risk his discovery by the troopers and result in his instant arrest, but it would also endanger the liberty of the brave men who have agreed to smuggle him to Geelong. Besides which, despite his agony, he has a rising sense of excitement. Tonight – *tonight!* – he will see once more the love of his life: sweet Alicia. She knows he is coming, knows he needs a safe place to stay, to recuperate, to get stronger, and has passed word back that she is more than ready for him.

Alas, Lalor's agonised reverie of what it will be like to be with her again is suddenly shattered by a shout from ahead.

'We are looking for Lalor,' he can now clearly hear a voice call out, belonging, he correctly presumes, to a member of the mounted police. 'There is a £200 reward on his head – dead or alive.'[2]

Lalor's heart nearly stops. His every breath sounds ragged and, to him, *very loud*, as he instinctively curls into the foetal position in the corner of the dray, trying to make himself small.

'Musha,'[3] replies Carroll in his thick brogue, using the Irish word for 'indeed' as he gets down from the wagon, slowly scratching his bushy beard. 'The English are always liberal when they want to book a man, and that's a real fine reward ye are offering for Lalor, and by the same token, if we get a glimpse of him, ye can depend upon us coming back and letting yez know.'[4]

At this point, Tommy Marks, ignoring for a moment that he is a devout Methodist unaccustomed to lying, chimes in, 'See 'ere, you, we know Peter, and will not forget the £200 if we get a sight on him on the road to Geelong.'[5]

A trooper doesn't need to be experienced to know these are good, honest men who want to help, and so they are allowed to proceed on their way . . . as Lalor breathes again.

That evening, well after dark, at a time when even prying eyes can make no headway in the thick stygian gloom, there is a muffled *knock-knock-kn* . . . on the door of the double-fronted wooden cottage at 188 McKillop Street, Geelong, before it is instantly opened.

After a small female cry of delight or anguish – it is hard to tell – the two fall into each other's arms. At least, Peter Lalor falls into Alicia's arms . . .

She is shocked by his emaciated form – as is her uncle, Father Dunne – but more than grateful to have him safely with her. As soon as the young woman and the priest can, they organise for a local surgeon to perform another operation on Lalor at Geelong's Young Queen Hotel, where the remaining bullet is removed from his shoulder. And then it is quickly back to bed in Alicia's house, where she devotes herself to nursing her love back to full health.

————

Back on the goldfields, though there was relief when Commissioner Rede 'asked to be relieved'[6] and returned to Melbourne, tension remains. And that tension is never higher than when, in the second week of January, to the 'unfeigned astonishment of everyone',[7] the diggers hear that the license-hunts are to resume!

The new Commissioner does indeed appear with six policemen, but it all proves to be just for show. These worthies have no sooner appeared to do a little prancing about – let that be a lesson to all you diggers that the government is still in charge – than they retreat to the Camp and are heard from no more.

8–10 January 1855, in Melbourne, at Toorac House, Hotham holds fast

Some more gentlemen to see you, Your Excellency . . .

It proves to be men from the Goldfields Commission of Enquiry that Sir Charles set up a month earlier, and they have come with a clear message. Though their voluminous official report will not be ready for many more weeks, they feel justified in telling His

Excellency immediately that they are 'unanimous in recommending the abolition of the license fee.'[8] After conducting open hearings in Melbourne and across the major goldfields, they have no doubt that the major cause of the Eureka disaster was the maladministration of those goldfields and, most particularly, the manner in which the license fee was collected.

In effect, the Commission is affirming that everything the diggers have been petitioning is legitimate, and it is the *government* that has been in the wrong – something that is quite shocking to Her Majesty's representative who has been primarily and demonstrably responsible for the whole state of affairs.

Out of the question, gentlemen. Good day to you, sirs. I said, good day.

And so they go.

Two days later, however, the men of the Goldfields Commission write the Lieutenant-Governor a formal letter, whereby they make clear: '[We] consider it would be both a wise and human policy on the part of Your Excellency to proclaim at once a general amnesty as regards the past in the late proceedings, including within its scope all persons now awaiting trial for their part in the outbreak . . .'[9]

A nice idea. Alas, another two days on again, the Commission receives a rather stiff note from the newly installed Colonial Secretary, William C. Haines, after consultation with the Executive Council: 'I have now to inform you that the Lieutenant-Governor, with the concurrence of the Council, declines to accede to your suggestion.'[10]

His Excellency has determined upon his course of action – and intends to follow through, come what may.

Come . . . what . . . may.

Sir Charles feels some vindication for this decision when, just a short time later, a jury pronounces itself unimpressed with Henry Seekamp's claims that he did not personally write the articles in question and finds him guilty of seditious libel – subsequently to be sentenced to six months in gaol – but the Lieutenant-Governor equally knows that this conviction is not remotely the test. Seekamp, who had been bailed for £2200 in early December, was not involved in the military defence of the Stockade, and in terms of the 13 prisoners charged with High Treason who have all of the public's attention, Seekamp is no more than a noisy sideshow at Row's Circus. In a similar vein, Arthur Purcell Akehurst's acquittal by a Melbourne jury of the 'manslaughter'[11] of Henry Powell, on the technicality that Powell had not been sworn in by Inspector Evans before taking his statement, is a small boon for Sir Charles and the conservative forces arrayed behind him, but no more than that.

There is no doubt that as the time for the trial proper approaches, public agitation for the release of the State trial prisoners is increasing. Two protest meetings in quick succession in mid-January, held in the vacant space adjacent to St Paul's Church in Swanston St, call for amnesty 'to all concerned in the recent disturbances at Ballarat'.[12] They are so passionately anti-government and sympathetic to the accused that the Sheriff of Melbourne, Claud Farie, feels it 'possible that some attempt might be made to rescue the prisoners in the event of a conviction'.[13]

There are some uplifting moments, despite it all. At the second meeting, a young Irish lawyer by the name of Butler Cole Aspinall brings joy to the crowd by insisting that the time for granting amnesty has now gone!

'Gentlemen,' he declares in richly educated tones, 'I am prepared to say that I consider it far better for these men and for the ultimate liberties of Victoria that they should be acquitted by their fellow citizens than that they should be pardoned by their "Owner".' *(Laughter and cheers.)* 'We want no pardon for them now, for I believe that their pardon is in the breasts of the jury who are to try them. They will be acquitted and not only that, but have the glorious privilege of pardoning those who put them on their trial.'[14] *(Cheers.)*

Cheers aside, the overall mood remains dangerous. Sheriff Farie secures no fewer than 500 sandbags, which he places strategically around Her Majesty's Gaol, so that in the event of a serious attack, he and his men will be able to defend themselves and the premises. As expressed in that new upstart newspaper *The Age*, which has been newly joined by the fiercely pro-digger campaigner Ebenezer Syme, civil war had been a real possibility. Now, even though the likelihood of that has diminished; even though thousands of special constables have been sworn in and there has been an endless blathering of loyalty by the propertied classes who have a stake in preventing violent political disorder, *The Age* is firm in its view.

All of this, it editorialises, 'weighs as nothing against the overwhelming expressions of contempt towards the authorities, of sympathy for the Diggers – ay, and admiration too – and, what is still more worthy of notice, the open assertion of republican principles, and the confident anticipation of speedy freedom and independence for the Australian colonies which one hears frequently expressed . . .'[15]

A letter to the editor that appears in the newspaper on 5 February, signed by 'An Australian', sets the tone, calling on 'every Australian who honours the men who have sacrificed their lives for their country [to] adopt their faith, and swear allegiance to republicanism'.[16] Ebenezer Syme couldn't agree more had he written it himself . . . and there would be speculation that he had done exactly that.

And this feeling is not only apparent in Victoria. So strong is the mood that an article in Sydney's *Empire* begins with the statement, 'In a city like Melbourne, so recently threatened with all the horrors of civil war . . . the triumphant unfolding of the banner of the Southern Cross, may not be so far distant as is popularly imagined.'[17]

6 February 1855, Her Majesty's Gaol, Melbourne, rough justice

The prisoners' situation in Melbourne Gaol has been intolerable, leavened only by the splendid mimicry of John Jeffreys as he takes off perfectly the walk and talk of their various turnkeys, and the fact that sometimes one of the guards might give them a stick of tobacco to share when Carboni sings some piece from an Italian opera. But that is it. The rest is just one wearisome day dragging itself into the next, and though on this day they collectively pen and sign a letter complaining to the Sheriff of their appalling treatment – 'We appeal to you, and ask, was there ever worse treatment, in the worst days of the Roman inquisition, for men whose reputation had never been sullied with crime?'[18] – they are destined to receive no reply.

22–24 February 1855, Victorian Supreme Court, Goodenough just ain't

At last!

The 13 prisoners are manacled, placed in drays and driven under tight guard through the streets of Melbourne to the Supreme Court, where they are placed in the dock before the baleful eye of Chief Justice Sir William à Beckett. (He, for one, is unlikely to be sympathetic to the diggers' cause. After all, three years earlier he had told the Melbourne Total Abstinence Society: 'Distinctions and grades, there will always be in any constitution of civilized society ... "Equality", as has well been said, "is the dream of a madman, or the passion of a fiend".')[19]

If it pleases, m'lud, the Attorney-General William Stawell – all wig, sideburns, black robes and the scent of slightly too much talc amid an air of great superiority – would like to file the formal charges against the dirty prisoners before him. And yes, for all his obvious superiority, the Attorney-General does look rather intense before this standing-room-only public gallery, but that is only because the stakes are so high. This trial is not simply a determination of the guilt or innocence of these particular diggers, but the guilt or innocence of the entire system that has caused them to take arms against it. Not only is all of Victoria watching this trial closely, but all the other colonies on the great red continent.

If the prisoners come to be acquitted, it will be a slur on the said system and effectively mean the rebels were justified in taking up arms against it. It is doubly important, therefore, that they be found guilty! And so to the charges, which are now read aloud by the Chief Justice's Associate, as not only the prisoners but the public gallery and every press man there strain forward to gather in every syllable . . .

'Prisoners at the bar,' the court functionary intones with the slightly bored air of the legal professional, an air totally at odds with the crackling excitement all around, 'the charge against you in the first count of the information to which you are now called to plead is, that you did, on the 3rd December, 1854 (being at the time armed in a warlike manner,) traitorously assemble together against our Lady the Queen; and that you did, whilst so armed and assembled together, levy and make war against our said Lady the Queen, within that part of her dominions called Victoria, and attempt by force of arms to destroy the Government constituted there and by law established, and to depose our Lady the Queen from the kingly name and her Imperial Crown . . .

'Having devised and intended to deprive our said Lady the Queen of the kingly name of the Imperial Crown in Victoria, you did express and evince such treasonable intention by the four following overt acts:—

'First. That you raised upon a pole, and collected round a certain standard, and did solemnly swear to defend each other, with the intention of levying war against our said Lady the Queen.

'Second. That being armed with divers offensive weapons, you collected together and formed troops and bands under distinct leaders, and were drilled and trained in military exercise, to prepare for fighting against the soldiers and other loyal subjects of the Queen.

'Third. That you collected and provided arms and ammunition, and erected divers fences and Stockades, in order to levy war against our said Lady the Queen.

'Fourth. That being armed and arrayed in a warlike manner, you fired upon, fought with, wounded, and killed divers of the said soldiers and other loyal subjects then fighting in behalf of our said Lady the Queen, contrary to your duty and allegiance.

'In the fourth count the charge against you is, that having devised and intended to levy war against the Queen, in order to compel her by force and constraint to change her measures and counsels, you did express and evince such treasonable intentions by divers overt acts . . .'[20]

William Stawell listens with some satisfaction to this account of the legal grievances the Queen has versus these State prisoners. It is he who, with Sir Charles Hotham, insists on charging them with High Treason from the beginning rather than something much easier to prove, like riot and affray. He has no doubt that such a dire offence – *betraying one's country by aiding and abetting another state* – is exactly what they have committed, and they must be held to account, come what may. This notwithstanding, he has already made an exception for the American James McGill who, after negotiations via an intermediary, presented himself to Sir Charles Hotham to express his regret.

Sir Charles, dismayed by McGill's youth, made no promises but at least did not have him arrested on the spot. Afterwards, he put out the word that if McGill quietly slipped away he would not be interfered with. Such leniency to McGill and his countrymen – for not long after the battle Sir Charles had also ordered the release of all Americans bar John Joseph – caused resentment among some of the diggers, feeling that they had received favourable treatment because of the sensitivity of relations between the British and Americans. But so be it.

As to those in the dock now, though they are under no illusions as to just how perilous their situation is, there remains among them a great sense of relief that after nearly three months of waiting they can at least – and *at last* – answer such charges. Yet, while every man must have his day in court, the most pressing question on this day is . . . which man?

Attorney-General Stawell and his legal counsellors wish to start with the most senior insurgent captured, Timothy Hayes, but their learned friends defending those on trial for their lives have other ideas. Through a series of legal manoeuvres focusing on minor technicalities, the defence manages to delay the trial of Hayes on the grounds that several material witnesses are absent. Other similar technicalities are invoked on other defendants until they arrive at the defendant the defence team has wanted to start with all along. His papers are in order, his witnesses are present. He is ready to go to trial. In the end the Attorney-General has no choice but to agree as the other prisoners are led away to the holding cells.

Step forward, John Joseph, the man characterised in the press variously as 'the nigger-rebel'[21] and the 'nigger martyr'.[22]

And so the black American does, even if the wheels of justice continue to move only very slowly from there. The Crown objects to all potential Irish jurors, all publicans and all others of dubious character, while to the amusement of the gallery – the nigger speaks! – John Joseph himself desires to have neither merchants nor gentlemen sitting in judgement upon him and says so. His drawling voice is rich as molasses, resonant and thickly accented.

Nevertheless, after no fewer than 30 prospective jurors are rejected by Joseph, assisted by his Lead Counsel, the former Colonial Secretary of Van Diemen's Land, Henry Chapman – who had been dismissed from that post because of his opposition to transportation – and his Junior Counsel, Butler Cole Aspinall, the two sides have finally agreed on 12 good men and true.

As all the legal manoeuvres have taken the better part of a day, the court is adjourned until the following morning, at which point the Attorney-General is not long in making what he considers to be an extremely strong case against the American.

There is no doubt that John Joseph was with the rebels from the start – he was there when they raised their flag and built their Stockade.

'They met under that flag,' Stawell says in his clipped tones, 'and patrolled together. Many of them were armed; indeed most of them were armed; and they all appeared to be marshalled, and they selected certain officers . . .

'Under this flag all those who really wished to volunteer, as it was termed, for this service, undertaking, as they called it, to fight for their rights and liberties, came forward, took their hats off, and knelt down and swore to defend each other, kneeling under this flag . . .'[23]

And this, of course, was only the beginning of the treasonous acts subsequently committed when those same rebels fired on Her Majesty's soldiers! As many witnesses will attest, John Joseph was in the Stockade in the days leading up to the battle, attended all the meetings and participated in all the drills, carrying a double-barrelled gun. And as it happens, members of the jury, we have the *very gun* that Joseph was subsequently seen firing at Captain Henry Wise of the 40th Regiment, giving that brave officer in Her Majesty's service a wound from which he subsequently tragically died.

For his first witness for the prosecution, William Stawell calls none other than Police Trooper Henry Goodenough, who, disguised in plain clothes, was inside the Stockade in the days leading up to the event. Strangely, however, the trooper's evidence is only of the most general variety, detailing the Stockade building and the drilling conducted therein, without actually positively identifying the defendant as being a part of it.

At least the next witness for the prosecution, Goodenough's fellow spy Andrew Peters, is able to give testimony that Joseph was in the Stockade on the early morning of 3 December, but, once again, could you trust the word of a spy? Joseph's counsel thinks not.

Peeved at this line of attack, the Attorney-General is at least able to bring forward several Redcoats who also testify to Joseph's presence in the Stockade *and* that he shot at Captain Wise.

'The soldiers were so impressed with the conviction that this man shot their officer,' Stawell says, 'that a desperate rush was made at the Stockade, and he was afterwards seen to go into a large tent in the Stockade known as "the guard tent".'[24]

Let us begin with Private Patrick Lynott, of the 40th Regiment.

'Do you swear to tell the truth, the whole truth and nothing but the truth, so help you God?'

'I do.'

'You are, I believe in the 40th Regiment?' the Attorney-General begins.

'Yes . . .'

'Did you go out on the morning of Sunday the 3rd December?'

'I did.'

'About what hour?'

'Between three and four o'clock.'

'How many went out?'

'I think between the 12th and 40th we amounted to 164 . . .'

Private Lynott then describes approaching the Stockade and being fired upon first.

'What distance were you from the Stockade when the volley was fired at you?' the Attorney-General asks.

'We might be about 300 yards . . .'

'When you got to the Stockade, did you go inside?'

'Yes.'

'Did you see anybody inside that you recognise?

'Yes, I saw the prisoner . . . He had a double-barreled gun, and he raised it and fired immediately . . . He discharged it, and in the direction in which he fired I saw Captain Wise lying wounded.'

At this point Henry Chapman objects strenuously: 'I would submit to your Honour that this is merely a matter of aggravation because in a melee of this sort, where, as the witness has described, firing was taking place pretty sharply on either side, it would be utterly impossible to ascertain from which particular bullet Captain Wise unfortunately fell. I submit that it is not evidence in the matter, it is utterly impossible for any witness to know that.'[25]

'The witness states it as a *fact,* your Honour,' Stawell interrupts, rather peeved at the presumption of his legal adversary. 'It is for the jury to say whether they think it worth attending to or not.'

In cross-examination, Chapman is at least able to shake the soldier a little.

'You are aware that this is a very serious charge against the prisoner, putting his life at risk, and I am quite sure you would not give testimony as to identity unless you felt certain of it. Had you ever seen the prisoner before that occasion?'

'No.'

'Were there other black men about the Camp there?'

'There were a good many black men.'

'Are you quite certain this was the one you saw there?'

'I am positive, I assisted to escort him out of the Stockade.'

Which is one thing, but Lynott's testimony amounts to no more than that he saw one black man among many black men fire only 'in the direction' of Wise. It is a long way from proof positive that he was the one who killed him.

The key witness in this regard is the 40th Regiment's Private Patrick O'Keefe. For, gentlemen of the jury, this man, *this* man, actually witnessed John Joseph firing at Captain Wise. Tell them, Private O'Keefe.

'Just as you got to it,' Stawell asks, 'did you see any one whom you now recognise?'

'Yes, that coloured man there.'

'What distance might you be from him?'

'It might be about five or six yards, and I saw him discharge one barrel of a double-barrelled piece.'

'Where was he when he fired, and where were you when you saw him?'

'I was within about six paces of the entrance of the Stockade where he was. He was inside the Stockade.'

'In what direction did he fire?

'He fired in the direction that I was coming up, both me and Captain Wise. Captain Wise fell, but I cannot say it was from the shot he delivered . . .'[26]

At these words the Attorney-General is seen to slump a little because it is clearly going to be impossible to prove beyond reasonable doubt that Joseph fired the fatal shot when the key witness 'cannot say'.

What makes matters worse is that, as Henry Chapman cross-examines the soldier, it is quickly established that besides Joseph – and more or less right beside him – 'two or three' other men were also firing! So who can say which shot from which gun killed Wise, most particularly when you know that the brave captain was wounded by *two* shots.

Hopefully the next witness, Thomas Allen – known to one and all as 'Old Waterloo' – might be able to provide some more cogent testimony?

The old man shuffles forward and is dutifully sworn in.

'What is your Christian name?' the Attorney-General begins.

'Yes, that is the prisoner,' says Old Waterloo, nodding towards John Joseph, as a laugh is raised in the gallery.

'What is your *name?*' repeats William Stawell, a little annoyed.

'No; I have no pension at all; you see I am rather deaf . . .'[27]

It is hopeless – even when the old man *does* understand the question, he proves unable or perhaps even unwilling to provide testimony that truly incriminates the American.

After some more legal manoeuvring, it is time for Henry Chapman to sum up the case for the defence, assisted by Butler Cole Aspinall. And it is now that Chapman truly comes into his own as he begins by dealing with the issue of the flag. After all, can it really be *High Treason,* to raise a flag bearing the Southern Cross? While some say it was a very peculiar kind of flag, this barrister does not.

'I believe,' he says with the flourish of one who is about to unveil a masterstroke, 'that it may be the very flag that was hoisted and produced when the Anti-Transportation League paid a visit – that is, the delegates from Van Diemen's Land, paid a visit to this Colony; and if I mistake not my learned friend the Attorney-General himself, who was always (and I think it highly to his credit that he was so) an opponent of transportation to these colonies, himself has acted under that very banner . . .'[28]

On a roll now, while Stawell stares, shocked, in the manner of a man who is powerless to get out of the way of a runaway train before it hits him, Chapman now flourishes the very thing . . .

'I must put this piece of physical evidence before your eyes, and ask you whether it was not the very flag[29] . . . that was hoisted here in the anti-transportation days, and if the fact of hoisting that flag be at all relied upon as evidence of an intention to depose Her Majesty, then I can only say that my learned friend and myself ought to be included in this indictment.'[30]

As it happens, so sickly does the Attorney-General look at this point that it would be a very hard-hearted jury indeed that would so indict him, but Chapman goes on for some time – deliciously, devastatingly – wondering just what the difference is between the so-called treasonous Eureka flag and the flag William Stawell was proud to gather under? Finally, however, even for the indefatigably merciless, there is no recourse but to be at least a little merciful, and he moves back to the diggers.

'Suppose they did intend to bring their licenses to burn them, what effect would that have? It would be injuring themselves, it would have just the foolish effect, I may say, upon the license fee that I might produce by burning some of the notes of the Union Bank of Australia which I may happen to have in my pocket; it would be simply injurious to myself.'[31]

As to the testimony heard from the likes of Henry Goodenough, who has identified John Joseph as being a part of the fight, this must be put in perspective. Chapman is completely merciless, his words lashing the English trooper in much the same manner that a gentleman might take his horsewhip, sir, to a cad, a cur and a . . . a . . . bounder! And what is worse, Goodenough was in the Stockade as a spy, which makes him *by definition* morally duplicitous!

'There is positive evidence,' Chapman thunders, 'that four men were sent forth disguised in various ways: Goodenough was disguised as a digger, Peters as a storekeeper, and for what purpose?

'For the purpose of acting as spies upon these men. Now, men who will be guilty of that extreme meanness of being spies under these circumstances, I say, are men who will not be very scrupulous of telling a lie when they come into the witness box. I believe it indicates a low moral condition which an honest mind naturally revolts from.'[32]

In short, in this man named 'Goodenough' we have one who is nothing of the kind, and the same can be said of those other low beings pretending to be diggers while actually in the employ of this perfidious government.

The testimony of witnesses like Private O'Keefe, identifying a black man at a distance before dawn, along with other shooters standing beside him, has already been demonstrated to be completely unreliable.

'It is quite clear, therefore,' the fiery barrister says, 'that no evidence whatever can be received that either one of these wounds was the cause of Captain Wise's death.'[33]

Beyond all the mechanics of who did what to whom and when, however, Chapman draws the jury's attention to the ludicrous nature of all four counts of the indictment against the accused.

'Now, gentlemen, look at that man at the bar. Do you suppose that that man, present as he may possibly have been, was present for the purpose of deposing Her Majesty from her rank and authority and station and kingly title in this Colony? Do you suppose that such an intention ever entered into his mind? Do you suppose that there was any intention in his mind to induce Her Majesty generally to change her measures? No, he never thought of such a thing.'[34]

John Joseph, under strict instruction to look as stupid as possible – though he is not that – stares blankly back at him, blinking slowly.

For let the jury look at the whole picture here. Perhaps it is wrong then to meet in large numbers . . .? Well, it depends which way you look at it.

'These men were driven to hold meetings that certainly afterwards became unlawful. They were induced to hold meetings at which they armed. They were unlawful meetings, I admit, but they were not High Treason. They might have been indicted for holding unlawful meetings; they might have been indicted for conspiracy; they might have been indicted for sedition, if their speeches were of that nature; but there was no treason in those speeches; they were unlawful, but not treasonable.'[35]

Criminal to build a Stockade . . .? How could that possibly be? For what would any reasonable group of people do, when finding themselves fired upon?

'Why would they raise a Stockade for the purpose of guarding themselves from the attacks that were apprehended? What does that prove? The only evidence given as to intention throughout the whole of this case is the words attributed to Lalor, and what does he say? Why, he says, "If the soldiers attack you, resist them," and that is what they did; and I say the soldiers marched up there without showing sufficient authority, and that want of authority stripped the case altogether of its treasonable character. It was an attack made on the part of men who were behind the Stockade, for the purpose of defending themselves against troops who had not put themselves in a lawful position, either by reading the Riot Act or by showing some authority under which they acted . . .'[36]

Yes, Chapman will reluctantly allow that Joseph's conduct might have been something less than proper, but that is not the issue at hand. For Joseph has not been charged with merely acting improperly, and the task of the jury is to determine whether he is innocent or guilty of what he *has* been charged with.

'Gentlemen, I ask you therefore once more, upon the whole of this testimony, whether you will deliberately upon your oaths as twelve reasonable men come to the conclusion that that man's intention was to upset the Queen's authority in this Colony, or to induce her to change her measures; because unless you can come to that conclusion, however culpable that man's conduct may have been, it certainly does not amount to High Treason.'[37]

Does the Junior Counsel Butler Cole Aspinall have anything he might like to add?

He certainly does.

'Gentlemen,' he starts in, 'there he is accused of an intention to subvert the British Constitution and depose Her Majesty, set up here as a sort of political Uncle Tom, and you must look upon him, I suppose, either as a stupid negro, a riotous nigger from down south who had no conception of treason in his head, or as being actuated by the eloquence of Lalor on the top of this stump, and actually prepared to defend himself, and that he had some idea, that though a negro, in any British possession he was entitled to his liberties . . .'[38]

It is a point well made, for the edition of *The Age* that very morning has confessed itself impressed with Joseph, despite his race.

'Here is a poor nigger charged with "ulterior designs" of a character to him quite incomprehensible,' it notes. 'Treason is rather a respectable crime, and is generally associated with political partisanship and intellectual energy. Not that we depreciate Joseph. He may be . . . a very respectable individual in his way. He is, at all events, a man of strength and courage, as shown by the fact that he "challenged" thirty men before quietly resigning himself to his trial.'[39]

The fact that he has black skin, however, is actually a key part of the defence's case. Aspinall goes on to point out in this closing address, to murmurings of wide agreement around the court, 'There are plenty of black men on the goldfields, and it is almost impossible for anybody but a slaveholder to know a negro from his fellow.'[40]

The dark mood among the remaining prisoners in their holding cells lifts as, at the lunch break, John Joseph is able to rejoin them and provide hilarious mimicry of the court proceedings. Oh, the fun of it!

Chapman, in the American's account, becomes 'old Chappyman' while Aspinall is 't'other smart'un of spin-all' and between the two of them, as Joseph evocatively describes it, they 'did fix that there mob of traps, especially that godammed hirpocrit of a sergeant, I guess!'[41]

And it is not just the words, it is the American way he does it, 'with such eye-twinklings, widening of nostrils, trumping up the lips, scratching all the while his black wool so desperately',[42] that they all fall about with laughter. Things are looking up!

But it is now time for Joseph to head back to court – he composes himself to look blank, blinking slowly once more – for the Attorney-General's closing address.

On the subject of John Joseph's supposed lack of intelligence, William Stawell will have none of Aspinall's line of reasoning and is crisply disapproving of this approach.

'One learned counsel's defence,' he says, staring bleakly at Aspinall, 'seemed to consist of this – that he supposed the prisoner now before you, because he happened to be a man of colour, was a man utterly devoid of intellect, utterly without education, a man who really did not entertain one single idea in his head. Gentlemen, I know no such thing – you know no such thing . . .'[43]

That, however, would remain to be seen. For now, all Stawell can do is to conclude the formal proceedings by bidding farewell to the jury on their deliberations and saying, 'Gentlemen, I leave this case fearlessly in your hands.'[44]

After Chief Justice à Beckett gives a long summation of the case to the jury – finishing with, 'Having discharged my duty, I now leave you to discharge yours'[45] – they retire to consider the verdict.

The jury returns just one hour later to an immediate stirring of the public gallery as all try to adduce the verdict from their looks alone. The stirring turns into a positive gust as the gallery thinks they spot it. And they like it!

Order! *Order!*

'Have you reached a unanimous decision?'

'We have, Your Honour . . .'

'What say you?'

'Your Honour, on the charge of Treason, we find the defendant, John Joseph . . . *not guilty.*'[46]

The roar from the crowd is so strong, so shattering, so entirely uncontrolled and improper in a judicial environment that Chief Justice à Beckett – 'Order! *Order!* ORDER!' – has no hesitation in putting two of the more uproarious members of the gallery in gaol a week for their trouble.

No matter! The calamitous commotion is soon turned outside the court as the cheering throng bear the stunned American upon their shoulders and out into the fresh air of freedom, tearing off down Swanston Street.

(Free at last, free at last, thank God almighty, he is free at last!)

What might have happened had he been found guilty? That is not certain, though one view later expressed by a carrier, John Chandler, who passed by the 3000-strong crowd outside the court every day, is that among them are many 'secretly'[47] armed men ready to forcibly release any man the court might find guilty and sentence to hang.

In the wake of John Joseph's acquittal, it is perhaps *The Age* – pushed along by Ebenezer Syme and campaigning editor David Blair – that is most strident in its criticism of the Hotham administration's handling of the case. The paper eloquently puts in black and white what the vast majority of the population is clearly thinking.

'There remains, then, only one safe and honourable course for the government,' it states flatly. 'They should at once ABANDON

THE STATE PROSECUTIONS . . . We repeat, and again repeat, ABANDON THE STATE PROSECUTIONS.[48]

To the far north, however, a few days later, *The Sydney Morning Herald*, disgusted that such a verdict could have been achieved in such a clear-cut case of treason, will have none of it.

'We are quite aware,' the august journal sneers, 'that a strong feeling exists in Victoria in favour of separation from the old country . . . Where there is a large foreign element, a strong democracy, and many who have "the little learning" which attaches infinite moment to a popular idea, it will of course exist in great and growing strength. We do not pretend to represent this notion as criminal in itself – it is held by every section of politicians as a thing to be looked for – to be met by rational, and therefore gradual preparation. But there are persons who anticipate this separation with mad impatience!

'Their real duty is, to press the claims of society and of the law to the last moment. If the Melbourne jurors chose to perjure themselves under the intoxication of popular passion, that is their concern. The Government should not abate one jot of its devotion to its duty, because it is met by a hostile influence, where it had a right to look for intrepidity and uprightness.'[49]

Sadly for the authorities, however, the case against the next man on trial for his life, John Manning, goes no better and is all over in one day. There is no evidence that shows him to have been actively fighting against government troops in the Stockade on the Sunday morning. (Even though he had, in fact, been as active as any man there.) Though he is strongly suspected of having written some of the more inflammatory diatribes in *The Ballarat Times,* there is no proof of that either. It is the nature of such diatribes that they go out under the banner of the paper itself, rather than the name of the individual.

So what have they got? Not much. Manning, too, is found not guilty!

The joyous commotion outside the court is matched only by the celebrations on the goldfields, as the mighty *Ballarat Times* reports: 'On Wednesday evening . . . in compliance with instructions from the committee of the Reform League, a large number of diggers fired salutes in honour of the acquittal of the two State prisoners, Joseph and Manning. Several large fires were lighted on the hills, and volley after volley was discharged. A band of music perambulated through the township in the afternoon, and played some lively tunes. There was a feeling of triumph and satisfaction in the breasts of all the sons of liberty at the acquittal of the prisoners and the defeat of the government.'[50]

That throbbing sound?

It is either the pulsating excitement running through much of the colony at the prospect of the government's total humiliation, or the veins in the temples of the Attorney-General and Lieutenant-Governor, who have now registered two major defeats. The pressure on them both is now enormous. It is one thing for the government forces to have stormed the Stockade, but with so many deaths they need to demonstrate that the assault was justified. Such grave consequences require that a charge of equally tremendous gravity be proven against the rebel leaders – to show it was their fault – and the only one that fitted was High Treason. With two of the accused now found not guilty of that charge, it is now *imperative* that the Attorney-General achieve a conviction against most or all of the remaining rebels.

How to do that? What is the problem?

There are three possibilities: there is a flaw in the law; they are flawed in the way they are arguing their case; or the judge and juries are simply getting it wrong. Stawell is not long in identifying the third possibility as the one that must be addressed, and he immediately orders a month's stay in proceedings so that an entirely new pool of jurymen can be identified and sworn in, and a different judge assigned.

Most of the Melbourne press, however, roundly condemn the

Attorney-General's move. In the words of *The Argus*, 'He sets aside broad and general principles, essential to the welfare of the community, in order to meet a particular evil; and this is precisely what the diggers are charged with having done.'[51]

7 March 1855, Prussia, full Marx

All over Prussia, the readers of *Neue Oder-Zeitung* – the most radical newspaper in the land – are reading an article by the paper's London correspondent, Karl Marx, who has become fascinated by an episode in a faraway land, an episode to do with a place called the Eureka Stockade . . .

NEWS FROM AUSTRALIA
BY KARL MARX

The latest news from Australia adds a new element to the general discomfort, unrest and insecurity. We must distinguish between the riot in Ballarat (near Melbourne) and the general revolutionary movement in the State of Victoria. The former will by this time have been suppressed; the latter can only be suppressed by far-reaching concessions. The former is merely a symptom and an incidental outbreak of the latter . . .[52]

This is more than just another article for Marx. The episode fascinates him. His good friend Friedrich Engels told him that Australia was no more than a United States of 'murderers, burglars, ravishers and pickpockets'[53] and not worth worrying about, but Marx disagrees. He is certain that it is yet one more example of workers rising against their oppressors, just as he had predicted.

12 March 1855, hoorays and hoots in Melbourne

The delay in the State trials in order to find a jury willing to convict the remaining prisoners causes such public discontent that, on this afternoon, there is yet one more public meeting on the open ground near St Paul's Church.

This is not a 'monster meeting', as had been held previously, but a smaller gathering of just 200 people to discuss the postponement of the State trials and raise money for the ongoing legal defence of the remaining prisoners.

One speaker, medical practitioner and Bendigo goldfields leader, Dr John Downes Owens, is particularly well received as he moves the key resolution, asserting that the conduct of the Attorney-General in postponing the State trials is so appalling that it can 'be expiated only by his resignation'.[54]

Hurrah! Cheers! Owens has summed up their mood exactly.

Though the authorities have a reserve guard on call, ready to move instantly if the crowd gets out of hand, there is no need. The meeting is conducted in a very orderly manner, and as the sun sinks low and an autumnal chill fills the air, most people start to drift homewards.

Still, there are some 50 who linger at the end of the meeting, and who should happen to pass by on his way back to Toorac House? Why, it is none other than His Excellency, Sir Charles Hotham himself. And yet the people do not treat him as 'His Excellency'. Quite the contrary . . .

No sooner have they seen his strangely withered form – it is odd how much bigger he had looked when he had landed in Melbourne only nine months earlier – than, as reported by the officer on watch, Sub-Inspector Thomas Langley. 'Some of the people assembled "hooted" him, but as they ceased as soon as he was out of sight no notice was taken of it.'[55]

19 March 1855, Melbourne Supreme Court, days of Hayes

At last the Attorney-General is ready with his new pool of 178 jurors from which the court will hopefully be able to find 12 good men who will agree to find guilty the next man on trial. And the prospects are good, for that man is none other than Timothy Hayes, against whom the authorities can provide *dozens* of witnesses able to attest to his role as one of the key agitators from the beginning – the very 'Chairman', no less, of the so-called Ballarat Reform League.

Hayes's counsel is an Irish lawyer working pro bono, Richard Ireland, who has already been heavily involved in the court cases coming from Ballarat. Curiously, he represented both Bentley *and* subsequently the three men held responsible for burning down Bentley's Eureka Hotel. With a head like a hammer and a tongue like the devil's poker, Ireland now sets to with a will to free his countryman so Hayes can return to the bosom of his wife and six children, now watching from the gallery. (And none more intensely than the fiery Anastasia, whose glare drills every man in turn who would speak or bear witness against her husband.)

Surveying them all from the bench is none other than the venerable Redmond Barry, a personal friend of William Stawell's, with whom he had been at Trinity College in Dublin – the same tertiary education as Magistrate Hackett *and* Peter Lalor – before travelling through Europe together on holiday. Judge Barry is a straight shooter, and rightly revered as one of Melbourne's leading citizens.

The Attorney-General's opening address is straightforward enough. Going to the heart of the matter – the two meetings on 29 and 30 November – there is no doubt that Timothy Hayes engaged in treasonous behaviour.

'Gentlemen,' Stawell begins in that curiously clipped accent of the well-educated Irishman, 'the first meeting was held to abolish by compulsion the existing license fee. Gentlemen, that meeting was called, it was attended by the prisoner now before you and several others, he was present, and I believe at one portion of it, he himself presided.'[56]

And not only was Hayes present at that first crucial meeting, the Attorney-General professes sorry to report – despite the gleam in his eye – he was also present throughout the entire decline into full rebellion. He was there at the meeting the next day when violence was first planned, took command of a body of armed men, saluted the rebel flag with all the rest and was present throughout all the treasonous drilling. He was arrested near the Stockade on the Sunday morning, carrying ammunition!

And now all William Stawell needs to do, is prove it.

The first witness for the prosecution is Henry Goodenough, who is equally forthright, affirming under oath that at the meeting on 29 November, when the Eureka flag first flew, he saw Hayes there, front and centre, and at the conclusion of the meeting Hayes said, 'It was no use to petition the Governor any longer, but to come forward and stand up for their rights and liberties, and he for one would do so.'[57] And then the next day, Hayes had been there again, as Lalor administered the oath to swear allegiance to the Eureka flag.

Interesting. Very interesting.

But, in cross-examination, Richard Ireland would just like to know of this fellow the *exact* words Hayes had said when speaking at the two digger meetings. He challenges Goodenough on his previous testimony that he heard Hayes say at one of the mass meetings that it was 'necessary to take the law into their own hands'.[58]

'He used words to that effect . . .'[59] Goodenough returns, falteringly.

'Then what you swore on the last trial is not true?'

'I will swear that Hayes said what I have said.'

'I ask you again, did Hayes state that to the meeting?'

'He did not.'

'Then if you said he did, did you say what was true or false?'

'I did not say so.'

'Will you swear to that?'

'I will not swear to that . . .'[60]

Perhaps you could tell us then, m'learned friend asks pleasantly enough, what you were wearing at the Stockade?

'I was dressed in plain clothes.'

'Why . . ?'

'Because I was ordered to.'

'For what purpose?'

'I cannot say.'

'Will you swear you cannot say?'

'I was ordered to go in plain clothes, and I went to see and be seen – to see what I could . . .'

'In fact, you went as a *spy* – was it not so?'

'If you like to call it so.'[61]

Mr Ireland does like to call it so, and intends to remind the jury with as much frequency as would make a sensitive man's nose bleed that Goodenough is a lowly hypocrite of a spy whose testimony cannot be counted on. And he may as well start now . . .

'You saw this process of kneeling under the flag. Did you kneel down, as you were doing the hypocrite?'

'I did.'

'Did you swear allegiance to the flag?'

'No.'

'Did you pretend to do so?'

'I did not swear.'

'You knelt down?'

'I knelt down.'

'Perhaps you said "Amen"?'

'No.'

'Are you sure of that?'

'Yes.'[62]

The barrister, his huge whiskers bristling at the indignity of having to even be in the same room as such a cur, appears far from sure that that is the truth, but again moves on. While perhaps Goodenough didn't swear allegiance, he would like the spy to admit that he, personally, had also urged the miners 'to stand up for their rights and liberties',[63] just as Hayes is said to have done! Reluctantly acknowledging that to be the truth, Goodenough nevertheless tries to defend having said it on the ground that he was there with two fellow policemen, similarly disguised. 'I did not want the diggers to know that I was a policeman.'[64]

But the fact is, he said it. Whatever is left of Goodenough's credibility has just been shredded. Perhaps they'll go better with the next witness?

No, not really. Andrew Peters, too, is like a sick rabbit before a ravenous dingo and is no match for the barrister. He had also been there as a *spy!*

'Did you hear anything said against the British Constitution?' Ireland asks him.

'I will not swear I did.'

'Did you hear anything about establishing a Republic?'

'There was a great deal said backwards and forwards . . .'[65]

No doubt. But Peters is unable to confirm positively that they had talked of a republic.

'On the Thursday, was there a search for licenses?'

'Yes, there was.'

'Did you go . . .?'

'No . . .'

'Did you know that there were shots fired by the troopers?'

'Not by the troopers, no, by the foot police, I heard them say so . . .'

'If a man should state that his license is in his tent, and he is at his hole, what do you do with him?'

'I go back to his tent with him.'

'Will you swear that such is a general practice?'

'I will not swear it is the general practice . . .'[66]

By the time Ireland has finished with him, Peters looks incapable of swearing as to what his own name is and leaves the dock shakily.

Next!

Police Inspector Henry Foster is called and recounts how, after Hayes's arrest outside the Stockade, he had personally searched the Irishman and found two gold licenses, a note in code, five bullets and some percussion caps.

This time Ireland is rather like a seemingly friendly python turning rogue – and squeezing tighter with every coil.

The five bullets, for example . . .

'I believe what you found on Hayes were the ordinary contents of a digger's pocket?'

'I cannot say . . .' [67]

Of course he cannot say, but the point is not lost on the jury. If carrying bullets in your pocket was treasonous of itself, then every man jack on the diggings was likely treasonous! But now, let us return to the licenses also found on Hayes

'Both those licenses were made out to Hayes, the prisoner?'

'Yes.'

'Then he evidently had not burnt his licenses?'

'No, evidently not . . .'[68]

After the court is adjourned for the day, it is reconvened the following morning, and Ireland is at least able to introduce credible testimony conclusively demonstrating both that the troopers had fired their weapons at the diggers on the morning of the 30 November digger hunt *and* that Hayes had not been in the Stockade at the time of the attack. And he most certainly had not fired a shot in anger.

One of Ireland's witnesses is a digger by the name of John O'Brien, who gives honest testimony that at the time of the attack on the Stockade he had gone to Hayes's tent to find his friend had just risen from bed and was on his way to Father Smyth's presbytery

– a fact that Father Smyth himself corroborates. Hayes had come to him, Father Smyth then recounts from the witness box, to tell him that they must both go together to the Stockade, where they will be needed.

With the act of firing upon Her Majesty's troops no longer possible to prove, the key remaining charge is that Hayes was treasonous by whipping up the mob against Her Majesty. And yet Loftus Grey, *The Argus* correspondent, swears on oath, so help him God, that he had been there at the meeting on 29 November with notebook in hand, listening intently and documenting it all.

Junior Counsel Thomas Spencer Cope addresses him in reference to that meeting. 'Now, was anything said at that meeting by Hayes of his intention to take the law into his own hands?'

'Decidedly not.'

'Did you hear Hayes saying anything about a "common enemy"?'

'No.'

'Goodenough stated that Hayes said they must stand up for their rights and liberties and fight. Is that correct?'

'I did not hear him use the word "fight".'[69]

'Did you see the digger hunt?'

Before he can answer, however, the somewhat flustered Attorney-General doth protest vigorously. 'I object, Your Honour, to the use of the term "digger hunt". It is not a proper form of expression.'

With an impatient wave of the hand, in the manner he might shoo a blowfly, Cope carefully rephrases: 'Did you see on the Thursday a search for licenses, commonly called on the diggings, a "digger hunt"?'

A wave of merriment rolls through the gallery.

Order! *Order!*

'Yes.'

'Will you describe it?'

'A party of 25 mounted police came down from the Camp.'

'Were they armed?'

'Yes, the mounted police had their swords drawn, and the foot police had their bayonets fixed.'

'Is that the customary method of collecting licenses?'

'I have seen the foot police with bayonets fixed, but not the troopers with their swords drawn.'[70]

Finally, it is time for Cope's *pièce de résistance* . . .

Over the fierce protestations of the Attorney-General, he now draws the jury's attention to Captain Thomas's report to Lieutenant-Governor Hotham, including the words, 'Early on the 2nd [December] information was received that the rebels were forming an entrenched camp at the Eureka diggings . . . I determined to attack their camp at daylight the next morning.'[71]

'You will remark, gentlemen,' Cope begins, 'that early on the 2nd December, Captain Thomas had made up his mind to attack the diggers, and not they him, and the reason of his determining to attack was, because they had entrenched themselves in the Eureka Stockade. Now, I have yet to learn that entrenching yourself in a Stockade is High Treason? The cause of these men retiring into the Stockade was in order to protect themselves . . . After being fired upon on the Thursday, they said, "We'll have no more of this, we'll have some place to go to, and not be shot down like dogs at a digger hunt . . ."'[72]

It is a devastating point, all the more damaging to the Crown's case because the fact that the government intended to attack them all along is nothing more than the simple truth, and all of it *in their own words*.

At this point Hayes's defence team would have loved nothing better than to call Sir Charles Hotham himself to demonstrate that the real blame lay not with those on Ballarat but with the man living in Toorac House. Alas, on the advice of his senior legal counsel, Sir Charles had already given notice that he declined to attend, on the grounds that his testimony might 'disclose that which public policy requires to be concealed'.[73]

Although Hotham does not escape unscathed.

Warming to a theme, Ireland now notes how well His Excellency had been welcomed to Victoria at a time when the colony had been 'loyally mad'.[74]

Ah, but that loyalty extended had not been *returned*.

'Gentlemen, the diggers at this time, no doubt suffering under a great deal of misgovernment and oppression, continued peaceably to bear it until the death of Scobie . . . They found a murder perpetrated, and when the man charged with it was brought before the authorities he was discharged and the Government took no notice of it . . . Gentlemen, in order to vindicate the law, the law was violated. The Eureka Hotel, worth £27,000, was burnt to the ground, and then and not till then Bentley was brought before a magistrate . . . tried at the Supreme Court, and sent to gaol for three years.'[75]

Ireland's theme is strong, the words of his summation confident.

'Gentlemen,' he continues, 'you are to connect the violence of 3rd December, not with the meeting on the 29th November, which was a legal, constitutional agitation, but you are to connect it with the firing on the people on the Thursday morning, and the apprehension that a repetition of the same thing would take place. Accordingly, you find them on the afternoon of that day drilling and re-drilling, marching and counter-marching . . . and on the Saturday you find them behind a Stockade, which they had erected, consisting of a few slabs thrown up in a few hours. And where? Why, actually around their own habitations!

'Gentlemen, does that show you an intention of deposing Her Majesty from her royal crown and dignity? Does it not rather show you that it was an organisation on the part of the people to resist aggression upon them in the shape of digger hunting? If it was, then I tell you, and His Honour will bear me out in so telling you, that this is not high treason. You may make it a riot; and why did not the Crown do so, and indict the prisoner for that offence? Why, because it is very desirable to make everybody opposed to the Government hate the Queen, instead of being opposed to the local Government.'[76]

Ireland is very strongly of the view that not just this State trial, but *all* of the State trials must be abandoned.

'I remind you gentlemen,' he concludes, 'that it is no act of treason merely to fire upon the Queen's troops. These men erected a Stockade in case of another diggers hunt. A place where they would not be shot down like dogs. The learned Attorney-General hopes you will see treason where it is seen by no-one else. I trust that justice is safe with you.'[77]

It is now that Judge Barry sums up, and after carefully going through the case – the evidence for and against a guilty verdict – his final words to the jury stun the Attorney-General: 'Recollect, gentlemen, that when I say this I am giving an opinion from which you may differ, [but] . . . my opinion is not to convict the prisoner . . .'[78]

Stawell slumps back in his chair. It has come to this!

Just 30 minutes later, the jury is back.

'Have you reached a verdict?'

'Yes, your Honour, we have.'

'How do you find the defendant?'

'*Not guilty.*'

Uproar. Through the court, down the corridors and out into the streets where no fewer than 5000 people are gathered.

'NOT GUILTY!'

The explosion of relief, of savage exultation, goes up and, in the now traditional fashion, Hayes is carried through the streets of Melbourne upon the worthy shoulders of his supporters, the roar growing louder as others join in.

And it is a roar that is not long in making it all the way to Toorac, where Sir Charles Hotham broods, more humiliated than ever before. He is, after all, the man who has presided over the massacre, who has ordered the troops to Ballarat, and if the ringleaders are not guilty of treason, then what were they guilty of? If *they* are innocent, it means that innocents were massacred – and he is the man responsible. It is obvious that the accused have broad public support and nowhere more so than among the 12 jurors who are successively selected to try them.

21 March 1855, Melbourne Supreme Court, Do you find the prisoner at the bar guilty or not guilty?

The only upside to the government's otherwise bleak legal landscape at this point is that at least the next defendant is Raffaello Carboni – of them all, perhaps the easiest to convict. As Stawell reviews the evidence going into this trial, he takes comfort in the fact that he has no fewer than eight solid witnesses who can swear on the Bible that they saw the noisy Italian in the Stockade, armed with a pike, and that he had attacked one of the witnesses and driven that witness outside its barriers before being fired upon by the rebels.

The Argus reports that Carboni on this day appears 'more self-composed than he has hitherto appeared, the former acquittals having evidently given him confidence. There was, however, a strange excitability, manifested by him throughout the trial, which his professional adviser could scarce restrain'.[79]

That professional adviser, James Grant, is nevertheless another reason for Carboni's growing confidence. As promised, the worthy Scot who had first visited him three months before to offer his services has assiduously prepared the Italian's defence and, most importantly, secured the services of Richard Ireland as Lead Counsel.

But to the business at hand. After the members of the jury have been agreed upon by both sides and sworn in, the Attorney-General delivers the opening address, covering now-familiar ground to the court, promising to prove beyond reasonable doubt that the foreign anarchist had been with the rebellion from the beginning, that he had not only helped to incite it but trained rebels and took up arms himself when the battle began. It is a reasonable, though rather brief address, which *The Age* would note the following day, observing that 'the learned Attorney-General . . . seemed labouring under severe indisposition'.[80]

And so, too, does the first witness, Henry Goodenough, seem a little out of sorts. His testimony has been shredded in the previous trials, and so it is again on this occasion, just as is the evidence of his fellow spy, Peters, after him.

Now it is the turn of the venerable magistrate, Charles Hackett, to take the stand. A careful, considered man, he tells the court that he remembers well the evening of 30 November, when the defendant had been one of a party of three, together with Father Patrick Smyth and George Black, who had come to the Camp as a delegation of diggers, seeking ways to avoid disaster.

And do you remember, sir, what Carboni had said that night?

Yes, he does. Hackett recalls the Italian telling them that the diggers were not animated by any 'spirit of rebellion'[81] but simply wanted an end to the exorbitant license fee.

Hardly the words of a man who went on to commit treason? That, at least, appears to be the mood of the gallery, as there is a happy sigh of relief at these words.

But let's focus, Ireland says, on the consequences of the jury returning a guilty verdict. As he notes – using clever lawyerly hyperbole to shock the members of the jury – the law is very severe on those who are found guilty of treason. The cruelly condemned man would be taken to the place of execution first, hanged by the neck, disembowelled and quartered – his body cut into four pieces. His severed head would then be affixed to a pole. Oh, yes, *that* would be the result of a guilty verdict. Is that a worthy fate for this man, who had only been reacting to hideous injustice, and who had certainly done no more than three other defendants who have been found 'not guilty' by three separate juries? Ireland would also take this opportunity to remind the jurors that he, personally, was not to blame for this enormous waste of time and money. That would be the Crown.

Ireland has complete faith in these honest men, that they will deliberate wisely and well and come back with the only verdict possible on the evidence presented: not guilty.

From the looks on the faces of the jury, they seem to be impressed by the argument as they gaze upon the Italian benignly at worst, perhaps even warmly. At nine o'clock the jury retires and, while Carboni prays to the Lord his God and Redeemer, they deliberate.

Mercifully, one way or another, it does not take long – the jurors are back just 20 minutes later. .

The Clerk of the Court takes over and speaks up: 'Gentlemen of the Jury, have you considered your verdict?'

'We have.'[82]

'Do you find the prisoner at the bar guilty or not guilty?'

'NOT GUILTY!'[83]

Hurrah!

Just a minute later, Raffaello Carboni is standing on the steps of the Supreme Court, a free man, completely smothered in hugs, handshakes and pats on the back from his supporters. The feeling is overwhelming, and yet the Italian still has the presence of mind to raise his right hand to the heavens and utter a quick public prayer, finishing with, 'in Thy mercy save this land of Victoria from the curse of the "spy system".'[84]

Right next to him, Timothy Hayes – a free man himself, of course – responds with, 'Amen', a word and sentiment repeated by all and sundry gathered before them.

With the jury's announcement the next day that the Nederlander Jan Vannick is also 'not guilty', *The Age* places its story prominently, beginning:

THE FIFTH DEFEAT!

Vannick, another of 'the foreign anarchists,' is acquitted! Go on Mr Attorney! You are very hoarse, but you are doing

more in a week to bring the Government into contempt than *The Age* could do in a year.[85]

The following day, with Raffaello Carboni in ecstatic attendance, encouraging them with many gestures and smiles in his Latin way, both Michael Tuohy and James Beattie are also acquitted.

Of course, with each acquittal the likelihood increases that all the remaining prisoners will also be freed. Once it has been established that the actions of the others are not treasonable, the task of the prosecutors will be to prove that one or all of the remaining prisoners has done something different. It is perhaps for this reason that on 26 March the Sydney-born Thomas Dignum is released without trial on the prosecutors' reckoning that they simply don't have enough evidence of sufficient weight and difference to convict him. (Which is alright for some, for it is on this very morning that the one-time editor of the seditious *Ballarat Times*, Henry Seekamp, begins to serve his six-month sentence.)

What of the other five cases? To most observers it is obvious that the government is never going to get a conviction, and as Sir Charles Hotham would later advise the now Home Secretary Sir George Grey in his report to his superior, after the acquittal of Carboni, 'it became a subject of discussion whether the trials should be proceeded with; it was urged that justice was held up to derision and mockery, and that it would be most prudent to desist.'[86]

Sir Charles, however, will hear none of it, as he would later tell Sir Grey: 'But in this opinion I do not share. If juries would not do their duty I could discover no reason why I should not do mine. I deemed it of the highest importance to prove that the common law of the land in political cases was insufficient.'[87]

So it is that the trials go ahead, with all five remaining prisoners brought to the court together.

On this very morning, *The Age*, with Ebenezer Syme and David Blair in their finest form, sets the tone:

'To-day,' it reports, 'the familiar farce of "State Prosecutions; or, the Plotters Outwitted" will be again performed, and positively for the last time; on which occasion that first-rate performer, Mr. W. F. Stawell, will (by special desire of a distinguished personage) repeat his well-known impersonation of Tartuffe, with all the speeches, the mock gravity, &c., which have given such immense satisfaction to the public on former occasions. This eminent low comedian will be ably supported by Messrs. Goodenough and Peters, so famous for their successful impersonations of Gold-diggers; and it is expected that they will both appear in full diggers' costume, such as they wore on the day when they knelt before the "Southern Cross," and swore to protect their rights and liberties. The whole will be under the direction of that capital stage manager, Mr. R. Barry, who will take occasion to repeat his celebrated epilogue, in which he will – if the audience demand it – introduce again his finely melodramatic apostrophe to the thunder.

'With such a programme, what but an exceedingly successful farce can be anticipated? A little overdone by excessive repetition, it may be said; but still an admirable farce; and, as we have said, this is positively the last performance. Therefore, let it go on; or as Jack Falstaff says, "play out the play".'[88]

And so it does go on, with the five prisoners all arraigned and tried together . . . for the widely expected result.

The next morning, after just seven minutes of deliberation, the jury delivers their verdict and . . . all are acquitted!

27 March 1855, alone, so very alone, in Toorac House

Never more isolated from Melbourne proper than now, Governor Hotham receives the news with a heavy heart, his morale and moral authority destroyed in equal measure. Even his legal authority is now looking shaky.

It is on this same day that the Goldfields Commission presents to the Lieutenant-Governor its report of their inquiry into the conditions of the Victorian goldfields, confirming everything that it had forewarned in early January.

It is their official view that the license fee is the primary cause of the revolt, and it should be abolished immediately, replaced by an export duty on gold at two shillings and sixpence an ounce. The diggers themselves would not be let off scot-free: although the whole license-fee system and Gold Commission should be abolished, they should pay for a license called a 'Miner's Right' at a fee of £1 annually, but with that license they would also have the right to vote. Who for? The Commission recommends that the Legislative Council should have eight members elected specifically from the gold-digging communities across Victoria, and another four nominated members. As to the administration of the law, it suggests that local miners' courts should be established on the goldfields, with local miners elected to them, just as local wardens could be appointed to replace the gold commissioners. What is more, the report finds, 'This land monopoly must be completely broken down. If the lands by hundreds and thousands of acres yearly are insufficient for that purpose, they must be brought forward by millions.'[89]

In short, the Commission's recommendations are that all the grievances held by the diggers are justified, and the best way forward is to grant all the things they have requested.

Yes, it is only a report at this stage, but the findings come with the imprimatur of having been issued by a qualified body that, at the Lieutenant-Governor's behest, has thoroughly investigated all the issues – and their findings clearly concur with what is the broad view of all of Victoria, with the exception of the squatters . . . who now matter less and less as democracy starts to take hold. The Lieutenant-Governor could only ignore the people and the findings of this Commission at his peril. Given the events at Eureka, that is unthinkable.

The days of Sir Charles Hotham ruling Victoria in splendid isolation are over.

Less than 12 months after his glorious arrival, he has lost the confidence of the people, his Executive Council and – though he has not yet received the letter confirming it – the confidence of his masters in London.

That letter, when it comes, is devastating in its own way. In a confidential dispatch, the British Secretary of State for the Colonies, Lord John Russell, does not mince words: 'In further acknowledgment of your dispatch No. 38 of 28th February last, respecting the trial of the prisoners taken at Ballarat, I wish to say that although I do not doubt you have acted to the best of your judgement, and under advice, yet I question the expediency of bringing these rioters to trial under a charge of High Treason, being one so difficult of proof, and so open to objections of the kind which appear to have prevailed with the Jury . . .'[90]

For the moment, however, it is *The Age* that puts it rather well, when it comes to Sir Charles: 'In the short period of seven or eight months, he has managed to alienate the sympathies of every class in the colony . . . earned a character for contemptible official trickery and evasion, and has brought the good faith of the Government into disrepute by a systematic breach of contract . . . [and] a disgraceful system of espionage.'[91]

———

Peter Lalor couldn't agree more as he continues to closely follow the unfolding events while recuperating under the care of Alicia. His love!

'I need not speak of Alicia,' he would soon write to his brother Richard, now back in Ireland. 'Every misfortune of mine seems to add new vigour to her affection. When I believed I was dying for some days, my only earthly trouble was Alicia. The diggers and inhabitants of Melbourne love her for her conduct towards me . . .'[92]

For the moment Lalor stays hidden but, in the light of the acquittals and the complete vindication of everything that he and his fellow diggers had fought for, the one-armed, one-time rebel leader eventually writes a statement for *The Argus*. Published on 10 April 1855, it includes words that Fintan Lalor himself would surely have been proud to pen . . .

'From the steps now being taken by the Government, I have no doubt but that we shall have many measures of useful reform carried into effect. Why were not these measures adopted before? Why did not the Government take steps to alter the land system, to amend the mode of collecting the gold revenue, and to place the administration of justice in the hands of honest men before this bloody tragedy took place? Is it to prove to us that a British Government can never bring forth a measure of reform without having first prepared a font of human blood in which to baptise that offspring of their generous love? Or is it to convince the world that, where a large standing army exists, the Demon of Despotism will have frequently offered at his shrine the mangled bodies of murdered men?

'Whatever may have been the object of our rulers in adopting the line of policy they have pursued, the result has been deplorable, and such, I hope, as a civilised people will never again have to witness.'[93]

5 May 1855, an auspicious day on the diggings of Ballarat

After a preliminary release of land the year before, some more prize land near Ballarat goes on sale at a public auction, allowing diggers and others a choice of lots of varying sizes to buy and have title to – some of it close to Ballarat. One particularly coveted bit of terrain boasts 160 acres of fertile fields at Glendaruel, just 20 miles northwest of the diggings, and the bidding is intense.

In the end, though, the man who wins it is a strapping fellow with a roundish face and beard who looks to be in his late 20s, standing at the back of the auction room with a coat curiously draped across his left shoulder.

The auctioneer knocks the land down to him and then says, 'Yours, sir. What is your name, please?'

'My name, sir,' says he, 'is Peter Lalor.'[94]

As one the room gasps and peers more closely, and it is indeed him! And he has the money to pay for it, too. Knowing Lalor's intent, many of his friends on Ballarat have gathered together to raise money to get him back on his two feet again, and have put together over £1000 for him to buy this land. It is Lalor's aim to try his luck raising crops and cattle – incapacitated as he now is, further gold-digging is out of the question, even if he wanted to. So grateful are the mass of diggers that even more money is now being raised to pay for a house to be built on that land and to establish the farm.

No move is made to arrest Lalor. Even though there officially remains a £200 reward on his head, it is tacitly understood, by the authorities at least, that there is to be no more pursuing those involved with the Eureka Stockade. In fact, four days after Lalor reappears in public, the government announces that the mooted reforms will indeed be made, and also makes a proclamation revoking the rewards that had been offered for the likes of Friedrich Vern, George Black and Peter Lalor. With 13 acquittals from 13 imprisoned, there is no point, nor strength left, to try the 14th, 15th and 16th, even if the government could find them.

For everything, but everything, is now changing rapidly.

———————

On 12 June, the *Goldfields Act 1855* – incorporating most of the Commission of Inquiry proposals – is passed. The whole system of license fees and collection is abolished, and, as had been suggested by the Commission, is replaced by the Miner's Right, which for an annual £1 fee gives the diggers the right to dig for gold, to vote for their eight members of the Legislative Council, and to build a home and develop a garden on a piece of land known as a 'Residence Area'. It is in this manner that the country towns of Central Victoria – stable, urban environments – suddenly spring up.

As to the judicial power previously borne by the Gold Commissioners as mini-dictators, that now passes to local courts presided over by men who have been elected by the diggers them-selves, *á la* the American system. And who should be one of the ten such magistrates so elected for the first time, on 14 July 1855?

It is none other than Raffaello Carboni, gone in the space of just a few short months from being in the dock as an accused prisoner to now presiding over the entire court from the big chair behind the magisterial bench. On the first day that the Italian turns up to the courthouse, he pauses beneath the shady gum tree outside and recognises it as the same spot where, on the night of 30 November the year before, he, George Black and Father Smyth had tried to convince Commissioner Rede to do everything possible to prevent bloodshed. A shadow of sorrow and regret passes over him, as it always does when he thinks of those terrible events, followed by cold rage. If only the three men could have succeeded . . .

Yet, as 1855 progresses, this newfound thing beneath the Southern Cross called 'democracy' still has some way to go to demonstrate its true wonders. This includes Henry Seekamp being released from gaol three months early, on 28 June, a month after Governor Hotham had been presented with a monster petition signed by 30,000 people. In the meantime, the first two men proposed by Ballarat to represent them in Victoria's Legislative Council this year are John Basson Humffray and . . . Peter Lalor!

Lalor's election manifesto is clear.

'I am in favour of such a system of law reform,' he states, 'as will enable the poor man to obtain equal justice with the rich one, which at present I believe to be impossible.'[95]

Both men stand unopposed and, on 10 November 1855, before the crowd gathered at the Ballarat Local Court, they are formally elected to take their place in the newly enlarged[96] Legislative Council as two of the eight representatives from five electorates of the goldfields.

In his acceptance speech, after being cheered as wildly to the echo as he is to the podium, Lalor is typically eloquent.

'Gentlemen and fellow diggers,' he begins, 'not twelve months ago a reward was offered by Government for my apprehension, and now by your suffrage I am going into the Legislative Council to meet that Government, and depend upon it I shall not shrink from my duty . . .

'I wish briefly to allude to the affair of the "Eureka Stockade" – not that I intend to vindicate the course of action, for I am free to confess that it was a rash act; nevertheless the most honourable man might have acted under similar circumstances as I did then. You are my witnesses that I never harangued the diggers to take up arms against the Government, and therefore, never would I have entertained the idea of becoming their commander-in-chief any more than I do this day expect to be made the Governor of Victoria. On the Thursday, I was present at the meeting, and one of my mates, James Brown, who was killed in that sad affair, asked me to get up, and having so done I could not conscientiously turn back having once put my hand to the plough – that hand which Signor Raffaello has said, "was never polluted by treachery or cowardice" – I could not, would not, retreat. It has been said that nothing was ever yet obtained by physical force, but there is something to be learnt from past historical events . . .

'When King John granted to England that memorable institution the great Magna Carta, it was to the Barons of England, with arms in their hands, and not to the petition of the people . . .

'And I will affirm,' he continues, 'that, if Sir Charles Hotham had ruled in Victoria in accordance with the principles of the British Constitution, the diggers of Ballarat would not have taken up arms – the Eureka Stockade would never have been erected, and, instead of standing here a mutilated man, should now be an unknown, but a happy digger . . .'[97]

More thunderous applause.

And so it is that Peter Lalor, who is also soon to be a father – for he had married Alicia on 10 July 1855 at St Mary's Church, Geelong, and she had all but instantly fallen pregnant – heads off to take his place in the very chamber that only a year earlier he had led the revolt against.

On Tuesday, 27 November 1855, just three days shy of a year after he had led 500 rebels in raising their right hand to the Southern Cross to swear their solemn oath – and 343 days after having a reward placed on his head for having done exactly that – Peter Lalor raises his right hand once more, to swear an entirely different kind of oath. In the august chambers of the Victorian Legislative Council, under full magisterial sail, he is ushered forward by none other than John Pascoe Fawkner, to swear an oath to take his own place there.

'I, Peter Lalor, do sincerely promise and swear that I will be faithful and bear true allegiance to Her Majesty Queen Victoria, as lawful Sovereign of the United Kingdom of Great Britain and Ireland, and of this Colony of Victoria. So help me God.'[98] The transformation from one swearing to the other is, of course, breathtaking.

And yet, in that last year, Lalor has not changed – his new home-land has, because of the very action he and his fellow rebels had taken.

And it would never be the same again . . .

EPILOGUE

Just 18 months after Sir Charles Hotham made his grand entrance
to Victoria with more pomp and pageantry than he had ever previously been accorded in his life, and certainly as much as the colony
had ever been able to muster, on the last day of 1855 he prepared to
make his exit in rather less-exalted circumstances.

Isolated, discredited and *tired*, he had written and dispatched his
letter of resignation the month before, and it had been his intention
to return to England. Yet, just in the week before Christmas, he had
fallen ill after catching a chill at the opening of the Melbourne gas-
works and steadily deteriorated from there with what was thought to

be a combination of influenza, dysentery, epilepsy and perhaps even a stroke.

At 11 o'clock that oppressively hot morning, lying in a mess of his own making, he fell into a coma so deep that he could see eternity from there. At 12.30 pm he shuffled off this mortal coil. He was just 49 years old.

In the Legislative Council on 10 January 1856, it was none other than the colony's most famous politician, John Pascoe Fawkner, who rose to propose a motion that the Council accord a sum 'not exceeding £1500 to defray the expenses of the public funeral of the late Governor, and to erect a monument over his tomb – the design for the monument to be subjected to the approval of the widow'.[3]

Acknowledging that the memory of Sir Charles was not universally revered, Fawkner added generously that he, at least, believed that the public was satisfied that at all times Sir Charles wished to do right, even if 'his want of knowledge of the constitutional forms of Government prevented him giving that satisfaction which otherwise he would have done'.[4]

Peter Lalor, however, sitting in that same august chamber, would have none of it.

'While I am willing to accede to the proposition of £500 for the funeral,' he said, 'I am unwilling to sanction the expense of erecting a monument over Sir Charles Hotham. I do not wish to offend the living or insult the character of the dead, but I must say that there is a sufficient monument already existing in the graves of the thirty individuals slain at Ballarat. These tombs form a standing monument . . .'[5]

Lalor was supported in this contention by his fellow member of the Legislative Council, John Basson Humffray, and though they were making what was surely no more than a fair point, Fawkner proved to be on the winning side of the argument and the motion was passed.

Sir Charles Hotham was buried in Melbourne General Cemetery, and an impressive monument now lies above his grave, bearing the relatively neutral inscription:

To the memory of Sir Charles Hotham Captain in the Royal Navy and one of Her Majesty's naval aides de camp Knight Commander of the Most Honourable Military Order of The Bath and the first Captain-General and Governor-in-Chief of Victoria.

———

As we have seen, while travelling to Australia aboard *Scindian* in the middle of 1852, Peter Lalor had told his shipmate William Craig that, 'I intend to have a voice in its government before two years are over . . . and I intend to sit in the Victorian Parliament after I find out where improvements are needed.'[6] Despite having led Australia's most famous revolt in the interceding period, Peter Lalor very nearly kept to that timetable, and his nomination to the Legislative Council was no more than the bare beginning of a very long and successful political career. His voice would be heard for decades afterwards in the Victorian parliament, just as it was once heard when standing on a stump, exhorting his fellow diggers to 'stand truly by each other and to fight to defend our rights and liberties . . .'[7]

Lalor remained as the Member for Ballarat in the Legislative Council until March 1856, and then in November of that year, once the new *Electoral Act* was passed, he moved to the newly established Legislative Assembly – a body that the diggers who held Miner's Rights had the franchise for – representing Ballarat's seat of North Grenville.

Despite his role at Eureka, Lalor did not prove to be the voice of 'the common man' that many had expected him to be.

In late 1856, Peter Lalor voted in favour of reforms to the

Electoral Act that included continuing to allow plural voting (giving a man as many votes as he has properties valued at £50 in different districts), while placing a six-month residency restriction on the Legislative Assembly franchise! His apparent turncoat attitude caused bitter scorn to be heaped upon him from all quarters, most particularly from his constituents on Ballarat, who had put him into parliament in the first place. They now found – at least those itinerants without property – that they were threatened with continued disenfranchisement.

In the words of one of Lalor's fellow rebels at Eureka, John Lynch, referring to the property qualification for the franchise and Lalor's support for it, 'This relic of effete feudalism, brought in as a ruling factor in future legislation, was more than true democracy could bear, and a howl of indignation admonished him of the revulsion setting in. The semi-Chartist, revolutionary Chief, the radical reformer thus suddenly metamorphosed into a smug Tory, was surely a spectacle to make good men weep.'[8]

Lalor stuck to his guns regardless – as he was always wont to do – maintaining that those itinerants who did not put down roots in a community should not have a say in how it is run. Still not content with that – but upping the ante, as was also his instinct – Lalor then went on to speak in favour of a nominee Upper House.

What on earth was going on?

So great was the outcry, with a 'Lalor Resignation Committee' being formed and a petition with over 2000 signatures upon it calling upon him to stand down circulating widely, that Lalor felt obliged to publicly respond. In an open letter in *The Argus* to 'The Electors of North Grenville', he attacked in turn those constituents and journalists who had claimed that he had gone from ultra-democrat before his election to base Tory now – and so was no longer worthy of the people's trust.

'I would ask these gentlemen,' he wrote, 'what they mean by the term "democracy". Do they mean Chartism or communism or republicanism? If so, I never was, I am not now, nor do I ever intend to be, a democrat. But if a democrat means opposition to a tyrannical press, a tyrannical people or a tyrannical government, then I have ever been, I am still, and will ever remain a democrat.'[9]

The feeling against Lalor was so strong that at a meeting back in Ballarat in January 1857 there was such uproar – and even a threat of violence – that Lalor told the baying crowd straight: 'If anything can disgrace human nature it is the tyranny of a mob towards the man who has suffered for them. You may murder me, but you can't frighten me!'[10]

Though mercifully no murder took place, there seemed little doubt that Lalor would be murdered at the coming polls if he stood for re-election for this particular seat, and so he wisely swapped to the electorate of South Grant. He continued to be elected there for almost all of the next three decades, losing just one election in 1871 before retaking it at the next poll.

Outside parliament, however, controversy still attended him, and never more so than when, in December 1873, in his role as the director of the Lothair goldmine at Clunes, he attempted to break a union strike lasting 14 weeks – the issue was the miners wanting to knock off the working week by midday on Saturday – by reportedly hiring Chinese labourers from Creswick to do the work instead.

As noted by author Geoff Hocking, 'On 9 December 1873, the miners barricaded the Ballarat and Clunes roads and pelted the Chinese with stones and bricks in a scene reminiscent of the entry of the 40th Regiment to the Eureka lead twenty years earlier.'[11] As it turned out, the miners were victorious on both counts. They succeeded in keeping the Chinese workers out of town and mine management backed down – the miners were granted a shorter working week.

Oddly, none of the controversy affected Lalor's parliamentary career, and just two years later he rose to the position of Minister of Trade and Customs and Postmaster-General before becoming the Speaker of the House in 1880, a position he held through three successive parliaments throughout the 1880s. So highly esteemed was he that on two occasions he was offered a knighthood by the very Queen he had once been accused of committing High Treason against, but twice he did refuse the Queenly crown.

Throughout the decades his one unshifting rock of support was his wife, Alicia, and their family of three children, though tragedy befell them in August of 1885 when their third child, Annie, died at her parents' home of consumption, aged just 29. Alicia Lalor herself became ill shortly afterwards, dying in May 1887 at 55, to be laid in the grave alongside her beloved Annie.

'She died on the 14th as she had lived,' Peter Lalor wrote sorrowfully to Alicia's sister, Anne, in Ireland, 'in perfect sanctity.'[12]

Suffering from diabetes himself, Lalor resigned as Speaker of the Legislative Assembly on 27 September 1887 and went on medical leave soon afterwards, hoping that a trip to California might help revive him.

It didn't. After returning to Melbourne he became progressively more frail and finally arrived at the house that held his death bed in early 1889 – the home of his son, Dr Joseph Lalor, in Church St, Richmond.

''Tis better as it is now,' Lalor said as he lay dying, looking back on his colourful life, and of course focusing on its most colourful episode. 'We not only got what we fought for, but a little more. It is sweet and pleasant to die for one's country, but it is sweeter to live and see the principles for which you have risked your life triumphant. I can look back calmly on those days. We were driven to do what we did by petty malice and spite.'[13]

He died at the age of 62 on 9 February 1889.

One who mourned him was his then five-year-old grandson Peter, who was destined to die as a Captain of G Company, 12th Battalion, Australian Imperial Force, on the first day of the landing at Gallipoli, 25 April 1915. The official history of his battalion recorded that he 'rallied his men and, waving his arms, shouted, "Come on, the 12th",' just before the fatal bullet hit, depriving the 12th of 'one of its most gallant and capable officers'.[14]

In a tight piece of Australian historical symmetry, further legend has it that he died holding the sword his grandfather had brandished at Eureka. Many years later *The Sydney Morning Herald* would report that 'contrary to regulations, he smuggled the famous sword in his kit. At the landing on Gallipoli, Captain Lalor unsheathed it and charged up the hill against the Turks. He was found dead at one of the foremost points reached by the Australians. Around him were the bodies of 10 dead Turks.'[15] In 1945, according to a contemporary newspaper story, 'Australian authorities in London asked the co-operation of the Turkish Government in finding the sword and the Turks showed great interest in the search, but it has now been given up without result.'[16]

As to John Basson Humffray, as the member for Grenville and the Minister of Mines for the first couple of years in the Richard Heales government, he remained in parliament until defeated in 1864. He was re-elected in 1868 and then defeated twice, in 1871 and 1874, at which point he retired from politics.

After losing a great deal of money in failed mining speculations, Humffray lived out the rest of his days quietly in Ballarat, relying a great deal on charity, and died on 18 March 1891, aged 66. At his request, his modest grave – which soon enough fell into disrepair – is located in Old Ballarat Cemetery, no more than a stone's throw from many of the graves of the rebels who had died in the Stockade 40 years earlier.

Many other key characters in the saga of the Eureka Stockade did not match Lalor and Humffray's long and productive lives, most particularly the perceived villains . . .

The one-time proprietor of the Eureka Hotel, James Bentley, came to a bad end. After being released from Pentridge Prison on 18 March 1856, his capital was gone, as were his job prospects. All that was left was, effectively, the bottle. Finally, on 10 April 1873, while living in Ballarat Street, Carlton, he took his own life by poisoning himself with laudanum.[17] The investigating constable was told by Catherine Bentley, 'My husband has never been quite right since he lost his property at the Ballarat Riots. He has never recovered from the effects of it, and for the last two years he has never ceased to talk about it. He has been low spirited . . .'[18]

He was just 54 when laid beneath the sod.

As E. B. Withers, one of the first of the Eureka writers, rather poignantly commented, 'Let us hope that Scobie's ghost, so romantically referred to by one of the Eureka orators one day, is at rest with his revenge now.'[19]

In another touch of odd historical synchronicity, the man whose corruption had helped to facilitate the Bentleys' fall, John Dewes, met a similar fate. After losing his commission in 1854, Dewes was not long in leaving Australia and soon took up a position as Acting Postmaster of Victoria on Vancouver Island, Canada, before suddenly disappearing in October 1861, owing money all over town and taking with him around £600 in post office funds.

He reappeared in England, but in April 1862 it was reported by the *British Colonist* that he had committed suicide, 'blowing out his brains, at Homburg, a watering place in Germany . . . Mr Dewes, it will be remembered, was a defaulter to the Government and fled from the Colony about eight months ago to avoid a criminal prosecution.'[20]

The troubled Dr Alfred Carr, whose loyalty to the cause of the digger was never sure, also came to an unhappy end. Upon his return to England for a holiday in March 1855, Dr Carr was devastated to have it reported in *The Liverpool Times* that he was 'one of the Ballarat rioters who had turned approver, and so escaped the just punishment that was due to him'.[21] At Dr Carr's highly anguished insistence, the editor published an unqualified apology, but was subsequently sued for libel anyway.

In 1857, by which time Dr Carr had returned to Australia, he had become so mentally ill that he was placed in the Yarra Bend Lunatic Asylum, where his condition deteriorated to the point that he was described as the most dangerous man there. He was eventually confined to a small cell in a straitjacket before being transferred to the infamous Ararat Asylum where – in that curious cosmic quirk that sometimes keeps the most deeply unhappy alive for the longest time, while taking the happiest at a young age – he stayed for many decades until he at last mercifully died on 26 June 1894, aged 78.

In Bendigo, on 24 July 1858, John Joseph, the black American who had been the first to be put on trial for treason after Eureka, aged just 41, suddenly succumbed to a heart condition and is now buried in an unmarked grave in White Hills Cemetery. (This is not right, in my view. The final resting place of such a significant man in Australian history should at least be honoured with a tombstone or plaque. The Embassy of the United States, in Canberra, is looking to rectify that.)

After his acquittal, the one-time Chairman of the Ballarat Reform League, Timothy Hayes, returned to his family in Ballarat and soon took up a post as town inspector of Ballarat East, overseeing new constructions and the like, before becoming a special constable

– with the role of helping to maintain the peace! And yet, restless and unhappy, he decided that perhaps the Americas might be a better place for him and departed, sadly without his wife, Anastasia, or their children. After working in Chile and Brazil, Hayes drifted north to San Francisco, where he settled for a time, working as a military engineer, helping to construct military field works. He drifted back to Melbourne in 1866, where he remained, still separated from his family. He died on 31 August 1873.

Anastasia continued to raise their children alone, working and living in Ballarat as a schoolteacher, right to the end. She died in her home, alone, on 6 April 1892, at the age of 74. (I weep!)

Henry Seekamp's time in prison did nothing to curb his volatile ways. When the great Irish-born dancer and courtesan Lola Montez visited Ballarat in February 1856, he took an extremely dim view of her dancing, which he thought crossed the border from exotic to erotic, and penned his vitriolic views for *The Ballarat Times*. Lola Montez took an even dimmer view of these views being so publicly expressed and, after lying in wait for him, famously took to him with a horsewhip in the main street. Seekamp whipped her back and the result was a sensational public scandal, with the two accusing each other in the courts of assault and libel.

The cases were dismissed, though Seekamp lost in the court of public opinion. In October of that same year, he and his wife, Clara, sold their paper and moved north to Sydney, before going further afield to Queensland. It was there, at the Drummond diggings, Clermont, on 19 January 1864, that Henry Seekamp – still only 35 years old – died of 'natural causes accelerated by intemperance'.[22]

Clara, though ten years his senior, lived another 44 years and died in Melbourne on 22 January 1908, at the age of 87.

And Raffaello Carboni?

The Eureka Stockade was but one fascinating episode in his supremely peripatetic life. After penning a colourful book on the whole episode, which he released on the first anniversary of the attack, Carboni left Australia just six weeks later, on 18 January 1856 – his ticket purchased with some gold he had mercifully found at Ballarat – as the only passenger on *Empress Eugenie*. (This, of course, was the ship that had brought the second division of the 12th Regiment to Melbourne in November 1854.) After spending time in India and the Middle East, including such holy places as Jerusalem and Bethlehem, he returned to Italy in time to again fight for Garibaldi in his campaign for the unification of Italy. Thereafter, Carboni settled in Naples and continued writing everything from plays to libretti – though none of them ever made it to the stage. His most appreciated writings were to his friend, Peter Lalor, in faraway Melbourne.

He died at the age of 58 in Rome on 24 October 1875, with his death certificate recording him as 'unmarried' and a 'man of letters.'[23]

On Monday, 28 January 1974, Gough Whitlam's equally flamboyant Immigration Minister, Al Grassby, visited Carboni's hometown of Urbino to honour him and unveil a plaque on the house where he was born. Minister Grassby noted his visit and the plaque were 'a tribute from the Australian Government and people', while describing him as a 'leader of the rebel forces which fought at the Eureka Stockade in a battle described as the birth of Australian democracy'.[24]

Fare thee well, Raffaello. You were a beaut.

And what of the 'long-legged' Vern?

After having escaped Ballarat dressed as a woman, the Hanoverian emerged from hiding at much the same time as Peter

Lalor and returned to mining. He again came to public notice when, as recorded by E. B. Withers, in 1856 he was put on trial in Ballarat for 'rioting at Black Lead on the 7th April',[25] a charge which, once proved, saw him sentenced to three months in the lockup.

In fact, this riot had nothing to with anything that had occurred on the Eureka in 1854, as it was a fight between diggers over who had the right to which claims, rather than a fight against the authorities. Little more is known of Vern's fate after this episode, apart from having his offer of service to the Burke and Wills expedition of 1860–61 turned down, and the fact that he was reported to have lived in the New South Wales town of Forbes in later years.

After being found 'not guilty' at his trial, the Irish firebrand and writer John Manning moved to New Zealand, where, after working as a journalist, he co-founded the *New Zealand Celt* in October 1867, supporting the Fenians and Irish nationalism. After writing supportively in 1868 of the attempted assassination in Sydney of Queen Victoria's son, Prince Alfred, he was arrested and charged with – goodness, can that be the time again? – seditious libel. After a stern warning by the judge, he was released and moved to the United States, where he continued writing, mostly stories with Australian and Maori themes. His last recorded writings are as late as 1892, but it is not known when he died.

Despite Sir Charles Hotham's quiet word that he should leave the colony, Lalor's American second-in-command at the Stockade, James McGill, had declined – hiding out instead at the Quarantine Station on the shores of Port Phillip Bay until the amnesty had been declared, whereupon he returned to mining. Yet the controversy concerning Eureka never quite left him, with allegations that he had been missing in action when the shooting started. Vern even went so far as to slanderously suggest that McGill had been bribed £800 by the government to abandon the diggers. In my view, this is demonstrably untrue as Lalor had been in complete agreement with McGill that he and his men position themselves at Warrenheip to intercept the Redcoats coming from Melbourne. It would later be McGill's widow's curious claim that her husband had left the Stockade on the specific instruction of the US Consul, James Tarleton, though this also seems highly unlikely.

For a time, McGill prospered in his second stint at mining, though – perhaps unable to shake off the allegations of desertion – he eventually descended into alcoholism and finally died destitute in Melbourne in 1883, not long after his 50th birthday. He is buried in an unmarked grave in Melbourne General Cemetery.

As to Tarleton, the US Consul who had been the key representative of the American Government during Eureka, he came to an equally sad, strange end. As reported in *The Washington Post* on 24 December 1880, after staying on as Consul in Melbourne until near the end of James Buchanan's administration, he returned to the United States and soon thereafter fell on hard times. Such hard times, in fact, that on the eve of Christmas Eve, 1880, the 72-year-old was found in the streets of Washington DC and died just hours later.

The editor and proprietor of *The Diggers' Advocate and Commercial Advertiser*, George Black, made good his escape after the battle of the Eureka Stockade, and only re-emerged after the announcement of the amnesty. He then twice stood for parliament against John Basson Humffray, and failed both times. What he did after this is something of a mystery beyond a partial return to mining, for it is known that with another brother, William, he was the owner of the Homeward Bound Quartz Crushing Company in Ballarat, where their third brother, Alfred, Lalor's 'Secretary of War' and the author of the long-winded Declaration of Independence – was killed in a mining accident on 25 June 1859. The next time that George Black showed up on the public record was when he died in Kew, Victoria, in May 1879, aged 62.

For all his fine oratory, Tom Kennedy – who never licked any lugs at Eureka – did not go on to particularly great things. He drove a bullock team for a time after the battle and died in Ballarat on 7 March 1859 at the age of just 32. He is buried in the old Ballarat Cemetery, though his grave is unmarked.

Father Smyth left Ballarat in October 1856 after being transferred to St Mary's Catholic Church in Castlemaine. Sadly, he too, was destined to die too young, just like many of the diggers he had tried to save at Eureka. After falling ill with tuberculosis, he died on 14 October 1865 at the age of just 41.

As to the finder of gold in Victoria, James Esmond stayed in mining and, typical of that generation, made and lost several fortunes – sadly with the latter finally prevailing. Near the end of his life, in the latter part of the 1880s, he was so impoverished that the people of Ballarat raised a public subscription for him, which was £150 to the good when he died of a kidney disease on 3 December 1890. There were few mourners at the 68-year-old's funeral, though at least his widow and nine children were there.

And then there are Esmond's contemporary great discoverers, Edward Hargraves, James Tom and the Lister brothers in New South Wales.

The dispute between them concerning who was the first discoverer of 'payable gold' in Australia would go on for decades, through courts, parliamentary inquiries and the popular press – very nearly until the turn of the century. Hargraves remained steadfast in his denial that *he* had ever considered *them* as his partners – they were no more than his guides, pure and simple. And he was still the one who had chosen the spot to search for gold.

While Tom and the Listers were given an initial £1000 by the government in 1853 in recognition of their input, they remained profoundly dissatisfied. They published their own account of what had happened in 1871, entitled *History of the Discovery of the first Pay-able Gold-field (Ophir)*. Hargraves did not emerge well from it, being described as one well habituated to having 'played the part of deception',[26] as well as one who had recorded 'extraordinary failures'[27] until such times as Tom and the Listers had told him where the gold was to be found. Still nothing changed in the official stance and the frustration of the younger men continued for another two decades.

Finally, however, in 1890, a committee of the New South Wales Parliament conducted an inquiry as to whom the credit properly belonged. Alas, on the very day he was due to give evidence, 17 September 1890, John Lister died. Nevertheless, at the conclusion of the process, the parliament found that Lister and Tom's April 1851 discovery of four ounces was indeed the first discovery of 'payable gold' in New South Wales, and they deserved better reward.

Hargraves's own feelings were firm: 'Now as to the "honour of the discovery," I have always thought it of trifling importance, as any person of ordinary observation might have done the same as myself; but the impudent pretensions put forward by persons for the purpose of gain, only on a mere speculation, is to be deplored. I look upon it as a disgrace to the country to have rewarded such charlatans in any way.'

The strangest thing? It was only a week after Hargraves died at the age of 75 on 29 October 1891 – leaving an estate worth around £375 to be divided between his two sons and three daughters – that an assembly of the New South Wales Parliament rejected the findings of the committee, which left the late Edward Hargraves *still* acknowledged as founding finder of payable gold in New South Wales. The epitaph on Hargraves's tombstone in Waverley Cemetery was firm in its own conclusions:

EDWARD HAMMOND HARGRAVES
BORN ENG. 7/10/1816
DIED 29/10/1891
THE ORIGINAL DIGGER WHOSE
GOLD DISCOVERY STARTED THE
GREAT AUSTRALIAN GOLD RUSH IN 1851

Nevertheless, there was a last word etched on the matter, and it was unveiled 72 years after the discovery of payable gold when, on 28 December 1923, no fewer than 300 people journeyed down '15 miles of the roughest road in the Orange district' to witness the unveiling of a commemorative obelisk at Ophir, on which the inscription read:

THIS OBELISK WAS ERECTED BY THE NEW SOUTH WALES
GOVERNMENT TO COMMEMORATE THE FIRST DISCOVERY IN
AUSTRALIA OF PAYABLE GOLD, WHICH WAS FOUND IN THE CREEK
IN FRONT OF THIS MONUMENT. THOSE RESPONSIBLE FOR THE
DISCOVERY WERE
EDWARD HAMMOND HARGRAVES
JOHN HARDMAN AUSTRALIA LISTER
JAMES TOM
WILLIAM TOM
FROM EXPERIENCE GAINED IN CALIFORNIA, HARGRAVES FORMED
THE IDEA THAT THE DISTRICT WAS AURIFEROUS AND HE FOUND

THE FIRST GOLD ON 12TH FEBRUARY, 1851, ABOUT TWO MILES UP LEWIS PONDS CREEK. HE EXPLAINED TO THE OTHERS HOW TO PROSPECT AND MAKE USE OF A MINER'S CRADLE, AND LISTER AND W. TOM FOUND PAYABLE GOLD BETWEEN 7TH AND 12TH APRIL, 1851.[28]

And let that be an end to it! (But if you go looking for it, get to the Ophir camping ground, cross the creek, walk 50 metres to the north, go up the stairs and you will see it there. Take some metho – the plaque needs a scrub.)

Sir Robert Nickle did not long survive his strenuous exertions at Ballarat. After falling ill in early 1855, Sir Robert applied for leave to return to his homeland, but he did not even get close. On 26 May of that year, at his home of *Upper Jolimont House* – one of the houses first brought to Victoria by Charles La Trobe – the old soldier died. He is buried at Melbourne General Cemetery.

Captain John Wellesley Thomas, who was promoted to Major shortly after the battle of the Eureka, went on to a glittering military career, in which his performance at Eureka was just one of many jewels. He served in North China in 1860 with the 67th Regiment of Foot and was both mentioned in dispatches and wounded while in command of a half-battalion attacking the North Taku Forts. Recovering, two years later he was promoted to Colonel and commanded the 67th Regiment and a brigade at the second capture of Khading during the Taiping Rebellion in China, which proved to be his last active service. Promoted to Major-General in 1877, he retired in 1881 with the honorary rank of Lieutenant-General. In 1882 he was appointed to the colonelcy of the Hampshire Regiment, and in 1904 was made a Knight Commander. He lived until the age of 85,

dying in February 1908. He never had a family and left no widow
to grieve.

After the seat on the Legislative Council of Captain Thomas's
second-in-command, Charles Pasley, was withdrawn in 1855 (with
the introduction of the *Victorian Constitution Act*, the old Legislative
Council was replaced with the new Legislative Council and an
elected Legislative Assembly), he decided that he would stand himself, winning the seat of South Bourke in 1856 in the Legislative
Assembly, thus taking his place in the same chamber as Peter Lalor
and John Basson Humffray! William Stawell was briefly there at the
same time, as one of the members for Melbourne, and he was the
Attorney-General of the first elected ministry before taking up his
post as Chief Justice when Sir William à Beckett retired.

Pasley's time in politics was only short-lived, however, as he
resigned in March 1857 and soon returned to his military career,
serving first in the Maori War in New Zealand in 1860, where
he was wounded. After convalescing in England, he returned to
Melbourne, where he served in a vast array of civil and military posts
that required his engineering expertise. He finally returned to Great
Britain in 1880 as Victoria's Agent-General, where he was appointed
a civil C.B. – the Order of the Bath Companions Decoration –
shortly before being promoted to Major-General. He died, aged 66,
on 11 November 1890 at his home in Chiswick, survived by his wife,
who was also his cousin. They had no children.

Two more players in the saga of Eureka who made their way into
that first Victorian Legislative Assembly in 1856 were the notable
barristers for the defence in the John Joseph case, Henry Samuel
Chapman and Butler Cole Aspinall. (With such a cast of characters in the Victorian Parliament who had first laid eyes on each

other across the rampart, or from the prisoner's dock, one can only imagine what crossways looks were exchanged as they passed in the corridors.)

As to Aspinall, he rose to the position of Solicitor-General in John MacPherson's ministry by 1870. He was very much the man about town and said to be the most coveted dinner guest in Melbourne, revered for his wit, intellect, aristocratic looks and – in some quarters – his ability to burn the candle at both ends. Alas, it was not only the candle that was burnt and, after suffering a complete mental breakdown in 1871, he had to resign all his posts before returning to England, where he died on 4 April 1875.

Judge Redmond Barry, who presided over the latter Eureka trials, went on to ever great respect as one of Victoria's most prominent judicial figures, though there was great surprise after Sir William à Beckett retired as Chief Justice of Victoria in 1857 that Barry did not succeed him. Instead, the post went to none other than William Stawell. Barry felt that this was because of political manoeuvres by Stawell, and their friendship never recovered.

Nevertheless, in 1860 Barry was knighted and was even more highly honoured with a Knight Commander of St Michael and St George in 1877, awarded to those regarded as having rendered extraordinary or important non-military service in a foreign country. His most famous trial involved the sentencing of Australia's most notorious bushranger, Ned Kelly, to death for the murder of three Victorian police constables, uttering the traditional words on such occasions, 'May God have mercy on your soul.'[29]

Kelly calmly replied, 'I will go a little further than that, and say I will see you there when I go.'[30]

As it happened, just twelve days after Kelly was hanged at the Old Melbourne Gaol on 11 November 1880, Sir Redmond Barry, at the age of 67, suddenly died, reportedly from congestion of the lungs. He was buried in Melbourne General Cemetery, where the chief mourner was the mother of his children, Mrs Louisa Barrow, the woman he never married but who was nevertheless buried beside him when she died in 1888.

A small example of the internecine relationships that bound many of the key protagonists of the events of the Eureka Stockade for decades afterwards was the fact that just as none other than Arthur Akehurst – the one-time Clerk of the Peace accused but not convicted of killing Henry Powell – had been the magistrate who had first fined Ned Kelly's mother, Ellen, with affray, so too was the foreman of the jury that convicted Ned Kelly the former auctioneer on the Eureka, Samuel Lazarus. The Melbourne Sheriff who presided over the hanging of the bushranger was Robert Rede himself.

After the Royal Commission into the Eureka massacre barely criticised Rede at all, his life in the public service continued. Recalled from Ballarat early in 1855, he had a year off on full pay before Lieutenant-Governor Hotham arranged for him to become Deputy Sheriff of Geelong and Commandant of the Volunteer Rifles. By 1857 he had become Geelong's sheriff, a post he retained for the next decade before returning to Ballarat, where he occupied the same post – becoming one of the foundation members of that worthy retreat for the distinguished gentlemen of the town, the Ballarat Club – and then had another decade as Sheriff of Melbourne, starting in 1877.

Rede finally retired from all positions in 1889, and when he died of pneumonia at the age of 87 in Melbourne on 13 July 1904 and was buried in St Kilda Cemetery, it was as a highly respected member of the community.

Though William Stawell had no involvement in the Kelly case, he did remain as Chief Justice of Victoria until 1886 and was equally a highly esteemed figure in both the legal and wider community. After having been knighted in 1857, he was even more highly honoured upon retirement from the law in 1886 – at which point he became Lieutenant-Governor of Victoria – when Queen Victoria also recognised his service with a Knight Commander of St Michael and St George. Stawell died aged 73 in Naples, in the land of Raffaello Carboni, on 12 March 1889. He was survived by his wife, Mary, and their only offspring, Dr Richard Stawell.

After resigning his post as Gold Commissioner at Eureka, Gilbert Amos first moved to Van Diemen's Land, where he married Isabella MacLachlan, before coming back to Victoria to become the Warden of Creswick in 1858. Alas, after the couple returned to England in 1862, they were both subsequently drowned in 1866, along with 218 others, when the steamship *London* was shipwrecked in the Bay of Biscay on its way from Gravesend to Melbourne.

John Pascoe Fawkner stayed in parliament as member for Central Province LC, until his death as the grand old man of the colony on 4 September 1869, aged 77. No fewer than 15,000 people paid their respects at his funeral, and his cortege boasted over 200 carriages. He, too, is buried at Melbourne General Cemetery.

While Charles La Trobe continued to grieve for the loss of his wife, Sophie, some balm was provided by the fact that just a couple of years later he proposed to her sister, Rose Isabelle de Meuron. As it was illegal under civil law and forbidden by the church to marry your deceased wife's sister in England, they were married in Switzerland on 3 October 1855 and were delighted to have two daughters of their own in quick succession. The two lived out the rest of their days in Switzerland, as La Trobe would never work for the British Government again, after what the authorities judged as his less-than-satisfactory performance in Victoria. No matter, he is unlikely to have missed it. Charles La Trobe died in 1875, aged 74. There are many institutions in Victoria that bear his name, most particularly the prestigious La Trobe University.

The second-last man left standing is the young lad, Barnard Welch, who gave such devastating testimony against Bentley and his associates. He lived until the ripe old age of 90, and a newspaper cutting from 1933 reveals that at the time he was living happily in Western Australia in a 'little, old-fashioned weatherboard cottage, opposite West Subiaco Railway Station'.[31] He died 8 May 1934.

Just six days later, and only a short distance away, William Edward Atherden of Western Australia – likely the youngest of those arrested in the Stockade – died, at the age of 96. He had returned to gold-mining and enjoyed great success a short time later, taking a small fortune to England in 1856 before returning to Perth shortly afterwards. He is buried in Karrakatta Cemetery.

The Eureka flag that was dragged down from the flagpole on that terrible December morn of 1854 had an interesting fate. For many years it remained in the possession of the family of the trooper who first claimed it, John King, until after his death, when his wife presented it to the Ballarat Art Gallery on permanent loan. There it remained, still on loan, right up until 2002 when the King descendants very kindly ceded ownership to the gallery. When I first gazed upon it, encased at that gallery, I was stunned, firstly, by its size. Secondly, though, I was gnawed by the sense that, instead of looking at it alone while sipping on a cup of tea, I should have been being jostled by a crowd of dozens of my fellow Australians, with two security guards staring at me sternly for bringing tea within 100 metres of it, even if it is behind glass.

The Aboriginal people of Victoria, of course, never recovered their traditional ownership of the land.

In Tim Flannery's book *The Birth of Melbourne*, their haunting fate is recorded by one of the Aboriginal men, Derrimut – the one-time headman of the Boonwurrung people – who had saved the infant settlement from massacre in October 1835 by warning of 'up-country tribes':

> *'You see, Mr Hull,' he told a magistrate he met on the street some years later, 'Bank of Victoria, all this mine, all along here Derrimut's once; no matter now, me tumble down soon.'*
>
> *Hull asked if Derrimut had any children, at which the enraged Aborigine replied, 'Why me have lubra? Why me have piccaninny? You have all this place, no good have children, no good have lubra, me tumble down and die very soon now.' A fragment of Derrimut's vast tribal estate was at last regained by him when, in 1864, he was buried in the Melbourne General Cemetery. The generosity of the settlers even extended to a headstone.*[32]

There was, however, one small bit of justice well over a century later that bears recounting. The first recognition of Aboriginal land rights came in 1975, when the Australian Prime Minister, Gough Whitlam, flew to Daguragu (Wattle Creek) in the Northern Territory to meet the Aboriginal elder of the Gurindji people, Vincent Lingiari. On the way there, Mr Whitlam told me in 1993 when I was conducting an interview for *The Sydney Morning Herald*, he was told by Cabinet Minister 'Nugget' Coombs the story of John Batman having the Aboriginal elders place the soil in his hands to indicate that the land now belonga'd a'him.

Inspiration struck, as it so often did with Gough Whitlam. Upon formally advising Vincent Lingiari that the government recognised his land claim, the two kneeled down on the red dirt and, as the cameras rolled and clicked, the Prime Minister picked up some handfuls of soil and placed it in Vincent Lingiari's hands.

Now the government recognised that the land had belonged to him and his people all along.

How would Eureka be remembered in the short to medium term? Well, we have it on the authority of E.B. Withers that on the second anniversary of the battle, a small procession made its way through Ballarat to the site where the Stockade once stood, with a total of 200 people gathering.

Here, one of Lalor's captains, John Lynch, stood on a tree stump and made a speech, beginning, 'Sensible of the debt of gratitude we owe to the memories of the brave men who fell victims on the fatal 3rd December, 1854, in their efforts to resist the oppression and tyranny of the then existing Government, we meet here to-day, the second anniversary of that disastrous day, in solemn procession, to pay to their names the only tribute in our power, the celebrating with due solemnity the sad commemoration of their martyrdom.'[33]

At the conclusion of the speech, a march of 300 people was made to the cemetery, led by James Esmond, with Henry Seekamp in tight behind.

Reported *The Ballarat Star*, as recorded in the pages of Withers,

'Arrived at the cemetery, the procession walked round the spot where the bodies of the men who fell on the fatal Sunday morning are interred, and, returning to the monument erected to their memory, the apex of the monument was crowned with the garlands borne in procession.'[34]

On the 50th anniversary of the attack, in 1904, a much larger crowd assembled in the rough area where the Stockade had stood – the precise area had been lost to the passage of the buffeting years – and there, again, was John Lynch, this time a far more withered form, though still proud, as he leaned upon the arm of his son, the even prouder Captain Lynch of the 3rd Battalion, Victoria Rifles. As he does so, 'The crowd stood back to allow him to pass and many of the older men doffed their hats.'[35]

That 50th anniversary saw the last great gathering of those who had fought from inside the Stockade, and the photo of the 60 or so men and women who came is an Australian classic. Old now, but almost to a man they have huge beards, bushy hair, and very, very, proud looks. They had been *there*, they had *fought*, they had stood against the Redcoats and never flinched!

———————

As to the overall significance of the battle, beyond the effect on the lives of those who were actually intimately involved, that is, of course, much more problematic – and the subject of endless debate.

The first and most obvious phenomenon is that many of the specific reforms sought by the Ballarat Reform League were ushered in around Australia over the next few years. Eureka happened too late in the piece to directly affect the different constitutions of the colonies but, against that, as eminent historian Geoffrey Blainey has noted, 'the first Parliament that met under Victoria's new Constitution was alert to the democratic spirit of the goldfields, and passed laws enabling each adult man in Victoria to vote at elections, to vote by secret ballot and to stand for the Legislative Assembly'.[36]

By 1857, in Victoria, a universal male franchise was in place, whereby all British, male citizens of sound mind and record, 21 years of age or over, could vote for the Legislative Assembly, regardless of their income or property, so long as they could read and write. And they could do so by secret ballot! (For the moment, the Legislative Council kept its severely restricted franchise, requiring that Council members have property worth £5000, while the property qualification for its electors was £1000.)

And, yes, those who seek to downplay the significance of Eureka do note that South Australia preceded these reforms in Victoria by a year, though as South Australia never had convicts and has always been a haven for liberal, social and political ideals, theirs was a far smaller step to take and a far less influential example to set.

It remained the reforms in the far more populous, powerful and turbulent Victoria that stood as the benchmark, demonstrating how democracy could soothe the savage breast of even the most passionate insurgent. New South Wales, acknowledging the mass democratic tides, followed suit in 1858 with its own reforms, with the other states also falling into line over the course of the next four decades.

The bottom line was that after all the struggles throughout Europe for the democratisation of the political process had been quashed in the two decades leading up to 1848, in Australia, in the three years after the Eureka Stockade, the better part of those struggles were won in Victoria at least. As a result of the political reforms ushered in by Eureka, Australia became nothing less than one of the key 'lights on the hill' for democratic movements around the world, most particularly when it came to secret ballots, known as the 'Australian ballot', with Tasmania, followed by Victoria and South Australia, introducing the world's first such ballot for an election in 1856. The country would remain at the forefront of those reforms for decades to come. By 1859, a law was passed in Victoria requiring there to be elections every three years, and in 1870 the last of the major Chartist demands was realised in Victoria with the *Payment of Members Act*, which saw a salary for members of both Houses for the first time, allowing poor men to be in positions of power, at least in the Legislative Assembly. Allowing women to both vote and sit in parliament would take another three decades, but, again, Australia was near the front of the movement, along with New Zealand.

Staggeringly, it would not be until 1918 that Great Britain would grant even the male suffrage that the two principal Australian colonies had been enjoying for the last six decades.

And yet, equal to the landmark political reforms won at Eureka was the emotional effect of the conflict on the people at large. That really did change Australia forever. Noted Eureka author John Molony, in his paper for the Federal Parliament on the occasion of Eureka's 150th anniversary in 2004, put it singularly well.

'Democracy,' he said, 'is much more than a system. It is an ideal and a spirit born day by day in those who believe in it. Eureka had its brief and bloody day 150 years ago. Eureka lives on in the heart and will of every Australian who understands, believes in and acts on the principle that the people are "the only legitimate source of all political power".'[37]

Such a principle had, of course, been first enunciated by the moral-force Chartists in Great Britain in the early 1830s, affirmed by the Ballarat Reform League in 1854 and even asserted by Charles Hotham shortly after arriving in Victoria that same year. But the battle of the Eureka Stockade aptly demonstrated the truth of it, and thereafter the example was before all the governments of all the colonies on the continent that the common people had political *rights* – and they were more than prepared to fight for them. Any denial of those rights could lead to dreadful consequences. The battle in Australia between the English elite who felt themselves born to rule in this new land and the muddied mass who felt that not only was Jack as good as his master but wanted a say in who that master *was* – and maybe even *be* that master himself – Eureka was a definitive victory for the mass and weakened the ability of the elite to resist change.

The degree to which Eureka has been celebrated for this in the time since has varied.

The shearers at Barcaldine, for example, flew the Southern Cross in 1891 as a symbol of their preparedness to – as the revered oath went – 'stand truly by each other and fight to defend our rights and liberties',[38] as both unionism and the Labor Party were formed. And on the 100th anniversary in 1954, there was a three-day festival at Ballarat, with no fewer than 70,000 attending, climaxing in a re-enactment of the event where the people jeered as the 'Redcoats' and 'Police' attacked – and it all became so heated that it had to be broken up.

It was all a lot quieter on the 150th anniversary, however, as 700 people gathered around a small lake down from the Eureka Centre – built on the site of the old Stockade – at dawn of 3 December 2004. Many were unionists with their modern trade union flags, chanting, 'A union, united, will never be defeated!'

Meanwhile, however, on this same day the Prime Minister, John Howard, declined to allow the Southern Cross to fly above Parliament House – despite the fact that it flew above every state and territory parliament and myriad town halls around the country – and did not attend any commemorative events himself.

'Ah, it's, part of the Australian story,' he carefully allowed to the ABC on the day, 'not quite the big part that some people give it, but equally a significant part.' For all that, not a single member of Mr Howard's Cabinet attended the 150th anniversary at Ballarat, and it is the claim of then Opposition Leader Mark Latham that the PM had even *banned* them from attending – though, to be fair, parliament was sitting at the time.

Nevertheless, Labor Senator Gavin Marshall criticised the Prime Minister individually, and the Coalition generally, for their overall attitude.

'Howard is an arch monarchist,' he told the *Sun-Herald*, 'and clearly they are running from what the Eureka flag represents; independence and people determined to fight for their rights.'[39] John Howard did release a short statement, noting that 'the events at Eureka 150 years ago were central to the development of Australia as an independent democratic country', but that was it. At the same time, however, the Victorian Premier Steve Bracks could find a great deal of inspiration when, in his own 150th anniversary address, he observed, 'I believe Eureka was a catalyst for the rapid evolution of democratic government in this country – and it remains a national symbol of the right of people to have a say in how they are governed. I am not saying there would be no democracy without Eureka. However, I doubt our democracy would have come as quickly – and I suspect our democracy would not be as egalitarian – without Eureka.'[40]

As Geoffrey Blainey noted in 1963, 'Eureka became a legend, a battlecry for nationalists, republicans, liberals, radicals, or communists, each creed finding in the rebellion the lessons they liked to see.'[41] The surprising thing, however, is that the Liberals specifically and the Conservative side of politics in general, at least in the modern era, has not embraced Eureka strongly – given that one could look at the whole uprising as a collection of small businessmen/entrepreneurs rising against iniquitous taxes and over-regulation that was stifling their creation of wealth. Right up the Libs' alley!

A devotee of the above view is the conservative columnist Gerard Henderson. In a *Sydney Morning Herald* column in 2004, he decried the lack of John Howard's involvement in the sesquicentenary, and finished, 'Let's hope that, by 2054, the federal Liberal leadership recognises that the battle for the Eureka legend requires more than a brief written message. After all, culture wars can be fun – and they are important.'[42] To be fair, even some senior Labor figures can downplay the significance of Eureka. Early in the course of my writing this book, one famous identity of the ALP – let's call him

Bob Carr – waved a dismissive hand, and said, "Eureka? Local tax revolt . . ."'

I passionately believe it was a lot more than that.

Personally, from the perspective of 2012, I think there is enormous inspiration to be found in Eureka for Australians of all political persuasions, pursuits and backgrounds.

Firstly, and most obviously, it is a great story of democracy, of a group of brave people fighting for, and *winning*, their democratic rights. Yes, it is right that we honour those men who fell at Gallipoli and elsewhere, but surely at least an equal debt is owed to those who died fighting for the 'liberties' we all enjoy today?

Obviously, those of us who believe that it is archaic that Australia should, in the 21st century, still be politically aligned with the British monarchy, even to the extent of having the British flag on our flag, can and do find great inspiration in Eureka, and I also agree with former ALP leader Mark Latham that it was one of the first great moments of multiculturalism in this country. (Notwithstanding the widespread mistreatment of Aborigines and Chinese in other parts of the goldfields.)

Let's hear from you, Raffaello Carboni, as you reflect on a gathering of native-born Australians, Irish, Swedes, Germans, black and white Americans, Canadians, Italians, French and Jamaicans, all acting as one for the greater good: 'We were of all nations and colours.'[43] The diggers had come together, 'irrespective of nationality, religion or colour to salute the Southern Cross as a refuge of all the oppressed from all countries on Earth'.[44]

Witness Peter Lalor, as he mounts the stump beneath the Southern Cross and focuses on the vast sea of his fellow rebels, not unified by a common race but by something else entirely: 'I looked around me. I saw brave and honest men, who had come thousands of miles to labour for independence. I knew that hundreds were in great poverty, who would possess wealth and happiness if allowed to cultivate the wilderness that surrounded us. The grievances under which we had long suffered, and the brutal attack of the day, flashed across my mind; and with the burning feelings of an injured man, I mounted the stump and proclaimed "Liberty".[45]

All put together, I entirely concur with the words written by Macgregor Duncan, Andrew Leigh, David Madden and Peter Tynan for their book *Imagining Australia: Ideas for Our Future*, which appeared in *The Sydney Morning Herald* for the 150th Anniversary of Eureka, in a piece entitled 'Time to reclaim this legend as our driving force'.

They wrote: 'Australia should re-elevate Eureka to its previous position as a central legend of Australian nationalism, standing for those distinctly Australian values – egalitarianism, mateship, fairness – together with democracy, freedom, republicanism and multiculturalism . . .

'Obviously, Australian nationalism can never be reduced to just one legend, but Eureka offers great potential to a nation floundering for a national story.'[46]

And their idea that I love most of all: 'Our rather limp citizenship oath could be revitalised with a fragment of the bold Eureka oath: "We swear by the Southern Cross to stand truly by each other and to defend our rights and liberties." And when we become a republic – as we surely some day must – what better flag to choose than the Eureka flag?'[47]

Say it loud. Say it proud. *Exactly!*

At the beginning of writing this book, as I mentioned in my introduction, I fancied that the image of the Eureka flag was too associated on the one hand with a certain right-wing, redneck, racist element – those who ludicrously brandish it as a symbol of white Australia – and on the other hand with the hard left of the trade union movement for it ever to be embraced by Australia as a whole.

But no more. Now that I *get* it, I understand that the Eureka story really is the great Australian story; that we can take enormous inspiration from what occurred and that the Eureka flag more truly represents what is great about Australia than our current flag, which states to the world that we are still Great Britain in the South Seas. (Cue Jerry Seinfeld on his visit here in 2000: 'I love your flag – Great Britain, at night!')

The reason I added *'the unfinished revolution'* to the title is because, though those who fought at Eureka accomplished a great deal for this country, the last part of the job that Lalor enunciated as his goal on the eve of the battle – 'Independence' – has *still* not occurred.

But it will come. And when it does so, I believe that the story of Peter Lalor and the valiant men and women of the Eureka Stockade will rightly take their place at the very forefront of Australian history.

They were good and brave people, fighting for a great cause, laying the very foundation stones on which modern Australia has been built.

I salute them. And their flag.

Our flag.

Notes and References

PROLOGUE

1. *The British Critic,* Volume I, No. 62, 1793, p. 80.
2. Rusden, p. 159.
3. Ibid.
4. Whitaker, p. 97.
5. McBrien, p. 60.
6. Horne, Donald, p. 35.
7. Batman, p. 29, SLV, MS13181.
8. Ibid., p. 31.
9. Ibid., pp. 33–5.
10. Ibid., pp. 36–9.
11. Author's note: This was the Saltwater River, now known as the Maribyrnong River.
12. Batman, John, p. 53, SLV, MS13181.
13. Van Toorn, p. 82.
14. Batman, p. 62, SLV, MS13181.
15. Ibid., pp. 63–4.
16. Ibid., p. 67.
17. Ibid., p. 70.
18. Shillinglaw, p. 111.
19. *The Courier*, 9 August 1851, p. 2.
20. Morgan, p. xiv. Author's note: There are alternative explanations for the origin of the expression.
21. John Batman to John Montagu, 30 November 1835, *Historical Records of Victoria*, p. 21.
22. Billot, *John Batman*, p. 105.
23. Billot, *Melbourne's Missing Chronicles*, p. 10.
24. Clark, p. 109.
25. Ibid.
26. Ibid.
27. MacDougall, p. 136.
28. Strange, pp. 6–8.
29. Withers, p. 8.

30. Toghill, p. 273, p. 280.
31. *Launceston Advertiser*, Thursday, 31 October 1839, p. 1S.
32. Strange, pp. 6–8.
33. *The Argus*, 1 October 1851, p. 2.
34. Cochrane, p. 93.
35. Marx, Engels, *Manifesto*, p. 5.
36. Marx, Engels, *Werke*, p. 21.
37. Lovett, *People's Charter*, p. 11.
38. Napier, p. 30.
39. Farwell, pp. 27–31.
40. Napier, p. 40.
41. *Lovett, Life and Struggles,* p. 252.
42. Section III, *An Act for the Better Security of the Crown and Government of the United Kingdom*, p. 127.
43. Hansard's, pp. 1175–76.
44. *The Irish Felon*, 24 June 1848, p. 65.
45. *The Irish Felon*, 1 July 1848, p. 85.
46. Ibid.
47. *The Irish Felon*, 24 June 1848, p. 57.
48. *The Irish Felon*, 22 July 1848, p. 111.
49. Ibid., p. 115.
50. O'Brien, p. 40.
51. *The Observer*, 16 October 1848, p. 6.
52. Mayer, p. 95.

CHAPTER ONE: FROM GOLDEN FLEECE TO GOLD ITSELF . . .

1. Withers, p. 18.
2. *The Sydney Morning Herald*, 23 December 1848, p. 3.
3. La Trobe letter from *Jolimont en Murs* to sister Charlotte, 2 March 1840. SLV, HS279.
4. McCrae, p. 236.
5. Ibid.
6. *The Melbourne Morning Herald*, 11 November 1850.
7. King, p. 7.
8. Davison, p. 52.
9. Hargraves, p. 114.
10. Ibid., p. 115.
11. Ibid., p. 116.

12. Ibid., p. 117.
13. Ibid., p. 140.
14. Ibid.
15. Davison, p. 469.
16. Hargraves, p. 116.
17. Davison, pp. 480–1.
18. Ibid., p. 470.
19. Ibid., p. 471.
20. King, p. 6.
21. Hargraves, pp. 119–20.
22. Author's note: The full title was Secretary of State for War and the Colonies. In 1854 the office was divided into Secretary of State for War and Secretary of State for the Colonies. For readability I have abbreviated this to Secretary of State throughout.
23. Tom, p. 4.
24. *The Sydney Morning Herald,* 2 May 1851, p. 3.
25. *Bathurst Free Press*, 10 May 1851, p. 5.
26. Ibid.
27. Ibid.
28. Ibid., p. 4.
29. Ibid.
30. Ibid.
31. *The Sydney Morning Herald*, 15 May 1851, p. 3.
32. Ibid.
33 Ibid., p. 2.
34. Ibid., p. 4.
35. Stutchbury to Colonial Secretary, 19 May 1851, Correspondence Relative to the Discovery of Gold in Australia, 3 February 1852, p. 2.
36. *Bathurst Free Press*, 28 May 1851, p. 3.
37. *Supplement to the NSW Government Gazette*, 22 May 1851, p. 831.
38. *The Sydney Morning Herald*, 24 May 1851, p. 5.
39. Mundy, p. 316.
40. Ibid.
41. *The Maitland Mercury*, 28 May 1851.
42. FitzRoy to Grey, 22 May 1851, Correspondence Relative to the Recent Discovery of Gold in Australia, 3 February 1852, p. 1.
43. Stutchbury to the Colonial Secretary, 25 May 1851, Correspondence Relative to the Recent Discovery of Gold in Australia, 3 February 1852, p. 21. *The Hobart Town Courier*, 14 June 1851, p. 3.

44. Stutchbury to the Colonial Secretary, 25 May 1851, Correspondence Relative to the Recent Discovery of Gold in Australia, 3 February 1852, p. 20.
45. *The Sydney Morning Herald*, 28 May 1851, p. 2.
46. *The Sydney Morning Herald*, 7 June 1851, p. 2.
47. Ibid.
48. *The Perth Gazette,* 22 August 1851.
49. Blainey, p. 20.

CHAPTER TWO: VICTORIA

1. Peach, p. 43.
2. *The Sydney Morning Herald*, 20 June 1851, p. 3.
3. Bonwick, p. 25.
4. *The Argus*, 11 June 1851, p. 4.
5. Ibid.
6. Ibid.
7. Ibid.
8. Ibid.
9. Ibid.
10. Ibid.
11. Ibid.
12. Ibid.
13. *The Argus*, 17 June 1851, p. 1.
14. *The Argus,* 8 July 1851, p. 2.
15. Author's note: While most accounts, including that of Manning Clark and the newspapers of the day, credit one Tommy Kerr with finding the nugget, I think this account more likely, as it originates from an eye witness who was there on the day, and was published in a book called *Australian Stories Retold* by W. H. Suttor, who was none other than the brother-in-law of Dr Kerr.
16. *The West Australian*, 13 August 1938, p. 3; Suttor, p. 36.
17. *Bathurst Free Press*, 19 July 1851, p. 2.
18. *Geelong Advertiser*, 7 July 1851. Author's note: Further investigation would show that there were many other contenders for being the first discoverer of gold in Victoria – including William Campbell, Louis John Michel and a Dr Bruhn – and there would even be later claims that Esmond himself had discovered gold many months earlier but had kept it secret so as to have it to himself. It is, however, broadly agreed that howsoever it might have happened,

Esmond was the first to discover gold that led to the establishment of a productive goldfield.

19. *The Argus*, 10 July 1851, p. 2.
20. Ibid.
21. *The Argus*, 1 July 1851, p. 4.
22. Ibid.
23. *The Sydney Morning Herald*, 18 July 1851, p. 2.
24. *Geelong Advertiser*, 25 July 1851.
25. Ibid.
26. *The Argus*, 22 July 1851, p. 2.
27. *The Sydney Morning Herald*, 23 July 1851, p. 2.
28. *The People's Advocate*, 9 August 1851, p. 8.
29. The *Southern Cross*, 19 August 1851, p. 2.
30. Ibid.
31. Ibid.
32. *The Argus*, 18 August 1851, p. 2.
33. La Trobe Despatch to Earl Grey, 25 August 1851, Correspondence Relative to the Discovery of Gold, 3 February 1852, p. 50.
34. *Supplement to the Victorian Government Gazette* (No. 6), 16 August 1851, p. 209; *The Sydney Morning Herald*, 25 August 1851, p. 3.
35. *The Victorian Government Gazette* (No. 8), 27 August 1851, p. 307.
36. *Geelong Advertiser*, 26 August 1851, p. 2.
37. Ibid.
38. Ibid.
39. Ibid.
40. Ibid.
41. Bate, p. 2.
42. Ibid., p. 9.
43. Stacpoole, p. 11.
44. Ibid.
45. *The Argus*, 27 August 1851, p. 2.
46. Author's note: The going rate for gold at this time was around 65 shillings for an ounce in the city, and around 60 shillings an ounce if sold at the goldfields.
47. *The Argus*, 27 August 1851, p. 2.
48. *The Argus*, 30 August 1851, p. 2.
49. Ibid.
50. Gold, p. 10.
51. Withers, p. 31.
52. *Bathurst Free Press*, 20 September 1851, p. 7.

53. Scott, p. 253.

CHAPTER THREE: THE GOLDEN GLOBE

1. Sharkey, p. 282.
2. Earp, *The Gold Colonies of Australia*, p. 2.
3. *The Times*, 2 September 1851, p. 4.
4. *The Argus*, 8 September 1851, p. 2.
5. *Geelong Advertiser*, 9 September 1851.
6. Ibid.
7. Bates, p. 8.
8. Hall, p. 10.
9. *The Argus*, 24 September, p. 2; Sutherland, *Tales of the Goldfields*, p. 44.
10. Sutherland, p. 44.
11. Gold, p. 13.
12. *Geelong Advertiser*, 26 September 1851.
13. *The Argus*, 25 September 1851, p. 2.
14. Clacy, p. 205.
15. Mayer, p. 104.
16. *The Argus*, 25 September 1851, p. 2.
17. *The Argus*, 8 November 1851, p. 2.
18. *The Argus*, 19 September 1851, p. 2.
19. Westgarth, p. 135.
20. Ibid.
21. Withers, p. 31.
22. *Launceston Examiner*, 11 October 1851, p. 3; *The Argus,* 13 October 1851, p. 2.
23. La Trobe to Earl Grey, 10 October 1851, 'Further Papers Relative to the Recent Discovery of Gold in Australia', 14 June 1852, p. 45.
24. La Trobe to Earl Grey, 3 December 1851, 'Further Papers Relative to the Recent Discovery of Gold in Australia', 14 June 1852, p. 51.
25. Flannery, p.171.
26. Cochrane, p. 93.
27. La Trobe to Earl Grey, 3 December 1851, 'Further Papers Relative to the Recent Discovery of Gold in Australia', 14 June 1852, p. 52.
28. Goodman, p. 42.
29. Elliott, Walter Woodbury to Ellen Woodbury, 20 June 1853, letter no. 6, p. 1.
30. Thomas Pierson Diary, 26 August 1853, SLV, MS 11646, Box

2178/4, p. 154.

31. Withers, p. 55.
32. Ibid.
33. Clacy, p. 56.
34. Ibid., p. 259.
35. *The Argus*, 10 November 1851.
36. Ibid., p. 2.
37. Ibid.
38. *The Argus*, 10 November 1851, p. 2.
39. Ibid.
40. Ibid.
41. *The Illustrated London News,* 22 November 1851, p. 620.
42. Craig, p. 1.
43. *The Argus*, 14 July 1904, p. 5.
44. *The Argus*, 29 November 1851, p. 3.
45. Sturt to Colonial Secretary, 15 December 1851, VPRS 1189, 51/1396, Box 8.
46. Shaw, p. 15.
47. La Trobe to Lord Grey, 3 December 1851, 'Further Papers Relative to the Recent Discovery of Gold in Australia', 14 June 1852, p. 53.
48. *The Argus,* 12 December 1851, p. 2.
49. La Trobe to Earl Grey, 3 December 1851, 'Further Papers Relative to the Recent Discovery of Gold in Australia', 14 June 1852, p. 52.
50. Howitt, p. 166.
51. *Victoria Government Gazette* (No. 22), 3 December 1851, p. 825.
52. *The Argus*, 12 December 1851, p. 2
53. *The Argus*, 10 December 1851, p. 2.
54. Bate, p.26.
55. *The Argus*, 18 December 1851, p. 2.
56. Ibid.
57. Ibid.
58. Ibid.
59. Ibid.
60. *Victoria Government Gazette* (No. 24), 17 December 1851, p. 864.

CHAPTER FOUR: EXODUS

1. W. Forlonge to C. Barnes, 30 December 1851, pp. 3–4, SLV, MS Box 111/5.
2. Blake, p. 12.

3. Dickens, *Household Words*, pp. 405–6.

4. Dickens, *David Copperfield*, pp. 814–15.

5. Capper, p. 6.

6. Ibid.

7. Ibid., p. 62.

8. Earp, p. 9.

9. Sidney, p.11.

10. MacFarlane, p. 74.

11. *Geelong Advertiser*, 10 September 1852, p. 2.

12. Gold, *Eureka*, p. 25.

13. *The Times*, 17 June 1852, p. 7.

14. Hugill, pp. 524–25.

15. La Trobe to Earl Grey, 8 July 1852, 'Further Papers Relative to the Recent Discovery of Gold in Australia', 28 February 1853, p. 210.

16. William Peters to the Earl of Malmesbury, 30 August 1852, Enclosed in: 'Pakington to La Trobe, Despatch from Downing Street', 30 September 1852, SLV, MS 7662, Box 74/3, no. 501.

17. Ibid.

18. Craig, p. 248.

19. *Otago Witness*, (*Sydney Bulletin*), 'In the Early Days', 9 Poutūterangi 1904, p. 65.

20. Craig, p. 250.

21. Craig, p. 250.

22. Ibid., p. 251.

23. Serle, p. 103.

24. *The Argus*, 28 October 1852, p. 3.

25. Craig, p. 4.

26. Ibid., p. 5.

27. Ibid., p. 6.

28. Ibid., pp. 7–8.

29. Ibid., p. 8.

30. Hill, p. 153.

31. Kelly, p. 29.

32. Ibid., p. 30.

33. Howitt, p. 6.

34. Carboni, p. 3.

35. *The Argus*, 20 October 1852, p. 4.

36. Kelly, p. 30.

37. Clacy, p. 17.

38. Fauchery, p. 22.

39. Howitt, p. 11.
40. Fauchery, p. 27.
41. Ibid.
42. Craig, p. 15.
43. Ibid.
44. Clacy, p. 23.
45. Foster, J. F. Leslie, p. 10.
46. Clacy, p. 23.
47. Ibid.
48. Ibid.
49. Ibid., p. 135.
50. Ibid., p. 23.
51. Howitt, p. 43.
52. Ibid., p. 201.
53. Ibid., p. 43.
54. Clacy, p. 127.
55. Goodman, p. 42.

CHAPTER FIVE: TO THE DIGGINGS

1. Sherer, p. 10.
2. Howitt, p. 25.
3. Kelly, p. 180.
4. *The Argus*, 25 June 1852, p. 3.
5. Ibid.
6. *Empire*, 22 October 1851, p. 2.
7. *The Sydney Morning Herald*, 27 December 1851, p. 2.
8. *The Argus*, 4 June 1852, p. 3.
9. *The Sydney Morning Herald*, 25 April 1851, p. 3.
10. Clacy, p. 51.
11. Craig, p. 36.
12. Sir John S. Pakington to Governor-General Sir Charles FitzRoy, 15 December 1852, 'Further Papers Relative to the Alterations in the Constitutions of the Australian Colonies', 14 March 1853, p. 44.
13. Sir John S. Pakington to La Trobe, 15 December 1852, 'Further Papers Relative to the Alterations in the Constitutions of the Australian Colonies', 14 March 1853, p. 57.
14. Author's note: The formal name of the Act is *An Act for the better Government of the Australian Colonies (5th August 1850)*.
15. Waugh, p. 331.

16. Carboni, p. 3.
17. Author's note: While several of these institutions had not started construction by this date, La Trobe has been working towards their establishment. The foundation stones for the Melbourne Public Library, now become the State Library of Victoria, and the University of Melbourne were laid the same day, 23 July 1854, by Lieutenant-Governor Sir Charles Hotham.
18. Author's note: Known as the Melbourne Athenaeum since 1873, it is one of the oldest public institutions in Victoria.
19. Author's note: Established in 1853, it is reportedly Australia's oldest surviving cultural organisation.
20. Bleissbarth, p. 28.
21. Hancock, p. 151.
22. Abbott, pp. 280–28. Author's note: The author, Edward Abbott, reports that, 'This was a Colonial beverage in use in the earlier days of Tasmania, and was named and drank by an eccentric governor, who had a stronger head than most of his subordinates. A wattle hut used to be improvised within a few miles of the capital, and temporary chairs and a strong table being fixed, the governor would take the seat of honour, having in front of him a barbecued pig, and on his honour's right hand, a cask of "blow my skull" – sufficient for all comers – no special invitation being necessary . . .
    "No heeltaps!" called out the governor in a voice of authority, and the unfortunate stranger was at once *hors de combat*; while the governor having an impenetrable cranium, and an iron frame, could take many goblets of the alcoholic fluid . . .'
23. Read, p. 172.
24. Craig, p. 219.
25. Clacy, p. 83.
26. Carboni, p. 4.
27. Ibid.
28. Ibid.
29. Hancock, p. 151.
30. Ibid.
31. *The Manchester Guardian*, 11 June 1853, p. 9.
32. Ibid.
33. Fauchery, p. 77.
34. Potts, p. 362.
35. Samuel Lazarus Diary, 24 September 1853–21 January 1855; Monday, 13 November 1853 [Monday November 21], SLV, MS

Box1777/4, p. 61.

36. Howitt, p. 185.
37. Clacy, p. 65.
38. Lang, *The Australian Emigrant's Manual*, p. 5.
39. Carboni, p. 4.
40. Ibid., p. 14.
41. Craig, p. 214.
42. Withers, p. 75
43. Ibid.
44. *The Sydney Morning Herald*, 25 December 1852, p. 4.
45. *The Sydney Morning Herald*, 12 February 1853, p. 1S.
46. Cahir, p. 123.
47. Ibid.
48. Bonwick, *Notes of a Gold Digger and Gold Digger's Guide*.
49. *Empire*, 12 February 1853, p. 5.
50. Ibid.
51. Ibid.
52. *The Sydney Morning Herald*, 12 February 1853, p. 1.
53. *Empire*, 12 February 1853, p. 5.
54. Ibid.
55. Howitt, p. 378.
56. Clacy, p. 54.
57. Ibid.
58. Craig, p. 300.
59. Ibid., p. 301.
60. Ibid., p. 303.
61. Ibid., p. 195.
62. Ibid., p. 196.
63. Gold, p. 23.
64. La Trobe to Newcastle, 1 June 1853, *Letter Book, 1851 June 30–1854 Apr. 7*, p. 17, SLV, MS 12618.
65. Ibid.
66. Ibid., pp. 18–19.
67. Ibid.
68. Ibid.

CHAPTER SIX: TROUBLE BREWS

1. Hill, p. 42.
2. Carboni, p. 6.

3. Younger, p. 264.
4. Clacy, p. 113.
5. La Trobe to Newcastle, 3 May 1853, 'Further Papers Relative to the Discovery of Gold', February 1854, p. 81.
6. La Trobe to Newcastle, 12 September 1853, 'Further Papers Relative to the Discovery of Gold in Australia', February 1854, p. 160.
7. *The Sydney Morning Herald*, 16 July 1853, p. 6.
8. Author's note: Despite this claim, the surviving petition in the State Library of Victoria has no more than 6,000 signatories and La Trobe writes to Newcastle of 5,000. A robbery of the escort at McIvor Diggings had denied the petition that region's signatures.
9. The 1853 Bendigo Goldfields Petition
10. Ibid.
11. Ibid.
12. The 1853 Bendigo Goldfields Petition; *The Sydney Morning Herald*, 16 July 1853, p. 6.
13. Ibid.
14. *The Argus*, 19 August, p. 4.
15. Hocking, p. 69.
16. *The Argus*, 19 August 1853, p. 4.
17. Howitt, p. 284.
18. Ibid., p. 285.
19. Ibid., p. 286.
20. *The Argus*, 5 August 1853, p. 4.
21. Ibid.
22. *The Argus,* 10 August 1853, p. 5.
23. La Trobe's reply to Bendigo Goldfields Petition, 20 August 1853, 'Further Papers Relative to the Discovery of Gold in Australia', February 1854, p. 170.
24. Ibid., p. 172.
25. Author's note: Where that darling of the Australian gold fields, Lola Montez, was to debut in Australia with her famous 'Spider Dance' in 1855.
26. *The Sydney Morning Herald*, 16 August 1853, p. 4.
27. Ibid.
28. Macdougall, p. 177.
29. *The Sydney Morning Herald*, 16 August 1853, p. 4.
30. *The Sydney Morning Herald*, 17 August 1853, p. 5.
31. *The Sydney Morning Herald*, 16 August 1853, p. 4.
32. Anderson, Hugh, 'Fawkner, John Pascoe (1792–1869)', Australian

Dictionary of Biography.

33. *The Sydney Morning Herald*, 16 August 1853, p. 4.

34. *The Argus*, 8 August 1853, p. 4.

35. *The Argus*, 2 September 1854, p. 4

36. Author's note: Extraordinarily, despite the major advances made in democracy so soon after Eureka, the property restrictions on the franchise for the Victorian Legislative Council would last until the early 1950s.

37. *The Argus*, 2 September 1854, p. 4.

38. *The Argus*, 29 August 1853, p. 5.

39. Carboni, p. 5.

40. Ibid.

41. *The Argus*, 10 September 1853, p. 6.

42. Bate, p.52.

43. Wright to Colonial Secretary Foster, 28 August 1853; La Trobe despatch to Newcastle, 12 September 1854, 'Further Papers Relative to the Discovery of Gold in the Australian Colonies', February 1854, p. 177.

44. La Trobe despatch to Newcastle, 12 September 1854, 'Further Papers Relative to the Discovery of Gold in the Australian Colonies', February 1854, p. 165.

45. Wright's report recommending reduction of license fee, 28 August 1853, 'Further Papers Relative to the Recent Discovery of Gold in Australia', February 1854, p. 177.

46. *The Argus*, 21 September 1853, p. 7.

47. *The Argus*, 23 November 1853, p. 4.

48. Ibid.

49. Ibid.

50. *The Times*, 13 December 1853, p. 6.

51. Serle, p. 155.

52. Roberts, p.89.

53. Ibid.

54. Captain Kay's evidence, 2 July 1867, 'Report from the Select Committee upon Mr. J. F. V. Fitzgerald's Case', p. 21.

55. Molony, 38; Serle, p. 156.

56. Carboni, pp. 83–84.

57. Withers, p. 143.

58. Withers, p. 84. Author's note: An alternative spelling, as used by the Public Records Office Victoria, is D'Ewes. But as the man himself signed his name Dewes, I have gone with that.

59. Dewes, p. 64.
60. Bates, p.16.
61. Withers, p. 36.
62. Clacy, p. 113.
63. Author's note: A third member of this group was Duncan Gillies, who would later go on to be the Premier of Victoria.
64. Carboni, p. 45.
65. Ibid., p. 8.
66. Ibid., p. 8.
67. Ibid., p. 8.
68. Ibid., p. 9.
69. Fauchery, p. 98
70. Ibid.
71. Ibid.
72. Craig, p. 230.
73. Ibid.
74. Clacy, p. 56.
75. Horne, Richard, *Australian Facts and Prospects*, London, 1859, p. 28.
76. La Trobe to Newcastle, 25 March 1854, 'Further Papers Relative to the Alterations in the Constitutions of the Australian Colonies', 31 July and 10 August 1854, George Edward Eyre and William Spottiswoode, Her Majesty's Stationery Office, London, 1854, p. 100.

CHAPTER SEVEN: ENTER HOTHAM

1. Withers, p. 57.
2. *The Argus*, 24 June 1854, p. 5.
3. Craig, pp. 273–4.
4. *The Argus*, 24 June 1854, p. 5.
5. Ibid.
6. Ibid.
7. Ibid.
8. Hotham to the Duke of Newcastle, 'Duplicate Despatches from the Governor to the Secretary of State', 26 June 1854, VPRS 1085/P0000/7, Despatch No. 79, pp. 6–7.
9. *The Argus*, 24 June 1854, p. 5.
10. Ibid.
11. Ibid.
12. Ibid.

13. Ibid.
14. Ibid.
15. Hotham to the Duke of Newcastle, 'Duplicate Despatches from the Governor to the Secretary of State', 26 June 1854, VPRS 1085/P0000/7, Despatch No. 79, pp. 8–9,
16. *The Argus*, 24 June 1854, p. 5.
17. Ibid.
18. Hotham to the Duke of Newcastle, Enclosure No. 1, 'Duplicate Despatches from the Governor to the Secretary of State', 26 June 1854, VPRS 1085/P0000/7, Despatch No. 79, pp. 1–2.
19. *The Argus*, 24 June 1854, p. 5.
20. Thomas Pierson Diary, 25 June 1854, SLV, MS 11646, Box 2178/4, p. 208.
21. Dewes, p. 87.
22. Letter from John Manning to the Secretary of the Denominational Schools Board, 17 July 1854, *Denominational Schools Board Inward Correspondence*, VPRS 61, 54/399.
23. Ibid.
24. 'Comparative Statement of the Population and Number of Licenses Issued Quarterly from 1st January 1853, with the Amount of Revenue Collected', Enclosures in No. 16, Gold returns contained in the Lieutenant-Governor's Despatch, No. 31, 21 July 1854, 'Further Papers Relative to the Discovery of Gold in the Australian Colonies', December 1854, p. 175.
25. Charles Wright's evidence, 18 June 1867, 'Report from the Select Committee upon Mr. J. F. V. Fitzgerald's Case', p. 10.
26. Ibid.
27. *The Sydney Morning Herald*, 20 March 1854, p. 4.
28. Ibid.
29. Ibid.
30. Author's note: That son became the prominent Sydney jeweler Charles Augustus FitzRoy Fitzsimons. And, thank you, I've checked – no relation!
31. Hirst, pp. 227–228.
32. *People's Advocate*, 18 February 1854.
33. Carboni, p. 18.
34. Ibid.
35. Ibid.
36. Ibid.
37. Ibid.

38. William Carroll's evidence to the Board of Inquiry, No. 27, 7 November 1854, 'Report of the Board into the Circumstances Connected with the Late Disturbances at Ballarat', p. 9.

39. Carboni to W. H. Archer, 18 October 1854, *Letters to W. H. Archer*, NL, MS 26414, p. 18.

40. *The Diggers' Advocate*, 19 August 1854, p. 4.

41 *The Ballarat Times*, 2 September 1854.

42. *The Argus*, 17 August 1854, p. 4.

43. Kelly, p. 71.

44. Kelly, p. 71.

45. Carboni, p. 16.

46. Molony, p. 47.

47. *The Ballarat Times*, 2 September 1854.

48. Sutherland, *Victoria and its Metropolis*, p. 360.

49. *The Ballarat Times*, 2 September 1854.

50. Bate, *Lucky City*, p.55.

51. Dewes, p. 87.

52. Hotham to Grey, 'Reporting Official Visit to the Goldfields of Victoria', 18 September 1854, Dispatch No. 112, VPRS 1085/P, Unit 8.

53. Ibid.

54. Ibid.

55. Ibid.

56. Ibid.

57. Ibid.

58. Ibid.

59. John Foster's (Fitzgerald) evidence, 13 June 1867, 'Report from the Select Committee upon Mr. J. F. V. Fitzgerald's Case', p. 21.

60. Captain Kay's evidence, 13 June 1867, 'Report from the Select Committee upon Mr. J. F. V. Fitzgerald's Case', p. 21.

61. Ibid.

62. John Foster's (Fitzgerald) evidence, 13 June 1867, 'Report from the Select Committee upon Mr. J. F. V. Fitzgerald's Case', p. 3

63. Ibid., p. 2.

64. Mrs James Grant to Hotham, 27 September 1854, VPRS 4066, No. 4, Box 1.

65. Ibid.

66. *The Argus*, 21 September 1854, p. 3.

67. Ibid.

68. *The Argus*, 22 September 1854, p 3.

60. *Geelong Advertiser*, 23 September 1854, p. 4.
70. Ibid.
71. *The Ballarat Times*, 30 September 1854.
72. Carboni, p. 17.
73. Thomas Pierson diary, 10 October 1854, SLV, MS 11646, Box 2178/4, pp. 232–233.
74. Additional deposition taken from Michael Welsh, 22 October 1854, for the inquest investigating the murder of James Scobie, VPRS 5527/P Unit 1, Item 2.
75. *The Argus*, 20 November 1854, p. 6.
76. MacFarlane, p 41.
77. *The Argus*, 20 November 1854, p. 6.
78. Ibid.
79. Ibid.
80. Author's note: Though there is no record of Dr Carr doing these things, it is consistent with what a doctor would do at this time with a person for whom the best hope is that they are on the point of death – and not actually dead.
81. Molony, *Eureka*, p. 51.
82. Deposition of James Bentley, Inquest into James Scobie's murder, 7 October 1854, VPRS 5527/P0, Unit 1, Item 1.
83. Deposition of Thomas Mooney, Inquest into James Scobie's murder, 7 October 1854, VPRS 5527/P, Unit 1, Item 1.
84. *The Ballarat Times*, 14 October 1854.
85. Deposition of Barnard Welch, Inquest into James Scobie's murder, 7 October 1854, VPRS 5527/P0, Unit 1, Item 1.
86. Ibid.
87. Peter Lalor's evidence to the Board of Inquiry, No. 19, 4 November 1854, 'Report of the Board into the Circumstances Connected with the Late Disturbances at Ballarat', p. 6.
88. Statement of the jury following the inquest into James Scobie's murder, 7 October 1854, VPRS 5527/P0, Unit 1, Item 1.
89. Peter Lalor's evidence to the Board of Inquiry, No. 19, 4 November 1854, 'Report of the Board into the Circumstances Connected with the Late Disturbances at Ballarat', p. 6.
90. *The Ballarat Times*, 14 October 1854.
91. Chief Commissioner [Wright] to Resident Commissioner [Rede], 9 October 1854, SLV, MS 11490, Box 59/2, Letter 3.
92. *The Ballarat Times*, 14 October 1854.
93. Ibid.

94. Ibid.
95. Ibid.
96. Carboni, p. 28.
97. Author's note: Also variously spelt in the original documents as Johnson and Johnston.
98. *The Ballarat Times,* 14 October 1854.
99. Carboni, p. 28.
100. *The Ballarat Times,* 14 October 1854.
101. Peter Martin deposition, brief for the prosecution in the trial of James and Catherine Bentley, W. Stance and John (or Thomas) Farrell and others, VPRS 5527/P Unit 1, Item 5.
102. *The Ballarat Times,* 14 October 1854.
103. Ibid.
104. Howitt, p. 421.
105. *Geelong Advertiser,* 10 October 1854, p. 5.
106. *Geelong Advertiser,* 11 October 1854, p. 4.

CHAPTER EIGHT: FIRE'S BURNING, FIRE'S BURNING, DRAW NEARER

1. *The Ballarat Times,* 28 October 1854.
2. Carboni, p. 4.
3. Withers, p. 73.
4. Thomas Pierson diary, 16 October 1854, SLV, MS 11646, Box 2178/4, p. 233.
5. *The Ballarat Times,* 14 October 1854.
6. James Bentley letter to Dewes, 16 October 1854, VPRS, 1189/P Unit 92, H54/11605.
7. Robert Rede's evidence, 10 January 1855, 'Report of the Commission Appointed to Enquire into the Condition of the Goldfields of Victoria', p. 306.
8. Ibid.
9. Thomas Pierson Diary, Monday, 16 October 1854, SLV, MS 11646, Box 2178/4, p. 234.
10. Carboni letter to W. H. Archer, 18 October 1854, NLA, MS 264/14, p. 80.
11. *The Ballarat Times,* 21 October 1854.
12. Ibid.
13. Carboni, p. 20.
14. *The Ballarat Times,* 21 October 1854.

15. Ibid.
16. Ibid.; *The Argus*, 23 October 1854, p. 5.
17. *The Ballarat Times*, 21 October 1854.
18. 'Report of the Board into the Circumstances Connected with the Late Disturbance at Ballarat', p. 5.
19. *The Argus*, 23 October 1854, p. 5.
20. MacFarlane, p. 50.
21. Carboni, p. 21.
22. Samuel Lazarus Diary, September 24 1853 – 21 January 1855, Wednesday, 25 October 1854, SLV, MS Box1777/4, p. 95.
23. Ximenes's evidence, 3 November 1854, 'Report of the Board into the Circumstances Connected with the Late Disturbance at Ballarat', p. 2.
24. *The Argus*, 23 October 1854, p. 5.
25. Thomas Pierson diary, Tuesday, 17 October 1854, SLV MS 11646, Box 2178/4, p. 235.
26. Thomas Pierson diary, Sunday, 5 November 1854, SLV MS 11646, Box 2178/4, p. 237.
27. McIntyre letter to his brother, 29 March 1855, SLV MS 8077, Box 956/2, p. 3. Author's note: This quote is not word for word, but it can be construed from McIntyre's letter to his brother, where he writes, 'The Commissioners were up in one of the broken windows trying to pacify the people telling them they had been diggers themselves, and they would see justice done to the diggers . . .'
28. MacFarlane, p. 52.
29. McIntyre letter to his brother, 29 March 1855, SLV MS 8077, Box 956/2, p. 3.
30. Carboni, p. 22.
31. Ibid.
32. Ibid.
33. Ibid.
34. Thomas Conboy deposition, 27 October 1854, 'Depositions Taken Against Albert Hurd for Rioting at Bentley's Hotel', VPRS 5527/P Unit 1, Item 7.
35. Thomas Wood deposition, 27 October 1854, 'Depositions Taken Against Albert Hurd for Rioting at Bentley's Hotel', VPRS 5527/P Unit 1, Item 7.
36. *The Ballarat Times*, 21 October 1854.
37. *The Argus*, 25 October 1854, p. 5.
38. Ibid.

39. Bate, p. 60.
40. *The Argus*, 25 October 1854, p. 5.
41. Samuel Huyghue diary, *The Ballarat Riots 1854*, SLV, MS 7725, Box 646/9, pp. 5–6.
42. Ibid., p. 6.
43. Dewes, p. 64.
44. Ibid., p. 96.
45. Carboni, p. 23.
46. Ibid.
47. Hotham to George Grey, 'Reporting the Burning of the Eureka Hotel on the Ballaarat Gold Field', Duplicate despatches from the Governor to the Secretary of State, VPRS 1085/P0, Duplicate despatch No. 148, Unit 8.
48. *The Argus*, 21 November 1854, p. 5.
49. Samuel Lazarus diary, 24 September 1853–21 January 1855, Wednesday, 25 October 1854, SLV, MS Box 1777/4, p. 98.
50. Acting Chief Police Commissioner MacMahon report to Foster, 22 October 1854, VPRS 1189/P Unit 92, K54/11823.
51. Ibid.
52. *The Ballarat Times*, 28 October 1854.
53. Thomas Pierson diary, Sunday, 22 October 1854, SLV, MS 11646, Box 2178/4, p. 236.
54. McIntyre letter to his brother, 29 March 1855, SLV, MS 8077, Box 956/2, p. 5.
55. Ibid, p. 6.
56. Hotham note on 'The Resident Commissioner Ballarat Report to the Chief Commissioner of the Goldfields', Melbourne, 20 October 1854. Collected papers regarding treatment of Smyth's servant, VPRS 1189/P Unit 92, J54/12201.
57. Rede report to Wright, 'The Resident Commissioner of Ballarat to Chief Commissioner of the Goldfields', Melbourne, 26 October 1854, VPRS 1189/P Unit 92, J54/12201.
58. *The Ballarat Times*, 21 October 1854.
59. Carboni, pp. 30–31.
60. Ibid., p. 46.
61. McFarlane, p. 56.
62. Ballarat Miners' Petition addressed to Lieutenant Sir Governor Charles Hotham, 23 October 1854, VPRS 5527, Eureka Stockade – Historical Collection P0, Unit 1.
63. Withers, p. 138.

64. Carboni, p. 29.
65. *The Ballarat Times*, 28 October 1854.
66. *The Ballarat Times*, 28 October 1854.
67. Bate, p. 44.
68. *The Argus*, 27 October 1854, p. 6.
69. Lynch, p. 11.
70. *The Argus*, 27 October 1854, p. 6.
71. *The Ballarat Times*, 28 October 1854.
72. Ibid.
73. Resident Goldfields Commissioner Robert Rede to Colonial Secretary Foster, 22 October 1854, VPRS 1189/P Unit 92, K54/11826.
74. MacFarlane, p. 11.
75. *The Maitland Mercury & Hunter River General Advertiser*, 4 November 1854, p. 4.
76. Ibid.
77. Lynch, p. 10.
78. Molony, p. 106.
79. *Captain Thomas's Plan of Defense for the Government Camp, Ballarat.*
80. *The Ballarat Times*, 28 October 1854.
81. *The Sydney Morning Herald*, 7 November 1854, p. 4.
82. Bate, p. 63.
83. *The Sydney Morning Herald*, 7 November 1854, p. 4.
84. Thomas Pierson diary, Sunday, 5 November 1854, SLV, MS 11646, Box 2178/4, p. 237. Author's note: Though Pierson did not specify that this remark was made at this specific meeting, it is the nearest major meeting to his diary notation.
85. *The Argus,* 7 November 1854, p. 6.
86. Lynch, p. 11; *The Argus*, 7 November 1854 p. 6.
87. Smith, p. 22.
88. *The Argus*, 7 November 1854, p. 6.
89. Charles Hotham to Sir George Grey, 18 November 1854, 'Duplicate Despatches from the Governor to the Secretary of State', VPRS 1085/P0, Unit 8, Duplicate despatch No. 148.
90. Peter Lalor's evidence to the Board of Inquiry, No. 19, 4 November 1854, 'Report of the Board into the Circumstances Connected with the Late Disturbances at Ballarat', p. 6.
91. Ballarat Reform League Letter to the Board, 10 November 1854, 'Report of the Board into the Circumstances Connected with the Late Disturbances at Ballarat', p. 19.

92. Ibid., pp. 19–20.
93. *Empire,* 7 November 1854, p. 4.
94. Robert Rede to Hotham, 7 November 1854, 'Correspondence with Office of the Chief Commissioner of Goldfields, Melbourne and Resident Gold Commissioner at Ballarat', 1854–1855, SLV, MS 11489-11490, Box 59/2–3, Letter 27.
95. Ibid.
96. Ibid.
97. Ibid.
98. Lynch, p. 13.
99. *The Ballarat Times,* 18 November 1854.
100. Ibid.
101. *The Argus,* 16 November 1854, p. 6.
102. Ibid.
103. *The Ballarat Times,* 18 November 1854.
104. *The Argus,* 16 November 1854, p. 6. Author's note: I have put the quotes recorded by *The Argus* into the present tense.
105. *The Ballarat Times,* 18 November 1854.
106. *The Argus,* 16 November 1854, p. 6.
107. Ibid., p. 6.
108. Ibid.
109. *The Ballarat Times,* 18 November 1854.
110. Thomas Pierson diary, 12 November 1854, SLV, MS 11646, Box 2178/4, p. 238.
111. Carboni, p. 30.
112. *The Ballarat Times,* 18 November 1854.
113. Section III, 'An Act for the Better Security of the Crown and Government of the United Kingdom', p. 127.
114. *The Argus,* 16 November 1854, p. 6.
115. *The Ballarat Times,* 18 November 1854, p. 2.
116. Molony, p 110.
117. John Foster's evidence, 'Report from the Select Committee upon Mr. J. F. V. Fitzgerald's Case', p. 2.

CHAPTER NINE: ALL RISE

1. Withers, p. 73.
2. Clark, pp. 68–69.
3. Author's Note: The Melbourne Public Library is now the State Library of Victoria – an institution that I relied on heavily for this

book and was always there for me!

4. *The Argus*, 20 November 1854, p. 6.

5. *The Age*, 20 November 1854, p. 5.

6. *The Argus*, 20 November 1854, p. 6.

7. Ibid.

8. Ibid.

9. Ibid., p. 4.

10. Foster to Wallace, 20 November 1854, VPRS 3219, Vol. 20, pp. 430–1.

11. *The Ballarat Star*, 4 March 1870, p. 4.

12. Ibid.

13. Carboni, p. 34.

14. Ibid.

15. Ibid.

16. Inflammatory poster, produced by Seekamp's press, VPRS 5527/P Unit 4, Item 1.

17. Lynch, p. 15.

18. Withers, pp. 141–42. *The Argus*, 8 July 1899, p. 4.

19. 'Report of the Board into the Circumstances Connected with the Late Disturbance at Ballarat', p. viii.

20. Ibid., p. xi.

21. Ibid., p. xiii.

22. Ibid., p. xi.

23. Ibid., p. xv.

24. Ibid., p. xi.

25. Record of meeting between Lieutenant-Governor Hotham and a deputation from the diggers, led by J. B. Humffrays and George Black, 27 November 1854, VPRS 1095/P Unit 3, Bundle 1, No. 16.

26. Ibid.

27. Ibid.

28. Ibid.

29. Ibid.

30. Ibid.

31. Ibid.

32. Ibid.

33. Ibid.

34. Ibid.

35. Ibid.

36. *The Argus,* 28 November 1854, p. 4.

37. Commissioner Robert Rede letter to Mr Furnell, 27 November

1854, VPRS 1189/P Unit 92, J55/14458.

38. MacFarlane, p. 38.

39. Commissioner Robert Rede letter to Mr Furnell, 27 November 1854, VPRS 1189/P Unit 92, J55/14458.

40. Commissioner Robert Rede to Colonial Secretary Foster, 27 November 1854, VPRS 1189/P Unit 92, J55/14458.

41. Inflammatory poster produced by Seekamp's press, VPRS 5527/P Unit 4, Item 1; Gold, p. 29.

42. *The Argus*, 28 November 1854, p. 4.

43. Charles Pasley letter to his father, 27 June 1855, p. 51, ML, B1564.

44. Ibid.

45. Ibid.

46. Ibid.

47. *Geelong Advertiser*, 30 November 1854, p. 4.

48. Gold, *Eureka*, p. 32.

49. *The Ballarat Times*, 3 December 1854.

50. Author's note: Confirmation that there were 600 Americans on the Ballarat diggings at the time of Eureka can be found In: L. G. Churchward, 'Americans and Other Foreigners at Eureka', in *Historical Studies: Eureka Supplement* (1954), p. 80.

51. *The Ballarat Times*, 3 December 1854.

52. Rede to Chief Commissioner of Goldfields, 28 November 1854, VPRS 1189/P Unit 92, J54/14459.

53. Potts, *Young America and Australian Gold*, p. 184.

54. Rede to Chief Commissioner of Goldfields, 28 November 1854, VPRS 1189/P Unit 92, J54/14459.

55. Turner, p. 55.

56. Ibid.

57. Ferguson, pp. 281–2.

58. *Geelong Advertiser*, 2 December 1854, p. 4.

59. *The Ballarat Times*, 3 December 1854.

60. Lynch, p. 29. Author's note: Lynch, among others, had it that Egan was killed outright; however, this has been proved otherwise by Ballarat historian Dorothy Wickham as Egan appears to have gone on to live a long and happy life.

61. Samuel Lazarus diary, 24 September 1853–21 January 1855; Tuesday, 28 November 1854, p. 116, SLV, MS Box 1777/4.

62. Samuel Huyghue diary, *The Ballarat Riots 1854*, SLV, MS 7725, Box 646/9, p. 1.

63. Ibid., pp. 10–11.

64. Carboni, p. 35.
65. Sameul Huyghue diary, *The Ballarat Riots 1854*, SLV, MS 7725, Box 646/9, p. 11.
66. Ibid., p. 12.
67. Commissioner Robert Rede letter to the Chief Commissioner of the Goldfields, 30 November 1854, VPRS 1189/P Unit 92, J54/14460.
68. Ibid.
69. Author's note: Though in his 1885 account Wilson does not specify Captain Ross being there, this is my assumption as other accounts have Ross as 'Father of the Flag', and it stands to reason that he would have been present.
70. Wickham, *The Eureka Flag*, p. 25.
71. Ibid.
72. Ferguson, p. 280.
73. Author's note: For an interesting discussion on the making of the flag, see Fox, L. *The Eureka Flag*, pp. 47–54. In this book, it is possibly an Anastasia Catherine Withers who is instrumental.

CHAPTER TEN: READING THE RIOT ACT

1. *The Argus,* 7 December 1904, p. 4.
2. *Geelong Advertiser*, 2 December 1854, p. 4.
3. Wilson, p. 7.
4. *The Ballarat Times*, 3 December 1854.
5. Ibid., p.
6 Thomas Pierson diary, Wednesday, 6 December 1854, SLV, MS 11646, Box 2178/4, p. 241.
7. Carboni, p. 36.
8. *The Ballarat Times*, 3 December, 1854.
9. *Empire*, 6 December 1854, p. 5.
10. Macdougall, p. 180.
11. *Empire*, 6 December 1854, p. 5.
12. Lynch, p. 26.
13. Ibid., p. 24.
14. Carboni, pp. 38–39.
15. *The Argus,* 7 December 1904, p. 4.
16. Author's note: Those remarks were recalled by a digger who seemingly was there at the time, in a letter to *The Argus*, some 50 years after the event. In the letter he states that Vern made these remarks a fortnight before the massacre, which positions it around

19 November, but as there appears to have been no significant meeting at Bakery Hill at this time I think that this is the meeting meant, as opposed to the meeting on 11 November, which was comparatively calm.

17. *The Argus*, 7 December 1904, p. 4.
18. *Empire*, 6 December 1854, p. 5.
19. *Daily Southern Cross*, 'Outbreak at Ballarat', 22 December 1854, p. 3.
20. Carboni, p. 40.
21. *The Ballarat Times*, 3 December 1854.
22. Carboni, pp. 40–41.
23. Thomas Pierson diary, Wednesday, 6 December 1854, SLV, MS 11646, Box 2178/4, p. 239.
24. Carboni, *The Eureka Stockade*, p. 41.
25. Wilson, p. 5.
26. Lynch, p. 25.
27. Pasley report to Hotham, 29 November 1854, VPRS 1189/P Unit 92, K/5413511.
28. *Geelong Advertiser*, 1 December 1854, p. 4.
29. *The Ballarat Times*, 3 December 1854.
30. Lynch, *Story of the Eureka Stockade*, p. 15.
31. Pasley report to Hotham, 29 November 1854, VPRS 1189/P Unit 92, K/5413511. Molony, p. 125.
32. Author's note: It is my assumption that the views expressed by Pasley to Hotham in his report are the same as the views he expresses to Rede and Thomas on this occasion.
33. *The Argus*, 2 December 1854, p. 5.
34. Robert Rede's evidence, 10 January 1855, 'Report of the Commission Appointed to Enquire into the Condition of the Goldfields of Victoria', p. 308.
35. Rede's report to the Colonial Secretary, 30 November 1854, VPRS 1085/P Unit 8, Duplicate 162 Enclosure no. 4.
36. *The Argus*, 2 December 1854, p. 5.
37. Ibid.
38. *The Argus*, 2 December 1854, p. 5.
39. Ibid.
40. Bohn, p. 644.
41. Lynch, p. 27.
42. Robert Rede's evidence, 10 January 1855, 'Report of the Commission Appointed to Enquire into the Condition of the

Goldfields of Victoria', p. 309.

43. Ibid.

44. *The Argus*, 2 December 1854, p. 5.

45. *Empire*, Wednesday, 6 December 1854, p. 5.

46. *The Argus*, 2 December 1854, p. 5.

47. Ibid.

48. *The Argus*, 2 December 1854, p. 5.

49. Ibid.

50. Ibid.

51. *The Argus*, 2 December, p. 5.

52. Samuel Lazarus diary, 24 September 1853–21 January 1855, Tuesday, 30 November 1854, SLV, MS Box 1777/4, p. 121.

53. Pasley report to the Colonial Secretary, 30 November 1854, VPRS 1189/P Unit 92, K54/13512.

54. Samuel Huyghue Diary, *The Ballarat Riots 1854*, SLV, MS 7725, Box 646/9, p. 15.

55. *Geelong Advertiser*, 2 December 1854, p. 5.

56. *The Argus*, 10 April 1855 p. 7.

57. *The Argus*, 10 April 1855, p 7.

58. Carboni, p. 43.

59. *The Argus*, 10 April 1855 p. 7.

60. Ibid.

61. Samuel Lazarus diary, 24 September 1853–21 January 1855; Thursday, 30 November 1854, SLV, MS Box 1777/4, p. 122.

CHAPTER ELEVEN: 'WE SWEAR BY THE SOUTHERN CROSS . . .'

1. Hotham despatch to Sir George Grey, 'Reporting a Serious Riot and Collision at the Ballarat Gold Field' 20 December 1854, VPRS 1085/P0, Duplicate despatches from the Governor to the Secretary of State, Unit 8, Duplicate Ddespatch No. 162.

2. *The Argus*, 10 April 1855, p. 7.

3. Queen v. Hayes, p.73.

4. Carboni, p. 44.

5. Author's note: One of Hanrahan's descendants is Mike Walsh, the television identity and cinema impresario.

6. Carboni, p. 50.

7. Lynch, p. 28.

8. Ibid.
9. Carboni, p. 50.
10. Ibid.
11. Queen v. Hayes, p. 29.
12. Author's note: An anomaly with many of the accounts of how big the Stockade was is that while the most authoritative accounts have it as about 200 yards long by 100 yards wide, they also have it as just one acre. But both statements cannot be correct.
13. Author's note: I am aware that Peter Lalor later downplayed the defensive nature of the Stockade, saying it was no more than a gathering point. However, at the time, it was very much in his interests to so downplay it.
14. Lynch, p. 11.
15. *The Argus*, 5 December 1854, p. 5.
16. *The Austral Light*, January 1896, p. 30.
17. Queen v. Hayes, p. 85.
18. Blake, p. 25.
19. Carboni, p. 64.
20. Ibid.
21. Ibid.
22. Ibid., p. 51.
23. Carboni, p. 64.
24. *The Ballarat Courier*, 20 July 1889, p. 5.
25. Ibid.
26. Rede's account of the Gravel Pit riots and call for martial law to be proclaimed, 30 November 1854, VPRS 1085/P Unit 8, Duplicate 162, Enclosure No. 4.
27. Rede to Colonial Secretary Foster, 30 November 1854, VPRS 1085/P Unit 8, Duplicate 162, Enclosure No. 4.
28. Pasley report to the Colonial Secretary, 30 November 1854, VPRS 1189/P Unit 92, K54/13512.
29. Author's note: He is also referred to as John Diamond.
30. Hotham to George Grey, 20 December 1854, 'Further Papers Relative to the Discovery of Gold in Australia', July 1855, p. 66.
31. Carboni, p. 45.
32. *The Argus,* 7 December 1904, p. 4.
33. Carboni, p. 47.
34. Ibid., p. 48.
35. Lynch, p. 28.
36. Carboni, p. 48.

37. Author's note: This is my assumption.
38. Nicholls, W. H., 'Reminiscences of the Eureka Stockade', *The Centennial Magazine*, Vol. 2, No. 10, May 1890, p. 748.
39. Ibid.
40. Carboni, p. 52.
41. Ibid., p. 53.
42. Ibid., p. 54.
43. Ibid.
44. Ibid.
45. Ibid., p. 55.
46. Ibid., p. 52.
47. Ibid., p. 55.
48. Ibid.
49. Ibid., p. 52.
50. Carboni, p. 55.
51. Ibid., p. 56.
52. Robert Rede's evidence, 10 January 1855,'Report of the Commission Appointed to Enquire into the Condition of the   Goldfields of Victoria', p. 309.
53. Ibid.
54. Carboni, p. 56.
55. Ibid.
56. Ibid.
57. Ibid.
58. Robert Rede's evidence, 10 January 1855, 'Report of the Commission Appointed to Enquire into the Condition of the Goldfields of Victoria', p. 309.
59. Ibid.
60. Carboni, p. 57.
61. Turnbull, p. 61.
62. Robert Rede's evidence, 10 January 1855, 'Report of the Commission Appointed to Enquire into the Condition of the Goldfields of Victoria', p. 309.
63. Resident Goldfields Commissioner Robert Rede to the Chief Commissioner of the Goldfields, 2 December 1854, VPRS 1189/P Unit 92, J54/14462.
64. Patrick Smyth letter to Hotham requesting temporary suspension of license fee to avoid bloodshed, 30 November 1854, VPRS 4066/P Unit 1, December 1854, no. 3.

CHAPTER TWELVE: 'AUX ARMES, CITOYENS!'

1. Resident Goldfields Commissioner Robert Rede to the Chief Commissioner of the Goldfields, 2 December 1854, VPRS 1189/P Unit 92, J54/14462.
2. Samuel Huyghue Diary, *The Ballarat Riots 1854*, SLV, MS 7725, Box 646/9, p. 19.
3. Carboni, p 51.
4. Ibid., p. 58.
5. *The Argus*, 5 December 1854, p. 4.
6. Housman, p. 39.
7. Carboni, p. 58.
8. Carboni, p. 59.
9. Nicholls, W. H., 'Reminiscences of the Eureka Stockade', *The Centennial Magazine*, Vol. 2, No. 10, May 1890, p. 746.
10. Ibid., p. 749.
11. Ibid., p. 746.
12. Ibid.
13. Ibid.
14. MacFarlane, p. 156.
15. Nicholls, W. H., 'Reminiscences of the Eureka Stockade', *The Centennial Magazine*, Vol. 2, No. 10, May 1890, p. 746.
16. Craig, pp. 265–266.
17. Withers, p. 103.
18. Ibid.
19. Carboni, p. 69.
20. *The Argus*, 10 April 1855, p. 7.
21. Withers, p. 103.
22. Ibid.
23. Ibid., p. 119.
24. *The Ballarat Courier*, 20 July 1889, p. 5.
25. Ibid.
26. Nicholls, W.H., 'Reminiscences of the Eureka Stockade', *The Centennial Magazine*, Vol. 2, No. 10, May 1890, p. 746.
27. Ibid., pp. 746–747.
28. Ibid., p. 746.
29. *The Ballarat Star*, 11 July 1860, p. 3.
30. Nicholls, W. H., 'Reminiscences of the Eureka Stockade', *The Centennial Magazine*, Vol. 2, No. 10, May 1890, p. 747.
31. *The Argus*, 2 December 1854.
32. Author's note: A cylindrical or truncated cone, military cap with

visor and plume or pompon.

33. Samuel Lazarus diary, September 24 1853–21 January 1855; Friday, 1 December 1854 [Monday November 21], SLV, MS Box1777/4, p. 127.

34. Wright, C., 'An Indelible Stain: Gifts of the Samuel Lazarus diary', *History Australia,* Vol. 6, No. 26, p. 45.

35. Pasley letter to father, 27 June 1855, SLV, MS Box 94/4.

36. Ibid.

37. Ibid.

38. Pasley letter to father, 27 June 1855, SLV, MS Box 94/4.

39. Ibid.

40. Assistant Colonial Secretary Moore on behalf of Hotham to Rede, 1 December 1854, VPRS 3219/P Unit 2, 3430.

41. Gold, p. 37.

42. Lynch, p. 28.

43. Samuel Lazarus diary, September 24 1853–21 January 1855; Saturday, 2 December 1854 [Monday November 21] pp. 128–129, SLV, MS Box 1777/4.

44. *The Melbourne Herald,* 5 December 1854, p. 4.

45. Carboni, p. 62.

46. MacFarlane, p. 159.

47. Carboni, p. 60.

48. Author's note: My source for much of this account is from Raffaello Carboni, page 60 onwards.

49. Withers, p. 105.

50. Robert Rede's evidence, 10 January 1855, 'Report of the Commission Appointed to Enquire into the Condition of the Goldfields of Victoria', p. 309.

51. Ibid.

52. Ibid., p. 310.

53. Ibid.

54. Samuel Huyghue diary, *The Ballarat Riots 1854,* SLV, MS 7725, Box 646/9, p. 21.

55. Queen v. Joseph, p. 85.

56. *The Ballarat Times,* 3 December 1854.

57. Ibid.

58. Carboni, p. 62. Author's note: I have modified the words 'they' and 'will' and 'victory' for 'zey' and 'vill' for 'wictory' to fit in with the way Vern is documented to have pronounced those words.

59. Gold, p. 37.

60. Author's note: Though this is what is claimed of McGill, it seems unlikely. He did have military experience, but there is no James McGill who appears on the enrolment lists at West Point in the period when he might have trained there.

61. Gold, p. 37.

62. Carboni, p. 63.

63. Corfield, p.25.

64. Ibid.

65. Carboni, p. 66.

66. Ibid.

67. Ibid.

68. Craig, p. 270.

69. Author's note: Variously referred to by Carboni as 'the Council for the Defence', 'the Committee for the Defence' and 'the Council-of-War for the Defence'.

70. Author's note: I am aware of Lalor's later statement that 'in plain truth it [the Stockade] was nothing more than an enclosure to keep our men together, and was never erected with an eye to military defence', but most other accounts are of the view that the Stockade really was exactly as I describe it here. It was in Lalor's interest at the time to describe it as he did.

71. Queen v. Joseph, p. 28.

72. Withers, p. 103.

73. Molony, p. 150.

74. Carboni, p. 65.

75. Commisioner Rede report to Chief Commissioner Wright, 2 December 1854, VPRS 1189/P Unit 92, J54/14462.

76. Robert Rede's evidence, 'Report of the Commission Appointed to Enquire into the Condition of the Goldfields of Victoria', p. 310.

77. Captain Thomas reports on the attack on the Eureka Stockade to the Major Adjutant General, 3 December 1854, VPRS 1085/P Unit 8, Duplicate 162, Enclosure No. 7.

78. Robert Rede's evidence, 10 January 1855, 'Report of the Commission Appointed to Enquire into the Condition of the Goldfields of Victoria', p. 310.

79. Ibid.

80. Captain Thomas reports on the attack on the Eureka Stockade to the Major Adjutant General, 3 December 1854, VPRS 1085/P Unit 8, Duplicate 162, Enclosure No. 7.

81. Charles Pasley letter to his father, 27 June 1855, ML, B1564, p. 54.

82. Nicholls, W. H., 'Reminiscences of the Eureka Stockade', *The Centennial Magazine*, Vol. 2, No. 10, May 1890, p. 749.
83. Carboni, p. 70.
84. Nicholls, W. H., 'Reminiscences of the Eureka Stockade', *The Centennial Magazine*, Vol. 2, No. 10, May 1890, p. 749.

CHAPTER THIRTEEN: THE QUEEN'S PEACE IS DISTURBED

1. Hotham to Sir George Grey, 20 December 1854, 'Further Papers Relative to the Discovery of Gold in Australia', July 1855, p. 66.
2. Charles Pasley letter to his father, 27 June 1855, ML, B1564, p. 54.
3. Thomas Pierson diary, Wednesday, 6 December 1854, SLV, MS 11646, Box 2178/4, p. 233.
4. *The Examiner*, 9 December 1854, p. 780.
5. Author's note: The 40th had reportedly brought 140 gallons of rum to Ballarat, which had been accessed before and after the attack; MacFarlane, p. 92.
6. Charles Pasley letter to his father, 27 June 1855, ML, B1564, p. 55.
7. Blake, pp. 141–142.
8. Charles Pasley letter to his father, 27 June 1855, ML, B1564, p. 55.
9. Robert Rede to Chief Commissioner of the Goldfields, 2 December 1854, VPRS 1189, 54/J14462, Box 92.
10. Withers, p. 126.
11. Samuel Huyghue Diary, *The Ballarat Riots 1854, SLV*, MS 7725 Box 646/9, p. 23.
12. Withers, p. 124.
13. Charles Pasley letter to his father, 27 June 1855, ML, B1564, p. 55.
14. Lynch, *Story of the Eureka Stockade*, p. 30.
15. Ferguson, *Experiences of a Forty-niner in Australia and New Zealand*, p. 284.
16. Ibid.
17. *The Argus*, 10 April 1855, pp. 14–16.
18. Withers, p. 118.
19. Author's note: There are other candidates as to who fired the first shot, and it all depends on which account you judge to be most credible, but this is my conclusion.
20. *Eureka Encyclopaedia*, p. 452.
21. Lynch, *Story of the Eureka Stockade*, p. 30.
22. Thomas report on the attack on the Eureka Stockade to the Major

Adjutant General, 3 December 1854, VPRS 1085/P Unit 8, Duplicate 162, Enclosure No. 7

23. Hackett to Chief Gold Commissioner, 3 December 1854, VPRS 1085/P Unit 8, Duplicate 162, Enclosure No. 9.
24. Carboni, p. 71.
25. Withers p.117.
26. Ferguson, p. 282.
27. Charles Pasley letter to his father, 27 June 1855, ML, B1564, p. 55.
28. Carboni, p. 71.
29. Ferguson, p. 285.
30. Lynch, p. 30.
31. Withers, p. 117.
32. Author's note: In the subsequent trials, Harris went under the name of James.
33. Carboni, p. 71.
34. Ibid.
35. Ibid., p. 72.
36. Sameul Huyghue diary, *The Ballarat Riots 1854,* State Library of Victoria, MS 7725, Box 646/9, p. 30.
37. *Geelong Advertiser,* 6 December 1854, p. 4.
38. Sameul Huyghue diary, *The Ballarat Riots 1854,* State Library of Victoria, MS 7725, Box 646/9, p. 30.
39. Blake, p. 161.
40. Queen v. Joseph, p. 21.
41. Lynch, p. 30.
42. Carboni, p. 71.
43. Ibid.
44. Ferguson, p. 285.
45. Lynch, p. 12.
46. Ibid., 11.
47. Macdougall, p. 182.
48. *Corfield,* p. 317.
49. Blake, p. 394.
50. Craig, p. 267.
51. Ibid.
52. Ibid.
53. Lynch, p. 34.
54. Ferguson, p. 285.
55. Ferguson, p. 286.
56. Author's note: There is a 4 December (p. 5) report in *The Argus,*

subsequently picked up by many other newspapers, reporting that 'the flag of the diggers, "The Southern Cross", as well as the "Union Jack", which they had to hoist underneath, were captured by the foot police'. However, in my opinion, this report of the Union Jack being on the same flagpole as the flag of the Southern Cross is not credible. There is no independent corroborating report in any other newspaper, letter, diary or book, and one would have expected Raffaello Carboni, for one, to have mentioned it had that been the case. The paintings of the flag ceremony and battle by Charles Doudiet, who was in Ballarat at the time, depicts no Union Jack. During the trial for High Treason, the flying of the Southern Cross was an enormous issue, yet no mention was ever made of the Union Jack flying beneath.

57. Carboni, p. 72.
58. Author's Note: There is a strong and well-known story to the effect that Hafele had the top of his head cleaved off with a single blow by a Lieutenant Richards, as detailed by Henry GylesTurner in his book *Our Own Little Rebellion* (p. 73). It is the strong view of Gregory Blake, however, after comparing first-hand accounts for two years for his book *To Pierce the Tyrant's Heart*, that it did not happen – and on the evidence presented, I agree with him.
59. Gold, p.46.
60. *The Argus*, 27 February 1855, p. 5.
61. Carboni p. 74.
62. Lynch, p. 41.
63. O'Brien, p. 99.
64. Deposition of William Wills, 11 December 1854, Trial Brief for Arthur Purcell Akehurst for the manslaughter of Henry Powell, VPRS 30/P Unit 40, Case no.2, Criminal Sessions Melbourne.
65. Thomas Pierson diary, Wednesday, 6 December 1854, p. 244, SLV, MS 11646, Box 2178/4.
66. Samuel Lazarus diary, 24 September 1853–21 January 1855; Sunday, 3 December 1854, p. 136, SLV, MS BOX 1777/4.
67. Carboni, p.83.
68. *Geelong Advertiser*, 6 December 1854, p. 4.
69. Johnson, pp. 40–41.
70. Ibid., p. 41.
71. Carboni, p. 74.
72. Ibid.
73. Ibid.

74. *Geelong Advertiser*, 6 December 1854, p. 4.

75. Charles Pasley letter to his father, 27 June 1855, ML, B1564, p. 56.

76. Ibid.

77. Withers, p.117.

78. *The Ballarat Times*, 3 December 1854.

79. Carboni, p. 75.

80. Samuel Lazarus diary, 24 September 1853–21 January 1855; Sunday, 3 December 1854, SLV, MS Box 1777/4, p. 132.

81. Sameul Huyghue diary, *The Ballarat Riots 1854*, SLV, MS 7725 Box 646/9, p. 37.

82. *Geelong Advertiser*, 6 December 1854, p. 6. Author's note: The correspondent does not name Hafele, but with 15 wounds it is quite likely the same man.

83. *Geelong Advertiser*, 6 December 1854, p. 4.

84. Withers, p. 124. The manner of this 'dispatching' is not recorded, only that it occurred.

85. Carboni, p. 75.

86. Samuel Huyghue diary, *The Ballarat Riots 1854*, SLV, MS 7725 Box 646/9, p. 32.

87. Ferguson, p. 287.

88. Carboni p. 76.

89. Ibid.

90. Ferguson, p. 287

91. Ibid.

92. *Geelong Advertiser*, 6 December 1854, p. 4

93. Captain Thomas reports on the attack on the Eureka Stockade to the Major Adjutant General, 3 December 1854, VPRS 1085/P Unit 8, Duplicate 162, Enclosure No. 7.

94. *Geelong Advertiser*, 6 December 1904, p. 4.

95. *Geelong Advertiser*, 4 December 1854, p. 4.

96. *Geelong Advertiser*, 6 December 1854, p. 4.

97. *The Melbourne Morning Herald*, 5 December 1854, p. 4.

98. Sameul Huyghue Diary, *The Ballarat Riots 1854*, SLV, MS 7725 Box 646/9, p. 32.

99. Lynch, p. 31.

100. Benjamin Welch's evidence, 20 December 1854, 'Report of the Commission Appointed to Enquire into the Condition of the Goldfields of Victoria', p. 112.

101. Ibid.

102. Samuel Huyghue Diary, *The Ballarat Riots 1854*, SLV, MS 7725 Box

646/9, p. 32–33.

CHAPTER FOURTEEN: AFTER THE TEMPEST

1. Lawson, *A Camp-fire Yarn*, p. 117.
2. Queen v. Hayes, p. 75.
3. Ibid., p. 77.
4. Craig, pp. 268–69.
5. Withers, p. 119.
6. Ibid.
7. Ibid.
8. Ibid.
9. Carboni, p. 82.
10. *The Argus*, 4 December 1854, p. 5.
11. Lynch, p. 32.
12. Ibid., p. 31.
13. Ibid.
14. *The Ballarat Times*, 3 December 1854.
15. Wickham, p. 35.
16. Author's footnote: It is difficult to determine precisely the number of diggers who immediately died as a result of the battle or later from their wounds. The government kept no strict figures on the number of insurgent deaths. Macfarlane (p. 92) lists 16 immediate digger deaths and nine later from their wounds. Captain Thomas in his report to the Major Adjutant General (VPRS 1085/P Unit 8, Duplicate 162, Enclosure No. 7), states 'no less than thirty killed on the spot, and I know that many have since died.' However, as MacFarlane notes, 'this figure probably included military casualties as well. From the eyewitness journalist accounts on the morning of 3 December, between 15 and 20 bodies were counted in the Stockade. Gregory Blake notes that there were a large number of unidentified digger bodies buried and numbers these as high as 21 and that together with MacFarlane's figure of 23, 44 insurgents died as a result of the battle. Towards the end of the battle, wounded escaped south-east towards Warrenheip and as McFarlane notes (p. 104) at least 3 bodies were buried in locations other than Ballarat.
17. Samuel Lazarus diary, 24 September 1853–21 January 1855; Thursday, 30 November 1854, SLV, MS Box 1777/4, p. 122.
18. Samuel Lazarus diary, 24 September 1853–21 January 1855; Sunday,

4 December 1854, SLV, MS Box 1777/4, p. 138.

19. Lynch, p. 32.

20. Samuel Huyghue diary, *The Ballarat Riots 1854,* SLV, MS 7725, Box 646/9, p. 41.

21. Carboni, p. 83.

22. Samuel Huyghue diary, *The Ballarat Riots 1854,* SLV, MS 7725, Box 646/9, p. 39.

23. Captain Thomas reports on the attack on the Eureka Stockade to the Major Adjutant General, 3 December 1854, VPRS 1085/P Unit 8, Duplicate 162, Enclosure No. 7.

24. *Victorian Government Gazette Extraordinary* (No. III), 4 December 1854, p. 2753.

25. Hotham to Denison, Enclosure 11 in No. 7, 4 December 1854; Hotham despatch to Grey, 20 December 1854, 'Further Papers Relative to the Discovery of Gold in Australia', July 1855, p. 85.

26. Ibid.

27. Ibid.

28. Hotham's military report to the Secretary of State, 22 December 1854, British National Archives, CO309/28.

29. Foster to Rede, Enclosure 12 in No. 7, 4 December 1854; Hotham despatch to Grey, 20 December 1854. 'Further Papers Relative to the Discovery of Gold in Australia', July 1855, p. 86.

30. Ibid.

31. *The Ballarat Times,* 3 December 1854.

32. Charles Jeffries Carter's evidence, State Trials, Queen v. Seekamp, VPRS 30/P Unit 40, Case No. 23, Criminal Sessions Melbourne.

33. Carboni, p. 84.

34. Hill, p. 185.

35. Johnson, p.40.

36. Ferguson, p. 290.

37. Carboni, p. 86.

38. Carboni, p. 86.

39. Author's note: Such, I am expertly advised, would be the result of having received a musketball in that spot the day before.

40. *The Argus,* 11 February 1889, p. 8.

41. Peter Lalor letter to his brother Richard, 1855, SLV, AJCP M Series M2039, p. 2.

42. Author's note: Such, I am expertly advised, would be how amputating the arm at the shoulder would have been done on a man in Lalor's condition at that time on the gold fields.

43. *The Argus*, 4 December 1854, p. 4.
44. Samuel Huyghue diary, *The Ballarat Riots 1854,* SLV, MS 7725 Box 646/9, p. 40.
45. Samuel Lazarus diary, 24 September 1853–21 January 1855; Monday,
    4 December 1854, p. 141, SLV, MS Box 1777/4.
46. Ibid. Author's note: Sameul Huyghue's diary contains a happier outcome for mother and child, namely that, 'They miraculously escaped with their lives, their clothes being actually riddled with bullet holes.' Nevertheless, on 7 December 1854, *The Argus* (p.4) reported that, 'The real harm done is the death of one woman and child.'
47. *Geelong Advertiser*, 6 December 1854, p. 4. Author's note: Again, I believe this to be a report only, without substance. And yet the point remains – such reports were circulating on the gold fields and enraged the diggers.
48. Samuel Lazarus diary, 24 September 1853–21 January 1855; Monday,
    4 December 1854, SLV, MS Box 1777/4, p. 141.
49. *The Melbourne Morning Herald*, 5 December 1854, p. 4.
50. *The Age,* 5 December 1854, p. 4.
51. *The Argus*, 6 December 1854, p. 7.
52. Ibid.
53. Ibid.
54. Ibid.
55. *The Age,* 6 December 1854, p. 5.
56. *The Argus*, 6 December 1854, p. 7.
57. Withers, p. 112.
58. *The Argus*, 6 December 1854, p. 7.
59. *Victoria Government Gazette Extraordinary* (No. III½), Monday, 4 December 1854, p. 2755.
60. Samuel Huyghue diary, *The Ballarat Riots 1854,* SLV, MS 7725 Box 646/9, p. 43.
61. Craig, p. 272.
62. Ibid.
63. The Argus, 5 December 1854, p. 5.
64. *The Melbourne Morning Herald*, 9 December 1854, p.6.
65. *Geelong Advertiser*, 12 December 1854, p. 4.
66. *The Melbourne Morning Herald*, 7 December, p. 6.
67. *The Argus,* 7 December 1854, p. 4.

68. Ibid.
69. Ibid.
70. Ibid.
71. *The Argus*, 7 December 1854, p. 5.
72. Hotham dispatch to Grey, 20 December 1854, 'Further Papers Relative to the Discovery of Gold in Australia', July 1855, p. 67.
73. *The Argus*, 7 December 1854, p. 5.
74. Ibid.
75. Record of public meeting held near St Paul's Church, 8 December 1854, VPRS 4066/P Unit 1, December 1854, No. 50.
76. *The Argus*, 7 December 1854, p. 5.
77. Ibid.
78. Withers, p. 119.
79. Lynch, p. 33.
80. Carboni, p. 86.
81. *The Argus*, 11 December 1854, p. 5.
82. Carboni, p. 86.
83. William Revell deposition to E. P. Sturt, 9 December 1854, VPRS 5527/P Unit 2, Item 4.
84. Hotham despatch to Sir George Grey, 28 February 1855. Further papers, July 1855, p. 103.
85. Molony, *Eureka*, p. 175.
86. Hotham to George Grey, 20 December 1854, 'Further Papers Relative to the Discovery of Gold in Australia', July 1855, p. 69.
87. *Geelong Advertiser*, 6 December 1854, p. 4.
88. MacFarlane, p. 113.
89. Ibid., p. 115.
90. *The Argus,* 15 December 1854, p. 6.
91. Ibid.
92. Ibid.
93. Ibid.
94. Deposition of William Wills, 11 December 1854, Trial Brief for Arthur Purcell Akehurst for the manslaughter of Henry Powell, VPRS 30/P Unit 40, Case No. 2, Criminal Sessions Melbourne.
95. Deposition of Gordon Evans, 11 December 1854, Trial Brief for Arthur Purcell Akehurst for the murder of Henry Powell, VPRS 30/P Unit 40, Case No. 2, Criminal Sessions Melbourne.
96. *The Argus*, 20 January 1855 p. 4.
97. *Geelong Advertiser*, 13 December 1854, p. 4.
98. Withers, p. 130.

99. McCombie, p. 277.

100. Stoney, p. 90.

101. Carboni, p. 92.

102. Ibid., p. 93.

103. Ibid., p. 98.

104. 'Report of the Commission Appointed to Enquire into the Condition of the Goldfields of Victoria', p. vii.

105. Carboni, p. 104. Author's note: This James Grant is quite distinct from the aforementioned James Grant, the digger imprisoned for being without a license.

106. Ibid.

107. Corfield, p.452.

108. Samuel Huyghue diary, *The Ballarat Riots 1854,* SLV, MS 7725 Box 646/9, p. 47.

CHAPTER FIFTEEN: TRIALS AND TRIBULATIONS

1. *The Sydney Morning Herald,* 1 January 1855, p.5.

2. *Barrier Miner,* 16 March 1899, p.3. Author's note: The mounted policeman may well have been overstating the reward and its conditions to elicit assistance. A £400 reward had been offered by the Victorian Government on 18 December 1854 for the apprehension of Lalor and Black (£200 per man) and there was no mention of 'dead or alive'. In the article it says £500, but this was a mistaken recollection by Carroll. At the time the reward was £200.

3. Author's note: Musha, actually spelt 'muise', means somewhere between 'indeed!' and 'well, well!' in Irish.

4. *Barrier Miner,* 16 March 1899, p.3.

5. Ibid.

6. *The Argus,* 14 July 1904 p.5.

7. Samuel Huyghue Diary, *The Ballarat Riots 1854,* SLV, MS 7725, Box 646/9, p. 49.

8. 'Report of the Commission Appointed to Enquire into the Condition of the Goldfields of Victoria', p. lxiv.

9. 'Report of the Commission Appointed to Enquire into the Condition of the Goldfields of Victoria', pp. lxv–lxvi.

10. Ibid., p. lxvi.

11. Author's note: The initial charge against him of 'willful murder' was downgraded once he was placed in the hands of the Melbourne legal authorities.

12. MacFarlane, p. 132.
13. Ibid.
14. *The Argus*, 16 January 1855, p. 5.
15. *The Age*, 3 January 1855, p. 3.
16. *The Age*, 5 February 1855, p. 6.
17. *Empire*, 26 December 1854, p. 4.
18. *The Age*, 14 February 1855, p. 5.
19. David Goodman, p. 42.
20. Queen v. Joseph, p. 3.
21. MacFarlane, p. 140.
22. *Geelong Advertiser,* 27 February 1855, p. 2.
23. Queen v. Joseph, p. 10.
24. Ibid., p. 11.
25. Ibid., p. 19.
26. Ibid., p. 25.
27. Ibid., p. 35.
28. Ibid., p. 43.
29. The Anti-Transportation League flag, was designed in 1849 and used from 1851. The flag is very close to the current Australian flag, with the Union Jack in the top left-hand corner and the five stars of the Southern Cross in yellow across the fly. (It did not have the seven-pointed star beneath the Union Jack.) It is thought to be the oldest known flag to feature a representation of the Southern Cross with the stars arranged as seen in the sky. While both flags bear stars, in actuality they look quite different, the Eureka flag bearing a star at the four end-points of a central cross.
30. Queen v. Joseph, p. 43.
31. Ibid.
32. Ibid., p. 44.
33. Ibid., p. 46.
34. Ibid.
35. Ibid., p. 47.
36. Ibid.
37. Ibid.
38. Ibid., p. 48; *The Age,* 26 February 1855, p. 5. Author's note: This passage is exactly as it appears in the trial transcript, with the exception of the words 'riotous nigger from down south', which is how it appeared in *The Age*, instead of the words 'down south man'.
39. *The Age*, 23 February 1855, p. 4.
40. Queen v. Joseph, p. 50.

41. Carboni, p. 91.
42. Ibid.
43. Queen v. Joseph, p. 52.
44. Ibid., p. 53.
45. Ibid., p. 59.
46. Author's note: Though that is not recorded in the official transcript, the verdict certainly is, and according to my research this was the verbal form used at the time.
47. Hocking, p. 168.
48. *The Age*, 24 Feburary 1855, p. 4.
49. *The Sydney Morning Herald*, 1 March 1855, p. 4.
50. *The Ballarat Times*, 10 March 1855, p. 2.
51. *The Argus*, 28 February 1855, p. 4.
52. *Neue Oder-Zeitung*, 7 March 1855, p. 3.
53. Mayer, p. 94.
54. *The Argus*, 13 March 1855, p. 5.
55. Acting Chief Commissioner of Police to Governor Charles Hotham, Reporting a Public Meeting, 15 March 1855, No. 29, Inward Correspondence, VPRS 4066, Box 2, p. 4.
56. Queen v. Hayes, p. 64.
57. Ibid., p. 65.
58. Ibid., p. 67.
59. Ibid., p. 68.
60. Ibid.
61. Ibid., p 69.
62. Ibid.
63. Ibid., p. 71.
64. Ibid.
65. Ibid., 73.
66. Ibid., p. 74.
67. Ibid., p. 78.
68. Ibid.
69. Ibid., p. 98.
70. Ibid.
71. Ibid.
72. Ibid., pp. 115–116.
73. Molony, p.187.
74. Queen v. Hayes, p. 93.
75. Ibid.
76. Ibid., p. 94–95.

77. Ibid., p. 116.
78. Ibid., p. 142.
79. *The Argus*, 22 March 1855, p. 5.
80. Ibid.
81. Molony, p. 189.
82. *The Argus*, 22 March, 1855.
83. Carboni, Pg. 117.
84. Carboni, p. 118.
85. *The Age*, 23 March 1855, p. 4.
86. Hotham despatch to Sir George Grey, 3 April 1855. 'Further Papers Relevant to the Discovery of Gold in Australia', February 1856, p. 64.
87. Ibid.
88. *The Age*, 26 March 1855, p. 5.
89. 'Report of the Commission Appointed to Enquire into the Condition of the Goldfields of Victoria', p. xix.
90. Secretary of State to Governor Hotham, Confidential Despatch, 2 June 1855, VPRS 1090, P0000/1, pp. 187–188.
91. *The Age*, 3 April 1855, p. 7.
92. Peter Lalor letter to his brother Richard, 1855, SLV, AJCP M Series M2039, p. 4.
93. *The Argus*, 10 April 1855, p. 7.
94. Johnson, p. 12.
95. Withers, p. 166.
96. Author's note: Hotham issued writs for the creation of new electoral districts (that included Ballarat and the other major gold districts) on 19 October 1855.
97. *The Argus*, 13 November 1855, p. 4.
98. *Victorian Government Gazette* (No.117), Friday, 23 November 855, p. 3077.

EPILOGUE
1. Smith, p. 89.
2. Molony, 'Eureka and the Prerogative of the People', Papers on Parliament, No. 42, December 2004.
3. *The Argus,* 11 January 1856, p. 4.
4. Ibid.
5. Ibid.
6. Craig, p. 251.

7. Lynch, p. 28.
8. Lynch, p. 37.
9. *The Argus*, 31 December 1856, p. 6.
10. Lynch, p. 128.
11. Hocking, p. 125.
12. Johnson, p. 12.
13. *Illustrated Australian News*, 9 March 1889, p. 43. Author's note: Lalor's obituary was written by the famed observer of the Australian colonies John Stanley, better known as 'The Vagabond'. Stanley interviewed Lalor in the week before his death.
14. Newton, p.73.
15. *The Sydney Morning Herald*, 6 August 1947, p. 3S.
16. *Cairns Post*, 17 April 1946, p.1.
17. *The Age*, 14 April 1873, p. 4.
18. MacFarlane, p. 110.
19. Withers, p. 89.
20. *The British Colonist*, 30 April 1862, p. 3.
21. Bowden, pp. 30–31.
22. Beggs Sunter, Anne. 'Seekamp, Henry (1829–1864), Australian Dictionary of Biography..
23. *The Sydney Morning Herald*, 28 December 1975, p. 30.
24. *The Sydney Morning Herald*, 29 January 1974, p.8.
25. Withers, p. 150.
26. Tom, p.8.
27. Ibid. p.7.
28. *The Sydney Morning Herald*, 28 December 1923, p. 8.
29. Cox, p. 37.
30. Ibid.
31. *The Daily News* [Perth], 11 August 1933, p. 5.
32. Flannery, p. 11.
33. Lynch, p. 11.
34. Withers, p. 154.
35. O'Brien, p.122.
36. Blainey, p. 57.
37. Molony, 'Eureka and the Prerogative of the People', Papers on Parliament, No. 42, December 2004.
38. Lynch, p. 28.
39. *The Sun Herald*, 28 November 2004, p. 16.
40. *The Age*, 3 December 2004, p. 15.
41. Blainey, p. 56.

42. *The Sydney Morning Herald,* 30 November 2004, p. 13.
43. Carboni, p. 51.
44. Ibid., p 39.
45. *The Argus,* 10 April 1855, pp. 14–16.
46. *The Sydney Morning Herald*, 29 November 2004, p. 15.
47. Ibid.

BIBLIOGRAPHY

Acronyms used:
AJCP   Australian Joint Copying Project
ML   The Mitchell Library, Sydney
NLA   National Library of Australia
SLV   The State Library of Victoria
VPRS   Public Record Office Victoria

Published Sources

Books

Abbott, Edward, The English and Australian Cookery Book: Cookery for the many, as well as for the upper ten thousand by an Australian aristologist, Sampson Low, Son, and Marston, London, 1864

Bate, Weston, *Lucky City: The First Generation at Ballarat 1851–1901*, Melbourne University Press, 1979

Billot, C. P. (ed.), *Melbourne's Missing Chronicles by John Pascoe Fawkner*, Globe Press Limited, Melbourne, 1982

Billot, C. P., *John Batman: the Story of John Batman and the Founding of Melbourne*, Hyland House, Melbourne, 1979

Blainey, Geoffrey, *The Rush That Never Ended*, Melbourne University Press, Melbourne, 1963

Blake, Gregory, *To Pierce the Tyrant's Heart*, Australian Military History Publications, Loftus, 2009

Bleissbarth, E. (ed.), *Charles Joseph La Trobe, Australian Notes 1839–1854*, Tarcoola Press, State Library of Victoria and Boz Publishing, Melbourne, 2006

Bohn, H. G., *The Standard Library Cyclopaedia: Political, Constitutional, Statistical and Forensic Knowledge*, Vol. IV, Harrison and Sons, St Martin's Lane, 1855

Bonwick, J., *Notes of a Gold Digger and Gold Digger's Guide*, The Hawthorn Press, Melbourne, 1942

Bowden, Keith Macrae, *Goldrush Doctors at Ballarat*, Magenta Press,

Victoria, 1977

Stoney, Henry B., *Victoria: With a Description of its Principal Cities, Melbourne and Geelong*, Smith, Elder & Co., London, 1856

Canon, Michael (ed.), *Historical Records of Victoria, Victorian Government Printing Office, Melbourne, 1981–2002*

Capper, John, *The Emigrant's Guide to Australia: Containing the Fullest Particulars Relating to the Recently Discovered Gold Fields, the Government Regulations for Gold Seeking*, George Philip and Son, Liverpool, 1852

Carboni, Raffaello, *The Eureka Stockade: The Consequence of Some Pirates on Quarter-Deck Wanting a Rebellion*, J. P. Atkinson and Co., Melbourne, 1855

Historical Studies: Eureka Centenary Supplement, Melbourne University Press, Melbourne, 1964

Clacy, Ellen, *A Lady's Visit to the Gold Digging of Australia in 1852–53*, Lansdowne Press, Melbourne, 1963

Clark, Charles Manning Hope, *A History of Australia, Vol. 4: The Earth Abideth Forever, 1851–1888*, Melbourne University Press, Melbourne, 1991

Clarke, William B., 'Araminta' *Emigrant Ship, 1852*, W. B. Clarke, Bicheno, Tasmania, 2003

Cochrane, Peter, *Remarkable Occurrences: The National Library of Australia's First 100 Years, 1901–2001*, National Library of Australia, Canberra, 2001

Corfield, Justin; Wickham, Dorothy and Gervasoni, Clare, *Eureka Encyclopaedia*, Ballarat Heritage Services, Ballarat, 2004

Cox, Leonard B., *The National Gallery of Victoria, 1861 to 1968: A Search for a Collection*, National Gallery of Victoria, Melbourne, 1970

Craig, William, *My Adventures on the Australian Goldfields*, Cassell and Company, London, Melbourne, 1903

Davison, Simpson, *The Discovery and Geognosy of Gold Deposits in Australia with Comparisons and Accounts of the Gold Regions of California, Russia, India, Brazil, &c.*, Longman, Green, Longman and Roberts, London, 1860

Dewes, John, *China, Australia, and the Pacific Islands, in the Years 1853–56*, R. Bentley, London, 1857

Dickens, Charles, *The Personal History and Experience of David Copperfield*, A. L. Burt Company Publishers, New York, (Undated)

Earp, George B., *The Gold Colonies of Australia and Gold Seeker's Manual*, George Routledge & Co., London, 1852

Elliott, A. F., (ed.), *The Woodbury Papers: letters and documents held by the Royal Photographic Society*, A. F. Elliot, South Melbourne, 1996

Farwell, Byron, *Queen Victoria's Little Wars*, W. W. Norton & Company, New York, 1985

Fauchery, Antoine, *Letters from a Miner in Australia*, Georgian House, Melbourne, 1965

Ferguson, Charles D., *The Experiences of a Forty-niner During Thirty-four Years' Residence in California and Australia*, The Williams Publishing Company, Cleveland, 1888

Flannery, Tim (ed.), *The Birth of Melbourne,* Text Publishing, Melbourne, 2002

Fogarty, L., *James Fintan Lalor: Patriot and Political Essayist*, Talbot Press Ltd, Dublin, 1919

Foster, John F. Leslie, *Three Letters to Hon. James Frederick Palmer*, James J. Blundell & Co., Melbourne, 1855

Fox, L., *The Eureka Flag*, Southwood Press, Marrickville, 1992

Gold, Geoffrey M. (ed.), *Eureka: Rebellion Beneath the Southern Cross*, Bigby Limited, Adelaide, 1977

Goodman, David, *Gold Seeking: Victoria and California in the 1850s*, Stanford University Press, Stanford, 1994

Serle, Grant, *The Melbourne Scene 1803–1956*, Melbourne University Press, Melbourne, 1957

Hall, William H., *Practical Experiences at the Diggings of the Goldfields of Victoria,* Effingham Wilson, London, 1852

Hargraves, Edward Hammond, *Australia and Its Gold Fields: A Historical Sketch of the Australian Colonies from the Earliest Times to the Present Day with a Particular Account of the Recent Gold Discoveries,* Ingram and Co, London, 1855

Hill, David, *The Gold Rush: The Fever that Forever Changed Australia,* William Heinemann Australia, Sydney, 2010

Hirst, John B., *Freedom on the Fatal Shore: Australia's First Colony*, Black Ink, Melbourne, 2008

Hocking, Geoff, *Eureka Stockade: The Events Leading to the Attack in the Pre-dawn of 3 December 1854*, The Five Mile Press, Rowville, Victoria, 2004

Horne, Donald, *The Story of the Australian People*, Reader's Digest, Sydney, 2010

Horne, Richard H., *Australian Facts and Prospects*, Smith, Elder & Co., London, 1859

Housman, A. E., *A Shropshire Lad*, International Pocket Library, Boston, 1989

Howitt, William, *Land, Labour, and Gold, or Two Years in Victoria with Visits to Sydney and Van Diemen's Land*, Longman, Brown, Green and Longman, London, 1855

Hugill, Stan, *Shanties from the Seven Sea Shipboard Work Songs and Songs Used as Work Songs from the Great Days of Sail*, Routledge and Kegan Paul, London, 1984

Jenks, Edward, *The Government of Victoria (Australia)*, MacMillan and Co., London, 1891

Johnson, Laurel, *Women of Eureka*, Brown Door Productions, Ballarat, 1995

Kelly, William, *Life in Victoria, or, Victoria in 1853 and Victoria in 1858*, Vol. I, Chapman and Hall, London, 1859

King, John, F. A., *Edward Hammond Hargraves Esq: An Exuberant Biography of the 'Discoverer' of Payable Gold in Australia*, Summit Books/Paul Hamlyn, Sydney, 1977

Lang, J. D., *An Historical and Statistical Account of New South Wales*, Vol. II, Longman, Brown, Green and Longmans, London, 1852

Lang, J. D., *The Australian Emigrant's Manual, or A Guide to the Gold Colonies of New South Wales and Port Phillip*, Partridge and Oakey, London, 1852

Lawson, Henry, *Selected Poems of Henry Lawson*, Angus and Robertson, Sydney, 1918

Lawson, Henry, Cronin, Leonard (ed.), *A Camp-Fire Yarn: Henry Lawson Complete Works 1885–1900*, Lansdowne, 1984

Lovett, William, *Life and Struggles of William Lovett in His Pursuit of Bread, Knowledge and Freedom,* Vol. II, G. Bell and Sons Ltd, London, 1920

Lovett, William, *The People's Charter: With the Address to the Radical Reformers of Great Britain and Ireland, and a Brief Sketch of Its Origin*, Working Men's Association, C. H. Elt, C. Fox, Islington, 1848

Lynch, John, *The Story of the Eureka Stockade: Epic Days of the Early Fifties at Ballarat*, Australian Catholic Truth Society, Melbourne, (undated)

Macdougall, Anthony K., *Australia: An Illustrated History: From Dreamtime to the New Millennium*, The Five Mile Press, Rowville, Victoria, 2004

MacFarlane, Ian, (ed.), *Eureka: From the Official Records*, Public Record Office of Victoria, Melbourne, 1995

Marx, Karl and Engels, Friedrich, *The Communist Manifesto*, Echo Library, Middlesex, 2009

Marx, Karl and Engels, Friedrich, *Werke*, Vol. 19, Dietz-Verlag, Berlin, 1962

Mayer, Henry (ed.), *Marx, Engels, and Australia*, University of Sydney, Department of Government and Public Administration, Sydney, 1964

McCombie, Thomas, *The History of the Colony of Victoria: From its Settlement to the Death of Sir Charles Hotham*, Sands and Kenny, Melbourne, 1858

McCrae, Georgiana Huntly Gordon, *Georgiana's Journal: Melbourne 1841–1865*, Angus and Robertson, Sydney, 1966

Molony, John, *Eureka*, Melbourne University Press, Carlton South, 2001

Morgan, John, *The Life and Adventures of William Buckley*, Archibald Macdougall, Hobart, 1852

Mundy, Godfrey Charles, *Our Antipodes; or, Residence and Rambles in the Australian Colonies: With a Glimpse of the Gold Fields*, Richard Bentley, London, 1852

Napier, Sir William F. P., *The Life and Opinions of General Sir Charles James Napier*, Vol. II, John Murray, London, 1857

Newton, L. M., *The Story of the Twelfth, a Record of the 12th Battalion, AIF, During the Great War of 1914–1918*, J. Walch and Sons, Hobart, 1925

O'Brien, Bob, *Massacre at Eureka: The Untold Story*, Sovereign Hill Museums Association, Ballarat, 1973

Peach, Bill, *Bill Peach's Gold*, Macmillan for Australian Broadcasting Commission, Melbourne, 1983

Potts, Eli D. and Potts, Annette, *Young America and Australian Gold: Americans and the Gold Rush of the 1850s*, University of Queensland Press, St Lucia, 1974

Quaife, Geoffrey Robert, *Gold and Colonial Society, 1851–1870*, Cassell Australia, Stanmore, 1975

Read, C. Rudson, *What I heard, saw and did at the Australian Goldfileds*, T. & W. Boone, London, 1853

Roberts, Shirley, *Charles Hotham: a Biography*, Melbourne University Press, Melbourne, 1985

Rusden, George W., *History of Australia*, Vol. I, Cambridge University Press, Cambridge, 2011

Scott, Ernest (ed.), *Australia*, Cambridge University Press, Cambridge, 1988

Serle, Geoffrey, *The Golden Age: A History of the Colony of Victoria, 1851–1861*, Melbourne University Press, Melbourne, 1963

Sharkey, Lawrence L., *Australia Marches On*, New South Wales Legal Rights Committee, Sydney, 1942

Shaw, Alan G. L. (ed.), *Gipps–La Trobe Correspondence 1839–1846*, Melbourne University Press at the Miegunyah Press, Melbourne, 1989

Sherer, John, *The Gold-Finder of Australia: How He Went, How He Fared, and How He Made his Fortune*, Clarke, Beeton & Co., London, 1853

Shillinglaw, John J., *Historical Records of Port Phillip, the First Annals of the Colony of Victoria*, Heinemann, Melbourne, 1972

Sidney, Samuel, *The Three Colonies of Australia*, Ingram, Cooke and Co., London, 1853

Smith, F.B. (Preface), *Historical Studies: Eureka Centenary Supplement*, Melbourne University Press, Carlton, 1965

Smyth, Robert B., *The Goldfields and Mineral Districts of Victoria*, John Ferres, Government Printer, Melbourne, 1869

Smythies, Capt. Raymond H., *Historical records of the 40th (2nd Somersetshire) Regiment, now 1st Battalion the Prince of Wales's Volunteers (South Lancashire Regiment)*, A. H. Swiss, Devonport, 1894

Stacpoole, Henry J., *Gold at Ballarat: The Ballarat East Goldfield, Its Discovery and Development*, Lowden Publishing Co., Kilmore, 1971

Stoney, Henry B., Victoria: With a description of its principal cities, Melbourne and Geelong: and remarks on the present state of the colony; including an account of the Ballaarat disturbances, and the death of Captain Wise, 40th Regiment, Smith, Elder & Co., Dublin, 1856

Strange, Albert W. S. and Strange, B., *Ballarat: The Formative Years*, (self-published), Ballarat, 1982

Sutherland, Alexander, *Victoria and its Metropolis: Past and Present*, Vol. I, McCarron, Bird & Co., Melbourne, 1888

Sutherland, George, *Tales of the Goldfields*, Walker, May and Co., Melbourne, 1880

Suttor, W. H., *Australian Stories Retold and Sketches of Country Life*, Whalan, Bathurst, 1887

Toghill, Jeff, *The Great Dividing Range*, Reed, Frenchs Forest, 1982

Tom, William and Lister, John, *History of the Discovery of the First Payable Gold-field (Ophir) in Australia*, Western Examiner Office, 1871 (online, Cultural Collections, University of Newcastle)

Tuckey, James Hingston, *An Account of a Voyage to Establish a Colony at Port Philip in Bass's Strait: on the South Coast of New South Wales in His Majesty's Ship Calcutta, In the Years 1802–3–4*, Longman, Hurst, Rees and Orme, and J. C. Mottley, Portsmouth, 1805

Turnbull, Clive, *Australian Lives*, F. W. Cheshire, Melbourne, 1965

Turner, Henry Gyles, *Our Own Little Rebellion: the Story of the Eureka Stockade*, Whitcombe & Tombs, Melbourne, 1913

Twain, M., *Following the Equator*, Harper and Brothers, New York, 1925

Van Toorn, Penny, *Writing Never Arrives Naked: Early Aboriginal Cultures of Writing in Australia*, Aboriginal Studies Press, 2006

Westgarth, William, *Personal Recollections of Early Melbourne and Victoria*, George Robertson and Co., Melbourne, 1888

Whitaker, Anne-Maree, *Unfinished Revolution: United Irishmen in NSW 1800–1810*, Crossing Press, Sydney, 1994

Wickham, D., *Deaths at Eureka*, Dorothy Wickham, Ballarat Heritage Services, 1996

Wickham, D.; Gervasoni, D. and D'Angri, V.; *The Eureka Flag: Our Starry Banner*, Ballarat Heritage Services, 2000

Wilson, J. W., *The Starry Banner of Australia: An Episode in Colonial History*, Brian Donaghey, Brisbane, 1963

Withers, W. B., *History of Ballarat: From the First Pastoral Settlement to the Present Time*, F. W. Niven and Co., Ballarat, 1887

Younger, Ronald M., *Australia! Australia! The Pioneer Years*, Vol. I, Rigby, 1975

Journal articles

Cahir, David and Clark, Ian D., 'Why should they pay money to the Queen? Aboriginal Miners and Land Claims', *Journal of Australian Colonial History*, Vol. 10, No. 1, 2008

Clark, Ian D., 'You have all this place, no good have children . . . Derrimut: traitor, saviour, or a man of his people?' *Journal of the Royal Australian Historical Society*, Vol. 91, No. 2, December 2005

Dickens, Charles, *Household Words*, Vol. 5, No. 121, 17 July 1852, Office 16, Wellington Street North, London, 1852

Franklin, William E., 'Governors, Miners and Institutions: The Political Legacy of Mining Frontiers in California and Victoria', *California History*, Vol. 65, No. 1, March, 1986

Hancock, Marguerite, 'News from *Jolimont*: The Letters of Charles Joseph and Sophie La Trobe to their Daughter Agnes, 1845–1854', *Victorian Historical Journal*, Vol. 73, No. 2, September 2002

Harvey, J. T., 'Locating the Eureka Stockade: Use of a Geographical Information System (GIS) in a Historiographical Research Context: Computers and the Humanities', Vol. 37, No. 2, May 2003

McCrae, George Gordon, 'Some Recollections of Melbourne in the "Forties"', *Victorian Historical Magazine*, Vol. 2, No. 3, November 1912

Molony, John, 'Eureka and the Prerogative of the People', Papers on

Parliament, No. 42, December 2004

Potts, Eli D., and Potts, Annette, 'The Negro and the Australian Gold Rushes', *Pacific Historical Review*, 1852–1857, Vol. 37, No. 4, November 1968

Taylor, Greg, '*Two Refusals of Royal Assent in Victoria*', Sydney Law Review, Vol. 29, 2007

Waugh, John, 'Framing the First Victorian Constitution, 1853–5', *Monash University Law Review*, Melbourne Law School, Vol. 23, No. 2, 1997

Wright, Clare, 'An Indelible Stain: Gifts of the Samuel Lazarus diary', *History Australia*, Vol. 6, No. 2

Newspapers and periodicals

The Age

The Argus

The Austral Light

Barrier Miner

Bathurst Free Press and Mining Journal

The Ballarat Courier

The Ballarat Star

The Ballarat Times: Buninyong & Creswick's Creek Advertiser

The British Colonist

The British Critic: A New Review

Cairns Post

The Centennial Magazine

The Courier

The Daily News

Daily Southern Cross

Empire

The Examiner (Launceston)

Geelong Advertiser and Intelligencer

The Gold Diggers' Advocate and Commercial Advertiser

The Hobart Town Courier

Illustrated Australian News

The Illustrated London News

The Irish Felon

Launceston Advertiser

The Maitland Mercury and Hunter River General Advertiser

The Manchester Guardian

The Melbourne Morning Herald and General Daily Advertiser
Neue Oder-Zeitung
The Observer
Otago Witness
The People's Advocate
The Perth Gazette and Independent Journal of Politics and News
The Southern Cross
The Sydney Morning Herald
The Times
The Washington Post
The West Australian
Victorian Government Gazette

Government publications

Gazettes
NSW Government Gazette
Victoria Government Gazette

Parliamentary papers
'Further Papers Relative to the Alterations in the Constitutions of the
    Australian Colonies', 14 March 1853, George Edward Eyre and
    William Spottiswoode, Her Majesty's Stationery Office,
    London, 1853
'Correspondence (and Further Papers) Relevant to the (Recent)
    Discovery of Gold in Australia, 1852–1856' in *Votes and Proceedings of
    the Legislative Council of Victoria 1851–1856*, John Ferres, Government
    Printer, Melbourne, 1852–1856
Hansard's *Parliamentary Debates (Great Britain), Third Series, Vol. IV*,
    published by T.C., Hansard, Pater Noster Row, 1831

Reports
'Report of the Board into the Circumstances Connected with the
    Late Disturbances at Ballarat', John Ferres, Government Printer,
    Melbourne, 1854
'Report of the Commission Appointed to Enquire into the Condition
    of the Goldfields of Victoria', John Ferres, Government Printer,
    Melbourne, 1855
'Report from the Select Committee upon Mr. J. F. V. Fitzgerald's

Case Together with the Proceedings of the Committee, Minutes of Evidence, and Appendices', John Ferres, Government Printer, Melbourne, 1867

Others
Victorian Supreme Court State Trials, March 1855. Queen v. Joseph. Queen v. Hayes. John Ferres, Government Printer, Melbourne, 1855
'An Act for the Better Security of the Crown and Government of the United Kingdom', Section III, 22 April 1848, Eyre and Spottiswoode, Printers to the Queen's most Excellent Majesty.

Unpublished material

Note: The Public Record Office of Victoria holds a large volume of unpublished material relevant to the Victorian goldfields 1851–1855 and in particular the Eureka Rebellion, accession details for which appear in the endnotes. Many of these records have been made available online at: http://wiki.prov.vic.gov.au.

The majority of government correspondence &c. has been sourced from the government series of collected papers, published under the title(s) 'Correspondence (and Further Correspondence) Relevant to the Discovery of Gold in Australia' and, unpublished, from the Public Records Office of Victoria. The majority of unpublished diggers' correspondence has been sourced from the Public Records Office of Victoria and the State Library of Victoria. Full accession details for all correspondence is to be found in the relevant endnote.

Correspondence
Forlonge to Barnes, SLV MS Box 111/5
Foster to Wallace, VPRS 3219, Vol. 20
Grant (Mrs) to Hotham, VPRS 4066, No. 4, Box 1
Lalor to his brother Richard, SLV, AJCP, M2039
Manning to the Secretary of the Denominational Schools Board, VPRS 61, 54/399
McIntyre to his brother, SLV, MS 8077 Box 956/2
Pasley to his father, ML, B1564
Pasley to Hotham, VPRS 1189/P Unit 92, K/5413511

Pasley to the Colonial Secretary, VPRS 1189/P, Unit 92, K54/13512
Peters to Malmesbury, SLV, MS 7662, Box 74/3, No. 501
Revell to Sturt, PROV VPRS, 5527/P Unit 2, Item 4
Smyth to Hotham, VPRS 4066/P Unit 1, December, 1854, No. 3
Sturt to Colonial Secretary, 51/1396, VPRS, 1189, Box 8I

Diaries and journals

Batman, John, journal, SLV, MS13181
Huyghue, Samuel Douglas Smyth, diary, *The Ballarat Riots 1854*, SLV, MS 7725, Box 646/9
Lazarus, Samuel, diary, 24 September 1853–21 January 1855, SLV, MS Box 1777/4
McBrien, James, field book 205 – *Traverse of Road from Emu Plans to Bathurst, Survey of Portion of Macquarie and Fish Rivers*, 1823 (http://www.baseline.nsw.gov.au/exhibitions/fieldbooks/fieldbook3.html)
Pierson, Thomas, diary, SLV, MS 11646, Box 2178/4

Other

Captain Thomas's Plan of Defense for the Government Camp, Ballarat, 27 October 1854, St. Ives Library, Sovereign Hill, Ballarat
1853 Bendigo Goldfields Petition, courtesy of the State Library of Victoria, *The Sessional Papers printed by Order of the House of Lords, or Presented by Royal Command, in the Session 1854*
Ballarat Miners' Petition to Lieutenant Sir Governor Charles Hotham, 23 October 1854, VPRS 5527 Eureka Stockade – Historical Collection P0, Unit 1
Bentley, James, deposition, inquest into James Scobie's murder, 7 October 1854, VPRS 5527/P0, Unit 1, Item 1
Carter, Jeffries, evidence, State Trials, Queen v. Seekamp, VPRS 30/P, Criminal Sessions Melbourne, Unit 40, Case No. 2
Conboy, Thomas, deposition against Albert Hurd for rioting at Bentley's Hotel, 27 October 1854, VPRS 5527/P Unit 1, Item 7
Evans, Gordon, deposition, 11 December 1854, trial brief for Arthur Purcell Akehurst for the murder of Henry Powell, VPRS 30/P Unit 40, Case no. 2, Criminal Sessions Melbourne
Martin, Peter, deposition, brief for the prosecution in the trial of James and Catherine Bentley, W. Stance, and John (or Thomas) Farrell and others, VPRS 5527/P Unit 1, Item 5
Mooney, Thomas, deposition, inquest into James Scobie's Murder, 7 October 1854, VPRS 5527/P, Unit 1, Item 1

Record of meeting between Lieutenant-Governor Hotham and a
deputation from the diggers, led by J. B. Humffrays and George Black,
27 November 1854, VPRS 1095/P Unit 3, Bundle 1, No. 16

Record of public meeting held near St Paul's Church, 8 December 1854,
VPRS 4066/P Unit 1, December 1854, No. 50

Rede, Robert, Account of the Gravel Pit riots and call for martial law to
be proclaimed, 30 November 1854, VPRS 1085/P Unit 8, Duplicate
162, Enclosure No. 4

Report of meeting between Lieutenant-Governor Hotham and a
deputation from the diggers, led by J. B. Humffrays and George Black,
27 November 1854, VPRS 1095/P Unit 3, Bundle 1, No. 16

Seekamp's press, inflammatory poster, VPRS 5527/P Unit 4, Item 1

Statement of the jury following the inquest into James Scobie's murder, 7
October 1854, VPRS 5527/P0, Unit 1, Item 1

Thomas, Plan of Defense for the Government Camp, 27 October 1854,
St. Ives Library, Sovereign Hill, Ballarat

Thomas, report on the attack on the Eureka Stockade to the Major
Adjutant General, 3 December 1854, VPRS 1085/P Unit 8, Duplicate
162, Enclosure 7

Welch, Barnard, deposition, inquest into James Scobie's murder, 7
October 1854, VPRS 5527/P0, Unit 1, Item 1

Welsh, Benjamin, additional deposition for the inquest investigating the
murder of James Scobie, 22 October 1854, VPRS 5527/P Unit 1, Item
2

Wills, William, deposition, 11 December 1854, 'Trial Brief for Arthur
Purcell Akehurst for the Manslaughter of Henry Powell', VPRS 30/P
Unit 40, Case No. 2, Criminal Sessions Melbourne

Wood, Thomas, deposition, 27 October 1854, 'Depositions Taken
Against Albert Hurd for Rioting at Bentley's Hotel', VPRS 5527/P
Unit 1, Item 7

Websites

Australian Dictionary of Biography (http://adb.anu.edu.au/)

Ballarat & District Genealogical Society (www.ballaratgenealogy.org.au)

Ballarat Heritage Services
(http://www.ballaratheritage.com.au/eureka/eureka.html)

Ballarat Historical Society (http://www.ballarathistoricalsociety.com/
index.php?option=com_content&view=frontpage&Itemid=1)

Ballarat Reform League Inc. (www.ballaratreformleague.org.au)

BIBLIOGRAPHY

Defending Victoria (http://users.netconnect.com.au/~ianmac/ross.html)

The C. J. La Trobe Society (www.latrobesociety.org.au)

eGold (www.egold.net.au)

The Eureka Centre (www.eurekaballarat.com)

Engels Internet Archive (http://www.marxists.org)

Heretic Press – Eureka Stockade
(http://www.hereticpress.com/Dogstar/History/eureka.html)

The Historic Shipping Website (www.historic-shipping.co.uk)

Museum of Australian Democracy (www.foundingdocs.gov.au)

Public Record Office of Victoria (www.prov.vic.gov.au)

Public Record Office Victoria Wiki (www.wiki.prov.vic.gov.au)

Reason in Revolt (www.reasoninrevolt.net.au)

Ship's Passengers Lists (Victoria) (http://www.access.prov.vic.gov.au/
public/PROVguides/PROVguide050/PROVguide050.jsp)

SurgiCat, The Royal College of Surgeons of England
(www.surgicat.rcseng.ac.uk)

Soldiers at Eureka Genealogy
(http://freepages.history.rootsweb.ancestry.com/~garter1/eureka.htm)

Sovereign Hill/Gold Museum
(http://www.sovereignhill.com.au/?id=gmuseum)

Victoria Government Gazette (www.gazette.slv.vic.gov.au)

Index